A Companion to Digital Literary Studies

D A

Blackwell Companions to Literature and Culture

This series offers comprehensive, newly written surveys of key periods and movements and certain major authors, in English literary culture and history. Extensive volumes provide new perspectives and positions on contexts and on canonical and post-canonical texts, orientating the beginning student in new fields of study and providing the experienced undergraduate and new graduate with current and new directions, as pioneered and developed by leading scholars in the field.

A COMPANION TO

DIGITAL LITERARY STUDIES

EDITED BY

RAY SIEMENS AND SUSAN SCHREIBMAN

WILEY-BLACKWELL

A John Wiley & Sons, Ltd., Publication

This paperback edition first published 2013
© 2013 Blackwell Publishing Ltd, except for editorial material and organization
© 2013 by Ray Siemens and Susan Schreibman

Edition history: Blackwell Publishing Ltd (hardback, 2007)

Registered Office
John Wiley & Sons, Ltd, The Atrium, Southern Gate, Chichester, West Sussex, PO19 8SQ, UK

Editorial Offices
350 Main Street, Malden, MA 02148-5020, USA
9600 Garsington Road, Oxford, OX4 2DQ, UK
The Atrium, Southern Gate, Chichester, West Sussex, PO19 8SQ, UK

For details of our global editorial offices, for customer services, and for information about how
to apply for permission to reuse the copyright material in this book please see our website at www.wiley.com/
wiley-blackwell.

Library of Congress Cataloging-in-Publication Data

A companion to digital literary studies / edited by Ray Siemens and Susan Schreibman.
    p.   cm.—(Blackwell companions to literature and culture)
  Includes bibliographical references and index.
  ISBN 978-1-4051-4864-1 (cloth) – 978-1-118-49227-7 (pbk)
1. Literature and the Internet.   2. Electronic publications.   3. Literature—Computer network resources.
4. Digital libraries.   5. Hypertext systems.   I. Siemens, Raymond George, 1966–   II. Schreibman, Susan.
  PN56.I65C66 2007
  802.85—dc22

                                        2007003822

A catalogue record for this book is available from the British Library.

Cover image: William Blake, *Newton*, color print finished in ink and watercolor, 1795/c. 1805;
© Tate, London 2006
Cover design by Richard Boxall Design Associates

Set in 11/13pt Garamond Three by SPi Publisher Services, Pondicherry, India
Printed in Malaysia by Ho Printing (M) Sdn Bhd

1   2013

Contents

Notes on Contributors

Editors

Ray Siemens is Canada Research Chair in Humanities Computing and Professor of English at the University of Victoria. He is President (English) of the *Society for Digital Humanities / Société pour l'étude des médias interactifs*, Visiting Senior Research Fellow at the Centre for Computing in the Humanities at King's College London, and Visiting Research Professor at Sheffield Hallam University. Director of the Digital Humanities Summer Institute, and founding editor of the electronic scholarly journal *Early Modern Literary Studies*, he is also author of works chiefly focusing on areas where literary studies and computational methods intersect, is editor of several Renaissance texts, is series co-editor of *Topics in the Digital Humanities* (University of Illinois Press) and is co-editor of several book collections on humanities computing topics, among them the *Blackwell Companion to Digital Humanities* (2004) and *Mind Technologies* (University of Calgary Press, 2006).

Susan Schreibman is Assistant Dean and Head of Digital Collections and Research at University of Maryland Libraries. She received her PhD in Anglo-Irish Literature and Drama from University College Dublin (1997). She is the founding editor of *The Thomas MacGreevy Archive, Irish Resources in the Humanities*, and principle developer of *The Versioning Machine*. She is the author of *Collected Poems of Thomas MacGreevy: An Annotated Edition* (1991), co-editor of *A Companion to Digital Humanities* (Blackwell, 2004), co-translator of *Siete poetas norteamericanas* (1991); and co-series editor of *Topics in the Digital Humanities* (University of Illinois Press).

Contributors

David Bamman is a computational linguist for the Perseus Project at Tufts University, focusing especially on natural language processing for Latin. David received a BA in Classics from the University of Wisconsin and an MA in Applied

Linguistics from Boston University. He is currently leading the development of the Latin Dependency Treebank.

Belinda Barnet (belinda.barnet@gmail.com) is Lecturer in Media and Communications at Swinburne University of Technology, Melbourne. She has a PhD in Media and Communications from the University of New South Wales, and research interests in digital media, the evolution of technology, convergent journalism, and the mobile internet. Prior to her appointment at Swinburne, Belinda was Service Delivery Manager at Ericsson Australia. Her work has been published in a variety of books and journals, including *CTHEORY*, *Continuum*, *Fibreculture*, *The American Book Review*, and *Convergence*.

Marc Bragdon is Electronic Services Librarian with the University of New Brunswick Libraries Electronic Text Centre. Marc plays a lead role in the ongoing development of digital preservation strategies for UNB Libraries that incorporate international standards in digital imaging and information exchange as well as associated networked indexing and search/retrieval applications.

Alan Burk (burk@unb.ca) is the Associate Director for the Libraries at the University of New Brunswick and was the founding director of the Electronic Text Centre from 1996–2005. His broad research interests are in the areas of Humanities Computing and Electronic Publishing. He has been involved in many grants, including a recent Canada Foundation for Innovation award for $11,000,000 to build a Pan-Canadian electronic publishing and research infrastructure. One of his main research interests, supported by a research agreement with Elsevier and a grant from the New Brunswick Innovation Fund, is in using applications of machine learning to automatically build metadata to describe scholarly information on the Web.

Lisa Charlong is Assistant Director and Coordinator of XML and SGML Initiatives at The Electronic Text Centre at University of New Brunswick Libraries. Lisa has been involved with numerous scholarly communications and publishing projects, including: The Atlantic Canada Portal and the Chadwyck-Healey-published *Canadian Poetry* online collection. Lisa's background is in information technology, education, archives, and art. Her current research interests revolve around the creation and use of structured data and digital collections as educational resources.

G. Sayeed Choudhury (sayeed@jhu.edu) is the Associate Director for Library Digital Programs and Hodson Director of the Digital Knowledge Center at the Sheridan Libraries of Johns Hopkins University. He serves as principal investigator for projects funded through the National Science Foundation, Institute of Museum and Library Services, and the Mellon Foundation. He has oversight for the digital library activities and services provided by the Sheridan Libraries at Johns Hopkins University. Choudhury has served on program committees for Open Repositories, the Joint

Conference on Digital Libraries, Web-Wise, the ISMIR music retrieval conference, Document Analysis for Image Libraries, and the IEEE Advances in Digital Libraries. He has provided presentations at the following conferences or meetings: Digital Curation Centre, American Library Association, Association of College and Research Libraries, the International Federation of Library Associations, Educause, Coalition for Networked Information, the Digital Library Federation, American Society for Information Science and Technology, and Web-Wise. Choudhury has published papers in *D-Lib*, the *Journal of Digital Information*, and *First Monday*.

Tanya Clement (tclement@umd.edu) is an English PhD candidate at the University of Maryland, College Park. Her focus of study is textual and digital studies as it pertains to applied humanities computing and modernist American literature. She has an MFA in Fiction from the University of Virginia, and was trained in Humanities Computing at Virginia's Electronic Text Center and the Institute for Advanced Technology in the Humanities. At the University of Maryland, she was a program associate at the Maryland Institute for Technologies in the Humanities from 2002 to 2005. Presently, she is the project manager for the *Dickinson Electronic Archives* and a research associate for MONK (Metadata Offers New Knowledge), a Mellon-funded project which seeks to integrate existing digital library collections and large-scale, cross-collection text mining and text analysis with rich visualization and social software capabilities.

Gregory Crane (gregory.crane@tufts.edu) is Winnick Family Chair of Technology and Entrepreneurship, Professor of Classics, and Director of the Perseus Project at Tufts University. Originally trained as a classicist, his current interests focus more generally on the application of information technology to the humanities.

James Cummings (james.cummings@computing-services.oxford.ac.uk) works for the Oxford Text Archive at the University of Oxford which hosts the UK's Arts and Humanities Data Service: Literature, Languages, and Linguistics (AHDS:LLL). His PhD from the University of Leeds was in the field of medieval studies on records of early entertainment. He is on the Executive Board and Editorial Committee of the Digital Medievalist project. He has been elected multiple times to the Technical Council of the Text Encoding Initiative, where he has worked hard to further the development of the *TEI Guidelines*. In his work for AHDS:LLL he advises UK funding applicants on recommended practices in text encoding. He lectures on both medieval and humanities computing topics at a number of institutions, and publishes in both these disciplines.

Peter Damian-Grint (peter.damian-grint@voltaire.ox.ac.uk) is Correspondence Editor of *Electronic Enlightenment*, a Web 2.0 e-publishing research project of the University of Oxford; he previously worked for the *Oxford Dictionary of National*

Biography and *Studies on Voltaire and the Eighteenth Century*. A medievalist by training, he teaches Old French at the University of Oxford and has written widely on Old French literature, especially historiography. He is the author of *The New Historians of the Twelfth-Century Renaissance* (1999) and editor of a collection of essays, *Medievalism and manière gothique in Enlightenment France* (2006).

Johanna Drucker (jrd8e@virginia.edu) is the Robertson Professor of Media Studies at the University of Virginia. She has published and lectured widely on topics in the aesthetics of digital media, graphic design, experimental typography, artists' books, and contemporary art. Her most recent title, *Sweet Dreams: Contemporary Art and Complicity*, was published by the University of Chicago Press in 2005. She is currently finishing work on a critical history of graphic design, with collaborator Emily McVarish, which will appear in 2008 from Prentice Hall. With Jerome McGann she co-founded SpecLab at the University of Virginia and was involved in developing the prototypes for several key projects, including Temporal Modeling and IVAN-HOE. Her current digital project is <http://www.ArtistsBooksOnline.org>.

Poet, editor, multimedia artist, and critic **Christopher Funkhouser** (funkhouser@adm.njit.edu), an Associate Professor at New Jersey Institute of Technology, was awarded a Fulbright Scholarship to lecture and conduct research on "hypermedia writing" in Malaysia in 2006, where his CD-ROM e-book, *Selections 2.0*, was issued by Multimedia University. In 2007 two books, *Prehistoric Digital Poetry: An Archaeology of Forms, 1959–1995*, and a bilingual collection, *Technopoetry Rising: Essays and Works*, will be published.

Bertrand Gervais (gervais.bertrand@uqam.ca) is full Professor in Literary studies at the University of Québec in Montréal (UQAM). He is the director of Figura, the Research Center on Textuality and the Imaginary, and of NT2, the Research Laboratory on Hypermedia Art and Literature (<http://www.labo-nt2.uqam.ca>). He teaches American literature and literary theories, specializing in theories of reading and interpretation. He has published essays on literary reading and twentieth-century American literature. His current work focuses on obsession, on the apocalyptic imagination, as well as on the Labyrinth in contemporary literature and film. He is also a novelist.

Gretchen Gueguen (ggueguen@umd.edu) is a member of the Digital Collections Library in the Digital Collections and Research Department of the University of Maryland Libraries. She has worked at the Maryland Institute for Technology in the Humanities on *The Thomas MacGreevy Archive* and as an assistant in the Digital Collections and Research division of the University of Maryland Libraries. Most recently, she has co-edited (with Ann Hanlon) *The Library in Bits and Bytes: A Digital Publication*, the proceedings of *The Library in Bits and Bytes: A Digital Library Symposium*.

Carolyn Guertin (guertin@uta.edu) is Assistant Professor of Digital Media and Director of the eCreate Lab, a graduate student research and development laboratory, in the Department of English at the University of Texas at Arlington. During the 2004 to 2006 academic years, she was a Senior McLuhan Fellow and SSHRC Postdoctoral Fellow in the McLuhan Program in Culture and Technology at the University of Toronto, and most recently gave the closing keynote address at "Re-Reading McLuhan: An International Conference on Media and Culture in the 21st Century" at the University of Bayreuth in Germany. She does both theoretical and applied work in cyberfeminism, digital narrative, digital design, media literacy (or postliteracy) and performance. She is a founding editor of the online journal *MediaTropes*, curator and founder of *Assemblage: The Women's Online New Media Gallery*, and a literary advisor to the Electronic Literature Organization. She has written textbooks on hypertext and literature and information aesthetics, and is working on a new book called *Connective Tissue: Queer Bodies, Postdramatic Performance and New Media Aesthetics*.

David L. Hoover (david.hoover@verizon.net) is currently Professor of English at New York University, and has been working in the areas of humanities computing, linguistic stylistics, and text alteration for twenty years. He has published two books, both of which use computer-assisted techniques: *A New Theory of Old English Meter* and *Language and Style in The Inheritors* (on William Golding's style). His current research is focused on authorship attribution, statistical stylistics, and corpus stylistics.

Alison Jones is a researcher at the Perseus Digital Library. She has a BA in History from Mount Holyoke College and an MLS from Simmons College. Her current research interests include digital library interfaces and the digitization of historical collections.

Ian Lancashire (ian@chass.utoronto.ca), Professor of English at the University of Toronto, founded the Center for Computing in the Humanities there in 1986 and co-developed *TACT* (*Text Analysis Computing Tools*). He is currently editing *Representative Poetry Online* (1994–), *Lexicons of Early Modern English* (2006–), and a volume of essays about online teaching for the Modern Language Association of America. His historical research treats the growth of Early Modern English vocabulary, and his theoretical writings concern cybertextuality. He presided over a Canadian learned society, now called the Society for Digital Humanities (SDH-SEMI), from 1992 to 2003 and is now active in the TAPoR and Synergies consortia.

John Lavagnino (John.Lavagnino@kcl.ac.uk) studied physics at Harvard University and English at Brandeis University, where he took his PhD in 1998; he is now Senior Lecturer in Humanities Computing at the Centre for Computing in the Humanities, King's College London. He and Gary Taylor are general editors of *The Collected Works* *of Thomas Middleton*, and he is also collaborating with Peter Beal and Henry Woudhuysen on the *Catalogue of English Literary Manuscripts 1450–1700*.

Mark Leahy (m.leahy@dartington.ac.uk) is a writer and curator who works with text, objects, and performance. Recent critical essays include "Plantation and Thicket: A Double (Sight) Reading of Sir Thomas Browne's 'Garden of Cyrus'," in *Performance Research* 10.2; "'I might have been a painter': John James and the Relation between Visual and Verbal Arts" in *The Salt Companion to John James*, edited by Simon Perrill (due summer 2007). He is curator of the exhibition "Public Pages" as part of the conference Poetry and Public Language at the University of Plymouth (April 2007). Since September 2005 he has been Director of Writing at Dartington College of Arts, England.

Alan Liu (ayliu@english.ucsb.edu) is Professor in the English Department at the University of California, Santa Barbara. He is the author of *Wordsworth: The Sense of History* (Stanford University Press, 1989); *The Laws of Cool: Knowledge Work and the Culture of Information* (University of Chicago Press, 2004); and *Local Transcendence: Essays on Postmodern Historicism and the Database* (forthcoming, University of Chicago Press). He is principal investigator of the UC Multi-campus Research Group, Trans-literacies: Research in the Technological, Social, and Cultural Practices of Online Reading; principal investigator of the UCSB Transcriptions Project (Literature and the Culture of Information); and co-director of his English Department's undergraduate specialization on Literature and the Culture of Information. His other online projects include *Voice of the Shuttle* and (as general editor) *The Agrippa Files*. Liu is also a member of the Board of Directors of the Electronic Literature Organization (ELO). He is Editor of the UC New Media directory.

Andrew Mactavish (mactavish@mcmaster.ca) is Director of Humanities Media and Computing and Associate Professor of Multimedia in the Department of Communication Studies and Multimedia at McMaster University. He researches theories and practices of digital games, humanities computing, and multimedia. He currently holds a research grant from the Social Sciences and Humanities Research Council of Canada to study the cultural politics of digital game play.

Willard McCarty (PhD, Toronto) (willard.mccarty@kcl.ac.uk) is Reader in Humanities Computing, Centre for Computing in the Humanities, King's College London, recipient of the 2006 Richard W. Lyman Award and, with Jean-Claude Guédon, of the 2005 Award for Outstanding Achievement, Society for Digital Humanities / Société pour l'étude des médias interactifs. He is the founding editor of *Humanist* (1987–) and author of *Humanities Computing* (Palgrave, 2005). The aim of his work is to build the theoretical basis for diverse and vigorous research programmes in the digital humanities. His primary focus is on modeling, with a particular interest in the *Metamorphoses* of Ovid.

Nick Montfort (nickm@nickm.com) is Assistant Professor of Digital Media at MIT. He writes and programs interactive fiction, including *Book and Volume* ([auto mata], 2005), and frequently collaborates on online literary projects, including *Implementation* (2005) and *2002: A Palindrome Story* (2002). His recent work is on the human and machine meanings of code, on the role of computing platforms in creative production, and on how the narrative discourse can be varied independently of the content in interactive fiction. He wrote *Twisty Little Passages: An Approach to Interactive Fiction* (MIT Press: 2003) and co-edited *The New Media Reader* (MIT Press: 2003).

Aimée Morrison (ahm@uwaterloo.ca) is Assistant Professor of English at the University of Waterloo. Her research focuses on the materialities of digital culture, from videogaming, to linguistic nationalism, to preservation. She teaches courses in media, multimedia, and electronic text and has recently published on the pedagogy of humanities computing and the rhetoric of internet democracy.

Jason Nugent is the Senior Programmer and Database Developer at the Electronic Text Centre at University of New Brunswick Libraries. He has been heavily involved with web and database development for over a decade, and is a regular contributor to open-source software projects on SourceForge. Before working with the ETC, he taught web development, UNIX administration, and relational database theory at Dalhousie University, and also worked in the private sector, developing innovative web solutions for a number of organizations. He holds an honors degree in Chemistry.

Daniel Paul O'Donnell (daniel.odonnell@uleth.ca) is Department Chair and Associate Professor of English at the University of Lethbridge. He publishes primarily in Anglo-Saxon studies and Digital Humanities. His digital-and-print edition of the earliest known English poem, *Cædmon's Hy*mn, was published by D. S. Brewer in 2005. He also writes a regular column on humanities computing for *Heroic Age*. He is currently director of the Digital Medievalist Project and Co-editor of the associated scholarly journal *Digital Medievalist*. Since the fall of 2006 he has been Chair of the Text Encoding Initiative.

Kenneth M. Price (kprice@unlnotes.unl.edu) is University Professor and Hillegass Chair of American literature at the University of Nebraska, Lincoln. He is the author of *Whitman and Tradition: The Poet in His Century* (Yale UP, 1990) and *To Walt Whitman, America* (University of North Carolina Press, 2004). He recently co-authored with Ed Folsom *Re-Scripting Walt Whitman: An Introduction to His Life and Work* (Blackwell, 2005). He is the co-editor of *The Walt Whitman Archive* and co-director of the Center for Digital Research in the Humanities at Nebraska.

Stephen Ramsay (sramsay@arches.uga.edu) is Assistant Professor of English and a Fellow at the Center for Digital Research in the Humanities at the University of Nebraska, Lincoln. He specializes in text analysis and visualization, and has lectured widely on subjects related to the computational analysis of literary texts and software design for the humanities.

Marie-Laure Ryan (marilaur@gmail.com) is an Independent Scholar specializing in how (new) media influence narrativity. Her *Narrative as Virtual Reality: Immersion and Interactivity in Literature and Electronic Media* (2001) has won the MLA Comparative Literature award. She is the editor of the *Routledge Encyclopaedia of Narrative Theory* (2005) and member of the editorial board of the book series *Frontiers of Narrative*, published by the University of Nebraska Press. She has published widely on narratology, possible worlds theory, and cyberculture. Marie-Laure Ryan was born in Geneva, Switzerland and currently resides in Bellvue, Colorado.

David Z. Saltz (saltz@uga.edu) is Associate Professor of Drama at the University of Georgia. He is Principal Investigator of Virtual Vaudeville: A Live Performance Simulation System, funded by the NSF, and has published essays about performance theory and interactive media in scholarly books and journals, including *Theatre Research International*, *Performance Research*, and the *Journal of Aesthetics and Art Criticism*. He is also a practicing director and installation artist whose work focuses on the interaction between digital media and live performance.

David Seaman (david.seaman@dartmouth.edu) is Associate Librarian for Information Management at Dartmouth College Library, and was until December 2006 the Executive Director of the Digital Library Federation (DLF). David joined the DLF in 2002 from the Electronic Text Center at the University of Virginia Library, where he was the founding Director (1992–2002). In this role, he oversaw the creation and development of an online archive of XML and SGML texts, of which many are available in multiple e-book formats. In addition, he has lectured and published extensively in the fields of humanities computing and digital libraries, and since 1993 has taught e-text and internet courses at the annual summer Book Arts Press Rare Book School at UVA.

Matthew Steggle (m.steggle@shu.ac.uk) is Reader in English at Sheffield Hallam University. He has published extensively on early modern literature, including the books *Richard Brome: Place and Politics on the Caroline Stage* (2004) and *Laughing and Weeping in Early Modern Theatres* (2007). He is the editor of the peer-reviewed e-journal *Early Modern Literary Studies*.

Darren Tofts (dtofts@groupwise.swin.edu) is Associate Professor of Media and Communications, Swinburne University of Technology, Melbourne. His most recent book is *Interzone: Media Arts in Australia* (Thames & Hudson, 2005).

Christian Vandendorpe (cvanden@uottawa.ca) is full Professor in the Department of Lettres françaises at the University of Ottawa, and Director of the Writing Centre.

Specialized in the theory of reading, he was a pioneer in research on the changes in reading habits caused by the arrival of hypertext and new media for the display of texts. His essay *Du papyrus à l'hypertexte* (1999), published in Paris and Montréal, has been translated into Spanish and Polish, and an English version is forthcoming. He is the editor of *Hypertextes. Espaces virtuels de lecture et d'écriture* (2002) and *Les défis de la publication sur le web : hyperlectures, cybertextes et méta-éditions* (2004). He is also responsible for a large publicly accessible database of dream narratives (<http://www.reves.ca/>). For more information: <http://www.lettres.uottawa.ca/vanden.html>.

Dirk Van Hulle (vanhulle@uia.ua.ac.be) is Associate Professor of Literature in English at the James Joyce Centre, University of Antwerp, Belgium. He is editor of the online journal *Genetic Joyce Studies*, member of the editorial board of *Samuel Beckett Today / Aujourd'hui*, and author of *Textual Awareness*, a genetic study of late manuscripts by Joyce, Proust, and Mann (University of Michigan Press, 2004) and *Joyce and Beckett, Discovering Dante* (National Library of Ireland, 2004). He edits the *Beckett Endpage* (<http://www.ua.ac.be/beckett>) and is currently working on a genetic edition of Samuel Beckett's last bilingual works.

John A. Walsh (jawalsh@indiana.edu) is an Assistant Professor in the School of Library and Information Science at Indiana University, where he teaches and conducts research in the areas of digital humanities and digital libraries. His research interests include the application of digital technologies and media formats to transform traditional humanities scholarship and to create new modes of scholarly discourse; semantic web and metadata technologies as tools for the discovery and analysis of humanities data; and digital editing, markup, and textual studies. Current projects include the *Swinburne Project* (<http:// www.swinburneproject.org/>), the *Chymistry of Isaac Newton* (<http://www.dlib.indiana.edu/collections/newton/>), and *Comic Book Markup Language* (<http://www.cbml.org/>).

Noah Wardrip-Fruin (nwf@ucsd.edu) of Brown University approaches digital media as a humanist and as a writer/artist. He has recently edited three books: *The New Media Reader* (2003, with Nick Montfort); *First Person: New Media as Story, Performance, and Game* (2004, with Pat Harrigan); and *Second Person: Role-Playing and Story in Games and Playable Media* (2007, also with Harrigan), all published by The MIT Press. His writing/art for digital media has been presented by galleries, arts festivals, scientific conferences, DVD magazines, VR Caves, and the Whitney and Guggenheim museums – as well as discussed in books such as *Digital Art* (2003) and *Art of the Digital Age* (2006). He is currently an Assistant Professor in the Communication department at UC San Diego as well as a Vice President of the Electronic Literature Organization and a relatively active blogger at <http://grandtextauto.org>.

William (Bill) Winder (winder@interchange.ubc.ca) is Assistant Professor of French at the University of British Columbia's French, Hispanic, and Italian Studies

Department. He is on the board of directors of the Consortium for Computers in the Humanities and the editorial board of *TEXT Technology*, and he co-edits *Computing in the Humanities Working Papers*. His interests lie in computational and formalist approaches to the semantics of language and literature. See his website (<http://www.fhis.ubc.ca/winder>) for recent publications and research.

Christian Wittern (wittern@kanji.zinbun.kyoto-u.ac.jp) is Associate Professor at the Documentation and Information Center for Chinese Studies, Institute for Research in Humanities, Kyoto University. He holds a PhD in Chinese Studies from Göttingen University. His research interests include history of thought and religion in medieval China, encoding of premodern Chinese texts, and methods of Humanities Computing. He has been a member of the TEI Technical Council since 2002.

Editors' Introduction

Intended to suggest a broad range of interests found in the field of literary studies and their confluence with the creative activities, analytical methodologies, and disseminative possibilities presented by computation and the electronic medium... intending to suggest all this, the phrase "digital literary studies" does little justice to what is a meeting of interests that, it may be argued, represents the most important change occurring in the field of literary studies today. That change is not driven by theoretical concerns, although it clearly is informed by them as much as it is, in turn, informing them; it is not posited solely by the necessities of bibliographic pursuits, though quite certainly the computational tractability of such pursuits has strongly encouraged material, textual, and other bibliographic endeavor; and it is not championed only by professional interests, although the pragmatics of our profession do play a large role. Rather, the change is driven chiefly by that which has always driven key aspects of society's engagement with text: the socially accessible technologies that govern the storage, transmission, and reception of textual material.

The way in which one might approach the engagement of computing in literary studies – a discipline as vast as it is deep – is through a multifaceted approach, understanding its relationship not only to the wider concerns of literary studies, which one might argue is its own present, but also to its own past. The origin of digital literary studies is typically located at the mid-point of the last century with the work of Father Roberto Busa, the Jesuit priest who used computational means to create the *Index Thomisticus*. The *Index Thomisticus* is, in itself, both a pre-history of the field as well as an active participant in contemporary technologies and theoretical perspectives. The raw material which formed the palimpsest of the published volumes (first to print formats, and most latterly in digital form) was migrated over a 49-year period onto a variety of media, from punch cards, to tape, to CDs, to the internet and, ultimately, to DVD. With each migration, the data was reformatted and its output re-visualized for a new generation of readers. Busa's engagement with one text across many generations of computer hardware and software forms a pre-history for the rich and varied methodologies, theoretical perspectives, and computational means that today comprise the field of digital literary studies: text encoding, e-literature, linguistic analysis, data mining, new media studies, hypertext studies, and well beyond.

Other perspectives abound. There are, indeed, many further acknowledged milestones to which one could draw attention amongst those in a recent history; one that could be seen to begin with John Smith's seminal article, "Computer Criticism" (1978), and extend through Roseanne Potter's *Literary Computing and Literary Criticism* (1989), Gregory Colomb and Mark Turner's "Computers, Literary Theory, and the Theory of Meaning" (1989), Charles Faulhaber's "Textual Criticism in the 21st Century" (1991), Paul Delany and George Landow's *Hypermedia and Literary Studies* (1991), Landow's *HyperText* (1992), Delany's "From the Scholar's Library to the Personal Docuverse" (1993), Geoffrey Nunberg's "The Place of Books in the Age of Electronic Reproduction" (1993), Richard Finneran's *The Literary Text in the Digital Age* (1996), Janet Murray's *Hamlet on the Holodeck* (1997), Espen Aarseth's *Cybertext* (1997), Jerome McGann's *Radiant Textuality: Literary Studies after the World Wide Web* (2001), N. Katherine Hayles' *Writing Machines* (2002) and so on, up to this day; but here, already, the documentation of such an energetic and, from our current perspective, resounding engagement – a thing of beauty in itself – reflects quite significantly the literary-critical perspective, the eye, of the beholder.

Even so, far from a *Busa*ian past, and the largely textual focus of scholarship at the end of the previous century, are the perspectives of game studies, social and ubiquitous computing, e-literature, and visualization, among many others. It is *all* these methodologies, perspectives, and means that intersect to form a roadmap through this dynamically evolving and richly experimental field. Yet, the sum of the chapters in this volume is much more than a survey of current concerns, which is, perhaps, best reflected in one's specific approach to, and entry into, the discipline itself. From our current perspective, we have the considerable luxury of being able to draw upon any number of the contemporary points of engagement being actively pursued in digital literary studies and seeing active representation in this volume. Thus, as we cast our eyes backward, we can construct a number of rich, informative histories while, at the same time, pointing toward new paths for future research. This meeting of past and future is nowhere more evident than in the introductory chapter to this volume, Alan Liu's "Imagining the New Media Encounter."

Upon Liu's foundation, the remainder of the volume is divided into three broad sections, *Traditions*, *Textualities*, and *Methodologies*; it concludes with a useful annotated bibliography, a starting point for the consideration of a number of the many exemplary initiatives in the area. The first section, *Traditions*, views digital literary studies much as our academic units do, from the perspective of disciplinary periodicity: classical, medieval, early modern, eighteenth-century, nineteenth-century, and twentieth-century and contemporary. Contributions to *Textualities* embrace notions of that ever-problematized entity, the "text," as those who engage literary text do so within the context of the manifold possibilities presented by new media. Lastly, *Methodologies* explores the new ways in which we engage in such pursuit.

The editors express their most sincere gratitude to all those involved in the conception, the shaping, and the production of this volume. Particular thanks go to Emma Bennett, our editor at Blackwell who embraced the idea for the volume and whose support throughout the production process has been unwavering, Annette Abel, who firmly and kindly oversaw the copyediting and page-proofing associated with the collection, and to Sean Daugherty (Maryland), Karin Armstrong (Victoria), and Anne Correia (Victoria), who assisted with many of the pragmatics of getting the volume ready for the press.

Ray Siemens
Susan Schreibman

Works Cited

Aarseth, Espen (1997). *Cybertext: Perspectives on Ergodic Literature.* Baltimore: Johns Hopkins University Press.

Busa, Roberto (Ed.). (1974–). *Index Thomisticus; Sancti Thomae Aquinatis operum omnium indices et concordantiae; consociata plurium opera atque electronico IBM automato usus digessit Robertus Busa.* Stuttgart: Frommann Verlag.

Colomb, Gregory, and Mark Turner (1989). "Computers, Literary Theory, and the Theory of Meaning." In Ralph Cohen (Ed.). *The Future of Literary Theory.* New York: Routledge, pp. 386–410.

Delany, Paul (1993). "From the Scholar's Library to the Personal Docuverse." In *The Digital Word: Text-Based Computing in the Humanities.* Cambridge, MA: MIT Press, pp. 189–199.

Delany, Paul, and George P. Landow (Eds.). (1991). *Hypermedia and Literary Studies.* Cambridge, MA: MIT Press.

Faulhaber, Charles B. (1991). "Textual Criticism in the 21st Century." *Romance Philology* 45: 123–148.

Finneran, Richard J. (Ed.). (1996). *The Literary Text in the Digital Age.* Ann Arbor: University of Michigan Press.

Hayles, N. Katherine (2002). *Writing Machines.* Cambridge, MA: MIT Press.

Landow, George P. (1992). *HyperText: The Convergence of Contemporary Critical Theory and Technology.* Baltimore: Johns Hopkins University Press.

McGann, Jerome (2001). *Radiant Textuality: Literary Studies after the World Wide Web.* New York: Palgrave/Macmillan.

Murray, Janet (1997). *Hamlet on the Holodeck: The Future of Narrative in Cyberspace.* New York: Free Press.

Nunberg, Geoffrey (1993). "The Place of Books in the Age of Electronic Reproduction." *Representations* 42: 13–37.

Potter, Roseanne (Ed.). (1989). *Literary Computing and Literary Criticism: Theoretical and Practical Essays on Theme and Rhetoric.* Philadelphia: University of Pennsylvania Press.

Smith, John B. (1978). "Computer Criticism." *Style* 12.4: 326–56.

Part I
Introduction

1

Imagining the New Media Encounter

Alan Liu

This volume in the Blackwell Companion series convenes scholars, theorists, and practitioners of humanities computing to report on contemporary "digital literary studies." Perhaps the best way to characterize their collective account is to say that it depicts a scene of encounter. *A Companion to Digital Literary Studies* is fundamentally a narrative of what may be called the scene of "new media encounter" – in this case, between the literary and the digital. The premise is that the boundary between codex-based literature and digital information has now been so breached by shared technological, communicational, and computational protocols that we might best think in terms of an encounter rather than a border. And "new media" is the concept that helps organize our understanding of how to negotiate – which is to say, mediate – the mixed protocols in the encounter zone.[1]

But if the *Companion* is an account of new media encounter, then it also belongs to a long lineage of such "first contact" narratives in media history. New media, it turns out, is a very old tale.

To help define the goals of this volume, it will be useful to start by reviewing the generic features of this tale. There are more and less capable imaginations of the new media encounter moment, and it is important to be able to tell the difference before we turn specifically to the digital literary studies scene.

{

Leonard Doob, in his report *Communication in Africa*, tells of one African who took great pains to listen each evening to the BBC news, even though he could understand nothing of it. Just to be in the presence of those sounds at 7 P.M. each day was important for him. His attitude to speech was like ours to melody – the resonant intonation was meaning enough. In the seventeenth century our ancestors still shared this native's attitude to the forms of media. . . . (Marshall McLuhan, "The Medium is the Message" [1994: 20])

No new media experience is fully imaginable, it appears, without the help of what may loosely be called narratives of new media encounter such as this Caliban moment of media enchantment/media colonization in McLuhan's essay.[2] Whether told from the perspective of the native of old media or the ambassador of new media, such tales are a staple of epochs undergoing media change. Two other paradigmatic examples are Plato's myth in the *Phaedrus* of the inventor of writing giving his demo and Claude Lévi-Strauss's account in *Tristes Tropiques* of the tribal chief who imitated the anthropologist's writing:

> But when they came to letters, This, said Theuth, will make the Egyptians wiser and give them better memories; it is a specific both for the memory and for the wit. Thamus replied: O most ingenious Theuth, the parent or inventor of an art is not always the best judge of the utility or inutility of his own inventions to the users of them. And in this instance, you who are the father of letters, from a paternal love of your own children have been led to attribute to them a quality which they cannot have; for this discovery of yours will create forgetfulness in the learners' souls, because they will not use their memories; they will trust to the external written characters and not remember of themselves. The specific which you have discovered is an aid not to memory, but to reminiscence, and you give your disciples not truth, but only the semblance of truth; they will be hearers of many things and will have learned nothing; they will appear to be omniscient and will generally know nothing; they will be tiresome company, having the show of wisdom without the reality. (Plato 2005)

> I handed out sheets of paper and pencils. At first they did nothing with them, then one day I saw that they were all busy drawing wavy, horizontal lines. I wondered what they were trying to do, then it was suddenly borne upon me that they were writing or, to be more accurate, were trying to use their pencils in the same way as I did mine. . . . The majority did this and no more, but the chief had further ambitions. No doubt he was the only one who had grasped the purpose of writing. So he asked me for a writing-pad, and when we both had one, and were working together, if I asked for information on a given point, he did not supply it verbally but drew wavy lines on his paper and presented them to me, as if I could read his reply. (Lévi-Strauss 1973: 333–4)

One might also think of such similar cross-historical pairings as Augustine's account of coming upon Ambrose engaged in the new practice of silent reading ("when we came to see him, we found him reading like this in silence, for he never read aloud" [VI.3]) and W. J. T. Mitchell's pedagogical exemplum of "showing seeing" (a simulation of new media contact in which "I ask the students to frame their presentations by assuming that they are ethnographers who come from, and are reporting back to, a society that has no concept of visual culture. . . . Visual culture is thus made to seem strange, exotic, and in need of explanation" [Mitchell 2002: 97]).

Many more instances could be cited; and, indeed, narratives of new media encounter in the form of first contact with the Word, Book, Law, Image, Music, and (more recently) Code are deeply embedded in the entire historiography of Early Modern religious or imperial conquest, Enlightenment and industrial "modernization," twentieth-century "control through communication" (coupled with "mass entertain-ment"), and postindustrial "informating" or "knowledge work."³ It might be hypothesized that all major changes in the socio-cultural order are channeled symbolically and/or instrumentally through narratives of media change – to the point, indeed, that such narratives often take on the significance of conversion experiences. New media encounters are a proxy wrestle for the soul of the person and the civilization. Augustine's conversion ("take it and read," the child sings nearby in one of history's most potent stagings of random-access reading [VIII.12] is not unique). Dramatizations of the instant when individuals, villages, or nations first wrap their minds around a manuscript, book, telephone, radio, TV, computer, cell phone, iPod, etc., are overdetermined. McLuhan spoke of "electric" media as if it were the incandescent star of a new nativity. And adepts of digital media today reverence the "born digital" with something of the conviction of the "born again."

Or, more accurately, "conversion" connotes too right-angled a change. The better term is indeed "encounter," indicating a thick, unpredictable zone of contact – more borderland than border line – where (mis)understandings of new media are negotiated along twisting, partial, and contradictory vectors. To adapt Jean-François Lyotard's concept, we may say that media contact zones are like the *pagus* in classical times: the tricky frontier around a town where one deals warily with strangers because even the lowliest beggar may turn out to be a god, or vice versa.⁴ New media are always pagan media: strange, rough, and guileful; either messengers of the gods or spam. Narratives of new media are thus less objective accounts than speculative bargaining positions. Encountering a new medium, one says in essence: "what do I get if I deal with this as if it were really a scroll, book, TV, phone, radio, or surveillance instrument (and so on) in disguise?" In addition, since any speculation has its risk-averse side, narratives of new media encounter are also in part conservative. Like photographic vignettes in the nineteenth century, they have rounded, gradient contours that blur the raw edge of new media into the comfort zone of existing techno-social constraints, expectations, and perceptions.⁵

At once descriptive and interpretive, speculative and wary, proselytizing and critical, and visionary and regulatory, narratives of new media encounter are the elementary form of media theory – the place from which all meta-discourse about media starts. Or again, they are *intra*-discursive: part of the self-mediating discourse or feedback by which media "ecologies," as they have recently been called, adapt systemically when new forces swarm across the border.⁶

}{

The above overview of how cultures tell themselves about new media would in a larger treatment invite more detailed, historically organized evidence. But on the present occasion, it is most useful to focus synoptically on the basic logic of such tellings.

The following four propositions outline something like the overall narrative genome of the new media encounter, particular aspects of which may dominate or recede:

(

1. Narratives of new media encounter are identity tales in which media at once projects and introjects "otherness." At the end of his borrowed anecdote of the African listening to the BBC, McLuhan concludes: "In the seventeenth century our ancestors still shared this native's attitude to the forms of media." Even as he projects the otherness of new media onto the cultural other, he introjects that otherness into the cultural self. It is really the Westerner (genealogically: Renaissance man) who passes as African. A similar identity chiasmus can be detected in other rehearsals of new media encounter. Mitchell's "showing seeing," for example, requires students to imagine exotic others, but also to exoticize themselves. The general function of any narrative of new media encounter, we may say, is to depict new media as the perpetual stranger or (*pace* Lyotard) pagan in our own midst. Such a mirror moment participates in the broader logic of cultural and interpersonal encounters, which are meaningful only to the extent that the self, at least for a piercing moment, becomes other to itself.

) (

2. Narratives of new media encounter emplot their identity tale as a life cycle of media change. The three primary moments in this life cycle – the building blocks of the new media narrative – are the following:

Media enchantment/colonization. Again, what I called McLuhan's "Caliban" moment is instructive. In the media studies field, the mysterious process of enchantment/ colonization that brings the African under the spell of the Prospero BBC goes by the name of "media determinism." For better or worse, media changes us. We are changelings of media.

Media disenchantment. This is the moment of critique/resistance. One thinks, for example, of the sly way in which the tribal chief in Lévi-Strauss's anecdote beards the anthropologist while pretending to be able to write:

> This farce went on for two hours. Was he perhaps hoping to delude himself? More probably he wanted to astonish his companions, to convince them that he was acting as an intermediary agent for the exchange of goods, that he was in alliance with the white man and shared his secrets. We were eager to be off. . . . So I did not try to explore the matter further. (Lévi-Strauss 1973: 334)

Here, the anthropologist's question, "Was he perhaps hoping to delude himself?" has a curious, self-canceling logic, since it is hard to conceive of intentional self-delusion without undermining the meaning of intent and veering from ethnography into psychoanalysis. This strange question is an indicator that something odd is happening in the experience of media during the contact moment: the "native" is not just enchanted with new media ("deluded" by its magical illusion) but able to see through the magic to its reality, which turns out to be the same-old-same-old of social power ("More probably he wanted to astonish his companions . . ."). The Caliban moment collapses into the Machiavellian moment. Media enchantment entails disenchantment and, ultimately, resistance. The Frankfurt School critique of the media "culture industry" is paradigmatic, as is more recent critique of the same industry by the conservative right. In the case of Lévi-Strauss's anecdote, the now canonical rebuttal from a disenchanted viewpoint is Jacques Derrida's discussion of *Tristes Tropiques* (tinged, one might think, by Derrida's own neo-Caliban childhood as an Algerian Jew during the run-up to World War II) (Derrida 1976: 107–40).

Media surmise. I take the word "surmise" from the last line of Keats's "On First Looking into Chapman's Homer": Cortez "star'd at the Pacific" while "all his men / Look'd at each other with a wild surmise." But my thought is borrowed from such recent media theorists as Matthew Fuller, who sees in such media as pirate radio "ways in which 'hidden' dimensions of invention and combination are embedded and implicit in particular dynamics and affordances of media systems and their parts" (2005: 8); and Ronald J. Deibert, whose analysis of media "ecology" supposes the opposite of media determinism ("once introduced a technology becomes part of the material landscape in which human agents and social groups interact, having many *unforeseen effects*" [1997: 29]).[7] The basic idea is that media – as befits a creature of the *pagus* – is/are wily. Indeed, the very uncertainty of singular versus plural (medium/media) is to the point.[8] Media is/are not a monolithic, one-way determinism but a buzzing, unpredictable "ecology." There are niches for both the established media aggregators (church, state, broadcast or cable TV, Microsoft, Google, iTunes, YouTube, etc.) and newer species, or start-ups, that launch in local niches with underestimated general potential. In the eighteenth century, for example, the novel was a start-up.

) (

3. *The life story of the new media encounter plays out in the key registers of human significance:*

Historical. The very phrase "new media," of course, stages an exaggerated encounter between *old* and *new.* No media change, it seems, is imaginable without staging such a temporal encounter, where the bias usually inclines toward *à la mode.* This means that narratives of new media are ipso facto narratives of modernization, whether configured as progress ("Enlightenment"), differentiation (the specialization of once unified cultural sensibilities and institutions into bureaucratically insulated modern functions), disruption (as in Joseph Schumpeter's economic model of "creative destruction"), or globalization (the most recent variation on all the above).

Socio-political. Since new media encounter narratives are modernization narratives, they are also big with the agendas of social identity that have attended the Western understanding of modernization from the Enlightenment through at least the apparent convergence of neo-liberalism and -conservatism that Francis Fukuyama, in the year of the fall of the Berlin Wall, famously called the "end of history." We need not review the extensive literature on the modernizing social effects of print, for example, to identify the Westernizing, post-Enlightenment program behind such recent new media claims as: *information wants to be free, the internet is decentralized,* or (most recently) *Web 2.0 = collective intelligence.*[9] Socio-political claims about new media inherit a longstanding assumption that media reconfigures one-to-many and many-to-many relations through what McLuhan described as "the new scale that is introduced into our affairs by each extension of ourselves, or by any new technology" (1994: 7). Racial, gender, class, age, and other social relations also figure in representations of new media encounter, including – as the work of such critics as Wendy Chun, Jennifer González, and Lisa Nakamura argues – those specifically focused on encountering the cultural other in the digital new world.

Subjective (cognitive, psychological, psychosomatic, phenomenological, "personal"). Here it is useful to recall the full context of the McLuhan dictum about the "new scale" and "extension of ourselves." The canonical passage from the opening of "The Medium is the Message" is as follows:

> In a culture like ours, long accustomed to splitting and dividing all things as a means of control, it is sometimes a bit of a shock to be reminded that, in operational and practical fact, the medium is the message. This is merely to say that *the personal and social consequences of any medium* – that is, of any extension of ourselves – result from the new scale that is introduced into our affairs by each extension of ourselves, or by any new technology. (1994: 7, italics added)

"The personal and social" is a typical McLuhan doublet for the impact of new media. New media may be a collective social-cultural experience, but it is also psychologically, corporeally, phenomenologically, and subjectively personal. As McLuhan put it in sound-bite form in his collaboration with graphic designer Quentin Fiore, *The Medium is the Massage*:

electric circuitry,

an extension of
the
central
nervous
system

And on the facing, recto page,

> Media, by altering the environment, evoke in us
> unique ratios of sense perceptions. The extension
> of any one sense alters the way we think and act –
> the way we perceive the world.
> **When**
> **these**
> **ratios**
> **change,**
>
> # men change.[10]

We see similar telescopings between collective and personal ratios in accounts of new media as old as Plato's *Phaedrus*, where the Egyptian king foresees the total effect of writing on his people in internalizing, psychological terms ("they will not use their memories; they will trust to the external written characters and not remember of themselves"). Similarly, accounts of so-called "Web 2.0" today turn upon paradigms such as MySpace.com: both "social networked" and intensely personal.

) (

4. When fully realized in their historical, socio-political, and personal entanglements, the identity tales created by narratives of new media encounter are unpredictable. The real interest in narratives of new media encounter – the underlying reason I describe them in such unmoored terms as "borderlands," "otherness," and "surmise" – is that the historical, socio-political, and subjective registers of media identity described above are not just neutral substrates (like pure silicon) on which programs of determinism and resistance run. Instead, they are doped with human contingencies that switch, bend, refract, refocus, and otherwise mediate the very experience of media in ways that kink any easy plot of old to new, centralized to decentralized, or embodied to tele-virtual. While narratives of new media encounter are modernization narratives, alternative visions of modernity and its complex identities emerge.

The weaker form of this thesis may be put this way: new media encounters are messy.[11] "Messy" means that right-angled historical, socio-political, or psychological distinctions between old and new media typically do not survive concrete acts of narration. Instead, binary distinctions open out into overlapping, contradictory, or otherwise thick affordances between media regimes. Raymond Williams's argument about coexisting "residual," "dominant," and "emergent" social forces is paradigmatic (1997: 121–7). Equally suggestive are many other intellectual models of messy cultural transition – ranging, for example, from Fernand Braudel's layered historiography of long, intermediate, and short durations to Fredric Jameson's forthrightly untidy definition of the transition from modernism to postmodernism as a reshuffling of emphases (1983: 123). In formal studies of media, such messiness characteristically surfaces in the recognition that media shifts have an impact only after long temporal and institutional lags full of indirection. Thus historians of writing demonstrate that multiple generations were needed to convert oral peoples into people who thought in terms of writing (e.g., who can read silently). So, too, as M. T. Clanchy shows in his *From Memory to Written Record, England 1066–1307*, the introduction of writing only became socially meaningful through the massive accretion of later institutions, practices, forms, and technologies that scaled up the initial invention into a cultural force (as in the case of the proliferation of documents in the years Clanchy studies).[12]

But there is also a strong version of this thesis that will provide an appropriately dramatic finish to this synopsis of the new media encounter: *narratives of new media encounter are reversible*. Indeed, reversibility is the fundamental reason why it is appropriate to call such narratives modally "narrative" even if they are generically as diverse as anecdote, memoir, autobiography, travelogue, prophecy, critical essay, and so on. After all, deep narratives – those like tragedy that we think come near to exposing the kernel of narrative experience – do only three essential things. They expose the reversibility of the underlying relations of human reality (one thinks, for example, of the antithetical claims made by collective society and personal ethics on the "great," "good" Aeneas, who – as when he leaves Dido – can be "great" or "good" but not simultaneously both). They arbitrarily break the symmetry of these relations to move the plot down an irreversible course (the classical authors called it Fate.) And they then reach closure by restoring some faux-equivalent of the original reversibility at a different level (e.g., in a marriage of opposites).

In the paradigmatic Aristotelian analysis, for instance, narrative turns upon a moment of "reversal" big with "recognition." Protagonist and antagonist (sometimes the same, as in the case of Oedipus) face off symmetrically, armed with equivalent, if incommensurable, claims and powers. Then the story breaks the symmetry to distribute the contested claims and powers along the irreversible time arrow so that, for example, he who was high is brought low. Yet at the end, tragedy leaves its audience haunted by a sense of transport back to the reversible crux where, eternally, fateful agony hangs in the balance. In the Shakespearean version, therefore, we leave the theater haunted by Lear's "no, no, no life?" because the very repetition of the question suggests that the only humanly meaningful answer to the existential binary calculation ("to be or not to be"; Richard II's "ay, no; no, ay") is not a reckoning at all but the suspension of decision in eternal, reversible abeyance.

So, too, structuralist approaches to narrative are on the same page with Aristotle. One of the key insights of Lévi-Strauss's structural anthropology, for instance, is that powerful myths express the irremediable bivalence of such great, existential structures of human identity as nature versus culture, hunting versus agriculture, and life versus death. Like all stories, however, myths break the symmetry so that life can happen. And so great warriors and brave maidens live and die. Yet, ultimately, myths mediate between the binaries in a way that – always with the ghostly touch of ancestors – reverts from fateful diachrony to reversible synchrony. Myths are not just about life and death, therefore, but also about how such tricksters as Coyote and Crow (whose animal totems split the difference between eating live and dead things) scam the normal symmetry-breaking of existence. Such trickster myths, we might say, are the ancestors of media because their constitutively human drive to mediate between polarities may well be the origin of the media drive. (Media today, after all, is where dead things live on, animals act like men, the poor and rich star as each other, and so on. Our great contemporary tricksters are all media-creatures – pop idols, stars, DJs, artists, terrorists, and politicians.)

Poststructuralism, it may be added, radicalized such mediation further, as when Derrida tells tales of Western philosophy starring such typically trickster concepts as *pharmakon* (poison and cure).[13] Or again, we might invoke an alternate tradition of thought by going back to Freud on the uncanny or *unheimlich*. The Freudian "unhomely" (as in the case of the Oedipus story that Aristotle and Lévi-Strauss thought about, too) is a tricky, reversible tale that at last reveals with all the shock of Aristotelian recognition only the "homely" in the strange, and the strange in the homely.[14]

The key point to take away is that narratives of new media encounter, like all narratives, *have no one necessary story, even if necessity is what seems to make their story go.* In the narratological universe, necessity – once called Fate, now renamed media determinism – does not dictate just a single plot line. Instead, necessity is better called "arbitrariness" or its poststructuralist variant "contingency." Earlier I suggested that media stories are pagan stories. One might also, at the end of the genealogy of theoretical approaches cited above, say with Hélène Cixous that they are "women's" stories. They are a "laugh of the Medusa." I know of no better messy, reversible account of the brilliant fury of media than the following passage from Cixous's essay, where it is possible to read not just "voice" and "speech" but "body" and "flesh" as "medium":

> Listen to a woman speak at a public gathering (if she hasn't painfully lost her wind). She doesn't "speak," she throws her trembling body forward; she lets go of herself, she flies; all of her passes into her voice, and it's with her body that she vitally supports the "logic" of her speech. Her flesh speaks true. She lays herself bare. In fact, she physically materializes what she's thinking; she signifies it with her body. In a certain way she *inscribes* what she's saying, because she doesn't deny her drives the intractable and impassioned part they have in speaking. Her speech, even when "theoretical" or political, is never simple or linear or "objectified," generalized: she draws her story into history. (Cixous 1998: 1457–8)

This story is also the history of encounter with new media. In Cixous's account, even one of our oldest media, the voice, is ever and again new.

) |

Revisiting the historical, socio-political, and subjective registers of new media encounter outlined earlier, we can now see that the effects of messiness and reversal – of insisting that there is always another plot fork in media history – can be quite compelling. Media identity, it turns out, is manifold and dynamic. The particular messy and contrary effects I refer to can be captioned:

(

New media are old; and old media new. When new media is understood to be fully embedded in history rather than (as when it is facilely said that the internet makes books obsolete) *post*-historical, then it appears to be trickily both before and after its time, both (to borrow from Peter Krapp's analysis) *avant la lettre* and *déjà vu.*[15]

The *déjà vu* haunting of new by old media is clear enough. The description of the World Wide Web as new media, for example, does not survive even an instant's examination before we discover revenants of past media: we "scroll" down web "pages" of "text," "photos," "videos," and so on. McLuhan – and, more recently, Jay David Bolter and Richard Grusin – get a handle on this phenomenon through the idea of "remediation." According to the remediation thesis, the "content" of any new medium is old media, as when McLuhan says that "the content of writing is speech, just as the written word is the content of print, and print is the content of the telegraph" (1994: 8). In the digital age when, as Lev Manovich says, we witness a "second stage of a media society, now concerned as much with accessing and reusing existing media objects as with creating new ones" (2001: 35–6), the remediation thesis is perhaps even more in force even if its concept needs to be updated. The container/content framework was already inadequate in McLuhan's mid-twentieth-century analog milieu, when the formalists made a Klein-bottle out of the form/content distinction. Now it is even more out of kilter in a digital environment that constructs both container and content as "objects" whose being – resident within, but not coincident with, physical being – is constructed relationally as what Matthew G. Kirschenbaum calls "formal materiality."

Just as powerful in recent media studies has been the *avant la lettre* or "back to the future" haunting of old media by new media perspectives. I refer to the conjunction of two of the most influential research approaches in recent media studies. One is "media archaeology" (sometimes called *Schriftlichkeitsgeschichte* and "materialities of communication"), as exemplified in Friedrich Kittler's and Wolf Kittler's post-McLuhan, -Shannon, -Turing, and -von Neumann meditations on early media technologies or philosophies (e.g., gramophone, typewriter); Lisa Gitelman and Geoffrey B. Pingree's collection of essays titled *New Media, 1740–1915*; Wendy Hui Kyong Chun and Thomas Keenan's collection of essays on *New Media Old Media*; William Warner's research into "Enlightenment new media" (e.g., correspondence societies in the American Revolution that bear a resemblance to the internet); Peter Krapp's research into "hypertext *avant la lettre*," Wolfgang Ernst's research; and many other such arche-media projects. The result of the media archaeology approach is that it is now difficult to imagine clicking a typewriter or telegraph key – all the way back, perhaps, to the silhouettes of hands on the cave walls in Chauvet, France – without envisioning a phantom relay connecting all those earlier digital manipulations with what our finger most itches to click now: a web link. Abstracting the logic of recent technology and generalizing it historically, media archaeology encourages us to see old media as beta-releases of computability, digitality, random access, Turing machines, Von Neumann architecture, databases, programming, hypertext, and so on. (Thus *I Ching*, the Oulipo group's writings, William Burrough's "cut-ups," Jorge Luis Borges's "Garden of the Forking Paths," Vannevar Bush's Memex, Ted Nelson's Xanadu, etc., are now stock examples of "pre-hypertext.")

The other research field I mention is "history of the book," which in the aftermath of McLuhan is definitely a branch of media studies on a par with media archaeology. Leading scholars in the field, for example, include Elizabeth L. Eisenstein (whose *The Printing Revolution in Early Modern Europe* explicitly acknowledged the influence of McLuhan), Roger Chartier (who in recent years has increasingly juxtaposed the history of the book to digital developments), and Adrian Johns (whose interest in print "piracy" recently sent him off to Asia to study digital piracy operations).[16] The history of the book field, of course, is about the specificity of the codex. But it is also about the codex as what Walter Ong called the "technologizing" of the word. The book is an early, and now highly advanced, media instrument.

) (

The socio-politics of new media cut both ways. This fact becomes clear when we realize that there is not a single modernization narrative about new media that cannot with equal conviction and evidence be reversed.

In the case of digital media, for example, the early, politically progressive narrative of the BBS, personal-computer, and internet cyberlibertarians (repeated today by Web 2.0 wiki-utopians) was that centralized or hierarchical information systems would cede irresistibly to hypertextuality, interactivity, peer-to-peer, and – to cite the Web 2.0 slogans – "open source" and "collective intelligence."

But in today's time of governmental and corporate information monitoring, of course, the reverse tale is just as persuasive and equally (post)modern. In my *Laws of Cool*, I named this contrary narrative "distributed centralization," as witnessed in "the implantation of dynamic packet-filtering firewalls, ever more complex permission levels, increasingly rigorous (and encrypted) login processes, burgeoning access logs that track users by IP number or domain name, proliferating spyware and monitoring programs, and innumerable other presence-points of control and accountability scattered throughout the lateral network" (Liu 2004: 148). Such neo-authoritarian protocols are "lite" – as when Web 2.0 proponents speak of "lightweight program-ming models" such as PHP, AJAX, and other duct-tape methods that do no more than combine proprietary data systems into bricolage "mashups" making users feel they are masters of their domain. But it is like Gulliver tied down by the light, distributed threads of the Lilliputians. Leaving aside the heavies that still exist (e.g., the US National Security Agency), today's Lilliputians are the people of "standards." Open source, for example, is all about democracy, except when it is about code-correctness or design-correctness. Pity the author of an ad hoc website or blog who inserts hand-crafted source code in an open-source environment, only to run up against code puritans who say, "Thou shalt not transgress against XHTML and CSS."[17] As Jaron Lanier has put it in extreme form in his critique of the total Web 2.0 mind set ("Digital Maoism: The Hazards of the New Online Collectivism"): "history has shown us again and again that a hive mind is a cruel idiot when it runs on autopilot. Nasty hive mind outbursts have been flavored Maoist, Fascist, and religious."

) (

The subjective experience of new media is profoundly reversible. By way of shorthand (an apt metaphor), I will settle on an aspect of this issue that may be called the paradox of "notation versus presentation" – one of the deepest problems in media theory.

"Notation" denotes experiencing new media as a kind of script or programming language that needs to be mentally decoded. "Presentation" means rendering the script intuitively or immediately. Wittgenstein formulates the problem as follows (in a passage that Mitchell discusses at length in his *Iconology*):

> At first sight a proposition – one set out on the printed page, for example – does not seem to be a picture of the reality with which it is concerned. But neither do written notes seem at first sight to be a picture of a piece of music, nor our phonetic notation (the alphabet) to be a picture of our speech. And yet these sign languages prove to be pictures, even in the ordinary sense, of what they represent.[18]

How is it, for example, that sight-reading changed historically from a mental-contortionist's act of translating alphabetic characters into oral performance to *being* the experience of the text? (As James J. O'Donnell puts it, "the manuscript was first conceived to be no more than a prompt-script for the spoken work, a place to look to find out what to say. The arrangement of words on the page, without punctuation or word division, was as user-hostile as DOS could ever hope to be, and was meant for the technician, who knew how to use it to produce the audible word" [1998: 54].) How did proficient telegraph and punch-card operators later make the transition from deciphering abstract patterns of dot-and-dash sounds or holes to directly understanding those patterns?[19] And in our current milieu: how will we ever change from clumsy searching, sampling, and text- or data-mining to directly grokking the data patterns (e.g., through new interfaces or visual-verbal representations)?

There are no easy answers to such questions, only better or worse descriptions of the problem. McLuhan himself tended merely to assert that new media impinge directly on the sensorium as an "extension of man" (rather than, for example, a Nam June Paik video installation offering a decoding of TV culture). The post-McLuhan media archaeology and history of book movements I mentioned are far more historically detailed, but in the end no less descriptive. The great quest in the landmark works of Eisenstein, Chartier, Johns, and (most recently) William St. Clair, therefore, is to describe how a strange alphabetic-mechanical notation system became not just knowledge but "print culture" and print "mentality" – that is, part of core social and individual experience. Reading these works, one is struck by the mismatch between the intimate goal of the quest – no less than to get inside the head of media experience – and the remoteness of the available historical or statistical observational methods. It is like recent astronomers telling us about planets around distant stars: no one can see them, but we infer their presence through complex calculations upon intricate meshes of indirect data (representing, for example, the slight wobble of a star). Even the nuanced models and software that psycholinguists and cognitive psychologists (the astronomers of the human mind) have developed to discern which texts appear "coherent" as opposed to complexly coded are in the end primarily descriptive (as in the case of the influential Coh-Metrix project). In all these approaches, we run up against the fact that beyond a certain point humans are still black boxes.

But instead of an explanation, media studies has a counter-description or counter-narrative. Educators call this reverse tale full "literacy" and postindustrial businesses call it "knowledge work," both of which concepts require users not just to render notation into presentation but the exact reverse: *to return presentation to the status of notation that can be thought about off-line, analyzed, manipulated, and otherwise actively or critically engaged.* While grade-school literacy means learning to read fluently, therefore, advanced literacy means learning to read analytically by mentally annotating, or otherwise reverse-engineering, presentation. The same applies mutatis mutandis to electronic and digital media. The Institute for Multimedia Literacy at the University of Southern California, for example, takes as its mission expanding "the notion of literacy to include learning how to author and analyze visual, aural, dynamic, and interactive media."[20]

Of course, if the gestalt shift to presentation is a mystery, then the return to notation is too. Yet it is happening around us all the time – as when bloggers and wikiers learn not just to <em>*envision*</em> but <em debug</em> the code that makes the Web go.

<p style="text-align:center">) }</p>

So what is a good story about encountering new media?

While the "narrative" trope has thus far served us well, the very direction – or, rather, multiple directions – in which I have taken it mean that we may now need to expand upon the concept. I led off by suggesting that "there are more and less capable imaginations of the new media encounter moment." In the end, *imagination* is a more capacious term than *narrative* for what is involved. For, if my propositions are correct, then it follows that the best stories of new media encounter – emergent from messy, reversible entanglements with history, socio-politics, and subjectivity – do not go from beginning to end, and so are not really stories at all. To recur to the "media ecology" trope cited earlier, good narratives of new media encounter are in the end less stories than whole imaginative environments or, as I termed them, borderlands of surmise. Good accounts of new media encounter imagine affordances and configurations of potentiality. We don't want a good story of new media with a punch line giving somebody the last word. We want a good *world* of new media that gives everyone at least one first word (as in "folksonomical" tagging systems). We want a way of imagining our encounter with new media that surprises us out of the "us" we thought we knew.

Thus the mandate of the Blackwell *Companion to Digital Literary Studies* is clear. Its goal is to tell a good story of new media encounter that has the maturity of a good world of messy, reversible, and imaginative possibilities. To do so, the volume has really just one trick to play – but what a powerful Coyote or Crow trick it is. The trick is to play the "old" and "new," "codex" and "digital," and "literary" and "informational" off each other in ways that thwart any facile modernization narrative and foster surprising recognitions about the scholarly and cultural potential of new media.

The *Companion* therefore starts off with a section on "Traditions" *before* it proceeds to sections on "Textualities" and "Methodologies." This means that everything is first of all staked on staging the encounter between literary studies and computing in a tricky, shared contact zone called "tradition," which – contrary to the usual connotation of the term – is a *pagus* full of surprises. Literary studies and computing bump up against each other in a common genealogy of mediated experience – bookish, online, or otherwise – that shuttles uncannily between old and new. In the first section of the volume, for example, Matthew Steggle discusses not just digital scholarship in Renaissance and seventeenth-century literary studies (methods that extend the uniquely information-intensive activities of print and microfilm-based cataloguing, bibliography-making, textual scholarship, and so on that had attended this field through much of the twentieth century) but also the emergence of a new "Renaissance information" approach that sees the early modern era as itself a precursor information revolution (the time of *The Renaissance Computer*, as the title of one precedent-setting volume of essays he cites would have it). John Walsh similarly frames digital scholarship in the Romantic and Victorian fields within the hypothesis of a special, elective affinity between the industrial nineteenth century and postindustrial contemporaneity. Not only did both periods witness rapid social, economic, political, and cultural upheaval, but both required "ever more sophisticated and flexible technologies for representing and managing . . . information" to drive and witness such change. "The Child is father of the Man," Walsh says, "the nineteenth century and the industrial revolution are in large part the parents of the digital age." And to jump to Chapter 11 of the volume, Johanna Drucker's article on "THE VIRTUAL CODEX FROM PAGE SPACE TO E-SPACE" sends us back to the future by asserting that digital new media invite us to reconsider – and, perhaps for the first time, really understand – how the traditional print codex actually works. Far from being an inert material or formal construct that "*is*," the codex was always a "program" that "*does*" and "*works*"; and it is such functional dynamism that new electronic reading environments should take as their baseline for extending, augmenting, and varying the history of the book. The book is the parent of the program.

The payoff from refusing to foreclose the negotiation between the old and new is that the volume throughout provides plenty of surmise about the possibilities that emerge from the encounter zone. The essay by Gregory Crane et al. thus imagines an "ePhilology" that would reapproach classical literature through "documents that learn from each other... learn from their audiences... and adapt themselves to their users" so as to create "a dynamic space for intellectual life as different from what precedes it as oral culture differs from a world of writing" (the latter analogy, we recognize, constituting a whole narrative of new media encounter in miniature). Stephen Ramsay envisions a new mode of "algorithmic criticism" able to convene computational techniques and literary works not just to enumerate properties in a scientific way but to be a "methodological project of *inventio*," a way of defamiliarizing works and corpuses, unfolding new "interpretive possibilities," and furthering the "radical transformation" necessary to any truly critical reading. Keeping to the key of surmise, he concludes, "It is not that such matters as redemptive world views and Marxist readings of texts can be arrived at algorithmically, but simply that algorithmic transformation can provide the alternative visions that give rise to such readings." Similarly, Willard McCarty outlines the alternative visions that digital methods might offer the humanities through access to an exploratory research paradigm previously more at home in the natural sciences: "modeling." Computation, he argues, can create models of literary discourse that have the phenomenological status of "models of" rather than "for" – where the suspensive, open-ended syntax of "model of" (seeming almost to look out over a Keatsian sea or Wordsworthian mood of "possible sublimity") precisely captures the air of surmise.

Inspired by such surmise, many other essays in this volume offer look-over-the-hill scouting reports about specific new computational algorithms, protocols, forms, and principles. On the side closer to computation as such (algorithms, protocols), essays by Marc Bragdon et al., James Cummings, David Hoover, Ian Lancashire, Bill Winder, and Christian Wittern provide rich discussions of topics related to automated text processing, quantitative analysis, text generation, encoding, markup, and so on: in essence a handbook of some of the most essential areas of computational research in the humanities. As pertains to forms, Bertrand Gervais, Carolyn Guertin, and Dirk Van Hulle study "hypertext" as it developed from what Belinda Barnet and Darren Tofts call an "image of potentiality" surmised by the early pioneers Vannevar Bush, Douglas Engelbart, and Ted Nelson. Guertin focuses on the "postnarrative" narratives that have arisen from such hypertext and other digital forms. In the same narrative vein, Nick Montfort studies the genre of interactive fiction, and Marie-Laure Ryan scales up the concept of digital fiction to "world building." Beyond narrative,

Christopher Funkhouser surveys the variety of digital poetry, while David Z. Saltz considers the new use of digital technology in performance. And then there are the new, born-digital genres: Aimée Morrison studies the blog, for example, and Andrew Mactavish considers not just digital gaming but the distinctive new imaginative genre of game "modding" or community-based game modification. Finally, no inventory of digital literary forms would be complete without mentioning the "electronic edition" and today's print/digital research "library." In the essays of Ken Price and Sayeed Choudhury/David Seaman, respectively, the edition and the library come alive as new media forms in their own right as rich with creative possibility as any of the genres listed above.

And to close on the side closer to what I above called "principles": several contributors probe the fundamental principles of digital computation as they drive the entire ferment of algorithms, protocols, and forms. John Lavagnino, for instance, discusses the complex relation between the orders of the "digital" and "analog"; while Noah Wardrip-Fruin looks closely at James Meehan's 1976 story-generation program, *Tale-Spin*, to theorize expansively about the "interplay" between a digital work's "surface, data, and process" that at last expresses its undergirding "logic of operations" and so its overall world view, ethos, or meaning (in this case, a world view of "planning" that exceeds the status of computational method per se). Digital literature, Wardrip-Fruin argues, is "expressive processing." Thus the surmise continues.[21]

What is the ultimate surmise prepared for by the Blackwell *Companion to Digital Literary Studies*? It is the imaginative surmise that all people today who both love *literature* and practice *new media* (or vice versa) attempt. Here we at last come to the most specific mission of this volume, which is not to explore the general encounter with digital new media but, in particular, the encounter of literary studies with digital new media. How can literature be digital? And how can the digital (the home territory, after all, of office files, databases, and spreadsheets as well as mass entertainment special effects) be literary? Does literature really have a future in a new media ecology where the fiercest, deepest, and most meaningful identity tales of our young people seem to be beholden to iPods and other I-media of music, video, chat, and blogs?

These questions also have no easy answer. I wrote a whole book recently that started out by aiming for an answer, only to be diverted into studying the proto-aesthetic of information "cool" from which, I hypothesized, any understanding of information answerable to my old love, literature, must eventually come. In lieu of an answer, let me here conclude simply by being clear about the immense stakes involved in the mission of the present volume, which, as I suggested, is not just to narrate but to prepare to imagine.

Let me tell an open-ended story. Once upon a time, "literature" in the general sense of "letters" was the darling of the great new medium of its time, writing, which – like any medium – organized and served as the interface between new technological, communicational, and computational protocols. Technologically, the protocol was the print codex and related forms (previously, the manuscript). Communicationally, it was rhetoric adapted to new graphic layouts. And computationally, it consisted of new logical processing apparatuses such as tables of contents, chapter or section titles, indexes, and so on that ramified classically mnemonic, analytical, and rhetorical routines (e.g., "my first point is … my second point is") into unsuspected new processing methods (including search, rapid random access, comparative reading of the Gospels, etc.). By the time "literature" was honed into its narrower, modern sense of aesthetic discourse, it was the operator of an advanced technological, communicational, and computational medium that was rapidly being extended via lithography, photography, and other means into a fully modern media mix.

But that fuller media sphere was also a problem for literature. In successive stages between the 1920s and 1970s, literature and literary studies – provoked in part by competition with the new audiovisual media apparatuses – assumed difficult avant-garde, formalist, structuralist, and poststructuralist avatars that at once stood off from info-media ("heresy of paraphrase," Cleanth Brooks called it) and assimilated its mind set.[22] Close reading in the Joycean, New Critical, structuralist, or post-structuralist manners was thus not exactly the same as modern technology, communication, or computation, where "not exactly the same" was its pride of aesthetic difference. But it had features of all these in unsettling ways. Cutting literature off from the old, high transcendental truths (located in the divine or the romantic self), these movements sequestered literariness in a peculiarly modern, academic, or know-ledge-work version of rhetoric and logic. Literature became a self-contained "form" whose internally programmed complexity had to be "closely read" with technical attention.[23]

Today, "digital" is the great new medium, and – as the modern to postmodern lineage outlined above anticipated – literature is certainly not its darling. The star today is "media" in a larger and more promiscuous sense that intermixes literature (when it includes it at all) with music, film, TV, animation, journalism, and so on to concoct an evolutionary stew of hot bits fighting against, and with, each other to create the new media ecology. Not coincidentally, therefore, *new media studies* is the title that in the academy has now won more general cultural and theoretical cachet than such narrower phrases rooted in specific disciplines as "digital humanities," "humanities computing," "electronic arts," "electronic literature," and "computer-mediated communications."[24] *New media* is the concept under which we now organize and interface with the current configuration of technology, communication, and computation. It is shorthand, for example, for technological innovations at the hardware and software levels; new communication paradigms (as studied in the social-science field of "computer-mediated communication"); and new computation methods (including data-mining and -generation).

Yet, to keep the story open-ended, all the while the question of imagination has been left open like a vulnerable port in a firewall through which literature might still hack its way. Of course, "imagination" is a distinctively romantic phrasing. (The Aeolian harp that exercised Coleridge's and Percy Shelley's imagination, perhaps, was really a special kind of algorithmic computational instrument on a par with the

Babbage machines and Jacquard looms of the time ancestral to the digital computer.) Let me generalize, therefore, by reaching all the way back to classical literary roots. Let me designate imagination *poiesis*, in the sense of the original concept for blended *technē* and aesthetic "making" (inclusive of narrative, drama, and poetry) generative of surmise. *Poiesis* is not the same as technology, communication, or computation. But it combines all these to imagine the identity tales – tragic, utopian, or messily mixed – that mediate "us" in relation to the others who are part of our generative kernel.[25]

We need today a *poiesis* of digital literary studies able to imagine how old and new literary media together allow us to imagine. In such a poetics, everything old and new is up for grabs again as we negotiate the contact zone between such paired terms as the following:

Writing	Encoding
Reading	Browsing
Publishing	Transmitting
Preservation	Migration
Absorption	Immersion
Mimesis	Modeling
Imagination	Simulation

We thought we knew what "writing" means, but now "encoding" makes us wonder (and vice versa). So, too, "reading" and "browsing" (as well as related activities like searching, data-mining, and data-visualization) destabilize each other. The same applies to all the other pairs in this list, and many others that could be added. The task of studying new media, it might be said, is to help us better to understand what it meant to write, read, and imagine in the past; while, inversely, that of studying old media is to help us appreciate what it now means to encode, browse, simulate, etc. "Digital literary studies" should make that possible.

"We" are always mediated creatures, and as such are fully alive in culture when old and new media – the ancestors and children of our self images – collaborate to allow us to encounter the imagination that we could be other.

NOTES

1 Lisa Gitelman writes in the introduction to her *Always Already New: Media, History, and the Data of Culture*: "new media are less points of epistemic rupture than they are socially embedded sites for the ongoing negotiation of meaning as such. Comparing and contrasting new media thus stand to offer a view of negotiability in itself – a view, that is, of the contested relations of force that determine the pathways by which new media may eventually become old hat" (2006: 6).

2 "Narrative" is here an elastic term whose scope expands or narrows as discussed below.

3 The phrases "control through communication" and "informating" are JoAnne Yates's and Shoshana Zuboff's, respectively.

4 "In other words, I think that the relation between gods and humans is to be thought of in terms of boundaries. And *pagus* always indicates the country, the region.... It is the place where one *compacts* with something else.... It is a place of boundaries. Boundaries are not borders. And the relation with the gods, including the pragmatic relation of discourses, does not obey a pragmatics of border to border, between the two perfectly defined blocks or two armies, or two verbal sets, confronting each other. On the contrary, it is a place of ceaseless negotiations and ruses. Which means that there is no reference by which to judge the opponent's strength; one does not know if s/he is a god or a human. It is a beggar, but it may be a god, since the other is metamorphic, and one will have to judge therefore by opinion alone, that is, without criteria" (Lyotard and Thébaud 1985: 42–3).

5 The following from Lisa Gitelman and Geoffrey B. Pingree's introduction ("What's New About New Media") to their edited collection, *New Media, 1740–1915*, seems to me very wise: "we might say that new media, when they first emerge, pass through a phase of identity crisis, a crisis precipitated at least by the uncertain status of the given medium in relation to established, known media and their functions. In other words, when new media emerge in a society, their place is at first ill defined, and their ultimate meanings or functions are shaped over time by that society's existing habits of media use (which, of course, derive from experience with other, established media), by shared desires for new uses, and by the slow process of adaptation between the two. The 'crisis' of a new medium will be resolved when the perceptions of the medium, as well as its practical uses, are somehow adapted to existing categories of public understanding about what that medium does for whom and why" (xii). In general, I would be proud if my own present introduction could find a place on the still relatively short shelf of historically reflective works about the meaning of "new media" next to Gitelman and Pingree's thought-provoking introduction. (See also the introduction go Gitelman's more recent monograph, *Always*

Already New: Media, History, and the Data of Culture.)

6 The notion of "media ecology" is now of increasingly broad provenance. I am aided in particular by Ronald J. Deibert; Matthew Fuller; and Bonnie A. Nardi and Vicki L. O'Day.

7 Also apropos is Jerome McGann's notion of "deformance," according to which technological apparatuses or Oulipo-like textual constraints can expose surprising, hidden logics in the processing of old by new media technologies (especially the chapter in *Radiant Textuality* on "Rethinking Textuality" as well as the chapter co-written with Lisa Samuels on "Deformance and Interpretation").

8 McLuhan fairly consistently respected the usage difference between "medium" (singular) and "media" (plural). It appears that sometime in the 1960s the singular usage of "media" gained currency. (The OED cites Kingsley Amis observing the singular usage of "media" in 1966.) It may be that the word blurred between plural and singular at roughly the time it came to designate, or discover, a *general* concept as opposed to discrete media forms. It is cognate, in other words, with the recognition of "media culture," "media theory," and so on. Something of a similar pattern appears to apply to the word "data," now commonly also blurred between plural and singular usages.

9 I several times in this essay invoke the concept of "Web 2.0," which came into vogue in digerati and information technology circles after 2005. Tim O' Reilly's "What is Web 2.0" (and the conferences that led up to it) was especially influential in putting the term into play.

10 McLuhan and Fiore 1967: 40–1.

11 Lisa Gitelman's characteristic word for this is "muddy" – e.g.:

"media are unique and complicated historical subjects. Their histories must be social and cultural, not the stories of how one technology leads to another, or of isolated geniuses working their magic on the world. Any full accounting will require, as William Ulricchio puts it, 'an embrace of multiplicity, complexity and even contradiction if sense to be made of such' pervasive and dynamic cultural phenomena.

Defining media this way admittedly keeps things muddy" (Gitelman 2006: 7).

12 In less formal studies, it may be added, the messiness of media change tends to come out more accidentally. It is very bizarre, for example, that McLuhan's "The Medium is the Message" contains a sustained sequence of strained analogies between electronic media and Shakespeare passages, including a comparison of the light that breaks through Juliet's window to television (1994: 9–10). Such symptoms are an indicator that the break between old and new media is not clean, that there is instead a linkage, but that the linkage cannot be fully rationalized. In this case, the accident that McLuhan happened to start as a scholar of English Renaissance literature stands in haphazardly for the deeper historical, social, and other continuities that link the rise of print to the rise of electronic media.

13 For a list of such Derridaean trickster philosophemes or "undecidables," see Derrida 1981: 43.

14 For Lévi-Strauss on Oedipus, see Lévi-Strauss 1963.

15 I borrow these terms from Krapp, but without the full complexity with which he develops them (especially *déjà vu*).

16 Since writing his *The Nature of the Book*, Adrian Johns has researched contemporary media piracy in preparation for his next project on the history of intellectual piracy from the invention of printing to the internet. Johns has just completed the manuscript for his book entitled *Piracy: Creativity, Commerce, and Crime from the Invention of Print to the Internet*, which includes a chapter on "Gutenberg and the Samurai" (personal communication from Johns).

17 Based on much personal experience, which will not be documented here.

18 *Tractatus*, 4.01; quoted in Mitchell 1986: 20. Cf., Johanna Drucker and Jerome McGann's "Images as the Text: Pictographs and Pictographic Logic": "The signs [in such invented pictographic systems as those of Joachim Becher and Bishop John Wilkins] were a code of a code, too complex for easy reading, too reductive to carry the semantic richness of ordinary language or the pictorial repleteness of visual images."

19 I borrow this observation from Kirschenbaum, MS, p. 44.

20 For a review of research literature on digital, online, and multimedia literacy, see Monica Bulger's research paper for the University of California Transliteracies Project on online reading practices (Bulger 2006).

21 I have mentioned most, but not all of the contributors to this volume in the discussion above. Omissions are purely an artifact of the need to capture a kind of "lossy," reduced-information image of the volume as a whole not redundant with the volume's table of contents. Even the shape of my image, of course, is rough; other possible thumbnail sketches of the content of this volume would emphasize a different subset of the many contributors.

22 I discuss the explicit aversion of Brooks to information and media in Liu 2005.

23 On the relation between formalist close reading and the technical, see Liu 1994: 401–2 n. 14.

24 On the emergence and fortunes of the term "new media," see Wendy Hui Kyong Chun's introduction ("Did Somebody Say New Media?") to Chun and Keenan.

25 See Liu 2003 and Liu 2006 for discussion of *poiesis*, *technē*, and the humanities as a technical profession.

References and Further Reading

Aristotle (1958). *The Poetics*. In *On Poetry and Style: Aristotle* (G. M. A. Grube, Trans.). Indianapolis: Bobbs-Merrill, pp. 400–6.

Augustine (1961). *Confessions*. (R. S. Pine-Coffin, Trans.). Harmondsworth, Middlesex, England: Penguin.

Bolter, J. D., and R. Grusin (1999). *Remediation: Understanding New Media*. Cambridge, MA: MIT Press.

Braudel, F. (1980). *On History* (S. Matthews, Trans.). Chicago: University of Chicago Press (Original work published 1969).

Bulger, Monica (2006). "Beyond Search: A Preliminary Skill Set for Online Literacy." September 8. Transliteracies Project, University of California. <http://transliteracies.english.ucsb.edu/post/research-project/research-clearinghouse-individual/research-papers/beyond-search-a-preliminary-skill-set-for-online-literacy>. Accessed September 9, 2006.

Chartier, R. (1993). "Libraries without Walls." *Representations* 42 (Spring 1993): 38–52.

—— (1995). *Forms and Meanings: Texts, Performances, and Audiences from Codex to Computer*. Philadelphia: University of Pennsylvania Press.

Chun, W. (2003). "Orienting Orientalism, or How to Map Cyberspace." In R. C. Lee and S. C. Wong (Eds.). *Asian America.net: Ethnicity, Nationalism, and Cyberculture*. New York: Routledge, pp. 3–36.

——, and T. Keenan (Eds.) (2006). *New Media Old Media: A History and Theory Reader*. New York: Routledge.

Cixous, H. (1998). "The Laugh of the Medusa" (K. Cohen and P. Cohen, Trans.). In D. H. Richter (Ed.). *The Critical Tradition: Classic Texts and Contemporary Trends*, 2nd edn. Boston: Bedford, pp. 1454–66 (Original work published 1975).

Clanchy, M. T. (1993). *From Memory to Written Record, England 1066–1307*, 2nd edn. Oxford: Blackwell.

Coh-Metrix Project. Home Page. Department of Psychology, University of Memphis. <http://cohmetrix.memphis.edu/cohmetrixpr/>. Accessed September 9, 2006.

Deibert, R. J. (1997). "Medium Theory, Ecological Holism, and the Study of World Order Transformation." In R. J. Deibert, *Parchment, Printing, and Hypermedia: Communication in World Order Transformation*. New York: Columbia University Press, pp. 17–44.

Derrida, J. (1976). *Of Grammatology* (G. C. Spivak, Trans.). Baltimore: Johns Hopkins University Press (Original work published 1967).

—— (1981). *Positions* (A. Bass, Trans.). Chicago: University of Chicago Press (Original work published 1972).

Drucker, J., and J. McGann (n.d.). "Images as the Text: Pictographs and Pictographic Logic." Institute for Advanced Technology in the Humanities, University of Virginia. <http://www.iath.virginia.edu/%7Ejjm2f/old/pictograph.html>. Accessed September 9, 2006.

Eisenstein, E. L. (1983). *The Printing Revolution in Early Modern Europe*. Cambridge: Cambridge University Press.

Ernst, W. (2000). *M.edium F.oucault: Weimarer Vorlesungen über Archive, Archäologie, Monumente und Medien*. Weimar: Verlag and Datenbank für Geisteswissenschaften.

Freud, S. (1958). "The 'Uncanny.'" In B. Nelson (Ed.). *On Creativity and the Unconscious: Papers on the Psychology of Art, Literature, Love, Religion*. New York: Harper and Row, pp. 122–61.

Fukuyama, F. (1989). "The End of History?" *The National Interest* 16 (Summer): 3–18.

Fuller, M. (2005). *Media Ecologies: Materialist Energies in Art and Technoculture*. Cambridge, MA: MIT Press.

Gitelman, L. (2006). *Always Already New: Media, History, and the Data of Culture*. Cambridge, MA: MIT Press.

——, and G. B. Pingree (Eds.) (2003). *New Media, 1740–1915*. Cambridge, MA: MIT Press.

González, J. (2000). "The Appended Subject: Race and Identity as Digital Assemblage." In B. E. Kolko, et al. (Eds.). *Race in Cyberspace*. New York and London: Routledge, pp. 27–50.

Institute for Multimedia Literacy. "About Us." <http://iml.usc.edu/html/about_us/>. Accessed September 9, 2006.

Jameson, F. (1983). "Postmodernism and Consumer Society." In H. Foster (Ed.). *The Anti-Aesthetic: Essays on Postmodern Culture*. Rpt. New York: New Press, 1998, pp. 111–25.

Johns, A. (1998). *The Nature of the Book: Print and Knowledge in the Making*. Chicago: University of Chicago Press.

Kirschenbaum, M. G. (forthcoming). *Mechanisms: New Media and Forensic Imagination*. Cambridge, MA: MIT Press.

Kittler, F. A. (1990). *Discourse Networks, 1800/ 1900* (M. Metteer with C. Cullens, Trans.). Stanford: Stanford University Press (Original work published 1985).

—— (1999). *Gramophone, Film, Typewriter* (G. Winthrop-Young and M. Wutz, Trans.). Stanford: Stanford University Press (Original work published 1986).

Kittler, W. (1990). "Schreibmaschinen, Sprechmaschinen: Effekte technischer Medien im Werk Franz Kafkas." In W. Kittler and G. Neumann (Eds.). *Franz Kafka: Schriftverkehr.* Freiburg: Rombach, pp. 75–163.

Krapp, P. (2004). *Déjà Vu: Aberrations of Cultural Memory.* Minneapolis: University of Minnesota Press.

—— (2006). "Hypertext *avant la lettre.*" In W. Chun and T. Keenan (Eds.). *Old Media, New Media: A History and Theory Reader.* London: Routledge, pp. 357–71.

Lanier, Jaron (2006). "Digital Maoism: The Hazards of the New Online Collectivism." *Edge.* Edge Foundation, Inc. 30 May. <http:// www.edge.org/3rd_culture/lanier06/lanier06_ index.html>. Accessed September 9, 2006.

Lévi-Strauss, C. (1963). "The Structural Study of Myth." In *Structural Anthropology* (C. Jacobson and B. G. Schoepf, Trans.). New York: Basic Books, pp. 206–31 (Original book published 1958).

—— (1973). *Tristes tropiques* (J. and D. Weightman, Trans.). New York: Washington Square (Original work published 1955).

Liu, A. (2003). "Sidney's Technology: A Critique by Technology of Literary History." In C. Jacobs and H. Sussman (Eds.). *Acts of Narrative.* Stanford: Stanford   University   Press, pp. 174–94.

—— (2004). *The Laws of Cool: Knowledge Work and the Culture of Information.* Chicago: University of Chicago Press.

—— (2005). "Understanding Knowledge Work." *Criticism* 47: 249–60.

—— (2006). "The Humanities: A Technical Profession." In M. Hanrahan and D. L. Madsen (Eds.). *Teaching, Technology, Textuality: Approaches to New Media.* Houndmills, Basingstoke,   Hampshire: Palgrave   Macmillan, pp. 11–26.

Lyotard, J.-F., and J.-L. Thébaud (1985). *Just Gaming* (W. Godzich, Trans.). Minneapolis: University of Minnesota Press (Original work published 1979).

Manovich, L. (2001). *The Language of New Media.* Cambridge, MA: MIT Press.

McGann, J. (2001). *Radiant Textuality: Literature after the World Wide Web.* New York: Palgrave.

McLuhan, M. (1994). "The Medium is the Message." In M. McLuhan, *Understanding Media: The Extensions of Man.* Cambridge, MA: MIT Press, pp. 7–21.

——, and Q. Fiore (1967). *The Medium is the Massage.* Rpt. New York: Touchstone, 1989.

Mitchell, W. J. T. (1986). *Iconology: Image, Text, Ideology.* Chicago: University of Chicago Press.

—— (2002). "Showing Seeing: A Critique of Visual Culture." In N. Mirzoeff (Ed.). *The Visual Culture Reader,* 2nd edn. London: Routledge, pp. 86–101.

Nakamura, L. (2002). *Cybertypes: Race, Ethnicity, and Identity on the Internet.* New York: Routledge.

Nardi, B. A., and V. L. O'Day (1999). *Information Ecologies: Using Technology with Heart.* Cambridge, MA: MIT Press.

O'Donnell, J. J. (1998). *Avatars of the Word: From Papyrus to Cyberspace.* Cambridge, MA: Harvard University Press.

Ong, W. J. (1982). *Orality and Literacy: The Technologizing of the Word.* London: Methuen.

O'Reilly, T. (2005). "What is Web 2.0: Design Patterns and Business Models for the Next Generation of Software." September 30, 2005. O'Reilly Media, Inc. <http://www.oreillynet. com/pub/a/oreilly/tim/news/2005/09/30/what- is-web-20.html>. Accessed September 8, 2006.

Plato (2005). *Phaedrus.* In *The Dialogues of Plato* (B. Jowett, Trans.). Oxford: Clarendon, 1892. Excerpted in H. Adams and L. Searle (Eds.). *Critical Theory since Plato,* 3rd edn. Belmont, CA: Thomson Wadsworth, pp. 36–8.

Schumpeter, J. A. (1942). *Capitalism, Socialism and Democracy.* Rpt. New York: Harper and Row, 1975.

St. Clair, William (2004). *The Reading Nation in the Romantic Period.* Cambridge: Cambridge University Press.

Warner, W. B. (2005). "Communicating Liberty: The Newspapers of the British Empire as a Matrix for the American Revolution." *ELH* 72: 339–61.

Williams, R. (1977). *Marxism and Literature*. New York: Oxford University Press.

Yates, J. (1989). *Control Through Communication: The Rise of System in American Management*. Baltimore: Johns Hopkins University Press.

Zuboff, S. (1988). *In the Age of the Smart Machine: The Future of Work and Power*. New York: Basic Books.

Part II
Traditions

2
ePhilology: When the Books Talk to Their Readers[1]

Gregory Crane, David Bamman, and Alison Jones

Writing, Phaedrus, has this strange quality, and is very like painting; for the creatures of painting stand like living beings, but if one asks them a question, they preserve a solemn silence. And so it is with written words; you might think they spoke as if they had intelligence, but if you question them, wishing to know about their sayings, they always say only one and the same thing. (Plato, *Phaedrus* 275d)

Introduction

This chapter suggests directions in which an ePhilology may evolve. Philology here implies that language and literature are the objects of study but assumes that language and literature must draw upon the full cultural context and thus sees in philological analysis a starting point for the *scientia totius antiquitatis* – the systematic study of all ancient culture. The term ePhilology implicitly states that, while our strategic goal may remain the *scientia totius antiquitatis*, the practices whereby we pursue this strategic goal must evolve into something qualitatively different from the practices of the past.

Digital technology is hardly new in classics: there are full professors today who have always searched large bodies of Greek and Latin, composed their ideas in an electronic form, found secondary sources online and opportunistically exploited whatever digital tools served their purposes.[2] Nevertheless, the inertia of prior practice has preserved intact the forms that evolved to exploit the strengths and minimize the weaknesses of print culture: we create documents that slavishly mimic their print predecessors; we send these documents to the same kinds of journals and publishers;[3] our reference works and editions have already begun to drift out of date before they are published and stagnate thereafter; even when new, our publications are static and cannot adapt themselves to the needs of their varying users; while a growing, global audience could now find the results of our work, we embed our ideas in specialized language and behind subscription barriers which perpetuate into the twenty-first century the miniscule audiences of the twentieth.[4]

This chapter makes two fundamental arguments. First, it assumes that the first generation of digital technology has only laid the groundwork for substantive change in classics and the humanities. Second, it advances arguments about what form an optimal digital future should assume. While Greek and Latin provide the focus for this chapter, the arguments apply in various ways to many areas within the humanities.

At least six features distinguish emerging digital resources: (1) they can be delivered to any point on the earth and at any time; (2) they can be fundamentally hypertextual, supporting comprehensive links between assertions and their evidence; (3) they dynamically recombine small, well-defined units of information to serve particular people at particular times; (4) they learn on their own and apply as many automated processes as possible, not only automatic indexing but morphological and syntactic analysis, named entity recognition, knowledge extraction, machine translation, etc., with changes in automatically generated results tracked over time; (5) they learn from their human readers and can make effective use of contributions, explicit and implicit, from a range of users in real time; (6) they automatically adapt themselves to the general background and current purposes of their users.

Print culture gave us expensive distribution by which we could send static documents to a few thousand restricted locations. If we can deliver information to any point on the earth and we can tailor that information to the varying backgrounds and immediate purposes of many people, we can thus address audiences far beyond the physical and, indeed, cultural limitations which communication – oral and print – has imposed.

In the *Phaedrus*, Plato's Socrates, a fictive rendering of a historical character scratched into life by pen and preserved as a pattern of ink, critiques writing – and thus the very medium in which he exerts a living presence to this day. A generation ago, Derrida famously expanded upon the observation that writing is not so much a cure as a poison for memory[5] – in a look-up culture not only do our memories decay but we lose in some measure that instant and deep recognition which integrated knowledge alone can spark. The critique in the *Phaedrus* is profound and addresses all technologies which represent information abstracted not only from the brain but also from the personal context in which much learning occurs. Plato's arguments have been echoed ever since, consciously or not – many of us in the first generation of a television society heard similar criticisms from our parents and, in turn, directed these to our net-oriented children.[6]

The quote that begins this essay, however, directs a criticism which is just as trenchant but has attracted less attention. All products of information technology – paintings and poems, novels and newspapers, movies and music – have been static since our ancestors first scratched diagrams in the dirt or pressed visions of their world on the walls of caves. Other human hands could add or destroy, but the products of our hands could do nothing but decay, prey to the scorching sun, the worm, or the slow fires of acid within. We can direct our questions to the written word or to the most lifelike painting, but we can expect only silence.

Now, however, we have created cultural products that can respond, systems that can change and adapt themselves to our needs. Millions of people around the world will, on the day that I compose these words, seek directions from a mapping service. Natural language, mathematical formulae, and visual representations of space will interact to generate tailored itineraries, with estimates of time and customizable maps illustrating the journey from one point to another, in some cases speaking their directions in an expanding suite of languages. We should not confuse the humble and well-defined goals of such tools with their significance in the evolution of humanity and indeed life.

The great question that we face is not what we can do but what we want to accomplish. The tools at our disposal today, primitive as they may appear in the future, are already adequate to create a dynamic space for intellectual life as different from what precedes it as oral culture differs from a world of writing. At one level, little will change – the Homeric epics, products of an oral culture ironically preserved in writing, are arguably as successful as cultural products as anything that followed: the ceiling of human creativity has not changed in three thousand years of increasingly sophisticated information technology – an observation that we should consider as we fret over the codex and print.[7]

Nevertheless, we can now plan for a world where ideas cross from language to language and from culture to culture with a speed and authenticity far beyond what we have ever experienced. Consider curious minds in Beijing or Damascus a generation from now who encounter something that sparks their interest in the Greco-Roman world. It could be a film or a popular novel translated into Chinese or Arabic or a game that carries them through a virtual space. It could even be something in their formal education which, as occasionally happens, fires their imagination. The internet as we have it has already increased the chances for such encounters and provided unprecedented opportunities for Beijing and Damascus to learn about ancient Greece and Rome or other cultures.

We can, however, do more. The intellectually alive mind asks about a Greek author, perhaps a widely translated one (such as Homer) or perhaps not. Background information and the text itself are translated into the Chinese or Arabic. The inquirer has developed a profile, not unlike her medical history, which can record the classes she has taken, the books she has read, the movies she has seen, the games she has played, and the questions that she has posed.[8] The personal reading agent can compare this profile, eagerly developed and shared only in part and under strict conditions, against the cultural referents implicit in the author or text of interest, then produce not only translations but personalized briefing materials – maps, timelines, diagrams, simulations, glossary entries – to help that reader contextualize what she has encountered. As the reader begins to ask questions, the system refines its initial hypotheses, quickly adapting itself to her needs.[9] As the system changes, it inspires new kinds of inquiry in the reader, creating a feedback loop that encourages their conversation to evolve.

Far from the static and one-sided interaction of Plato's complaint, this is the definition of dialectic.

As this chapter will suggest, we already possess the technology to build a system of this type that will be effective in many cases: the professional classicist moving into early modern Latin or even tracking developments in his or her own field, with text mining identifying trends in the secondary literature or phenomena in the source texts.[10]

The question that we face is much deeper than the challenge of producing more or, preferably, better articles and monographs. We must more generally ask what kind of space we wish to produce in which to explore the linguistic record of humanity – whether we are contemplating the *Odyssey*, administrative records from Sumer, or tracing mathematical thought through Greek and Arabic sources. More important perhaps than the question of what we can do may be the opportunity to redefine who can do what – to open up intellectual life more broadly than ever before and to create a fertile soil in which humanity can cultivate the life of the mind with greater vigor and joy.

Background

The systematic application of computing technology to classical languages began in 1968, when David Packard had toiled with primitive computing in the basement of Harvard's Science Center to produce a full concordance to Livy. The resulting massive print volumes were both a fundamental new tool and a staple at Harvard University Press remainder sales of the 1970s, illustrating both the potential of even simple electronic tools and the limitations of the codex. Three fundamental developments quickly followed.

First, the *Thesaurus Linguae Graecae* (TLG),[11] founded in 1972, began developing what would be called a digital library of classical Greek literature. A third of a century later, the TLG has completed its initial goal of digitizing all published Greek literature up through AD 600 and has extended its coverage through the Byzantine period and beyond.[12] The TLG thus provided the first digital well-curated collection of digital resources in classics.

Second, David Packard began in the 1970s to develop a system not only to work with collections such as the TLG but to provide the first computerized typesetting and word processing for Greek.[13] At the Boston APA convention of 1979, for example, Packard could show a working Ibycus computer system. Based on a Hewlett-Packard minicomputer, the Ibycus included a unique operating system designed for classics. The Ibycus was, by the standards of the early twenty-first century, astonishingly expensive – it cost tens of thousands of dollars – but it provided scholars with services they needed not only to exploit the TLG but to write and publish. Its contributions were so important that more than a dozen departments raised the necessary capital.

Third, the TLG and Ibycus system were the products of two distinct organizations, thus promoting a separation of data from service providers and opening the way for a range of entrepreneurs to create additional services and solutions.[14] The TLG website lists more than a dozen packages that were developed to work with the CD ROM texts.

A generation later, classicists still depend upon texts and services designed in the 1970s. Figure 2.1 illustrates the results from a sample search of the TLG in May 2006 as suggested on the TLG website. The system reflects decades of investment, both from subscriptions and from grants (e.g., a $235,000 grant in 2000 from the National Endowment for the Humanities that provided partial support for "restructuring of data and development of an online search and retrieval system for the Thesaurus Linguae Graecae."[15]) The resulting in-house system provides a fast, reliable service on which Hellenists depend, especially since the TLG no longer updates its CD ROM and thus does not generally distribute source texts published after the February 2000 TLG E Disk.[16]

It would be hard to overstate the importance of searchable text corpora. Classicists are also fortunate to have access to the Packard Humanities Institute CD ROM for Latin literature, as well as proprietary commercial databases such as the Biblioteca Teubneriana Latina.[17] Classicists have become accustomed to scanning wide swathes of Greek and Latin literature, with full professors today who have never known a

Figure 2.1   TLG Search, May 17, 2006.

world without searchable texts. Many take for granted this core infrastructure and, when asked, admit that these tools have had far more impact upon the questions that they ask and the research that they conduct than they readily articulate. An analysis of primary source citations in the classics journals of JSTOR would give us a better appreciation of the impact which these collections have had upon published scholarship.

In the past thirty years more texts have been added but the essential services and underlying data model visible to the classical community have not changed. The TLG, as it appeared in May 2006, is selected for analysis because it has successfully served, and continues to serve, the field and provides a standard of excellence, in terms of continuity and quality of service, but the analysis offered below applies to many efforts in classics and the humanities. The goal is not to diminish the importance of what TLG and projects like it have contributed but, by describing the state of the art as it existed when this chapter was written, to suggest future movements for classics and the humanities.

- *String based searching*: As this chapter is being written, users do not search for a lexeme (e.g., APODEIKNUMI) but for strings with which to find inflected forms.[18] This reduces precision (the string above would, for example, locate not only forms of the verb APODEIKNUMI but the noun APODECIS) and recall (to locate all forms of the verb one would need to search for other strings, e.g., APEDEC, APODEIKN, APODEIC, APODEXQ, etc.)

  Users need to find many other patterns and we need research and development on a range of searches.[19] Lemmatized searches allow users to query a dictionary entry and identify all known inflected forms. Collocational analysis allows users to find words that co-occur with unusual frequency and thus to uncover idiomatic expressions.[20] Users also need to be able to locate syntactic patterns: e.g., what subjects and objects does a particular verb take? How often does the verb actually take the dative in a given corpus? What adjectives modify particular nouns? They need to search for people and places, identifying not only all Alexanders and Alexandrias but also be able to locate references to the particular Alexander and Alexandria in which they are interested. They should be able to find basic propositional patterns: e.g., at what locations does person X appear within the corpus?[21] They should be able to apply intelligent clustering, automatic summarization, and text mining to searches that produce thousands of results.[22] They should be able to search for secondary sources that talk about directly or are generally relevant to any given passage.

- *Texts are encoded as page surrogates*: Beta code markup tags the speakers in the Euripides search results pictured above. In the Thucydides and Plutarch results, the electronic text faithfully reproduces the line-breaks (including hyphenization) of the print original. Users cannot exploit semantic markup (e.g., search and compare results from the language of Helen and Menelaus in the *Helena* of Euripides, separate results from spoken vs. narrative text in Thucydides). Even the section breaks are only approximately encoded, with section breaks, for example, simply inserted at the start of the line rather than in their proper position.[23] It is not difficult to convert the page layout Beta encoding of the TLG into TEI-compliant SGML or XML,[24] but fuller conversion requires substantial editing with enough human interpretation of the meaning implicit in the page layout for a true XML version to appear as a new edition in its own right. The cost of analyzing and formatting a complex document (such as a play) is comparable to the cost of double-keyed professional data entry.[25]

- *Texts represent only a single, isolated edition*: After consulting with the scholarly community, the TLG chose to encode only the consolidated text, leaving aside variants and providing only a single edition of each author.[26] At the time, the added cost and complexity were determining factors. This initially reluctant measure has become policy: the TLG suppressed older editions, removing them from circulation and replacing them completely.[27] Rather than letting users search both the Murray (which was on the D Disk) and the Diggle edition (which took its place on the E Disk), users received just the one, more recent edition and (to use the TLG's own language) "suppressed" the older editions.[28]

- *Limited interoperability*: The TLG does build in some measure on third party efforts: the TLG can, for example, add links to the open access morphological and lexicographic data at the Perseus Digital Library but there are no clear methods whereby third party systems can interact with the TLG. Even sites that erect subscription barriers around their data do not have to be data silos. The TLG Canon could be distributed, at least in part, via the Open Archives Initiative (OAI), a low-barrier approach well suited to distributing cataloguing data.[29] This would allow pointers to TLG texts to appear in library catalogues and for third party searching and text mining to add value to the base data. At a more advanced level, even if the TLG does not choose to distribute its newer texts, it could make search results available via an application programming interface (API) so that subscribing third parties could efficiently analyze the results of searches and/or create custom-ized front ends. The emerging Classical Texts Services protocol[30] would provide a consistent method whereby systems could extract labeled chunks of text – a crucial function as dynamically generated documents emerge.

- *Texts cannot be readily repurposed or circulate freely*: Publishers assert copyright to the editions which they publish. The legality of this claim is by no means clear,[31] and publisher claims represent aspiration rather than settled law – Norton went so far as to claim copyright to the through line numbers in their published facsimile of the First Folio (Hinman 1968) – in fact, a computer program will generate the through line numbers by mechanically counting lines and thus no recognizable "original expression" is in play. Publishers have, however, traditionally charged permission fees for materials that were in the public domain and an exploration of rights and practices would provoke interesting lines of inquiry.[32] The threat of legal action, however frivolous, has exercised a chilling effect upon scholarship. The publishing institutions that exist to facilitate the exchange of ideas thus choke the circulation of primary materials, constrain the fundamental moral right of academic authors to reach the broadest possible audience, and restrict scholarly activity.[33] With no new TLG CD ROMs, an emphasis on a single propriety site, and no interoperability (not even an OAI harvestable version of the TLG Canon), Hellenic studies have, if anything, taken a step backwards.

The limitations described above have been acceptable because they support the practices of print culture. Textual corpora such as the TLG, whether on the web or on CD ROM, are immense, dynamic, flexible concordances. They thus support traditional work but also provide no incentive for innovative forms of publication. The monolithic website isolates classicists from the electronic infrastructure which supports them. If our goal is to produce more and better researched articles and monographs – if we think that the answer to the crisis in academic monographs is to produce more content – then the status quo will serve us well.[34]

The Future in the Present

At this point, we return to the six features that, at least in part, distinguish digital from print publication. While work remains at an early stage of development, progress is being made in all six areas. The following section illustrates these points primarily with work done associated with Perseus for classics, but Perseus and the field of classics are only components of a much larger process.[35]

Global access

Library subscription budgets shield many scholars – especially those at the most prestigious institutions – from the economic realities with which libraries struggle. Many – probably most – do not realize that the scholarly resources – much of it in the public domain – on which they daily rely are available only through expensive subscriptions. Various open access movements have attacked this problem – rarely with support, not infrequently with scorn, from academics: Project Gutenberg began in 1971 (one year before the TLG), hosts a library of 18,000 public domain books and downloads two million of these each month.[36] More recently, Google Library and the Open Content Alliance (OCA) have set out to digitize the entire published record of humanity. Each pursues contrasting rights regimes: Google retains its collection for its proprietary use, while the OCA is building an open source collection: Yahoo and Microsoft are both backing OCA, with each planning to provide its own set of unique services to the shared content. Both Google Library and the OCA are, however, open access – the business models of Google, Yahoo, and Microsoft all depend upon maximizing their audiences.[37] Open access seems to them to be a better engine for revenue generation than subscription models.[38]

Within classics, the Latin Library dramatized the hunger for open-source primary materials. Frustrated by proprietary text corpora, members of the community, most from outside of academia, have spontaneously digitized almost all classical Latin, and a growing body of post-classical Latin literature and made it freely accessible at a single site.[39] It is easy to criticize this work: original scholarship resides along with texts bearing the unnerving label "from an unidentified edition," while other texts combine multiple editions without substantive documentation.[40] The site reflects a widespread and heart-felt desire to assemble a critical mass of freely accessible Latin texts. While professional scholars can criticize some of the texts, we should also ask ourselves why the community felt it necessary to do so much work to establish such a basic service. Were the publications that we composed with proprietary databases a greater contribution to intellectual life than a universally accessible library of primary texts?

From the beginning of its web presence in 1995, Perseus provided open access to all of its holdings not otherwise restricted by third party rights.[41] More recently, members of the community – especially the rising generation of classicists – have argued forcefully that all core materials should be available under an open-source license, allowing third parties to repurpose what we have begun. We have thus moved beyond open access and to open source for all materials to which we have rights. We chose a Creative Commons attribution/share-alike/non-commercial license.[42] Third parties may thus freely create new resources based on what we provide but they must make their additions available under the same terms and they cannot restrict access to these resources behind a subscription barrier. The non-commercial license does not exclude advertising-based revenue and we hope that internet services such as Google, Yahoo, and Microsoft will load everything that we produce into their collections.

Since spring 2005, we have provided a web service that exposes well-formed chunks of our data to third parties. In March 2006, we have made available under a Creative Commons license the TEI-compliant XML files for the Greek and Latin source texts that we have created that were based upon public domain editions: c. 13,000,000 words of text. While this collection is much smaller than the 76,000,000 words on the 2000 TLG E Disk or the 91,000,000 words on the spring 2006 TLG website, it does already contain most of classical Greek and many classical Latin source texts. All of our unencumbered lexica, encyclopedias, commentaries, and other reference materials will follow suit and be released under the same license. Likewise, all components of the new digital library system that underlies Perseus are being written for open source distribution and will, we hope, be integrated into the next generation of digital library systems.

Hypertextual writing

As with access, hypertextual documents depend upon policy – even web links, primitive though they may be, provide a starting point. Classicist Christopher Blackwell has produced what may be the best example of a publication that bridges the gap between traditional print and densely hypertextual web publication. He produced an electronic publication as his tenure book, a website that surveys Athenian democracy.[43] Figure 2.2 illustrates a snapshot of this site. The site includes not only PDF

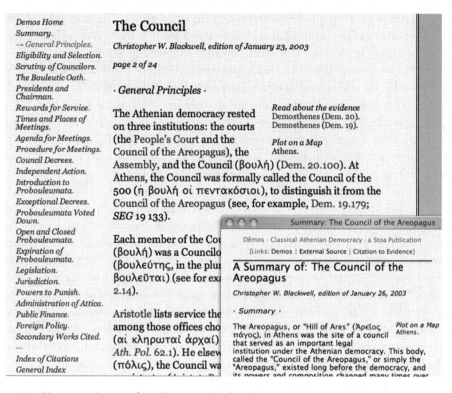

Figure 2.2   Hypertextual writing from Christopher Blackwell's *Demos*, which illustrates a genuine step beyond print monographs.

visualizations of the text optimized for print but also HTML representations of the same documents. The HTML documents contain a dense set of primary source citations that are filtered out of the print-oriented PDF publications. Blackwell has striven to provide the primary source evidence behind every significant assertion. The secondary scholarship on this subject has grown so tangled that many publications simply cite other secondary scholarship, leaving readers to dig through multiple sources before they can assess the underlying evidence. Blackwell's publication assumes the presence of a stable, comprehensive digital library to make the citations actionable links.

Hypertextual writing builds on ubiquitous access to source materials. We can create hypertextual documents with links to subscription-based resources, but in so doing we implicitly define an audience of academics and a handful of committed non-professionals with access to good libraries. Hypertextual writing hidden from the outside world behind subscription barriers cannot, of course, reach beyond academic elites. Dense hypertextual links that are in open-access publications but that point to academic subscription-based sources have no more impact on society as a whole than citations to print-only resources. Only open access publications with links to open-access sources can increase the transparency of what we in the humanities do and engage a broader audience in the intellectual discourse that we pursue.[44]

Aside from the content, Blackwell's work demonstrates the potential of the form and exhibits a scholarly leadership badly needed within the humanities. Had he worked with a conventional academic publisher he might have earned greater conventional prestige, but he would have reached a smaller audience and would probably not have had the freedom to create expository texts so well adapted to the digital environment.

Fine-grained, repurposable digital objects

We need compound documents, dynamically generated to serve particular users at particular times, that draw upon materials from a range of sources to create a new, unified whole.[45] Such documents have two requirements:

- *Rights agreements that provide access to source objects and their constituent parts* (e.g., TEI XML, the measurements underlying a 3D model) rather than their derivatives (e.g., HTML, QuickTime VR). This reflects a simple, but profound, commitment that differs from the rights regimes that predominate in the web.
- *Well-structured source objects*: Access to the digital text of a dictionary does us little good if the text does not mark the headwords and the beginnings and the senses and other components of individual articles.[46] Most SGML/XML documents available online have very simple structures that do not capture crucial data (e.g., the entries in the book index, which allow us to draw on human, rather than machine, decisions as to whether a particular Salamis is part of Athens or Cyprus).[47]

Figure 2.3 illustrates an entry from the Liddell Scott Jones Greek English Lexicon (LSJ 9)[48] Notice that the mention of "Pi. Pae." has not been expanded to a textual form but has been linked instead to an authority list (in this case, the numeration of the TLG Canon[49]) unambiguously stating that "Pi. Pae." denotes Pindar's *Paean odes*. Such links are fundamental as collections grow larger and increasingly ambiguous. The beginnings and ends, not only of the article as a whole but of each sense within it, are clearly marked and each has a unique identifier with which other documents can cite it.

Third parties can dynamically extract well-formed fragments of XML from the Perseus Digital Library, including canonical chunks of source texts, articles from various reference works, as well as the entire contents or individual senses from lexica. Figure 2.4 shows the same article as it appears in <http://www.dendrea.org/>, a third party site separate from the Perseus source collection: because it has access to the XML source, this site has been able to generate services (such as a browser for etymologically related terms, synonyms and antonyms) not available at Perseus.

Documents that learn from each other

The artificial intelligence pioneer Marvin Minsky suggested that the time would come when no one will imagine that the books in a library did not talk with one

```
- <TEI.2>
  - <text>
    - <body>
      - <div0 n="*s111" type="alphabetic letter" org="uniform" sample="complete">
        - <entryFree id="n102117" key="sw/frwn" type="main" opt="n">
            <orth extent="full" lang="greek" opt="n">SW/FRWN</orth>
            ,
          - <gramGrp opt="n">
              <gram type="dialect" opt="n">Ep.</gram>
            </gramGrp>
            and poet.
            <orth extent="full" lang="greek" opt="n">SA^O/FRWN</orth>
            (as in
          - <bibl default="NO">
              <author>Hom.</author>
            </bibl>
            ,
            <abbr>v.</abbr>
            infr.,
          - <bibl n="Perseus:abo:tlg,0033,005:9:46" default="NO">
              <author>Pi.</author>
              <title>Pae.</title>
              <biblScope>9.46</biblScope>
            </bibl>
            ),
            <orth extent="full" lang="greek" opt="n">ONOS</orth>
            ,
            <gen lang="greek" opt="n">O(</gen>
            <foreign lang="greek">, H(</foreign>
            : neut.
            <foreign lang="greek">SW=FRON</foreign>
            :—prop.
          - <sense id="n102117.0" n="A" level="1" opt="n">
              <tr opt="n">of sound mind</tr>
```

Figure 2.3   XML entry from LSJ 9 on the Perseus website.

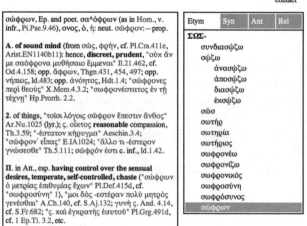

Figure 2.4   LSJ entry from Dendrea website.

another. While Minsky may have envisioned very powerful artificial intelligence spawning conversations between books far beyond what is currently possible, our books are already beginning to converse in simple but substantive ways.[50] Put another way, so much material is already online that only machines can scan more than a tiny fraction of what is available. Smart books are already beginning to appear to provide knowledge-intensive services and offer up more information about themselves than any reader might have thought to ask.

Figures 2.5, 2.6, 2.7, and 2.8 illustrate four dynamically generated views based on the interaction of different books within the Perseus digital collection.

Figure 2.5 is a "basic report" from the Perseus website that lists various translations, editions, commentaries, and other resources about a particular passage of classical Greek – Thucydides' *History of the Peloponnesian War*, Book 1, chapter 86. While it resembles the page of a book, it reflects the fact that many books have been analyzed and relevant sections extracted to create a dynamic view that would be not feasible in print. Different works represent Thucydides as "Th.," "Thuc.," "T.," "Thucyd.," etc., the history as "Hist.," "H.," "Pel. War," etc., and the citation as "I, 86," "I.86," "1,86," "1.86." All of these representations are mapped onto a single canonical reference around which we can then cluster a range of information. When the user calls up one translation, the translation calls out to the library for other translations, Greek editions, commentaries, lexica, grammars, and other reference works which cite words in this passage. The text in focus thus interacts with a range

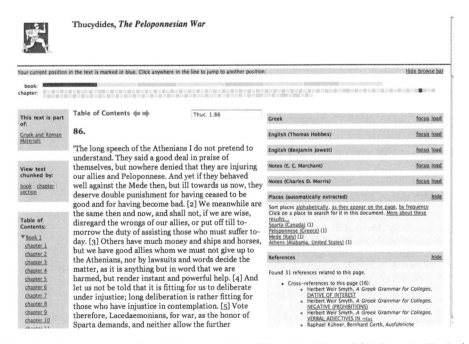

Figure 2.5   Basic report: A user has called up a translation of Thucydides, *History of the Peloponnesian War*, Book 1, chapter 86.

empire	dominion	power	government
office	government	magistrates	people
command	Mindarus	Tissaphernes	Laches
power	Eurystheus	king	Atreus
dominion	power	rule	Hellenes
magistrates	Theseus	people	council
government	power	Hippias	Pharnabazus
ancient	descendants	temples	Pythian
whom	beginning	pits	just
called	Zancle	Pangaeus	originally
Harmodius	originally	basket	Cyclopes
Philip	brother	government	Sitalces

Figure 2.6   Parallel text analysis: word clusters associated with uses of the Greek word *arche* in Thucydides' *History of the Peloponnesian War* (c. 150,000 words) and five English translations. Translation equivalents are underlined.

of other related resources, which align themselves in real time, ready to provide background information or to become themselves the focus of attention.

Figure 2.6 displays the word clusters associated with uses of the Greek word *arche* in Thucydides' *History of the Peloponnesian War* (c. 150,000 words) and five English translations. By comparing the English translations with the source text, the automatic process identified clusters of meaning associated with various Greek words – in effect, creating a rough English/Greek lexicon and semantic network. The clusters capture the senses "empire," "government," "political office," and "beginning." The cluster headed "ancient" (marked in bold) captures a distinct word that happens to share the stem *arch*. Such parallel text analysis can update its results as new translations and source texts appear within the system, providing dynamic conclusions based on interaction of books within the digital library.

Likewise, Figure 2.7 shows the results of automatic named entity identification. In this case, a translation of Thucydides compares its vocabulary to authority lists such as encyclopedias and gazetteers to determine possible names and then uses the context in

```
9 <milestone unit="sentence" n="974" /></seg> </p>
0 <p> <milestone n="108" unit="chapter"/> <milestone unit="section" n="1"/>
0 <seg> <milestone unit="para" ed="P" />About the same time <persName
0 n="Alcibiades,,,,," id="n-0001.0000.00000.01912"
0 reg="mostcommon:Alcibiades,nomatch:0" ><surname>Alcibiades </surname></persName
0 > returned with his <num value="13">thirteen </num> ships from <placeName
0 key="perseus,Caunus" >Caunus</placeName> and <placeName reg= "Phaselis, Antalya
0 Ili, Akdeniz kiyisi" key= "tgn,7002612">Phaselis </placeName> to <placeName
0 key="tgn, 7002673">Samos </placeName>, bringing word that he had prevented the
```

Figure 2.7   Named entity tagging: an XML fragment of Thucydides with all named entities automatically extracted and disambiguated.

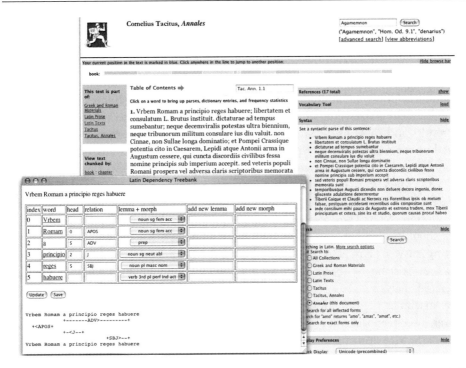

Figure 2.8 A prototype of a basic report of Tacitus' *Annales* where users have the option to see automatically generated syntactic parses of the sentences. Users can contribute to the system by correcting the automatic parse (e.g., *Romam* should not be in apposition to *Vrbem*) and transforming the partial parse into a complete one (here, by assigning tags to *Vrbem* and *habuere*).

other books to resolve ambiguous references in actual text[51] (e.g., does "Salamis" designate the island near Athens, a place in Cyprus or some other location?).

Figure 2.8 shows the results of automatic syntactic parsing. Here a parser assigns tags to words by comparing the current text to other texts that have been syntactically analyzed by hand. By communicating with other texts in this way, the parser can determine the likelihood that a given morphological sequence (e.g., accusative noun, preposition, ablative noun) has a given syntactic parse. In the prototype shown in the figure, only tags with a reasonably high probability are assigned (allowing the system to have higher precision at the expense of greater coverage). If errors arise (as shown at the bottom of the figure, where *Romam* should not modify *Vrbem* as an apposition), users can correct the syntactic dependencies to improve the overall system, providing a valuable feedback mechanism whereby both the user and the text can productively learn from each other.

The figures above thus provide initial examples of books interacting with each other to create new forms of publication. These examples point the way toward increasingly intelligent collections which become more powerful and sophisticated as their size and internal structure improve – the more books communicate with each other, the more information about themselves they can provide.

Documents that learn from their audiences

Documents can learn from each other and drive automated processes to identify people and places in full text, analyze the contents of collections to provide integrated reports drawing on multiple information sources and perform similar tasks to apply existing classification or mine new potential knowledge.[52] But even when such processes address questions with discrete, decidable answers, users will want to refine the results and these user-contributed refinements are important not only for other users but for improving the quality of subsequent automated analysis.[53] Thus, an automated system may incorrectly identify "Washington" in one passage as Washington, DC, when it is in fact Washington state. Or it may simply fail because its gazetteer does not include an entry for the right Washington in a given passage (e.g., Washington, NC). Thus, even when working with very simple conceptual systems, users should be able to correct system conclusions whether by selecting a different existing answer or by adding a new possible answer to the existing set. Figure 2.9 shows an existing feedback mechanism whereby users can vote against a machine-generated analysis.

As machines perform more sophisticated analyses where there is no single right answer, user feedback may be even more important: lexicographers do not always agree on how to describe the senses of a word.[54] Machines can infer possible senses by

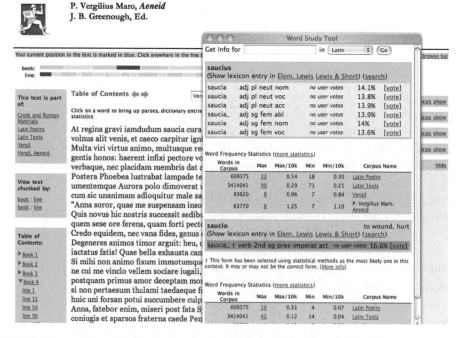

Figure 2.9   A morphological analysis system: this system has calculated the possible analyses for a given form. A simple machine learning system has ranked the possibilities of each analysis in the given context. Users can now vote for the analysis which they see as correct.

studying the contexts in which a word appears but we still want to be able to modify the suggested word senses, even if experienced lexicographers would not agree on any one final configuration of senses.

Documents that adapt themselves to their users

Customization and personalization constitute two other methods by which machines respond dynamically to user behavior. In customization, users explicitly set parameters to shape subsequent system behavior. Personalization generally implies that the system takes action on its own, comparing the behavior of a new user to that of other users that it has encountered in the past.[55] Some of us create our own customized versions of internet portals (e.g., "My Yahoo!"). Most humanists had, by 2006, encountered the personalization on sites such as Amazon, which inform us that people who bought the book that we just chose also bought books X, Y, and Z.[56]

Both customization and personalization have great potential within the humanities.[57]

Figure 2.10 illustrates how a user profile can help filter information, showing readers what terms they have and have not encountered. A reader has informed the system that she has studied Latin from Wheelock's fifth edition. The system has then compared a passage from Suetonius against the vocabulary in the textbook (drawing upon the morphological analysis system which can match inflected words to their dictionary entries). Of the 115 possible dictionary words in this passage, the reader has probably encountered 54 and will find 61 that are new. These new words are then listed according to their frequency in the given passage. Alternate sorting orders could stress words that would be important in readings that have been assigned for the rest of the semester, for Suetonius in general or for some particular topic

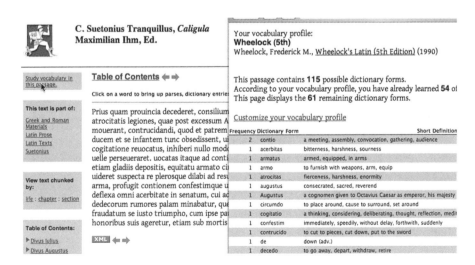

Figure 2.10   Customization in the Perseus Digital Library. This work was done by David Mimno and Gabriel Weaver, Perseus Project, Tufts University.

(e.g., military events) of interest to the reader. The technology can be based on straightforward principles of ranking and filtering from information retrieval but have a significant impact. The example given addresses language learning but the same techniques are applicable to technical terms. The key to this approach would be the development of learning profiles which track the contents of many textbooks, handouts, and assigned readings over different learning which we pursue throughout our lives.[58]

Figure 2.11 illustrates an example of personalization from the Perseus Digital Library. Once a user has asked for information on four or five words in a 300-word passage of Ovid, we can then predict two-thirds of the subsequent words that will elicit queries. This recommender system is similar in principle to the systems that Amazon and other e-commerce systems use to show consumers new products based on the products purchased by people who also bought product X. The application, however, reduces the search space of a language passage, suggesting words for study rather than products for purchase.[59]

Customization and personalization are fundamental technologies. While the examples given above address the needs of intermediate language learning, the same techniques would support professional researchers working with source materials outside of their own areas of specialization (e.g., an English professor with a background in classical Latin working through sixteenth-century English Latin prose). Customization and personalization have potential for filtering and structuring information for experts within their own field of expertise. They are core services for any advanced digital infrastructure underlying ePhilology.

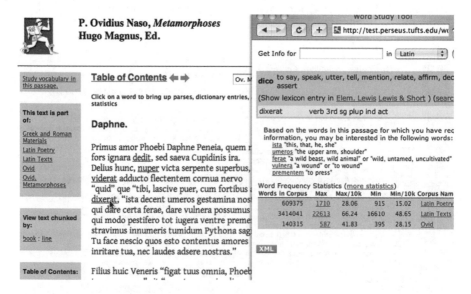

Figure 2.11 Personalization in the Perseus Digital Library. This work was done by D. Sculley, PhD candidate in Computer Science at Tufts University under the supervision of Professor Carla Brodley, with help from Gabriel Weaver of the Perseus Project.

Building the Infrastructure for ePhilology

The examples in the preceding section illustrate current steps toward future possibilities. This section describes an infrastructure to move the field forward. On the one hand, we need to exploit emerging technologies. This not only includes downloading applications and compiling source code but reading research publications and implementing suitable algorithms. At the same time, in the long run we in classics and in the humanities may primarily contribute the knowledge sources whereby developed tools can analyze historical materials. Thus, named entity systems applied to texts about the Greco-Roman world will perform much better if they have access to information about the people and places of the Greco-Roman world than if they must rely wholly on resources which describe the contemporary world.[60]

Primary sources and reference materials that evolve in real time should include the following features:

- *Open source/polyphonic*: We need encoded knowledge that can be maintained in real time and that can incorporate multiple points of view. Core resources should not be held restricted by rights agreements but should serve as a common resource to which others may add and from which others may generate new resources.[61] New variations on traditional review will emerge, with ongoing usage within the scholarly community complementing – and perhaps in some measure supplanting – the hit or miss preparatory edits of static documents necessary for print. In a digital world, capital information sources such as editions and reference works evolve: where print publication freezes documents, digital publication only begins its functional life after publication. We can easily preserve versions of the document as it appeared at any one time (thus allowing us to see what an author saw when the citation was added to an argument) and track who contributed what and at what time.
- *Readable by machines and people alike*: Our dictionaries should be able to search new texts for the varying senses claimed for each word; our encyclopedias should scan secondary sources for, and then summarize the results of, new discussions of the people, places, and topics which they cover; our texts should collate themselves against other witnesses and editions as these come online. The more machines can understand, the more effectively they will be able to support the questions that we pose and to provide the personalized background that we need.[62] The need to add the greater structure and consistency needed for machine processing only highlights the need for materials that we can freely reformat.

These features have at least one profound implication. Once documents become dynamic and can evolve over time, we must evaluate them according to their potential for growth – their state at any one time constitutes only a single data point. In classics, editions and reference works more than a century old but which are in the public domain and can be freely updated may thus prove more valuable in an electronic environment than the best current resources if these are either static or even updated according to a traditional editorial process.

A range of community-driven reference works has emerged in recent years. The most famous, Wikipedia, arguably constitutes the most important intellectual development of the early twenty-first century: a new form of intellectual production, community driven and dynamic, has produced more than 1,000,000 general articles in five years.[63] If and when the need for new articles diminishes, it will be interesting to see whether this vast resource enters a phase of refinement, thus suggesting a two-fold model: an open phase of development to bootstrap the system, followed by a period of revision. Criticizing this work is important, but only insofar as such criticism helps us to draw upon and contribute to this flood of intellectual energy.[64] Other community-driven systems with more centralized editorial control have appeared for math and physics.[65] A 2005 grant from the National Endowment for the Humanities has even provided support for Pleiades, a community-driven project on Greco-Roman geography.[66]

An infrastructure for ePhilology would contain two fundamental components: the primary sources and a network of reference works, linked to and constructed from the sources. Dynamic and intelligent links should connect all components of the infrastructure. When changes are suggested to a text, the effects of these changes upon associated reference works should be tracked and all affected places in all reference works should automatically report the change. Conversely, work based on analysis of a particular reference work should be noted in the text (e.g., a new study of a particular person that suggests reading one name vs. another).

Technically, this environment needs two things: a set of data structures and data. The Text Encoding Initiative (TEI) provides serviceable structures for texts themselves.[67] Text mining can identify many patterns latent within these texts,[68] but once we have ways of identifying people, places, organizations, and other entities within texts we need methods to reason, at least in rudimentary fashion, about them. Knowledge bases differ from databases in that they are designed to support inferencing: thus, if the system knows that no events in Herodotus postdate 400 BCE, that Alexander the Great was born after 400 BCE and that Alexander the Great was a king of Macedon, then it can avoid identifying the Alexander, king of Macedon, in Herodotus as Alexander the Great. Fortunately, the slowly emerging Semantic Web is designed to support such reasoning. Promising formats exist for geographic information[69] and for museum objects,[70] and we now have a well-developed set of guidelines for ontology production in OWL (Web Ontology Language).[71] Ontologies, however, rapidly grow idiosyncratic and their development is as much a social as a technical process.[72] To drive that development, however, we need enough data for serious experimentation – data structures and data will need to evolve, however cautiously, in tandem. We need services of interest to attract long-term user communities and enough data to raise issues of scale if we are to engineer solutions that will support intellectual life over time.

The Google Library and especially the Open Content Alliance, which has an open source policy, will help provide access to image books of virtually all useful public domain materials. These will provide immediate access to Latin and Roman script publications, with searchable OCR (optical character recognition) for classical Greek probably not far behind. These texts will provide the foundation on which we can build a dynamic knowledge base that evolves and grows more intelligent.

Moving from print to knowledge involves three steps:

1. Initial markup to capture the basic structural elements: we need the headwords for dictionaries/lexica/gazetteers, clear separation of headers, footnotes and text, and other basic elements not present in raw OCR.[73]
2. Semantic analysis: classification of proper names (e.g., is Peneius the river or the river god?) and identification of basic propositional statements (e.g., "a REGION of PLACE," "PERSON born at PLACE in DATE").[74]
3. Alignment against pre-existing entries common list and identification of new entries: Alexander-12 in encyclopedia-1 may be equivalent to Alexander-32 in encyclopedia-2 or it may represent an entirely new Alexander not yet attested.[75]

Automated methods can address all three of the above phases but all methods are imperfect and print sources differ just enough that methods still need to be tuned for most reference materials. The three steps above constitute the most important and probably the most difficult work that we face, but they are essential and foundational to any serious infrastructure.

Classicists are fortunate in having a well-developed set of public domain print resources with which to begin their work.

- *Texts*: These can take older editions as their initial base texts but should then (1) be collated with other editions, both older and new, and (2) provide an initial database of variants and conjectures that can be expanded over time.[76] One well-tagged edition could help automatically identify and provide preliminary tagging for other online editions.[77] Perseus contains c. 70 percent of the corpus of classical and Hellenistic Greek and 50 percent of the corpus of classical Latin in TEI-compliant XML. Both collections are expanding, with coverage of Latin being particularly cost effective: we should be able to provide coverage of 96 percent of the text on the PHI CD ROM, with later authors not in that collection (e.g., Ammianus, Sidonius) and a substantial postclassical collection.
- *Translations*: Scholars working with any historical language should, as a matter of principle, ensure that (1) translations are readily available and (2) flag those places where the new edition would impact at least one standard translation. Translations are, however, not only useful for those with little or no knowledge of the source language: parallel text analysis is a major component for machine translation (necessary where translations do not exist), automated lexicography, cross-language information retrieval etc.[78] Multiple translations of a single text strengthen statistical analysis. Translations are thus a high priority to any infrastructure for an ePhilology. In Perseus we have collected at least one translation for most of our sources.

- *Morphology*: The ability to connect a dictionary entry with its inflected forms is a fundamental service for any language. While the code needed to recognize legal combinations of stem and ending is challenging in Greek (where we must also consider augments, preverbs, accent, and diacritics), morphological analysis is a data-intensive process that depends upon lists of endings and especially stems. Since stems are, in practice, an unbounded set, assembling suitable databases of morphological data is the greatest challenge to morphological analysis in Latin and Greek. Dictionaries have provided the best general source for the stems, with Liddell, Scott, Jones (LSJ), and Lewis and Short helping us create databases with 52,700 Greek and 19,800 Latin stems. In 1990, we provided 100 percent coverage for the one million words of Greek included in Perseus 1.0. Many low frequency words and most proper nouns are not in these source lexica and only modest progress was made in extending this coverage. The need to improve morphological analysis provided one, though by no means the only, reason to identify, digitize, and mine more comprehensive reference works with people and places.

- *People and places*: For classical texts, the nineteenth-century three-volume *Dictionary of Greek and Roman Biography and Mythology* (Smith 1873) and Smith's two-volume *Dictionary of Greek and Roman Geography* (Smith 1854) are more than a century older than the third edition of the *Oxford Classical Dictionary* (OCD3) (Hornblower and Spawforth 1996). Anyone looking for a survey of standard views from the late twentieth century must, of course, consult OCD3. Nevertheless, the older Smith dictionaries are better sources for ePhilology because they are more extensive and contain tens of thousands of machine-extractable source citations. Both dictionaries set out, with reasonable success, to document all significant people and places mentioned in the literary corpus,[79] with 20,000 and 10,000 entries in the bio-graphical and geographical dictionaries. Equally important, we have been able to extract 37,500 and 25,800 citations, respectively. Each citation not only associates a particular passage with a particular topic but provides more materials whereby text-mining software can learn to distinguish the various Alexanders and Alexandrias when they appear elsewhere in primary and secondary sources alike. The original Smith articles can be mined for information about birth/death dates, family relations, place locations, and other quantifiable data that can be used for intelligent information retrieval and general text mining.

- *Authors, works, and their citation schemes*: Authors comprise a key subset of people, with their works often listed in biographical entries of Smith's biographical dictionary, as well as good coverage for more than three and a half centuries of printed editions. The TLG and PHI Institute each have produced up-to-date catalogues of recent editions, as well as lists of author works. Lexica such as LSJ and Lewis and Short include extensive bibliographies of authors, works, and older editions. While the *Oxford Latin Dictionary* is a relatively recent publication, it began work in the 1930s and the editions which it cites are almost all in the public domain today – thus providing an excellent starting point for digitization. Other materials can provide other categories of background: (Hall 1913), for example, describes the textual traditions for all major classical authors as it was understood in the early twentieth century (and thus as it appears in most public domain editions). Authors and works that have appeared as separate editions also have standard names: once we associate Marcus Tullius Cicero, M. Tullius Cicero, and Cicero, for example, with the canonical name authority form "Cicero, Marcus Tullius," we can automatically search standard library catalogues. Online texts generally provide one citation scheme. Some authors, however, have multiple citation schemes and we need to manage them all if we are to exploit the full range of citations. These should be included when the electronic editions are created, with alternate citation schemes added to existing texts as image books with the alternate citations become available.

- *Lexicography*: We want to be able to identify not only particular forms and dictionary entries but the distinct senses of particular words in particular passages. Parallel corpora, with source texts in one language aligned with translations in one or more languages, have allowed machine translation to make substantial progress in recent years. The machine translation systems can look for statistical associations between words in the two languages to identify probable translation equivalents for particular words in particular passages. Machine-readable dictionaries remain crucial tools for machines as well as for human readers.[80] Online lexica not only provide reading support but provide a foundation for semantic analysis through comparison of dictionary definitions and an open inventory of documented senses. LSJ 9 and Lewis and Short,[81] augmented by more specialized lexica, provide a reasonable starting point for an electronic infrastructure.

- *Syntax*: We also want to be able to identify the syntactic relations within a sentence – at the simplest, answering the question "what does this word depend on and what is its function?" Generating accurate parse trees for complete sentences is difficult in any case and increasingly difficult the larger and more complex the sentence. Nevertheless, even if the complete sentence parse is not correct, enough individual word-to-word relations are usually correct to detect patterns such as which nouns go with which adjectives, what cases a verb takes, etc. Grammars are the logical starting point for syntactic data: we have thus digitized the extensive Kühner-Gerth Greek Grammar,[82] as well as the shorter Smyth[83] and Allen and Greenough[84] grammars for Greek and Latin. Highly inflected languages store much of their syntactic information in word forms that less heavily inflected languages may express in word order. Greek and Latin lexica thus contain much – and arguably more – syntactic information than conventional grammars, since the constructions associated with individual words may be key to determining the correct parses for a sentence.

- *Specialized reference materials*: Larger works may contain specialized glossaries on particular topics. (Hall 1913) contains a very useful glossary that explains the Latin names for manuscripts in many editions; (Smyth 1920) contains a glossary of rhetorical terms. Specialized lexica cover the language of particular authors, such as Slater's Pindar lexicon.[85] Once again, the Smith dictionary series provided us with a foundational resource on which to build: the two-volume *Dictionary of Greek and Roman Antiquities* (Smith, Wayte et al. 1890) contains 3,400 entries and (as of this writing) 25,000 extracted citations covering law, architecture, religion, rhetoric, and other aspects of life.

- *Events*: One can easily enter a philosophical funk trying to define what is and is not an event, but modern timelines and ancient chronologies show us what others chose to identify as significant events and provide us with an objective record of what others have chosen to label and recall.[86]

The role of the editor in a digital world

The digital world makes possible a new kind of editor: the corpus editor occupies a middle ground between the algorithm-heavy, knowledge-light approaches of computer science and the wholly manual practices of traditional editing. The corpus editor works with thematically coherent bodies of text that are too big to be processed and checked by hand and that therefore demand automated methods. The corpus editor combines knowledge bases and automated methods to apply automated markup and/or extract information. The corpus editor cannot check every automated decision but is able both to document how the automated decisions were made and to provide statistical measures for the accuracy of those decisions.[87]

The role of the traditional editor also changes in an electronic environment. The traditional editor becomes responsible for preparing documents for use not only by people but by machines. The ePhilologist reviews a high percentage – and ideally all – of the automated decisions that link a particular text to knowledge sources such as those listed above: the editor manages the automated processes and reviews the results. The editor checks the morphological analyses and parse trees, comments on passages where the identification of a person or place is ambiguous, etc. The edited documents in the digital library provide crucial training sets that improve the performance of automated methods generally: thus, careful work on a few lives of Plutarch should improve results on the other lives and on similar Greek prose generally.

Cultural Informatics

Digital culture already dominates serious intellectual life, even if its dominance still subordinates itself to the superficial – and, to a classicist, quite recent – forms of print culture. The previous section described one partial survey of what form classics might take as a digital culture matures and intellectual practice begins to exploit this digital world for its own strengths. The examples given reflect substantive work with existing technologies applied to questions common to all students of historical languages. All of the examples above either are, or could become, general services.[88] Nevertheless, they constitute a few first steps in a much larger process.

Much of the above work was possible because the National Science Foundation and the National Endowment for the Humanities collaborated on the Digital Library

Initiative Phase II, a program which supported a range of humanities projects. We cannot expect such levels of support in the future.[89] If we are to move forward as a field, we must use what we have learned from what worked and what did not work in the past to develop a strategy to help us move forward in the future. Classics may or may not pursue the particular directions suggested in the previous section, but passively drifting along a broader current of academic practice is a dangerous course. The Mellon Foundation and American Council on Learned Societies recently funded a "Commission on Cyberinfrastructure for Humanities and Social Sciences."[90] A PhD in English (John Unsworth) chaired the commission, which included five humanists, including another person from English literature (Jerome McGann), an American historian (Roy Rosenzweig), an art historian (Sarah Fraser), and the director of an archaeological research collection (Bruce Zuckerman). The draft report available in May 2006 makes cursory mention of classics. Classicists cannot expect colleagues who work primarily in English and with relatively recent sources to anticipate the problems of working with historical languages. Classics – and all disciplines which draw upon languages of the past – must tirelessly engage in larger conversations and be prepared to defend the significance of language.

One effective solution is the creation of a new area of informatics designed to bridge the gap between a discipline and current research in computer science – a demanding task, if performed well, because it requires a command of emerging, as well as established, issues in two radically different disciplines. The field of biology, confronted with overwhelming amounts of raw data, produced the field of bioinformatics, thus creating an intellectual space, primarily grounded in biology, to connect research in computer science with biology research.

Classics probably cannot command a hundredth part of the resources on which biological research depends. We cannot call forth a major new discipline with the funding to attract the attention of grant-driven computer scientists. Nevertheless, we can accomplish a great deal.

- *All philological inquiry, whether classical or otherwise, is now a special case of corpus linguistics*: Its foundational tools should come increasingly from computational linguistics, with human and automated analysis. Vague statements such as "typical of Greek prose," "common in early Greek," etc. must give way to dynamically generated measurements of well-mapped corpora. Human judgment must draw upon and work in conjunction with documented mathematically grounded models. The salaries which support Classics faculty are the one resource which we, as a field, collectively allocate. As at least some, if not most, members of the field begin to see themselves as computational linguists with a particular focus on Latin and/or Greek, we will soon mobilize over a long period of time far more intellectual capital than the most generous grants could provide for limited periods.
- *We need to rethink what we study*: Tasks which we as human readers take for granted often demand substantial analysis when we transfer them to automated systems. Classicists cannot manually fit all 91,000,000 words in the current TLG into parse

trees. Some tasks, such as concordance generation or even more sophisticated problems such as morphological analysis, can follow well-defined results: e.g., display all possible instances of the Latin verb *facio* in the Catilinarians of Cicero. We soon reach problems for which rule sets provide much less accurate results: is a given instance of the form *faciam* a subjunctive or future? Which "Alexander" does a particular passage cite? Which accusative noun is the subject of the infinitive and which the object? We need a foundational work on the problem of resolving ambiguities, producing the best possible results and providing accurate information as to the accuracy of automated results. We need to take a step and work on the tools on which research will rely.

- *We must distinguish programming from computer science*: We will need quite a bit of advanced programming, even if we are only gluing together tools developed by our colleagues in computational linguistics. Nevertheless, we must separate analysis of our methods from the code by which we test them. We need the patience to evaluate multiple methods to solve the same problem and to produce results from which others can learn – a patience that will become more common as we develop a community of research. We also need to consider our skills: crucial as programming may be, philologists who wish to draw effectively upon the emerging tools of our world must become familiar with linear algebra and probability.

- *ePhilology is part of a larger, cultural informatics*: ePhilology represents one particular approach to a comprehensive analysis of earlier culture: we may center our attention on words, but our questions will soon lead us to the evidence of material culture. Classics may be big enough to sustain its own classical informatics, but we would be much better served by contributing to a larger cultural informatics. We should aggressively establish alliances with partners with similar needs and limit, as much as possible, ourselves to those problems which only classicists can address. We have developed our own morphological analyzers, syntactic analyzers, and named entity recognition systems, but it would be much better for us to concentrate on the databases of stems and endings, the grammar, and the knowledge bases of people, places, etc. Our natural collaborators include not only all of those working with historical languages but also those struggling to analyze the thousands of languages spoken in our contemporary world. Where cultural informatics would embrace all sources of information – natural language, relational databases, images, GIS, 2D and 3D models, simulations – ePhilology implies a focus upon linguistic sources.

- *We need to identify what structures we need to institutionalize*: A generation ago, classicists could get jobs, tenure, and promotion at leading institutions as editors and authors of scholarly commentaries. Almost all classics faculty under the age of fifty in US departments have, however, made their careers by producing articles and monographs, with far less emphasis on editing and work on the intellectual infrastructure of the field. A generation of ePhilologists may emerge to play prominent roles in our departments as the field realizes that we are not just copying print into digital form but creating a wholly new, qualitatively distinct infrastructure. The changes before us may exceed those spawned by movable print and may be more comparable to the invention of writing itself. We also need new libraries to help us maintain into the future the resources that we create. Libraries will need to develop new skills to manage digital libraries and new ways to use their acquisition budgets to support the creation of content with the structure and the right regimes needed by humanists.[91] We may need new departmental and research structures – combinations of Classics and computer science may become common, to the benefit of both fields. We need to establish relationships with major commercial entities such as Google, Yahoo, and Microsoft, if these continue to evolve into the public libraries of the twenty-first century and provide us with new channels to society as a whole.

Conclusion

Some emerging technologies could, if applied to classics and to other philological disciplines, have a swift and dramatic impact upon the questions that we pursue: machine translation, parallel text analysis, named entity identification, syntactic analysis, cross-language information retrieval and a range of text mining methods are well suited to a range of needs. The impact of digital technology will, however, be far broader and more pervasive than any particular tools we can deploy in the immediate future. The future of classics depends less upon particular tools than upon an emerging digital environment that integrates an increasing number of tools together into a dynamic world, constantly evolving to answer our questions and support the life of the mind. From the nineteenth century through the twentieth, we were able to take our scholarly infrastructure for granted: we had our publishers and libraries, our editions, commentaries, lexica, journals, monographs, and encyclopedias. We now have the merging of print, broadcast media, and gaming, new commercial entities planning universal access to a better library than the wealthiest academic institution on earth could provide to its faculty; we have new forms of intellectual production such as blogs and wikis; we have ontologies and knowledge bases at the core of reference materials; we have a world of dynamic information – books that read and learn from each other and from their human readers. The challenge now – and it is perhaps the greatest challenge classicists have faced since they found themselves pushed out of the center of the academy – is to shape this world and negotiate a new place for classical studies within it.

NOTES

1 The work described here builds on support from a variety of sources, including the Digital Library Initiative, Phase 2, the National Endowment for the Humanities, the National Science Foundation, and the Institute for Museum and Library Services. Many individuals have contributed. We mention in particular Carla Brodley, Lisa Cerrato, David Mimno, Adrian Packel, D. Sculley, and Gabriel Weaver.

2 For some reviews of how technology has been used within classics, please see: Crane 2004, McManus 2003, Latousek 2001, and Hardwick 2000.

3 Classicists were quick to embrace the Bryn Mawr Classical Review (<http://ccat.sas.upenn.edu/bmcr/>), which began publication in 1990 as a mailing list. BMCR was successful for three reasons: first, it used email to speed up the pace of scholarly communication, thus addressing a single, nagging problem; second, the electronic form allowed BMCR greater flexibility than its print counterparts, allowing it to accept a greater range of reviews, thus encouraging a wider range of submissions; third, its articles were, and remain, electronic analogues of print: they do not challenge their authors to rethink the substantive form of their work. The Stoa publishing consortium, by contrast, began in 1997 and has supported a range of more innovative projects (including the Demos project described below).

4 For some recent overviews of the issues with scholarly publishing, please see Unsworth 2003.

5 Derrida 1972.

6 For a discussion of fears that Google and the digitization of libraries will lead to serious decontextualization of learning, see Garrett 2006.

7 Dino Franco Felluga discusses this issue as well in regards to literary studies; please see Felluga 2005.

8 The idea of a permanent personal digital archive or storehouse of lifetime memories and knowledge has been well articulated by the creators of MyLifeBits (Gemmell 2006). Neil Beagrie has also explored this concept (Beagrie 2005).

9 A wealth of research has been conducted into how systems can best automatically adapt themselves to the needs of different readers, such as Russell 2003, Dolog 2004, Niederee 2004, Rouane 2003, Wang 2004, and Terras 2005.

10 Text mining is increasingly being used in humanities applications; see, for example, Kirschenbaum 2006 and Xiang 2006.

11 <http://www.tlg.uci.edu/>.

12 For one exploration of the impact of the TLG on classical scholarship, please see Ruhleder 1995.

13 For a discussion of some of this work, see Packard 1973.

14 Crane 2004.

15 <http://www.neh.gov/news/awards/preservation2000.html>.

16 <http://www.tlg.uci.edu/CDROME.html>.

17 Biblioteca Teubneriana Latina 2004.

18 Maria Pantelia, the director of the TLG, reported (private communication, September 2006) that lemmatized searching was in active development and would become part of the core TLG functionality.

19 There is a growing body of research into the need for more complex linguistic querying capabilities, particularly with historical language materials, please see de Jong 2005, Egan 2005, and Gerlach 2006.

20 See, for example, (Church 1989 and Justeson 1995).

21 The Perseus Digital Library has done extensive research in terms of the importance of named entity recognition and searching; please see Crane and Jones 2006a, Smith 2001.

22 For an example of a prototype system that supports many of these features, please see Ignat 2005.

23 A search for –pemp– turns up "(4.) OI)KH/ TORAS A)POPE/MPEIN. OI(DE\ *) EPIDA/MNIOI OU)DE\N AU)TW=N U(P-" with the label Thucydides "Book 1 chapter 26 section 4 line 1." In fact, the word is part of section 3, with section four beginning in the middle of the print line after the period. Simple programming can capture most of these section breaks, although some lines have more than one full stop and editors may use commas – or nothing – to mark the divisions of established units.

24 In the late 1990s, while Theodore Brunner was director of the TLG, David Smith of the Perseus Project created an SGML version of the TLG that validated against the TEI DTD. Mark Olsen of ARTFL also created a similar experimental version at the University of Chicago. In both cases, understanding the idiosyncratic reference encoding of the TLG proved the major barrier.

25 The largest Greek dramas are, with extensive XML markup, just over 120,000 bytes and would cost $120 to $180 to enter, depending on the vendor.

26 Research into variant editions and how best represent this information digitally has received a growing amount of attention, for example see Dekhytar 2005, Pierazzo 2006, Schmidt 2005, Audenaert 2005, and Riva 2005, and for an example in classics Bodard 2006.

27 <http://www.tlg.uci.edu/CDEworks.html#supp>.

28 The online TLG does not seem to provide any information about the texts that have been "suppressed," in effect consigning these editions to an electronic *damnatio memoriae*. A print copy of the second edition of the TLG Canon preserves the fact that the TLG had originally contained the Murray edition of Euripides. The online TLG canon simply lists the Diggle edition of Euripides now included in the TLG.

29 <http://www.openarchives.org/>.

30 Blackwell 2005. For some examples of how the CTS protocols are being used, please see Porter et al. 2006.

31 According to at least one participant at the international gathering of Hellenists which launched the TLG in the early 1970s, the experts in the field assumed that the texts of ancient authors, as published in editions, were not copyrightable. We need automated methods with which not only to compare but to quantify the differences between various electronic editions of the same text. Preliminary analysis suggests that changes from one edition to another are comparable to copy-editing. The best model for editors employed by academic institutions may thus be a work-for-hire, with the rights holders more properly being institutions who paid their salary.

32 The representative of one UK publisher stopped at Perseus years ago en route, as he informed us, to assert rights to electronic versions of texts that a third project had entered. We paid $7,000 for rights to two editions – only to discover that those editions had unambiguously gone into the public domain by UK law and had never been under copyright in the US. Another US publisher that had knowingly published materials in the public domain reportedly charges permissions fees for these materials for which it has no legal rights.

33 For more on the issue of the public domain and copyright issues in the face of mass digitization, please see Thatcher 2006 and Travis 2005.

34 Classicists define their own conventions of what does and does not count, and we can accept monographs published in emerging institutional repositories – in effect, we would return to a scholarly publication model, separate from university and commercial presses, that has served us well in the past.

35 For further discussion of Perseus examples, please see Crane et al. 2006a.

36 <http://www.gutenberg.org/wiki/Main_Page>.

37 For discussion of the Google Library project, please see MacColl 2006, for the Open Content Alliance please see Tennant 2005.

38 For a comprehensive look at the open access movement, please see Willinsky 2005.

39 <http://www.thelatinlibrary.com/>.

40 <http://www.thelatinlibrary.com/readme>.

41 <http://www.perseus.tufts.edu/hopper/>.

42 <http://creativecommons.org/>.

43 <http://www.stoa.org/projects/demos/home>.

44 The work of the Public Knowledge Project attempts to link scholarship to freely available sources in order to support reading by a broader audience; see Willinsky 2003.

45 This need for reusable digital objects that can draw upon a range of services is a major theme of the recent Mellon-funded study to support interoperability between digital repositories (Bekaert 2006).

46 For a good overview of the possibilities inherent in better exploiting the semantic content of digital objects, please see Bearman and Trant, 2005.

47 A similar issue is often raised by those researchers who wish to analyze Wikipedia, but find its unstructured data requires a great deal of work to support automated processing. See Volkel 2006.

48 Liddell et al. 1940.

49 Berkowitz and Squitier 1990.

50 For more on the potential of what can happen when the knowledge within digitized books interacts, please see Kelly 2006, Crane 2005a, Crane 2005b.

51 Smith 2001. For more on the technical details of this system, see Crane and Jones 2005.

52 A variety of work is beginning to explore how best to exploit both the structured and unstructured knowledge already present in digital library collections to train other systems with document analysis and machine learning; see for example Nagy and Lopresti 2005 and Esposito et al. 2005.

53 Research into how to capture the knowledge of users to drive both machine learning processes and personalization is growing rapidly, see for example Chklovski 2005, Carrera 2005, Gilardoni 2005, Kruk 2005.

54 Some initial work in having user contributions assist in automated word sense disambiguation has been reported in Navigli and Velardi 2005.

55 For an expansion of these definitions see Russell 2003, and for a particular application see Bowen and Fantoni 2004.

56 For more on the Amazon system, please see Linden et al. 2003.

57 There is growing body of literature as to how these technologies might be applied within the humanities, most often digital libraries, for an overview please see Smeaton and Callan 2005,

58 Developing accurate user models and profiles to support and track learning is a topic of significant study, for some recent work please see Brusilovsky 2005 and Kavcic 2004.

59 Work on how personalization, particularly recommender systems, might be used within humanities environments has been explored by Bia 2004, Kim 2004, to name only a few.

60 On the need for historical knowledge sources, see Crane and Jones 2006b and also Siemens 2006.

61 For some recent work on creating reference works that allow users to both edit and create

materials, please see Witte 2005 and Kolbistch 2005.

62 For an intriguing exploration of the potential of "machines as readers", see Shamos 2005.

63 As of May 23, 2006, the count for English articles on <http://www.wikipedia.org> stands at 1,145,000.

64 For example, see Rosenzweig 2006.

65 <http://planetmath.org/>;   <http://planet physics.org/>.

66 <http://www.unc.edu/awmc/pleiades.html>.

67 <http://www.tei-c.org/>.

68 This is the approach of the Nora text mining project: <http://nora.lis.uiuc.edu/description. php>; Plaisant et al. 2006.

69 <http://www.alexandria.ucsb.edu/gazetteer/ ContentStandard/version3.2/GCS3.2-guide. htm>.

70 <http://cidoc.ics.forth.gr/>.

71 <http://www.w3.org/TR/owl-features/>.

72 For some particular applications of ontologies in the humanities, see Nagypal 2004, 2005, Mirzaee 2005, and for the merging of various efforts, see Eide 2006 and Doerr 2003.

73 For some lengthier discussion of these issues see Bearman and Trant 2005 and Sankar 2006.

74 Named entity recognition and semantic classification have large bodies of literature, but the use of theses applications in the humanities is receiving more examination; see Hoekstra 2005 and Shoemaker 2005.

75 For interesting work in this area, see Barzilay 2005.

76 For some previous work in this vein see Spencer 2004.

77 If we have "arma virumque cano Troiae qui primus ab oris" tagged in one text as Aen. 1.1, then we locate other instances of this line and apply the same markup. This strategy draws upon the fact that runs of repeated words are surprisingly uncommon, even in large corpora.

78 For a recent exploration of the uses of parallel texts, see Mihalcea 2005, and their use in machine translation Smith 2006.

79 Smith 1873: ix: "Some difficulty has been experienced respecting the admission or

rejection of certain names, but the following is the general principle which has been adopted. The names of all persons are inserted, who are mentioned in more than one passage of an ancient writer: but where a name occurs in only a single passage, and nothing more is known of the person than that passage contains, that name is in general omitted. On the other hand, the names of such persons are inserted when they are intimately connected with some great historical event, or there are other persons of the same name with whom they might be confounded"; (Smith 1854: viii: "Separate articles are given to the geographical names which occur in the chief classical authors, as well as to those which are found in the Geographers and Itineraries, wherever the latter are of importance in consequence of their connection with more celebrated names, or of their representing modern towns,–or from other causes. But it has been considered worse than useless to load the work with a barren list of names, many of them corrupt, and of which absolutely nothing is known. The reader, however, is not to conclude that a name is altogether omitted till he has consulted the Index; since in some cases an account is given, under other articles, of names which did not deserve a separate notice."

80 For more on machine translation and WSD see Smith 2006, Marcu 2005, and Carpuat 2005.

81 Liddell et al. 1940, Andrews et al. 1879.

82 Kühner et al. 1890.

83 Smyth 1920.

84 Allen et al. 1904.

85 Slater 1969.

86 The use of HEML Historical Event Markup Language could be applicable in this area; see Robertson 2006.

87 For more on the role of corpus editors, see Crane 2000.

88 For examples of potential services, please see Patton 2004 and Crane et al. 2006b.

89 For a discussion for the future of digital library funding, see Griffin 2006.

90 <http://www.acls.org/cyberinfrastructure/cyber.htm>.

91 For more on the needs of new library services and infrastructures, see Dempsey 2006.

BIBLIOGRAPHY

Allen, J. H., J. E. Greenough, et al. (1904). *Allen and Greenough's New Latin Grammar for Schools and Colleges, Founded on Comparative Grammar*. Boston, MA, and London: Ginn & Company.

Andrews, E. A., W. Freund, et al. (1879). *A Latin Dictionary Founded on Andrews' Edition of Freund's Latin Dictionary*. Oxford and New York: Clarendon Press.

Audenaert, N., et al. (2005). "Integrating Collections at the Cervantes Project." *Proceedings of the 5th ACM/IEEE-CS Joint Conference on Digital Libraries* (Denver, CO, USA, June 7–11, 2005). JCDL '05. New York: ACM Press, pp. 287–8.

Barzilay, R., and N. Elhadad (2003). "Sentence Alignment for Monolingual Comparable Corpora." *Proceedings of the Conference on Empirical Methods in Natural Language Processing* (EMNLP 2003), pp. 25–32.

Beagrie, N. (2005). "Plenty of Room at the Bottom? Personal Digital Libraries and Collections." *D-Lib Magazine* 11 (6, June). <http://dlib.anu.edu.au/dlib/june05/beagrie/06beagrie.html>.

Bearman D., and J. Trant (2005). "Converting Scanned Images of the Print History of the World to Knowledge: A Reference Model and Research Strategy." *RDLP* 8 (5). <http://www.elbib.ru/index.phtml?page=elbib/eng/journal/2005/part5/BT>.

Bekaert, J., and H. Van de Sompel (2006). "Augmenting Interoperability across Scholarly Repositories." <http://eprints.rclis.org/archive/00006924/>.

Berkowitz, L., and K. A. Squitier (1990). *Thesaurus Linguae Graecae Canon of Greek Authors and Works*. New York: Oxford University Press.

Bia, A. C., I. Garrigós, and J. Gómez (2004). "Personalizing Digital Libraries at Design Time: The Miguel De Cervantes Digital Library Case Study." *ICWE 2004*, pp. 225–9.

Bibliotheca Teubneriana Latina, BTL-3 (2004). Turnhout: Brepols; Munich: K. G. Saur.

Blackwell, C., and N. Smith (2005). *A Guide to Version 1.1 of the Classical Text Services Protocol.* Digital Incunabula: a CHS site Devoted to the Cultivation of Digital Arts and Letters. <http://chs75.harvard.edu/projects/diginc/techpub/cts-overview>.

Bodard, G. (2006). "Inscriptions of Aphrodisias: Paradigm of an electronic publication." *CLiP 2006*. <http://www.cch.kcl.ac.uk/clip2006/content/abstracts/paper33.html>.

Bowen, J. P., and S. F. Fantoni (2004). "Personalization and the Web from a Museum Perspective." *Museums and the Web 2004*. <http://conference.archimuse.com/biblio/personalization_and_the_web_from_a_museum_perspective>.

Brusilovsky, P., S. Sosnovksy, and O. Shcherbinina (2005). "User Modeling in a Distributed E-Learning Architecture." *User Modeling 2005*, Lecture Notes in Computer Science 3538, pp. 387–91.

Carpuat, M., and D. Wu (2005). "Word Sense Disambiguation vs. Statistical Machine Translation." *Proceedings of the Association for Computational Linguistics 2005*, pp. 387–94.

Carrera, F. (2005). "Making History: An Emergent System for the Systematic Accrual of Transcriptions of Historic Manuscripts." *Eighth International Conference on Document Analysis and Recognition (ICDAR '05)*, pp. 543–9.

Chklovski, T., and Y. Gil (2005). "Improving the Design of Intelligent Acquisition Interfaces for Collecting World Knowledge From Web Contributors." *Proceedings of the 3rd International Conference on Knowledge Capture, K-CAP '05*, pp. 35–42.

Church, K., and P. Hanks (1989). "Word Association Norms, Mutual Information, and Lexicography." *Proceedings of the 27th Annual Meeting of the Association for Computational Linguistics*, pp. 76–83.

Crane, G. (2004). "Classics and the Computer. An End of the History." In Susan Schreibman, Ray Siemens, and John Unsworth (Eds.). *A Companion to the Digital Humanities*. Oxford: Blackwell Publishing, pp. 46–55.

Crane, G. (2005a). "No Book is an Island: Designing Electronic Primary Sources and Reference works for the Humanities." In H. van Oostendorp, Leen Breure, and Andrew Dillon (Eds.). *Creation, Use, and Deployment of Digital Information*. Hillsdale, NJ: Erlbaum, pp. 11–26.

Crane, G. (2005b). "Reading in the Age of Google: Contemplating the Future with Books That Talk to One Another." *Humanities* 26 (5, September/October). <http://www.neh.gov/news/humanities/2005–09/readingintheage.html>.

Crane, G., and A. Jones (2005). "The Perseus American Collection 1.0." <http://www.perseus.tufts.edu/~gcrane/americancoll.12.2005.pdf>.

Crane, G., and A. Jones. (2006a). "The Challenge of Virginia Banks: An Evaluation of Named Entity Analysis in a 19th Century Newspaper Collection." *Proceedings of the 6th ACM/IEEE-CS Joint Conference on Digital Libraries*, pp. 31–40.

Crane, G., and A. Jones (2006b). "Text, Information, Knowledge and the Evolving Record of Humanity." *D-Lib Magazine* 12 (3, March). <http://purl.pt/302/1/dlib/march06/jones/03jones.html>.

Crane, G., and J. A. Rydberg-Cox (2000). "New Technology and New Roles: the Need for 'Corpus Editors'." *Proceedings of the Fifth ACM Conference on Digital Libraries*, pp. 252–3.

Crane, G. et al. (2006a). "Beyond Digital Incunabula: Modeling the Next Generation of Digital Libraries." *Proceedings of ECDL 2006*, pp. 353–66.

Crane, G. et al. (2006b). "Services Make the Repository." Paper presented at JCDL 2006 Workshop: *"Digital Curation and Trusted Repositories."* <http://www.ils.unc.edu/tibbo/JCDL2006/Jones-JCDL Workshop2006l.pdf>.

de Jong, F. et al. (2005). "Temporal Language Models for the Disclosure of Historical Text." *XVIth International Conference of the Association* for History and Computing. <http://eprints.eemcs.utwente.nl/7266/01/db-utwente-433BCEA2.pdf>.

Dekhytar, A., et al. (2005). "Support for XML Markup of Image Based Electronic Editions." *International Journal on Digital Libraries* 6 (1): 55–69.

Dempsey, L. (2006). "The (Digital) Library Environment: Ten Years After." *Ariadne* <http://www.ariadne.ac.uk/issue46/dempsey/>.

Derrida, J. (1972). "La Pharmacie de Platon." In *La Dissemination*. Paris: Éditions du Seuil, pp. 69–196.

Doerr, M., J. Hunter, and C. Lagoze (2003). "Towards a Core Ontology for Information Integration." *Journal of Digital Information* 4 (1). <http://jodi.tamu.edu/Articles/v04/i01/Doerr/>.

Dolog, P., et al. (2004). "The Personal Reader: Personalizing and Enriching Learning Resources Using Semantic Web Technologies." *Proceedings of the 3rd International Conference on Adaptive Hypermedia and Adaptive Web-Based Systems*, pp. 85–94.

Eide, O., and C. E. Ore (2006). "TEI, CIDOC-CRM and a Possible Interface between the Two." *Proceedings of the ALLC-AHC 2006*.

Egan, G. (2005). "Impalpable Hits: Indeterminacy in the Searching of Tagged Shakespearian Texts." Paper delivered on March 17 at the *33rd Annual Meeting of the Shakespeare Association in America*, in Bermuda. <http://hdl.handle.net/2134/1294>.

Esposito, F., et al. (2005). "Intelligent Document Processing." *Proceedings of Eighth International Conference on Document Analysis and Recognition*, pp. 1100–4.

Felluga, D. F. (2005). "Addressed to the NINES: the Victorian Archive and the Disappearance of the Book." *Victorian Studies* 48 (2): 305–19.

Garrett, J. (2006). "KWIC and Dirty? Human Cognition and the Claims of Full Text Searching." *Journal of Electronic Publishing*, 9 (1). <http://hdl.handle.net/2027/spo.3336451.0009.106>.

Gemmell, J., G. Bell, and R. Lueder (2006). "MyLifeBits: A Personal Database for Every-thing." *Communications of the ACM* 49 (1, January): 88–95.

Gerlach, A. E., and N. Fuhr (2006). "Generating Search Term Variants for Text Collections with Historic Spellings." *ECIR 2006*, pp. 49–60.

Gilardoni, L. et al. (2005). "Machine Learning for the Semantic Web: Putting the User into the Cycle." *Proceedings of the Dagstuhl Seminar on Machine Learning for the Semantic Web*, February 13–18, 2005, Dagstuhl, Germany. <http://www.quinary.com/pagine/downloads/files/Resources/QuinaryDagstuhl.pdf>.

Griffin, S. (2005). "Funding for Digital Libraries: Past and Present." *D-Lib Magazine* 11 (7/8). <http://www.dlib.org/dlib/july05/griffin/07griffin.html>.

Hall, F. W. (1913). *A Companion to Classical Texts*. Oxford: Clarendon Press.

Hardwick, L. (2000). "Electrifying the Canon: The Impact of Computing on Classical Studies." *Computers and the Humanities* 34: 279–95.

Hinman, C. (1968). *The First Folio of Shakespeare: The Norton Facsimile*. New York: W. W. Norton.

Hoekstra, R. (2005). "Integrating Structured and Unstructured Searching in Historical Sources." *Proceedings of the XVI International Conference of the Association for History and Computing*, pp. 149–54.

Hornblower, S., and A. Spawforth (1996). *The Oxford Classical Dictionary*. New York: Oxford University Press.

Ignat, C., et al. (2005). "A Tool Set for the Quick and Efficient Exploration of Large Document Collections." *Proceedings of the 27th Annual ESARDA Meeting*. <http://arxiv.org/abs/cs.CL/0609067>.

Justeson, J. S., and M. K. Slava (1995). "Technical Terminology: Some Linguistic Properties and an Algorithm for Identification in Text." *Natural Language Engineering* 1: 9–27.

Kavcic, A. (2004). "Fuzzy User Modeling for Adaptation in Educational Hypermedia." *IEEE Transactions on Systems, Man and Cybernetics* Part C, 34 (4, November): 439–49.

Kelly. K. (2006). "Scan This Book!" *New York Times Magazine*. <http://www.nytimes.com/2006/05/14/14publishing.html>.

Kim, S., and E. A. Fox (2004). "Interest-Based User Grouping Model for Collaborative Filtering in Digital Libraries." *7th International Conference of Asian Digital Libraries*, pp. 533–42.

Kirschenbaum, M. (2006). "The NORA Project: Text Mining and Literary Interpretation." *Digital Humanities 2006*, pp. 255–6.

Kolbitsch, J., and H. Maurer (2005). "Community Building around Encyclopaedic Knowledge." *Journal of Computing and Information Technology* 14 (3): 175–90.

Kruk, S. R., S. Decker, and L. Zieborak (2005). "JeromeDL – Adding Semantic Web Technologies to Digital Libraries." *DEXA 2005*, Lecture Notes in Computer Science 3588, pp. 716–25.

Kühner, R., F. Blass, et al. (1890). *Ausführliche Grammatik der Griechischen Sprache*. Hannover: Hahnsche Buchhandlung.

Latousek, R. (2001). "Fifty Years of Classical Computing: A Progress Report." *CALICO Journal* 18 (2): 211–22.

Liddell, H. G., R. Scott, et al. (1940). *A Greek–English Lexicon*. Oxford: The Clarendon Press.

Linden, G., B. Smith, and J. York (2003). "Amazon.com Recommendations: Item-to-Item Collaborative Filtering." *Internet Computing* 7 (1): 76–80.

MacColl, J. (2006). "Google Challenges for Academic Libraries." *Ariadne* 46. <http://www.ariadne.ac.uk/issue46/maccoll/>.

Marcu, D., and K. Knight (2005). "Machine Translation in the Year 2004." *Proceedings of Acoustics, Speech and Signal Proceedings (ICASSP 2005)*, vol. 5, pp. 965–8.

McManus, B. F., and C. A. Rubino (2003). "Classics and Internet Technology." *American Journal of Philology* 124 (4): 601–8.

Mihalcea, R., and M. Simard (2005). "Parallel Texts." *Natural Language Engineering* 11 (3, September): 239–46.

Mirzaee, V., et al. (2005). "Computational Representation of Semantics in Historical Documents." *Proceedings of AHC 2005*.

Nagy, G., and D. Lopresti (2006). "Interactive Document Processing and Digital Libraries." *Proceedings of the Second International Conference on Document Images, Analysis for Libraries (DIAL 2006)*, pp. 2–11.

Nagypal, G. (2004). "Creating an Application-Level Ontology for the Complex Domain of History: Mission Impossible?" In *Proceedings of Lernen – Wissensentdeckung – Adaptivitat (LWA 2004)*, FGWM 2004 Workshop, Berlin, Germany, pp. 287–94.

Nagypal, G., et al. (2005). "Applying the Semantic Web: The VICODI experience in Creating Visual Contextualization for History." *Literary and Linguistic Computing* 20 (3): 327–49.

Navigli, R., and P. Velardi (2005). "Structural Semantic Interconnections: A Knowledge-Based Approach to Word Sense Disambiguation." *IEEE Transactions on Pattern Analysis and Machine Intelligence* 27(7): 1075–86.

Niederée, C., et al. (2004). "A Multi-Dimensional, Unified User Model for Cross-System Personalization." *Proceedings of Advanced Visual Interfaces International Working Conference (AVI 2004) – Workshop on Environments for Personalized Information Access*, pp. 34–54.

Packard, D. W. (1973). "Computer-Assisted Morphological Analysis of Ancient Greek." *Proceedings of the 5th Conference on Computational Linguistics*, Pisa, Italy, pp. 343–55.

Patton, M. S., and D. M. Mimno (2004). "Services for a Customizable Authority Linking Environment." *Proceedings of the 4th ACM/IEEE-CS Joint Conference on Digital Libraries*, p. 420.

Pierazzo, E. (2006). "Just Different Layers? Stylesheets and Digital Edition Methodology." *Digital Humanities 2006*.

Plaisant, C., J. Rose, et al. (2006). "Exploring Erotics in Emily Dickinson's Correspondence with Text Mining and Visual Interfaces." *Proceedings of the 6th ACM/IEEE-CS Joint Conference on Digital Libraries*, pp. 141–50.

Porter, D., et al. (2006). "Creating CTS Collections." *Digital Humanities 2006*, pp. 269–74.

Riva, M., and V. Zafrin (2005). "Extending the Text: Digital Editions and the Hypertextual Paradigm." *Proceedings of the Sixteenth ACM Conference on Hypertext and Hypermedia*, pp. 205–7.

Robertson, B. (2006). "Visualizing an Historical Semantic Web with HEML." *Proceedings of the WWW 2006*, pp. 1051–2.

Rosenzweig, Roy (2006). "Can History Be Open Source: Wikipedia and the Future of the Past." *Journal of American History* 93 (1): 37–46.

Rouane, K., C. Frasson, and M. Kaltenbach (2003). "Reading for Understanding: A Framework for Advanced Reading Support." *Proceedings of the 3rd IEEE International Conference on Advanced Learning Technologies*, pp. 394–5.

Ruhleder, K. (1995). "Reconstructing Artifacts, Reconstructing Work: From Textual Edition to On-Line Databank." *Science, Technology, & Human Values* 20 (1, Winter): 39–64.

Russell, J. (2003). "Making it Personal: Information That Adapts to the Reader." *SIGDOC '03: Proceedings of the 21st Annual International Conference on Documentation*, pp. 160–6.

Sankar, K. P., et al. (2006). "Digitizing a Million Books: Challenges for Document Analysis." *Document Analysis Systems VII, 7th International Workshop, DAS 2006*, pp. 225–36.

Schmidt, D., and T. Wyeld (2005). "A Novel User Interface for Online Literary Documents." *Proceedings of the 19th Conference of the Computer–Human Interaction Special Interest Group (CHISIG) of Australia on Computer–Human Interaction*, pp. 1–4.

Shamos, M. I. (2005). "Machines as Readers: a Solution to the Copyright Problem." *Journal of Zhejiang University Science* 6A, 11: 1179–87.

Shoemaker, R. (2005). "Digital London: Creating a Searchable Web of Interlinked Resources on Eighteenth Century London." *Program: Electronic Library and Information Systems* 39 (4): 297–311.

Siemens, R. (2006). "Knowledge Management and Textual Cultures? Work Toward the Renaissance English Knowledgebase (REKn) and its Professional Reading Environment." Paper delivered at *CASTA 2006*.

Slater, W. J. (1969). *Lexicon to Pindar*. Berlin: de Gruyter.

Smeaton, A. F., and J. Callan (2005). "Personalisation and Recommender Systems in Digital Libraries." *International Journal of Digital Libraries* 5: 299–308.

Smith, D. A. (2006). "Debabelizing Libraries: Machine Translation by and for Digital Collections." *DLib Magazine* 12 (3, March). <http://www.dlib.org/dlib/march06/smith/03smith.html>.

Smith, D. A., and G. Crane (2001). "Disambiguating Geographic Names in a Historical Digital Library." *Proceedings of the 5th European Conference on Research and Advanced Technology for Digital Libraries (ECDL '01)*, Lecture Notes in Computer Science, pp. 127–36.

Smith, W. (1854). *Dictionary of Greek and Roman Geography*. Boston: Little Brown & Co.

Smith, W. (1873). *A Dictionary of Greek and Roman Biography and Mythology*. London: J. Murray.

Smith, W., W. Wayte, et al. (1890). *A Dictionary of Greek and Roman Antiquities*. London: J. Murray.

Smyth, H. W. (1920). *A Greek Grammar for Colleges*. New York, Cincinnati [etc.]: American Book Company.

Spencer, M., and C. Howe (2004). "Collating Texts Using Progressive Multiple Alignment." *Computers and the Humanities* 38 (3, August): 253–70.

Tennant, R. (2005). "The Open Content Alliance." *Library Journal* December 15. <http://www.libraryjournal.com/article/CA6289918.html>.

Terras, M. (2005). "Reading the Readers: Modelling Complex Humanities Processes to Build Cognitive Systems." *Literary and Linguistic Computing* 20 (1): 41–59.

Thatcher, S. G. (2006). "Fair Use in Theory and Practice: Reflections on its History and the Google Case." *Journal of Scholarly Publishing* 37 (3): 215–29.

Travis, H. (2005). "Building Universal Digital Libraries: An Agenda for Copyright Reform." Forthcoming, *Pepperdine Law Review*. <http://papers.ssm.com/sol3/papers.cfm?abstract_id=793585>.

Unsworth, J. (2003). "The Crisis in Scholarly Publishing in the Humanities." *ARL Bimonthly Report* 228 <http://www.arl.org/newsltr/228/crisis.html>.

Volkel, M., et al. (2006). "Semantic Wikipedia." *Proceedings of the 15th International Conference on World Wide Web*, pp. 585–94.

Wang, C. Y., and G. D. Chen (2004). "Extending E-Books with Annotation, Online Support and Assessment Mechanisms to Increase Efficiency of Learning." *SIGCSE Bulletin* 36 (3): 132–6.

Willinsky, J. (2003). "Opening Access: Reading (Research) in the age of Information." In C. M. Fairbanks, J. Worthy, B. Maloch, J. V. Hoffman, and D. L. Schallert (Eds.). *51st National Reading Conference Yearbook*. Oak Creek, WI: National Reading Conference, pp. 32–6.

Willinsky, J. (2005). *The Access Principle: The Case for Open Access to Research Scholarship.* Cambridge, MA: MIT Press.

Witte, Rene (2005). "Engineering a Semantic Desktop for Building Historians and Architects." *SemDesk 2005 Workshop Proceeding.* <http://www.semanticdesktop.org/xwiki/bin/download/Wiki/EngineeringASemantic DesktopForBuildingHistoriansAndArchitects/34_witte_engineeringsd_final.pdf>.

Xiang, X., and J. Unsworth (2006). "Connecting Text Mining and Natural Language Processing in a Humanistic Context." *Digital Humanities 2006.*

3

Disciplinary Impact and Technological Obsolescence in Digital Medieval Studies[1]

Daniel Paul O'Donnell

In May 2004, I attended a lecture by Elizabeth Solopova at a workshop at the University of Calgary on the past and present of digital editions of medieval works. The lecture looked at various approaches to the digitization of medieval literary texts and discussed a representative sample of the most significant digital editions of English medieval works then available: the *Wife of Bath's Prologue* from the *Canterbury Tales Project* (Robinson and Blake 1996), Murray McGillivray's *Book of the Duchess* (McGillivray 1997), Kevin Kiernan's *Electronic Beowulf* (Kiernan 1999), and the first volume of the *Piers Plowman Electronic Archive* (Adams et al. 2000). Solopova herself is an experienced digital scholar and the editions she was discussing had been produced by several of the most prominent digital editors then active. The result was a master class in humanities computing: an in-depth look at markup, imaging, navigation and interface design, and editorial practice in four exemplary editions.

From my perspective in the audience, however, I was struck by two unintended lessons. The first was how easily digital editions can age: all of the CD-ROMs Solopova showed looked quite old fashioned to my 2004 eyes in the details of their presentation and organization and only two, Kiernan's *Beowulf* and McGillivray's *Book of the Duchess*, loaded and displayed on the overhead screen with no difficulties or disabled features.

For the purposes of Solopova's lecture these failures were not very serious: a few missing characters and a slightly gimpy display did not affect her discussion of the editions' inner workings and indeed partially illustrated her point concerning the need to plan for inevitable technological obsolescence and change at all stages of edition design. For end users consulting these editions in their studies or at a library, however, the problems might prove more significant: while well-designed and standards-based editions such as these *can* be updated in order to accommodate technological change, doing so requires skills that are beyond the technological capabilities of most humanities scholars; making the necessary changes almost certainly requires some post-publication investment on the part of the publisher and/ or the original editors. Until such effort is made, the thought and care devoted by the original team to editorial organization and the representation of textual detail presumably is being lost to subsequent generations of end users.

The second lesson I learned was that durability was not necessarily a function of age or technological sophistication. The editions that worked more or less as intended were from the middle of the group chronologically and employed less sophisticated technology than the two that had aged less well: they were encoded in relatively straightforward HTML (although Kiernan's edition makes sophisticated use of Java and SGML for searching) and rendered using common commercial web browsers. The projects that functioned less successfully were encoded in SGML and were packaged with sophisticated custom fonts and specialized rendering technology: the Multidoc SGML browser in the case of the *Piers Plowman Electronic Archive* and the Dynatext display environment in the case of the *Canterbury Tales Project*. Both environments were extremely advanced for their day and allowed users to manipulate text in ways otherwise largely impossible before the development and widespread adoption of XML- and XSL-enabled browsers.

Neither of these lessons seems very encouraging at first glance to medievalists engaged in or investigating the possibilities of using digital media for new projects. Like researchers in many humanities disciplines, medievalists tend to measure schol- arly currency in terms of decades, not years or months. The standard study of the Old English poem *Cædmon's Hymn* before my recent edition of the poem (O'Donnell 2005a) was published nearly seventy years ago. Reference works like Cappelli's *Dizionario di abbreviature latine ed italiane* (first edition, 1899) or Ker's *Catalogue of Manuscripts Containing Anglo-Saxon* (first edition, 1959) also commonly have vener- able histories. In the case of the digital editions discussed above – especially those already showing evidence of technological obsolescence – it is an open question whether the scholarship they contain will be able to exert nearly the same long- term influence on their primary disciplines. Indeed, there is already some evidence that technological or rhetorical problems may be hindering the dissemination of at least some of these otherwise exemplary projects' more important findings. Robinson, for example, reports that significant manuscript work by Daniel Mosser appearing in various editions of the *Canterbury Tales Project* is cited far less often than the importance of its findings warrants (Robinson 2005: §11).

The lesson one should *not* draw from these and other pioneering digital editions, however, is that digital projects are inevitably doomed to early irrelevance and undeserved lack of disciplinary impact. The history of digital medieval scholarship extends back almost six decades to the beginnings of the *Index Thomisticus* by Roberto Busa in the mid-1940s (see Fraser 1998 for a brief history). Despite fundamental changes in focus, tools, and methods, projects completed during this time show enough variety to allow us to draw positive as well as negative lessons for future work. Some digital projects, such as the now more than thirty-year-old Dictionary of Old English (DOE), have proven themselves able to adapt to changing technology and have had an impact on their disciplines – and longevity – as great as the best scholarship developed and disseminated in print. Projects which have proven less able to avoid technological obsolescence have nevertheless also often had a great effect on our understanding of our disciplines, and, in the problems they have encountered, can also offer us some cautionary lessons (see Keene n.d. for a useful primer in conservation issues and digital texts).

Premature Obsolescence: the Failure of the Information Machine

Before discussing the positive lessons to be learned from digital medieval projects that have succeeded in avoiding technological obsolescence or looking ahead to examine trends that future digital projects will need to keep in mind, it is worthwhile considering the nature of the problems faced by digital medieval projects that have achieved more limited impact or aged more quickly than the intrinsic quality of their scholarship or relevance might otherwise warrant – although in discussing projects this way, it is important to realize that the authors of these often self-consciously experimental projects have not always aimed at achieving the standard we are using to judge their success: longevity and impact equal to that of major works of print-originated and disseminated scholarship in the principal medieval discipline.

In order to do so, however, we first need to distinguish among different types of obsolescence. One kind of obsolescence occurs when changes in computing hardware, software, or approach render a project's content unusable without heroic efforts at recovery. The most famous example of this type is the *Electronic Domesday Book*, a project initiated by the BBC in celebration of the nine-hundredth anniversary of King William's original inventory of post-conquest Britain (Finney 1986–2006; see O'Donnell 2004 for a discussion). The shortcomings of this project have been widely reported: it was published on video disks that could only be read using a customized disk player; its software was designed to function on the BBC Master personal computer – a computer that at the time was more popular in schools and libraries in the United Kingdom than any competing system but is now hopelessly obsolete. Costing over £2.5 million, the project was designed to showcase technology that it was thought might prove useful to schools, governments, and museums interested in producing smaller projects using the same innovative virtual reality environment. Unfortunately, the hardware proved too expensive for most members of its intended market and very few people ended up seeing the final product. For sixteen years, the only way of accessing the project was via one of a dwindling number of the original computers and disk readers. More recently, after nearly a year of work by an international team of engineers, large parts of the project's content finally have been converted for use on contemporary computer systems.

The Domesday Project is a spectacular example of the most serious kind of technological obsolescence, but it is hardly unique. Most scholars now in their forties and fifties probably have disks lying around their studies containing information that is for all intents and purposes lost due to technological obsolescence – content written using word processors or personal computer database programs that are no longer maintained, recorded on difficult-to-read media, or produced using computers or operating systems that ultimately lost out to more popular competitors. But the Domesday Project did not become obsolete solely because it gambled on the wrong technology: many other digital projects of the time, some written for mainframe computers using languages and operating systems that that are still widely understood, have suffered a similar obsolescence even though their content theoretically could be recovered more easily.

In fact the Domesday Project also suffered from an obsolescence of approach – the result of a fundamental and still ongoing change in how medievalists and others working with digital media approach digitization. Before the second half of the 1980s, digital projects were generally conceived of *information machines* – programs in which content was understood to have little value outside of its immediate processing context. In such cases, the goal was understood to be the sharing of results rather than content. Sometimes, as in the case of the Domesday Book, the goal was the arrangement of underlying data in a specific (and closed) display environment; more commonly, the intended result was statistical information about language usage and authorship or the development of indices and concordances (see for example, the table of contents in Patton and Holoien 1981, which consists entirely of database, con-cordance, and statistical projects). Regardless of the specific processing goal, this approach tended to see data as raw material rather than an end result.[2] Collection and digitization were done with an eye to the immediate needs of the processor, rather than the representation of intrinsic form and content. Information not required for the task at hand was ignored. Texts encoded for use with concordance or corpus software, for example, commonly ignored capitalization, punctuation, or *mise-en-page*. Texts encoded for interactive display were structured in ways suited to the planned output (see for example the description of database organization and video collection in Finney 1986–2006). What information was recorded was often indicated using ad hoc and poorly documented tokens and codes whose meaning now can be difficult or impossible to recover (see Cummings 2006).

The problem with this approach is that technology ages faster than information: data that require a specific processing context in order to be understood will become unintelligible far more rapidly than information that has been described as much as possible in its own terms without reference to a specific processing outcome. By organizing and encoding their content so directly to suit the needs of a specific processor, information machines like the Domesday Project condemned themselves to relatively rapid technological obsolescence.

Content as End-product: Browser-based Projects

The age of the information machine began to close with the development and popular acceptance of the first internet browsers in the early 1990s. In an information machine, developers have great control over both their processor and how their data is encoded. They can alter their encoding to suit the needs of their processors and develop or customize processors to work with specific instances of data. Developers working with browsers, however, have far less control over either element: users interact with projects using their own software and require content prepared in ways compatible with their processor. This both makes it much more difficult for designers to produce predictable results of any sophistication and requires them to adhere to standard ways of describing common phenomena. It also changes the focus of project design: where once developers focused on producing results, they now tend to concentrate instead on providing content.

This change in approach explains in large part the relative technological longevity of the projects by McGillivray and Kiernan. Both were developed during the initial wave of popular excitement at the commercialization of the internet. Both were designed to be used without modification by standard internet web browsers operating on the end-users' computer and written in standard languages using a standard character set recognized by all internet browsers to this day. For this reason – and despite the fact that browsers available in the late 1990s were quite primitive by today's standards – it seems very unlikely that either project in the foreseeable future will need anything like the same kind of intensive recovery effort required by the Domesday Project: modern browsers are still able to read early HTML-encoded pages and Java routines and are likely to continue to do so, regardless of changes in operating system or hardware, as long as the internet exists in its current form. Even in the unlikely event that technological changes render HTML-encoded documents unusable in our lifetime, conversion will not be difficult. HTML is a text-based language that can easily be transformed by any number of scripting languages. Since HTML-encoded files are in no way operating system or software dependent, future generations – in contrast to the engineers responsible for converting the Electronic Domesday Book – will be able to convert the projects by Kiernan and McGillivray to new formats without any need to reconstruct the original processing environment.

SGML-based Editions

The separation of content from processor did not begin with the rise of internet browsers. HTML, the language which made the development of such browsers possible, is itself derived from work on standardized structural markup languages in the 1960s through the 1980s. These languages, the most developed and widely used at the time being Standard General Markup Language (SGML), required developers to make a rigid distinction between a document's content and its appearance. Content and structure were encoded according to the intrinsic nature of the information and interests of the encoder using a suitable standard markup language. How this markup was to be used and understood was left up to the processor: in a web browser, the markup could be used to determine the text's appearance on the screen; in a database program it might serve to delimit it into distinct fields. For documents encoded in early HTML (which used a small number of standard elements), the most common processor was the web browser, which formatted content for display for the most part without specific instructions from the content developer: having described a section of text using an appropriate HTML tag as <i> (italic) or <b> (bold), developers were supposed for the most part to leave decisions about specific details of size, font, and position up to the relatively predictable internal style sheets of the user's browser (though of course many early web pages misused structural elements like <table> to encode appearance).

SGML was more sophisticated than HTML in that it described how markup systems were to be built rather than their specific content. This allowed developers to create custom sets of structural elements that more accurately reflected the qualities they wished to describe in the content they were encoding. SGML languages like DocBook were developed for the needs of technical and other publishers; the Text Encoding Initiative (TEI) produced a comprehensive set of structural elements suitable for the encoding of texts for use in scholarly environments. Unfortunately, however, this flexibility also made it difficult to share content with others. Having designed their own sets of structural elements, developers could not be certain their users would have access to software that knew how to process them.

The result was a partial return to the model of the information machine: in order to ensure their work could be used, developers of SGML projects intended for wide distribution tended to package their projects with specific (usually proprietary) software, fonts, and processing instructions. While the theoretical separation of content and processor represented an improvement over that taken by previous generations of digital projects in that it treated content as having intrinsic value outside the immediate processing context, the practical need to supply users with special software capable of rendering or otherwise processing this content tended nevertheless to tie the projects' immediate usefulness to the lifespan and weaknesses of the associated software. This is a less serious type of obsolescence, since rescuing information from projects that suffer from it involves nothing like the technological CPR required to recover the Domesday Project. But the fact that it must occur at all almost certainly limits these projects' longevity and disciplinary impact. Users who must convert a project from one format to another or work with incomplete or partially broken rendering almost certainly are going to prefer texts and scholarship in more convenient formats.

XML, XSLT, Unicode, and Related Technologies

Developments of the past half-decade have largely eliminated the problem these pioneering SGML-based projects faced in distributing their projects to a general audience. The widespread adoption of XML, XSLT, Unicode, and similarly robust international standards on the internet means that scholars developing new digital projects now can produce content using markup as flexible and sophisticated as anything possible in SGML without worrying that their users will lack the necessary software to display and otherwise process it. Just as the projects by Kiernan and McGillivray were able to avoid premature technological obsolescence by assuming users would make use of widely available internet browsers, so to designers of XML-based projects can now increase their odds of avoiding early obsolescence by taking advantage of the ubiquity of the new generation of XML-, XSLT-, and Unicode-aware internet clients.[3]

Tools and Community Support

The fact that these technologies have been so widely accepted in both industry and the scholarly world has other implications beyond making digital projects easier to distribute, however. The establishment of robust and stable standards for structural markup has also encouraged the development of a wide range of tools and organizations that also make such projects easier to develop.

Tools

Perhaps the most striking change lies in the development of tools. When I began my SGML-based edition of *Cædmon's Hymn* in 1997, the only SGML-aware and TEI-compatible tools I had at my disposal were GNU-Emacs, an open source text editor, and the Panorama and later Multidoc SGML browsers (what other commercial tools and environments were available were far beyond the budget of my one-scholar project). None of these were very user-friendly. Gnu-Emacs, though extremely powerful, was far more difficult to set up and operate than the word processors, spreadsheets, and processors I had been accustomed to use up to that point. The Panorama and Multidoc browsers used proprietary languages to interpret SGML that had relatively few experienced users and a very limited basis of support. There were other often quite sophisticated tools and other kinds of software available, including some – such as TACT, Collate, TUSTEP, and various specialized fonts like Peter Baker's original Times Old English – that were aimed primarily at medievalists or developers of scholarly digital projects. Almost all of these, however, required users to encode their data in specific and almost invariably incompatible ways. Often, moreover, the tool itself also was intended for distribution to the end user – once again causing developers to run the risk of premature technological obsolescence.

Today, developers of new scholarly digital projects have access to a far wider range of general and specialized XML-aware tools. In addition to GNU-Emacs – which remains a powerful editor and has become considerably easier to set up on most operating systems – there are a number of full-featured, easy to use, open source or relatively inexpensive commercial XML-aware editing environments available including Oxygen, Serna, and Screem. There are also quite a number of well-designed tools aimed at solving more specialized problems in the production of scholarly projects.

Several of these, such as Anastasia and Edition Production and Presentation Technology (EPPT), have been designed by medievalists. Others, such as the University of Victoria's Image Markup Tool and other tools under development by the TAPoR project, have been developed by scholars in related disciplines.

More significantly, these tools avoid most of the problems associated with those of previous decades. All the tools mentioned in the previous paragraph (including the commercial tools) are XML-based and have built-in support for TEI XML, the standard structural markup language for scholarly projects (this is also true of TUSTEP, which has been updated continuously). This means both that they can often be used on the same underlying content and that developers can encode their text to reflect their interests or the nature of the primary source rather than to suit the requirements of a specific tool. In addition, almost all are aimed at the developer rather than the end user. With the exception of Anastasia and EPPT, which both involve display environments, none of the tools mentioned above is intended for distribution with the final project. Although these tools – many of which are currently in the beta stage of development – ultimately will become obsolete, the fact that almost all are now standards compliant means that the content they produce almost certainly will survive far longer.

Community support

A second area in which the existence of stable and widely recognized standards has helped medievalists working with digital projects has been in the establishment of community-based support and development groups. Although Humanities Computing, like most other scholarly disciplines, has long had scholarly associations to represent the interests of their members and foster exchanges of information (e.g., Association for Literary and Linguistic Computing [ALLC]; Society for Digital Humanities/Société pour l'étude des médias interactifs [SDH-SEMI]), the past half-decade has also seen the rise of a number of smaller formal and informal Communities of Practice aimed at establishing standards and providing technological assistance to scholars working in more narrowly defined disciplinary areas. Among the oldest of these are Humanist-l and the TEI – both of which pre-date the development of XML by a considerable period of time. Other community groups, usually narrower in focus and generally formed after the development of XML, Unicode, and related technologies, include MENOTA (MEdieval and NOrse Text Archive), publishers of the Menota handbook: Guidelines for the encoding of medieval Nordic primary sources; MUFI (Medieval Unicode Font Initiative), an organization dedicated to the development of solutions to character encoding issues in the representation of characters in medieval Latin manuscripts; and the Digital Medievalist, a community of practice aimed at helping scholars meet the increasingly sophisticated demands faced by designers of contemporary digital projects, which organizes a journal, wiki, and mailing list devoted to the establishment and publication of best practice in the production of digital medieval resources.

These tools and organizations have helped reduce considerably the technological burden placed on contemporary designers of digital resources. As Peter Robinson has argued, digital projects will not come completely into their own until "the tools and distribution . . . [are] such that any scholar with the disciplinary skills to make an edition in print can be assured he or she will have access to the tools and distribution necessary to make it in the electronic medium" (Robinson 2005: abstract). We are still a considerable way away from this ideal and in my view unlikely to reach it before a basic competence in Humanities Computing technologies is seen as an essential research skill for our graduate and advanced undergraduate students. But we are also much farther along than we were even a half-decade ago. Developers considering a new digital project can begin now confident that they will be able to devote a far larger proportion of their time to working on disciplinary content – their scholarship and editorial work – than was possible even five years ago. They have access to tools that automate many jobs that used to require special technical know-how or support. The technology they are using is extremely popular and well supported in the commercial and academic worlds. And, through communities of practice like the Text Encoding Initiative, MENOTA, and the Digital Medievalist Project, they have access to support from colleagues working on similar problems around the globe.

Future Trends: Editing Non-textual Objects

With the development and widespread adoption of XML, XSLT, Unicode, and related technologies, text-based digital medieval projects can be said to have emerged from the incunabula stage of their technological development. Although there remain one or two ongoing projects that have resisted incorporating these standards, there is no longer any serious question as to the basic technological underpinnings of new text-based digital projects. We are also beginning to see a practical consensus as to the basic generic expectations for the "Electronic Edition": such editions almost invariably include access to transcriptions and full color facsimiles of all known primary sources, methods of comparing the texts of individual sources interactively, and, in most cases, some kind of guide, reading, or editorial text. There is still considerable difference in the details of interface (Rosselli Del Turco 2006), *mise en moniteur*, and approach to collation and recension. But on the whole, most developers and presumably a large number of users seem to have an increasingly strong sense of what a text-based digital edition should look like.

Image, sound, and animation: return of the information machine?
Things are less clear when digital projects turn to non-textual material. While basic and widely accepted standards exist for the encoding of sounds and 2D and 3D graphics, there is far less agreement as to the standards that are to be used in presenting such material to the end user. As a result, editions of non-textual material

often have more in common with the information machines of the 1980s than contemporary XML-based textual editions. Currently, most such projects appear to be built using Adobe's proprietary Flash and Shockwave formats (e.g., Foys 2003; Reed Kline 2001). Gaming applications, 3D applications, and immersive environments use proprietary environments such as Flash and Unreal Engine or custom-designed software. In each case, the long-term durability and cross-platform operability of projects produced in these environments is tied to that of the software for which they are written. All of these formats require proprietary viewers, none of which are shipped as a standard part of most operating systems. As with the BBC Domesday Project, restoring content published in many of these formats ultimately may require restoration of the original hard- and software environment.

Using technology to guide the reader: three examples[4]

Current editions of non-textual material resemble information machines in another way, as well: they tend to be over-designed. Because developers of such projects write for specific processors, they – like developers of information machines of the 1980s – are able to control the end-user's experience with great precision. They can place objects in precise locations on the user's screen, allow or prevent certain types of navigation, and animate common user tasks.

When handled well, such control can enhance contemporary users' experience of the project. Martin Foy's 2003 edition of the Bayeux Tapestry, for example, uses Flash animation to create a custom-designed browsing environment that allows the user to consult the Bayeux Tapestry as a medieval audience might – by moving back and forth apparently seamlessly along its 68-meter length. The opening screen shows a section from the facsimile above a plot-line that provides an overview of the Tapestry's entire contents in a single screen. Users can navigate the Tapestry scene-by-scene using arrow buttons at the bottom left of the browser window, centimeter by centimeter using a slider on the plot-line, or by jumping directly to an arbitrary point on the tapestry by clicking on the plot-line at the desired location. Tools, background information, other facsimiles of the tapestry, scene synopses, and notes are accessed through buttons at the bottom left corner of the browser. The first three types of material are presented in a separate window when chosen; the last two appear under the edition's plot-line. Additional utilities include a tool for making slideshows that allows users to reorder panels to suit their own needs.

If such control can enhance a project's appearance, it can also get in the way – encouraging developers to include effects for their own sake, or to control end-users' access to the underlying information unnecessarily. The British Library *Turning the Pages* series, for example, allows readers to mimic the action of turning pages in an otherwise straightforward photographic manuscript facsimile. When users click on the top or bottom corner of the manuscript page and drag the cursor to the opposite side of the book, they are presented with an animation showing the page being turned over. If they release the mouse button before the page has been pulled approximately

40 percent of the way across the visible page spread, virtual "gravity" takes over and the page falls back into its original position.

This is an amusing toy and well suited to its intended purpose as an "interactive program that allows museums and libraries to give members of the public access to precious books while keeping the originals safely under glass" (British Library Board n.d.). It comes, however, at a steep cost: the page-turning system uses an immense amount of memory and processing power – the British Library estimates up to 1 GB of RAM for high quality images on a standalone machine – and the underlying software used for the internet presentation, Adobe Shockwave, is not licensed for use on all computer operating systems (oddly, the non-Shockwave internet version uses Windows Media Player, another proprietary system that shares the same gaps in licensing). The requirement that users drag pages across the screen, moreover, makes paging through an edition unnecessarily time- and attention-consuming: having performed an action that indicates that they wish an event to occur (clicking on the page in question), users are then required to perform additional complex actions (holding the mouse button down while dragging the page across the screen) in order to effect the desired result. What was initially an amusing diversion rapidly becomes a major and unnecessary irritation.

More intellectually serious problems can arise as well. In *A Wheel of Memory: The Hereford Mappamundi* (Reed Kline 2001), Flash animation is used to control how the user experiences the edition's content – allowing certain approaches and preventing others. Seeing the Mappamundi "as a conceit for the exploration of the medieval collective memory...using our own collective *rota* of knowledge, the CD-ROM" (§ I [audio]), the edition displays images from the map and associated documents in a custom-designed viewing area that is itself in part a *rota*. Editorial material is arranged as a series of chapters and thematically organized explorations of different medieval Worlds: World of the Animals, World of the Strange Races, World of Alexander the Great, etc. With the exception of four numbered chapters, the edition makes heavy use of the possibilities for non-linear browsing inherent in the digital medium to organize its more than 1,000 text and image files.

Unfortunately, and despite its high production values and heavy reliance on a non-linear structural conceit, the edition itself is next-to-impossible to use or navigate in ways not anticipated by the project designers. Text and narration are keyed to specific elements of the map and edition and vanish if the user strays from the relevant hotspot: because of this close integration of text and image it is impossible to compare text written about one area of the map with a facsimile of another. The facsimile itself is also very difficult to study. The customized viewing area is of a fixed size (I estimate approximately 615×460 pixels), with more than half this surface given over to background and navigation: when the user chooses to view the whole map on screen, the 4-foot-wide original is reproduced with a diameter of less than 350 pixels (approximately 1/10 actual size). Even then, it remains impossible to display the map in its entirety: in keeping with the project's *rota* conceit, the facsimile viewing area is circular even though the Hereford map itself is pentagonal: try as

I might, I never have been able to get a clear view of the border and image in the facsimile's top corner.

Future standards for non-textual editions?

It is difficult to see at this point how scholarly editions involving non-textual material ultimately will evolve. Projects that work most impressively right now use proprietary software and viewers (and face an obvious danger of premature obsolescence as a result); projects that adhere to today's non-proprietary standards for the display and manipulation of images, animation, and sound currently are in a situation analogous to that of the early SGML-based editions: on the one hand, their adherence to open standards presumably will help ensure their data is easily converted to more popular and better supported standards once these develop; on the other hand, the lack of current popular support means that such projects must supply their own processing software – which means tying their short-term fate to the success and flexibility of a specific processor. Projects in this field will have emerged from the period of their technological infancy when designers can concentrate on their content, safe in the assumption that users will have easy access to appropriate standards-based processing software on their own computers.

Collaborative Content Development

The development of structural markup languages like HTML were crucial to the success of the internet because they allowed for unnegotiated interaction between developers and users. Developers produce content assuming users will be able to process it; users access content assuming it will be suitable for use with their processors. Except when questions of copyright, confidentiality, or commerce intervene, contact between developers and users can be limited to little more than the purchase of a CD-ROM or transfer of files from server to browser.

The past few years have seen a movement toward applying this model to content development as well. Inspired by the availability of well-described and universally recognized encoding standards and encouraged no doubt by the success of the Wikipedia and the open source software movement, many projects now are looking for ways to provide for the addition and publication of user-contributed content or the incorporation of work by other scholars. Such contributions might take the form of notes and annotations, additional texts and essays, links to external resources, and corrections or revision of incorrect or outdated material.

An early, pre-wiki, model of this approach is the Online Reference Book for Medieval Studies (ORB). Founded in 1995 and run by a board of section editors, ORB provides a forum for the development and exchange of digital content by and for medievalists. Contributors range from senior scholars to graduate students and interested amateurs; their contributions cover a wide variety of genres: encyclopedia-like articles, electronic primary texts, on-line textbooks and monographs, sample syllabi, research guides, and resources for the non-specialist. Despite this, the project itself is administered much like a traditional print-based encyclopedia: it is run by an editorial board that is responsible for soliciting, vetting, and editing contributions before they are published.

More recently, scholars have been exploring the possibilities of a different, unnegotiated approach to collaboration. One model is the Wikipedia – an on-line reference source that allows users to contribute and edit articles with little editorial oversight. This approach is frequently used on a smaller scale for the construction of more specialized reference works: the Digital Medievalist, for example, is using wiki software to build a community resource for medievalists who use digital media in their research, study, or teaching. Currently, the wiki contains descriptions of projects and publications, conference programs, calls for papers, and advice on best practice in various technological areas.

Other groups, such as a number of projects at the Brown Virtual Humanities Laboratory, are working on the development of mechanisms by which members of the community can make more substantial contributions to the development of primary and secondary sources. In this case, users may apply for permission to contribute annotations to the textual database, discussing differences of opinion or evidence in an associated discussion form (Armstrong and Zafrin 2005; Riva 2006).

A recent proposal by Espen Ore suggests an even more radical approach: the design of unnegotiated collaborative editions – i.e., projects that are built with the assumption that others will add to, edit, and revise the core editorial material: texts, introductory material, glossaries, and apparatus (Ore 2004). In a similar approach, the Visionary Rood Project has proposed building its multi-object edition using an extensible architecture that will allow users to associate their own projects with others to form a matrix of interrelated objects, texts, and commentary (Karkov et al. 2006). Peter Robinson has recently proposed the development of tools that would allow this type of editorial collaboration to take place (Robinson 2005).

These approaches to collaboration are still very much in their earliest stages of development. While the technology already exists to enable such community participation in the development of intellectual content, questions of quality control, intellectual responsibility, and especially incentives for participation remain very much unsettled. Professional scholars traditionally achieve success – both institutionally and in terms of reputation – by the quality and amount of their research publications. Community-based collaborative projects do not easily fit into this model. Project directors cannot easily claim intellectual responsibility for the contributions of others to "their" projects – reducing their value in a profession in which monographs are still seen as a standard measure of influence and achievement. And the type of contributions open to most participants – annotations, brief commentary, and editorial work – are difficult to use in building a scholarly reputation: the time when a carefully researched entry on the Wikipedia or annotation to an on-line collaborative edition will help scholars who are beginning or building their careers is still a long way away (see O'Donnell 2006 who discusses a number of the economic issues involved in collaborative digital models).

Conclusion

Digital scholarship in Medieval Studies has long involved finding an accommodation between the new and the durable. On the one hand, technology has allowed scholars to do far more than was ever possible in print. It has allowed them to build bigger concordances and more comprehensive dictionaries, to compile detailed statistics about usage and dialectal spread, and to publish far more detailed collations, archives, and facsimiles. At the same time, however, the rapidly changing nature of this technology and its associated methods has brought with it the potential cost of premature obsolescence. While few projects, perhaps, have suffered this quite so spectacularly as the BBC's Domesday Book, many have suffered from an undeserved lack of attention or disciplinary impact due to technological problems. The emphasis on information as a raw material in the days before the development of structural markup languages often produced results of relatively narrow and short-term interest – often in the form of information machines that could not survive the obsolescence of their underlying technology without heroic and costly efforts at reconstruction. Even the development of early structural markup languages like SGML did not entirely solve this problem: while theoretically platform-independent and focused on the development of content, SGML-based projects commonly required users to acquire specific and usually very specialized software for even the most basic processing and rendition.

Of the projects published in the initial years of the internet revolution, those that relied on the most widely supported technology and standards – HTML and the ubiquitous desktop internet browsers – survived the best. The editions by Kiernan and McGillivray showcased by Solopova in her lecture that summer still function well – even if their user interfaces now look even more old fashioned two years on.

In as much as the new XML- and Unicode-based technologies combine the flexibility and sophistication of SGML with the broad support of early HTML, text-based medieval digital scholarship is now leaving its most experimental period. There remain economic and rhetorical issues surrounding the best ways of delivering different types of scholarly content to professional and popular audiences; but on the whole the question of the core technologies required has been settled definitively.

The new areas of experimentation in medieval digital studies involve editions of non-textual material and the development of new collaborative models of publication and project development. Here technology both has even more to offer the digital scholar and carries with it even greater risks. On the one hand, the great strides made in computer-based animation, gaming, and 3D imaging in the commercial world offer projects the chance to deal with material never before subject to the kind of thorough presentation now possible. We already have marvelous editions of objects – maps, tapestries, two-dimensional images – that allow the user to explore their subjects in ways impossible in print. In the near future we can expect to see a greater use of 3D and gaming technology in the treatment of sculpture, archaeological digs, and even entire cities. With the use of wikis and similar types of collaborative technologies, such projects may also be able to capture much more of the knowledge of the disciplinary experts who make up their audiences.

For projects dealing with non-textual objects, the risk is that the current necessity of relying on proprietary software intended for the much shorter-term needs of professional game designers and computer animators will lead to the same kind of premature and catastrophic obsolescence brought on by the equally-advanced-for-its-day Domesday Project. Sixteen years from now, animation design suites like Director (the authoring suite used for producing Shockwave files) and gaming engines like Unreal engine (an authoring engine used to produce current generations of video games) are likely to be different from, and perhaps incompatible with, current versions in a way that XML authoring technologies and processors will not. While we can hope that reconstruction will not be as difficult as it proved to be in the case of the Domesday Project, it seems likely that few of today's non-textual editions will still be working without problems at an equivalent point in *their* histories, two decades from now.

In the case of experimentation with collaborative software, the challenge is more economic and social than technological. In my experience, most professional scholars initially are extremely impressed by the possibilities offered by collaborative software like wikis and other forms of annotation engines – before almost immediately bumping up against the problems of prestige and quality control that currently make them infeasible as channels of high-level scholarly communication. Indeed at one recent conference session I attended (on the future of collaborative software, no less!) the biggest laugh of the morning came when one of the speakers confessed to having devoted most of the previous month to researching and writing a long article for the Wikipedia on his particular specialism in Medieval Studies.

That current text-based digital editions seem likely to outlive the technology that produced them can be attributed to the pioneering efforts of the many scholars responsible for editions like those by Adams, Kiernan, McGillivray, and Robinson discussed by Solopova in her lecture. The current generation of scholars producing editions of non-textual objects and experimenting with collaborative forms of scholarship and publication are now filling a similar role. The solutions they are developing may or may not provide the final answers; but they certainly will provide a core of experimental practice upon which the final answers most certainly will be built.

NOTES

1 The focus of this chapter is on theoretical and historical problems that have affected digital scholarship in Medieval Studies in the past and are likely to continue to do so for the foreseeable future. Scholars seeking more specific advice on technological problems or best practice have access to numerous excellent Humanities Computing societies, mailing lists, and

internet sites. For some specific suggestions, see Part IV, "METHODOLOGIES," pp. 389–576, below. I thank Roberto Rosselli Del Turco for his help with this chapter.

2 Exceptions to this generalization prove the rule: pre-internet-age projects, such as the Dictionary of Old English (DOE) or Project Gutenberg, that concentrated more on content

than processing, have aged much better than those that concentrated on processing rather than content. Both the DOE and Project Gutenberg, for example, have successfully migrated to HTML and now XML. The first volume of the DOE was published on microfiche in 1986 – the same year as the BBC's Domesday Book; on-line and CD-ROM versions were subsequently produced with relatively little effort. Project Gutenberg began with ASCII text in 1971.

3 Not all developers of XML-encoded medieval projects have taken this approach. Some continue to write for specific browsers and operating systems (e.g., Muir 2004a); others have developed or are in the process of developing their own display environments (e.g., Anastasia, Elwood [see Duggan and Lyman 2005: Appendix]). The advantage of this approach, of course, is that – as with information machines like the BBC Domesday Book – developers acquire great control over the end user's experience (see for example McGillivray 2006 on Muir 2004b); the trade-off, however, is likely to be more rapid than necessary technological obsolescence or increased maintenance costs in the future.

4 The discussion in this section has been adapted with permission from a much longer version in O'Donnell 2005b.

References and Further Reading

Organizations and support

Digital Medievalist. An international web-based Community of Practice for medievalists working with digital media. Operates a mailing list, peer-reviewed journal, and wiki <http://www.digitalmedievalist.org/>.

Humanist-l. An international electronic seminar on humanities computing and the digital humanities <http://www.princeton.edu/humanist/>.

MENOTA (MEdieval and NOrse Text Archive), publishers of the *Menota handbook: Guidelines for the encoding of medieval Nordic primary sources* <http://www.menota.org/>.

MUFI (Medieval Unicode Font Initiative), an organization dedicated to the development of solutions to character encoding issues in the representation of characters in medieval Latin manuscripts <http://gandalf.aksis.uib.no/mufi/>.

TEI (Text Encoding Initiative). An international and interdisciplinary standard that enables libraries, museums, publishers, and individual scholars to represent a variety of literary and linguistic texts for online research, teaching, and preservation. Also operates a mailing list <http://www.tei-c.org/>.

Further Reading

Adams, Robert, Hoyt N. Duggan, Eric Eliason, Ralph Hanna III, John Price-Wilkin, and Thorlac Turville-Petre (2000). Corpus Christi College Oxford MS 201 (F) [CD-ROM]. Ann Arbor: University of Michigan Press.

Armstrong, Guyda, and Vika Zafrin (2005). "Towards the Electronic *Esposizioni*: The Challenges of the Online Commentary." *Digital Medievalist* 1.1 [Online Journal]. <http://www.digitalmedievalist.org/article.cfm?RecID=1>.

British Library Board (n.d.). "Turning the Pages: Welcome" [Webpage]. <http://www.armadillosystems.com/ttp_commercial/home.htm>.

Cummings, James (2006). "Liturgy, Drama, and the Archive: Three Conversions from Legacy Formats to TEI XML." *Digital Medievalist* 2.1 [Online Journal]. <http://www.digitalmedievalist.org/article.cfm?RecID=11>.

Duggan, Hoyt N. (2005). "A Progress Report on *The Piers Plowman Electronic Archive*" with a contribution by Eugene W. Lyman. *Digital Medievalist* 1.1 [Online Journal]. <http://www.digitalmedievalist.org/article.cfm?RecID=3>.

Finney, Andy (1986–2006). "The Domesday Project" [Website]. <http://www.atsf.co.uk/dottext/domesday.html>.

Foys, Martin K. (2003). *The Bayeux Tapestry: Digital Edition* [CD ROM]. Leicester: SDE.

Fraser, Michael (1998). "The Electronic Text and the Future of the Codex I: The History of the Electronic Text" [Unpublished Lecture]. History of the Book Seminar, Oxford University. January 1998. <http://users.ox.ac.uk/~mikef/pubs/hob_fraser_1998.html>.

Karkov, Catherine, Daniel Paul O'Donnell, Roberto Rosselli Del Turco, James Graham, and Wendy Osborn (2006). "The Visionary Cross Project" [Webpage]. <http://www.visionarycross.org/>.

Keene, Suzanne (n.d.). "Now You See It, Now You Won't" [Webpage]. <http://www.suzannekeene.info/conserve/digipres/index.htm>.

Kiernan, Kevin S. (1999). *Electronic Beowulf* [CD ROM]. London: British Library.

McGillivray, Murray (2006). [Review of Muir 2004b]. *Digital Medievalist* 2.1 [Online Journal]. <http://www.digitalmedievalist.org/article.cfm?RecID=14>.

—— (1997). *Geoffrey Chaucer's Book of the Duchess: A Hypertext Edition* [CD-ROM]. Calgary: University of Calgary Press.

Muir, Bernard James (2004a). *The Exeter Anthology of Old English Poetry: An Edition of Exeter Dean and Chapter MS 3501*. Rev. 2nd [CD ROM] edn. Exeter: Exeter University Press.

—— (2004b). *A digital facsimile of Oxford, Bodleian Library MS. Junius 11*. Software by Nick Kennedy. Bodleian Library Digital Texts 1. Oxford: Bodleian Library.

O'Donnell, Daniel Paul (2004). "The Doomsday Machine, or, 'If You Build It, Will They Still Come Ten Years From Now?': What Medievalists Working in Digital Media Can Do to Ensure the Longevity of Their Research." *Heroic Age* 7 [Online Journal]. <http://www.mun.ca/mst/heroicage/issues/7/ecolumn.html>.

—— (2005a). *Cædmon's Hymn: A Multimedia Study, Archive and Edition*. Society for early English and Norse electronic texts A.7. Cambridge: D.S. Brewer in association with SEENET and the Medieval Academy.

—— (2005b). "O Captain! My Captain! Using Technology to Guide Readers Through an Electronic Edition." *Heroic Age* 8 [Online Journal]. <http://www.mun.ca/mst/heroicage/issues/8/em.html>.

—— (2006). "Why Should I Write for Your Wiki: Towards a New Economics of Academic Publishing." Unpublished Lecture: "New Technologies and Renaissance Studies IV: Publication and New Forms of Collaboration," 52nd Annual Meeting of the Renaissance Society of America, San Francisco, CA, March 23.

Ore, Espen S. (2004). "Monkey Business – or What Is an Edition?" *Literary and Linguist Computing* 19: 35–44.

Patton, Peter C. and Renee A. Holoien, Eds. (1981). *Computing in the Humanities* Lexington, MA: Lexington Books.

Reed Kline, Naomi (2001). *A Wheel of Memory: The Hereford Mappamundi* [CD ROM]. Ann Arbor: University of Michigan Press.

Riva, Massimo (2006). "Online Resources for Collaborative Research: The Pico Project at Brown University." Unpublished Lecture: "New Technologies and Renaissance Studies IV: Publication and New Forms of Collaboration," 52nd Annual Meeting of the Renaissance Society of America, San Francisco, CA, March 23.

Robinson, Peter (2005). "Current Issues in Making Digital Editions of Medieval Texts – or, Do Electronic Scholarly Editions Have a Future?" *Digital Medievalist* 1.1 [Online journal]. <http://www.digitalmedievalist.org/article.cfm?RecID=6>.

——, and N. F. Blake (1996). *The Wife of Bath's Prologue on CD-ROM. Canterbury Tales Project*. Cambridge: Cambridge University Press.

Rosselli Del Turco, Roberto (2006). "After the Editing Is Done: Designing a Graphic User Interface for Digital Editions" [Unpublished lecture]. Delivered at: Session 640 "Digital Publication," 41st International Congress on Medieval Studies, Western Michigan University, May 6.

4
"Knowledge will be multiplied": Digital Literary Studies and Early Modern Literature
Matthew Steggle

The paradox of digital literary studies is that it takes a discipline notorious, in lay circles, for its suspicion of "fact," and its emphasis on the importance of interpretation and ambiguity rather than raw data, and it gives that discipline a set of tools which are, above all, about accessing, searching, and manipulating large amounts of raw data. As Douglas Adams puts it, *à propos* of the related discipline of philosophy, there is no point sitting up all night arguing that there may, or may not, be a God, if a computer can give you his phone number in the morning. Of course, literary studies are far more complex in their relation to factuality than such a reductive analysis would suggest, but all the same, in the ensuing survey of projects which have sought to develop a digital dimension to studies of early modern literature, relatively little will be said about the development of "new" raw primary data. Instead, a recurring theme will be the ways in which data which already, in some sense, exist, are repackaged, resorted, made searchable, and, above all, made accessible by the tools of digital literary studies.

In the first section, I argue that the digital "revolution" is made possible by, is shaped by, and must be considered in relation to the major scholarly projects of the pre-digital age. This proposition could perhaps be applied, to some extent, to most academic disciplines, but a number of converging factors make it particularly important in the field of early modern literature. The first part of my argument discusses some of these factors, relative to the projects, many of them Victorian in origin, which shaped, and shape through digital resources, our sense of the early modern.

If much of the digital revolution is about providing new ways of accessing existing data, then the ease of access itself is a crucial factor. The second section of the article surveys the development of e-texts of early modern literature, from single-handed labors of love to *Early English Books Online*, relative to themes of availability and usability; authority and completeness; and the opportunities raised by new ways of searching existing data, especially in the field of attribution studies. The third section moves on to online scholarship and discussion, broadly defined, in electronic lists, electronic forms of journal, and blogs. Many of the themes of the earlier sections – problems of authority, opportunities of novel ways of searching, and above all, questions of access – recur in the histories of exemplary projects in this section. Thus, the questions raised by the emerging discipline of digital literary studies in this field are both theoretical and practical.

The piece concludes by considering one theoretical, and one practical, extension of those questions. The theoretical extension is the emerging field of "Renaissance information": scholarly work which considers early modern literature and culture in terms of contemporary discourses of information and knowledge. The practical extension is a case study of one of the *causes célèbres* of Shakespearean studies in the past ten years, the controversy around the attribution to Shakespeare of the poem *A Funeral Elegy* (1612). This controversy was most obviously digital in that computer-aided analysis was used on both sides of the argument about the poem: but it was also digital in that many of the arguments themselves were conducted online, or in forms which show the increasing complication and interdependence of print and electronic media. Through the *Funeral Elegy* affair, I will argue, one can see a transition from traditional scholarship to a new, and in many ways less exclusive, order in which online texts and tools make knowledge, of all sorts, more easily accessed, more quickly searched, and more widely shared.

Developing a Canon

There is no scholarly agreement on exactly when the digital revolution in Renaissance and seventeenth-century literature got under way. Some trace its origins back to the early 1970s, and the first e-text of *Paradise Lost*: others consider that it only became mainstream in the past five years, with the arrival, in the form of *EEBO*, of an application which so obviously not merely supplemented, but entirely supplanted, a standard existing non-electronic method. The truth is that, informally at least, most academics tend to trace the start of the digital revolution in early modern studies to the moment when they themselves first adopted an email account. But in the case of early modern literature – the phrase I will use here in place of the more mouth-filling alternative term, Renaissance and seventeenth-century literature – the origins of the revolution go back into the early twentieth century and beyond.

What is distinctive about the early modern period, compared to the others under consideration in these essays, is the extent to which its literary canon is made finite and describable, first, by the invention of printing during that period, and second, by the relatively small numbers of books printed. As a general principle, every extant book printed in England or in English in the early modern period is likely to be recorded in one of two great catalogues, A. W. Pollard and G. R. Redgrave's *A short-title catalogue of books printed in England, Scotland, & Ireland and of English books printed*

Matthew Steggle

abroad, 1475–1640, which appeared in its first version in 1926, and Donald Godard Wing's *Short-title catalogue of books printed in England, Scotland, Ireland, Wales, and British America and of English books printed in other countries, 1641–1700,* which first appeared in 1945. Guided by the first of these two catalogues, generally now known as *STC I,* and later by Wing's (or *STC II* as it is now referred to), Eugene Power's University Microfilms project was able to gain access to the great American and British libraries – access to the latter made easier by the threat of impending war in the 1930s – and produce a series of microfilms aiming to reproduce every page of every book listed in Pollard and Redgrave and in Wing. The first microfilm units of this epic publication were issued in 1938, and it is due for completion in the next five or ten years.[1]

We will turn in a later section of this article to the digitization of the University Microfilms project as *Early English Books Online* (EEBO), but what is important to note for the moment is that *STC I* and *II* together hold out the prospect of representing the whole canon of English printed books from the period. Clearly, *STC I* and *II* are imperfect, even in their revised forms. Most obviously, *STC II* is deficient in its representation of ephemera, and *EEBO,* for instance, augments them with the catalogue of the Thomason tracts and with the *Early English Books Tract Supplement.* Nonetheless, in principle, one would be surprised to come across an early modern book – particularly an early modern book in public hands – which is *not* in *STC I* or *II,* and such a find would be worth publishing with a view to ensuring its incorporation in the next revision of *STC.* The *STC* catalogues hold out the possibility of perfectibility.

Clearly, too, printed books are not the whole story. The vibrant manuscript culture of the early modern period remains largely outside the panopticon-like view of such catalogues of printed material. But for printed books, thanks to labor before and during the early decades of the twentieth century, the early modern period is describable much more securely than either the medieval period (where they do not feature) or the later periods where the books are simply more numerous and more varied.

In ways other than the purely bibliographical, early modern literature is unusually well described, thanks, once again, to work which took place well before the digital revolution made it possible to interrogate that work in new ways. Early English printed drama is particularly well charted, thanks to a series of catalogues, each building on their predecessors, and stretching back from more recent incarnations such as G. E. Bentley's *The Jacobean and Caroline Stage* all the way to works like Gerard Langbaine's *A new catalogue of English plays containing all the comedies, tragedies, tragi-comedies, opera's, masques, pastorals, interludes, farces, &c. both ancient and modern, that have ever yet been printed, to this present year 1688.* This set of catalogues offers, in effect, successive refinements of a dataset of early modern drama, in which each play is associated with sets of data such as date of composition, authorship, company, venue, and genre. This long run of cumulative scholarly work has ensured that English drama was particularly well represented in *The Cambridge Bibliography of English*

Literature (1941), which means, in turn, that there is an almost comprehensive collection in the Chadwyck–Healey database *Literature Online*.[2] Similarly, printed English poetry and fictional prose are well documented in a series of secondary works.

Biographical data about those involved in literature and drama in this period is also easily available to the electronic researcher. The number of actors documented in connection with early modern theater is sufficiently small that sources such as Nungezer's *Dictionary of Actors* (1929) could aim for completist coverage, and just as Nungezer was succeeded by G. E. Bentley's list in *The Jacobean and Caroline Stage*, so Bentley's is already, *de facto*, in the process of being succeeded by David Kathman's ongoing project, the *Biographical Index of English Drama Before 1660*.[3] As for writers, the original *Dictionary of National Biography*, published between 1885 and 1900, appears to have had a policy of including every creative writer of the early modern period who was able to get a poem into print. As a result, even a writer of the stature of Dunstan Gale (*fl.* 1596), almost unknown to biographical history and the author of a single poem pithily and accurately described by Kenneth Muir as "both dull and bad," gained an entry in the *DNB*.[4] The effects of that continue to propagate, thanks to the *Oxford Dictionary of National Biography*'s policy not to exclude anyone who was included in the original *DNB*, with the result that there is a fresh entry on Gale in the new version, completed in 2004 and available not just in print but in a magnificent and fully searchable online edition.[5] The work done by the writers of Victorian printed sources continues to be felt, directly and indirectly, in the digital data now available to researchers.

Indeed, what is true of bibliography, and of biography, for this period, holds true for lexicography as well, in the form of the *Oxford English Dictionary*, a project begun in 1857 and published in its first form between 1884 and 1928. The distorting factor here, as so often in early modern studies, is Shakespeare: the enormous prestige attached to the language of Shakespeare in the nineteenth century, and the enormous energy devoted then to its glossing, means that early modern English (albeit, perhaps, a particularly "literary" flavor of early modern English) is unusually well represented in the *OED*. And whereas the Victorian *DNB* bequeathed to its successor the *Oxford DNB* its shape and outlines, and some small sections of its text, the first edition of the *OED* still, at the time of writing, makes up the bulk of the text of its subsequent incarnations. The second edition, completed in 1989, was a matter of adding new entries rather than reshaping the existing ones, and the first edition entries will remain in place until the completion of the third edition, currently under way. Thus the product which became available in CD-ROM form in 1992, and in subscription website form in 2000, traces not merely its origins but most of its fabric back to the work of James Murray's team.[6] Of course, the data in the *Oxford English Dictionary* are accessible in ways never before imaginable to researchers of early modern literature, thanks to full-text searches of the dictionary, and tools such as proximity searching and wildcard searching: but the skeleton of that data derives from a much older research effort. The stress on the novelty of electronic resources should not disguise the extent to which they are built out of preceding research.

Electronic Texts

If one of the themes of this chapter is that the electronic revolution in early modern studies stands on the shoulders of much earlier work, another theme is that it is only the very easy availability of the resources that has made that revolution possible, a point which can be illustrated, with regard to electronic texts, by a personal anecdote. In 1993, as a graduate student interested in Renaissance constructions of Aristophanes, I went to my university's computing service to ask if I could do a search across the electronic texts that they held in order to locate occurrences where Aristophanes was referred to by name. The computing services staff explained to me that they did indeed have a collection of literally dozens of early modern electronic texts, in various markup formats and on various media, each donated by a researcher who had prepared it in connection, usually, with a project of linguistic analysis or concordance-making. However, although they held these texts, there was no convenient way of making the whole database available at once for cross-searching. They offered, instead, to give me any one text of my choice on a diskette. Although these electronic texts were available – in one sense of that word and for certain sorts of analysis – they weren't available for the sort of unsophisticated and speculative one-off cross-search that I wanted to perform on them.

By the time I completed my doctoral thesis, and by dint of much reading, I had amassed a collection of perhaps three dozen early modern texts which make reference by name to Aristophanes, references which formed the basis for my assertions in that thesis about the cultural currency of Aristophanes in the period. By contrast, in autumn 2004, a brief full-text search on *Early English Books Online* – a check which took under a minute – showed up 136 texts published before 1660 which make reference to Aristophanes by name. Even worse, these numbers do not stay static as *EEBO*'s provision of full-text continues to progress. The same search, repeated in spring 2006, revealed, just as quickly, 205 texts that name the Greek comedian.[7] The sheer brute force of these resources entirely changes one's ability to find certain sorts of data in early modern literature. But before giving proper consideration to *EEBO*, it is necessary to review the other ways by which electronic texts of the Renaissance became available and searchable.

As well as the resources which are likely to be featured in other discussions in this volume of the rise of e-texts – *Project Gutenberg*, the *Internet Public Library*, *Representative Poetry Online*, and so forth – some initiatives have been of particular interest to early modern studies, and this chapter will survey them briefly, concentrating on ones which have survived the test of time and are still generally available.[8]

Risa Bear's Renascence Editions project has been an inspiration to many working in the field for its combination of scholarly care and aesthetic sensibility. Its origins lie, firstly in Bear's career as a typographer, and secondly, in the experience of being a student: " While working on the M.A. in English at the University of Oregon, in 1992, I became interested in producing texts for internet distribution as an alternative to writing term papers." Bear ended up spending a year of her spare time typing the entire *Faerie Queene* into a computer, and then going through and adding in, before and after every italicized word, the tags <i> and </i>:

> I ... created the *Faerie Queene* as an HTML coded text, hand coding with macros in a program called PCWrite on a 286 computer, uploading to the University's server via XMODEM at 300 baud, and checking my work with LYNX, the text-based browser available on the mainframe. My first HTML project, then, was a single work, in eight files, comprising some two million characters.[9]

Bear's *Faerie Queene* was published in 1995, and has been in constant use ever since. Alongside it there are now around two hundred other early modern texts, edited by Bear and a team of volunteers, and all prepared with the belief that HTML is a form of typography and deserves the respect given to other forms of that craft. Bear's project has also provided a home for work whose roots go back much further, such as Judy Boss's transcription of the ten-book version of *Paradise Lost*, originally made in 1971. In a world where the innovations heralded by Renascence Editions have become so much the norm, it is worth stressing how strange and intoxicating an idea it seemed, at the time of its inception, that early modern texts not necessarily available in an academic's local library could be downloaded, for free, in minutes, onto a computer anywhere.

There are several points of contact between *Renascence Editions* and Anniina Jokinen's *Luminarium* project, a mine of online information on medieval, Renaissance, and seventeenth-century literature, based around a series of author-centered pages.[10] First, and perhaps most conspicuously, neither is concerned with revenue generation, nor with the gaining of "conventional" academic authority. Jokinen, indeed, calls her site a labor of love. Perhaps a cause of that is a similarity in their origins: like *Renascence Editions*, *Luminarium* started not out from the experience of being a teacher, but from the experience of being a student. Jokinen writes: "The site started in early 1996. I remember looking for essays to spark an idea for a survey class I was taking at the time."[11] A page of links to online essays quickly grew into a site containing author quotations and biographies. As for electronic texts, the power of *Luminarium* lay in the combination of a careful list of links to e-texts scattered around the web, together with *Luminarium*'s own project of easily accessible HTML texts mostly based on Victorian editions (so that, again, the new technologies are, in effect, propagating the work of nineteenth-century scholars). For instance, in the case of Ben Jonson, Jokinen's combination of links to other sources together with her own transcriptions of William Gifford's modern-spelling edition made accessible large chunks of Jonson's work to anyone with a modem. *Renascence Editions* and *Luminarium* are representative examples of a class of projects which might also include Dana F. Sutton's *Philological Museum*, specializing in neo-Latin works, and elegantly juggling text, translation, and commentary; *The Milton Reading Room*, a site of texts and commentary developed by Thomas H. Luxon and his students at Dartmouth College from 1997 onward and now covering much of Milton's poetry and prose; the *Early Modern English Dictionaries Database*, under the guidance of Ian Lancashire, providing a searchable reference tool; and the Memorial web edition of Alciato's *Book of Emblems*, combining text, translation, image, and cross-reference to other emblem series and other emblem sites.[12] All four of these projects date back to the 1990s; all four are still online; I've personally used all four as the best ways of answering research questions.

Projects like these, like *Luminarium* and *Renascence Editions*, were important because they made electronic texts of early modern literature easily available, in numbers, and – a supplementary consideration – generally made them visible to search engines. None of them, though, aimed to be comprehensive. On the other hand, one resource which did have that aim – within its self-set limits – was Chadwyck-Healey's *Literature Online*, also known as *LION*, which relied not on labors of love, or on dubious automatic optical character recognition (OCR), but on large-scale, industrial-style data entry. The *LION* procedure was to take the earliest version of a text, and have a professional operator type it into a computer; meanwhile another operator would be typing in the same text, and discrepancies between the two would be examined as a way of weeding out errors. Using this double-keyboarding technique, *LION* claimed an accuracy rate of 99.97 to 99.995 percent in its transcriptions.[13] *LION* had its first incarnation in a series of CD-ROMs, but it gained a new level of power when it became available through IP recognition, thus ridding the user of all the inconveniences of engaging with the discs on which the data were stored. (A review by Catherine Alexander, for *EMLS*, catches the start of the online version in 1999.[14]) *Literature Online*'s texts were, of course, old-spelling, and marked up with various forms of metadata identifying, for instance, the difference between stage directions and dialogue within a play, although this metadata is generally invisible to the end user. Building on the comprehensive bibliographies discussed in Section 1 above, *Literature Online* aimed to provide e-texts, edited to a single consistent standard, of almost everything conventionally classified as early modern literature. For the first time, there was a corpus on the basis of which it seemed possible to make reasonably definitive pronouncements.

One use of this work is exemplified by articles such as Gabriel Egan's "Hearing or Seeing a Play?: Evidence of Early Modern Theatrical Terminology."[15] Egan uses *LION* to demonstrate that, in spite of the often-repeated statement that early modern theater was thought about as primarily an auditory, rather than a visual appearance, the phrase "hear a play," and its myriad variants of spelling and phrasing, is much rarer than the equivalent phrase "see a play," and all its myriad variants of spelling and phrasing, across the literary writing of early modern England as represented in *LION* in 2001. This is, on the one hand, an interesting result, from the point of view of how one thinks about early modern attitudes to theater. On the other hand, it also asks questions about the wider methodology of corpus search using *LION* and similar resources. One subset of these problems relates to the variability of early modern spelling, most obviously "u/v," "i/j," and terminal "e," but also all the other variants of orthography. Egan's answer in this piece is to methodically list all the plausible combinations and work through them. Similarly, a researcher searching the full-text for passing references to the brothel "Holland's Leaguer" must work through variant spellings of the second word alone including "leagver," "leagure," "leagar," and "leager." Such tasks are now facilitated by to some extent by *LION*'s "include typographical variants" option. This recently introduced option works methodically and mechanically through a series of permutations of the search term, based on the combinations of substituting u/v, i/j/y, w for vv or uu, and s for f; it thus offers a shortcut for certain sorts of search, but, equally, does not claim to be a panacea, since in the case of "leaguer" it would only catch the first of the four variant spellings listed above.[16] In addition, Egan's article raises all sorts of questions about the selection biases that have operated ever since some works were printed and some not; that have continued throughout the processes that have seen some publications survive in numbers, and some fail to survive in even a single copy; and that are still felt in the decisions about "literary" status made by the *CBEL* which determine whether or not a text is represented in the starting corpus.

Such issues are particularly pressing to scholars wishing to make statements based on negative evidence adduced from *LION*: statements about what *LION* appears *not* to contain. Early modern attribution studies, for instance, adopted *LION* with enthusiasm, as offering a large database of texts to act as controls, particularly for statistical approaches based on multivariate analysis of the relative frequencies of common words.[17] More will be said later about attribution studies, but for the moment it is worth noting that *LION*, which serves as one of the principal staples of such work, is also an important and powerful resource in the provision of texts of all sorts, for all purposes, to scholars and students of the early modern period.

While *LION* is limited by its definition of the literary, it is empowered by its broad chronological sweep. This doesn't merely mean that it is possible to compare plays and poems from across the centuries, although it does: it is also particularly useful in dealing with early modern literature, in that it allows the reach of a scholar to extend into the manuscripts of the period. Thus, it is possible to search *LION* for all the plays performed (according to its metadata) between 1620 and 1630, and that search pulls out results (such as the anonymous *The Fatal Marriage*) which remained in manuscript until the twentieth century.

I have argued that *LION*'s usefulness compared to collections on the scale of *Luminarium*, *Renascence Editions*, and *Representative Poetry Online* lies not just in the fact that it offers more texts than them, but also in its ambitions to comprehensive coverage – in the fact that it aims there should be no texts, within its self-imposed limits, which it does not cover. The same is already partly true of the most powerful single resource for early modern studies, *Early English Books Online*. At the time of writing, *EEBO* contains page images of every page of around 95,000 books, out of the approximately 125,000 listed in *STC I* and *II*, so that it can provide instant access to a large majority of the surviving printed texts of early modern Britain. As noted at the start of this chapter, *EEBO* is the end-product of microfilming efforts which began before World War II, and in one sense there is nothing in the "original" *EEBO* which is not in that microfilm collection. However, as anyone who ever used the micro-film will attest (and it is a sign of *EEBO*'s position of dominance that one can even write that sentence), it was not a user-friendly medium. It required, first, finding a library that had it; secondly, negotiating the torturous collation of the appropriate *STC* catalogue with the cross-index, a book consisting solely of two columns of numbers; finding the microfilm, whether by locating it in one of its cabinets or by putting in a request form to a librarian; loading the microfilm onto the spindle; whirring or creaking it through to the required book and the required pages (assuming, that is, that it turned out to be the right film); and attempting to print it on a reader-printer, a device that took the fallible moving parts of a microfilm reader and added to them the fallible moving parts of a photocopier. When I think of using the *STC* microfilms, I think of perishing rubber bands, uncoiling films, the smell of toner, and headaches behind the eyes. *EEBO* is simply a faster, better, and more flexible way to get at the images originally committed to the microfilm, enabling a researcher to spend less time locating pages of the book and more time reading them.

That product – essentially, *EEBO* as originally released – was at once recognized as an "invaluable research tool," even though the execution of it then was crude compared to the speed and fluency with which it works for most university users now.[18] Also deserving of mention here as a comparably powerful resource is *Gallica*, the digital arm of the French *Bibliothèque Nationale*.[19] *Gallica* offers facsimile images of hundreds of books from the early modern period, mostly in French and Latin. While the terms of reference of the catalogues on which *EEBO* is founded encourage an insular view of England's relation to continental Europe, a project like *Gallica* offers wider horizons. Indeed *Gallica* is in one respect more path-breaking even than *EEBO*, certainly for academics who are not actually physically based in the Biliothèque Nationale. The microfilms from which *EEBO* takes its images are, as discussed above, hard to find and inconvenient to take copies from, but they are accessible in numerous libraries around the world. But in opening up to worldwide readers the riches of the Biliothèque Nationale, *Gallica* makes available texts which before were even harder to find and to copy.

This is not to deny, though, the power of *EEBO*, a power which has continued to increase with the advent of the Text Creation Partnership. This is a project based around a methodology of double keyboarding similar to that used by *LION* to create full-text transcripts of, in the first instance, 25,000 of the books in *EEBO*. At the time of writing, 11,055 books have been completed, and the result is a large and constantly expanding corpus of fully searchable text which is already having revolutionary effects both on research projects, such as that on Aristophanes described at the start of this section, and on teaching. Of course, *EEBO* does not make, and will never make, *LION* redundant: rather, the two databases offer different ways of examining the data. If *EEBO*'s self-imposed restrictions relate to its date range and to its limitation to print culture, its strength is the range of print culture it enables a reader to get at – not merely literary texts, but sermons, cookery books, guides to arithmetic, and factual material of all sorts. *EEBO* holds out the prospect of getting a truer sense of proportion than ever before about the extant print culture of early modern Britain.

So far, the discussion has focused on a series of projects to create corpora of texts. One thing that *Renascence Editions*, *Luminarium Editions*, *LION*, *Gallica*, and *EEBO* all have in common is that they are none of them concerned with adding value by annotating the texts they compile into their corpora. The final part of this section will consider electronic editing and commentary as an activity.

An exemplary project here is the Internet Shakespeare Editions project, under the leadership of Michael Best.[20] Best set out in 1996

> to create a website with the aim of making scholarly, fully annotated texts of Shake-speare's plays freely available in a form native to the medium of the internet. A further mission was to make educational materials on Shakespeare available to teachers and students: using the global reach of the internet, I wanted to make every attempt to make my passion for Shakespeare contagious.
>
> This seemingly simple set of objectives becomes interestingly complicated as we look at what is involved. What do we mean by a "scholarly" text? What is "full annotation"? And, most challenging of all, what kind of text is "native to the medium of the internet"?[21]

Best's project uses peer-review to ensure scholarly quality:

> the central metaphor is a Library, a virtual space in which only peer-reviewed materials are published. To take advantage of the more informal traditions of the internet, however, we also have an Annex to the Library where materials valuable to the scholarly community – but not yet fully reviewed – can be published.[22]

In order to ensure a consistency of markup and annotation across the edition as a whole, in which each play is being edited by a separate editor, *ISE* has extensive and detailed editorial guidelines, against which the submitted work is measured in the process of peer-review central to the *ISE* model. In an adaptation to the requirements of different users of the text, *ISE* has three different "levels" of annotation – level one, reflecting the needs of school students, and offering straightforward word-for-word glosses; level two, offering full scholarly annotation, as in a standard print edition, but enhanced by opportunities to link to images, video, and other forms of multimedia representation; and level three, offering opportunities for detailed discussion of the sort that a print edition would be forced to handle in an appendix.

Just as there is more than one level of scholarly annotation in *ISE*, so there is also more than one version of the text being annotated, depending upon the requirements of the reader. The *ISE* project views Shakespeare's texts as documents existing in multiple forms – old-spelling and modernized spelling; quarto and folio versions; and page-by-page pictorial facsimile of those originals. All of these versions are tied to one another for easy comparison. The markup is in XML, and this, too, can be output in various forms to create TEI-compliant XML documents. *ISE* is a work in progress, which promises to be one of the most serious and scholarly contributions to online editing. It is a benchmark for the current generation of heavyweight editions of Renaissance texts, in which an electronic component is fast becoming a *sine qua non*. The *Cambridge Works of Ben Jonson*, for instance, will be published with the texts and ancillary material also available through a subscription-only website, while the *Complete Works of Richard Brome*, currently in preparation, is to be published in electronic form as its primary medium, and intends to make extensive use of multimedia possibilities such as video clips in the course of that electronic edition.[23]

A taste of what might be achievable in such an edition can be gained from the *Interactive Shakespeare Project*, prepared by the Theatre Department of Holy Cross College, Worcester, Massachusetts.[24] At the heart of this project is a modern-spelling text of *Measure for Measure*, with hotlinked annotation which appears in a separate frame on the screen, while yet a third frame contains stills from a production of the play. The text is also enriched with a series of red-boxed links in the left margin to secondary materials: to suggestions for exercises; and to questions to prompt a reader. A video clip of the whole scene in production is also accessible. The whole thing is carefully produced, beautifully executed, robust, and still accessible to anyone seven years after its completion (Figure 4.1). What the *Interactive Shakespeare Project* does for

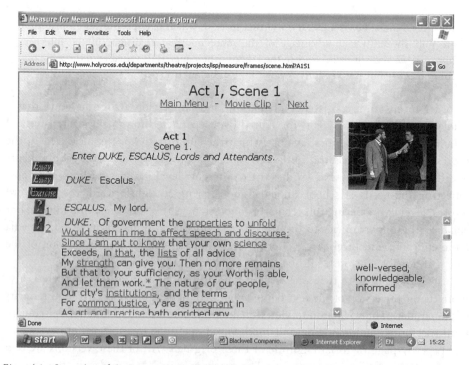

Figure 4.1   Screenshot of the Interactive Shakespeare Project. Source: http://www.holycross.edu/departments/theatre/projects/isp/measure/frames/scene.html?A1S1.

explicitly pedagogical purposes may give a glimpse into what scholarly editions of the future will look like. With electronic texts becoming increasingly a part of the scholarly landscape, exercises like the Interactive Shakespeare Project point the way to the next great challenge: not mere availability, but usability.

Literary Scholarship and Criticism Online

Discussion lists

Discussion lists were early, and important, factors in the development of an online community of early modern scholars. Lists such as HUMANIST were influential in shrinking the distance between scholars in institutions separated widely by geography and other factors. A particularly interesting example, and one which might serve as an exemplary case study, is provided by the long-running and still extant list, SHAKSPER, "the global electronic Shakespeare conference." SHAKSPER was established in July 1990, with a dozen members, under the editorship of Ken Steele, who, indeed, cited HUMANIST as a model in his first message to the list. Steele's opening message also implies that the original intention of the list was to seek some sort of formal affiliation to the Shakespeare Association of America, which did not materialize, but in other ways what is surprising is how modern the early correspondence of the list feels, with announcements of performances; debates about historical fidelity; and, lurking in the background at once like the snake in the garden of Eden, the shadowy presence of anti-Stratfordians.[25] Only the list's name, in which Shakespeare's surname had to be rendered in an eight-letter form in order to meet the requirements of the early operating systems, obviously indicates the difference in technology from today, a difference which is also elided by the ease with which the archives may now be accessed and navigated. Whereas the archives of the list are now accessed through a clear and well-laid-out website, designed by Eric Luhrs for a readership for whom web browsing is intuitive, the SHAKSPER archives were previously accessible only through an arcane series of listserv commands (for instance, by writing an email consisting of the wonderful phrase GET SHAKSPER BIOGRAFY), or through downloading and searching an entire year's records as a text file.

In 1992 Hardy M. Cook took over as list owner and moderator, a post which he still holds, reading and reformatting each contribution before sending it out to the list – a policy which, although guaranteeing the list is spam-free, is labor-intensive. As SHAKSPER grew in numbers of subscribers, so questions of community, audience, and etiquette became more intense. In one respect, the lists were recapitulating the experience of early print journals, such as *Notes and Queries*, which offered a "medium for intercommunication" between a virtual community of scholars, and whose early history can itself be described using the terminology of lurkers and flame wars; in another, they were reenacting the experiences of non-virtual Shakespeare societies, in which questions of seriousness versus pleasure, exclusivity versus inclusivity, and cohesion versus competition are repeating themes.[26]

In the case of SHAKSPER, the most obvious source of friction in terms of all three of the above categories is anti-Stratfordianism. As Cook has written,

> I tried to be as patient as I could with the primarily Oxfordians, who were generally non-academics and who had begun to flood the list with posting. However, after a while, I deemed as a responsible Shakespearean firmly ensconced in academia that I could no longer tolerate the misleading, conspiracy-laden ramblings and banned further discussion on the topic.[27]

The result was the establishment in 1995 of a usenet group, humanities.lit.authors. shakespeare or HLAS, which is open to all aspects of "alternative" theory and authorship conspiracy, as well as more conventional questions, and which has been receiving over a thousand posts per month for the past eight years. This compares with an average, for SHAKSPER over the past few years, of between two and three thousand posts per year. HLAS is thus a far more active forum than SHAKSPER, even though it does not gain the academic recognition of its elder sibling. In the words of Gary Allen, writing on SHAKSPER in 2001, "Think of SHAKSPER as the lovely gardens where esthetes in Grecian garments wander at their ease, then think of HLAS as the concert hall where 140 ill-paid musicians are flailing away at 'The Ride of the Valkyries'."[28] Among the worthwhile consequences of HLAS, incidentally, is Terry Ross and David Kathman's *Shakespeare Authorship Page*, "Dedicated to the proposition that Shakespeare wrote Shakespeare," which is to be celebrated as a clear and careful statement of how we know what we know about Shakespeare, and how scholarship actually works.[29]

Even without the Oxfordians, Baconians, Marlovians, Derbyites, and assorted other non-believers, most of whom migrated to HLAS, debate has continued on SHAKSPER about what are, and are not, acceptable topics of discussion. How often, for instance, is it necessary to have debates about in what sense, if any, Shakespearean characters can be thought of as real people? One large category of material ranges across reviews of Shakespeare films, announcements of Shakespeare theater productions, and detection of Shakespeare allusions in popular forms from sitcom to political cartoon to pornographic film. What does, and does not, constitute something worth drawing to the attention, however briefly, of SHAKSPER's 1,300 members? At the time of writing, SHAKSPER's editor has proposed to move, like the early editors of *Notes and Queries*, from the position of mere facilitator to something more like a gatekeeper: "the Editor only posts contributions that he believes are of interest to the academic Shakespearean community."[30] Thus, one might see the first step in the process of a discussion list turning into a reviewed publication.

Other long-lived and well-balanced lists of interest to scholars of early modern literature include MILTON-L, a list on Milton associated with a fine website.[31] SIDNEY-SPENSER is a particularly interesting example of a list which emerged from the combination of two separate lists, formerly SIDNEY-L and SPENSER-L. The combined identity has worked well, partly because of the list's strong sense of on- and off-line community, reflected in its frequent discussions of the festivities associated with the Sidney and Spenser sessions in the annual meetings at Kalamazoo. The Sidney-Spenser list, too, is associated with an excellent website, or rather two excellent websites, a relic, perhaps, of its bifurcated past: The Sidney Homepage, maintained by Andrew Zurcher, and The Spenser Homepage, maintained by Gavin Alexander.[32] Both host numerous documents, articles, and links, likely to be of interest to scholars of Spenser and Sidney. Significantly, both also host the homepages of associated print journals. The Sidney Homepage hosts an archive of tables of contents of issues of the paper *Sidney Journal*, while the Spenser homepage does the same for the paper journal *Spenser Studies* and also includes the abstracts. At the time of writing, one article in the *Sidney Journal* back catalogue has turned from a bare title into a blue underlined title, with the entire text of the article behind it, perhaps a sign of things to come in journals generally.[33] As with SHAKSPER, one can see the start of a process where the gap between listserv, website, and academic journal is starting to shrink.

E-journals and other scholarly e-publications

Some projects, however, have gone down a different path, and used the electronic medium to produce peer-reviewed e-journals which resemble, to a greater or lesser extent, their print equivalents. I will take as a test case in this section the history of the e-journal *Early Modern Literary Studies*, a history which exemplifies many of the wider questions and problems that have dogged the development of early modern e-journals.[34]

Early Modern Literary Studies is a peer-reviewed online journal, publishing articles on all aspects of early modern literature. No registration or subscription is required, and it is available for free to anyone anywhere in the world with access to a web browser. Since its foundation in 1995 *EMLS* has published over a hundred and fifty scholarly articles, and over two hundred and fifty reviews of books, films, plays, and multimedia products. In a typical week, its servers record around 6,000 different readers in eighty different countries.[35]

EMLS was originally set up by its founding editor, Ray Siemens, to be accessible not merely through a web browser, but also by gopher, and even as an email sent in ASCII form.[36] Siemens recruited a distinguished international editorial board to review the submissions; established norms for how to cite the journal; and arranged for the journal to have a PURL, or permanent URL, which would stay the same regardless of where, physically, the journal was hosted. The advantage of a PURL over a conventional domain name is that PURLs are administered by the OCLC, a worldwide federation of libraries, so that one doesn't have to be able to continue to pay fees to an internet service provider to keep it operative. In other respects, the journal set out to mimic the conventions of paper journals. It was assigned an ISSN, it set out to get indexed in the sources where scholars would normally look for details of print publications – sources like ABELL and the MLA; and it was published in three discrete "issues" per year, even though the website would have allowed continuous updating. Strikingly, although *EMLS* has made use of the multimedia properties of online publication – non-linear articles; images; sound clips; videos; even virtual reality fly-throughs of early modern theaters – its experiments in encroaching on the territory of the discussion lists have met with only limited success. Something about the analogy with a print journal deters academics from engaging in dialogue in the context of the e-journal, except in the format appropriate to print journals – namely, relatively slow-moving and carefully wrought exchanges of positions, in the "readers' forum" section of the journal.

In some ways, more pressing than the purely technical details of developing the journal have been the institutional issues: how the journal is supported; how people gain credit for publishing in the journal; and how to ensure the long-term availability and future of the journal. This piece will consider each of these in turn, using *EMLS* as an example.

EMLS is supported, in effect, by the university department of the academic who edits it. In the case of *EMLS*, as with SHAKSPER, the academic involved does all the editing and production work by themselves. Partly as a consequence, *EMLS* is published in HTML. More elegant and structured ways of encoding data are certainly technologic- ally feasible, but HTML is readable by even the most basic of web browsing software; it is accessible to search engine spiders; it is robust; and if anything goes amiss, the editor can solve the problem themselves rather than having to call for technical support. The journal's success, and its continued wide readership, is partly a product of this "tractor technology" approach to the basic architecture, with the technological innovations – images, sound, video, and others – sitting on top of a structure which is very simple for the reader to navigate through. On the other hand, the tractor technology approach also has an eye to the journal's long-term future. The fact that the editor can sustain it single-handed insulates the journal from threat of the crises that beset long-term projects when the funding dries up, or when institutional support is unavailable.

As for the question of the recognition gained from publishing in an online journal, there is a deep suspicion of something that is "only" digital, particularly among a profession so heavily invested in the printed word. According to a commonly held prejudice, online journals are seen as "write journals" – places which exist more for contributors than for readers.[37] In spite of *EMLS*'s rigid peer-review policy, and in spite of institutional statements proclaiming the validity of electronic publication, this is an issue the journal continues to contend with. The best form of reply, really, is to continue to publish high-quality material, and to collect admiring references to the work that the journal does.[38]

As for securing the long-term future of the journal: one part of this strategy, already identified, is *EMLS*'s low-tech approach. The content of the journal is archived at the University of Toronto and the National Library of Canada, and *EMLS* is also now involved in Stanford University's LOCKSS project, a project to create multiple and constantly updated caches of the journal's contents at research libraries around the world.[39] *EMLS* has syndication agreements with publishers including the Thomson

Gale group, which is one route by which *EMLS* articles, although born digital, are starting to appear alongside the electronic incarnations of print articles.

Otherwise, "true" e-journals devoted to the early modern field remain surprisingly thin on the ground. *Renaissance Forum*, based at the University of Hull, is one of the longest established, "an electronic journal of early-modern literary and historical studies." *Early Modern Culture* has a remit which leads it more into cultural studies, and is written in the format of an "electronic seminar," looking for dialogue with the papers under discussion. Honorable mention should be made of *Borrowers and Lenders: The Journal of Shakespearean Appropriation*, which although not strictly devoted to the early modern, is certainly of interest to anyone working on Shakespeare. The *Early Modern Journal*, a project based at Claremont Graduate University which aimed to publish work by graduate students, is not to be found at the moment of writing, its home page being replaced with advertisements for hypertension remedies.[40] In practice, though, what has happened is that it has become usual practice to cite print journals from electronic sources without mentioning the intermediate electronic source. Projects such as *LION*, *JSTOR*, and *Project Muse* offer either facsimile reproductions, or text which has gone through optical character recognition; individual publishers offer electronic access to their current and past journal issues, and even to extracts from current books, sometimes requiring subscription and sometimes not; old and current journal articles and books are being put online unofficially, and with varying degrees of rigor, by a host of independent contributors to the internet.[41] Indeed, in some areas of interest to literary scholars of the early modern, early secondary sources are turning up in the *Google Books* project and even *Eighteenth Century Collections Online*. Electronics is changing the face of the scholarly journal: however, the extent of this change is masked by the prevailing convention of still citing the paper "original," even when that original has only been seen through the medium of a facsimile.

The newest area of interest in early modern studies, and one where, again, the technology remains to be proven, is the early modern blog. Three early entrants into what will doubtless be a burgeoning field might be mentioned here: Adam Smyth's *Renaissance Lit* blog, the collaborative project *Blogging the Renaissance*, and Sharon Howard's *Early Modern Notes*.[42] At the time of writing, blogs are yet to prove themselves as respectable tools of the early modern researcher: but, given the trajectories followed by discussion lists and e-journals, it is surely only a matter of time.

Renaissance Information

Forecasting the future direction of a field is notoriously difficult, but if academic blogs are one possible Next Big Thing, another idea whose time is frequently said to be coming is the application to Renaissance studies of contemporary ideas about information and information revolutions. Many analogies, indeed perhaps too many analogies, can be made between the Renaissance and the contemporary world in this respect. Early modern manuscript publication is often described as offering the sort of informal hand-to-hand dissemination of documents now associated with email. Equally, though, the culture of electronic publication could be described as suffering, as discussed in the previous section, from something analogous to the much-debated idea of the Renaissance "stigma of print." A ground-breaking collection of essays published in the year 2000, *The Renaissance Computer*, started to explore Renaissance culture from the perspective of "knowledge technology." Renaissance works, in this account, could be read not as a single linear narrative, but as information-retrieval systems deploying an array of hypertextual features such as indices, marginalia, and illustrations. At the time, *The Renaissance Computer* seemed likely to herald a major new field of enquiry.[43] Since then, relatively little work has appeared in this interesting, and perhaps neglected, area of early modern studies.

Case Study – *A Funeral Elegy*

This chapter closes with a case study of a single controversy which has run through the online Shakespeare community over the past ten years. The story intersects with several of the themes of this chapter – the interrelation, and also rivalry, of print and online media; the rapid development of e-texts, both for the purposes of text analysis programs and for the purposes of flesh-and-blood readers; and questions of protocols of informal scholarly conversation, and of the status of online publication.

In 1612, there appeared in print, under the initials "W. S.," *A funerall elegye in memory of the late vertuous Maister William Peter of Whipton neere Excester* (London: G. Eld, 1612). To give a sample of the poem, here are the opening eight of its 578 lines:

> Since *Time*, and his predestinated end,
> Abridg'd the circuit of his hope-full dayes;
> Whiles both his *Youth* and *Vertue* did intend,
> The good indeuor's, of deserving praise:
> What memorable monument can last,
> Whereon to build his neuer blemisht name?
> But his owne worth, wherein his life was grac't?
> Sith as it euer hee maintain'd the same.
>
>   (A3r)

In 1989, Donald W. Foster published a book arguing, on the basis of parallel passages and other evidence, that "W.S." stood for William Shakespeare.[44] This discussion will not cover the pros and cons of that identification; nor the various rival identifications which have been proposed – John Ford generally now being regarded as the clear winner of the honor of having written the poem; nor the passage of the *Elegy* into and out of the Shakespeare canon as measured in publications of *Complete Works*. What interests me is the effect of digital technologies on scholars' abilities to talk about the poem.

Digital technologies were, indeed, important to Foster's claims about the *Elegy*, since between 1989 and 1986 he developed a database he called SHAXICAN, which counted the appearance of rare words in the Shakespeare corpus and in a corpus of assorted other available Renaissance e-texts, and measured the *Elegy* against them. This use of statistical analysis wasn't in itself new, but previously the counting had to be carried out manually – the automation of the process simply made it much more practicable. The unpublished database, and its results, fueled Foster's renewed claims, made at conferences and carried in the media, that the *Elegy* could be securely identified as a new item in the Shakespeare canon.[45] On January 12, 1996, in response to queries on the SHAKSPER discussion list, Foster made a modern-spelling e-text of the poem available on the SHAKSPER fileserver, which helped ignite a long and intense discussion of the *Elegy*, and of the criteria for establishing its authorship. To understand why posting this transcription had such a dramatic effect, it is important to remember how unavailable the *Elegy* was in 1996. It could be got at on microfilms, subject to the inconveniences of microfilm detailed above, and it could be found transcribed in Foster's book, but it was still the case that, as Foster wrote, "most SHAKSPERians will not have the text at their disposal."[46] Nowadays, with the page images accessible as a matter of course through *EEBO* – the source for the old-spelling transcription above – this would not be the case.

The ensuing debates make fascinating reading, as SHAKSPEReans apply a range of techniques – considerations of rare words, investigations of historical context, gut feelings about poetic style – to a common problem, in "real time," or at least over a timescale of days rather than years. Many of the posts appeal to vocabulary, using printed Shakespeare concordances: William Godshalk uses one, for instance, to note that line 8 quoted above is, if Shakespearean, "the first time in his undoubted writing that he's used 'Sith as that.' (Correct me if I'm wrong.)."[47] Another contributor has access to a CD-ROM of Shakespeare texts, which he can repurpose as an electronic concordance, but notes the limitations of the available materials:

> Unfortunately, I do not have Ford's plays in any database and so I cannot discover if the other words are present in Ford's works without carefully reading them. However, given the small sampling I have of Ford, compared to the entirety of Shakespeare, I cannot help but feel it is statistically significant that two of the ten words Shakespeare never used (again, according to my CD), appear in such a small sampling of Ford...[48]

Again, technology has simply moved on into the forms described earlier in this chapter, giving the researchers better tools. Debate about the *Funeral Elegy* on the discussion list (and on HLAS) paralleled a similar debate taking place in the letters column of the *Times Literary Supplement*, and fueled a series of projects and publications revolving around the development of computer-assisted statistical methods of assessing authorship. Foster's own tools, database, and results were to be published in their entirety on a website (although this never materialized due to difficulties of implementation), but the very fact that they might become open-access encouraged challenges to Foster based on the fact that they were not yet available, and also independent experimentation.[49]

Debate of the *Elegy* continued, on and off, on SHAKSPER, with the current of thought generally running against the attribution to Shakespeare, and with some arguments becoming increasingly bitter and *ad hominem*. In 2002, after years of further work and improving tools had made the grounds of the Shakespeare attribution look increasingly shaky, Gilles Monsarrat published an article in the prestigious, paper-based *Review of English Studies*, arguing, on the basis of parallel passages, that Ford might have written the *Elegy*. Monsarrat's approach sidesteps computers altogether, shelving any consideration of statistical text analysis, and declining to engage with the online debate. While Monsarrat is aware of the existence of SHAKSPER, he has not, it seems, read it himself, citing it only through other writers' allusions to it in print articles.[50] (An effect of this is that he doesn't really give much credit to the work of Richard J. Kennedy, who had pressed the case for Ford's authorship of the poem in a series of postings to SHAKSPER: Monsarrat's article still lingers in a world where online publication appears irrelevant to real scholarship[51].) On this article's publication, Don Foster and another of the theory's chief proponents, Richard Abrams, announced their acceptance of the idea that the author of the *Elegy* was John Ford. Wanting to publish his historical research on the Peter family while the matter was still reasonably topical, Abrams opted for the swift peer-review and production cycle of an online journal, *EMLS*.[52] Abrams and Foster also chose to make their recantations in online format:

> As Foster and I were quick to pounce on others' attributional errors, it seemed only fair to move the conversation along by expeditiously acknowledging our own. In light of the new evidence we posted endorsements of the Ford attribution to a venue in which we could control copy (it had been otherwise in our letters to the *TLS* years before): the online Shakespeare list, *Shaksper*.[53]

It could be said that, between 1996 and 2002, in this aspect of the affair, SHAKSPER had supplanted the *TLS* as the medium of record.

The *Funeral Elegy* may, in Ward Elliott's phrase, have proved to be "Fool's Gold" in the hunt for texts by Shakespeare (although still an interesting specimen of Jacobean elegy), and the role of SHAKSPER in the response to it emblematizes some of the downsides of being a digital humanist: the discussions were sometimes incompletely informed, repetitive, or long-winded, or else they veered into flame wars, and in any case they were, in effect, ignored in the article which is generally presented as providing the definitive conclusion to the affair. But, equally, the affair started to show some of the potential of even quite straightforward digital technology in a virtual community of humanities research.[54] Vickers criticizes Foster, in part, for playing fast and loose with processes of peer review, notably by justifying his assertions in terms of future as-yet-unpublished print articles, but the interesting thing about the SHAKSPER debates is that they provided, in a public forum, a *de facto* form of public peer review. It was an arena in which Foster could repeatedly be challenged for the non-appearance of the promised data. It was an arena in which nothing said could be unsaid, since as Richard Kennedy noted, "All of my early posts on John Ford can be retrieved from Hardy's archives, Foster's responses, etc."[55] It made much more visible the idea that scholarly writing is an act of persuasion, and made those involved question how that persuasion worked. Richard Abrams describes this aspect of the emerging new forum in calling the *Funeral Elegy* a "poem that has made many thoughtful people in the profession ask themselves what they listen for when they listen to Shakespeare."[56] (And not just, one might add, in the profession: SHAKSPER's remit is significantly wider than that.)

But the *Funeral Elegy* affair did more than just provide talk and discourse, acting as a heuristic device for readers and teachers of Shakespeare. It also marked a transition from a world in which few people were expected to have access – to the results of Foster's computer, to the primary texts, to the latest criticism – into a world in which electronic texts, tools, discussions, and electronic versions of publications both born-digital and born-paper were much more available, so that ultimately indefensible scholarship had, one might say, fewer places to hide. This represents perhaps the most powerful continuity between the digital revolution and traditions of scholarship dating back before the twentieth century and even to Renaissance humanism itself.

Digital projects, then, have widened access to the data which form the basis of factual and interpretive claims about early modern culture and literature. This applies to texts produced in that period, now available as e-texts and e-editions; to later scholarship, in particular to the datasets exemplified by the *OED* and the *Oxford DNB*; and to new secondary texts, in the forms of discussion lists, electronic publications, and blogs. Effective digital projects have been produced by a variety of agents, from individual enthusiasts to publishing multinationals, and at a variety of levels of technological sophistication. If this survey focuses mainly on internet-delivered resources providing access to text, then that is because these are the technologies which are making the most obvious practical difference to current researchers. It's here, I would argue, that we most see the multiplication of knowledge which gives this chapter its epigraph.

And yet, although that epigraph sounds like it comes from current information theory, its source is somewhat older, and more obviously in tune with the early modern: the Old Testament, mediated through a Renaissance library. Over the entrance to the Bodleian Library in Oxford is inscribed a quotation from the Book of Daniel: *Plurimi pertransibunt et multiplex erit scientia* [Many shall pass through, and knowledge will be multiplied]. What libraries like the Bodleian offer is also, in a sense, what the digital revolution offers to early modern studies.

NOTES

1 ProQuest Information and Learning website, <http://proquest.com/brand/umi.shtml>; *Early English Books Online*, "About *Early English Books Online*," <http://eebo.chadwyck. com/about/about.htm>. All references to

web pages are implicitly to those pages as they stood on May 10, 2006.

2 F. W. Bateson, *The Cambridge bibliography of English literature*, 5 vols (London: Macmillan, 1941), and subsequent revisions; among

projects which specifically seek to reorder the dataset in particular ways, one might cite the various revisions of Harbage's *Annals of English Drama*; Tom Dale Keever's *Early Modern Drama Database*, <http://www.columbia.edu/~tdk3/earlymodern.html>; and Gabriel Egan's *Non-Shakespearean Drama Database*, <http://www.gabrielegan.com>.

3   David Kathman, *Biographical Index of English Drama Before 1660*, <http://shakespeare authorship.com/bd/>.

4   Kenneth Muir, "*Pyramus and Thisbe*: a study in Shakespeare's method," *Shakespeare Quarterly*, 5 (1954), 141–53, qtn from 146.

5   Matthew Steggle, "Gale, Dunstan (*fl.* 1596)," *Oxford Dictionary of National Biography*, <http://www.oxforddnb.com/view/article/10290>.

6   See Jurgen Schäfer, *Documentation in the O.E.D: Shakespeare and Nashe as test cases* (Oxford: Clarendon Press, 1980); on the chronology of the *OED*, see K. M. Elisabeth Murray, *Caught in the Web of Words: James Murray and the Oxford English Dictionary* (Yale: Yale University Press, 1977), and the *Oxford English Dictionary*, "Dictionary Milestones: A Chronology of Events Relevant to the History of the *OED*," <http://www.oed.com/about/milestones.html>.

7   These are searches on *EEBO*, <http://eebo.chadwyck.com>, using the search term "Aristophan*."

8   Project Gutenberg, <http://www.gutenberg.org>; the Internet Public Library, <http://www.ipl.org>; Representative Poetry Online, <http://rpo.library.utoronto.ca/display/index.cfm>. This last project, which first appeared online in 1994 under the editorship of Ian Lancashire, also illustrates the importance of earlier work to later publication; it is an electronic descendant of a University of Toronto anthology which first appeared in print in 1912. For detailed information on the early evolution of online Shakespeare texts, as well as on some now-defunct or unavailable projects such as *Ardenonline*, see Michael Best, "Shakespeare and the Electronic Text," in Andrew Murphy, Ed., *A Concise Companion to Shakespeare and the Text* (Oxford: Blackwell, forthcoming).

9   Risa Bear, "Nexus: Renascence Editions and the Art of Online Publishing," paper delivered at the 2003 meeting of the Renaissance Society of America, online at <http://dark wing.uoregon.edu/%7Erbear/chron1.html>.

10 Anniina Jokinen, *Luminarium*, <http://www.luminarium.org>.

11 Anniina Jokinen, "Luminarium: A Letter from the Editor," <http://www.luminarium.org/letter.htm>.

12 Dana F. Sutton, Ed., *The Philological Museum*, <http://www.philological.bham.ac.uk/>; Ian Lancashire, Ed., *The Early Modern English Dictionaries Database*, <http://www.chass.utoronto.ca/english/emed/emedd.html>; *The John Milton Reading Room*, <http://www.dartmouth.edu/~milton/>; *The Memorial Web Edition of Alciato's 'Book of Emblems'*, <http://www.mun.ca/alciato/site.html>.

13 See the *LION* information page "From Source Text to Screen: The Digitization Process," <http://lion.chadwyck.co.uk/marketing/academics/textconv.jsp>.

14 Catherine Alexander, "Review of Chadwyck-Healey *English Poetry, Early English Prose Fiction, and English Verse Drama* CD-ROM Databases." *Interactive Early Modern Literary Studies* (October, 1999): <http://purl.oclc.org/emls/iemls/reviews/alexlion.htm>.

15 Gabriel Egan, "Hearing or Seeing a Play?: Evidence of Early Modern Theatrical Terminology," *Ben Jonson Journal* 8 (2001): 327–47.

16 The description of the "typographical variants" option is taken from *LION*'s help text, <http://lion.chadwyck.co.uk/help/texts_srch.jsp#typography>; in the case of "leaguer" and its variants, it may be suggested that a search for "leag*" would get round the problem, but this is unwieldy because of the large number of results for words like "league," "leagues," and "leagued."

17 For a discussion, see MacD. P. Jackson, "Editing, Attribution Studies, and 'Literature Online': A New Resource for Research in Renaissance Drama," *Research Opportunities in Renaissance Drama* 37 (1998): 1–15.

18 For this phrase, and reports of early glitches, see John Jowett and Gabriel Egan, "Review of the Early English Books Online (*EEBO*)." *Interactive Early Modern Literary Studies*

(January, 2001): <http://purl.oclc.org/emls/iemls/reviews/jowetteebo.htm>.

19 *Gallica*, <http://gallica.bnf.fr/>.

20 *Internet Shakespeare Editions*, <http://ise.uvic.ca/index.html>; for windows into the evolution of the project, see two Special Issues of *EMLS*; Michael Best, Ed., *The Internet Shakespeare: Opportunities in a New Medium, Early Modern Literary Studies* 3.3/Special Issue 2 (January, 1998): <http://purl.org/emls/03-3/03-3toc.html>; Michael Best and Eric Rasmussen, Eds., *Monitoring Electronic Shakespeares, Early Modern Literary Studies* 9.3/ Special Issue 12 (January, 2004), <http://purl.org/emls/09-3/ 09-3toc.htm>.

21 Michael Best, "The Internet Shakespeare Editions: History and Vision," cited from <http://ise.uvic.ca/Foyer/ISEoverview. html>; see also Best, "Shakespeare and the Electronic Text."

22 Best, "The Internet Shakespeare Editions: History and Vision."

23 Prospectus for the *Cambridge Works of Ben Jonson*, <http://www.cambridge.org/features/literature/cwbj/introduction/default.htm>.

24 The *Interactive Shakespeare Project*, <http://www.holycross.edu/departments/theatre/projects/isp/>.

25 See two emails by Ken Steele to SHAKSPER, 26 July 1990, <http://www.shaksper.net/archives/1990/0000.html>; and <http://www.shaksper.net/archives/1990/0002.html>.

26 Patrick Leary, "A Victorian Virtual Community," *Victorian Review* 25:2 (2000): 62–79, online at <http://www.victorianresearch.org/nandq.html>; my thinking about Shakespeare communities is influenced by the seminar "Shakespeare Forums," organized by Matt Kozusko and Robert Sawyer, which took place at the Shakespeare Association of America annual meeting 2006, papers from which are due to appear as a Special Issue of the e-journal *Borrowers and Lenders: the Journal of Shakespeare and Appropriation*, <http://atropos. english.uga.edu/cocoon/borrowers/>.

27 Hardy M. Cook, "Shaksper: The Politics of an Academic Discussion Group," paper written for the SAA, 1997, online at <http://www.shaksper.net/archives/files/saa1997.shaksper.html>; for another view of SHAKSPER from around this era, see Sean Lawrence, "'That Liberty and Common Conversation': A Review of the SHAKSPER List-serv Discussion Group." *Early Modern Literary Studies* 2.1 (1996): 16.1–16, <http://purl. oclc.org/emls/02-1/rev_law1.html>.

28 Gary Allen, email dated September 5, 2001, cited from <http://www.shaksper.net/archives/2001/2103.html>; HLAS is now accessible through a web browser, for instance at <http://groups.google.co.uk/group/humanities.lit.authors.shakespeare>, the source for the statistics on levels of usage; for more on HLAS see the *HLAS FAQ*, online at <http://www.shakespeare.handshake.de/>.

29 David Kathman and Terry Ross, *The Shakespeare Authorship Page*, <http://shakespeareauthorship.com/>.

30 Hardy M. Cook, current editorial statement at <http://www.shaksper.net/archives/files/shaksper.announce.html>.

31 *The Milton-L Website*, <http://www.urich.edu/~creamer/milton/>.

32 See, respectively, <http://www.english.cam.ac.uk/spenser/>; and <http://www.english.cam.ac.uk/sidney/>.

33 See the list of *Sidney Journal* contents for issue 17.1, online at <http://www.english.cam.ac.uk/sidney/17i.htm>.

34 *Early Modern Literary Studies*, <http://purl.org/emls>. I should, however, declare a vested interest here, being the current editor of the journal (while the journal's founder is one of the co-editors of the volume in which this piece appears).

35 For a review of *EMLS'* early history, and a previous stocktaking, see Paul Dyck, R. G. Siemens, Jennifer Lewin, and Joanne Woolway Grenfell, "The Janus-face of *Early Modern Literary Studies*: Negotiating the Boundaries of Interactivity in an Electronic Journal for the Humanities," *Early Modern Literary Studies* 5.3 / Special Issue 4 (January, 2000): 4.1–20, <http://purl.oclc.org/emls/05-3/dslwemls. html>.

36 Raymond G. Siemens, "*Early Modern Literary Studies*: An Editor's Prefatory Statement." *Early Modern Literary Studies* 1.1 (1995):

1.1–7,   <http://purl.oclc.org/emls/01-1/emls_int.html>.

37 For the term, and for many other interesting comments on the reception of e-journals, see Rod Heimpel, "Legitimizing Electronic Scholarly Publication: A Discursive Proposal," *Computing in the Humanities Working Papers* A.15 (October, 2000), <http://www.chass.utoronto.ca/epc/chwp/heimpel2/>.

38 See the page "Reviews of and Awards for *EMLS*," <http://purl.org/emls/revemls.htm>.

39 The LOCKSS project, <http://lockss.stanford.edu/>.

40 *Renaissance Forum*, <http://www.hull.ac.uk/renforum/>; *Early Modern Culture*, <http://emc.eserver.org/>; *Borrowers and Lenders: The Journal of Shakespearean Appropriation*, <http://atropos.english.uga.edu/cocoon/borrowers/>; the *Early Modern Journal*, <http://www.earlymodernjournal.com>; some of the content of the *Early Modern Journal* is recoverable through an important research tool, the *Internet Archive*, <http://www.archive.org>.

41 One example of these processes is the online self-archiving now practiced by many academics; another is *ITER*, a Renaissance-specific collection of online resources developed by a team led by William R. Bowen at <http://www.itergateway.org>; a third, outstanding, example is the University of Toronto's *Records Of Early English Drama* project, who have made their entire series of volumes so far available for free online in the "texts" section of the *Internet Archive*, <http://www.archive.org/details/texts>.

42 See, respectively, <http://earlymodern-lit.blogspot.com/>; <http://bloggingtherenaissance.blogspot.com>; <http://www.earlymodernweb.org.uk/emn/>.

43 Neil Rhodes and Jonathan Sawday, Eds., *The Renaissance Computer: Knowledge Technology in the First Age of Print* (London: Routledge, 2000); see also Philippa Berry and Margaret Tudeau-Clayton, Eds., *Textures of Renaissance Knowledge* (Manchester: Manchester University Press, 2003); Arthur F. Kinney, *Shakespeare's Webs; Networks of Meaning in Renaissance Drama* (London: Routledge, 2004), using an idea of linkage which draws both on ideas of hypertext and on cognitive theory.

44 Donald W. Foster, *Elegy by W.S.: A Study in Attribution* (Newark: University of Delaware Press, 1989); for a detailed account of the whole saga, see Brian Vickers, *'Counterfeiting' Shakespeare: Evidence, Authorship and John Ford's Funerall Elegye* (Cambridge: Cambridge University Press, 2002), especially the Epilogue, "The Politics of Attribution"; see also the helpful guide of Kathman and Ross at *The Shakespeare Authorship Page*.

45 The best description of SHAXICON is in a series of emails posted by Foster to SHAKSPER starting on February 11, 1998: <http://www.shaksper.net/archives/1998/0123.html>.

46 Donald W. Foster, email dated January 11, 1996,   <http://www.shaksper.net/archives/1996/0035.html>; the text of the poem also appeared in the print journal *Shakespeare Studies*, but not until the 1997 issue.

47 William Godshalk, email dated February 9, 1996,   <http://www.shaksper.net/archives/1996/0101.html>.

48 Patrick Gillespie, email dated August 7, 1996, <http://www.shaksper.net/archives/1996/0545.htm>.

49 See, for instances, Hugh Craig, "Common-words Frequencies, Shakespeare's Style, and the *Elegy* by W. S." *Early Modern Literary Studies* 8.1 (May, 2002): 3.1–42 <http://purl.oclc.org/emls/08-1/craistyl.htm>;   a series of publications by Ward Elliott and Robert Valenza, including "Smoking Guns and Silver Bullets: Could John Ford Have Written the *Funeral Elegy*?" *Literary and Linguistic Computing* 16 (2001): 205–32; SHAXICAN, an open-source project started by Gabriel Egan, which aims to provide something approaching an emulation of what SHAXICON would have done: <http://www.gabrielegan.com/shaxican>.

50 Gilles D. Monsarrat, "*A Funeral Elegy*: Ford, W.S., and Shakespeare," *Review of English Studies* 53 (2002): 186–203, esp. 187; naturally, this article is cited here from its electronic incarnation as a .pdf available from *Literature Online*.

51 Vickers argues that Foster's attacks on Kennedy were *ad hominem* (*Counterfeiting Shakespeare*, 437–9), especially in his allusions to Kennedy's anti-Stratfordianism; but Kennedy *was* an anti-Stratfordian, something manifested on HLAS, and sometimes visible on the edges of his postings to SHAKSPER. Given that Foster and Kennedy were arguing, among other things, about acceptable methods of attribution, this is surely a relevant factor. It does, however, speak to another of the running concerns of the online group: questions of "credentials" and community.

52 Richard Abrams, "Meet the Peters," *Early Modern Literary Studies* 8.2 (September,

2002): 6.1–39 <http://purl.oclc.org/emls/08-2/abrapete.html>; Lisa Hopkins, editor of *EMLS* 1998–2003, *pers. comm.*

53 Abrams, "Meet the Peters," 1; the emails, dated July 13, 2002, are at <http://www.shaksper.net/archives/2002/1484.html>.

54 Ward Elliott, email dated August 19, 2005, <http://www.shaksper.net/archives/2005/1358.html>.

55 Vickers, *Counterfeiting Shakespeare*, 425–6; Richard J. Kennedy, email dated June 21, 2002, <http://www.shaksper.net/archives/2002/1519.html>.

56 Abrams, "Meet the Peters," 39.

5

Eighteenth-Century Literature in English and Other Languages: Image, Text, and Hypertext

Peter Damian-Grint

Introduction

Although eighteenth-century studies are alive and well in European and North American university life, and there are many sites dealing with historical material of the period and online research projects such as scholarly editions of letters or papers, online access to resources linked to eighteenth-century *literature*, as opposed to other material, is surprisingly limited. Popular texts, particularly those figuring widely on syllabuses, are readily available: it is not hard to find sites providing certain major eighteenth-century works in English and one or two other languages (as well as English translations of works originally written in other languages). But other than these "classics," the number of works available is quite small. Any eighteenth-century literary text at all specialist – especially one in a language other than English[1] – is likely to be difficult or impossible to find online. Unless, that is, the text is not *only* literary but has other interest as a philosophical or political essay. If it is not hard to find examples of Rousseau's *Émile, ou de l'éducation*, it is less because it is a novel (of sorts) than because it had a significant influence on theories of education in the eighteenth and early nineteenth centuries.

In addition, as is generally true of the present generation of electronic resources, there is a clear focus on quantity over quality. Most available digital resources connected with eighteenth-century literature appear to be aimed at the secondary-level (high school) student, and the materials provided are generally unimpressive in both substance and presentation. There is little attempt at scholarship; critical annotation is often absent or basic, and the text itself (when it does not consist simply of page images) is frequently error-strewn. Even leaving aside the actual accuracy of the text, it is common to find that no information has been provided about the printed source from which it has been taken; when the source *is* known, it often proves to come from an uncritical popular edition of the nineteenth or early twentieth century – i.e., the digitizer has gone for material in the public domain, without any regard to reliability or accuracy. Texts are provided without contexts, and in their rawest and most technologically unsophisticated state; even the visual presentation is frequently uninviting.[2] Clearly we are still in the early stages of electronic provision, and more recent sites show the promise of more usability and a more sophisticated approach to literary works and their creators.

Bibliographies and Related Resources

Bibliographies

Most websites in eighteenth-century literary studies have a page or pages of bibliographical information – either citation references for the material presented on the site, or information about books, articles, and other studies related to the material – and another page containing links to related sites. There are also a small number of eighteenth-century sites whose primary purpose is to provide this information and in fact to point the user in other directions.

Sadly, many – perhaps most – online bibliographies of eighteenth-century literary studies clearly show their "book-bound" origins. They typically offer interminable and unstructured lists or large slabs of text, both of which are difficult to use unless searchers already know what they are looking for. A quote from a typical offender suggests (perhaps with unintentional irony) the disjunction that can exist between creator and user: "These bibliographies should help scholars lost in a flood of information to find helpful printed sources."[3] But they don't: instead the bibliographies take the form of over fifty print pages of single-spaced text without a single hotlink in sight. That is not to say that such lists do not have their value, for they do bring obscure and scattered information together and make it available in some shape; but they can hardly be seen as an example of how digital technology can aid study or scholarship, for the same or better could be (and frequently is) provided in printed format.[4] Even a site like Benoît Melançon's bibliographical journal *XVIIIᵉ siècle: bibliographie*, which provides an excellent up-to-date listing of eighteenth-century studies (of all kinds, not only literary), gives citations in just flat text, with the occasional link to a review. While reviews can be very useful, the logical next step – to provide links from the bibliography entries to the works themselves or to holding libraries – is almost never forthcoming, presumably for the simple reason that the amount of time and effort that would have to be invested to create direct links for all (or even a significant number of) entries in such bibliographies would make it prohibitively expensive. Just occasionally a bibliography site in a university may provide links to the university library; but it is clear that it will not happen on a wide scale until the technology is in place to permit the process to be automated.

Link sites

A step up technologically from the bibliographies, link sites or metapages frequently share the same defects of presentation: the lists, though they consist of links to related sites rather than citation references, are often similarly interminable and similarly hard to navigate through.[5] A major problem with these sites is "link rot": as digital resources – and not only the obscure ones – are migrated or taken offline, more and more of the links on the page become inactive or point to reroute pages.[6] This is of course a common problem with all kinds of online resources (though no less irritating for that); in the case of link sites, however, it is a problem that tends to neutralize the very raison d'être of the resource itself.

At the same time, it would be wrong to give an impression that all link sites are opaque and out of date. One such site should probably be among of the first stops for any searcher looking for digital resources in eighteenth-century literature: Jack Lynch's "labor of love," the *Eighteenth-Century Resources* site at Rutgers. The site as a whole is very user-friendly; and the *Literature* links page is comprehensive, well laid out and well signposted, and includes invaluable notes indicating the contents of the sites linked to, and any problems that might be expected. Lynch's claim to have "an up-to-date and nearly comprehensive list of e-texts available on the internet," if at first blush hardly over-modest, is in fact an accurate description of what he provides (he also provides a separate index for the e-texts). However, the other resources linked by Lynch are of no less interest, as they include aids such as bibliographies, chronologies, images, and guides of other sorts. It would not be an exaggeration to say that in most cases, a trip to *Eighteenth-Century Resources* will point academics and students at least in the direction of whatever they need, as long as it is actually in existence online. Another site that shows what can be done (though on a smaller scale, and not wholly dedicated to the eighteenth century) is *The Literary Gothic* website. Its pages on writers such as Addison, Beckford, and Walpole are elegant, clear, and, like Lynch's, apparently completely up to date, no mean feat.

Both these sites concentrate on literature in English. A first stop for those studying literature in other languages would be the ACRL's *Electronic Text Collections in Western European Literature* (*WESS WEB*). This site links to material in a relatively wide spread of (Western European) languages, ranging from Catalan and Provençal to Swedish and Romanian, though the lion's share is taken as ever by material in French, German, and Italian. A second stop for both – and one highly praised by Lynch – is the *Voice of the Shuttle*, which has links for both English and non-English literature. There is in fact only a limited amount of literature not in English, and as the site is not devoted solely to eighteenth-century literature and only the French section of the site provides a chronological division of the material, in most cases the searcher will need to hunt around. Link sites in other languages are fewer, although French again has a good number; among the most comprehensive are *Littérature francophone virtuelle* at Swarthmore University's ClicNet and Athena's *Textes Français*. The French Ministère des affaires étrangères and Ministère de la culture also provide numerous links to literature sites.[7] Again, these sites do not specialize in the eighteenth century, so that finding the site is only the first stage, as it will then be necessary to do further searches (typically by author name) to find the specific subset that is wanted. A third and no less important link site is *The European Library*,[8] which provides access to many of the national libraries of Europe – many of which have significant holdings of e-texts in their own languages, or links to digital libraries (see below).

Texts

The number of sites devoted specifically to eighteenth-century literature is vanishingly small. In general, eighteenth-century e-texts appear as a small subsection (or, quite frequently, simply mixed in with other material) in sites devoted either to literature in general, or to eighteenth-century history or culture. There are exceptions, the best known probably being *ECCO* (Thomson-Gale's *Eighteenth-Century Collections Online*), which is a wonderfully rich resource – at least for those whose institutions are able to afford it. Among the most important of the general literature sites are *Project Gutenberg* and the University of Virginia's *Electronic Texts Center*, both of which have plenty of eighteenth-century literary texts. However the sources, where known, are generally material in the public domain, derived from uncritical early (nineteenth-century) editions, with basic HTML tagging and no editorial notes. Other general sites are often more interesting, and some include a fair number of literary works. A good example is the Liberty Fund's *Online Library of Liberty*, with texts – many of them literary, including book-length essays – from some seventy-five eighteenth-century writers. However, although the editions are generally scholarly and plenty of biographical, historical, and bibliographical information is provided on the site, the texts themselves are PDF or flat HTML with relatively little in the way of linking either internal or external. The series of texts under the rubric *Storiografia, erudizione e filosofia nell'Europa settecentesca* in the *Electronic Library of Historiography* at the University of Florence,[9] fewer in number, are elegantly presented but provide only minimal scholarly annotation or background.

Text sites containing eighteenth-century literary resources cover the entire range from the very static to the very dynamic and interlinked. Many collections, including major ones such as *ECCO*, are primarily devoted to the provision of page images. This format (sometimes with basic OCR indexing) is a valuable substitute for rare books collections, but should not be confused with critical editions of eighteenth-century texts. Following on from the provision of page images is the transcription of the images with basic HTML formatting; hyperlinks, if there are any, are usually restricted to footnoting. They are ideal for word searches (assuming the text is accurate), but otherwise of limited usefulness. Happily, not all websites stop at page images or flat HTML. The up-and-coming generation of eighteenth-century literary sites show a more imaginative and integrated approach to texts, with more internal links – and external ones, too, to other material of different types;

but are only just beginning to explore the possibilities of mixed media and interactive approaches.

The primacy of the image

The fact that page scans give primacy to the book as an object is reflected in the
preference for this form of digitization above all by libraries that hold the books. A
number of major national libraries have modeled their digitization projects to a
greater or lesser extent on the *ECCO* format, although, taking advantage of technological progress in the meantime, their page images are often high resolution and in
color. The *Colecciones digitales* of the Biblioteca Nacional in Madrid contain a large set
of digitized material (though in this case the quality of the scans is not very high),
together with presentations of important authors from the eighteenth century as well
as other periods. The *Biblioteca Nacional Digital* from the Portuguese Biblioteca
Nacional has a more developed form of the same model, providing scans of over
1,000 eighteenth-century Portuguese literary works together with bibliographical
and historical information, and many internal and external library links. Icelandic
literature of the eighteenth century is almost too well served, with *two* official digital
library projects: *Timarit*, based on the Icelandic National Library's holdings, and
Saganet,[10] a joint project between the National Library and Cornell. Again, both
projects have chosen to give only page scans – of excellent quality and high resolution.
The Swedish *Project Runeberg* similarly provides scan images of a large number of
Swedish (and also some Icelandic, German, and other) writers, including some from
the eighteenth century, as does the *Polska Biblioteka Internetowa*, for eighteenth-
century Polish literature.[11] The Czech National Library's *Manuscriptorium* virtual
library,[12] though in its early stages, is more ambitious. At present the works are
presented as page scans only (with extremely detailed bibliographic information); but
the project information indicates that they intend to capture the text in "pragmatic
editions" with XML tagging, thus combining page images with something close to a
true digital edition.

Flat text provision

The great majority of e-text sites offer not page scans (or not *only* page scans) but
keyed or OCR'd texts of varying degrees of sophistication. The official sites providing
"national collections" or "digital libraries" of electronic texts tend to provide a fairly
flat text with basic HTML tagging and few links. This can be seen, for example, in
the official *Biblioteca Româneasca*, where the Romanian literary texts included lack
bibliographical information, chronologies and dates for writers or works, and no links
outwards. Much the same is true of the (still limited) eighteenth-century collections
of the Russian State Library's *Open Russian Electronic Library* (OREL) and the Serbian
Projekt Rastko,[13] as well as the Portuguese *Projecto Vercial*, which gives extracts from
the writings of many eighteenth-century authors under the rubric *Literatura Neoclassica*, but no links. The *Dansk Nationallitterært Arkiv*,[14] which forms part of the Dansk

Koniglige Bibliotheket website, provides a good collection of literature from the period (an important century in Danish letters) in an attractive and user-friendly interface; but again little is given other than the texts and basic bibliographic details. This style of provision, where an attractive presentation does not quite hide the fact that the texts are flat HTML with few or no notes and no links, can be seen in numerous other sites. Even literary sites as well known as the University of Augsburg's *Augustana*, which sets out to provide a wide range of European literature,[15] provide only bibliographical source information; others, such as the University of Gdansk's elegant *Wirtualna Biblioteka Literatury Polskiej*, which provides a large number of Polish works, give no bibliographical information and no notes, although in the University of Gdansk's case biographical information on the writers is provided, along with some illustrations.

The lack of additional information, either biographical or contextual (or, more rarely, bibliographical), may be due to the use of an uncritical base print edition; but sometimes it is a matter of editorial choice. In the case of an online literature project such as Bibliopolis's *Classiques Garnier* collection in *Gallica classique* (of which eighteenth-century French literature forms a small part of the whole), a deliberate decision has been taken not to have notes, as the works derive from the Garnier editions but all the critical apparatus has been removed.[16] The suspicion that this is for purely financial reasons, in order not to harm sales of the print edition, is hard to avoid. In other cases, like the elegantly presented collection of the French Ministère des affaires étrangères under the rubric *livre et écrit*, the complete lack of annotation, critical apparatus, or links of any kind is more likely to be in order not to put off the casual enquirers who appear to be the intended audience (to judge from the authors and texts provided).[17]

New generation

More recently, a small number of e-text sites have begun to reflect the possibilities offered by online presentation. The *digitale bibliotheek voor de Nederlandse letteren* (*DBNL*) is one of these next-generation sites. Beautifully presented and very friendly, it is easy to navigate straight to the texts in HTML, with PDFs of the page scans if wanted; and the large number of eighteenth-century Dutch texts (over 200 of them, in a separate section) is contextualized by a further listing of secondary literature, also available in HTML, and a "ladder" of links to more than seventy e-journals, together with images, bibliographies, maps (including plenty of contemporary ones), and even audio material (readings), as well as dense project pages linking authors and materials thematically.[18] Also worth watching is the *Project Laurens Janszoon Coster*, which aims to provide more interactive electronic editions of "klassieke Nederlandstalige literatuur"; a good start has been made on a broad range of Dutch literature, though as yet it is still relatively flat and there is not much eighteenth-century material.

The Bibliothèque nationale de France has its own "bibliothèque numérique," *Gallica*, one section of which (*Gallica classique*) contains an impressive selection of important eighteenth-century texts.[19] This is fully interlinked with the BNF's catalogue, so full bibliographical details are available. Some thought has also gone into the thematic linking, which works well. Even more interesting in some ways are the BNF/Gallica *Dossiers*, half a dozen mini-sites created with thematic cross-linkage between works; a fair number of the dossiers are connected with eighteenth-century themes. Slightly counter-intuitive at first, they are designed with great flair and clearly thought through with care to put together interesting and sometimes unexpected collections of texts. (The range of documents is broad, as befits a national library, and the emphasis is probably more documentary than literary, though many of the texts are literary works.)

One of the more interesting new-generation sites in this field – more interesting, among other reasons, because it gives an indication of the possibilities by coming at the texts from an unusual angle – is the British Library's *Literary Landscapes*, which associates various literary texts with the (British) geographical locations they are based in – though only a couple of eighteenth-century texts are reviewed, and the illustrations are frustratingly small.[20] Another interesting experiment in a different direction is the University of Sherbrooke's *Callisto*, which links together major eighteenth-century writers in English, French, and German; however, the material available (flat HTML with few links) does not quite live up to the clever introductory pages.

Another excellent example of what can be done, apparently aimed at a secondary/high-school level although it could in truth be of interest to undergraduates as well, is the *Norton Topics Online* website. Here we have what is in principle a hybrid work, as the topics are given with links indicated to the *Norton Anthology of English Literature* (NAEL); nevertheless, although they are there in the first place to provide context, they also include short texts themselves. The organization of the site repays examination. A side bar provides access to the material, either in a structured way via Topics, Review, or Archive or by a simple Search; within these come further subdivisions. It is intuitive and clearly signposted; the range of material is impressive, including both well-captioned contemporary images (engravings, paintings) and audio readings of some material as well as a multiple-choice quiz (technically simple, but cleverly thought out). The texts are well chosen, being of a length suitable for reading on screen; and they all have editorial notes.

Project Sites and E-journals

Genre is not (yet) a word that has much meaning in digital resources. Certainly there is no watertight division between the e-text sites discussed above, particularly the new-generation sites with their contextualization and interlinking, and what one might call "project" sites: websites based on teaching or research rather than simply the provision of texts. Particularly close to the new-generation e-text sites, to the extent that they shade imperceptibly into them,[21] the teaching sites properly speaking provide material for students and their teachers. They are usually built on broad themes; there are for instance a number of sites on such topics as Romanticism or theater.

Other project sites are created not so much for students as for groups doing research into either individuals or, more commonly, literary themes or areas. There is again little sharp distinction between research and teaching sites, particularly as many research sites also provide a good deal of general information and may even deliberately make available a large amount of material of a non-specialist nature in order to broaden interest in the project theme. Closely related to these research sites are the e-journals: indeed, the distinction between such sites and e-journals in the strict sense of the term is hardly more than one of point of view, given that a truly interactive research site will be encouraging (or at least welcoming) much the same kind of interaction between academics and teachers as takes place within the framework of a proper online journal.

Finally, those sites created by groups working on digital editions of the works of individual writers or individual works are among the most interesting, and have the potential to be the most technically advanced. However, there are very few sites of this sort in eighteenth-century literary studies; most eighteenth-century writers whose works are being edited digitally are better known as scientists or public figures – see, e.g., the *Rousseau Studies* website, Rousseau being incomparably better known as a philosopher and political theorist.

Teaching sites

Other project sites are designed for high-school or college students and follow a similar pattern to sites providing only texts. Many are relatively primitive and not particularly user-friendly. The *Johnson Society* site, though somewhat unfriendly in appearance, is more intelligent than most. On the other hand a project site like the University of Virginia's *British Poetry 1780–1910*, though it describes itself as a "hypertext archive of scholarly editions," in fact contains little material that could possibly qualify as hypertext. The links are basic; there are no annotations, and each hypertext page is linked to low-quality page scans or other images. Nor is there even much evidence that the editions are scholarly in any meaningful sense. A third site, *The Dictionary of Sensibility*, shows an intelligent approach to teaching the theme; it introduces the searcher to the concept through a list of a couple of dozen terms, each leading to a series of short readings with glosses to orient the reader. Although the organization and layout is not very attractive, the material is good; however, the site does not really live up to expectations as apart from a couple of indigestible bibliographies there is little additional material.

Research sites

A good example of the general research site in eighteenth-century literature is Barry Russell's *Le Théâtre de la Foire à Paris*.[22] Containing as it does a wealth of documentation of many different types, it is a resource of real value for those studying theater history; however, the primitive format makes it very unintuitive to use. Quite different is the larger research site to which it is linked, *CÉSAR* (the *Calendrier Électronique des Spectacles sous l'Ancien régime et sous la Révolution*), a "dynamic online database" which covers French theater right through to end of the eighteenth century. Considerable thought has obviously gone into putting structure into the immense amount of information available, and providing as comprehensive as possible a set of "entry points."[23] And there are links to further resources considered "external" to the historical data that lies at the heart of the resource: a number of e-books, some hyperlinked and others page images, "treatises" (books published during the period), and – potentially even more interesting – "press," i.e., contemporary press reviews of plays, though the reviews tend to take the form of very tightly cut "snippets" with no context. A serious effort has been made to explain at every stage what the searcher is looking at, but the information is presented in a rather unfriendly "database" style which is clearly aimed at the researcher, not the student.

Many other research sites are much more user-friendly. The University of Toronto's *Representative Poetry Online* provides a timeline with links to a wide range of (among others) eighteenth-century poets and their works, with impressively complete biblio-graphical information (including the rhyme scheme and the poetic form) about not only the original edition but the electronic edition as well. The search is well constructed, as are the cross-links between different poets who influenced one another, their biographies, their poems, the glossary, other poems by the same poet, and so on. There are few critical annotations to individual poems, but longer critical evaluations are easily reached.

A more advanced multimedia project site, Alexander Huber's exemplary *Thomas Gray Archive*, contains not only scrupulously edited and copiously annotated texts but also concordances, links to page images, and even audio-visual clips of recital of some of Gray's works. The two very different project sites within the *Blake Web*,[24] a kind of "umbrella" site by Steven Marx at Cal Poly University, also repay examination. *The Blake Multimedia Project*, a teaching project, uses a hypertext edition containing all the illustrations of several of Blake's works – an example of an intelligent approach to the author, given the importance of the image in Blake's work. However, the project is showing its age, as the hypertext edition is only in the format of downloadable HyperCard files. The second site, the hypermedia *William Blake Archive*, contains a broad range of resources on Blake, including biography, glossary, and articles, to-gether with many images. The material is well put together, with exhaustive anno-tations of all the editions, and transcriptions as well as images of the text; there are also (an unusual detail) detailed descriptions of each of the images, thus permitting searches of these as well as of the text.

Even more comprehensive is the project site *Romantic Circles*. This sophisticated website features a blog, scholarly resource links to texts, densely annotated image banks, chronologies, some very complex hypertext electronic editions (though most are of nineteenth-century texts), reviews, teaching guides, and a MOO[25] for "discus-sion, meetings and gaming." In Jack Lynch's words, *O si sic omnes!* It is perhaps telling that it is not devoted to a wholly eighteenth-century theme.

Online journals

Online journal or e-journal is an elastic term. Such e-journals as *Eighteenth-Century Life*,[26] or *Eighteenth Century Studies*,[27] provide their material in generated PDFs or in HTML with footnote links; but they are print journals that are stored electronically, rather than online journals in any real sense.[28] A more developed format of online journal with significant material on the eighteenth century is *Romanticism on the Net*, which is (as its name suggests) electronic only. Designed as it is for online delivery, it is easy to search, elegantly presented, and more readable than many other online publications; nevertheless, although it is all in HTML it has few links other than those to footnotes. Much the same can be said of another online journal containing eighteenth-century literary material, *Early Modern Literary Studies*, though it is not as friendly in appearance.[29]

Very different from all of these is the University of Maryland's *Romantic Circles Praxis Series*, the journal of the *Romantic Circles* project site discussed above, which has been created with a clear intention to make full use of the possibilities offered by the electronic medium. The series is described as aiming to use "computer technologies to investigate critically the languages, cultures, histories, and theories of Romanticism," which at first glance looks like a claim to some form of complex software-driven research into the text – a claim which is not obviously substantiated, and one which may divert the user from the sophisticated way the technology is used in the presentation of the e-journal. Although inelegant in layout and style, it is exceptionally integrated, with links from author to abstract to article and links within documents to popup notes.

Online editions

One of the few more sophisticated eighteenth-century edition projects, *The Spectator Project* is still in its early stages – it has got as far as providing high-resolution color images of the original newssheets. While these are of considerable interest from a literary and publishing history point of view, as the editors point out, a scholarly edition and further contextual information are still awaited; and the fact that a good proportion of the newssheets are not yet digitized limits their usefulness for the time being. If the editors' intentions are followed through, however, it will be a site to watch.

Conclusion

As we saw at the outset, the digitization of eighteenth-century literature – even in English where it is furthest advanced – is still in its early stages. The vast majority of text sites are quite primitive, delivering either PDFs of pages or little if anything more than minimally tagged, flat HTML pages of indefinite length. Structure is kept to a minimum; even headings are often tagged not as headings but simply as bold, indented, or (occasionally) centered text. The relationship between the text and the technology appears to follow the system of the cook in one of Saki's short stories, who "nourished an obstinate conviction that if you brought rabbit and curry powder together in one dish a rabbit curry would be the result."[30]

It is perhaps not surprising that little thought appears to have been given to the ways in which the texts might be used; it is clearly felt that it is enough to make the material available, in however rudimentary a form. In many cases this is true enough, and the digitizer has indeed done the academic community a real service simply in providing *any* sort of electronic version of these texts – texts which might otherwise be difficult of access, texts which can now be worked with and searched in a way not previously possible.

But while it is clear that academic work methods are changing and that electronic texts, even in their most rudimentary form, are opening up new possibilities to researchers and students, it is also becoming increasingly clear that this is no longer enough. Search for a quote from Addison's *Spectator* on the internet and you may find twenty answers – but they will not all be the same answer, and most will give only the bare details. It can be useful for a quick check that the quote is correct: but then, how can one even be sure which of the twenty versions is in fact accurate? And in most cases you can go no further: no editorial comment, no contextualization, no links, not even any bibliographical details. For different reasons, this "naked" text is in fact as useless to the student as it is to the researcher. Scholarship, however undemanding, needs some sort of background to the text if one is to avoid a sterile and facile subjectivity.

There is, besides, a danger in the old "more is better" paradigm that simply counts pages. For the time being, no literary text more than a couple of pages long (if that) can be comfortably read on-screen; and while it is true that longer texts can be printed out, there is a certain perversity in the concept of laboriously scanning or keying in long texts in order that they may be printed out again so that they can be used. That, surely, is a case of using the computer to do less well what the publishing industry can usually do far better and more efficiently.

There is more of a point to the exercise if the intention is to make available page scans of eighteenth-century publications, as *ECCO* has done on a grand scale; after all, even if they are not quite incunabula, eighteenth-century editions can be both expensive and rare. (Academics may of course be more interested in questions that can only be answered by reference to the physical volume, but these generally fall rather within the orbit of history of the book rather than strict literary criticism.) But here too it is not the fact that they are online that is important: a print-out – or a facsimile volume – would be much easier for most researchers to use. Unless the images are (for example) of such high resolution that they enable one to see details not visible to the naked eye, or the software makes it possible to examine the images in some way that cannot be done with the originals, they do not represent a technological step forward, but merely a convenient storage facility.

Where next for the online resource in eighteenth-century literature? Useful developments are likely to take place in two separate directions. The student and the more general reader will probably get most out of sites that give context to the text, through linkages to other related texts and a dense network of significant material (not only texts but images and audio), along the lines of *Romantic Circles* or *Norton Topics Online*. For the academic specialist, a truly interactive research site like the *Thomas Gray Archive* will facilitate new electronic editions and permit further annotation and collaboration between scholars. In fact the *Thomas Gray* site, which contains both scholarly and more general material, may be a paradigm of one type of next-generation online resource in the field. This new generation is already making it clear that not only is quality more important than quantity, it is also possible to have both. Though there will continue to be a place for *ECCO* and other page-image collections, particularly as a part of research library and archive sites where they will provide an important service to scholars and researchers of all kinds, the "never mind the quality, feel the width" style of online provision is going to look increasingly out of date over the next few years.

NOTES

1 Exception can possibly be made of French and German; nevertheless, even though the provision of e-texts of eighteenth-century works in these two languages is relatively good, it can hardly compare with what is available in English.

2 Common faults include the use of inelegant and hard-to-read typefaces such as Courier, and patterned or dark backgrounds that "lose" the text. The use of psychedelic colors is, mercifully, on the decrease.

3 *Jim May's Bibliographies*.

4 Bibliography sites often seem to be the work of individuals and to suffer from the effects of hobbyist's myopia: i.e., because the builders of such sites are so close to their subject, they can find it hard to appreciate that the information needs to be mediated in a way that makes sense to the non-expert.

5 A site like eserver's *Eighteenth Century Studies* gives a fair example of how user-unfriendly this can be.

6 As well as providing reminders for users to update their bookmarks, reroute pages sometimes underline the length of time since the last update of the link site by indicating when the site migrated to its new address.

7 The page *Livres et Littérature* of the site *Culture.fr* permits searches of a very wide range of

material – most of which, however, is not eighteenth-century.

8 The site distinguishes full members (who have direct links to their websites) from associated members, but there is a clear intention to have all European national libraries as full members sooner or later.

9 It is the largest of the collections in *ELIOHS*.

10 The project (as its name suggests) focuses on saga material, but includes eighteenth-century editions of, and material on, the sagas.

11 Cf. the Croatian National Library's very sophisticated digitized volumes (scans) on its *Digitalizirana baština* pages, although these include no eighteenth-century work as yet.

12 There are versions of the site in Czech and English.

13 The site also includes links to Montenegrin, Romanian, Albanian, and other Slav and Balkan literature.

14 *DNA* or *Danish National Archive of Literature*, drawn largely from the *Arkiv for Dansk Litteratur*.

15 It is, for example, one of the very few sites to provide literature in Yiddish; and it also provides material in Latin, Greek, and medieval languages. Many of the texts promised are, however, still on the stocks and the great

majority of texts it provides at the time of writing are in German.

16 *Bibliopolis* features just twelve texts (including four collections) by seven authors.

17 A few complete texts are provided in RTF; others are extracts in HTML. A single "star" text is presented as a separate section with images, detailed discussion, and links. At the time of writing, the section – entitled *La Quintinie et le potager du roi* – is based on La Quintinie's *Instructions* (1690) and includes extracts, descriptions, and links to related sites including Versailles and the École nationale supérieure du paysage. The page contains little eighteenth-century material.

18 At the time of writing there is just one theme page, on Antwerp, with images, text, and lots of links to authors and works.

19 Not always (possibly for copyright reasons) are the best editions available: thus the works of Voltaire in *Gallica* are taken from the Beuchot and Hachette editions, not the Moland or the ongoing Oxford *Œuvres complètes*.

20 The full images are so small that most of the detail is not distinguishable; they can be viewed in close-up, but only in very small sections at a time.

21 The decision to deal with the *Norton Topics Online* site under e-texts, for instance, is arguably largely arbitrary: the determining factor in this case was that the site is a commercial

one whereas project sites tend to be produced by academics and teachers.

22 The site contains mainly seventeenth-century material.

23 The complete set of entry points is: People, Troupes, Places, Titles, Dates, Publications, Publishers, Libraries, Images. For a less advanced English-language equivalent, see the student project run by Patricia Craddock, *The World of London Theater, 1660–1800*.

24 The site also contains an e-book, Marx's *Youth Against Age: Generational Strife in Renaissance Poetry*, in a surprisingly low-tech HTML version without even internal links to the footnotes.

25 Multi-user domain Object Oriented: a computer program that allows multiple users to connect via the internet to a shared database of "rooms" and other objects, and interact with each other and the database in synchronous time.

26 Hosted by HighWire.

27 Hosted by JStor, *LION*, and Project MUSE.

28 Benoît Melançon's e-journal *XVIIIe siècle: bibliographie* mentioned above is a more specialized example of the same thing.

29 At the time of writing there are problems with non-standard entities; non-roman scripts are given only as images.

30 "The jesting of Arlington Stringham," in *The Chronicles of Clovis* (1912).

WEBSITES CITED

Bibliographies and related sites

Eighteenth-Century Resources (Jack Lynch, Rutgers): <http://andromeda.rutgers.edu/~jlynch/18th/lit.html>.

Eighteenth Century Studies (eserver): <http://eserver.org/18th>.

Electronic Text Collections in Western European Literature (ACRL): <http://www.lib.virginia.edu/wess/etexts.html>.

The European Library: <http://libraries.theeuropeanlibrary.org/>.

Jim May's Bibliographies: <www.personal.psu.edu/special/C18/maytools.htm>.

The Literary Gothic: <www.litgothic.com/Authors/authors.html>.

Littérature francophone virtuelle (ClicNet, Swarthmore University): <http://clicnet.swarthmore.edu/litterature/litterature.html>.

Livres et Littérature (Ministère de la culture, France): <http://www.culture.fr/Groups/livre_et_litterature/>.

Textes Français (Athena): <http://un2sg4.unige.ch/athena/html/francaut.html>.

Voice of the Shuttle (VoS): <http://vos.ucsb.edu/>.

XVIIIᵉ siècle: bibliographie (Benoît Melançon): <http://mapageweb.umontreal.ca/melancon/biblio.tdm.html (ISSN 1207-7461)>.

Texts

Arkiv for Dansk Litteratur: <http://adl.dk/>.

Augustana (University of Augsburg): <http://www.fh-augsburg.de/~harsch/augustana.html>.

Bibliopolis (Garnier): [link to Gallica <http://gallica.bnf.fr/classique/>from which you can click.]

Biblioteca Nacional Digital (Portuguese Biblioteca Nacional): <http://bnd.bn.pt/>.

Biblioteca Româneasca: <http://biblioteca.euroweb.ro/autori.htm>.

Classiques Garnier (Bibliopolis): <http://gallica.bnf.fr/classique/>.

Colecciones digitales (Spanish Biblioteca Nacional): <http://www.bne.es/esp/catalogos/colecciones digitales.htm>.

Dansk Nationallitterært Arkiv (*DNA* or *Danish National Archive of Literature*, Dansk Koniglige Bibliotheket): <http://www.kb.dk/elib/lit/dan/>.

Digitale bibliotheek voor de Nederlandse letteren (*DBNL*): <http://www.dbnl.nl/>.

Digitalizirana bastina (Croatian National Library): <http://www.nsk.hr/Heritage.aspx?id=25>.

Eighteenth-Century Collections Online (*ECCO*, Thomson-Gale): <http://www.gale.com/Eighteenth Century/>.

Electronic Library of Historiography – Storiografia, erudizione e filosofia nell'Europa settecentesca (*ELIOHS*, University of Florence): <http://www.eliohs.unifi.it/collane.html>.

Electronic Texts Center (University of Virginia): <http://etext.virginia.edu/>.

Gallica classique (Bibliothèque nationale de France): <http://gallica.bnf.fr/classique/>.

Literary Landscapes (British Library): <http://www.collectbritain.co.uk/galleries/litlandscapes>.

Livre et écrit (French Ministère des affaires étrangères): <http://www.diplomatie.gouv.fr/fr/actions-france_830/livre-ecrit_1036/collection-textes_5281/>.

Manuscriptorium virtual library (Czech National Library): <http://www.manuscriptorium.com/Site/ENG/>.

Norton Topics Online (*Norton Anthology of English Literature*): <http://www.wwnorton.com/nael/>.

Online Library of Liberty (Liberty Fund): <http://oll.libertyfund.org/>.

Open Russian Electronic Library (*OREL*, Russian State Library): <http://orel.rsl.ru/book/2.html>.

Polska Biblioteka Internetowa: <http://www.pbi.edu.pl/>.

Project Gutenberg: <http://www.gutenberg.org/>.

Project Laurens Janszoon Coster: <http://cf.hum.uva.nl/dsp/ljc/>.

Projekt Rastko: <http://www.rastko.org.yu/>.

Project Runeberg: <http://runeberg.org/>.

Projecto Vercial – Literatura Neoclassica: <http://alfarrabio.di.uminho.pt/vercial/programas.htm>.

Saganet (National Library and Cornell University): <http://sagnanet.is/>.

Timarit (Icelandic National Library): <http://www.timarit.is/>.

Wirtualna Biblioteka Literatury Polskiej (University of Gdansk): <http://monika.univ.gda.pl/~literat/books.htm>.

Project sites and e-journals

The Blake Multimedia Project: <http://cla.calpoly.edu/~smarx/Blake/blakeproject.html>.

Blake Web (Steven Marx, Cal Poly University): <http://cla.calpoly.edu/~smarx/Blake/blakeweb.html>.

British Poetry 1780–1910 (Virginia University): <http://etext.lib.virginia.edu/britpo.html>.

Calendrier Électronique des Spectacles sous l'Ancien régime et sous la Révolution (*CÉSAR*): <http://www.cesar.org.uk/cesar2/home.php>.

The Dictionary of Sensibility (Virginia University): <http://www.engl.virginia.edu/enec981/dictionary/>.

Early Modern Literary Studies: <http://www.shu.ac.uk/emls/emlshome.html (ISSN 1201-2459)>.

Eighteenth-Century Life: <http://ecl.dukejournals.org/>.

Eighteenth Century Studies: <http://uk.jstor.org/journals/00132586.html>; <http://lion.chadwyck.co.uk/showPage.do?DurUrl=Yes&

TEMPLATE=/contents/abl_toc/Eighteenth CenturyStudiesAmerica/issues.jsp; http://muse. jhu.edu/journals/eighteenth-century_studies/>.

Johnson Society: <www.lichfieldrambler.co.uk>.

Representative Poetry Online (University of Toronto): <http://rpo.library.utoronto.ca/>.

Romantic Circles: <http://www.rc.umd.edu/editions/>.

Romantic Circles Praxis Series (University of Maryland): <http://www.rc.umd.edu/praxis/> (ISSN 1528-8129).

Romanticism on the Net: <http://www.ron.umontreal.ca/index.shtml> (ISSN 1467-1255).

Rousseau Studies: <http://rousseaustudies.free.fr/>.

Spectator Project: <http://meta.montclair.edu/spectator>.

Le Théâtre de la Foire à Paris (Barry Russell): <http://www.theatrales.uqam.ca/foires/>.

Thomas Gray Archive (Alexander Huber): <http://www.thomasgray.org/texts>.

William Blake Archive: <http://www.blakearchive.org/blake/>.

The World of London Theater, 1660–1800 (Patricia Craddock): <http://www.nwe.ufl.edu/~pcraddoc/lonmen1.html>.

6

Multimedia and Multitasking: A Survey of Digital Resources for Nineteenth-Century Literary Studies

John A. Walsh

Introduction

For any given literary period, it is easy to locate characteristics of the literature and circumstances of the historical moment that parallel in different ways the character-istics and circumstances of the digital age we now inhabit. The medieval scriptorium and the production of elaborate illuminated manuscripts, for instance, bear a curious resemblance to the contemporary digitization shop where classic texts are re-keyed and laboriously and intricately encoded, wrapped in a metatext that in its native form is often either invisible or opaque to all but the digital specialist. Similarly, Gutenberg's invention of moveable type in the fifteenth century and the cultural transformations engendered by this technological development may be seen as pre-cursors to the electronic text of the digital age and the significant societal developments, such as podcasting and social networking, enabled by digital communications and environments. Moveable type increased the bandwidth of communication in societies that adopted the mechanical technology. Transportation networks (canals, railways, highways, air routes) and communication technologies (the telegraph, telephone, radio and television) provide still more bandwidth. The communication bandwidth available now in the twenty-first century through contemporary digital technologies (internet, wireless, cellular networks) and communication devices (computers, cellular phones) dwarfs anything hitherto available. The number of recorded and documented human utterances, and the accessibility of these utterances, is unparalleled.

Among these many and diverse forms of expression – commercial websites, blogs, MySpace and Facebook pages, YouTube videos, newly created literature and art and performance – are thousands of examples of nineteenth-century literature, some carefully prepared by professional scholars, others enthusiastically, though perhaps less rigorously, prepared by fans and readers of great literature. Because of the digital publishing efforts of literary scholars, students, librarians, and enthusiasts, users can Google for "dance milkier sail" or "passions senses warble" and happen immediately upon these two stanzas from Tennyson's *In Memoriam*:

> Now dance the lights on lawn and lea,
> The flocks are whiter down the vale,
> And milkier every milky sail
> On winding stream or distant sea;
>
> ***
>
> Wild bird, whose warble, liquid sweet,
> Rings Eden thro' the budded quicks,
> O tell me where the senses mix,
> O tell me where the passions meet,

The poetry of Tennyson, along with other literature of the nineteenth century, has become part of the greater digital landscape, and when a web user searches the internet, he or she searches the nineteenth century (and other centuries) as well as the continually growing body of born-digital content. Many of these digitized texts (and related images) are freely available to all who have access to the appropriate networks and digital technologies. The availability of the texts is itself a great boon to literary scholarship. Many of these texts have been long out of print and are now available in versions edited by highly qualified and accomplished scholars, and the digital texts are accompanied by supplementary materials – page images, critical apparatuses, essays, and auxiliary primary source material – that would not practically fit into the confines of the traditional printed book. Beyond access to high-quality texts and digital reproductions of manuscript images and visual art by Blake, Whitman, Rossetti, Swinburne, and others, the digital environment provides new modes and media for interacting with and engaging these works, for commentary, collaborative scholarship, creative criticism, serendipitous discovery, and performance of critical and theoretical strategies. And of course the digital networked environment provides the advantage of allowing interaction with the cumulative body of these objects and tools in networked homes, offices, and cafés – free from the traditional confines of often remote archives and libraries.

While interesting parallels and precursors to the digital age may be found in all periods of literature, the nineteenth century has a preponderance of such features and so holds a special attraction for digital literary scholarship. It is the era nearest to our own, and so shares many similarities simply because of its chronological proximity. The industrial revolution of the nineteenth century is the closest analog to the rapid technological and social change of the digital age. And many features of the nineteenth century – increased literacy rates, the beginnings of mass media, the decreasing costs of publishing – led to ever-increasing volumes of information and the need for ever more sophisticated and flexible technologies for representing and managing that information. Chronologically, technologically, and figuratively, the nineteenth century and the industrial revolution are in large part the parents of the digital age: "The Child is father of the Man."

The nineteenth century is an extremely rich and diverse era that includes the Romantic and Victorian periods in Great Britain and, in the works of figures like Hawthorne, Whitman, Melville, Dickinson, and Twain, the flowering of a distinctively American literature in the United States. It was the last great age of poetry; that is, the last period in which great poetry was written, widely read, and culturally relevant. The eighteenth century saw the birth of the novel in the works of Richardson, Fielding, and Sterne, but the nineteenth century witnessed an incredible growth in the production of novels as prose fiction became the dominant literary form. Non-fiction prose is also well represented in the writings of Lamb, Hazlitt, De Quincy, Leigh Hunt, Emerson, Thoreau, Carlyle, and Ruskin. British literary periodicals such as the *Edinburgh Review*, *Quarterly Review*, and *Athenaeum* and American monthlies such as *Harper's New Monthly Magazine*, *Atlantic Monthly*, and *Southern Literary Messenger* contributed to the number and diversity of voices in the literary landscape and foreshadowed the mass media of the twentieth and twenty-first centuries. Nineteenth-century literature includes interesting hybrid forms, such as the dramatic monologue, combining elements of the lyric and dramatic, and Landor's "Imaginary Conversations," which combine elements of drama and prose fiction. Blake, Rossetti, and Morris unite textual and visual languages in innovative ways, providing a crucial analog for the multimedia and "new media" creative works found on the web and in other digital environments.

Along with this diversity of writers and genres, in the nineteenth century may be found the origins of the modern phenomenon of information overload, when the amount of recorded information produced – even in a focused discipline – becomes overwhelming and nearly impossible to process through traditional means, such as reading. The *English Short Title Catalog* (ESTC), a database of items printed in English from the beginnings of print to 1800, contains roughly 460,000 records. By contrast, the *Nineteenth-Century Short Title Catalog* (NSTC), a similar database with coverage from the beginning of the nineteenth century to the end of World War I, includes over 1.2 million records, three times as many titles as were published in the previous four centuries. Manipulation and full analysis of such a massive volume of textual (and other) data demand digitization, modern information retrieval techniques, and computer analysis.

As the temporal home of the industrial revolution, the nineteenth century claims a special place in the field of digital literary studies. The industrial revolution effected a shift from an agrarian to a manufacturing and industrial economy, a shift that led to or was accompanied by major societal upheavals, such as the American Civil War. In turn, the digital revolution has effected a shift from an industrial to a service- and information-based economy. Both the industrial and digital transitions are accompanied by varying, disproportionate, and unequal levels of prosperity and despair of the sort depicted by Dickens in *Oliver Twist* and *Hard Times*. Likewise, the digital age of the late twentieth and early twenty-first centuries is wracked by the shockwaves of globalization, the mass migration of industrial jobs, "outsourcing" of highly skilled technical positions to cheaper labor markets, and dot-com billionaires and bankrupts. Both the industrial and digital revolutions are attended by technologically enhanced and augmented modes of communication. Thus, artists, critics, scholars, and others from both periods are faced with transformative social change that necessitates reflection and commentary as they are simultaneously provided with conditions and tools (cheaper printing, growing literacy, word processors, the internet) that facilitate the communication of their ideas.

It is tempting to romanticize the digital revolution,[1] which one does merely by calling it a revolution, by referencing the iconoclasm and experimentation of digital publication and new media, by emphasizing the empowering reach the internet provides to the individual voice – scholarly or creative – freed from the physical constraints of print media and the economic barriers to print publishing, by noting the ease with which anyone or anything can become the subject of a documentary or creative work with instantaneous worldwide distribution, and by citing new opportunities for creative and experimental criticism made possible by digital technologies: opportunities to incorporate multimedia – image, audio, video, and animation – into traditional scholarship; opportunities to create dynamic scholarship that updates and changes as the scholar's ideas change and evolve, abandoning the constraints of the static monograph while retaining the ability to provide a static snapshot of any stage in the evolving scholarly process. One must guard against an overly enthusiastic application of Romantic idealism to the promises of digital technology and remain cognizant of negative consequences such as the digital divide, digitally induced isolation from physical interaction, and billions of deleted email messages with subjects like "Vi[agra, Levi@tra LOWEST Cost Ever!" Nonetheless, these romantic claims for the digital age provide yet another parallel with the literature and culture of the nineteenth century.

Nineteenth-Century Multimedia

In the nineteenth century it is possible to find many examples of what might today be termed multimedia, a reintegration of creative activities and a recognition that the individual artist might excel in various modes and formats, such as poetry (text), painting (image), science, and technology. A number of major literary figures in the nineteenth century were interested in both text and image, the integration of the two modes and media types, and the connections between the two. William Blake, John Ruskin, William Morris, and Dante Gabriel Rossetti were all accomplished writers and visual artists. Other major nineteenth-century literary figures, such as Swinburne and Pater, were primarily writers who also wrote passionately about the visual arts. Ruskin was a great polymath whose impressive knowledge of science added yet another dimension to the multimedia aspect of his work. And it was Ruskin who so vigorously championed the work of J. W. M. Turner, another progenitor of multimedia in the arts. As soon as he was allowed by a change in the Royal Academy's exhibition procedures in 1798, Turner began inserting verses in the catalog to accompany his pictures. In that first year, he included verses from Milton's *Paradise Lost* and James Thompson's *Seasons* to five of his exhibited works. Among approximately two hundred oil paintings exhibited by Turner, fifty-three have poetic epigraphs, and twenty-six of these were composed by Turner himself. In addition, many of his titles make reference to poetry (Landow 1971: 45–8).

Digital media, particularly the World Wide Web, are excellent platforms for presenting multimedia primary works and related scholarship. Not surprisingly, many of the early and well-known digital humanities projects focus on these nineteenth-century "multimedia" artists. In 1996 Cambridge University Press published a simple digitization, delivered on CD-ROM, of Cook and Wedderburn's early twentieth-century "Library Edition" of *The Works of John Ruskin*, a multimedia work featuring Ruskin's complete writings along with hundreds of his drawings and paintings. And two of the earliest web-based digital humanities projects, the *Rossetti Archive* and the *William Blake Archive*, focus on multimedia painter-poets.

It is worth noting that most of these projects are scholarly editing, "archive" projects, assembling digitized versions of authors' published works and manuscripts, together with significant and valuable scholarly treatment. Marcel O'Gorman, borrowing terminology from Derrida, has claimed that the field of digital humanities is particularly susceptible to "archive fever," an inordinate emphasis on textual editing and archiving at the expense of more adventurous, experimental, and creative uses of technology to transform humanities scholarship (O'Gorman 2006: 9). The early "archive" projects (e.g., *Blake, Whitman, Rossetti*)[2] do demonstrate a high level of creativity, both in their early adoption of digital technology and, in the case of the *Rossetti* and *Blake* archives, in their refusal to tolerate the traditional segregation of the textual and the visual. Furthermore, the archive projects provide the raw materials with which other scholars may apply computational or aesthetic creativity to attempt still more transformative and original modes of discourse and criticism. Nonetheless, those working in digital literary studies should take note of O'Gorman's cautionary tale:

> [S]omewhere in the early 1990s, the major tenets of deconstruction (death of the Author, intertextuality, etc.) were displaced into technology, that is, hypertext. Or to put it another way, philosophy was transformed, liquidated even, into the materiality of new media. This alchemical transformation did not result in the creation of new, experimental scholarly methods that mobilize deconstruction via technology, but in an academic fever for digital archiving and accelerated hermeneutics, both of which replicate, and render more efficient, traditional scholarly practices that belong to the print apparatus. (O'Gorman 2006: xv)

Explorations into digital archiving and accelerated hermeneutics should continue unabated. These efforts represent the first generation of digital humanities work, and provide a foundation for new and more experimental approaches.[3] Nonetheless, digital literary scholarship will expand both its content and its audience and more fully exploit digital tools and media by heeding O'Gorman's call to "shape a new apparatus" and to

> reclaim deconstruction [and theory generally] from the digital liquidation it underwent in the 1990s in order to apply it more carefully (though experimentally and radically) in the creation of discursive practices that are suitable to a culture that has internalized the primary tenets of postmodern theory, but has done so by way of popular culture and computing techniques. (O'Gorman 2006: xv–xvi)

Electronic Scholarship and the Digital Guild

The Victorians themselves were susceptible to a sort of "archive fever," illustrated in George Eliot's character from *Middlemarch*, Edward Casaubon, and his doomed *Key to All Mythologies*, an endless, meaningless, and ultimately futile effort to compile, integrate, and provide a single "key" to all the world's mythologies. Ruskin, Morris, and others reacted against such strains of nineteenth-century pedantry and overspecialization and encouraged a more holistic and interdisciplinary approach to art and life.

Electronic scholarship encourages interdisciplinary collaboration and gives scholars control over more aspects of the production and presentation of their work, from writing and editing to design, contextualization, and publication. Traditional literary scholarship is often a lonely pursuit – solitary work devoted to the production of a monograph. Digital literary scholarship, on the other hand, is generally social and collaborative with scholars, students, librarians, and technologists working together to produce a scholarly product with more functionality, further reach, and potentially wider appeal than the traditional monograph. One of the joys of digital scholarship is its social aspect and the real-time, face-to-face experience of knowledge sharing, teaching, and learning that takes place outside of the conventional classroom and outside the constraints of the teacher–student relationship. Individuals from diverse backgrounds, all experts in their respective fields, must work together to produce a complex digital scholarly project. All members of the group are simultaneously teachers and students.

Ruskin wrote famously on the division of labor and the "division of men":

> It is not, truly speaking, the labour that is divided; but the men: – Divided into mere segments of men – broken into small fragments and crumbs of life; so that all the little piece of intelligence that is left in a man is not enough to make a pin, or a nail, but exhausts itself in making the point of a pin or the head of a nail. (Ruskin 1903: 10: 196)

The point of the pin or the head of the nail – the words of a scholarly text are just that. As scholars such as D. F. McKenzie and Jerome J. McGann have persuasively argued, any text is a collaboratively, socially produced artifact, involving the contributions of authors, designers, typesetters, printers, publishers, etc. (McKenzie 1986; McGann

2006b). All the players contribute to the shape, form, and meaning of text. In digital scholarship, there may well be more players, more and different contributions (e.g., programming or document object modeling), and more confluence of roles (e.g., literary scholarship, systems development, visual design) within an individual contributor to a project.

The collaborative teams that are assembled to produce digital literary scholarship may be viewed as a humorously ironic, though vitally important and necessary answer to a particularly nineteenth-century concern, the anxiety – shared by Ruskin, Morris, and others – over the division of labor. As a traditional textual or bibliographic literary scholar could master the intricacies of the printing and publishing industries – folios, foolscap, gatherings, and duodecimo – so scholars working in the digital environment will find it useful to familiarize themselves with the tools and technologies – XML, TEI, XHTML, JavaScript, and CSS – for "printing" and publishing digital scholarship. In the digital environment, the scholar – often working with a team of students, developers, and designers – has more control of the whole process of generating and presenting the scholarship. The interaction of team members provides opportunities for debate, learning, and insights about the source material. As developers and designers struggle with how to adequately present on the web a particularly troublesome feature of the text – for instance, an infralinear insertion that winds its way around the margins of the recto and finds a stopping point in the middle of a another poem on the verso – they will ask questions of the text and of the other members of the team, and people will talk and generate ideas, many of which will be useful and insightful and lead to new understandings of the work. This sort of work results in true interdisciplinarity, a much-lauded goal of scholarship. The combination of, say, history and literary studies is after all a rather shallow pool of interdisciplinarity; the skills required to master each field are not all that different. But literary studies, computer science, graphic design, human–computer interaction design, digital publishing – these are all disparate though nonetheless complementary disciplines that combine in exciting ways to form the deep interdisciplinarity of digital literary studies.

The Nineteenth Century as the Final Frontier

Another attraction of the nineteenth century as a subject of digital literary scholarship is that it is perhaps the final age of literature for which the content is freely accessible and unencumbered by copyright restrictions. Due to increasingly draconian copyright laws in the United States and Europe, no works created since 1923 (that were still copyrighted in 1998) will enter the pubic domain until 2019.[4] And the threat exists that large, wealthy, and powerful copyright holders may have future successes persuading legislators to extend copyright even further. Thus, for at least another decade, the nineteenth century remains a final frontier of sorts for digital scholarship focused on the editing, reproduction, and manipulation of primary materials. Of course, one may seek permission to use and reproduce copyrighted works, but arranging such permissions places an extraordinary burden on the scholar and is unmanageable and impractical if one's work requires a large and diverse corpus representing multiple authors and potentially hundreds of copyright holders.

Survey

Below is a discussion of a number of exemplary digital projects focused on nineteenth-century literature. The list is by no means exhaustive; rather, I have attempted to discuss a representative selection of digital projects of various types – those devoted to single authors, reference works, online communities, and more comprehensive projects that seek to collect and integrate digital scholarship from a variety of sources and about a variety of subjects.

Individual authors

William Blake Archive *<http://www.blakearchive.org/>*
The *William Blake Archive*, edited by Morris Eaves, Robert Essick, and Joseph Viscomi, was launched in 1996 as a free website with a goal to become "an international public resource that would provide unified access to major works of visual and literary art that are highly disparate, widely dispersed, and more and more often severely restricted as a result of their value, rarity, and extreme fragility" (Eaves et al. 2005). The *William Blake Archive* has in large part fulfilled that mission by offering digital editions of multiple copies of all of Blake's nineteen illuminated works. The illuminated books are supplemented by additional materials such as commercial book illustrations; prints for other works, such as the illustrations for The Book of Job and Dante; drawings and paintings; and manuscript materials.

In the figure of William Blake, the nineteenth century provides one of the best arguments for digital scholarship. Blake was a multimedia artist, and it is only with the advent of digital technology that a comprehensive presentation of Blake's multi-media output becomes possible. As the editors of the *Archive* explain:

> The dominant tradition of Blake editing has been overwhelmingly literary. The historical Blake, a printmaker and painter by training who added poetry to his list of accomplishments, has been converted, editorially, into a poet whose visual art is acknowledged but moved off to the side where it becomes largely invisible, partly because of what one of Blake's first critics, the poet Swinburne, called "hard necessity" – the technological and economic obstructions that have prevented the reproduction of accurate images in printed editions. (Eaves et al. 2005)

The editors' discussion of their editorial principles persuasively argues for the transformative power of digital literary scholarship to overcome previous "technological and economic obstructions." These digital technologies and modified editorial principles make possible a reintegration of the textual and graphic components of Blake's work and will necessarily transform future perceptions and understandings of Blake.

An important achievement of the *Blake Archive* is the scholarly treatment of the digital images. The *Archive* would be a splendid and extraordinarily useful resource if it simply provided high-quality digital images of Blake's works, along with some basic descriptive metadata; however, the editors have augmented such basic function-ality with extensive descriptions of each image and with advanced image manipula-tion and annotation tools (Figure 6.1). Further, they have created a controlled vocabulary of image "characteristics" and assigned terminology to the images, allow-ing users to search the database of images. Grouped under the five general categories of figure, animal, vegetation, object, and structure are terms such as demon, knight, nymph, jailor, blacksmith, Cupid, Elijah, John the Baptist, Zoa, tiger, spider, snake, rose, thistle, thorn, coffin, cradle, kite, quill, skull, altar, dome, cottage, and tower. While some have argued that imposing such a controlled vocabulary on Blake's work is simplistic and reductive and betrays the richness and subtlety of his images,[5] on the contrary the controlled vocabulary is an excellent tool for finding what one wants to find. The controlled vocabulary serves a much-needed purpose, like an index or page

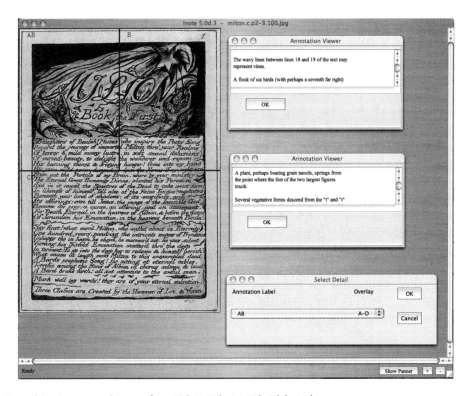

Figure 6.1 An annotated image (from Blake's *Milton*) in *The Blake Archive*.

numbers, for locating material of interest. Having then found interesting content, the scholar can reflect on the subtlety and richness, ambiguity and clarity of the work.

The Complete Writings and Pictures of Dante Gabriel Rossetti
(Rossetti Archive) <*http://www.rossettiarchive.org/*>

The *Rossetti Archive*, edited by Jerome J. McGann, is a long-running project devoted to the work of Victorian artist and poet Dante Gabriel Rossetti. Begun in 1992, before the widespread adoption of the World Wide Web, the *Rossetti Archive* is one of the earliest of the projects listed here and has served as a model for a great deal of subsequent digital scholarship. After the recent publication of the third of a projected four installments for the *Archive*, the project now includes page images and transcriptions of the 1861 book of translations, *The Early Italian Poets*; the 1870 edition of Rossetti's *Poems*; and the 1881 publications *Ballads and Sonnets* and *Poems. A New Edition*. Included with each volume are related pictorial works and other materials.

The *Rossetti Archive* is particularly noteworthy for its comprehensiveness. Recognizing that "Rossetti was a major figure in the rich cultural context of late Victorian England," McGann has added to the rich collection of Rossetti's works an impressive body of contextual material, including related texts, visual works, and contemporary periodicals.

Walt Whitman Archive <*http://www.whitmanarchive.org/*>

The *Walt Whitman Archive*, edited by Ed Folsom and Kenneth M. Price, "is an electronic research and teaching tool that sets out to make Whitman's vast work, for the first time, easily and conveniently accessible to scholars, students, and general readers" (Folsom, "Introduction"). Whitman's work, particularly *Leaves of Grass*, presents well-known and challenging textual difficulties. Unfettered by the constraints of word and page count or the weight of a massive bound volume, the *Whitman Archive* has the luxury of presenting a complex work such as *Leaves of Grass* in its various editions and formats as "distinct creations rather than as a single revised work" (Folsom, "Introduction"). In addition to the various editions and incarnations of *Leaves of Grass*, the *Archive* includes Whitman's notebooks, manuscript fragments, prose essays, letters, and journalistic articles. The *Archive* includes electronic text and page images for the six American editions of *Leaves of Grass* as well as the so-called "deathbed edition" of 1891–92, "a reprinting of the 1881–82 edition with 'annexes'" (Folsom). In addition to these important published texts, the Archive includes transcriptions and page images for nearly one hundred manuscripts, mostly poetry. The editors' discussion of what constitutes a "poetry manuscript" illustrates the importance of the *Archive* and the insights that may be gained by exploring its rich and subtle treasures:

> We have chosen to define "poetry manuscript" broadly, since it is often hard to determine the boundary between prose and verse in Whitman's manuscripts – especially in the pre-war years, Whitman habitually migrated his writing from prose to verse. For the purposes of this project, we consider as a poetry manuscript any writing in

Whitman's hand that either is written as verse, contains a key image or language that eventually made its way into a recognized Whitman poem, or discusses the making of a poem. (Folsom 2006)

A particularly useful component of the *Whitman Archive* is "An Integrated Finding Guide to Walt Whitman's Poetry Manuscripts," a resource that makes innovative use of the Encoded Archival Description (EAD) metadata standard. EAD is an XML format for encoding archival finding aids, documents that describe the background and contents of an archival collection, such as a collection of literary manuscripts. Whitman's manuscripts are dispersed across libraries, archives, and other institutions in the United States and United Kingdom. Each of these repositories has paper or digital finding aids describing their collections. The *Walt Whitman Archive* has worked with the many repositories and integrated these finding aids into one comprehensive EAD/XML-encoded "Finding Guide." The "Integrated Finding Guide" gathers the disparate findings aids, authored using the different conventions and standards of some thirty repositories, and presents the data in a single, unified, consistent manner.

Algernon Charles Swinburne Project *<http://www.swinburneproject.org/>*

My own *Swinburne Project* is a digital collection focused on the life and works of Victorian poet, critic, and novelist Algernon Charles Swinburne. The *Project* currently includes editions of Swinburne's four long, book-length poems, the classical verse dramas *Atalanta in Calydon* (1865) and *Erechtheus* (1876), and the Arthurian narrative poems *Tristram of Lyonesse* (1882) and *The Tale of Balen* (1896). Swinburne's most famous volume, the 1866 *Poems and Ballads*, is also included, along with later volumes *Songs before Sunrise* (1872), *Poems and Ballads*, Second Series (1878), *Songs of the Springtides* (1880), and *Studies in Song* (1880). The texts are all from the 1904 collected *Poems*, overseen by Swinburne and published by Chatto and Windus.

The *Swinburne Project* recently expanded its content to include current scholarship on Swinburne. Among the secondary scholarship currently available are John D. Rosenberg's essay "Swinburne and the Ravages of Time" (2005), a revision of his important 1967 essay "Swinburne" originally published in the journal *Victorian Studies*, and supplemental materials from Terry L. Meyers's important three-volume *Uncollected Letters of Algernon Charles Swinburne* (2005), which includes over 550 letters that were unavailable when Cecil Y. Lang published his landmark collection of Swinburne letters in the late 1950s and early 1960s.

Following the publication of his *Uncollected Letters*, Meyers approached the *Swinburne Project* about hosting additional materials related to the collection, including five additional letters that have surfaced since 2005. There was a forty-year wait between the publication of Lang's *Collected Letters* and Meyers's *Uncollected Letters*. Through the online publishing environment provided by the *Swinburne Project*, the *Uncollected Letters* is not a static collection, but an active, growing enterprise, and scholars need not wait months or years for the publication of newly edited Swinburne correspondence.

Aiming for comprehensiveness, future installments of the *Swinburne Project* will include the rest of the published poetry, the dramas, prose fiction and criticism, and manuscript materials.

Collaborative environments and integrated resources
VICTORIA *<https://listserv.indiana.edu/archives/victoria.html>*
As digital technologies and the capabilities of the web continue to advance at lightning speed, it is important not to lose sight of simpler, more fundamental functionalities provided by digital technology. A relatively early digital project that has contributed to literary scholarship is VICTORIA, a simple listserv (i.e., an electronic mailing list) that began in 1993 to facilitate online communication among scholars and students of Victorian studies. Because listserv software provides the functionality to maintain and search archives of the email messages shared among subscribers, VICTORIA is not only an important tool for collaboration and communication, but has become an important reference resource capturing over thirteen years of scholarly discussion and debate among graduate students, authors of historical fiction, widely published scholars, and others with an interest in Victorian studies.

Romantic Circles *<http:www.rc.umd.edu/>*
Romantic Circles, edited by Neil Fraistat and Steven E. Jones, is "a refereed scholarly Website devoted to the study of Romantic-period literature and culture." Unlike most of the projects discussed above, *Romantic Circles* is not devoted to a single author and presents a rich variety of content presented as the following categories:

- Electronic Editions.
- RC Blog, a weblog regularly updated with news and announcements of likely interest to Romanticists and *Romantic Circles* users.
- Praxis, original essays on Romanticism and Romantic literature.
- Scholarly Resources, reference resources such as chronologies, indexes, concordances, bibliographies, and links to related web resources.
- Pedagogy, teaching resources.
- Reviews, original reviews of print and online publications related to Romanticism.
- Romantic Circles MOO, an online, virtual environment for "discussions, meetings, and gaming." (Fraistat 2006)

The electronic editions include works by Southey, Wordsworth, Coleridge, Shelley, Keats, and a number of woman writers, including Mary Shelley, Betty T. Bennett, Felicia Hemens, Maria Jane Jewsbury, and Ana Laetitia Aikin.

Romanticism on the Net *<http://www.ron.umontreal.ca/>*
Romanticism on the Net, or *RoN*, is an international peer-reviewed electronic journal edited by Michael Eberle-Sinatra. *RoN* was first published in February 1996 and celebrated its tenth anniversary with a special issue in June 2006. With a distinguished

advisory board, a standard scholarly peer-review system, a quarterly publication schedule, and representation in the *MLA International Bibliography*, *RoN* has all the credentials of well-established print journals along with the many advantages of an online journal, including the timely promotion of relevant conferences and other journals; the ability to link to related online resources, such as *Romantic Circles*; and ready, unrestricted access to the full run of the journal.

NINES (Networked Interface to Nineteenth-Century Electronic Scholarship) <http://www.nines.org/>

NINES is an ambitious project to transform digital resources for the nineteenth-century beyond collections of texts, articles, reference material, etc. into an online, peer-reviewed environment for individual and collaborative research. NINES attempts to aggregate digital scholarship centered in nineteenth-century studies, British and American, and to provide digital scholarly tools for analyzing, exploring, collecting, and interacting with the aggregated content. Further, NINES is engaged in the development of tools designed to exploit the scholarly potential of the digital resources aggregated in the NINES environment. These tools include IVANHOE, Juxta, and Collex.

The first two tools, IVANHOE and Juxta, though developed and available under the auspices of the overall NINES project, are not necessarily tied to the NINES online environment, nor to the nineteenth century for that matter. The origins of the IVANHOE game lie in playful explorations of Scott's novel, and Juxta was developed with an eye toward the examination and editing of nineteenth- and early twentieth-century texts, but both tools may be run on a user's own computer with any text, regardless of whether it is a nineteenth-century text/resource or whether the text/resource has gone through the peer-review process and been incorporated into the NINES environment.

The IVANHOE game – a networked, Java-based desktop application – provides "a shared, online playspace for readers interested in exploring how acts of interpretation get made and reflecting on what those acts mean or might mean." The homepage for the INVANHOE game provides a detailed explanation of the functionality and aims of IVANHOE:

> The explorations come as active interventions in the textual field that is the target of the readers' interests. These interventions are then returned to the players in various kinds of visual transformations useful for critical reflection on the interpretative process. These reflections become computerized transformations of the discourse field into visualizations that expose interpretive relationships and possibilities. The visualizations are mapped to three interrelated coordinates: the players acting in the field; the moves executed by the players (comprising sets of multiple actions); and the documents that are acted upon. IVANHOE creates a formalized digital space where these three coordinates dynamically interact. Such interactions generate a complex interpretive space whose possibilities of meaning are returned to the interpretive agents in visualizations designed to provoke critical reflection and re-exploration. (*IVANHOE* 2006)

The IVANHOE game allows scholars to play with texts. Players assume a persona that may reflect an aspect of the text (e.g., a character from a novel or a biographical figure from the author's life), a theoretical approach to the text, or some other strategic critical intention. Players then make moves in the game; a move may be a written response to the text, a reaction to another player's response, or the introduction of a new text to the game/discourse field. The personas, the play, the texts, and the visualizations provided by IVANHOE all may serve, for the willing participant, to provoke "critical reflection and re-exploration," which of course is what scholars do — we reflect and explore and write and talk about our reflections and explorations. But in the context of IVANHOE this reflection and exploration may be done more collaboratively, and the visualizations and other aspects of the digital environment may provoke insights different than those that emerge from traditional modes of critical discourse.

Juxta is a Java-based textual analysis and editing tool for the comparison of textual objects. Any digitized text may be chosen as the base text and collated with any number of additional witnesses. Juxta provides multiple visualization options, including a side-by-side comparison of the base text with a witness text and a histogram displaying a graph of differences between the currently selected document and the other collated texts (Figure 6.2). Further, Juxta can generate a critical apparatus, in HTML format, detailing the textual variants in a set of compared texts. Juxta was primarily designed for editing nineteenth- and twentieth-century texts, but the developers are interested in making the tool useful for editing earlier texts as well (Juxta).

The third tool currently available as part of the NINES project is Collex, a "collections- and exhibit-builder designed to aid humanities scholars working in digital collections or within federated research environments like NINES" (Collex). Like IVANHOE and Juxta, Collex has the potential to be used in other projects and with other texts, but it is not a desktop tool and must be integrated with a more complex, server-based environment. Unlike many other projects discussed here, which more or less replicate print technology in the less restrictive online environment, Collex strives to exploit current information technologies (e.g., folksonomies and semantic web concepts) to provide a collaborative online scholarly environment with functionality extending far beyond that available in the print paradigm. Within the Collex environment, users may

> collect, tag, analyze, and annotate trusted objects (digital texts and images vetted for scholarly integrity); reorganize and publish objects in fresh critical perspectives; share these new collections with students and colleagues, in a variety of output formats; and, without any special technical training, produce interlinked online and print exhibits using a set of professional design templates. (*Collex* 2006)

Many of the projects, collections, and resources discussed in this essay are awaiting formal peer-review and inclusion in NINES; many are already available through the NINES/Collex interface. NINES has the potential to transform the way in which

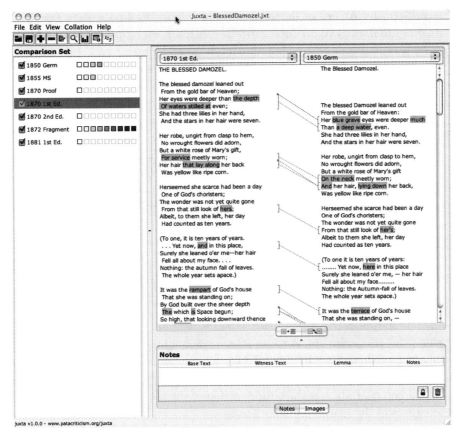

Figure 6.2   Screen shot of Juxta; a side-by-side comparison of the text of Rossetti's "Blessed Damozel" from the 1870 *Poems* (1st edn) and from the 1850 *Germ*.

these collections are used by allowing scholars to collect texts, images, and other objects from a variety of peer-reviewed sources and integrate them into a single user-defined exhibit or collection. Further, scholars may "tag" each item with keywords relevant to their own research. These tags may be shared with the public. As more and more users add tags to items within NINES, the NINES environment grows richer by reflecting the insights and interests of a larger and larger community of scholars. In addition to single word "tags" or "keywords," users may add more elaborate annotations to objects in their collections.

Additional Resources

As mentioned above, the nineteenth century is a rich source of material for digital scholarship, and I have selected only a few representative resources to discuss in detail. Many other noteworthy projects are available. Additional resources for nineteenth-century American literature include Stephen Railton's *Uncle Tom's Cabin and American Culture: A Multi-Media Archive* <http://www.iath.virginia.edu/utc/>, a comprehensive archive centered on Harriet Beecher Stowe's novel. In addition to multiple texts of *Uncle Tom's Cabin*, the collection includes "PreTexts" (Christian texts, anti-slavery texts, etc.) and "Responses" (American reviews, African-American responses, pro-slavery responses, etc.) as well as resources related to depictions of *Uncle Tom's Cabin* on stage and screen. The *Dickinson Electronic Archives* <http://www.emilydickinson.org/> includes writings by the Dickinson family and Emily Dickinson's correspondence, responses to Dickinson's writing, current scholarship on Dickinson, and teaching resources. *The Wright American Fiction Project* <http://www.letrs.indiana.edu/web/w/wright2/> includes both searchable electronic text and page images for over 2,800 titles of nineteenth-century American fiction, as listed in Lyle Wright's bibliography, *American Fiction, 1851–1875*.

Among the many additional resources for British literature is *The Victorian Women Writers Project* <http://www.indiana.edu/~letrs/vwwp/>, which includes nearly two hundred works of prose and poetry. George P. Landow, a scholar of John Ruskin and a leading theorist on hypertext, has developed *The Victorian Web* <http://www.victorianweb.org/>, a richly hypertextual general resource for the study of Victorian literature and culture. Patrick Leary, founder of the VICTORIA email discussion list, maintains the *Victorian Research Web* <http://victorianresearch.org/>, a listing of traditional and digital resources relevant to research and teaching about the Victorian period. The *Victorian Studies Bibliography* <http://www.dlib.indiana.edu/reference/victbib/> is the online version of the annual bibliography produced by the editors of the journal *Victorian Studies*.

The 1990s began with a few brave scholars turning from traditional modes of scholarship and risking reputations to explore how emerging technologies might be applied to the production of scholarly texts, the examination of those texts, and the discourse about the texts. In a couple of noteworthy cases, the technology was used to unite, in ways that were not previously possible, the visual and textual works of important figures like Blake and Rossetti. These early projects inspired others to adopt similar modes, provided exemplars for digital scholarship, and contributed the raw materials, in the form of a growing corpus of digital text and images, for experiments in computational literary analysis, digital annotation, and other innovative applications of technology. Well over a decade after these early projects began, scholars of nineteenth-century British and American literature are awash with an ever-growing number of high-quality digital resources, and initiatives likes NINES, building on the inherently collaborative nature of digital humanities scholarship, are attempting to aggregate disparate projects under a single interface coupled with a variety of digital tools that are likely to enhance the potential of existing archives and resources and to encourage and enable increasingly daring and creative scholarship and teaching about the nineteenth century.

NOTES

1 Richard Coyne's *Technoromanticism: Digital Narrative, Holism, and the Romance of the Real* (Cambridge: MIT Press, 2001) is a book-length study on the romanticization of digital technology.

2 Eaves, Morris, Robert N. Essick, and Joseph Viscomi (Eds.). *The William Blake Archive.* Accessed October 1, 2006. <http://www.blakearchive.org/>; Folsom, Ed, and Kenneth M. Price (Eds.). Overview of the Archive. *The Walt Whitman Archive.* <http://www.whitmanarchive.org/>. Accessed October 1, 2006; McGann, Jerome J. (Ed.). *The Complete Writings and Pictures of Dante Gabriel Rossetti (Rossetti Archive).* <http://www.rossettiarchive.org/>. Accessed October 1, 2006.

3 Jerome McGann's *Rossetti Archive*, for instance, provides an initial foundation for *NINES* (discussed below), a more recent project that integrates scholarly digital resources, provides tools for manipulating and interacting with the content, and implements emerging information retrieval methodologies, such as folksonomies (collaboratively generated categorization and tagging of content).

4 For an overview of US copyright see "Copyright Office Basics" published by the US Copyright Office and available at <http://www.copyright.gov/circs/circ1.html>.

5 See, for instance, Andrew Cooper and Michael Simpson's "The High-Tech Luddite of Lambeth: Blake's Eternal Hacking." *Wordsworth Circle* 30.3 (Summer 1999): 125–31.

REFERENCES AND FURTHER READING

Cooper, Andrew, and Michael Simpson (1999). "The High-Tech Luddite of Lambeth: Blake's Eternal Hacking." *Wordsworth Circle* 30.3: 125–31.

Collex (2006). Applied Research in Patacriticism. <http://www.nines.org/tools/collex.html>. Accessed October 1, 2006.

Coyne, Richard (2001). *Technoromanticism: Digital Narrative, Holism, and the Romance of the Real.* Cambridge, MA: MIT Press.

Eaves, Morris, Robert N. Essick, and Joseph Viscomi (Eds.) (2005). "Editorial Principles: Methodology and Standards in the Blake Archive." *The William Blake Archive.* <http://www.blakearchive.org/blake/public/about/principles/>. Accessed October 1, 2006.

——, Robert N. Essick, and Joseph Viscomi (Eds.) (2006a). "The Archive at a Glance." *The William Blake Archive.* <http://www.blakearchive.org/blake/public/about/glance/>. Accessed October 1, 2006.

—— (2006b). *Crafting Editorial Settlements. Romanticism on the Net*, 41–2. <http://www.erudit.org/revue/ron/2006/v/n41-42/013150ar.html>. Accessed October 1, 2006.

——, Robert N. Essick, and Joseph Viscomi (Eds.) (2006c). *The William Blake Archive.* <http://www.blakearchive.org/>. Accessed October 1, 2006.

Eberle-Sinatra, Michael (Ed.) (2006). *Romanticism on the Net.* <http://www.ron.umontreal.ca/>. Accessed October 1, 2006.

English Short Title Catalogue (2006). *The British Library.* <http://estc.bl.uk/>. Accessed October 1, 2006.

Feluga, Dino Franco (2006). "Introduction: *Skeuomorphs* and Anti-Time." *Romanticism on the Net*, 41–2. <http://www.erudit.org/revue/ron/2006/v/n41-42/013149ar.html>. Accessed October 1, 2006.

Folsom, Ed, and Kenneth M. Price (Eds.) (2006). "Overview of the Archive." *The Walt Whitman Archive.* <http://www.whitmanarchive.org/introduction/index.html>. Accessed October 1, 2006.

Fraistat, Neil, and Steven E. Jones (Eds.) (2006). *Romantic Circles.* <http://www.rc.umd.edu/>. Accessed October 1, 2006.

——, Steven Jones, and Carl Stahmer (1998). "The Canon, the Web, and the Digitization of Romanticism." *Romanticism on the Net* 10. <http://www.erudit.org/revue/ron/1998/v/n10/005801ar.html>. Accessed October 1, 2006.

IVANHOE (2006). Applied Research in Patacriticism. <http://www.nines.org/tools/ivanhoe.html>. Accessed October 1, 2006.

Jones, Steven E. (n.d.). "Digital Romanticism in the Age of Neo-Luddism: The Romantic Circles Experiment." *Romanticism on the Net* 41–2. <http://www.erudit.org/revue/ron/2006/v/n41-42/013152ar.html>. Accessed October 1, 2006.

Juxta (2006). Applied Research in Patacriticism. <http://www.nines.org/tools/juxta.html>. Accessed October 1, 2006.

Landow, George (1971). *The Aesthetic and Critical Theories of John Ruskin*. Princeton: Princeton University Press.

—— (2006). *The Victorian Web*. <http://www.victorianweb.org/>. Accessed October 1, 2006.

Leary, Patrick (2006). *Victorian Research Web (VRW)*. <http://victorianresearch.org/>. Accessed October 1, 2006.

Mandel, Laura (Ed.) (2006). *The Poetess Archive*. <http://unixgen.muohio.edu/~poetess/>. Accessed October 1, 2006.

McGann, Jerome J. (Ed.) (2006a). *The Complete Writings and Pictures of Dante Gabriel Rossetti (Rossetti Archive)*. <http://www.rossettiarchive.org/>. Accessed October 1, 2006.

—— (2006b). "From Text to Work: Digital Tools and the Emergence of the Social Text." *Romanticism on the Net* 41–2. <http://www.erudit.org/revue/ron/2006/v/n41-42/013153ar.html>. Accessed October 1, 2006.

—— (2006c). "Visible Language, Interface, IVANHOE." In *The Scholar's Art: Literary Studies in a Managed World*. Chicago: University of Chicago Press, pp. 148–71.

——, et al. (2006d). *NINES (Networked Interface for Nineteenth-Century Electronic Scholarship)*. <http://www.nines.org/>. Accessed October 1, 2006.

McKenzie, D. F. (1986). *Bibliography and the Sociology of Texts*. London: British Library.

Miller, Andrew H., and Ivan Kreilkamp (2005). *Victorian Studies Bibliography*. Bloomington: Indiana University Press and Indiana University Digital Library Program. <http://www.dlib.indiana.edu/reference/victbib/>. Accessed October 1, 2006.

Nineteenth-Century Short Title Catalogue (2004–2006). <http://nstc.chadwyck.com/>. Accessed October 1, 2006.

O'Gorman, Marcel (2006). *E-Crit: Digital Media, Critical Theory, and the Humanities*. Toronto: University of Toronto Press.

Railton, Stephen (2006). *Uncle Tom's Cabin and American Culture: A Multi-Media Archive*. <http://www.iath.virginia.edu/utc/>. Accessed October 1, 2006.

Rosenberg, John D. (2005). "Swinburne and the Ravages of Time." In *Elegy for an Age*. London: Anthem Press, pp. 163–86.

Ruskin, John (1903). "The Nature of Gothic." *The Stones of Venice*. Vol. 2. *The Works of John Ruskin*. (Ed.) E. T. Cook and Alexander Wedderburn. 39 vols. London: George Allen, 1903–12. 10, pp. 180–269.

Smith, Marth Nell, et al. (Eds.). *Dickinson Electronic Archive*. <http://www.emilydickinson.org/>. Accessed October 1, 2006.

Stauffer, Andrew (2006). "Romanticism's Scattered Leaves." *Romanticism on the Net* 41–2. <http://www.erudit.org/revue/ron/2006/v/n41-42/013155ar.html>. Accessed October 1, 2006.

Swinburne, Algernon Charles (2005). *Uncollected Letters of Algernon Charles Swinburne* (Ed. Terry L. Meyers). 3 vols. London: Pickering and Chatto.

Viscomi, Joseph (n.d.). "Blake's Virtual Designs and Deconstruction of *The Song of Los*." *Romanticism on the Net* 41–2. <http://www.erudit.org/revue/ron/2006/v/n41-42/013151ar.html>. Accessed October 1, 2006.

Walsh, John. A. (Ed.) (2006). *The Swinburne Project*. <http://www.swinburneproject.org/>. Accessed October 1, 2006.

Willett, C. Perry (Ed.) (2002). *Victorian Women Writers Project*. <http://www.indiana.edu/~letrs/vwwp/>. Accessed October 1, 2006.

Wright American Fiction 1851–1875. Committee on Institutional Cooperation (CIC). <http://www.letrs.indiana.edu/web/w/wright2/>. Accessed October 1, 2006.

Hypertext and *Avant-texte* in Twentieth-Century and Contemporary Literature

Dirk Van Hulle

Twentieth-century and contemporary literature are characterized by an increased attention to the writing process as an inherent part of the written product. This enhanced textual awareness is reinforced by a mutual influencing between literature in print and digital media, a development that is nicely captured in the 2001 revision of J. G. Ballard's *The Atrocity Exhibition* (1970). While the idea of working with short blocks of texts, constituting the 1970 "exhibition," may have had an impact on digital literature, the reverse process became noticeable some thirty years later: in the internet era Ballard wrote an "Author's Note" to the revised, expanded, and annotated edition (2001), presenting his book as a hypertextual structure:

> Readers who find themselves daunted by the unfamiliar narrative structure of *The Atrocity Exhibition* – far simpler than it seems at first glance – might try a different approach. Rather than start at the beginning of each chapter, as in a conventional novel, simply turn the pages until a paragraph catches your eye. If the ideas or images seem interesting, scan the nearby paragraphs for anything that resonates in an intriguing way. Fairly soon, I hope, the fog will clear, and the underlying narrative will reveal itself. In effect, you will be reading the book in the way it was written. (Ballard 2001: vi)

This form of what Roland Barthes called a "writerly" text (*texte scriptible*, *S/Z* 10) approximates the structure of hypertexts, which George Landow defined as "text composed of blocks of text – what Barthes terms a lexia – and the electronic links that join them" (Landow 1997: 3). These "lexias" or fragments of text reflect the emphasis on perspectivism and fragmentariness that characterizes numerous twentieth-century and contemporary works of literature, at least since Gertrude Stein's experimental literary equivalents of cubism and the fragments T. S. Eliot "shored against [his] ruins" in the last stanza of *The Waste Land* (1922). In many ways the experiments of the modernists prefigure literary aesthetics in the digital age. Notably the tendency to deviate from a linear narrative structure anticipates non-linear forms of writing and reading that characterize *hyperfiction* (digital literature that is marked by a hypertextual structure). Instead of representing or mirroring reality they tried to convey the experience of reality, resulting in complex studies of the ways in which human beings deal with time and space. Time became a dominant preoccupation to so many modernist authors in the wake of Marcel Proust's *A la recherche du temps perdu* that Wyndham Lewis started referring to them as "proustites" and worshippers of "the Great God Flux" (Lewis 1989: 335).

The modernist attempts to convey the *experience* of time and space resulted in formal experiments that may be regarded as proto-hypertexts. With reference to the treatment of Time (in Section 1 of this chapter), William Faulkner's *The Sound and the Fury* serves as an appropriate paradigm of such a proto-hypertext, especially since it has actually been translated into a freely accessible hypertext edition on the web. With regard to the treatment of Space (Section 2), Julio Cortázar's novel *Hopscotch* suggests a key metaphor to describe the reading process of these proto-hypertexts and their translatability to a digital medium. Thus, old ideas like the creation of a "hideous progreny" by assembling body parts *à la* Frankenstein are reinvigorated by translating them into hyperfiction (Section 3), as Shelley Jackson shows in *Patchwork Girl*.

The reverse translation is noticeable as well. Especially toward the end of the twentieth and the beginning of the twenty-first centuries, authors prove themselves increasingly skillful in applying characteristic features of electronic literature to print (Section 4). A paradigmatic work in this regard is Mark Z. Danielewski's *House of Leaves*, which manages to translate hypertextual multi-linearity to the leaves that constitute the house in which the reader is invited to actively participate in the creation of meaning. An important consequence of this evolution is the realization that texts are never quite finished. This awareness finds its expression in the decision to publish texts (both printed and digital) in the form of an unfinished product, as in the case of Toby Litt's *Finding Myself*, presented as a revised typescript with manuscript corrections by the publisher.

With hindsight, these contemporary writings have drawn attention to the importance their modernist predecessors attached to the writing process of their own writings. Given their preoccupation with Time, it was perfectly consistent with their poetics to acknowledge that their own writings did not escape the effects of Time: "the individual is a succession of individuals," as Samuel Beckett noted in his essay on Proust (Beckett 1999: 19); in a similar way the text consists of a succession of versions, a series of consecutive adaptations – which partly explains why so many modernist authors have carefully preserved their manuscripts and sometimes even donated them to university libraries, indicating the extent to which they considered the *avant-texte* (the whole collection of preparatory textual material) to be an integral part of the literary work. The intrinsically hypertextual structure of literary geneses (Section 5) – consisting of blocks of text that are shuffled around during the writing process – indicates how useful digital tools can be to map out literary composition histories. This involves yet another translation, this time from manuscript material to digital facsimiles and transcriptions encoded in markup languages, resulting in one of the most useful applications of digital media in literary studies: the study of the hypertextual nature of literary geneses.

1. Time

Time is one of the preoccupations of major modernist authors in the first half of the twentieth century, resulting in sometimes intricate narrative structures. For instance, the strokes of Big Ben as a motif in Virginia Woolf's *Mrs. Dalloway* do not merely emphasize the importance of time in this novel (whose provisional title in an early version was *The Hours*). They also indicate the tension between the human system-atization of time and the way it is experienced subjectively in the mind, i.e., "psychological time" measured by what Henri Bergson called "duration." Since a human being's thoughts are constantly interspersed with memories, his experience of time cannot be accurately conveyed by means of a chronological account of events. When for instance in *The Sound and the Fury* (1929) William Faulkner tries to present what goes on in the mind of the eldest son of the Compson family on the day he is going to commit suicide (June 2, 1910), the succession of unpleasant memories gradually accelerates until Quentin is ready to kill himself. Each of these flashbacks can be divided into fragments, scattered over the chapter. The size of these lexias ranges from just a few words to a few pages. The recollections of Quentin's youngest brother are different in that the mentally retarded Benjy truly relives them, to such an extent that he lives more in the past than in the present: only one-third of the first chapter takes place in the "present" (April 7, 1928, his 33rd birthday). The reader is challenged to follow the associative leaps in his mind and assemble a story by means of the scattered fragments of remembrances.

To analyze such an intricate narrative structure, hypertext can be a helpful tool, as the hypertext edition of William Faulkner's *The Sound and the Fury* (Ed. R. P. Stoicheff et al.) illustrates (Figure 7.1). The remembered scenes are color-coded (one color for all the fragments of one recollection) by means of a bar that flanks the reading text on the left-hand side. For instance, the paragraph starting with "You a big boy" is flanked by a colored bar with a number (9.2) corresponding to recollection 9.2, which is summarized on the right-hand side as "Benjy sleeps alone for the first time at 13 years old, 1908." The analysis of these recollections has resulted in an interesting observation: the fragments of a particular recollection may be scattered over the whole chapter, but they are scattered in a more or less chronological order. Still, it is sometimes hard to recall the preceding fragment. To link up both fragments, a clock icon (next to the color-coded bar, at the beginning of each fragment) takes the reader to the other fragments in chronological sequence.

When the reader arrives at fragment 9.2 ("You a big boy"), clicking on the clock icon makes it possible to link it to 9.1 ("Come on, now." Dilsey said. "You too big to

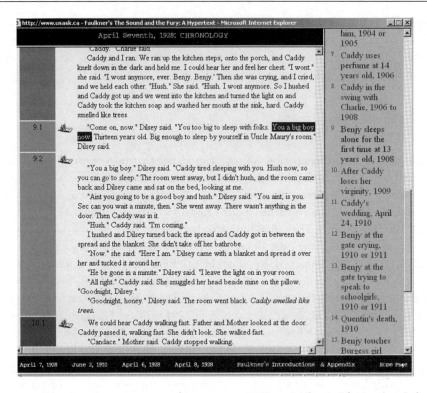

Figure 7.1 Chronological rearrangement of segments in William Faulkner's *The Sound and the Fury* (Ed. R. P. Stoicheff et al.).

sleep with folks. You a big boy now. Thirteen years old. Big enough to sleep by yourself in Uncle Maury's room." Dilsey said.) and reconstruct the flashback in its entirety (9.1 + 9.2).

The reader's attempt to translate Benjy's psychological time into clock time is facilitated by means of twenty scenes, summarized in a permanent frame on the right-hand side in the hypertext edition, and chronologically arranged from the grand-mother's (damuddy's) death to the present. These scenes can be regrouped into eight time slots: 1898 (damuddy's death when Benjy is 3 years old); 1900 (Benjy's name is changed); 1904–5 (his uncle's affair with Mrs. Patterson); 1905–10 (his sister's sexual adventures); April 1910 (his sister's wedding); May 1910 (his castration); June 1910 (his brother Quentin's suicide and subsequent death); April 7, 1928 (his 33rd birthday). But as Jean-Paul Sartre noted in his essay on "Time in the Work of Faulkner," reconstructing a chronological account of the events is "telling another story": "Jason and Caroline Compson have had three sons and a daughter. The daughter, Caddy, has given herself to Dalton Ames and become pregnant by him. Forced to get hold of a husband quickly..." (Sartre 1994 [1955]: 265). Whereas classical novels are built around a central complication, "we look in vain for such a complication in *The Sound and the Fury*": "Is it the castration of Benjy or Caddy's wretched amorous adventure or Quentin's suicide or Jason's hatred of his niece?" (265) Sartre is struck by the novel's "technical oddity," which is more than merely an exercise in virtuosity. Each episode hides other episodes. Unlike the chronological reconstruction, Faulkner's narrative gives access to a time without clocks. Notably Benjy's sense of time is clockless. When, at the very beginning of the novel, the golfers on the course next to the Compsons' house call for their caddie, Benjy is immediately reminded of scenes in the past with his sister Caddy.

The hypertext edition may give the impression of being designed merely as a tool to facilitate the reconstruction of chronology, and as Sartre suggested, to reconstruct the text in this fashion is a way of telling another story. But the edition facilitates many more alternative narrative paths. While the initial impulse might be a wish to re-establish order in the temporal disorder, the reader is also tempted into creating further disorder and invited to take part in the sound and the fury of the Compson chaos. Toward the end of the first chapter, when Benjy undresses, looks in the mirror and starts crying, the cook's grandson Luster says: *"Looking for them aint going to do no good"* (Figure 7.2).

By now the reader knows that "them" is a reference to Benjy's removed testicles, and even though *"Looking for them aint going to do no good"* the hypertext edition invites its users to do just that. The cruel mutilation of the sympathetic character may cause

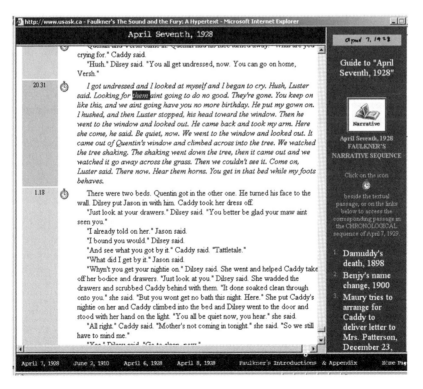

Figure 7.2 Faulkner's sequence of segments in *The Sound and the Fury* (Ed. R. P. Stoicheff et al.).

sufficient indignation to organize a search for Benjy's balls by means of the "search" function. This alternative narrative path allows the reader to follow this leitmotif in all its instantiations, notably in the form of the golf balls Benjy and Luster are looking for near the fence of the golf course. This simple search has remarkably complex consequences as it turns the reader simultaneously into an ally of Benjy (looking for golf balls and other leitmotifs) and into an accomplice in the act of castration (as the search highlights all the instantiations of "balls" and thus separates them from the text).

Every text requires a different approach, and this is even true for various chapters within the same novel. For Quentin's chapter, Faulkner changed his narrative technique. The mental processes that take place in Quentin's mind are more abstract and labyrinthine. As a result the temporal shifts occur even more suddenly, often in the middle of a sentence. For instance: "I carried the books into the sitting-room and stacked them on the table, the ones I had brought from home and the ones *Father said it used to be a gentleman was known by his books; nowadays he is known by the ones he has not returned* and locked the trunk and addressed it." (Faulkner 1994: 51) This different narrative technique required a different hypertextual treatment. Here, the editors have color-coded the text itself. One of the consequences of this color coding is that the text draws attention to what Rosalind Krauss calls the "grid."

2. Space

The spatial metaphor of the grid is "emblematic of the modernist ambition," according to Rosalind Krauss (1985: 9). Whereas the grid used to be employed by painters as a tool to create a successful reality effect by means of perspective, modern artists tend to focus on the discontinuity between reality and its representation: "Unlike perspective, the grid does not map the space of a room or a landscape or a group of figures onto the surface of a painting. Indeed, if it maps anything, it maps the surface of the painting itself. (. . .) Considered in this way, the bottom line of the grid is a naked and determined materialism." (Krauss 1985: 10). The same applies to literature. Instead of hiding the grid that marks most forms of composition, the modernist artist draws the reader's attention to it. And this tendency continued after World War II.

To examine some of the spatial preoccupations of postwar fiction, Julio Cortázar's *Hopscotch* (1963) is a suitable starting point. This masterpiece, which presents itself as child's play, is divided into three parts: "Del lado de allá" (From that side), "Del lado de acá" (From this side), and "De otros lados" (From other sides). The story does not end with the word "acabó" (finished), which concludes the second part. With reference to the other sides, a "Tablero de dirección" by Cortázar suggests that the reader can easily leave this last part unread, and just read the first two parts as they are presented in the book. But he or she can also follow an alternative narrative path. The 155 short, numbered chapters are conceived as mobile units of text. Changing the reading order results in a new book. So, as an alternative book, Cortázar suggests a particular reading order, starting with number 73, followed by 1, 2, 116, 3, 84, etc.

In case of confusion, it is always possible to return to the "Tablero de dirección" at the beginning of the book:

73 – 1 – 2 – 116 – 3 – 84 – 4 – 71 – 5 – 81 – 74 – 6 – 7 – 8 – 93 – 68 – 9 – 104 – 10 – 65 – 11 – 136 – 12 – 106 – 13 – 115 – 14 – 114 – 117 –...

In the reading text, the end of chapter 114 is followed by the suggestion "(–117)" indicating that chapter 117 is the next one in this alternative narrative. Although this alternative narrative is an equally linear path, the idea to work with mobile lexias and indicate the next lexia by means of a proto-hyperlink prefigures the first forms of hyperfiction and also makes this novel particularly amenable to digital manipulation and translation into hypertext. As Espen Aarseth has argued in *Cybertext: Perspectives on Ergodic Literature* – hypertextual structures do not need to be electronic. As a form of "ergodic literature," which urges the reader to complete the text, this novel already plays with the concept of "transclusion" before Ted Nelson had even coined the term: the same piece of information can be accessed in different contexts and from different perspectives. *Hopscotch* does not give shape to the desultory situation of Oliveira; it invites its readers to take part in this situation, and if they play along and follow the outlined track till the end, they are eventually sent back and forth between chapters 131 and 58. Like Oliveira in the open window (at the end of the second part), everything continues to be pending. The form matches and reflects the content.

Cortázar gives a few hints about the underlying poetics by means of a few chapters devoted to the character Morelli, an old writer who has had an accident in Paris. Morelli is said to justify the lack of coherence in his stories by arguing that we can never capture another person's life like a film, but only as a series of fragments. Hence Morelli's method of writing, which is comparable to a photo album. The link between two different moments has to be made by the reader. This appeal to the reader's involvement is a crucial aspect that many experimental works of fiction share with works of hyperfiction. As Cortázar indicates in the "Tablero de dirección," his book *is* multiple books: "este libro es muchos libros." The alternative narrative he suggests is only an invitation to try out other paths. The track he has outlined in the "Tablero de dirección" includes lexias from the third part and thus invites readers to look at the matter "From other sides," hopping from one chapter to another.

With this game of hopscotch, Cortázar offers an interesting spatial metaphor for hypertextual structures. What on the pavement looks like a single drawing is a multitude of combinations. Hypertext can be seen as an application of what authors such as Virginia Woolf, James Joyce, William Faulkner, and Julió Cortázar have suggested on paper with reference to the multiple ways in which we perceive time and space. Putting "Allspace in a Notshall," as Joyce called it in *Finnegans Wake*, is something readers need to do by themselves. This modernist idea underlies many works of hyperfiction; it is radicalized by means of its translation into a digital hypertext structure.

3. Toward Hyperfiction: Translation into a Digital Format

Other hypertexts on paper, such as Robert Coover's short story "The Babysitter," have turned out to be suitable for translation into an electronic format. This translatability is more than merely a technical issue. Samuel Beckett employed the notion of translation to stress that link between the idea that a "book is multiple books" and its existential equivalent by translating his own work from French into English or vice versa. In *How It Is* (his self-translation of *Comment c'est*) the phrase "ma vie dernier état" becomes another "version": "my life last state last version" (Beckett 2001: 2–3). The notion of perspectivism that is so central to twentieth-century fiction is probably the main reason why some of the texts from this period lend themselves particularly well to a translation from the printed medium to a digital format.

Some printed books not only contain elements that have the potential of being translated into a hypertext; they also give rise to digital rewritings or new creative hyperfiction, such as Shelley Jackson's *Patchwork Girl*, inspired by the different body parts of Victor Frankenstein's "monster" in Mary Shelley's bestseller. On the website of Eastgate Systems Inc. *Patchwork Girl* is recommended by Robert Coover as "[p]erhaps the true paradigmatic work of the era" (Jackson 1995). Shelley Jackson elaborates – among many other things – on Cortázar's hopscotch metaphor. One of the clickable words is "hop," leading to a lexia in which Patchwork Girl describes herself: "I am a discontinuous trace, a dotted line."

The formal structure of *Patchwork Girl* consists of multiple layers or levels. To move up or down in this structure, the reader can make use of upward and downward arrows in the toolbar, which shows a question mark, a two-way arrow, and a box with three dots, surrounded by four arrows in four directions (up, down, left, right).

In "Visual Structuring of Hyperfiction Narratives" Raine Koskimaa analyses how this visual device allows the reader to choose whether a text-screen or a map-screen will be shown uppermost. The map option shows a set of named boxes that can contain other constellations of texts, starting from an outline that contains the front picture, title page, and the main chapters. The arrows left and right of the three-dot button (in the toolbar) take the reader to the lexia either to the left or to the right within the current level of the map. Here, left and right refer to the spatial layout of the map. The role of the two-way arrow, on the other hand, is less strictly spatial.

Figure 7.3   Toolbar in Shelley Jackson's *Patchwork Girl*.

It takes the reader to the next lexia in the default narrative. The question-mark button shows the links that lead to and from the lexia currently read.

Many of the lexias in this hypertext are concerned with the problematic nature of identity, not only the identity of the protagonist (for which the etymology of the text – from Latin *textus*, woven – is further complicated in the central metaphor of the quilt), but also that of her author, Mary/Shelley & Herself. The ideas of authorship and of a singular origin are problematized, as Patchwork Girl notes with reference to her own birth: "My birth takes place more than once" (lexia: "birth"). The link with death is crucial, as the lexia "a graveyard" emphasizes: "I am buried here. You can resurrect me, but only piecemeal. If you want to see the whole, you will have to sew me together yourself (in time you may find appended a pattern and instructions – for now, you will have to put it together any which way, as the scientist Frankenstein was forced to do.) Like him, you will make use of a machine of mysterious complexity to animate these parts" (lexia: "a graveyard"). The text thus urges the reader to become a writer and assume the roles of Frankenstein, Shelley Jackson, and Mary Shelley. The composition of Patchwork Girl is described in two lexias that mirror the writing/ sewing metaphor:

> I had made her, writing deep into the night by candlelight, until the tiny black letters blurred into stitches and I began to feel that I was sewing a great quilt (...) (lexia: "written").

> I had sewn her, stitching deep into the night by candlelight, until the tiny black stitches wavered into script and I began to feel that I was writing (...) (lexia: "sewn").

Against the backdrop of the problematized issue of origins, it is somewhat paradoxical that the text retraces the origin of the *textus* metaphor: "At first I couldn't think what to make her of. I collected bones from charnel houses, paragraphs from *Heart of Darkness*, and disturbed, with profane fingers, the tremendous secrets of the human frame, but finally in searching through a chest in a solitary chamber, or rather cell, at the top of the house, I came across an old patchwork quilt, a fabric of relations, which my grandmother once made when she was young" (lexia: "research"). Even in the period of hypertext euphoria, when Deleuze and Guattari's notion of the rhizome was celebrated and any arboreal concept generally abhorred, the mention of the chest and the grandmother indicate that the problematized notions of origins and filiation apparently still hold great attraction.

The focus on the etymology of the word "text" indicates the extent to which digital literature can be defined as a "fabric," not just as a textile metaphor but also in the sense of a manufactured construction. In digital literature, this fabric of the text can be explored in more innovative ways than on paper, as Dan Waber and Jason Pimble show in *I, You, We*, with its six-dimensional words, plotted on the X, Y, and Z axes. Or Kenneth Goldsmith's *Soliloquy*, which fully exploits the blank space and allows the reader to experience the transitoriness of spoken language: moving over the white screen makes sentences appear and also disappear again as soon as the user moves the cursor. Since it is almost impossible to move the cursor in a straight horizontal line, the reading will automatically be multi-linear. Technically more sophisticated hyper-fictions, such as Mary Flanagan's [*the House*] (built with the open-source programming language called "processing") or *Cruising* by Ingrid Ankerson and Megan Sapnar (which are part of the *Electronic Literature Collection*), are not necessarily more sophis-ticated in terms of narrative structure but rather emphasize the possibilities of linking linear narratives to respectively architectural and cinematic concepts.

One of the characteristics of many forms of digital literature is the use they make of disorientation as an aesthetic quality. As Ziva Ben-Porath pointed out during the ICLA conference on comparative literature and hypertext ("Literatures: from text to hyper-text," Madrid, Universidad Complutense, September 21–22, 2006) this disorientation also has an effect on the reading process in that it urges the reader not to jump to interpretive conclusions. As soon as readers have formed an opinion on a passage, they are usually reluctant to revise it, even if new information seems to make the interpret-ation implausible. But the presence of a hyperlink (i.e., of potentially new information) may function as an invitation to suspend the formation of an opinion. To some readers this may be a cause of frustration, which goes some way to explain that up until now hyperfiction has not become "mainstream." Alexandra Saemmer, however, suggests that this may only be a characteristic of the first generation of hyperfiction authors, whose work can in many ways be seen as a continuation of the French *nouveau roman* or the experiments of Oulipo (Ouvroir de littérature potentielle). Several electronic literature projects, such as the interactive poetry or *Oulipoems* by Millie Niss, build on the notion of combinatorial literature initiated by Oulipo.

The tenth issue of the French journal *Formules* (June 2006), to which Saemmer contributed one of the essays, is devoted to "littérature numérique." Its central question is whether digital works of literature will remain in an experimental stage or whether they announce a new literary paradigm. While this is an important question, it also indicates a paradox that characterizes the poetics of the first gener-ations of hyperfiction authors. The first generation of hyper-poets and -writers have emphasized non-linearity and the empowerment of the reader, and this emphasis still pervades hypertext rhetoric – as the repetition of the word "libéré" in Eduardo Kac's definition of "holopoésie" illustrates: "L'holopoésie traite le mot comme une forme 'immatérielle', c'est-à-dire comme un signe qui peut changer ou se dissoudre dans l'air, en brisant sa rigidité formelle. *Libéré* de la page et *libéré* de tout autre matériau tangible, le mot envahit l'espace du lecteur et force celui-ci à le lire de façon dynamique" (*Formules* 10). But the recourse to this rhetoric of empowerment and liberation, combined with the wish to "force" the user to read in a particular way, may be symptomatic of the difficulty to "sell" experimental and sometimes high-brow digital literature to a broad audience. The central question of *Formules* 10 indicates the tension between the experimental nature of a majority of hyperfiction and the somewhat paradoxical desire to become more mainstream, or – in more dramatic terms – cause a "paradigm shift." In this respect the reverse translation from hyperfiction to print may prove to be of help.

4. The Interaction between Hyperfiction and Print

In many forms of hyperfiction the reader's space (or "l'espace du lecteur" as Eduardo Kac calls it) is not so much "invaded" but rather enlarged – for instance by making use of Google's image search engine – in the case of Gregory Chatonsky's *La révolution a eu lieu à New York*, in which Ben Saïd walks the streets of an American metropolis. As the readme file explains: "Some words are associated fragments of video and sound, images are turning into 'Manhattan' while walking toward Ground Zero, sounds are coming from sources of the account itself. Other words are being translated into images through Google (<http://www.google.fr/imghp?>). Associations of all those elements, produces a flowing narration, a narrative." A similar interaction between text and image is also realized in print in Jonathan Safran Foer's novel *Extremely Loud & Incredibly Close* by including the successive stills of a person falling from one of the Twin Towers. Foer's other typographic and visual experiments in the novel serve as tools to visualize the way the nine-year-old protagonist's mind functions: "That's how my brain was." (Foer 2005: 36) The interest in what goes on inside the human mind, which is one of the most prominent features of twentieth-century and contemporary fiction, is increasingly linked to the dominance of visual media and its importance in contemporary society.

The link between the processing of images and associative mental activity is the central focus of *Transitoire observable* (created in 2003), a group of so-called "numerical artists" interested in "the globality of systems which are using computers and not only on the forms of surface which can be observed on screen." In his creative work, one of the founders, Philippe Bootz, tries to simulate the mechanisms of information processing that take place inside the brain. Since the human brain is an open system, Alexandra Saemmer rightly wonders whether an electronic work can be equally open. This question is all the more relevant since there seems to be a link between "literatures of constraint" and digital literature, as Jean-Pierre Balpe points out. Again Oulipo serves as a hinge point, for many members of Oulipo took part in the founding of Alamo (Atelier de littérature assistée par la mathématique et les ordinateurs) in 1981. Another contributor to the *Formules* issue on "Littérature numérique" is Jan Baetens, who – together with Jan Van Looy – edited a volume on *Close Reading New Media: Analyzing Electronic Literature* (2003). Starting from a brief discussion of key works such as Marie-Laure Ryan's *Narrative as Virtual Reality* (2001) and Bolter and Grusin's *Remediation* (1999), the editors draw attention to the way electronic works of literature often turn the interior inside out.

With its tripartite structure, this first publication to apply the method of "close reading" to electronic literature clearly distinguishes between "Hypertext," "Internet Text," and "Cybertext." While Theodore Holm Nelson coined the term "hypertext" in his 1965 paper "A File Structure for the Complex, the Changing, and the Indeterminate," he defined it in *Literary Machines* (1987) as "non-sequential writing" (Nelson in Wardrip-Fruin and Montfort 2003: 452). In the meantime, the term multi-sequential writing is usually preferred. The first hypertext theorists (such as Jay David Bolter, Michael Joyce, George Landow, Stuart Moulthrop) were quick to relate the idea of the branching text to poststructuralist ideas, notably to Roland Barthes and Julia Kristeva's notion of intertextuality. Vannevar Bush's original interest was mainly of an encyclopedic nature, making associations between different sources of information; now, the disruptive potential of hyperlinking was recognized as well: "The dismantling effect of hypertext is one more way to pursue the typically postmodern challenge of the epistemologically suspect coherence, rationality, and closure of narrative structures, one more way to deny the reader the satisfaction of a totalizing interpretation" (Ryan 2001: 7).

But electronic literature is not limited to hypertextual works, as Baetens and Van Looy rightly point out. Raymond Federman's *Eating Books*, for instance, does not work with non-sequential writing, but is – on the contrary – radically linear in that the words are "consumed" and disappear as soon as they are read: The text appears as just one horizontal line and for each new letter one reads on the right-hand side of the screen another one disappears on the left-hand side. While a book still allows readers to page back and reread a passage, this "Internet Text" does not even grant them this slightest of non-sequential reading acts, since the words of *Eating Books* do not reappear once they are read. In Brian Kim Stefan's *Star Wars, one letter at a time* (part of the *Electronic Literature Collection*) the dimensions of the text are reduced to even less than a line: each letter disappears as soon as it is overwritten by the next.

Apart from Hypertext and Internet Text, the notion of Cybertext refers to both Espen J. Aarseth's work of that name and to Norbert Wiener's *Cybernetics* (1984). Stressing the importance not only of the text as a product but also as a process, a cybertext requires an interface and depends upon a human operator's action. The production of meaning implies a reader who has to work (Gr. 'ergon'). This eventually leads to increasingly interactive texts, of which Marie-Laure Ryan notes: "The critical discourse that will secure the place of interactive texts in literary history may still remain to be invented, but it is not too early to derive from the hypertext some cognitive lessons about the nuts and bolts of the reading process" (Ryan 2001: 226).

This renewed focus on the dynamic production of text also applies to the writing process and has resulted in an enhanced textual awareness, metafictional self-reflexiveness, and a different interpretation of the term "mimesis." In *Narcissistic Narrative* Linda Hutcheon makes a distinction between "product mimesis" and "process mimesis." The latter form implies more involvement on the part of the reader, because he or she is invited to participate in the creative process as a witness of the way the book analyses itself (Hutcheon 1984: 9). Readers are expected to do more than simply show their admiration for the credibility and verisimilitude of the fiction; they are involved in the creation of meaning by means of language (30). In metafiction, the mechanisms that are usually hidden in a traditional realist novel are uncovered and made functional (41), drawing attention to what Krauss referred to as "the grid."

A paradigmatic work of metafiction, indicative of the mutual impact of digital and printed literature, is Mark Z. Danielewski's *House of Leaves* (2000). The reader does not get to see a single shot of the movie that is the novel's central topic. Everything has to be reconstructed on the basis of the elaborate commentary of the old blind poet Zampanò, who is on a par with Jorge de Burgos in Eco's *The Name of the Rose* or Melquíades in García Marquez's *One Hundred Years of Solitude*. Apart from the possible reference to Cortázar's character Morelli, Zampanó pays homage to the blind Argentinian builder of labyrinths Jorge Luis Borges. The house with its empty rooms, endless corridors, and dead ends is a strong metaphor for this book about shifting immobility and surreal estate, full of meta-*Ficciones*. Borges is another author whose stories have had a serious impact on the development of hyperfiction. Noah Wardrip-Fruin and Nick Montfort rightly included Borges' story "The Garden of Forking Paths" in *The New Media Reader*, arguing that "many of new media's important ideas and influence first appeared in unexpected contexts" (Wardrip-Fruin and Montfort 2003: 29). One of the most explicit references to Borges in Danielewski's *House of Leaves* is a footnote about Pierre Menard. The note is a short comparative study of a passage about truth from, on the one hand, Miguel de Cervantes' *Don Quijote* ("... la verdad, cuya madre es la historia,...") and on the other hand the deceivingly identical passage by Pierre Menard ("... la verdad, cuya madre es la historia,..."). Borges prefigured the copy/paste function and the Nelsonian concept of transclusion by creating the perfect reflection of a narrative Narcissus. But Danielewski constantly disturbs this smooth mirror image, for instance by suggesting that the printed text is never identical with the text as it is "performed" by a reader. By projecting all kinds of hobby-horses into the text, the reader is the one who turns the house into a *House of Leaves*, i.e., a text that is bigger than what is on the pages. The book is always smaller than what people read into it.

What may seem a gratuitous literary experiment, mocking any interpretive effort, can also be seen as an attempt to find out how the human brain functions and creates meaning, especially when it is confronted with an overload of data. Hypertext suggest that the creation of meaning is a matter of making links, which is what this book invites the reader to do by means of footnotes, annotations, glosses, appendices, and comments. Between Zampanó's notes, Danielewski inserts long footnotes by Johnny Truant, who has edited Zampanó's manuscripts. Truant arranges, (mis)transcribes, edits, selects, censors, and distorts, so that – even though he is not as cunning as Charles Kinbote in Nabokov's *Pale Fire* – he cannot be trusted. The errors reflect Truant's own mental wandering, and thus illustrate an important aspect of Danielewski's poetics. By presenting the process of transcribing as part of the novel, he suggests both the implied identity of writer and scribe (Zampanó and Truant, "the blind man of all blind men, me" [117]), and the "non-self-identity" of the text, as Jerome McGann calls it in *Radiant Textuality*: "Texts are not self-identical" (McGann 2001: 149). Not unlike the house whose interior keeps changing, the interior of the text is constantly on the move. This process is part and parcel of the product: "If the work demanded by any labyrinth means penetrating or escaping it, the question of process becomes extremely relevant" (Danielewski 2000: 115). The book even provides its readers with some facsimiles of manuscripts to create the effect of authenticity and emphasize the inextricable link between the book and its textual memory. This way, the temporal and the spatial preoccupations characterizing twentieth-century literature intertwine, which opens up a fascinating aspect of digital literary studies: the use of digital tools to study writings as processes, rather than merely products.

5. Time and Space: the Hypertextual Structure of Literary Geneses

Modernist authors such as Marcel Proust and James Joyce were well aware that the effects of time, which they wrote about, also applied to their own writing processes. The hypertextual mechanisms underlying the composition history may have an unexpected impact on the published version of the text. This effect of the *avant-texte* is noticeable in the genesis of James Joyce's last work, *Finnegans Wake*. In its published form the text consists of four books, subdivided into seventeen chapters, and each chapter consists of several sections. The section is usually (in its first draft version) not longer than a few pages and may be treated as a lexia. This was Joyce's favorite working unit. Each of these lexias consists of multiple versions. Thus, for instance, the so-called red-backed copybook (British Library 47471b) contains – among many other sections – three versions of a letter (written by the main female character ALP, in defense of her husband HCE). It is preceded and followed by a philological commentary of this document. Within the context of this early phase in the writing process, this lexia is referred to as I.5§2 (Book I, Chapter 5, Section 2). After a few versions, however, Joyce decided to extract this letter from chapter 5. Not until the summer of 1938, i.e., fourteen years later, did he decide to reincorporate it, but in a heavily distorted way and at a completely different location: at the very end of the text, in Book IV. The shuffling of lexias is common practice in many composition histories, but this one has a special effect. Because of the extraction of the letter from its original context, the philological commentary discusses an early version of this letter (one of the versions in the red-backed copybook) instead of the one that is printed in Book IV. This way, the writing process becomes an inherent part of the published text.

In contemporary literature, the tendency to present the work's genesis as part of the text becomes even more overt, for instance in Toby Litt's *Finding Myself* (2003). By means of the interaction between the characters of the writer (Victoria) and the editor (Simona), Toby Litt is able to use the process of revision in a functional way to deal with themes such as self-censorship, social control, and perception. When the editor reads this final draft, she deletes several passages. Since the text is presented as a draft, some blocks of text are still considered to be mobile lexias, to be shuffled and inserted elsewhere. In a note to herself, Victoria adds this parenthesis after a long paragraph: "(Insert this earlier.)" But the editor disagrees, deletes the note "(~~Insert this earlier.~~)" and adds: "*Works better here, I think*" (66). To the title page of this final draft she sticks a Post-It to tell the author (and the reader at the same time): "This is what we're thinking of printing. Hope you can live with it."

On the title page, the title ~~*Finding Myself*~~ is replaced by *From the Lighthouse*. This kind of interaction between author and editor, writer and reader, text and *avant-texte* reflects an enhanced notion of the mutability of both the text and the self, suggesting a close link between textual and existential matters that is also explored in electronic literature. It is interesting to notice that pioneers of hyperfiction such as Michael Joyce and Shelley Jackson have recently published printed novels, which does not need to be interpreted as a loss of faith in the potential of hypertextual fiction, but rather as a sign of the applicability of hypertextual writing as a composition method. Conversely, the hypertextual structure of writing methods discussed with reference to modernist authors proves to be more than just a metaphor and is applicable to contemporary literature as well, even to authors of hyperfiction. An excellent example is Juan B. Guttiérrez' novel *Extreme Conditions*. This "adaptive literary hypertext" reconfigures itself according to the lexias the reader has read before. Depending on the reading history the links have different destinations.

This is a new response to the first generation of hyperfiction authors, who continued the tradition of experimental literature, exploiting a sense of disorientation. Guttiérrez does not indulge in the sense of fragmentation, which hypertext seems to enhance. Instead, he uses the new medium to "optimize the plot": "Are multilinearity and fragmentation the goal of hyperfiction, or are they the product of the state of the art when the first literary hypertexts were produced? Is fragmentation a paradigm that we want to preserve? We have the ability to produce a text that exploits the essence of digital media, and that at the same time preserves the essence of narrative in a classical sense: immersion" (Guttiérrez 2006). The "adaptive literary hypertext" interacts with the reader in that each lexia suggests different ways to continue reading. Thus, for instance, the text on the opening page or first lexia of *Extreme Conditions* is followed by three suggestions for further reading or "adaptive links," preceded by a percentage and accompanied by a short summary:

> 90% Tenth Decade: Miranda parked her car near a service station. (. . .)
> 85% End of Ninth Decade: Central Lab. Miranda at 22 enters (. . .)
> 85% Eighth Decade: The avatar children pummeled out of school in troops. (. . .)

A higher percentage indicates greater narrative continuity, so that more adventurous readers will probably be tempted by the latter links.

This work also indicates that genetic criticism is not necessarily limited to manuscript versions on paper. Guttiérrez provides the necessary links for "digital archaeology" with reference to his novel, and explains what is characteristic about each of the electronic versions:

> Extreme Conditions Version 3 – 2006 (English): This version was the first piece of digital narrative (. . .) in which the information system tries to optimize the reading process.

Condiciones Extremas Version 2 – 2000 (Spanish): This version tried to optimize the user interface and facilitate navigation through multiple entry points grouped by space, time and characters.

Condiciones Extremas Version 1 – 1998 (Spanish): This version was (. . .) a primitive hypertext; it was important, however, because it helped in the learning process.

Condiciones Extremas. Printed Version – 1998 (Spanish): *First Edition:* April, 1998.

Another initiative that emphasizes the continued interest in the writing process, even in a digital age without the aura of authorial manuscripts, is the *Digital Variants* archive, founded in 1996 by the Department of Italian at the University of Edinburgh. Several contemporary Italian authors have agreed to contribute to this project by preserving electronic versions of their works at different stages of the writing process and making them available on the internet. "The aim of the project is to make available on the internet texts of living authors at different stages of writing" (*Digital Variants*). Although this initiative is called *Digital Variants*, the different stages of the texts (for instance the three versions of chapter "666" from Angel García Galiano's novel *El mapa de las aguas*) are presented as a form of "versioning," without highlighting the variant readings. Here, the *Versioning Machine* might be a useful tool, the way it is applied in the *Thomas Macgreevy Archive*, for instance to the four versions of the poem "Nocturne, St. Eloi, 1918," which can be visualized in parallel juxtaposition. Clicking on a line in one of the versions makes it appear in bold in all corresponding versions, so that the user can follow the composition history of a particular line and see for instance how "Afraid, aware, ~~little~~ blundering, lonely thing" became "Alone, self-conscious, frightened, blundering" in the second version.

One of the most important challenges for digital literary studies is to try to give shape to what Peter L. Shillingsburg describes as "knowledge sites." In *From Gutenberg to Google: Electronic Representations of Literary Texts* (2006) Shillingsburg envisions what might be viewed as a scholarly interpretation of Ted Nelson's Xanadu (outlined in *Literary Machines*, 1981), shifting from a paradigm in which editorial control was paramount to a "new model edition," in which "control should be passed along with the edition to its users" (83). This implies an infrastructure for script acts that "provide[s] tools that allow individuals to personalize their own access to the work" (100). These knowledge sites would have to include, among many other things, a literary work's reception history (reviews, criticism, literary analyses, . . .). Although these theoretical ideas still meet with numerous practical problems, several modest but brave attempts have already been made to give shape to different aspects of such an electronic infrastructure. A laudable initiative is Raphael Slepon's *Finnegans Wake* Extensible Elucidation Treasury (FWEET), which links each line of Joyce's last work to the critical analyses that have been written about it. In theory, this reception history is also linkable to each line's textual prehistory, but copyright is a practical obstacle that impedes many digital projects dealing with twentieth-century literature. This copyright issue explains the lack of twentieth-century thematic research collections. It is related to a complex issue that was signaled for the first time by Walter Benjamin in his essay "Das Kunstwerk im Zeitalter seiner technischen Reproduzierbarkeit." The increased reproducibility of works of art may imply a loss of what Benjamin refers to as its "aura" (linked to the authenticity of the original). With reference to literature the aura of unique manuscripts determines to an important extent its value. The fear that this value may decrease by putting digital facsimiles online seems unfounded. In their capacity of cultural objects manuscripts may function in the same way as for instance paintings, and it seems more likely that their reproducibility will rather raise the value of the original document thanks to the greater interest aroused by a more general awareness of their existence and their importance.

Another solution is a combination of "in-house" and "hybrid" editions. A complete electronic edition with scans of all the manuscripts is made accessible in the holding libraries, so that the valuable originals do not need to be touched so often and are preserved in optimal conditions. Part of this edition, without the digital facsimiles but with both topographic and linear transcriptions, can be published in a so-called hybrid edition, combining the electronic texts (for instance on CD ROM) with a printed reading text and a genetic analysis. This way the philological research can be shared with a broader audience, while the complete "in-house" edition can constantly be updated.

The exposure of texts and *avant-textes* by making them available on the internet may put off literary estates. Peter Shillingsburg's suggestion to make knowledge sites self-sustaining by generating revenue with user fees revaluates a form of "micropayment" (suggested by Ted Nelson 1981), a system comparable to a utility charging the user a small amount for each piece of information accessed ("Proposal for a Universal Electronic Publishing System and Archive," a chapter from *Literary Machines*). A large portion of "micropayment" is returned to the owners of the viewed material's copyright. But apart from the financial aspect, the very idea of availability and general access to digital images of manuscripts on the internet among all kinds of data, not all of them equally trustworthy, may be even more deterring or discouraging to literary estates and holding libraries. Hence the importance of the attempts to build a scholarly environment on the internet, so that readers know that the information provided within this environment is peer-reviewed. In this respect Paolo D'Iorio's HyperNietzsche project <www.hypernietzsche.org> is an interesting initiative that will have an impact on digital literary studies with reference to twentieth-century literature, for this research group is trying to build an open scholarly community with so-called "crossing hypertexts" on several authors, including Virginia Woolf, Samuel Beckett, and Marcel Proust. The idea of integrating access to primary sources (digital images of manuscripts) with the publication of peer-reviewed scholarship is yet another way in which hypertext and *avant-texte* are combined in a useful way. The seemingly fixed nature of the printed text is confronted with the fluidity of the writing process – which may have been one of the reasons why twentieth-century authors such as Samuel Beckett donated their manuscripts to university libraries, to study their works as part of a poetics of process. With the support of the Beckett Estate a first electronic genetic edition of Samuel Beckett's last bilingual texts was completed during the Beckett centenary year (2006). This edition is a continuation of a project that was initiated during the last years of Beckett's life. The disadvantage of the printed medium was that the transcriptions of manuscript versions could only be presented by means of a synoptic apparatus with an intimidating amount of diacritical signs.

Digital technology makes it possible to present different transcriptions (both topographic and linear) of each of the extant manuscripts in their entirety and with a minimum of diacritical signs. Moreover, if the linear transcriptions are encoded in a markup language like XML, it becomes possible for the user to view the textual material from different perspectives (according to language; according to the order of the documents; in the order of the writing sequence; with a focus on abandoned sections or dead ends in the *avant-texte*). As in the case of the hypertext edition of Faulkner's *The Sound and the Fury* an electronic genetic edition allows the user to follow alternative narrative paths, such as the search for a particular leitmotif; the

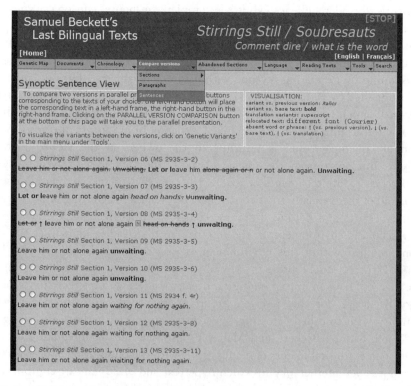

Figure 7.4   Comparison of versions of textual segments in the electronic genetic edition of Samuel Beckett's *Stirrings Still / Soubresauts*.

difference is that this search comprises both the synchronic and the diachronic structure of the work, i.e., the text as it was published as well as all its preceding and subsequent versions, editions, and self-translations up to the author's death.

A particular problem with reference to the study of different versions (especially of longer texts) is the danger of getting lost in the manuscripts. Here, the digital medium offers a solution in that it allows the user to compare all versions of a particular unit of text in different sizes: Large (sections); Medium (paragraphs); Small (sentences). This way an electronic genetic edition can facilitate a reading "through time," following for instance the sentence "Leave him or not alone again waiting for nothing again" through all the stages of its composition, highlighting the genetic variants between the versions (Figure 7.4).

In conclusion, digital literary studies seem to intensify the relation between a published work and its textual memory. Twentieth-century and contemporary literature show a sensitivity for the correlation between the idea that a text is a succession of versions and the notion of the individual as a succession of individuals, which Samuel Beckett explored in his self-translations. Digital literature radicalizes this notion of the text as a constantly adaptable and retranslatable set of lexias that only build a text thanks to the efforts of the reader to assemble or "sew together" a set of narrative fragments into a narrative. With reference to twentieth-century works, genetic criticism is one of the fields of research in which digital media prove to be quite useful for literary studies. Literary geneses often have a hyper-textual structure and digital tools prove to be of help in their examination. The preservation of manuscripts is indeed becoming less evident now that most authors use computers to write fiction, but the interest in the writing process and the tendency to thematize the composition history have not diminished in contemporary writing – on the contrary.

REFERENCES AND FURTHER READING

Alt-X Network: <http://www.altx.com/>.

BeeHive Hypertext / Hypermedia Journal: <http://beehive.temporalimage.com/departments/>.

Digital Variants: <http://www.digitalvariants.org/>.

Eastgate: <http://www.eastgate.com/Hypertext Now/>.

Electronic Book Review: <http://www.electronicbookreview.com/>.

Electronic Literature Collection: <http://collection.eliterature.org>.

Electronic Literature Organization: <http://www.eliterature.org/>.

Finnegans Wake Extensible Elucidation Treasury (FWEET): <http://www.fweet.org>.

Formules 10 (June 2006): <http://www.utc.fr/~bouchard/formules/index.html>.

Image {&} Narrative: Online Magazine of the Visual Narrative: <http://www.imageandnarrative.be/>.

Thomas MacGreevy Archive: <http://www.macgreevy.org/home.jsp>

trAce: <http://trace.ntu.ac.uk/>.

Transitoire observable: <http://transitoireobs.free.fr/to/>.

Versioning Machine: <http://www.v-machine.org/>.

Voice of the Shuttle: <http://vos.ucsb.edu>.

Aarseth, Espen J. (1997). *Cybertext: Perspectives on Ergodic Literature*. Baltimore: The Johns Hopkins University Press.

Baetens, Jan, and Koen Geldof (Eds.) (2002). *Literatuur en nieuwe media*. (ALW-cahier 23). Leuven: Vlaamse Vereniging voor Algemene en Vergelijkende Literatuurwetenschap.

Ballard, J. G. (2001). *The Atrocity Exhibition*. London: Flamingo (Harper Collins).

Barthes, Roland (1970). *S/Z*. Paris: Seuil.

Beckett, Samuel (1999). *Proust, and Three Dialogues with Georges Duthuit*. London: Calder.

—— (2001). *Comment c'est / How It Is. A Critical Genetic Edition*. Ed. Magessa O'Reilly. London: Routledge.

—— (2006). *Stirrings Still/Soubresauts & Comment dire/What Is the Word: Genetic Edition* (Dirk Van Hulle, Ed; Vincent Neyt, Technical Realization). Turnhout: Brepols (forthcoming).

Benjamin, Walter (1996). "Das Kunstwerk im Zeitalter seiner technischen Reproduzierbarkeit." *Ein Lesebuch*. Ed. Michael Opitz. Frankfurt am Main: Suhrkamp.

Birkerts, Sven (1994). *The Gutenberg Elegies: the Fate of Reading in an Electronic Age*. New York: Fawcett Columbine.

Bolter, Jay David, and Grusin, Richard (1999). *Remediation: Understanding New Media*. Cambridge, MA: The MIT Press.

Bush, Vannevar (1945). "As We May Think." *The Atlantic Monthly* 176.1 (July 1945): 101–8.

Chatonsky, Gregory. *La révolution a eu lieu à New York*. <http://www.incident.net/works/revolution_new_york/#>.

Cohn, Ruby (2000). *A Beckett Canon*. Ann Arbor: University of Michigan Press.

Cortázar, Julio (1998). *Rayuela*. Ed. Andrés Amorós. Madrid: Catedra.

Danielewski, Mark Z. (2000). *House of Leaves*. 2nd edn. New York: Pantheon Books.

Ellmann, Richard (1983). *James Joyce*. Rev. edn. Oxford: Oxford University Press.

Faulkner, William (1994). "An Introduction to *The Sound and the Fury*." In *The Sound and the Fury*. New York: Norton.

—— (2003). *The Sound and the Fury: A Hypertext Edition*. Eds. R. P. Stoicheff, Muri, Deshaye, et al. Updated Mar. 2003. University of Saskatchewan. <http://www.usask.ca/english/faulkner>. Accessed September 15, 2006.

Gaggi, Silvio (1997). *From Text to Hypertext: Decentering the Subject in Fiction, Film, the Visual Arts,*

and Electronic Media. Philadelphia, PA: University of Pennsylvania Press.

Guttiérrez, Juan B. (2006). *Extreme Conditions*. <http://www.literatronica.com/src/Nuntius.aspx?lng=BRITANNIA&nuntius=T_INTRO_DYNAMIC>.

Hulle, Dirk Van (2004). *Textual Awareness: A Genetic Study of Late Manuscripts by Joyce, Proust, and Mann*. Ann Arbor: University of Michigan Press.

Hutcheon, Linda (1984). *Narcissistic Narrative: The Metafictional Paradox*. New York: Methuen.

Jackson, Shelley (1995). *Patchwork Girl*. Watertown, MA: Eastgate Systems Inc. <http://www.eastgate.com/catalog/PatchworkGirl.html>.

Joyce, James (1992). *Finnegans Wake*. London: Penguin Books.

—— (1977–9). *The James Joyce Archive*. Eds. Michael Groden, et al. New York: Garland.

Joyce, Michael (1990). *Afternoon, A Story*. Electronic text. Watertown, PA: Eastgate, 1990.

Keep, Christopher, Tim McLaughlin, and Robin Parmar (1995). *The Electronic Labyrinth*, <http://jefferson.village.virginia.edu/elab/hfl0098.html>.

Koskimaa, Raine. (1997–8). "Visual Structuring of Hyperfiction Narratives." *Electronic Book Review* (EBR) 6 (Winter). <http://www.altx.com/EBR/ebr6/6koskimaa/6koski.htm>.

Krauss, Rosalind E. (1985). "Grids." *The Originality of the Avant-Garde and Other Modernist Myths*. Cambridge, MA: The MIT Press, pp. 9–22.

Landow, George P. (1997). *Hypertext 2.0: The Convergence of Contemporary Critical Theory and Technology*. Baltimore: Johns Hopkins University Press.

—— (2006). *Hypertext 3.0: Critical Theory and New Media in an Era of Globalization*. Baltimore: The John Hopkins University Press.

Lewis, Wyndham (1989 [1926]). *The Art of Being Ruled*. Santa Rosa: Black Sparrow Press.

Litt, Toby (2004). *Finding Myself*. London: Penguin.

Manovich, Lev (2001). *The Language of New Media*. Cambridge, MA: The MIT Press.

McGann, Jerome (2001). *Radiant Textuality: Literature After the World Wide Web*. New York: Palgrave.

Meriwether, James B., and Michael Millgate (Eds.) (1968). *Lion in the Garden: Interviews with*

William Faulkner, 1926–1962. New York: Random House.

Moulthrop, Stuart (1991). *Victory Garden*. Electronic text. Watertown, MA: Eastgate Systems.

Murray, Janet (1997). *Hamlet on the Holodeck: The Future of Narrative in Cyberspace*. New York: The Free Press.

Nelson, Theodor Holm (1965). "A File Structure for the Complex, the Changing, and the Indeterminate." In *Proceedings of the 20th National Conference*. New York: Association for Computing Machinery, pp. 84–100.

—— (1993 [1981]). *Literary Machines*. Sausalito, CA: Mindful Press.

Neyt, Vincent (2004). Review of Faulkner, William (2003). *The Sound and the Fury: A Hypertext Edition*. *Literary and Linguistic Computing* 19.1: 137–43.

Pountney, Rosemary (1987). "The Structuring of *Lessness*." *The Review of Contemporary Fiction* 7.2 (Summer): 55–67.

Proust, Marcel (1987–9). *A la recherche du temps perdu*. Ed. Jean-Yves Tadié et al. Paris: Gallimard Pléiade.

Ryan, Marie-Laure (Ed.) (1999a). *Cyberspace Textuality: Computer Technology and Literary Theory*. Bloomington: Indiana University Press.

—— (1999b). "Cyberage Narratology: Computers, Metaphor, and Narrative." In David Herman (Ed.). *Narratologies*. Columbus: Ohio State University Press, pp. 113–41.

—— (2001). *Narrative as Virtual Reality: Immersion and Interactivity in Literature and Electronic Media*. Baltimore: The Johns Hopkins University Press.

Safran Foer, Jonathan (2005). *Extremely Loud & Incredibly Close*. London: Hamish Hamilton/Penguin.

Sartre, Jean-Paul (1994). "On *The Sound and the Fury*: Time in the Work of Faulkner." In Faulkner, William. *The Sound and the Fury*. New York: Norton, pp. 265–71.

Shillingsburg, Peter L. (2006). *From Gutenberg to Google: Electronic Representations of Literary Texts*. Cambridge: Cambridge University Press.

Van Looy, Jan, and Jan Baetens (2003). *Close Reading New Media: Analyzing Electronic Literature*. Leuven: Leuven University Press.

Wiener, Norbert (1948). *Cybernetics; or, Control and Communication in the Animal and the Machine*. New York: Technology Press.

Wardrip-Fruin, Noah, and Nick Montfort (Eds.) (2003). *The New Media Reader*. Cambridge, MA: MIT Press.

Part III
Textualities

8

Reading Digital Literature: Surface, Data, Interaction, and Expressive Processing

Noah Wardrip-Fruin

Introducing Digital Literature

Digital literature – also known as electronic literature – is a term for work with important literary aspects that requires the use of digital computation. Such literature has been produced for more than fifty years, with the first known example being Christopher Strachey's 1952 love letter generator for the Manchester Mark I computer (Strachey 1954). It ranges from some of the bestselling software of the 1980s (Montfort, Chapter 14, RIDDLE MACHINES: THE HISTORY AND NATURE OF INTER-ACTIVE FICTION, this volume) to a current diversity of work that includes experimental installations, performance-based pieces, and more.

Critical study of digital literature has a somewhat shorter history. For example, the first known PhD dissertation is Mary Ann Buckles's 1985 study of the seminal interactive fiction *Adventure* (Buckles 1985; Crowther and Woods 1976). In fact, digital literature maintained a remarkably low critical profile until the early 1990s, when a series of publications focused on hypertext literature garnered wider attention. Especially notable among these were Jay David Bolter's *Writing Space*, George Landow's *Hypertext*, and Robert Coover's essays for *The New York Times* (Bolter 1991; Landow 1992; Coover 1992; Coover 1993). The most widely discussed works of hypertext literature include Michael Joyce's *afternoon*, Stuart Moulthrop's *Victory Garden*, and Shelley Jackson's *Patchwork Girl* (Joyce 1987; Moulthrop 1991; Jackson 1995). All three of these were created within the Storyspace software environment, which organizes text into discrete nodes with links between them. The meaning of the term "hypertext" is, however, significantly broader than nodes and links – including, according to an early definition, all texts that "branch or perform on request" (Wardrip-Fruin 2004).

After hypertext criticism brought digital literature to the attention of a wider group, in the late 1990s a number of publications sought to expand the discussion.

Of these, two particularly notable books were Janet Murray's *Hamlet on the Holodeck* and Espen Aarseth's *Cybertext* (Murray 1997; Aarseth 1997). While vastly different in their critical approaches, both books employed examples from previously-neglected forms of digital literature such as interactive fiction, story generation systems, and interactive characters. These forms grow out of a heritage of computer science research, especially in artificial intelligence. The work of both Murray and Aarseth has since had an influence on interpretations of another once-neglected form of digital media that grows out of computer science, often employs artificial intelligence, and can have important literary aspects: computer games. In the years since these publications, significant work in digital literature has continued, ranging from the first book-length examination of the form of interactive fiction (Montfort 2003) to new theoretical approaches such as "media-specific analysis" (Hayles 2002).

Models for Reading Digital Literature

The starting point for this chapter is an observation: When studying a work of digital literature, as with any cultural artifact, we must choose where to focus our attention. To put this another way, we must operate with some model (explicit or implicit) of the work's elements and structures – one which foregrounds certain aspects while marginalizing others.

Most critical work in digital literature – whether focused on hypertext or other forms – proceeds from an implicit model that takes audience experience to be primary. The main components of the model are the surface of the work (what the audience sees) and the space of possible interactions with the work (ways the audience may change the state of the work, and how the work may respond).

The primary competitors to this implicit model are Aarseth's explicit models presented in *Cybertext*. The most important of these is a typology for discussing textual media, consisting of *scriptons* (text strings as they appear to readers), *textons* (text strings as they exist in the text), and *traversal functions* (the mechanism by which scriptons are revealed or generated from textons). This model, here referred to as the "traversal function" model, has been highly influential.

This chapter will consider one of the most famous works of digital literature: James Meehan's *Tale-Spin* (1976). Meehan's project is the first major story generation program. It made the leap from assembling stories out of pre-defined bits (like the pages of a Choose Your Own Adventure book) to generating stories via carefully-crafted processes that operate at a fine level on story data. In *Tale-Spin*'s case, the processes simulate character reasoning and behavior, while the data defines a virtual world inhabited by the characters. As a result, while altering one page of a Choose Your Own Adventure leaves most of its story material unchanged, altering one behavior rule or fact about the world can lead to wildly different *Tale-Spin* fictions. For this reason Meehan's project serves as an example in the books of Bolter, Murray, and Aarseth, among others.

This chapter argues that *Tale-Spin* is not just widely discussed – it is also widely misunderstood. This is demonstrated in several stages, beginning and ending with readings of *Tale-Spin* (and its companion text generator, *Mumble*) that employ the implicit audience model. Between these readings, the chapter will, first, attempt to apply Aarseth's traversal function model, second, trace the operations of *Tale-Spin's* simulation, and, third, present a new model that helps clarify the issues important for a notion I call *expressive processing*. This new model differs from the audience model by, following Aarseth, including the work's mechanisms. It differs from Aarseth's model, however, by not assuming that the transition from textons to scriptons is either (a) readily identifiable or (b) the primary site of interest. Instead, after having identified the interplay between the work's *data, process, surface,* and possibilities for *interaction,* it is proposed that groupings of these may be considered as *operational logics* and explored both as authorial expressions (following Michael Mateas's notion of *Expressive AI* (2002)) and as expressing otherwise-hidden relationships with our larger society (particularly the cultures and materials of science and technology).

For *Tale-Spin* in particular, its primary operational logic is revealed to be that of the planning-based simulation. It is deeply connected to the cognitive science account of planning that has been extensively critiqued by scholars such as Lucy Suchman and Phil Agre (Suchman 1987; Agre 1997). It is also, more broadly, a "microworld" approach to AI of the sort that, by failing to scale up, resulted in the symbolic AI "winter" beginning in the 1980s. For the purposes of this chapter, it can be particularly valuable in two regards. First, it provides a legible example of the inevitably authored – inevitably fictional – nature of simulations of human behavior. Second, as we increasingly create human-authored microworlds as media (e.g., digital literature and computer games) it provides a fascinating example and cautionary tale.

Taking a step back, and realizing that none of this is visible from the audience's perspective, a new term is proposed. Just as the "*Eliza* effect" is used to describe systems that give the audience the impression of a much more complex process than is actually present, the "*Tale-Spin* effect" may be used to describe the obscuring of a complex process so that it cannot be perceived by the audience. The existence of these two effects helps demonstrate that the implicit audience model provides only a partial view of digital literature.

Reading *Tale-Spin's* Outputs

From an audience perspective, a story generation program such as *Tale-Spin* is mostly experienced through its outputs – through the texts it produces. Many critics agree that this is *Tale-Spin's* most famous output:

> Joe Bear was hungry. He asked Irving Bird where some honey was. Irving refused to tell him, so Joe offered to bring him a worm if he'd tell him where some honey was. Irving agreed. But Joe didn't know where any worms were, so he asked Irving, who refused to

say. So Joe offered to bring him a worm if he'd tell him where a worm was. Irving agreed. But Joe didn't know where any worms were, so he asked Irving, who refused to say. So Joe offered to bring him a worm if he'd tell him where a worm was.... (129–30)

Two things are curious here. First, this text is rather unimpressive for being the most famous output of one of the most widely discussed works of digital literature. It raises the question: Why does this work open nearly every computer science treatment (and many critical treatments) of digital fiction?

Second, and even more curiously, this is not actually an output from *Tale-Spin*. Rather, it is, as Meehan says, a "hand translation" (127) into English, presumably performed by Meehan, of an internal system state originally represented as a set of "conceptual dependency" (CD) expressions. Further, the output above was produced early in the creation of *Tale-Spin,* before the system was complete. To publish this as one of *Tale-Spin*'s tales is akin to printing a flawed photograph taken with a prototype camera, while it still has light leaks, and using this to judge the camera's function.

Let's begin with the second of these curiosities. Why would authors such as Aarseth and Murray present these hand-transcribed errors – what Meehan refers to as "mis-spun tales" – rather than actual *Mumble* outputs of *Tale-Spin* story structures? We can begin to get an idea by examining some of the system's actual output:

> George was very thirsty. George wanted to get near some water. George walked from his patch of ground across the meadow through the valley to a river bank. George fell into the water. George wanted to get near the valley. George couldn't get near the valley. George wanted to get near the meadow. George couldn't get near the meadow. Wilma wanted George to get near the meadow. Wilma wanted to get near George. Wilma grabbed George with her claw. Wilma took George from the river through the valley to the meadow. George was devoted to Wilma. George owed everything to Wilma. Wilma let go of George. George fell to the meadow. The End. (227–8, original in all caps.)

Now, here are two mis-spun tales from similar scenarios:

> Henry Ant was thirsty. He walked over to the river bank where his good friend Bill Bird was sitting. Henry slipped and fell in the river. He was unable to call for help. He drowned.

> Henry Ant was thirsty. He walked over to the river bank where his good friend Bill Bird was sitting. Henry slipped and fell in the river. Gravity drowned. (128–9, Meehan's parenthetical explanation removed.)

All three of these drowning ant stories are quite strange. But they're not strange in the same way. The first story – the successful story, from *Tale-Spin*'s perspective – might make one ask, "Why is this language so stilted?" or "Why are these details included?" or "What is the point of this story?" The second and third story – the mis-spun stories – on the other hand, elicit questions like, "Why didn't his 'good friend' save Henry?" or "How is it possible that 'gravity drowned'?"

To put it another way, the first example makes one wonder about the telling of the story, while the second and third make one wonder how such a story could come to be. These errors prompt readers to think about systems. And this, in turn, offers insight into the first curiosity mentioned after Joe Bear's story above. *Tale-Spin* begins so many computer science discussions of digital fiction because of the operations of its system – its processes – rather than any qualities of its output. Given this, it seems essential that an analysis of *Tale-Spin* at least consider these processes. This chapter will return, later, to the conclusions of those who read *Tale-Spin* employing an implicit audience model. The next section will attempt to employ Aarseth's traversal function model in studying *Tale-Spin* and *Mumble*.

Locating *Tale-Spin*'s Traversal Function

In order to employ Aarseth's traversal function model one must identify its three elements: *scriptons* (text strings as they appear to readers), *textons* (text strings as they exist in the text), and *traversal functions* (the mechanism by which scriptons are revealed or generated from textons). For example, when interacting with a simulated character such as *Eliza/Doctor,* the scriptons are the texts seen by audience members, the textons are the simple sentence templates stored within the system, and determining the traversal function provides a typological classification of how system operations and audience behavior combine to produce the final text (Weizenbaum 1966).

Aarseth, unfortunately, while he discusses *Tale-Spin,* does not analyze it employing his model. However, on a table on page 69 of *Cybertext* he does provide its traversal function. So to employ Aarseth's model one need only identify the scriptons and textons in *Tale-Spin/Mumble*. Finding the scriptons is easy. They are the sentences output by *Mumble* in stories such as those reproduced above.

Finding the textons is harder. *Tale-Spin* operates at the level of story structure, not story telling. In particular, *Tale-Spin* focuses on simulating a virtual world – its characters, its objects, and their histories and plans. As mentioned above, there are no English sentences inside *Tale-Spin*. Its virtual world, instead, is represented in the form of "conceptual dependency" (CD) expressions. These expressions were developed as a language-independent meaning representation in the "scruffy" branch of 1970s AI research, especially in efforts headed by linguist and computer scientist Roger Schank and psychologist Robert Abelson.

Schank was Meehan's dissertation advisor during the period of *Tale-Spin*'s completion. He outlines the basic form of CD expressions in *Conceptual Information Processing* (1975), presenting them as multidimensional diagrams. When used for projects such as *Tale-Spin,* however, CD expressions are generally represented as parenthesis-organized lists. So, for example, what *Mumble* outputs as "George was very thirsty" might be represented in a program like *Tale-Spin* as:

(WORLD '(THIRSTY (ACTOR GEORGE) (VAL (7))))

Similarly, what *Mumble* outputs as "George wanted to get near some water" might be represented in a manner such as this:

(GEORGE '(GOAL (ACTOR GEORGE) (AT GEORGE WATER)))

Are CD expressions the textons of *Tale-Spin/Mumble*? It seems unlikely. Aarseth's phrase "strings as they exist in the text" sounds more like *Eliza/Doctor*'s pre-existing sentence templates, rather than parenthesis-ordered lists created during *Tale-Spin*'s run.

Unfortunately, *Mumble* doesn't provide us with any better texton candidates. It contains no sentence templates or other recognizable texts. Instead, when presented with a CD expression for output, it first identifies the expression's main act, state, or connective. For example, in the expression above, that George has a goal. The first thing produced is a subject-verb pair, such as "George wanted..." Then nouns are inserted. If George wanted to go to particular water and the simulation indicated that, at that time, the water belonged to a particular character, then the possessive would be added (e.g., "get near Arthur's water"). If the simulation history indicated that George had already been there then *Mumble* would choose words to indicate this (e.g., "return to Arthur's water"). Once the main words are present in the correct order, *Mumble* goes through inserting articles and punctuation.

In other words, *Mumble* assembles sentences on the fly, using a body of knowledge about English and accessing information from *Tale-Spin*'s simulation. Each sentence is based on a CD expression, but not all CD expressions are employed, and most CD expressions used do not exist before the particular run for which they help form the output. Given this, it seems clear that *Tale-Spin/Mumble* does not provide us with a set of clear textons, of obvious "strings as they exist in the text." Nevertheless, we still have an idea of the elements that go into producing the system's scriptons, and this may be enough to allow a discussion of its traversal function.

Aarseth's presentation of traversal functions identifies a set of "variables" – the values of which define the function. These are a mixture of elements that include audience activity and system behavior. Specifically, drawing from Aarseth's pages 62–5: *Dynamics* describes whether the work's surface and data can change in particular ways – remaining static, with only surface variability, or also variability in the number of pieces of textual data in the system. *Determinability* describes whether the work's processes operate predictably in their production of textual output, or if the processes for producing surface texts can be influenced by unpredictable factors (e.g., randomness) and so yield different responses to the same audience actions. *Transiency* describes whether the work's processes cause surface texts to appear as time passes (e.g., as in textual animations). *Perspective* describes whether an audience member determines the strategic actions of a particular character. *Access* describes whether all possible surface texts are available to an audience member at any time (e.g., a book can be flipped through, so its surface texts are "random" access). *Linking* describes types of user-selectable connections that may be presented by the work's surface (such as links on World Wide Web pages) which may be always available, available under certain conditions, or simply not present. *User functions* are Aarseth's last variable. Every text makes available the "interpretive" user function to its audience. Other possible functions include the "explorative" (selecting a path), "configurative" (selecting or creating scriptons), and "textonic" (adding textons or traversal functions).

So the traversal function here is not simply the means by which *Tale-Spin* triggers English-language output from *Mumble*. Rather, the traversal function encompasses the work's operations in a number of manners. Given this, in order to go further one must investigate the operations of the *Tale-Spin* simulation.

Tale-Spin's Simulation

Tale-Spin was intended to be a storytelling system built on a veridical simulation of human behavior. As Meehan puts it:

> Tale-Spin includes a simulator of the real world: Turn it on and watch all the people. The purpose of the simulator is to model rational behavior; the people are supposed to act like real people. (107)

The basis of this simulation was the work being done Schank, Abelson, and the researchers working with them. For example, each *Tale-Spin* story begins with a character with a problem, what the group called a "sigma-state." A problem might be solved by a simple act (e.g., if a hungry character has food then she can eat it). But if a problem can't be solved by a basic act, then the character must plan to change the state of the world so that it can be. In the group's terminology such a plan was called a "delta-act." For example, if the character does not have food then she may plan to change the world so that she does have food.

However, things don't stop there. Any delta-act may, itself, have pre-conditions that aren't present in the current state of the world. For example, getting food may require knowing where some food is located, and a character may not know. Or a delta-act may include several "planboxes" that represent different approaches to a problem, which are considered serially.

Each time something is made true about the world ("asserted") *Tale-Spin* automatically works through many inferences from it. For example, if it is asserted that a character is thirsty (i.e., if a CD expression is added to the simulation that expresses this fact) then the inference mechanisms result in the character knowing she is thirsty, forming the goal of not being thirsty, forming a plan (a chain of delta-acts) for reaching her goal, etc. Crafting these inferences was an important part of authoring *Tale-Spin*. For example, in an early version of the system, when a character traveled to a place other characters nearby did not "notice." (The inference mechanism from the act of travel didn't give knowledge of the character's new location to those nearby.) This lack resulted in the mis-spun tale, quoted above, in which Henry Ant drowns while his friend Bill Bird sits nearby, unresponsive.

Take, for example, the beginning of an example story, drawn from Meehan's chapter 11. Initially, *Tale-Spin* asks what characters to use for the story, and the audience chooses a bear and a bird. *Tale-Spin* gives the characters names (Arthur Bear and George Bird), homes, basic physical characteristics, etc. Next the audience is given a list of possible miscellaneous items to create in the world, and chooses a worm. The audience is asked who knows about the worm, and chooses Arthur Bear. *Tale-Spin* then asks who the story will be about (the audience chooses Arthur) and what his problem is ("hunger" is chosen).

Through inference, Arthur forms the goal "Arthur has some food." *Tale-Spin* checks to see if it's already true, and it's not. Then *Tale-Spin* checks to see if it's already a goal. It's not, so it is added to Arthur's goal structure. This second check is performed for two reasons. Most obviously, because if it is already his goal (or a subgoal toward a higher goal) then it makes little sense to add it. But another reason to check for the goal's existence is that *Tale-Spin* also keeps failed goals, and the reasons for their failure, as part of a character's goal structure. Before this was added to the system it was easy to create mis-spun tales like the one quoted earlier in this chapter – *Tale-Spin*'s best-known product: Joe Bear forming the goal of bringing Irving Bird a worm over and over.

The first step in the plan Arthur forms, since he doesn't know where to find any honey, is to ask someone else where there is honey. He knows the location of George Bird, so the audience is asked how Arthur conceives of his relationship with George (e.g., does Arthur think that George likes him?). The answers are encouraging, so Arthur travels to ask George (after *Tale-Spin* creates the parts of the world that lie between them). Oddly enough, the CD expressions for this sort of travel seem to be sent to *Mumble* for output in full. The example quoted above, when the ant "walked from his patch of ground across the meadow through the valley to a river bank," is actually one of the less egregious.

When Arthur reaches George's tree he asks George to tell him the location of some honey. Again, the audience is asked for information about George and Arthur's relationship, this time from George's perspective. The answers lead to George believing that Arthur will believe whatever he says. Given this, George starts to speculate – the *Tale-Spin* inference mechanisms are used not to change the state of the world but for one character to "imagine" other possible worlds. George draws four inferences from Arthur believing there is honey somewhere, and then he follows the inferences from each of those inferences, but he doesn't find what he's after. In none of the possible worlds about which he's speculated is he any happier or less happy than he is now. Seeing no advantage in the situation for himself, he decides, relatively arbitrarily, to answer. Specifically, he decides to lie.

So George creates, in *Tale-Spin*'s memory, a set of CD expressions that aren't yet believed by anyone – including himself. These describe Ivan Bee, and Ivan's honey, which exist at a particular location (a location which *Tale-Spin* creates in support of George's plan). Of course, it must be a lie, because honey is not among the miscellaneous items that the audience chose to create at the outset of the story.

Observations on the Simulation

Arthur's saga continues, but enough has been said to allow a few observations. The first is that this *Tale-Spin* story contains quite a bit of psychological "action." Characters are weighing how they view their relationships with each other, spinning out many possible worlds to look for ones in which they achieve benefit, making multi-stage plans, telling elaborate lies, and so on. This is the material from which fiction is made.

However, in contrast to the detailed description of travel itineraries, the CD expressions that describe psychological action are almost never sent to *Mumble*. While Meehan doesn't provide the *Mumble* output for the story of Arthur and George, here is an excerpt from a story containing similar events:

> Tom asked Wilma whether Wilma would tell Tom where there were some berries if Tom gave Wilma a worm. Wilma was inclined to lie to Tom. (232)

All the psychological action described above between George and Arthur, in some version, took place for Wilma and Tom as well. But one would never know it from the output. Instead, by far the most interesting events of Wilma and Tom's *Tale-Spin* story take place in the gap between these two *Mumble* sentences. From an audience perspective Wilma's decision to lie might as well have been determined by a random number.

On the subject of randomness, it is also worth noting that George's decision to answer Arthur was not really arbitrary. Rather, seeing no advantage to any world about which he can speculate, *Tale-Spin* has George decide whether to answer based on his kindness. The audience is asked, and decides that George is "somewhat" kind. So, as Meehan puts it, he decides to answer "out of the goodness of his little heart" (183). But then the answer that George chooses to give, out of kindness, is a lie about honey that doesn't exist. This isn't a simulation of George thinking Arthur should diet, but a breakdown in the simulation. The component of *Tale-Spin* that determines what answer to give doesn't have any knowledge of the fact that the answer is being provided out of kindness.

There is much more that could be discussed about *Tale-Spin*'s simulation, but, for now, this is enough to return to this chapter's attempt to employ Aarseth's model.

Tale-Spin's Traversal Function

As noted above, Aarseth provides *Tale-Spin*'s traversal function to readers of *Cybertext*. Specifically, Aarseth reports that *Tale-Spin* has "textonic dynamics" (the number of textons is variable), is "indeterminable" (perhaps Aarseth identifies a random element in *Tale-Spin*), is "intransient" (it does nothing if not activated by the user), has an "impersonal perspective" (the user is not playing a strategic role as a character), has "controlled access" (not all the possible scriptons are readily available), has no linking, and has a "configurative user function."

This seems largely accurate. But it may also clarify why Aarseth doesn't employ his model in his discussion of *Tale-Spin*. This model doesn't turn attention to *Tale-Spin*'s most salient features. As seen above, the action in *Tale-Spin*'s simulation – its most telling operations – are in the formation, evaluation, and execution of plans. Most of this action is never output by *Mumble* – it never becomes scriptons. So a model that focuses on the traversal function "by which scriptons are revealed or generated from textons" is going to miss the primary site of action as well.

Further, the basic components of *Tale-Spin* and *Mumble* are hard to think about using Aarseth's model. We've already discussed the difficulty in recognizing textons within *Tale-Spin/Mumble*. The difficulty also runs the other direction. How should we think about *Tale-Spin*'s processes for inference making or character planning? They aren't mechanisms for turning textons into scriptons, except extremely indirectly. They aren't pointed at by "textonic dynamics" or a "configurative user function" or any of Aarseth's other variables.

Given this, I believe it is time to consider alternative models. As these models are developed it seems important to retain Aarseth's focus on system operations, such as the mechanisms by which surface text is produced. At the same time, it also seems necessary to abandon the particular focus and specific elements of his model in favor of concepts that will support consideration of a wider variety of digital literature.

A New Model

In developing a new model it may prove useful to diagram some of the alternatives, as in the diagram of an implicit audience model in Figure 8.1.

In this model the audience(s) can see the media object and engage with it through interaction. The interaction may produce some change visible to the audience(s), but what happens inside the object is unknown, as is the object's internal structure. Also, while it is known that the work is authored, the "author function" is represented in gray – author studies having been explicitly set aside by most critics. The focus is on the object as it is visible to (and can be acted upon) by the audience(s).

We might diagram Aarseth's traversal function model somewhat differently. Figure 8.2 shows an attempt.

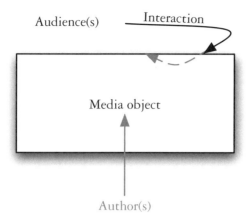

Figure 8.1 An implicit audience model of digital media.

In this model the audience(s) can see the scriptons and also work through the scripton surface to provide some of the variables of the traversal function that generates/reveals scriptons from textons (as well as, in some cases, contribute scriptons and/or textons). The textons, in most cases, along with some traversal function variables, are provided by the grayed out author(s).

Neither of these make a very good fit with the elements we've discussed of *Tale-Spin* and *Mumble,* which can be diagram in a manner such as in Figure 8.3.

This diagram represents the audience reading *Mumble*'s output on a teletype or terminal and typing replies to questions at the same point, creating a combined text. Audience responses to questions feed into *Tale-Spin*'s processes, leading to CD expressions being asserted, developing the facts and history of the simulated world.

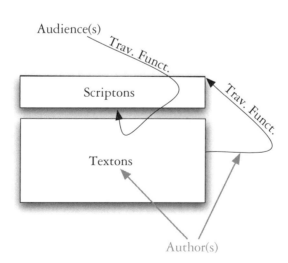

Figure 8.2 An attempt at diagramming Aarseth's traversal function model.

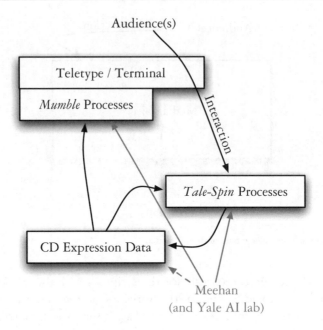

Figure 8.3   The elements of *Tale-Spin* and *Mumble*.

Inferences are drawn from assertions, using *Tale-Spin* processes, resulting in the assertion of further CD expressions (and possibly triggering character planning operations, world building operations, travel operations, etc.). A subset of CD expressions are sent to *Mumble*'s natural language generation processes, resulting in English-language output at the teletype or terminal. The *Tale-Spin* and *Mumble* processes, along with the structure of the CD data, were authored by Meehan (building on concepts then current at the Yale AI lab).

This is a quite complicated picture – and one may be inclined to think twice about it as the starting point for a model. And yet, as a work of digital literature, the structure of this system is in some ways quite simple. A brief comparison with two of my collaborative works as an author of digital literature may help to demonstrate this point.

First, in *Tale-Spin/Mumble*, audience display and interaction happen through a single, text-only device. But in a work like *Screen* (Wardrip-Fruin et al. 2003–5), created with collaborators at Brown University, the site of display and interaction includes a room-sized virtual reality display (the Cave), shutter glasses synchronized with the display via infrared pulses, and magnetic motion trackers attached to the audience member's body (Figure 8.4). This allows words (of short fictions exploring memory as a virtual experience) to appear to peel from the walls, fly around the reader, be struck with the hand, split apart, and return to the walls in new places to create altered versions of the original texts.

To take another example, the structure of *Tale-Spin/Mumble* is relatively simple because all of its processes and data can exist, self-contained, on one computer.

Figure 8.4   Screen, a digital fiction for the virtual reality Cave.

Another piece on which I collaborated, *The Impermanence Agent* (Wardrip-Fruin et al. 1998–2002) is significantly more complex in this regard (Figure 8.5). First, because it is a work for the World Wide Web that includes operations both on the server and on audience members' computers, its processes and data are split across two computers even for a single audience member. Further, while the work's processes were all defined by the authors, the work's data was different for each audience member. *The Impermanence Agent* monitored each reader's web browsing (presumably across many far-flung web servers) and incorporated parts of images and sentences from each individual's browsing into the version of its story (of documents preserved and destroyed) being performed for that reader. And it is important to realize that neither this work's split across multiple computers nor its indeterminacy of data is uncommon. They are also present for many other web works, as well as for other digital forms such as virtual worlds (e.g., massively multiplayer online games).

These two examples are only the proverbial tip of the iceberg in the complex and rapidly developing field of digital literature. Given this, how can one construct a model that will accommodate the variety of work being done in the field, provide a vocabulary useful for talking comparatively about different works, and help turn attention to the aspects significant to individual works? I offer a proposal here, but recognize that any such proposal should be preliminary, open to rejection or refinement by others, and perhaps most useful in helping us see how individual works differ from the generic. My model might be visualized as shown in Figure 8.6.

All works of digital literature are somehow presented to their *audiences* – whether on teletypes, in web browser windows, through immersive installations, or by other means. If the audience is able to interact with the work, the means for this are also

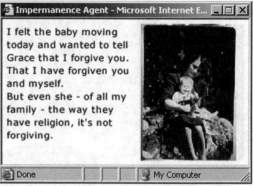

Agent before alteration

I felt the baby moving today and wanted to tell Grace that I forgive you. That I have forgiven you and myself.
But even she - of all my family - the way they have religion, it's not forgiving.

Agent after 1 alteration

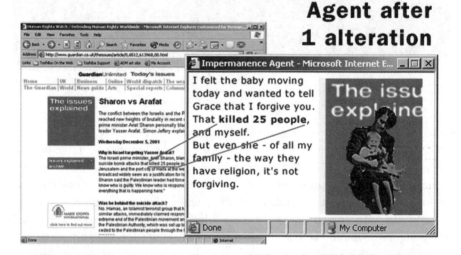

I felt the baby moving today and wanted to tell Grace that I forgive you. That **killed 25 people,** and myself.
But even she - of all my family - the way they have religion, it's not forgiving.

Agent after 3 alterations

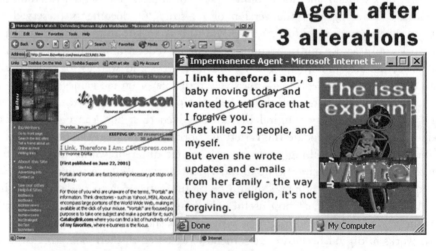

I link therefore i am , a baby moving today and wanted to tell Grace that I forgive you. That killed 25 people, and myself.
But even she wrote updates and e-mails from her family - the way they have religion, it's not forgiving.

Figure 8.5   The Impermanence Agent customizes its story of impermanence for each reader, using material from that reader's web browsing.

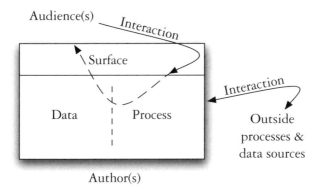

Figure 8.6   The proposed model of digital literature.

part of the work. I will call this site of presentation and (possible) interaction the work's *surface*. It may be as simple as a generic personal computer, consist of a large space or dizzying number of devices, or even take unexpected form (e.g., *The Impermanence Agent* makes all web browsing part of its interaction surface).

Works of digital literature also – whether they are organized as one or more systems, and whether they exist across one or more computers – operate via *processes* that employ *data*. This is not always obvious. For example, an email narrative may appear to consist entirely of data: the text of the email messages. But an email narrative cannot be email without the processes of the audience's email readers and at least one email server. Here the model follows Chris Crawford's vocabulary in his discussion of *process intensity* (1987) rather than the vocabulary of computer science (which might substitute a word such as *algorithm* for *process*).

While there are many definitions of *interaction,* for the purposes of this model I define it as a change to the state of the work, for which the work was designed, that comes from outside the work. Given this, the audience is not the only possible source of interaction. It is also worth noting that, in many cases, some trace of interaction is immediately apparent on the surface (e.g., an audience member types and the letters appear as they are typed, or an audience member moves her hand and a video image of her hand moves simultaneously) but this is not required. Interaction, while it always changes the state of the work, can be approached with the primary goal of communication between audience members.

The *author* is still present in this model, but the arrows representing attribution of different elements are gone. This is because we cannot predict which portions of a work will be created by authors. An installation-based work may present a physical surface almost entirely constructed by one or more authors, while an email narrative may be presented on a physical device, and using an email reading program, indi-vidually selected by each audience member. The data employed in a piece may be created by the author, contributed by the audience, generated through processes, or selected from pre-existing sources by the author, audience, or processes. Or it may be a mixture. The same is true of processes. An author may simply select among those provided by a tool such as Flash, or authors may write or modify programming language code, or the audience may be involved in process definition. The authorial status of a work may even be unknowable.

Employing the Model

As the above discussion suggests, this model can help us consider work comparatively. Just as Aarseth's model points us toward comparisons along variables such as linking, this model points us toward comparisons along variables such as the form the work's surface takes, the sources of the data employed, the state changes produced by interaction, and so on.

It also provides a structure for thinking about the operations of a work's processes – and the relationship of processes to data, surface, and interaction – more broadly than in terms of texton/scripton traversal functions. We can ask, "What is the work doing?" without expecting that we already know the answer ("turning textons into scriptons"). That is to say, in addition to comparison, I believe this model also helps us consider individual works specifically and give appropriate weight to their internal operations.

As readers have likely noticed, the work of viewing *Tale-Spin* through this model is already underway in this chapter. There has already been discussion of its processes, data, surface, and interaction. We've already seen – e.g., in the example of George Bird incoherently lying out of kindness – the way the specifics of the system operations can present revealing gaps between what the system is presented as doing (acting as "a simulator of the real world," in Meehan's words) and what it actually does. We've also seen how the most interesting operations of a work – e.g., George Bird imagining the many worlds in which Arthur believes there is honey somewhere, searching for his own advantage – may never be visible on the work's surface. Hopefully these are convincing demonstrations that tracing an algorithm's steps (watching the interplay between process and data over time) can be an important type of critical reading for digital literature. Putting this type of reading on a more equal footing with audience-perspective readings is a primary goal of this model.

What hasn't yet been explored is the wider view that this sort of examination can help develop. *Tale-Spin* has many fascinating processes, from its inference mechanisms to its simulation of interpersonal dynamics to its creation of virtual geography. I would argue that – by tracing the interplay between *Tale-Spin*'s surface, data, and process – one may be able to abstract from these to characterize the *logic* of operations such as inference. One can then discuss this operational logic itself, as well as identify this logic, and different approaches to this logic, in works with implementations (surface, data, and process) that differ from *Tale-Spin*'s. And, crucially, one can also go further, because there is a central operational logic that can be identified in *Tale-Spin*.

This central logic is *planning*. One can identify it by looking carefully at the contexts in which the other logics come into play. Consider those that create the geography of the virtual world. *Tale-Spin* does not begin by modeling a virtual world that includes all its characters and objects. Rather, many spaces, and the connections between spaces, only come into existence once one character begins to plan to travel from one place to another. The same is true of the logics that simulate interpersonal relationships. *Tale-Spin* does not create a world and then determine how all the characters feel about each other. Rather, none of the feelings that characters have about each other are determined until one of them begins to plan for interaction with the other. And characters have no feelings or other characteristics that are not those needed for *Tale-Spin*'s simulation of rational planning. Consider the following statement from Meehan's dissertation in terms of our culture's stories of love – for example, any Hepburn and Tracy movie:

> "John loves Mary" is actually shorthand for "John believes that he loves Mary." . . . I'm not sure it means anything – in the technical sense – to say that John loves Mary but he doesn't believe that he does. If it does, it's very subtle. (64)

In fact, it is not subtle at all. It is a significant plot element of the majority of romantic novels, television shows, and movies produced each year. But from within *Tale-Spin*'s central logic his conclusion is perfectly rational. If John doesn't know that he loves Mary, then he cannot use that knowledge in formulating any conscious plans – and in *Tale-Spin* anything that isn't part of conscious planning might as well not exist.

This blindness to all but planning – this assumption that planning is at the center of life – was far from unique to Meehan. Within the wider AI and cognitive science community, at the time of Meehan's work, the understanding and generation of plans was essentially the sole focus of work on intelligent action. Debate centered on what kind of planning to pursue, how to organize it, and so on – not on whether planning deserved its central place as a topic for attention. This was in part due to the field's technical commitments, and in part the legacy of a long tradition in the human sciences. Lucy Suchman, writing a decade later in her book *Plans and Situated Actions* (1987), puts it this way:

> The view, that purposeful action is determined by plans, is deeply rooted in the Western human sciences as the correct model of the rational actor. The logical form of plans makes them attractive for the purpose of constructing a computational model of action, to the extent that for those fields devoted to what is now called cognitive science, the analysis and synthesis of plans effectively constitute the study of action. (ix–x)

This view has, over the last few decades, come under widespread attack from both outside and within AI. As Suchman puts it, "Just as it would seem absurd to claim that a map in some strong sense controlled the traveler's movements through the world, it is wrong to imagine plans as controlling action" (189). As this has happened – and particularly as the mid-1970s theories of Schank, Abelson, and Meehan have moved into AI's disciplinary history – *Tale-Spin* has in some sense lost its status as a simulation. There's no one left who believes that it represents a simulation of how actual people behave the in the world.

As this has taken place, *Tale-Spin* has become, I would argue, *more* interesting as a fiction. Its logics can no longer be regarded as an accurate simulation of human planning behavior, with a layer of semi-successful storytelling on top of it. Rather, its entire set of operations is now revealed as an authored artifact – as an *expression*, through process and data, of the particular and idiosyncratic view of humanity that its author and a group of his compatriots once held. Once we see it this way, it becomes a new kind of fiction, particularly appreciable in two ways. First, it provides us a two-sided pleasure that we might name "alterity in the exaggerated familiar" – one that recalls fictions such as Calvino's *Invisible Cities* – which presents us with the both strange and recognizable image of life driven only by plans within plans. At the same time, it also provides an insight, and cautionary tale, that helps us see the very act of simulation-building in a new light. A simulation of human behavior is always an encoding of the beliefs and biases of its authors – it is never objective, it is always a fiction.

Resurfacing

Having spent most of this chapter on an examination of *Tale-Spin*'s internal operations (and on proposing a model of digital literature that provides space for such examinations) this chapter will now return to *Tale-Spin*'s surface by considering two examples of what has been written by those noted earlier in this chapter as operating via an implicit audience model.

Janet Murray, in her book *Hamlet on the Holodeck* (1997), writes of *Tale-Spin* in the context of her argument that writers "need a concrete way to structure a coherent story not as a single sequence of events but as a multiform plot" (185). Murray reprints the famous mis-spun tale of Joe Bear forming the failed goal, over and over, of bringing Irving Bird a worm, and then writes:

> The program goes into a loop because it does not know enough about the world to give Joe Bear any better alternatives. The plot structure is too abstract to limit Joe Bear's actions to sequences that make sense. (200)

In fact, as discussed earlier, *Tale-Spin* looped because – in its partially-completed state at the time this mis-spun tale was generated – its characters could reassert a goal that had already failed. Further, Joe Bear's problem had to happen at the character level – it could not happen at the level of "plot structure" – because *Tale-Spin* has no representation of plot at all. Murray's failure to understand *Tale-Spin/Mumble*'s operations leads to a missed opportunity. As the next chapter of her book demonstrates, she is very interested in systems that model the interior operations of fictional characters. And characters like Joe Bear and George Bird have quite complex interior operations, if one looks beyond the anemic events output by *Mumble,* making them a good potential example for arguments like Murray's.

In *Cybertext,* on the other hand, *Tale-Spin* is one of Aarseth's three primary examples for the argument that machine narrators should not be "forced to simulate" human narrators (129). *Tale-Spin* is presented as a failed example of such simulation, with its mis-spun tales its only claim to interest. From the viewpoint of AI, Aarseth's is an exceedingly strange argument. The primary critique of *Tale-Spin* in AI circles is precisely that it *does not* attempt to simulate a human narrator. *Tale-Spin* simulates characters – not narrators, not authors. We can overlook this, however, because Aarseth is arguing against simulating human narrators only as a proxy for their assumed poetics. He writes:

> To achieve interesting and worthwhile computer-generated literature, it is necessary to dispose of the poetics of narrative literature and to use the computer's potential for combination and world simulation in order to develop new genres that can be valued and used on their own terms. (141)

Of course, as our examination of its operations shows, *Tale-Spin* can be seen as precisely the sort of literature for which Aarseth is calling. The story structures it produces are almost never like those that a human storyteller would produce. Instead, it uses "combination and world simulation" to produce strange branching structures of plans within plans within plans. From this it is possible to see that, for Aarseth, too, *Tale-Spin* could serve as a strong positive (rather than misleading negative) example.

Aarseth's missed opportunity, combined with Murray's missed opportunity, helps to reveal something interesting. *Tale-Spin,* early as it was, stands at an important crossroads. If we choose to emphasize its continuities with traditional fiction and drama, via its characters, then it becomes a useful touchstone for views such as Murray's. If we choose to emphasize its complicated strangeness, its computational specificity, then it becomes an important early example for views such as Aarseth's. In either case, a close examination of the system's operations reveals something much more intriguing than either author assumed.

And there is also something further that can be learned from considering the readings of these two generally insightful scholars. Even dedicated, careful researchers were unable to see what might interest them about *Tale-Spin* by looking at the *Mumble* output. Its fascinating operations were completely hidden, when viewed from the surface perspective.

There is, in fact, a term for works that, when viewed from the surface, seem (at least at first) much more complex and interesting than they actually are: the "*Eliza* effect," in reference to Joseph Weizenbaum's early interactive character. I would like to propose a companion term, inspired by what we see here about *Tale-Spin/Mumble's* surface: the "*Tale-Spin* effect" which describes works that have complex and interesting internal processes that are hidden when the work is viewed from the surface.

I believe the *Tale-Spin* effect is important to consider for two reasons. First, scholars of digital literature must be aware that the surface may not reveal the aspects of a work that will be most telling for analysis (a case in which scholars may miss what a work's processes express). Second, and just as importantly, authors of digital literature must realize that an interesting, successful, *hidden* process will offer less to an audience even than the *visible* errors produced by a broken process, as can be seen with *Tale-Spin's* mis-spun tales (a case in which authors are not effectively employing processes in their expression through the work). In both cases, I believe that a model organized around the relations of surface, data, process, and interaction – and their interplay in operational logics – may provide fruitful insights into expressive processing.

REFERENCES AND FURTHER READING

Aarseth, E. J. (1997). *Cybertext: Perspectives on Ergodic Literature*. Baltimore: Johns Hopkins University Press.

Agre, P. E. (1997). *Computation and Human Experience*. Cambridge: Cambridge University Press.

Bolter, J. D. (1991). *Writing Space: The Computer, Hypertext, and the History of Writing*. Mahwah, NJ: Lawrence Erlbaum Associates, Inc.

Buckles, M. A. (1985). *Interactive Fiction: The Computer Storygame Adventure*. PhD thesis, University of California, San Diego.

Coover, R. (1992). "The end of books." *The New York Times Book Review* June 21: 1, 23–5.

—— (1993). "Hyperfiction: novels for the computer." *The New York Times Book Review*, August 29: 1, 8–12.

Crawford, C. (1987). "Process Intensity." *Journal of Computer Game Design* 1.5.

Crowther, W., and D. Woods (1976). *Adventure*. [Computer game].

Hayles, N. K. (2002). *Writing Machines*. Cambridge, MA: MIT Press.

Jackson, S. (1995). *Patchwork Girl*. Watertown, MA: Eastgate Systems Inc.

Joyce, M. (1987). *afternoon: a story*. Watertown, MA: Eastgate Systems Inc.

Landow, G. P. (1991). *Hypertext: The Convergence of Contemporary Critical Theory and Technology*. Baltimore: Johns Hopkins University Press.

Mateas, M. (2002). *Interactive Drama, Art and Artificial Intelligence*. PhD thesis, Carnegie Mellon University.

Meehan, J. R. (1976). *The Metanovel: Writing Stories by Computer*. PhD thesis, Yale University.

Montfort, N. (2003). *Twisty Little Passages: An Approach to Interactive Fiction*. Cambridge, MA: MIT Press.

Moulthrop, S. (1991). *Victory Garden*. Watertown, MA: Eastgate Systems Inc.

Murray, J. H. (1997). *Hamlet on the Holodeck*. New York: The Free Press.

Schank, R. C. (1975). "Conceptual Dependency Theory." In R. C. Schank (Ed.). *Conceptual Information Processing*. New York: Elsevier Science Inc., pp. 22–82.

Strachey, C. (1954). "The 'Thinking' Machine." *Encounter* III.4: 25–31.

Suchman, L. A. (1987). *Plans and Situated Actions: The Problem of Human-Machine Communication*. Cambridge: Cambridge University Press.

Wardrip-Fruin, N. (2004). "What Hypertext Is." In J. Whitehead and D. De Roure (Eds). *HYPERTEXT '04: Proceedings of the Fifteenth ACM Conference on Hypertext & Hypermedia*. New York: ACM Press, pp. 126–7.

——, A. Chapman, B. Moss, and D. Whitehurst (1998–2002). *The Impermanence Agent*. <http://www.impermanenceagent.com/>.

——, S. Becker, J. Carroll, R. Coover, S. Greenlee, and A. McClain (2003–5). *Screen*. Providence, RI: Brown University Center for Computation and Visualization.

Weizenbaum, J. (1966). "Eliza: A Computer Program for the Study of Natural Language Communication between Man and Machine." *Communications of the ACM* 9.1: 36–45. New York: ACM Press.

Is There a Text on This Screen? Reading in an Era of Hypertextuality

Bertrand Gervais

As the vibrant new field of electronic textuality flexes its muscle, it is becoming overwhelmingly clear that we can no longer afford to ignore the material basis of literary production. Materiality of the artifact can no longer be positioned as a sub-specialty within literary studies; it must be central, for without it we have little hope of forging a robust and nuanced account of how literature is changing under the impact of information technologies. (N. Katherine Hayles, *Writing Machines*. Cambridge, MA: MIT Press, 2002: 19)

Does a literary text retain the same status once it has become virtual? What is the status of any text in today's era of hypertexts and linked computers? What type of materiality are we dealing with? What forms of reading, what forms of knowledge?

We are confronted with increasingly different forms of texts produced with the aid of computers. More often than not, these texts exist only on the internet. They are often animated, filled with sounds and images, accessible through a network, related to one another by hyperlinks, and inscribed in complex environments. How do we manipulate texts that seem to be in a fluid state, that constantly shift; how do we understand them, interpret them?

Two examples will show both the diversity and the complexity of texts present in cyberspace. Stuart Moulthrop's *Hegirascope*, whose first version dates from 1995, offers, since 1997, a complex hypertext fiction consisting "of about 175 pages traversed by more than 700 links. Most of these pages carry instructions that cause the browser to refresh the active window with a new page after 30 seconds" (Moulthrop 1997). *Hegirascope* starts with the claim: "Where you're going there are no maps." It's a warning to the reader: you are now entering a labyrinth where you will not only be clueless as to where you are at any given point, but your own progression will be decided by the work itself. As readers, we are pressed into the position of Theseus who is initially blind to his own destiny. Likewise, we hope to acquire enough knowledge to get a clear view of the work itself through our exploration of its maze, thereby possibly arriving at Daedulus's perspective (Faris 1988: 4–5; Gervais 1998b: 32–3).

While *Hegirascope* provides us with the possibility to play with the flow of pages appearing on the screen, Gregory Chatonsky's *2translation* does not. In this Flash-based hypermedia work created in 2002, we are bombarded with words in both French and English which move toward us. We are invited to read the words, a French and English version of Alain Robbe-Grillet's *Topology of a Phantom City*, as they go by, one at a time. The screen is black, the words are in white or gray, the background music is electronic. Robbe-Grillet's text, like a phantom, haunts the browser's window. Can we read this text, or are we consigned to simply appreciate its iconic features? Is it a text or an image? Is it a *textual* figure?

What type of reading experience is being proposed in *Hegirascope* and *2translation*? How do we talk about it? Must we discuss the software used? Must we indicate the colors of the windows, as the words go by? In *Hegirascope*, the background color

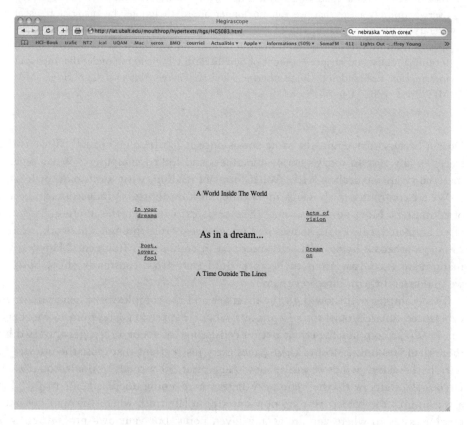

Figure 9.1   Hegirascope. Source: http://iat.ubalt.edu/moulthrop/hypertextx/hgs/HGSOB3.html.

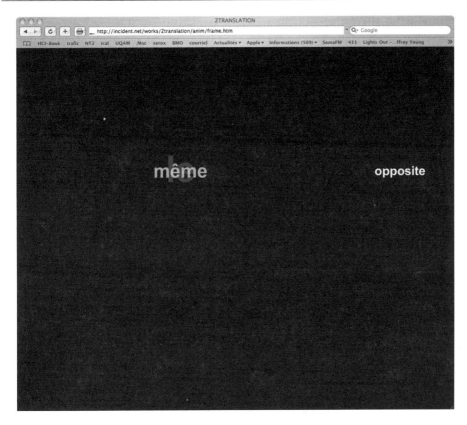

Figure 9.2   2translation. Source: http://incident.net/works/2translation/anim/frame.htm.

changes from one page to another. In *2translation*, the Macromedia Flash player uses our own integrated microphone and camera to change the tone of the screen (from black to various shades of gray).

It is clear that we require a new vocabulary to talk about this new textual reality. Georges Landow argues "Since hypertext radically changes the experiences that *reading*, *writing*, and *text* signify, how, without misleading, can one employ these terms, so burdened with the assumptions of print technology, when referring to electronic materials?" (Landow 1992: 41). Roger Chartier has made a similar case, arguing the current revolution "is a revolution of the structures of the material support of writing, and the ways we read" (Chartier 1997: 12–13). He argues that electronic representation of texts engenders new relationships with writing, where the materiality of the book has been substituted for the immateriality of texts "that lack their own space" and where "the whole of a complete work, rendered visible by the object that contains it" is replaced with "navigating rivers of textual islands with ever changing shore lines" (Chartier 1995: 275). Christian Vandendorpe asks if an internet user even reads, recognizing that "by navigating or surfing, reading is broken up, rapid, instrumental and oriented towards action" (1999: 208). Ollivier Dyens, working with the same metaphor, suggests "Clicking, surfing and zapping is the structure of learning on the Web. [...] learning, on the Web, is not acquired from the text itself, rather it is acquired in the act of navigation from one site to another, from one text to another" (Dyens 2002: 277). He also argues that "The Web is not a book. It is not a text. It is therefore useless to 'read' information" (Dyens 2002: 277).

It is becoming evident that the vocabulary related to the book and reading is no longer adequate. Various terms have been put forward – browsing, surfing, navigating – that appear to encapsulate the experience of acquiring knowledge on the internet (see Vandendorpe, Chapter 10, READING ON SCREEN: THE NEW MEDIA SPHERE, this volume). The marine metaphor seems somehow apt to describe the exploration of cyberspace, perhaps because it does actualize its spatial dimension. Recourse to this metaphor is not new. In fact, according to Hans Blumenberg (1996), it is as old as the world itself. Writers have regularly used as a metaphor sea travel with its inherent risks, like shipwreck and drowning, to speak of the movement of their life in its totality.

Navigating, browsing, and surfing are words that contribute to the overall aspect of this sphere of communication: uncharted, ill-defined, limits unknown, and, therefore, impossible to grasp in its entirety. It is a space whose limits and determinations are electronic, not human: it defines a new frontier, a limitrophe territory where mastery is ephemeral and no immutable laws yet exist.

Regardless of the term chosen, to browse, to surf, or to navigate the web, reading is always involved. Exploring cyberspace is an activity where texts play a major role. If we do not recognize it as a form of reading it is because we tend to forget that texts are omnipresent, and we misconstrue what reading is. Reading is not a single, constant act, the same every time – it is a complex practice bringing into play a large number of variables which determine its forms and functions. As an activity, reading brings into play relationships between manipulation, comprehension, and interpretation – acts that complement each other in our progression through texts, regardless of their particularities or their material aspects (Gervais 2001: 40–3). In this sense, to browse, to surf, or to navigate is to read because, and quite simply, our eyes *register* written words and texts. Our aims and objectives may vary from one context to another – from struggling to find information or hopping from site to site, to engaging in the study of a poem's stylistics or a novel's narrative structure – however, what is performed is always an act of reading.

In the following pages I will describe some of the constraints on the act of reading in an era of hypertextuality: first by proposing a definition of what a text is, one capable of embracing the various forms it can take; going on to describe the current context of our reading practices. This will provide the basis for an identification of the major difficulties we face while reading new textual forms. Before we begin, however, I want to look briefly at Richard Powers's short story "Literary Devices" (2003), which not only plays on our limited knowledge of cyberspace and its possibilities, it begs the question: what is the future of text in an era of increasing automation?

A Mythical Cyberspace

The computer and the internet radically change our relationship with texts, the methods of their production, and our ways of reading. But do we know the *real* capabilities of the instrument we use with such increasing frequency? Do we really understand what we're dealing with?

The computer is no longer simply a tool – it is a medium. Bolter and Gromala write: "For us today – and it's a realization that our culture has made gradually over the past thirty years – the computer feels like a medium. It is providing us with a set of new media forms and genres, just as printing, the cinema, radio, and television have done before" (Bolter and Gromala 2003: 5). So what exactly are the new possibilities with this medium? Are they in fact infinite? The most pervasive beliefs about cyberspace and the computer revolution revolve around the unlimited capabilities of digitalization to provide an ideal representation of the world and its ability to autonomously produce texts.

In "Literary Devices," Richard Powers provides an ironic portrait of this belief in autonomous text generation. In fact, he exploits our incredulity and our inability to distinguish between fact and fiction, and to understand the real status of texts in cyberspace. On the first of the year 2001, the most inauspicious of dates, Richard Powers, author, narrator, and character of this story, tells us how he received an intriguing email. A man he knows nothing about, called Bart, proposes nothing less than the alpha version of an incredible program, designed to automatically produce fictions, i.e., interactive fictions, as they are produced in an epistolary form. Concretely speaking, the program *Dialogos* produces *actants*, i.e., characters capable of acting according to precise schemas in narrative structures (Greimas 1984).

To start *Dialogos*, you merely open the downloaded program, whose interface is similar to email programs (Outlook, Eudora, Entourage), write to anyone you want – your dead father, a childhood friend, or even Rip van Winkle – and hit send, with no need to include a precise address. *Dialogos* does a search and answers the email as if it came from Rip van Winkle or your own dead father, maintaining the fiction of these characters through a dialogue with the sender.

Richard Powers, at first incredulous, sends his first letter to Bart. Impressed with the response he receives, he decides this time to write to the actress Emma Thompson, congratulating her on her last film role, an adaptation of Jane Austen's *Sense and Sensibility*. Emma, or what passes for her, quickly responds, providing details about her last film and current projects. Powers immerses himself in the game. He writes back to her and they exchange a number of letters. Emma, this *actant* without body or life, plays her role exceptionally through the letters, personifying with ease the British actress.

To further test the machine, which is performing beyond all expectations to the point of suggesting some form of trickery, Powers decides to send out a bunch of letters, three dozen in fact: he writes to Emily Dickinson, and to Goethe's Werther; he writes to old colleagues and friends, to actors and CEOs of different corporations, to fictional characters found in literature from around the world and current best-sellers, and even some characters wholly invented. In less than an hour, the responses start appearing on his screen:

> Few of the notes came close to passing the Turing Test for intelligent equivalence. But more of them amused me than even my unrepentant, strong-AI inner child could have hoped. Some of the message senders even claimed to have heard from one another, as if the burst of notes I'd sent out was already being traded and forwarded among all interested parties, triggering new memos that I wasn't even privy to. (Powers 2003: 12)

Powers finally settles on one specific epistolary relationship, the one he started with Werther, which goes on for months. He also keeps in touch with Charlotte, Albert, and Goethe. And the expected occurs. Werther commits suicide. But not without first convincing Richard Powers of the incredible autonomy of the program, of its capacity to generate completely independent fictions, fictions that produce their own story, a narration narrating itself and inventing its own program, thereby creating its own reality.

But how does such a generator of fictions and stories work? How could a machine slide into the skin of historical or fictional characters and succeed in convincing even the most skeptical author? It does so, in part, by becoming a *structuralist*, capable of transforming stories into narrative programs, and characters into functions or actants; it also does so in part by being connected to this vast ensemble of data and knowledge that is the internet. As Bart explains, his team has created a machine language capable of dealing with databases, the most unstructured of texts. This language is capable of processing the necessary information contained in the "two billion pages of collective unconscious" (Powers 2003: 11) that is the web. "Think of this thing," exclaims Bart, "as Google meet Babelfish" (Powers 2003: 11), as if these two names represented gods about to battle for the souls of humanity.

We are living in an age of digitalization and electric texts, and as Powers would add, an era of incredible alienation that forces us to take our hopes and dreams for reality. In "Being and Seeming: the technology of Representation," an essay published on the internet and closely related to his short story, Powers tells us that:

> Our dream of a new tool inclines us to believe that the next invention will give us a better, fuller, richer, more accurate, more immediate image of the world, when perhaps just the opposite is the case. Television does not improve on the verisimilitude of radio, nor photography on that of painting. The more advanced the media, the higher the level of mediation. (Powers 2000)

The myth of an ideal transparency, and of endless possibilities that cyberspace encapsulates, is a mere fiction, a myth per se: a story we want to believe because it explains what is happening and where we are going. Powers's "Literary Devices" is a persuasive example of these expectations, since it blurs the frontier between what is simply hypothetical and what is genuine. And the questions it raises are more real with each passing day. What is the status of an author in this universe of simulacra? What forms of reading are we engaging in with cyberspace, and its primary expression, hypertextuality?

Dialogos is a fiction: the fiction of a narrative written by no one, a completely automated narrative whose content has been culled from a sea of information. Roland Barthes would roll over in his grave! Here, recasting Barthes's well-known declaration (1977), the author is not simply dead, there is just no need for one anymore! This function – the author function, to use Michel Foucault's term (1977: 124–7) – has been taken over by an actant, a function in a structure, an anonymous relay.

The death of the author was never more than a theoretical principle, a symbolic death that should allow, or so Barthes suggests, the emergence of the reader; more specifically, the beginning of theories about texts and their reading. *Dialogos* transforms this symbolic death into an actual disappearance, leaving even the function of scribe, an automation. If Barthes can be said to have killed the author, Bart (an obvious pun by Powers) has not only done away with the author's body, but has removed any trace of his presence. No one is at the origin of the signs that are read. If the symbolic death of the author encouraged a figure of the reader to emerge, the complete elimination of the author leaves the reader an orphan, or a slave who has no one left to oppose, or in an even more apocalyptic scenario, becomes completely obsolete. Powers, the narrator, learns this the hard way in the short story: he finds himself on a site where he discovers a long list of messages that have been exchanged between Werther, Willhelm, Albert, Charlotte, and his father; and on a chat, he finds the same actants exchanging in a deluge of messages transmitted at a speed too fast for him to read. The very person who initiated the exchange of messages has become useless and obsolete. The story tells itself. And turning off the computer changes nothing – the story is happening in cyberspace, this limitrophe non-human space propelled by its own dynamic.

What Texts Are We Reading?

Leaving *Dialogos* and the myth of an omnipotent cyberspace, let's get back to our initial question: what forms of reading are electronic and digitalized texts generating? This requires of course an initial understanding of what constitutes a text. In literary theory, there has been a wide variety of responses to this question. One of the more widely accepted stances proposes that whatever can be interpreted or perceived as a totality is a text, whether this be the flight patterns of bees or human interactions. The more restrictive definitions have focused on writing in a natural language. A text is what you have before your eyes right now. But does this writing require a coherent totality, is it composed uniquely in a natural language excluding any schema, illustration, figure, or diagram?

Let us define a text, in its broadest possible view, as *an organized ensemble of signifying elements for a given community.* This definition delimits the status of the text by relating it to a set of conventions already set and established by an interpretive community, i.e., by a group of individuals sharing the same strategies for writing and reading texts, for establishing their properties and their intentions (Fish 1980). A text is what such a community decides it to be. With this premise in mind, it is possible to add a further definition, narrower in scope: *a text is a being of language transmitted by a medium and actualized in a specific situation.* As a *being of language* (Charles 1995: 47), a text is a set of utterances providing form for content. What such a set can be is open to discussion and can be specified whichever way seems fit. The important part of the definition is the presence of speech acts, recognized as such and interpreted as constituting an enunciation. A being of language, however, can only exist if it is actualized in a given situation. It requires a sender, evidently, but also and more importantly a receiver, a reader in this case, who will actualize in his or her own context and by way of his or her own experiences its form and content. A text, in this definition, does not exist alone, but only within its relation to a reader. It exists through the act of reading. A text is what we make it to be; and its legitimacy is a function of what we provide it through our diverse experiences and institutions.

The third aspect of this definition is the essential presence of a medium, the material support by which a text is transmitted. For the French theorist François Rastier, a text is, simply put, "an empirically attested linguistic suite, produced within a specific set of social practices, and affixed to some form of support" (2001: 21). Rastier considers this material support an essential part of the text's status and definition. And it is only by questioning this aspect of our textual experiences that we can investigate the concrete modalities by which a text is read, and the impact new media and forms of texts can have on our reading practices. Does it make a difference, in terms of reading, if a text is transmitted through a computer screen instead of a printed page? What does the presence of fixed or animated images change in our readings habits? What is the current cultural context of our reading experiences?

This context can be described as a "hyperextension" of our cultural practices (Gervais 1998a: 7). It is fundamentally new and corresponds to our linked computer culture, in contradistinction to the more traditional manuscript and book cultures.

The Linked Computer

Manuscript culture corresponds to what historians of literacy and reading refer to as an intensive reading situation (where few texts are read, but they play an essential role in the life of the reader), while book culture corresponds to an extensive reading situation (where many different texts are read, but in a superficial manner). In manuscript culture, books are important and of a religious nature, while they become cultural goods in book culture (Chartier 1996; Cavallo and Chartier 1999).

In our linked computer culture, texts are simply overflowing. It is a context of hyperconsumption of cultural goods, which the terms browsing, surfing, or even navigating especially evoke. The tendency is toward acceleration. Texts come in a wide variety of forms and formats, they are read rapidly and with little investment. With few exceptions, they are quickly left behind after the initial encounter. These texts often do not partake of any pre-established canon, they are selected with few prior motivations. We read as fast as we can what comes up on our screen, through the simple click of a mouse.

The internet pushes further the reading practices typical of popular culture, where magazines and newspapers are quickly read and then disposed of. Generic markers play an important role in defining initial reading strategies and reader involvement. One does not approach a literary text the same was as a news item. With the linked computer, these generic markers lose their relevance. Books and magazines, literary texts, and press releases share the same space, the window of a browser, and they are subject to the same initial reading strategies.

This context of cultural hyperextension has come about because two major tendencies converged, each amplifying the other. The first corresponds to the development of new technologies for storing and transmitting texts and is marked by the advent of cyberspace and its specific textuality. The second relates to modifications in the very structure of cultural relationships and the way identity is defined. For instance, both identity and cultural relationships are progressively moving from a logic of *tradition* to a logic of *translation*. This transition favors a shift from relationships expressing ties with a cultural center, ensuring permanence and value, to relationships expressing ties with the periphery and exchanges between cultures. Tradition as a cultural principle implies a certain stability, e.g., a literary canon that provides a community with its history, its habits and manners, its identity. Translation as a cultural principle implies accelerated transformations, the multiplication of ties that provide an ever-shifting identity. As Yuri Lotman has shown (1990), tradition does not exclude outside influences, translation, or exchange – however, its tendency to re-appropriate them is paramount. As an identity principle, translation places its emphasis on de-appropriation, with an a priori for the other. The movement is centrifugal – not centripetal.

The internet participates in the decentralizing of cultural exchanges – short-circuiting a number of social and cultural institutions by proposing a network that allows individuals to be connected to the world while never leaving their computers, and to participate in virtual communities grounded on speech acts, rather than cultural position. However, the increasing liberty of the individual, who can easily publish texts and have them read by whomever is interested, is paid for by a certain precariousness of the texts themselves. The internet escapes traditional modes and mechanisms for the institutionalization of texts. Nothing guarantees the authority, or even the authenticity of what is published on the web. Nothing guarantees its seriousness or quality. Its author is all but faceless. If we are still a far cry away from Richard Powers's automated text generator and its subsequent elimination of the author, the authority of texts, and therefore of its authors and readers, is already jeopardized by the sheer amount of texts available and the reorganization of the traditional modes of publication and distribution.

This context of cultural hyperextension and linked computers is a consequence of the convergence of two transformations: technological and cultural. We do not yet know how or what this context will provide, although we already feel its effects; we can, nonetheless, begin to identify certain factors that are influencing our reading practice and experiences. These are dealt in the next section by focusing on the new materiality of text, and the problems their manipulation generates.

Constraints on the Act of Reading

The question is simple: how do we manipulate a text that is "digitally demateri-alizing" (Rastier 2001: 21)? How do we handle what cannot be held, what literally slips through our fingers? What can be said about reading a text whose primary mode of being is now virtual, mediated by a computer device whose complexity we do not always master?

We know how to manipulate books. We learn to read in infancy, playing with books, turning their pages, looking at images and trying to figure what the words accompanying them mean. They become second nature. We do not have to think about the book, its design, or its constraints to be able to use it. But can the same thing be said about a digital text? Can we read a text on a linked screen the same way we read a text printed on paper? Can we engage in the same activities and with the same ease? More often than not, and the references to browsing, surfing, and navigating are revealing, we engage in a rapid form of reading, where the impetus is more on progression than comprehension, more on rapidity than density. Can we read a literary text on a screen? Can we analyze it, interpret it, and evaluate its formal and esthetic aspects (see Wardrip-Fruin, Chapter 8, READING DIGITAL LITERATURE: SURFACE, DATA, INTERACTION, AND EXPRESSIVE PROCESSING, this volume)?

Obviously the paper has disappeared; the text can no longer be examined in its entirety, at least not in the same way the book has conditioned us, with its weight, volume, and forms. The text is now nothing more than a bombardment of photons on a computer screen. How can this type of text be studied and analyzed? Over the past centuries reading has become progressively more interiorized, passing from oral reading to silent reading. The computer is provoking yet another transformation: an increased intellectualization of the reading act, where the technologizing of the word blurs the limits between what is or is not text.

Cyberspace, for instance, leaves the impression that the writing we find has dematerialized to the point of passing for something else, e.g., some form of oral derivative. It is regularly suggested we are finally witnessing a consummate expression of what Walter Ong has called a secondary orality (Ong 1988: 3), a term used to describe situations where oral communication is mediated by writing and print technology. However, this orality is first and foremost silent. It is an intellectualized orality that needs no ear to be listened to. By applying Ong's concept to the internet, Phillipe Hert demonstrates how "the temptation for a 'quasi oral' writing corresponds to the desire to fully explore a heterotopia" (1999: 100). However, this "non-spoken orality" (Hert 1999: 100) remains timid at best because it is tied to an impossible *transparency* of a writing that can never escape its own specificity, despite all the attraction of the heterotopic devices brought into play. Hert argues that, in the case of the internet, "the illusion of a more direct communication, more transparent, more immediate, without barriers or spatial-temporal limitations, so hyped by the utopias of cyberspace, is confronted with the writing it uses" (1999: 102).

We are in a period of transition, which must be understood not only in terms of the implantation of a new text technology, but also as a new configuration of our reading practices. The transition has been evoked through various oppositions: from papyrus to hypertext (Vandendorpe 1999), from codex to screen (Chartier 1995), or from the page to the screen (Autié 2000). As well, we either minimize the transition, or we fear it (Birkerts 1994); and we can also exaggerate its consequences and see hypertextuality as a new stage in the life of language (Lévy 2002). Whatever evaluation we make, a reconfiguration is taking place as we move toward a linked computer culture, and this forces us to reexamine the essential gestures involved in reading.

Every act of reading is comprised of three gestures: the overlapping and complementary acts of manipulation (the basic modalities of appropriation), comprehension (the act of understanding the text per se), and interpretation (the relationship established between the text being read and other texts explaining it). These gestures are present with every act of reading, and they are logically related to each other. Reading is always manipulating a text, understanding it, and interpreting it. Specific instances of reading can generate a greater emphasis on one of these gestures (interpretation in literary studies, for instance); however, their co-presence and overlapping constitute the foundation of every act of reading. Interpretation requires that some form of understanding be obtained. And comprehension necessitates that the text be manipulated with ease. If the last cannot be obtained, the whole edifice collapses. A text that cannot be manipulated, therefore be included in a genuine reading practice, will resist complex forms of understanding and become impermeable to interpretation. Evidently, with our move from text to digital and cybertext, with its implicit shift from paper to screens and linked computers, it is this very activity of manipulation that has yet to be completely assimilated.

Manipulation is usually taken for granted. The level of automatism involved in this act is reflected in the numerous theories and hypotheses about reading traditionally debated in literary studies: they almost never take into consideration the manipulation or the material aspects of texts being read (Hayles 2002: 19). It's not seen as necessary because the act has been so well learned. But, with texts available only through computer screens, this learning still remains to be completed. The very metaphor of browsing is an obvious sign that this manipulation is still imperfect. To browse is to move from one thing to another, to remain disconnected – like the act of shopping, browsing text is about texts not yet ours. Consequently, we need to learn to do more than browse, we need to learn to take possession, make these new texts our own, re-appropriate them.

So what types of difficulties are inherent in the manipulation of these new forms of texts? A number of problems have already been identified. Certainly, the first is their novelty. Another is their institutional instability, i.e., their status in a cyberspace still in transformation. Another four difficulties can be readily identified and are described next.

Risks of Manipulation

The first of these difficulties is the digitalization of the text – its dematerialization. In conjunction with this ephemeral way of being present, digitalization adds a new functionality. On the one hand, the words on the screen-page no longer just "say," they can also "act": they embody a computer function that allows them to activate hyperlinks, which appear to be a very new act of language not currently covered by the usual speech act categories. Certainly, this computer function of the words impacts their semiotic function in ways that we do not yet understand. Are hyperlink words read the same way as simple words? What about database-driven text? Should we read a *Dialogos*-generated text the same way as a traditional text, one produced for instance by Richard Powers?

The shift from one medium (the page) to another (the linked computer) has substantially modified our relation with linearity. In hypertextuality, linearity is no longer a limit or a constraint, a basic quality that literature often tried to escape, it has become an added feature. A hypertext is a non-linear text composed of nodes connected together by hyperlinks. It is not just written, it is imbedded, a HTML code. The electrified text flows in any direction it wants, establishing links independently from its user. In this context, linearity is a quality that we try to recuperate in order to maintain, among other things, the possibility of telling a story, which still requires a certain form of linearity. The hyperlink does not only change words and the way texts are structured, it also modifies the basic modalities of progression through texts, transforming it from a logic of discovery to one of revelation. I will come back to this argument in the last section of this chapter.

Again, digitalization implies the increased presence of an invisible writing, of a code organizing data and enabling functions. On a page, no part of the text is invisible. Everything is there, unless of course you adopt the genetic approach to texts, where what is present is only a small part of what could have been written. However, in terms of reading, nothing is hidden. The same cannot be said of a hypertext, or any text on a linked computer. These forms require an invisible writing: links already established and operational throughout the act of reading, a programming that structures and organizes the nature of the text albeit implicitly, transforming the constraint of linearity, for example, into an accidental property. How do we make room for this "extra" in the act of reading? (See Wardrip-Fruin, Chapter 8, READING DIGITAL LITERATURE: SURFACE, DATA, INTERACTION, AND EXPRESSIVE PROCESSING, this volume.)

A second difficulty is the ever-increasing number of texts available in our cultural context of hyperextension. Accessibility, an ideal in a capitalist society, pays tribute with an uncontrollable influx of texts. It is common knowledge that we are living in the age of a second flood, a flood of communication. This flood significantly changes our relationship with texts. They are no longer something rare (as in a manuscript culture) or usual (as in a book culture), they are almost a menace. We are less concerned with finding texts, and more concerned with stopping the flood of texts coming in. We need to construct dams capable of holding back this incredible mass. The situation of overabundance forces us to look for ways by which to reduce the amount of texts, to organize data, and make it manageable, with search engines and automated text analysis. In fact, we do not want to read texts, we want to erase most of them. The need for selection is preponderant. We need to learn to omit texts, to develop strategies of exclusion, albeit "intelligent" strategies that allow for a judicious exclusion. If we are entering a new cognitive era, it seems to have omission as its core structuring principle.

We can easily observe that research on reading and its processes these past two decades has been done less by literary scholars and more by linguists and researchers in cognitive science, looking to develop software capable of automatically analyzing texts, thereby accelerating their study. The supreme value in our context of hyper-extension is speed, hence the need for an accelerated progression through texts. However, this ever-increasing need for speed has its toll on comprehension, which still requires time. With the impetus on accelerated reading processes, comprehension is more and more reduced to its simplest forms: literal meaning and superficial interpretation.

Banality is the foremost danger of digitalized and easily accessed texts. They are no longer a rare commodity – they are objects easily reproduced with almost no symbolic value: "Digital text will never acquire the aura of the manuscript" (Rastier 2002: 86). A text on a screen has almost no value: the mediation by the computer has rendered its presence immaterial. With fragments read on internet sites, this immateriality is characterized by an absence of spatial-time determinations. Where is the text? What is the status of what appears on the screen? Instead of a corporeal text, the sheer materiality of page and book, we have the ghost text of cyberspace, a figure as untouchable as it is ephemeral. It's obvious this type of text will generate far less investment in the act of reading. The digitalization of text, with its easy access, its ability to be present on numerous screens simultaneously, results in a loss of symbolic value.

A third difficulty arises with the complexity of the text itself – its essentially hybrid quality. More and more, texts share their space with images, animated sequences, sounds, etc. The internet favors the development of iconotexts, i.e., texts where writing and images intersect through various modes, ranging from simple

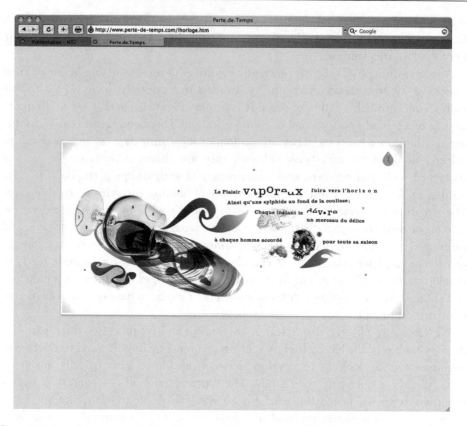

Figure 9.3   Perte de temps. *Source*: http://www.perte-de-temps.com/lhorloge.htm.

juxtaposition, as in comic books or newspapers, to fusion, as in calligrams or calligraphy (Hoek 2002; 1995). Iconotexts have always been part of literature, albeit in a marginal fashion. Now, with the development of computer graphic design, iconotextuality has become a standard.

Texts on the internet have a strong iconic component. Hypermedia pages are set as in a newspaper, words are sometimes immersed in images, their fonts vary, and they compose a complex reality. With such creations, we are confronted with "texts" that are now figures of texts, i.e., texts first and foremost seen as images instead of writing. They are no longer read, they are experienced as a spectacle.

Hypermedia experimentations such as Julie Potvin's "Perte de temps," a Flash-based adaptation of Charles Baudelaire's poem "L'Horloge" (<http://www.perte-de-temps.com/lhorloge.htm>), or Young-Hae Chang's animated texts that reveal themselves one word or one line at a time (witness the very funny "Cunnilingus in North Korea" or the more subtle "Rain on the Sea", <http://www.yhchang.com/>) are powerful examples of texts whose iconic aspect is put in the foreground. With such experimentations, we are pushed to the limits of our reading practices, where the text itself is no longer given to be read, but to be seen, to be contemplated as a figure.

It's the iconic value of the words that becomes significant, their formal aspects, their disposition on the page, their accumulation or the treatment they have received. It is the figure they constitute in their totality that now commands our attention.

This transformation subordinates the perception of the words and their signification, necessarily codified, to an intuitive perception of images. It is a textual figure, an artifact, that first imposes itself while the information contained in the text recedes. If we want to read these textual figures, if we want to go back to what they might be saying, we have to go beyond their iconic dimension. We have to accustom ourselves to their design and graphic aspects. Simply put, we must learn to manipulate them, until this first step of the reading process is mastered. Textual figures appear opaque, simply because our attention has been distracted by the glamour that images and linked screens have brought into the reading experience.

Our difficulty in reading the new forms of texts stems, at least in part, from the constraints that the overall iconic context imposes on the reader.

A Logic of Revelation

The fourth and last difficulty is related to the actual status of the signs brought into play with hypertextuality. Electricity changes the nature of text – it transforms it into a digital text. Through computer programming, a new function appears – one which operates at the frontier of semiotics and computers: it is the hyperlink. This sign, with its singular properties, seems to call us to discovery – at least on the surface – allowing us to move from text to text with ever-increasing ease. However, in doing so, it jeopardizes the very core of the reading process, which is discovery. The hyperlink is, surprisingly enough, a simulacrum of a sign – i.e., it is a language entity that acts like a sign without actually being a sign. Its uniqueness lies in the nature of the link it proposes and, to a certain extent, the role we play in establishing it. Are we its creators, or simply the users of the relationship set up by the link? The hyperlink in fact places us in the second role – users – which explains the logic of revelation it surreptitiously imposes.

A sign is essentially something which stands for something else for someone. In this triadic relationship, which finds its full development with C. S. Peirce (1992), the sign is not directly linked with its object. It is the interpreter, or more precisely the *interpretant*, that establishes the relationship by identifying the object. The object of the sign is not determined absolutely, its attribution depends on the knowledge and experience of the interpretant. With signs, we can always make mistakes. We can fail to fully understand the signification of a word and proceed to make a faulty attribution – e.g., if we don't know a presbyter is the house of a minister, we might believe it refers to a small yellow and black striped snail. This would be a faulty attribution. Because we are responsible for the attribution, it requires our interpretants to be effective – and they can prove themselves to be inadequate. The signification of a sign is the unique result of our action on it.

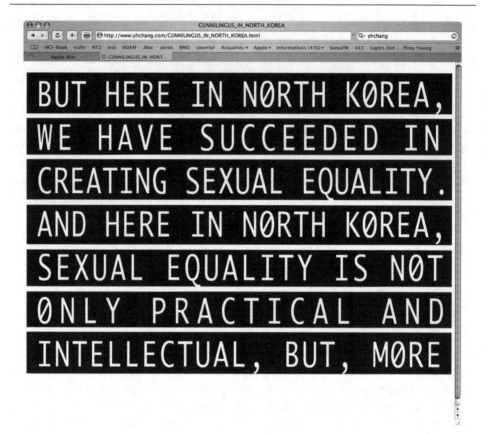

Figure 9.4 Cunnilingus in North Korea. *Source*: http://www.yhchang.com/CUNNILINGUS_IN_NORTH_
KOREA.html.

With the hyperlink, this logic is inverted: the link never varies, regardless of the interpreter who activates it. The hyperlink acts like a sign – it stands for something else for someone; however, once programmed, it does so identically in every case. The hypertext link, once activated, and this despite our interpretants, always goes to the next text to which it has been linked. It can never be faulty. Granted, it can be defective – in which case it is completely ineffective – however, it can never link to something else beyond what has been established. It is no longer operating in the order of the possible, it is a finished act only waiting for the push of a finger to reveal its true nature. We no longer hypothesize at the moment of activation – there is no risk of error as we content ourselves to follow instructions and passively watch the deployment of the link.

The possibility of error, inscribed at the very heart of our semiotic reality, is the essential condition for a process of discovery – and reading is one of our foremost processes of discovery. The hyperlink, because it can never vary, can never be wrong, places us in this respect in a logic of revelation – the apparition of truths stemming

Figure 9.4 Continued.

not from a quest for information, rather as a gift. The gift of a link revealed with its surprise and novelty. Hypertexts in this sense are not discovered, but revealed.

The difference between discovery and revelation, between searching for a truth and having one simply revealed without any effort, is the difference between a word and a word button, between a real sign and a hyperlink, between the semiosphere (Lotman 1990) and cyberspace. Hypertextuality, by its very structure, strings us along from revelations to revelations. For this reason, the medium is extremely exciting, it gives us our money's worth because it offers things we didn't even know existed. The unexpected and the spectacular impose their logic. Moreover, what we find is not the result of a quest – it is a search barely palpable because highly sophisticated search engines are able to discover for us, and reveal like truth the substance of our investigation no matter how summary. From the masters of inquiry, cyberspace transforms us into spectators of a miracle that never ceases to repeat itself, a spectacle of the appearance. It transforms us into believers, convinced that an exterior force controls our path, our destiny.

Hyperlinks transform the basic drive associated with reading: the discovery associated with progression through a text, the step-by-step process required to read sentences and to organize them into a totality, a specific being of language. They transform this active process into a more passive stance, which might explain the important adjustments required to develop complex modalities of reading, necessitating by definition a greater participation. It goes against the grain.

Conclusion

Obviously, these are only a few of the factors that explain our difficulty in reading the new forms of texts produced in our linked computer culture. The impact of the cultural transformations brought about by the new computer technologies is enormous and it calls forth a reconfiguration of our relations with texts. A new cultural space has been created, one we are slowly getting accustomed to.

Richard Powers's fable about the *Dialogos* text generator comes to mind again. Not only must we get accustomed to this new media and its environment – cyberspace is a "communicative environment" (Downes 2005: 3) –, we must also understand its real capacities, and not get lured by the myth it is drawn into. In "Being and Seeming," Powers warned us that "We dream that a new tool might put us closer to the thing that we are sure lies just beyond us, just outside the scale of our being. [...] New media have forever promised to take us to the place we can no longer get to" (Powers 2000). It is a Xanadu-like dream. One that can never be attained, even if it enthralls us.

Ironically, our entrance into this mythical cyberspace does not happen under the tutelage of Oedipus, the first philosopher, rather it transpires under the auspices of Oedipa Mass, the heroine of the 1966 Thomas Pynchon novel, *The Crying of Lot 49*. Much like us with our hypertexts, Oedipa moves from revelation to revelation; like us, it is in a state of wonder that she experiences a ballet of texts and symbols that come in an order she can never anticipate. And the novel finishes without us, readers, ever knowing the final word of the story. In the ultimate scene, Oedipa is attending an auction. She has an interest in lot 49, which is about to be put on the block. However, the novels ends abruptly at the very moment the auctioneer starts the auction. The last revelation is not presented – indefinitely suspended beyond the confines of the text. However, the logic of revelation requires precisely this type of suspense – the sequence cannot end. It is the expectation that creates the link. It is not the revealed truth that matters; it is the next that it anticipates, the revelation to come, the one always the more desirable insofar as it remains a promise. Cyberspace is such a promise.

BIBLIOGRAPHY

Autié, Dominique (2000). *De la page à l'écran: réflexions et stratégies devant l'évolution de l'écrit sur les nouveaux supports de l'information.* [From Page to Screen: Reflexions and Strategies Regarding the Evolution of the Written Form on the New Information Aids]. Montréal: ELAEIS.

Barthes, Roland (1977). "Death of the Author." In *Image-Music-Text* (Stephen Heath, Trans.). New York: Hill and Wang.

Birkerts, Sven (1994). *The Gutenberg Elegies. The Fate of Reading in an Electronic Age*. New York: Fawcett Columbine.

Blumenberg, Hans (1996). *Shipwreck with Spectator. Paradigm of a Metaphor for Existence*. Cambridge: MIT Press.

Bolter, Jay David, and Diane Gromala (2003). *Windows and Mirrors. Interaction Design, Digital Art, and the Myth of Transparency*. Cambridge: MIT Press.

Cavallo, Guglielmo, and Roger Chartier (Eds.) (1999). *A History of Reading in the West*. Amherst: University of Massachusetts Press.

Charles, Michel (1995). *Introduction à l'étude des textes*. [Introduction to the Study of Texts]. Paris: Seuil.

Chartier, Roger (1995). "Lecteurs dans la longue durée : du codex à l'écran." [Readers in the Long Run: From Codex to Screen]. In R. Chartier (Ed.). *Histoire de la lecture: un bilan des recherches* [History of Reading: a Research Account]. Paris: IMEC éd., Éd. de la maison des sciences de l'homme, pp. 271–83.

—— (1996). *Culture écrite et société. L'Ordre des livres (XIVe–XVIIIe siècle)*. Paris: Albin Michel.

—— (1997). *Le livre en révolutions*. [Revolutions of the Book]. Paris: Textuel.

Chatonsky, Gregory (2002). *2translation*. Incident. net. <http://incident.net/works/2translation/anim/frame.htm>. Accessed June 25, 2006.

Downes, Daniel (2005). *Interactive realism. The Poetics of Cyberspace*. Montreal: McGill-Queen's University Press.

Dyens, Ollivier (2002). "La texture de la nouvelle connaissance. " [The Texture of New Knowledge]. *éc/arts*. Paris: 2: 275–9.

Faris, Wendy B. (1988). *Labyrinths of Language: Symbolic Landscape and Narrative Design in Modern Fiction*. Baltimore: Johns Hopkins University Press.

Fish, Stanley (1980). *Is There a Text in this Class?* Cambridge: Harvard University Press.

Foucault, Michel (1977). "What Is an Author?" In Donald F. Bouchard (Ed.). *Language, Counter-Memory, Practice*. Ithaca, New York: Cornell University Press, pp. 124–7.

Gervais, Bertrand (1998a). "Une lecture sans tradition: lire à la limite de ses habitudes." [Reading without Tradition: To Read beyond Our Limits]. *Protée* 25.3: 7–20.

—— (1998b). "The Broken Line: Hypertexts as Labyrinths." *Sources. Revue d'études anglophones*. Orléans: Paradigm, pp. 26–36.

—— (2001). "Sans fin, les terres. L'occupation des sols au risque d'une définition des pratiques de lecture." [Reading as an Occupation: The Case of Jean Echenoz's *L'occupation des sols*]. In Catherine Thauveron (Ed.). *Comprendre et interpréter le littéraire à l'école et au-delà* [To Understand and Interpret Literacy in School and Beyond]. Paris: Institut National de Recherche Pédagogique, pp. 37–54.

Greimas, Algirdas Julien (1984). *Structural Semantics* (Daniele McDowell, Ronald Schleifer and Alan Velie, Trans.). Lincoln: University of Nebraska Press (Original work published 1966).

Hayles, N. Katherine (2002). *Writing Machines*. Cambridge, MA: The MIT Press.

Hert, Philippe (1999). "Internet comme dispositif hétérotopique." [Internet as a Heterotopic Device]. *Hermès* 25: 93–107.

Hoek, Leo H. (1995). "La transposition intersémiotique pour une classification pragmatique. " [Intersemiotic Transposition for a Pragmatic Classification]. In Leo H. Hoek and Kees Meerhoff (Eds.). *Rhétorique et image* [Rhetoric and Image]. Amsterdam: Rodopi, pp. 65–80.

—— (2002) "Timbres-poste et intermédialité. Sémiotique des rapports texte/image." *Protée* 30 (2): 33–44.

Landow, George P. (1992). *Hypertext: the Convergence of Contemporary Critical Theory and Technology*. Baltimore, London: Johns Hopkins University Press.

Lévy, Pierre (2002). "L'hypertexte, une nouvelle étape dans la vie du langage." [Hypertext, a New Step in the Life of Language]. *éc/arts* 2: 104–9.

Lotman, Yuri (1990). *Universe of the Mind. A Semiotic Theory of Culture*. Bloomington: Indiana University Press.

Moulthrop, Stuart (1997). *Hegirascope*. <http://iat.ubalt.edu/moulthrop/hypertexts/hgs/HGSAbout.html>. Accessed June 25, 2006.

Ong, Walter J. ([1982] 1988). *Orality and Literacy: The Technologizing of the Word*. New York: Routledge.

Peirce, Charles Sanders (1992). *The Essential Peirce. Selected Philosophical Writings. Volume 1 (1867–1893)*. Bloomington: Indiana University Press.

Powers, Richard (2000). "Being and Seeming: The Technology of Representation." *Context A Forum for Literary Arts and Culture*, no. 3. <http://www.centerforbookculture.org/no3/powers.html>.

—— (2003). "Literary Devices." *Zoetrope All Story* 6 (4): 9–15.

Pynchon, Thomas (1966). *The Crying of Lot 49*. Philadelphia: Lippincott.

Rastier, François (2001). *Arts et sciences du texte*. [Arts and Science of the Text]. Paris: PUF.

—— (2002). Écritures démiurgiques. *éc/arts* 2: 80–91.

Vandendorpe, Christian (1999). *Du papyrus à l'hypertexte. Essai sur les mutations du texte et de la lecture*. [From Papyrus to Hypertext. Essay on the Mutations of Text and Reading]. Montréal: Boréal.

10

Reading on Screen:
The New Media Sphere

Christian Vandendorpe

Far from being "natural," reading is a complex skill that is highly dependent not only on the way it has been learned, but also on the nature of the text to be read and the media on which the text is written. Even if it is not within the scope of this chapter to do a history of reading (Manguel 1996; Vandendorpe in print), it is necessary to highlight the main points of its evolution in the western world if we want to grasp the new context created by the advent of the computer and the internet.

The history of reading is closely related to the history of the book. In a nutshell, one might say that it is characterized overall by the evolution of the document from a linear and uniform flow of text to a tabular organization. In Rome, two thousand years ago, silent reading was unknown and people read out loud; or, if they were affluent enough, they listened to their slaves reading to them. Since then, reading has evolved from that "hearsay" model into the complex semiotic interaction of a variety of verbal and visual clues we know today.

The most important milestone in the history of the book was the adoption of the *codex* format – a Latin word meaning booklet– and the subsequent demise of the *volumen* or scroll. That revolution took place in Rome in the first century AD. The Christians were the first to adopt the codex, for a variety of reasons: the codex was cheaper than the scroll because the sheets could be written on both sides; it was also more compact and easier to conceal, an important feature for members of a forbidden religion who traveled a lot, and so this new medium was best adapted to a new religion preaching a revolutionary gospel. As the ascent of the codex followed that of the new religion, the new format of the book became progressively more common. It was dominant in Rome by the end of the fourth century AD, when the new religion was recognized as the official religion of the empire.

The passage from scroll to codex allowed important changes in the way texts were read. First, it freed the hands of the reader. The scroll was necessarily held with both hands; it was unrolled horizontally, and the readers might need to control the proper reenrolling of the scroll with their chin. The codex also made it easier to refer to a given portion of text. It gave more visibility to the content of the book and allowed artists to illuminate sacred manuscripts in order to foster a reverential attitude among believers. More importantly, various incremental improvements across the centuries would make the text easier to read: adoption of a minuscule script around 800, introduction of spaces between words (Saenger 1997), and of embryonic forms of punctuation (Parkes 1993), for example. Those developments would make silent reading easier to achieve and therefore fairly common in the monasteries' scriptoria of the twelfth century.

After the invention of the printing press, the book progressively gained its most modern features: page numbering, delineated paragraphs, secondary titles and tables, titles of chapters, etc. All these improvements made it easier for readers to control their reading activity, to retrieve a particular passage of a text and to share it with others. The book thus became ideally suited as a vehicle for the revolution in knowledge that characterized the Renaissance and ushered in the modern era.

According to the history of reading (Engelsing 1974), another important change in the habits of reading would occur in the eighteenth century. Until then, the book was thought of as an entity whose content a serious reader should assimilate through sessions of intensive reading, digesting and ruminating until it became part of him or her. With the multiplication of books and of all forms of printed material, a new attitude toward text called "extensive reading" would gain legitimacy. In place of percolating intensively a few books, the reader could choose to browse through vast amounts of material and content by reading only passages of particular interest. This attitude would foster the production of big encyclopedias like Chambers' *Cyclopaedia, or Universal Dictionary of Arts and Sciences* (1728) and the Diderot and D'Alembert's *Encyclopédie* in 33 volumes (1751–72).

Over the centuries, reading thus became a distinct cognitive experience autonomous from the spoken word. As a distinct media, the specificity of the printed text is that it allows readers to understand verbal content at their own pace.

From Print to Screen

The advent of the personal computer at the beginning of the 1980s made the writing process infinitely more fluid than it had ever been before. Being easy to correct, to format and to disseminate, digital writing was rapidly adopted by the many professions dealing with the production of text. But the adoption of the screen as a reading device was much less enthusiastic. For quite a few years the computer did not look like a real rival of the printed book, a fact that was partly due to the poor quality of monitors at the time. This situation began to change with the massive adoption of the web in the mid-1990s.

The internet solved elegantly and definitively the old problem of the portability of documents. In that aspect, we have come a long way from the bulky clay tablets of the Sumerians. As we have seen, the codex was adopted in part because it was more portable than the scroll. And the printers had the intelligence to invent through the ages very small books that were very handy for travelers. But with the web, documents no longer need to be transported: they can be stored in public repositories accessible from everywhere. Ubiquity is the perfect solution to portability.

Thanks also to improvements in display technologies, and to increasingly vast amounts of data available on the web, there has been, over the course of a dozen years, a steady increase in the time the general public spends in front of a screen, which in the USA was around fifteen hours per week in the spring of 2006. However, since not all of that time could be considered as "serious reading" by most people, it may be useful to introduce some distinctions between various modes of reading.

Heyer (1986) proposes three different modes of reading or gathering information, based on metaphors borrowed from the ways our ancestors gathered food: grazing, browsing, and hunting. In the grazing mode, the "reader" picks up everything coming out of the book. For this purpose, we shall call that mode "continuous reading," in the sense that the reader aims to construct a significant whole out of a long text, even if the reading spans many sessions. This mode of continuous reading is most typical of the novel where users have to immerse themselves in a book in order to create a fictional universe. It is also the case, albeit with significant differences, with long essays where the reader has to master a series of arguments and relationships, like Darwin's *On the Origin of Species* or Freud's *Interpretation of Dreams*. In browsing mode, readers pick up only what is of interest to them through the "scanning of a large body of information with no particular target in mind" (Heyer). That mode became fairly common with the advent of newspapers, magazines, big catalogues, and coffee table books. In hunting mode, the reader seeks specific information. This mode is relatively recent and became a real possibility only when alphabetical order was adopted for dictionaries, in around 1000, and then extended to indexes for scholarly books between 1200 and 1300. Naturally, this characterization of various modes of reading is only an approximation: there are many processes involved in reading just as there are in the process of understanding. These categories are useful, however, as guidelines.

These three modes of reading are not at all equal when it comes to implementing them on a computer screen. Significantly, the browsing mode was the first to define the activity of reading on the screen: it is so well adapted to the screen that the interface created for the web was aptly named a "*browser.*" It allows the user to navigate the web from one node of information to another, as is done with the titles of a newspaper. It should be no surprise, then, that printed magazines and newspapers were among the first to be digitally available through the web.

Next, the hunting mode became fairly common with the advent of sophisticated search engines and basic interactivity. The turning point occurred in 1999 with the appearance of Google, whose fast algorithms and page-ranking system greatly improved the results of any search. The search engine is to the book index what the internet is to portability: far from being limited to a small percentage of books, full text search is now available for all kinds of documents. By an effect known as a "virtuous loop," the more information there is on the web, the more probability there is that a user will get an elaborate answer to any given request. That, in turn, provides a greater incentive for people to put documents on the web, knowing that it may be found by someone looking for it. That powerful dynamic has led to the exponential growth of the web. Far from slowing down, this trend should continue in years to come.

By another interesting feedback effect, the reading sphere could well be profoundly affected by this new conjuncture. With the availability of ever more powerful search engines, a culture of questioning is now spreading to all categories of people. In other words, what was once considered as typical of a learned method of reading is now gaining in popularity and occupies a more important segment of reading time for many people.

Thanks to the ubiquity and searchability of documents, the screen is now the place of choice for the modes of reading related to browsing and searching, but it still lags well behind paper for continuous reading activities. Many people prefer the conviviality of the book or even photocopies when they have long documents to read attentively. This is due to a variety of reasons, notably the rigidity of the screen and the technological barriers posed by the mouse and the keyboard, which prevent readers from immersing themselves in a reading experience comparable to that offered by the book.

The Issue of Legibility

It took many years to adapt typography to the screen. Owing to the fact that the monitor is made of tiny little squares, it was necessary to develop sub-pixel addressing technologies in order to avoid ragging effects in the display of type. Even if that technology was pioneered as early as 1976 by Apple and later introduced in Acrobat Reader PDF format, it was not until 1998 that it was made available in the Microsoft world under the name ClearType. And even then, that method of smoothing the edges of screen fonts was not the default mode of the operating system until the latest versions of Windows XP. As poor font quality makes reading difficult and strenuous, it should be no surprise that the screen was generally discarded as a continuous reading device.

Meanwhile, new fonts were developed for enhancing legibility, such as Georgia and Verdana. While the later is sans serif, the former is a serif font, which means that each letter has a kind of small footprint at its base. The general effect of a page of text is very different depending on which type has been used for its display. The question of which family should be preferred has been the matter of many debates. There is no ideal font: choices are dependent on context and on the effect that is desired. In the world of printed books, serif fonts are largely dominant because they have been used since the Roman era and also because the decorative strokes of the serif tend to offset the dull effect otherwise produced by the extreme regularity of type across pages and pages of text. Many magazines, on the contrary, will favor sans fonts in order to make the text look light and "clean" in the midst of pages already heavily decorated by illustrations, color bars, and publicity.

On the screen, serif fonts were largely dominant in the nineties, due to their dominance in the printed world. For many years, Times was the font of choice because it looks better than Helvetica (or its clone Arial) when it is printed on paper. Increasingly, however, sans fonts are gaining followers, and rightly so: as screens and webpages are often cluttered by icons and graphical elements, sans fonts look cleaner, stay legible at a very small size and make for more appealing and more visually balanced screen pages.

The size of the letters is another thorny issue. Small typesize allows the display of more text in one screenshot, but if it is too small, many readers will have to resize it, which may be cumbersome, even impossible with certain browsers. If it is too large, the screen looks cluttered and as ugly as a billboard. Spacing between the lines creates white space, which is a relief for the eye: the closer the lines, the more strenuous will be the reader's effort. Again, however, a too large spacing reduces the amount of text displayed in the window. Generally, the longer the columns of text available on a single screen, the easier it is for the reader to grasp the context of what is being read.

Handling the Flow of Text

The codex took over from the scroll and sent it to the dustbin of history mainly because it gave the reader a better control over the reading process.

The main advantages of the codex were lost when text was converted to the screen. The main drawback of the screen lies in the fact that it is a two-dimensional object. As such, it can only show one "page" at a time. This is far different from the book whose structure allows the reader to leaf through the pages and, in doing so, gain some visual control over the content of the book, and be able to compare pages in one section with those in another one. It is also possible to browse through the book, search in the index for a word, or read the book from cover to cover. This flexibility of the book, which adapts easily to any of the three main modes of reading, helps to understand why the printed media was so successful and why it is still very much attached symbolically to the highest cognitive activities.

Therefore, we should not see the attempt to reproduce the qualities of the codex in the virtual world as backward longings for a dead past, but as a quite rational desire to ensure a smooth transition between the remarkable achievements of the book and the new possibilities offered by the digital world. A culture does not progress by erasing the past, but by weaving it into its future – like the humanists of the Renaissance did with the works from Greek and Roman antiquity. If the screen is the future of the page, governments and libraries should ensure that books from the past will be accessible in this new medium.

The first vision of a digital library was put forward by Michael Hart, who founded the Gutenberg Project in 1971. Twenty years later, some national libraries began to make available thousands of books on the web, but the real wake-up call came with the announcement at the end of 2004 that Google would digitize 15 million books. Even if this project has been attacked on legal grounds by various American publishers, its mere perspective has raised an incredible interest all around the world and incited various governments to enter the fray. The task is gargantuan. Kelly (2006) estimates that "humans have 'published' at least 32 million books [and] 750 million articles and essays" since the first Sumerian clay tablets appeared on the surface of the globe. This vast quantity of published texts represents the repository of human experiences in various cultures throughout history and it should be made available on the web for future generations. All over the world, various projects have been initiated and the pace of digitization is now estimated at one million books per year. The big question is how to make those books easily readable on screen.

The scroll and the codex are the two main metaphors available for displaying text on a computer screen. The vertical scroll format was adopted as a norm by the first word processors in the 1960s. In that metaphor, the text is seen as a continuous flow of words that the reader handles by clicking with the mouse on the scrollbar or by using keyboard controls (page up, page down). An important drawback of this solution is that the position of a specific sentence on the screen shifts with the scrolling movements, which excludes the participation of visual memory in the reading process.

Moreover, the scrollbar gives the user very poor control over the flow of text. The size and position of the scrollbar are very insufficient for handling large documents and make it difficult for the reader to build up a mental model of the entire text or to go directly to a specific position in the text. There is no small irony in the fact that the first attempt to naturalize the reading process on the screen reverted to the antiquated metaphor of the scroll and to an analogous way of handling the flow of text, in place of a digital one. But these shortcomings were considered as acceptable since the screen was seen as a transitory space, with the actual reading taking place when the text was printed on paper.

Progressively, some word processors would offer the possibility of seeing page breaks, margins, headers and page numbers, even when the user is scrolling through the text, and of displaying the layout of the pages in any format. Over the past twenty years, the dominance of Microsoft Word is due to the fact that it was the first word processor to give the user full visual control over the text, a control popularized by the acronym *wysiwyg* (*"what you see is what you get"*). The 2006 version of this program offers no fewer than five ways of visualizing the flow of text, each with its own strengths, depending of the user's goals: normal, web, page, plan, and double page (aptly called "reading mode"). Word processors are thus getting away from the "native" scroll format adopted at the beginning of the computer age, and they now tend to replicate many aspects of the codex format.

In that respect, PDF offers some of the closest approximations to the experience of reading a codex. It replicates the appearance of the printed page and offers many sophisticated features that enhance the navigation and the reading process by giving the reader various *tabular* controls over the text. He or she may flip through the pages laterally (codex-like) or vertically (scroll-like). Any page is accessible by its number or by clicking on thumbnails of pages on the left. Some features even surpass the functionalities of the codex. The search function displays in a window all the occurrences of a word in the document, with the page numbers and a short context. It is also possible to highlight, underline or cross-out portions of text, insert comments and place bookmarks, and even reorganize the document. Readers are thus able to appropriate the text as deeply as needed, check their progression in the text, easily compare two sentences positioned in different sections of the text, and find a specific occurrence without having to lose their position in the document. These features tend to make reading on a screen quite efficient.

The Advent of Hypertext

The reconciliation on a screen of the vertical scroll and the horizontal codex formats was unproblematic as long as the text was a closed linear entity. Things changed radically with the advent of hypertext. Hypertext is a way of linking any portion of a document to another one (see Belinda Barnet and Darren Tofts, Chapter 15, Too Dimensional: Literary and Technical Images of Potentiality in the History of Hypertext, this volume). The term "hypertext" was coined in 1965 by Ted Nelson (1974), who took his inspiration from the seminal paper "As we may think" written by Vannevar Bush (1945). In this paper, Bush envisioned a system where the users could access all books and scientific articles in microfilm format, combine sections of interest to them and record their reading sessions. This dream began to become reality when the necessity of handling enormous masses of documents on a small computer monitor led to the implementation of the SGML (Standardized Generalized Markup Language) in the mid-1980s. The concept of hypertext began to penetrate into the public domain in 1987 with the arrival of a new Macintosh equipped with HyperCard. It was fully realized with the creation of the World Wide Web by Tim Berners-Lee and Robert Cailliau in 1993.

Hypertext introduces a new metaphor for the representation of text, since it is conceptualized as a hierarchy or an arborescence of textual nodes linked together. The text is thus apt to be thought of as a purely logical structure.

The basic unit of a hypertext has received various names. Computer people first used the technical term "stacks," which refers to a series of addresses in the RAM memory of the computer. For some time, the term "hypercard" was very common, by metonymy with the software of the same name and the similarity between hypertext nodes and library cards. For the literary hypertext, George Landow (1994: 1) proposed the term "lexia," in reference to the way Roland Barthes names chunks of text in *S/Z*

(1970). Many hypertext writers published at Eastgate in the 1990 have adopted the term "writing space" derived from the software Storyspace.[1] Today, most people simply use the word "page."

This designation gained in popularity with the advent of the web. Within a few years, the hypertext became part of the mainstream experience and it showed its ultimate strength in its ability to link seamlessly billions of pages as if they were a single entity, a constantly evolving book. But its basic unit, the so-called page, has only a vague resemblance with its physical cousin. On paper, a page is a fixed spatial entity whose word-count is approximately the same for every page of a book. As a physical entity, it coincides only loosely with semantic content; on the screen, a page has no intrinsic limit and could include only one word or a million.

Only ten years after the web became a common experience for billions of people, the text on the screen has morphed into an interactive mix of text, images, sounds, and graphs. Not only the "page," but even the traditional notion of "text" does not seem any more adequate to name this hybrid, which is better designated as a "document." At the same time, the reading experience is changing. This experience was previously shaped by the physicality of the codex and the immense popularity of the novel during the past two centuries. For the average reader, a book was seen not just as a collection of pages bound together, but as an organic whole worth being read from cover to cover. With the web, pages accessed by the user are generally just fragments whose meaning depends on the context within which they are grasped. Hypertext links give an incredible lightness to the reader, who can easily jump from one idea to another one, shifting contexts as easily as in a conversation. This is not always a blessing, of course, since it distracts the reader from following a single thread of thought, as is normally required in reading a printed book.

Hypertext has, however, made possible easy access to a wealth of data that exceeds humanists' wildest dreams since the great vision that gave birth to the library of Alexandria in 300 BC.

The Disappearance of the Column

The advent of hypertext also makes more complex the task of displaying text on the screen in a way that would foster, or at least be compatible with, continuous reading. When Tim Berners-Lee and Robert Cailliau had to choose a language for designing a "distributed hypertext system for the management of general information," they opted for "an interchange format very similar to an SGML application" (Cailliau 1999). HTML was perfectly suited for the linkage of nodes of text, the display of lists, and for representing various hierarchical levels of titles, but it had only very basic tools for the layout of the page. The main drawback was, and still is, the lack of a fixed-width column of text, as the text in basic HTML is supposed to flow freely in the browser, going from one border to the other. As long as the monitors did not exceed 800 pixels of width, the width of the browser was adequately suited to reading.

Short columns of text are easier to read than large ones. This was already known in Greece, more than two thousand years ago. In the papyrus scroll, the width of the column of text varied between 8 and 12 centimeters, which corresponds to approximately 30 to 40 letters per line. Interestingly, those dimensions are still in use in today's newspapers and magazines. And it is so, not because they are imposed by cultural habit, but by the physiology of reading. In fact, experimental studies have shown that, in the reading activity, the eye does not proceed in a linear and smooth fashion. As Wikipedia puts it, "Eye movements are typically divided into fixations and saccades".[2] As the eye proceeds in a jerky fashion, the longer a line of characters, the greater the risk that the eye loses track of the line on which it is fixed. This is the reason why a column of text in a printed book usually stays under the upper limit of 70 characters per line. If it needs to be longer, like in art book, then the spacing between lines must increase, in order to facilitate reading and make the text more appealing.

In the past dozen years, we have witnessed steady progress in the quality and size of monitors. On a big screen, therefore, a web page that follows the World Wide Web Consortium (W3C) recommendations may well display a line of more than 300 characters. While practical for revising a software program where each line of code is an instruction, this "kilometric display" is quite inadequate for serious reading. In fact, as evidenced by many studies, it incites the reader to skim through the text rather than to read it attentively. Of course, the reader has always the possibility to resize the browser. But this process is cumbersome and tends to distract from the reading activity since it makes the screen more cluttered. Moreover, it does not give the reader the white space of the margins. Contrary to what one might think, margins are not just lost space. They give shape to the text and allow the eye to regenerate from the tension produced by the innumerable saccadic movements of the eye during the reading process. With the disappearance of margins, text is reduced to its content. This is the ultimate victory of the logical over the visual.

By reducing the text to a collection of bits of information that should flow freely on any screen, the engineers of the W3C broke away from the millennial tradition that saw the page as a semantico-visual space organized in order to procure a maximum of legibility. They were victims of the same illusion that McLuhan recognized in some of his students who were "prone to be concerned with book content and to ignore its form" (1962: 77).

Sure enough, the main providers of text for serious reading on the screen, like newspapers and magazines, in the main do not follow the W3C recommendations and calibrate precisely the width of the column of text at around 400 to 600 pixels using sophisticated *cascading style sheets*. It may be even less. For example, *The New York Times* displays text in columns of about 45 characters per line. That gap between official standards and real practices indicates that we are still in an era of transition, comparable in many ways to the fifty years that followed the Gutenberg invention, where books were still *incunabula*. We have to reconcile the logical with the visual, the fluidity of hypertext with the imperatives of a visual layout and the characteristics of the reading process desired.

The Birth of the E-book

The first attempt to naturalize the book for a digital media was the *Dynabook* designed by Alan Kay at Xerox Park in 1968. The design was very similar to what is known today as a laptop computer or a tablet PC. This kind of portable device, holding thousands of encoded books, was the inspiration for Neal Stephenson's novel *The Diamond Age*, in which a young girl is given a talking book as a companion and a tutor. As Beverly Harrison describes Kay's project, "This was one of the earliest reference designs that captured the notion of today's e-books – a portable, wireless, networked device that could act as a notebook and reading device while maintaining many useful affordances of a book" (2000: 35).

Owing to display technology, battery life, and miniaturization problems, it was not until the mid-1990s that we saw various attempts to design computers specifically and uniquely dedicated to replicating the book in a portable digital format, namely the e-book. The main models were the SoftBook Reader, the Rocket eBook, Cybook, and Gemstar eBook. In recent years, considerable advances have been made in display technologies, mainly with the invention of "digital paper," notably e-ink, which displays text using reflective light. The absence of backlighting translates into an enormous longevity of the battery, allowing some 10,000 pages to be read with the Sony's Librié, launched in 2005. Digital paper is also very light, making for better portability.

Ideally, the perfect e-book should also allow the user to manipulate documents as with Adobe Acrobat: highlighting, selecting, copying, commenting, and exchanging. The arrival of hypertext has opened doors that today's readers already appreciate too much to give them up.

The Future of Reading

It may be premature to make predictions for the future, since the display of documents on screen has not yet reached its maturity. History has shown, however, that a medium as widely used as the scroll could be completely replaced by the codex or book format in the course of three centuries.

Since our reading activity is shaped by the constraints of the media, we can forecast that the relationships between the various modes of reading will shift. While the grazing mode was the standard way of reading in the Gutenberg galaxy, it is now superseded by the browsing mode. And the hunting mode is also becoming fairly common due to the availability of answers to any given question a user might happen to think of. In the future, if this trend continues, the novel as a literary genre could well become an endangered species, despite its long history. There should be no surprise if today's novelists and publishers look at the web with some suspicion.

In a passionate plea for digitizing the millions of books presently in the various national libraries, Kevin Kelly (2006) suggested that such an accomplishment would allow those books to become part of the global hypertext:

> Turning inked letters into electronic dots that can be read on a screen is simply the first essential step in creating this new library. The real magic will come in the second act, as each word in each book is cross-linked, clustered, cited, extracted, indexed, analyzed, annotated, remixed, reassembled and woven deeper into the culture than ever before. In the new world of books, every bit informs another; every page reads all the other pages.

Such a vision is indicative of the appeal of hypertext and of its enormous power of transformation on the reading sphere. In Kelly's view, the main interest of digitizing these millions of books is not to make them readable on the screen in a continuous mode. On the contrary, he envisions a future where books would be reduced to "snippets of a page" and "These snippets will be remixed into reordered books and virtual bookshelves." Their contents would be linked and tagged so that they would become a single huge hypertext. In this anticipation of the future, the printed book is no longer seen as a universe, but as a separate entity, at best an island, at worst a prison.

It is therefore no wonder if Kelly's vision was anathema to the writer John Updike (2006), who labeled it "a pretty grisly scenario":

> In imagining a huge, virtually infinite wordstream accessed by search engines and populated by teeming, promiscuous word snippets stripped of credited authorship, are we not depriving the written word of its old-fashioned function of, through such inventions as the written alphabet and the printing press, communication from one person to another – of, in short, accountability and intimacy?

All too naturally, the novelist is not ready to accept a future where authors would be stripped of their status. In that respect too, the electronic text ushers us into a new era, just as the Gutenberg printing press did five hundred years ago. Writers gained a status that has been growing over the centuries: "printing tended to magnify the distance between the author and the reader, as the author became a monumental figure, the reader only a visitor in the author's cathedral" (Bolter 1991: 3.) The revolution brought in by the internet may well be seen by some as a barbaric invasion similar to the ones that marked the end of the Roman Empire and the beginning of the Middle Ages. It is evident that cyberspace favors anonymous collaboration over single authorship, be it by blogs, forums, or encyclopedias like Wikipedia.

As time goes by, however, the printed book will have more and more difficulty meeting the expectations of most readers; i.e., that all texts should share the characteristics of digital documents: ubiquity of access, fluidity of copy-paste and exchange operations, integral searchability, participatory interactivity and hypertext links.

It will become imperative that the millions of books printed up to now become available online.

It is true that in mid-2006 there was not yet a clear market for e-books. Sales were still a fraction of what printed books represent, and had not changed much from the previous year. In 2004, the market for e-books "accounted for an estimated 0.1% of the 2.3 billion books U.S. publishers sold worldwide" (Helm, 2005). Things could change rapidly, however, if a new device were to make digital reading as convenient as reading on paper. All over the world, publishers and newspapers are experimenting with electronic paper. It is now possible to envision a kind of truly electronic scroll the size of an open magazine where text would flow in parallel columns and that would display at least twice as much text as a big monitor. Such a device, that would combine the affordances of PDF format with those of the double page and of an extreme portability, would greatly enhance the readability of articles and long documents, since continuous reading comprehension greatly depends on the possibility for the reader to embrace a rather large quantity of text.

Ironically then, the foreseeable future of the book could well be in an electronic re-creation of the original scroll format, a development that would make digital reading as "natural" as reading a codex is today.

NOTES

1 Eastgate describes this software in these words: "Storyspace map shows each hypertext writing space and each of its links": <http://www.eastgate.com/storyspace/index.html>.

2 <http://en.wikipedia.org/wiki/Reading_%28 activity%29>.

REFERENCES AND FURTHER READING

Aarseth, E. (1997). *Cybertext. Perspectives on Ergodic Literature*. Baltimore: Johns Hopkins University Press.

Bolter, J. D. (1991). *Writing Space*. Hillsdale, NJ: Lawrence Erlbaum.

Bush, V. (1945). "As We May Think." *The Atlantic Monthly* 176 (July): 101–8.

Cailliau, R. (1999). "Hypertext in the Web – a History." *ACM Computing Surveys* 31.4 (December). <http://www.acm.org/surveys/Formatting.html>.

Engelsing, R. (1974). *Der Bürger als Leser: Lesergeschichte in Deutschland 1500–1800*. Stuttgart: Kohlhammer.

Harrison, B. L. (2000). "E-books and the Future of Reading." *IEEE Computer Graphics and Applications* 20.3: 32–9.

Helm, B. (2005). "Curling up with a Good E-book." *BusinessWeek Online* December 29. <http://www.businessweek.com/technology/content/dec2005/tc20051229_155542.htm?chan=search>.

Heyer, M. (1986). "The Creative Challenge of CD-ROM." In S. Lambert and S. Ropiequet (Eds.). *CD-ROM. The New Papyrus. The Current and Future State of the Art*. Redmond, WA: Microsoft Press, pp. 347–57.

Kelly, K. (2006). "Scan This Book!" *The New York Times Magazine* May 14, sect. 6, p. 43, col. 3.

Landow, G. P. (1994). *Hyper/Text/Theory*. Baltimore: Johns Hopkins University Press.

Manguel, A. (1996). *A History of Reading*. New York: Viking.

Manovich, L. (2001). *The Language of New Media*. Cambridge, MA: The MIT Press.

McGann, J. (2001). *Radiant Textuality: Literature after the World Wide Web*. New York: Palgrave.

McLuhan, M. (1962). *The Gutenberg Galaxy*. Toronto: The University of Toronto Press.

Negroponte, N. (1995). *Being Digital*. New York: A. Knopf.

Nelson, T. H. (1974). *Dream Machines: New Freedoms through Computer Screens – a Minority Report*. Chicago: Nelson/Hugo's Book Service.

Ong, W. (1982). *Orality and Literacy. The Technologization of the Word*. London: Methuen.

Parkes, M. B. (1993). *Pause and Effect. An Introduction to the History of Punctuation in the West*. Berkeley: University of California Press.

Saenger, P. (1997). *Space between Words. The Origins of Silent Reading*. Stanford: Stanford University Press.

Shneiderman, B., and G. Kearsley (1989). *Hypertext Hands-On! An Introduction to a New Way of Organizing and Accessing Information*. Reading, MA: Addison-Wesley.

Stoicheff, P., and A. Taylor (2004). *The Future of the Page*. Toronto: The University of Toronto Press.

Updike, J. (2006). "The end of authorship." *The New York Times* June 25. <http://www.nytimes.com/2006/06/25/books/review/25updike.html?ex=1156219200&en=24f36593b5c16137&ei=5070>.

Vandendorpe, C. (In print). *From Papyrus to Hypertext*. Illinois: Illinois University Press.

11

The Virtual Codex from Page Space to E-space

Johanna Drucker

The brief career of the "e-book" has been plagued with fits and starts. In the twenty-some years since desk-top computers, palms, hand-helds, pods, and other devices have come into widespread use, a whole host of surrogates for traditional books have been trotted out with great fanfare and high expectations. In almost every case, these novelties are accompanied by comparisons between familiar forms and their reinvented shape in an electronic context. That legacy can be traced in nearly every descriptive title: the expanded book, the super-book, the hyper-book, or, "the book emulator" – my personal favorite for its touching, underdog, sensibility. Such nomenclature seems charged by a need to acknowledge the historical priority of books and to invoke a link between their established cultural identity and the new electronic surrogates.

Nonetheless, the rhetoric that accompanies these hybrids tends to suggest that all of the advantages are on the electronic side. The copy written in support of what are frequently new products bidding for market share contains conspicuous promises of improvement. The idea that electronic "books" will "supersede the limitations" of paper-based books and overcome the "drawbacks" of traditional books features largely in such promotional claims. But why? On what grounds?

The promotional rhetoric presumes that books are static, fixed, finite forms that can be vastly improved through the addition of so-called "interactive" features. Testing those claims against the design of various means of text access and display in electronic formats one encounters a field fraught with contradictions. Electronic presentations often mimic the most kitsch elements of book iconography while for the longest time the newer features of electronic functionality seemed not to have found their place in the interface at all. So we see simulacral page drape but very little that indicated the capacity for such specifically electronic abilities as rapid refresh and time-stamped updates or collaborative and aggregated work. E-book "interactivity" was largely a matter of multiple options within fixed link-and-node hyperstructures. The iterative aspects of digital processing, however, are finally making themselves felt in tools that are genuinely interactive and intersubjective and result in material transformation of the text and knowledge produced through the activity they support.

The recent design of two authoring and editing environments, *Sophie*, currently being prototyped by Bob Stein, and Collex, being developed by Bethany Nowviskie and Jerome McGann at SpecLab at the University of Virginia, are addressing some of the issues that hindered e-spaces from coming into their own.[1] *Sophie* incorporates features of time-based, animated multimedia alongside texts and images in authoring software that is easy enough for classroom use, but multi-purpose in its applications. The design embodies certain residual legacies that echo book structures, particularly in the way it segments or modularizes its spaces and their sequencing. Collex is conceived entirely within digital functionalities (collecting, aggregating, making use of folksonomy technology and other networking capabilities) meant to support electronic publishing and scholarship. Its interface is strictly functional, with viewing areas for searching, display, and notation features rather than a global view of activity. Both projects are so new that issues of scale and sustainability, patterns of use, and graphical navigation issues have yet to reveal themselves. Both are highly promising. Still, I would argue, these and other electronic environments for reading and authoring expose our indebtedness to print culture at the conceptual level: what are the basic units for viewing and organizing text/image materials, how are relations among them ordered for reading and sequencing, how are they viewed and annotated? Understanding the way the basic spatio-temporal structure of the codex undergirds the conceptual organization of reading spaces is still important as we move forward with designing new environments for publication.

That the e-books were limited no one doubts. That newer projects are finding their way within a firmer understanding of the possibilities of electronic technology is evident. But my thesis is that the conception of these environments, from e-books to digital authoring environments for a range of purposes, could be informed by a different understanding of what traditional books are. This would be an understanding based less on a formal grasp of layout, graphic, and physical features and more on an analysis of how those format features effect the functional operation and activity of the work done by a traditional book. Or, to put it more simply, rather than think about simulating the way a book *looks*, we might consider extending the ways a book *works* as we shift into digital instruments.

A bit of review is in order as a way to begin. A glance at the literature on electronic books shows the persistence of hyperbolic claims spanning more than a decade. Stein's earlier experiment, Voyager, was an adventurous and frankly visionary early pioneer.[2] Their design of online formats for hypertext and other new media presentations of experimental works launched its "Expanded Book" in the early 1990s, before the web was in operation, using CDs and other storage devices. But Voyager finally abandoned this development, out of money and out of spirit for the task, leaving behind some exemplary prototype projects. From these ashes, and with telling residual features, Sophie, already mentioned above, has arisen.

Earlier forms, particularly CDs and the alternative reading practices of hypertext story structures, have not found large followings in the ways we earlier expected. Hypertext fiction and the once-much-sought chimera of interactive films seem like ancient models of modular chunks and links between nodes, more work than reward. The one area where branching narratives and experimental pathways have taken off dramatically is in the design of games, a field that rarely feels compelled to reference books as a point of historical or conceptual origin. The experiment to develop new reading formats would appear to have reached an impasse if we judge by continuing addictions to traditional fictional forms, or even the activity of online reading by scrolling through a single text. But of course, few of us read with such sustained linearity in a digital environment. We may read in that way for informational purposes, but not for prolonged entertainment or scholarship.

But during the same decade that hypertext fiction went the way of Kahotek, the Net has become a fixture in contemporary life. Links and hyperlinks abound. Reading along these networked structures has become a habit, like browsing a newspaper. The vision of a reconfigured reading environment has been realized, but not in the way the proponents of electronic book or story space imagined. Enthusiasm for experimental engagement with alternative structures and invention of new artistic, literary, graphic, or information forms has leveled off considerably while hypermedia have become familiar, integrated in a daily way with reading in electronic space. A disconnect exists between the windows-based experience of online reading and the e-book industry's attempt at designing a visual format that suggests an extension of the traditional book for presentation or re-presentation of materials once only avail-able in the bound codex. An even greater disjunction has existed between those designs and the conceptualization of formats suitable to the functions unique to electronic space. This is changing as new tools for assembling objects and promoting communications in virtual space are being developed. Textual, visual, graphic, navigational, and multimedia artifacts that are geographically dispersed in their original form can be aggregated in a single space for study and use, manipulated in ways that traditional means of access don't permit. The telecommunications aspect of new media allows creation of an inter-subjective, social space of shared use and exchange. Arguably, this latter is an extension of the social space of traditional scholarly or communicative exchange mainly by the change in rate, the immediacy, capacity to engage simultaneously in shared tasks or common projects. Concep-tualizing designs in response to prototypes of e-books and assessing their design limitations is useful as a start.

To begin, I would suggest that the slowness by which new formats have arisen is as much the result of conceptual obstacles as technical ones. The absence of an e-book with the same brand-recognition as Kleenex or Xerox isn't due only to the fact that the phrase "electronic document management and information display systems and spaces for inter-subjective and associative hyper-linked communication using aggregation, folksonomies, and real-time authoring and participatory editing" doesn't trip off the tongue. A stable nomenclature will no doubt emerge, and various palm-adaptation devices (Sony, IBM, etc.) are increasingly used for the display and reading of texts downloaded from a text-repository server source and kept for perusal or reference according to personal whim. But what aspects of the familiar book have any relevance for the design and use of information in this electronic environment? Are they the features that researchers such as IBM's Harold Henke refer to when they identify "metaphors" of book structure?[3] What is meant by these "metaphors"? What does the malleable electronic display of data whose outstanding characteristic is its mutability have to do with the material object known so familiarly to us as the codex book? These questions devolve towards a single core issue – what do we mean by the "idea of a book"?

A look at the designs of the graphical interfaces for e-books gives some indication of the way conventional answers to this question lead to a conceptual impasse. Ex-libris, Voyager's Expanded book, and other "superbook" and "hyperbook" formats have all attempted to simulate in flat screen space certain obvious physical character-istics familiar from traditional books. The IBM research suggested that readers "prefer features in electronic books that emulate paper book functions." Functions are not the same as formal features. The activity of page turning is not the same as the binary structure of either the two-page opening or the recto–verso relations of paper pages. But most of what is understood by a "book" in the design of "electronic books" is fairly literal simulation. For instance, a kitsch-y imitation of page drape from a central gutter is one of the striking signs of book-ness. This serves absolutely no purpose, like preserving a coachman's seat on a motorized vehicle. Icons that imitate paper clips or book marks allow the reader to place milestones within a large electronic document. As in paper formats, these serve not only for navigational purposes, but also to call attention to sections within a larger argument. The substitution of pages and volume with a slider that indicates the depth or place within the whole reinforces our necessity to understand information in a gestalt, rather than piecemeal. Finally, the reader's urge to annotate, to write into the text with responsive immediacy, has also been accommodated in electronic book designs as note-taking capabilities for producing e-marginalia have been introduced.

The many "drawbacks" of traditional books are, therefore, supposedly to be overcome by introducing into electronic ones features like a progress gauge, book-marks, spaces for annotation, search capabilities, navigation, and comments by the author. Such a list is easily ridiculed, since every feature described is already fully present in a traditional codex and, in fact, the very difficulty resides in simulating in another medium the efficient functionalities that exist in the traditional form. But other features of electronic space do add functionality – live links and real-time or frequent refresh of information. These are materially unique in digital media; even if linking merely extends the traditional reference function of bibliography or footnotes, it does so in a manner that is radically distinct in electronic space by the immediacy with which a surrogate can be called. Links either retrieve material or take the reader to that material, they don't just indicate a reference route. And the idea of rapid refresh materially changes the encoded information that constitutes a text in any state.

Date stamping and annotating the history of editions will be increasingly important aspects of the information electronic documents bear with them. The capacity to materially alter electronic surrogates, customizing actual artifacts, or, at the very least, specifying particular relations among them, presents compelling and unique opportunities.

So what possible function, beyond a nostalgic clue to the reader, do features like gutter and page drape serve in electronic space? The icon of the "book" that throws its long shadow over the production of new electronic instruments is a grotesquely distorted and reductive idea of the codex as a material object. The cover of the book that contains links and clues in the video game *Myst* is a perfect example of the pseudo-gothic, book-as-repository-of-secret-knowledge clichés that abound in the use of the codex as an icon in popular culture. Let's return to the design of electronic books for one more moment, however. If we ask what is meant by a "metaphor" in Henke's discussion and look at examples of e-book design, we see familiar formats, text/image relations, visual cues that suggest a book, and a number of other navigation devices (as per above) meant to make "use for novices" easy. The assumption that familiar forms translate into ease of use may be correct in the first iteration of electronic book-type presentations. But when we look at a table of contents, or an index, or even headers/footers or page numbers – or any of the other structuring elements of book design – it's difficult to imagine how we can consider these "metaphors" in Henke's sense. For these aren't figures of meaning, or presentations of an idea in an unfamiliar form. Quite the contrary, these are instruction sets for cognitive performance, along the lines of the assessment of cathedral spaces and memory theaters proposed by medievalist Mary Carruthers.[4] Her reassessment of the revised notion of memory theaters recast them as designs for enacting a cognitive task of remembering rather than as formal structures memorized for storage and retrieval. I would argue that as long as visual cues suggest a literal book, our expectations continue to be constrained by the idea that books are communication devices whose form has a static and formal, rather than active and functional, origin. But if we shift our approach we can begin to abstract that functional activity from the familiar iconic presentation. One place to begin this inquiry is by paying attention to the conceptual and intellectual motivations that led to these format features. From this we can extrapolate the design implications that follow for new media.

Instead of reading a book as a formal structure, then, we should understand it in terms of what is known in the architecture profession as a "program" constituted by the activities that arise from a response to the formal structures. Rather than relying on a literal reading of book "metaphors" grounded in a formal iconography of the codex, we should instead look to scholarly and artistic practices for an insight into ways the programmatic function of the traditional codex has been realized. Many aspects of traditional codex books are relevant to the conception and design of virtual books. These depend on the idea of the book as a performative space for the production of reading. This virtual space, like the e-space, or electronic space of my title, is created through the dynamic relations that arise from the activity that formal structures make possible. I suggest that the traditional book produces this virtual *e-space*, but this fact tends to be obscured by attention to its iconic and formal properties. The literal has a way with us, its graspable and tractable rhetoric is readily consumed. But concrete conceptions of the performative approach also exist. I shall turn my attention to these in order to sketch a little more fully this idea of a "program" of the codex.

We should also keep in mind that the traditional codex is as fully engaged with this "virtual" space as electronic works are. For instance, think of the contrast between the *literal* book – that familiar icon of bound pages in finite, fixed sequence – and the *phenomenal* book – the complex production of meaning and effect that arises from dynamic interaction with the literal work. My model of the phenomenal codex draws on cognitive science, critical theory, and applied aesthetics. The first two set some of the basic parameters for my discussion. Invoking "cognitive models" suggests that a work is created through interaction with a reader/viewer in a co-dependent manner. A book (whether thought of as a text or a physical object) is not an inert thing that exists in advance of interaction, rather it is produced new by the activity of each reading. This idea comports well with the critical legacy of post-structuralism's emphasis on performativity. We make a work through our interaction with it, we don't "receive" a book as a formal structure. Post-structuralist performativity is distinguished from its more constrained meaning in work like that of John Austin, for whom performative language is defined by its instrumental effect. Performativity in a contemporary sense borrows from cognitive science and systems theory in which entities and actions have co-dependent relations, rather than existing as discrete entities. Performance invokes constitutive action within a field of constrained possibilities, not only the use of fixed terms to achieve particular ends. Thus in thinking of a book, whether literal or virtual, we should paraphrase Heinz von Foerster, one of the founding figures of cognitive science, and ask "how" a book "does" its particular actions, rather than "what" a book "is."

With these reference frames in mind, I return to my original question: What features of traditional codex books are relevant to the conception and design of virtual books? My approach can be outlined as follows: (1) proceed through analysis of "how" a book "works" rather than by describing what we think a book "is"; (2) describe the "program" that arises from a book's formal structures; (3) discard the idea of iconic "metaphors" of book structure in favor of understanding the way these forms serve as constrained parameters for performance. The literal space of the book thus serves as a field of possibilities, waiting to be "intervened" by a reader. The *e-space* of the page arises as a virtual program, interactive, dialogic, dynamic in the fullest sense. Once we see the broader outlines of this program, we can extend it through an understanding of the specific functions that are part of electronic space.

Dramatic demonstration of these dynamic principles can be drawn from historical and artistic examples. An anonymous sixteenth-century painting of a book from the Uffizi Gallery collection, at first glance simply a depiction of an object, provides a vivid, if unexpected presentation of how a book *works*.[5] This image reveals a phenomenal book that arises from the material embodiment, showing its graphic elements as the means to enact dynamic functions. The book is arrayed in an odd position in the painting. Its pages, presumably vellum, fan out in an artifice of display. No book would hold this position without an elaborate device, so clearly this is a not a naturalistic depiction, but one motivated by another agenda. That singular display marks the first distinction between a realistic portrayal of an actual book, which this is not, and a conceptual investigation of a phenomenal book. This is a book whose identity is projected from its material forms, but isn't equivalent to them. The phenomenal book doesn't negate the formal properties of a physical object, quite the contrary. The phenomenal book can be envisioned as having the same

Figure 11.1 An anonymous sixteenth-century painting of a book from the Uffizi Gallery collection. Photograph: Scala/Art Resource, NY.

relation to a physical book as a musical performance of a work has to a score. The material substrate, and its formal particulars, are the instructions for that performance. In the sixteenth-century depiction, the book's manner of display exceeds the showing of literal pages in a sequence, and instead, creates an image of a full e-space of the book as a conceptual, relationally produced work.

The book in the Uffizi painting shows pages that are improbably varied. This in itself marks a move from the representation of a literal to that of a phenomenal object. A certain measure of visual unity is achieved by the fact that all the pages show the same script. We are certainly meant to imagine that this is a single object. But then the book's pages offer very varied kinds of information and graphical formats: double-columned text with a gold initial letter on black ground, musical notation on a page with a black majuscule on a gold ground, a page with interlinear rubrication that seems to stretch across the full page facing another double-columned text page in which red and black paragraphs alternate. Another page repeats elements of this format, reinforcing our expectations about the uniformity of design within a single work. The final sheet, of which we can glimpse just the lower right-hand edge, seems to bear a full-page illumination, bordered with floral motifs. A skull, the hem of a robe, a bit of architecture can be glimpsed in the edge of the image. These hold a promise never to be fulfilled, and we assume the existence of the entire page by virtue of the power of suggestion, another instance of phenomenal rather than literal representation. In fact, in this case as in the rest of these partially glimpsed openings and pages, we are offered an understanding of the relations among elements within the volume as much as of the individual parts. The suggestion of unity produced at the interplay graphical sameness and variety is just an *idea of continuity*, not its literal documentation. This is a virtual book. The literal "spaces" are shown in such a way as to create a figurative and phenomenal *e-space* of exchanges and relations. Even understanding what this book is in formal, literal terms, seems to require our being shown many of its parts in relation. Action and use are suggested by the individual elements – the musical score, place markers, the variety of textual presentations – and this suggestion is reinforced by the presentation of the volume as peculiarly suspended in movement. The improbable disposition of pages provides multiple points of view and insight. The image offers a veritable catalogue of possibilities. The painting isn't an image of *this* book, but of the many books comprised by a single work. The work flaunts Jerome McGann's assertion that a book is never "self-identical."[6] A book doesn't close on itself as a static, inert artifact between boards or covers.

The book we see in this sixteenth-century painting embodies many of the features we think of as defining the iconic image of the codex. But this idea is infused with different agendas of use that have morphed dramatically at particular historical moments under the pressures to perform different functions or meet specific needs. Roger Chartier, tracking the development of book culture, noted several crucial technological and cultural milestones.[7] The shift from scroll to codex in the second to fourth centuries and the invention of printing in the fifteenth century are possibly the two most significant transformations in the technology of book production.

Further substantive changes come with the industrialization of print production in the late eighteenth and nineteenth centuries and then with the electronic dissemination of texts. Other technological innovations mark important developments, but shifts of cultural attitude are not always coincident with technological changes. For instance, reading habits are transformed as monastic approaches are replaced by scholastic attitudes toward texts in the twelfth through fourteenth centuries bringing about dramatic changes in format. The textual apparatus and paratextual structures of indices, tables of contents, footnotes, and marginalia all emerge to enable the reading practices associated with scholastic culture. Recovering the reading practices that gave rise to these structures make them appear in a whole new light. No longer just format features, but structuring devices, they take on an active aspect.

The historian of medieval culture, Malcolm Parkes, described the way these transformations of format came about.[8] In earlier usage, books were the basis for linear, silent reading of sacred texts broken by periods of contemplative prayer. These habits gave way to the study and creation of argument as the influence of Aristotle on medieval thought brought about increased attention to rhetoric and the structure of knowledge. Readers began to see the necessity to create meta-textual structures for purposes of analysis. To facilitate the creation of arguments, heads and subheads appeared to mark the divisions of a text. Marginal commentary not only added a gloss, an authorial indication of instructions on how to read the text, but also created a summary outline in the margins of points visually buried in the linear text. Contents pages provided a condensed argument, calling attention to themes and structures and their order within the volume as a whole. The graphic devices that became conventions in this period are aspects of functional activity. They allow for arguments to be abstracted so they can be used, discussed, refuted. These elements are devices for engaging with texts in a manner radically distinct from that of reflection and prayer. Argument, not reading, is the purpose to which such works are put, and their formal features are designed to provide a reader with a schematic overview, but also with the means to use the work in rhetorical activity.

Obviously, using a book for prayer is an active engagement with the text. But the sequential, linear, reading style didn't require any extra apparatus as a guide. The development of graphical features used to provide an abstraction of the contents shows a radical change in its attitude toward knowledge. Ordered, hierarchical, with an analytical synthesis of contents, the book that arose as the instrument of scholastic *lectio* is distinct from that object which sufficed for monastic reading practices. Readers came to rely on multiple points of access and on navigational devices providing search capabilities through the meta-textual apparatuses of contents, indices, page numbers, running heads, and so on.

Parkes makes his point by contrasting a page from an early thirteenth-century manuscript of excerpted *auctoratates* with that of an early fifteenth-century page in order to trace the appearance of paratextual features. In his earlier example, the sources are noted in a graphical manner that is clumsily embedded in the overall text block lines. In the later work, the excerpts are organized alphabetically. Each section within the later book is marked by a letter that stands alone at the top of the page, and conspicuous rubrication reinforces the modeling of content with a graphical code.

The important point here is not just that format features have their origin within specific reading practices. The significant principle is relevant to all reading practices: that the visual hierarchy and use of space and color don't simply reference or reflect the existing hierarchy in a text, they make it, producing the structure through the graphical performance. Such approaches seem self-evident because they are so familiar to us as conventions. Conceptualizing the book in terms of its paratextual apparatus required a leap from literal, linear reading to the spatialized abstraction of an analytic meta-structure. Differentiating and identifying various parts of a codex went hand in hand with the recognition of separate functions for these elements. Function gives rise to form, but the form sustains activity as a program that arises from its structure.

We inherit that scholastic model, frequently oblivious of the dynamic agency of its graphic elements. We may find headers a delightful feature on a page, chapter breaks and subheads convenient for our reading in reference materials, but rarely do we shift from our notice of the graphic presence of such items to a more general observation about them as coded instructions for use. The modern table of contents abstracts the structural relations of the substance of a work into a condensed presentation. The lines of its text, and the accompanying page numbers, function as cognitive cues, pointers into the volume. The information space of a book appears as the structure of its layout. But the analytic synopses in the index and contents are organized to show something in their own right as well as to enable specialized reading tasks.

Various statistical analyses of content appeared as paratextual apparatuses, in medieval manuscripts and even their classical predecessors, sometimes motivated by the need to estimate fees (counting of lines) as much as from a studious purpose. The habit of creating commentary through marginal notes establishes a space of conversation within a single page. And the palimpsestic nature of such conversations has a rich lineage in commentaries upon sacred texts. An interwoven cultural document like the Talmud is in effect a record of directives for reading. The interpretive gloss is designed to instruct and guide, disposing the reader toward a particular understanding. By contrast, as Anthony Grafton points out, the footnote makes a demonstration of the sources on which a text has been constructed.[9] Justification and verification are the primary purpose of mustering a scholarly bibliography to the support of one's own work. Thus footnotes may occupy a humbler place, shrunk to the bottom of a page or transformed into endnotes at the finish of a section or work. Marginalia must be ready to hand, allowing the eye to take in their presence as visual adjunct if they are to be digested in tandem with the flow of the original text.

Other familiar features of the codex, such as page numbers, are linked to devices like the signature key and register list of first words on sheets. These originally functioned as instructions from printer to binder. The half-title is also an artifact of production history, having come into being with the printing press. Sheets already finished, folded, and awaiting binding needed protection on their outer layer, hence the half-title. Medieval manuscript scribes, keenly aware of the scarcity and preciousness of their vellum sheets, indicated the start of a text with a simple "Incipit" rather than waste an entire sheet on naming the work, author, or place of production.

The familiarity of conventions causes them to become invisible, and their origin within activity even more so. For instance, the complicated formal structure of a page of Euclid, printed by Ernst Ratdolt in Venice in 1482, doesn't bear conspicuous hallmarks of the processes by which its design elements have evolved. We can't recover the stages by which each of the elements in this page came to function as it does. But clearly, each element embodies decisions. The graphic forms carry information. Spacing, type size, hierarchy of titles to sections of proofs, divisions between image and text and the subdivisions therein are all structuring elements. Though not strictly semantic, these elements are the dynamic scaffolding from which the production of meaning arises and in which it is embodied. The relations among elements figure in the argument created on the page, and their origin in a step-by-step process of abstracting the rules of such arguments, codifying them into graphical forms, is visible in what appears to be a fixed and static format. The program of the Euclid pages is so complicated and conspicuous that it is still probably easier to see that it functions as an instruction sheet for dynamic production of reading than in the case of simpler-seeming pages of a classic reference or a garden-variety academic publication. I cite these less-conspicuous-seeming reference books only because the apparently unmarked seeming condition of their pages comes from their familiarity. A phenomenal book is latent in the pages of any text, and in this respect the Euclid and reference text all encode potential programs of activity. The conventions of codex format are a legacy. The metaphor of those formats, their figured presentation of meaning, is a condensation of an argument that is specific to the codex. That argument is made in material structure and graphical form as well as through textual or visual matter. Recovering the dynamic principles that gave rise to those formats reminds us that graphical elements are not arbitrary or decorative, but serve as functional cognitive guides.

This brief glance at the historical origins of familiar conventions for layout and design should also underscore the fundamental distinction between scroll and codex. The unified-seeming and very determinedly linear scroll format, in which navigation depended on markers (ribbons or strips protruding) and a capacity to gauge the volume of the roll on its handle, is striking in contrast to the flexibility and mobility of the reader's relation to information in codex format. When the paratextual features are added, the codex becomes a dynamic knowledge system, organized and structured for various routes of access. The replication of such features in electronic space, however, is based on the false premise that they function as well in simulacral form as in their familiar physical instantiation. In thinking toward a design of electronic textual instruments, we would do well to reflect on what the action is that every graphical feature can serve, as well as what informational reference it contains as part of production or reception history. But the electronic information space, I suggest, has other functionalities specific to the electronic medium, points I will touch on at the end of this piece in sketching our work on the Ivanhoe project. Even so, understanding the dynamic program of the codex is important for designing electronic work.

Artists and poets provide other conceptual understandings of the codex through their investigation of its material forms. For instance, the structure of a codex might well be grasped as a figure, as a spatialized shape with a dynamic form. The most remarkable achievement in this realm may still be that of Stéphane Mallarmé in his late-nineteenth-century vision of *Un Coup de Dès*. The graphical form of that work exploits the codex as a three-dimensional space. The relation of each page to the next accrues to create the work as a whole shape. The lines in this work, weighted by typographic style and size, hang like elements of a mobile, suspended in careful balance to each other. The paper almost disappears, as the figure of the poem rises. Mallarmé's poem offers a structuring means through which to experience the spatial form of a book. Between the original work and the interpretations to which it gives rise the process of interpretation intervenes in the potential field of the book, carving out a shape from points in relation to each other that have semantic, poetic, affective, and other dimensions to them.

By contrast, the equally striking work by OuLiPo writer Raymond Queneau, the author literally cut the pages of his 1961 Gallimard publication, *Cent Mille Milliard des Poèmes*, to provide access to the entire catalogue of lines within.[10] The physical effect of hyper-linking through these cuts is dramatic. The page surface can be delved into, connecting it to the deep space of the volume. The lines can be turned. The work is recomposed and remade by each turning. The possibilities, though not endless, are of a significantly high number, a factor of the combinatoric form. The format features actually establish parameters for performance of the work. This shifts the conceptualization from that of a poem as fixed artifact to that of a work whose existence is contingent on the active engagement of the reader. Always true, now demonstrated, this principle re-imagines the space of the book through artistic imagination, revealing the dynamic properties of the codex.

If Queneau enacts the performative potential of the physical book, contemporary book artist Brad Freeman also reveals the lie of the printed book as static artifact.[11] Shifting and contingent relations are registered on the table of contents page of Freeman's 1998 *Muzelink*, a work whose very title suggests the associative processes of artistic invention of which it is a striking example. The contents page was typeset initially at a formative stage of the project. The dummy book in which the original was bound became a journal for recording changes. The work changed through accretion, deletion, revision. The history of those changes is marked on the sheets. The prediction of the table of contents turned out to be continually subject to transformation throughout the production process. This book was not a fully formed artifact whose production merely brought it into being. The book shows the bringing into being as a highly self-conscious but emergent process which produces a printed work as a record of its making, rather than as a result. As an effect of accretion, the work suggests the continuing trajectory of linkages that keep producing the work from the book, the phenomenal e-space from the literal space.

The simultaneous existence of two kinds of spaces, phenomenal and literal, is evident in the interplay of levels of illusion in Janet Zweig's *Heinz and Judy* (1985).[12] Zweig separates the layers of spatial illusion into distinct registers, each appearing to occupy a discrete depth in relation to the flat surface of presentation of the page. Her theatrical staging within the layered text takes advantage of the dramatic potential of the page as a play of action. Where are we to locate the work in this instance? The surface of the page serves as a scrim, in an indeterminate place between projected shadow from behind, activity precipitated from above (scraps of paper laid, illusionistically, onto the page as if cut from another sheet), as a surface on which are scribbled, palimpsestic, traces of another reading. The sheets are also used to support a conventional text block, thus playing with the invisible or neutral status to which they are so often relegated. The effect of these various layers is to destabilize the sheet. No single identity can be assigned to it. The paper floats, is receptive, functions according to several codes of presentation simultaneously. And the space created is very much a virtual e-space constituted by relations among these modes and their capacity to produce effect. The reading of such a page necessarily results in a contingent work, one that uses the codex to advantage while undercutting its fixed identity.

Means of activating the codex form in imaginative ways are a favorite sport of artists making books. Innumerable devices have been engaged to demonstrate the virtual *e-space* of traditional book forms from the painting of fore-edges, the use of the gutter as a way to connect separate openings through the spine, the interconnection of elements across turnings so that the literal edge of pages is countermanded by the continuities within the structure of the work as a whole. This short list of examples could be amplified with innumerable others. Though these books are static artifacts in the conventional sense with the finite sequence of their pages fixed into the binding, they each demonstrate the way in which a book is as much a manifestation of what it *does* as what it presumably *is*. The distinction that supposedly exists between print and electronic books is usually characterized as the difference between static and inter- active forms. But a more useful distinction can be made between two ontologies – active and passive modes – that are relevant across media. Interactivity is not a function of electronic media. The capacity of a literal book to be articulated as a virtual dynamic space is exhaustible, while any attempt at reducing a work to its literal static form is probably almost impossible.

Media do matter, however, and the specific properties of electronic technology and digital conditions allow for the continual transformation of artifacts at the most fundamental level of their materiality – their code. The data file of an electronic document can be continually reconfigured. And an intervening act brings a work into being in each instance, operating on the field of potentialities. In digital files we can take advantage of the capacity of electronic instruments to mark such changes rather than merely registering them within the space of interpretation. In addition, two other functions mentioned above are given specific extension within electronic space: aggregation of documents (as documents and as data) and creation of an inter-subjective exchange. The calling of surrogates through a "portal" in electronic space (as pointed out by Joseph Esposito) not only allows materials from dispersed collections to be put into proximity for study and analysis.[13] The ability to resize, rescale, alter, or manipulate these documents provides possibilities that traditional paper-based documents simply don't possess. (Looking at a manuscript scanned in raked light, enlarging it until the fibers of the paper show, is a different experience from handling an autographic work in most special collections.) The electronic space engages these technological mediations of the information in a surrogate. But electronic space serves as a site of collaboration and exchange, generative communication in an inter-subjective community that is integral to knowledge production. Information, as Paul Duguid and John Seely Brown so clearly pointed out,[14] gains its value through social use, not through inherent or abstract properties. The virtual e-space we envision takes all of these features, themselves present in many aspects of the traditional codex, but often difficult to grasp clearly, and makes them evident. All those traces of reading, of exchange, or of new arrangements and relations of documents, or expressions of the shared and social conditions in which a text is produced, altered, received can be made evident within an electronic space. These very real and specific features of virtual space can be featured in a graphical interface that acknowledges the codex and traditional document formats as a point of reference, but conceives of this new format quite distinctly.

I'll conclude with a few notes on our recent attempts to conceptualize the design of just such a space in our Ivanhoe project. In thinking about this as an electronic tool for critical studies, we have intent to link these concepts with a functional design for their presentation. Linking identity to activity has been crucial in that process, so that the already several-times repeated theme here of replacing the identity of what a book *is* with what it *does* carries through into electronic space. The actions of calling a text, of declaring an edition, of creating a space for interpretation, of reflecting individually, and of intersubjective engagement with materials and a community are all essential to the act of interpretation. We begin with the notion of a discourse field, a domain of references and materials that form the productive ground from which a work emerges. This requires a very different presentation within an interface than simply creating simulacral bookmarks (that simulate their conventional form) or hyperlinked footnotes (that conjure a surrogate in record time). Neither call attention to the subjective nature of the interpretive act, even though both are instrumental-seeming devices for access or navigation. The real effect of such devices is to create a stream of relations.

Individual subjectivity, the personal act of interpretive reading, is evident in this space of configured connections. The mechanical efficiency of bringing a text or document onto a screen space isn't merely an act of technologized communication, but is able to be seen and marked as an interpretive act. The dynamic action encoded in a codex's program of text and paratext isn't merely a means of interconnecting static elements. That interpretive act, the creation of what I keep referring to as the phenomenal, virtual *e-space* of the codex, produces a work in each iteration. Making that fact evident requires vivid, graphic demonstration of what such a virtual *e-space* is as an emergent work, as the effect of interpretation. The capacity of electronic media to record and display reception histories, to produce them as an ongoing feature of a document, may prove to be the single most significant feature distinguishing e-books from their print precedent. An interface that creates a platform for interpretive acts to be noticed as such, called to our attention as performance. The idea is to mark the shift from the conception of books as artifacts, or documents as vehicles for delivery of content, and instead demonstrate the living, dynamic nature of works as produced by interpretive acts.

This brings me back to *Sophie* and Collex, their specific capabilities and designs. Sophie's authoring environment borrows from the modular sequence of page structures. Each screen is equivalent to an opening in a book. The software includes animation and real-time actions, borrowing the basics of Flash-type animation (elements, timelines, frames, and a library) in a "lite" version. Sophie documents look like HTML pages, whether sequenced or linked, and the robust character of the project permits it to be useful for authoring born-digital documents that incorporate time-based media or effects in a fairly intuitive interface. *Sophie* is a multimedia composition space that is meant to be as easy to use as a word processing program, and it bundles what have been rather more industrial-level skills into a usable format. Its strength is that it offers a suite of production tools for a non-technical user, familiar with special effects in the graphics and text universe and in need of an affordable and powerful application. Costs of licensing and use are minimal with *Sophie*, compared to the overhead on industry products from Macromedia or Adobe, since it was created with foundation backing and sponsorship specifically for educational use. As a tool, *Sophie* is itself interactive, that is, it produces iterative documents through activities that materially alter the text. The documents it produces can be interactive in the old sense, artifacts that have multiple options or special effects activated through use.

The Collex tool is being designed to facilitate online collections, exhibits, and publishing. It makes use of: aggregation of information (through data processing features like folksonomies and tag clouds); a networked collection (in which the objects are provided with Collex-specific metadata); a community of participants whose collections have varying degrees of openness and access; and high-level search capabilities (facilitated by Lucene to work with specific features in existing metadata of Collex objects as well as to perform more broad-based searches). Collex's design is born digital, which is to say, it uses interface features such as sliders, automated list generation, tag cloud hierarchies marked graphically, that are all enabled by data processing and interactivity. It is meant to support a community of commentary (in its current, initial application in the NINES project, the Networked Infrastructure for Nineteenth Century Electronic Scholarship, this is specifically a professional scholarly community with peer-review requirements, but those are imposed for this particular community and not a requirement of Collex's use) and exchange. Materials in Collex have to have specific metadata, and Collex can't freely acquire objects from the web (*Sophie* can). In that sense, Collex works within established collections and boundaries, while *Sophie* is eclectic and free-ranging. Published Collex documents can be produced in HTML, XML, and be put into RSS feeds. A Collex document can be viewed as a series of "pages" or in scroll form, with text/image elements present as live links. A facsimile manuscript image in a Collex document can be blown up and studied in detail. Collex objects collect commentary from many sources, and the commentary on them accretes.

The functions that digital technology affords more readily than print media are those of accretion (and processing) of data, aggregation (pulling things together in virtual space that are either separated in physical space or don't exist in physical space), real-time and time-based work, and community interactions in multi-authored environments. But the iterative aspect of digital work fostered by multiple-author environments is also a crucially distinctive feature. Developing a graphical code for representing these functions in an analytic and legible semiotics of new media will still take some time. *Ivanhoe* is one attempt in this direction, because it was meant to abstract and schematize information in diagrammatic form. Other information visualizations lie ahead, and the conventions for linking functionality and format are emerging.

Conclusion? The pernicious effect of introducing a new technology is that proponents of the invention tend to mis-characterize older forms. One wonders if typographers in the mid-fifteenth century said "script" with the same knowing tone, slight curl in the upper lip, smug with the secure sense that their metal faces were a superior invention over the hand-drawn efforts of traditional scribes. The balance sheet of history shows no such clear division among accounts. Writing persists, to this day, with its intimacy and immediacy, while print forms and other mass production technologies continue to carve up the space of communication according to an ever-more-complex division of ecological niches. Books of the future depend very much on how we meet the challenge to understand what a book is and has been.

The idea of "the book" guiding design of e-books has been a commonplace, grotesquely reductive and unproductive. No single book exists, so no "idea" of "the" book could be produced in any case. The multiplicity of physical structures and graphic conventions are manifestations of activity, returned to book form as conventions because of their efficacy in guiding use. The notion of a metaphor applied to an element like a table of contents is highly misleading. This is not a metaphor at all, but a program, a set of instructions for performance. By looking to scholarly work for specific understanding of varieties of attitudes towards the book as literal space and a virtual *e-space*, and to artists and poets for evidence of the way the spaces of a book work, we realize that the traditional codex is also, in an important and suggestive way, already virtual. But also, that the format features of virtual spaces of e-space, electronic space, have yet to encode conventions of use within their graphical forms. As that happens, we will witness the conceptual form of virtual spaces for reading, writing, and exchange take shape in the formats that figure their functions in layout and design.

NOTES

1 *Sophie*:   <http://www.futureofthebook.org/
content/Mellon.pdf>. Accessed March 17,
2006. Collex: <http://www.nines.org/about/
Nowviskie-Collex.pdf>. Accessed March 17,
2006.

2 Voyager references, including a discussion of
the history of the e-book, came from a site no
longer working, accessed November 20,
2004: <http://web.signet.com.sg/~abanergi/
sect3.htm>. However, current information
on Bob Stein and his work on the future
of the book can be found at: <http://www.
futureofthebook.org/blog/about.html>.
Accessed March 26, 2007.

3 Henke, H. A. <http://www.chartula.com/
0972786007_toc.pdf>. Accessed February
15, 2004.

4 Carruthers, M. (1998). *The Craft of Thought*.
Cambridge: Cambridge University Press.

5 Anonymous oil painting, Uffizi Gallery, Florence, Italy, encountered on a visit there in 2001.

6 McGann, J. (2001). *Radiant Textuality*. New
York: Palgrave.

7 Chartier, R. (1995). *Forms and Meanings*. Philadelphia: University of Pennsylvania Press.

8 Parkes, M. B. (1976). "The Influence of the
Concepts of *Ordinatio* and *Compilatio* on the
Development of the Book." In J. J. G. Alexander
and M. T. Gibson (Eds.). *Medieval Learning and
Literature*. Oxford: Clarendon, pp. 115–41. See
also Avrin, L. (1991). *Scribes, Scripts and Books*.
Chicago: American Library Association and
the British Library; Smith, M. M. (1994). "The
Design Relationship between the Mss. and the
Incunable." In R. Meyers and M. Harris (Eds.).
A Millennium of the Book. Delaware: Winchester;
Febvre, L., and H.-J. Martin (1997). *The Coming
of the Book*. London: Verso; McMurtrie, D.
(1943). *The Book, the Story of Printing and Book-
making*. New York: Dorset.

9 Grafton, A. (1997). *The Footnote*. Cambridge,
MA: Harvard University Press.

10 Queneau, R. (1961). *Cent Mille Milliards de
Poèmes*. Paris: Gallimard.

11 Freeman, B. (1999). *MuzeLink*. New York:
Varicose Productions.

12 Zweig, J. (1985). *Heinz and Judy*. Rochester:
Visual Studies Workshop Press.

13 Esposito, J. "The Processed Book." At First
Monday: <http://www.firstmonday.org/issues/
issue8_3/esposito/index.html>.   Accessed
February 17, 2004.

14 Brown, John Seely, and Paul Duguid (2000).
The Social Life of Information. Cambridge, MA:
Harvard Business School Press.

12

Handholding, Remixing, and the Instant Replay: New Narratives in a Postnarrative World

Carolyn Guertin

"We live in the age of the instant replay..." (Marshall McLuhan, "Art as Survival in the Electric Age" [1973]: 218)

Digital narrative is a battleground. The digital is granular, molecularized, particular. Narrative, on the other hand, has an arching, linear trajectory that pulls us along with it. The two are at war with each other as the drive for fragmentation threatens to shatter the rhythmic ebb and flow of the narrative impulse. Yet perhaps, as the adage says, opposites do attract, for the quest for narrative – even in such a hostile environment – is a prevailing human concern. What passes for narrative in the new born-digital storytelling forms is hyperactive, postmodern, postdramatic, self-reflexive, and repetitive. Instead of emulating the act of reading, what we perform in these spaces is a visual task of browsing. It is the act of pattern recognition in a spatialized form. As a result, the whole concept of "story" has been transformed by its migration into the spaces of digital media. The interactive or performative nature of the new media alters how and why we read. In the intervening years since the electronic hyperlink was born, many new innovations have continued to transform the nature of storytelling space and our expectations of it. Some exemplary emergent forms have arrived, including interactive fiction, narrative computer games, responsive environments, podcasting, and tactile and wireless interfaces, and we can see them as indicators of present and future trends.

To understand where we are going though, sometimes we first need to take a look at where we have been. In 1967 a revolutionary new way of seeing was introduced to televised sports: the instant replay (Schoenherr). Media guru and visionary Marshall McLuhan was so enthralled by this effect that he dubbed ours "the age of the instant replay" (1973: 218). The replay was revolutionary because of the way it spatialized time-based events and, for the first time, allowed the viewer to derive the meaning of an event without having lived the experience (McLuhan, 1973: 219). A kind of flashback, it foregrounded the notion of seeing again or of recognizing the familiar in the new. McLuhan dubbed this "pattern recognition" (1965: 63) in sympathy with the ability exhibited by artificial intelligences to identify voices or visual repetitions. The idea of seeing again or revisiting the place of known moments is integral to storytelling as much as it is to the new kinds of narrative that are emerging within digital culture.

As the fluidity of multi-linear narrative forms allow the reader or browser greater and greater freedom to replay a text, the more the browser returns to her recollections of the intertwining threads of the story. She follows links back to earlier readings to construct a narrative from the fragmentary nature of the literary text. Like the instant replay, the return to see a familiar passage in a text a second or third time alters our understanding of the meaning of the whole. This is not pastiche, which merely celebrates or reminds us of an earlier telling. Like the instant replay, in the digital narrative revisiting passages is, according to N. Katherine Hayles,

> a reshaping, a reconfiguration that changes what the text means precisely because what it means has already been established in the reader's mind. Rereading unsettles as much as it settles, an insight further emphasizing the exfoliating multiplicity of hypertext narrative. Given this multiplicity, it is not surprising that hypertext narrative also leads to a different sense of time than one that follows a more straight-forwardly linear progression. (1997: 574)

While Hayles is specifically concerned with the literary form called hypertext, rereading or replaying – revisioning – exposes our earlier perspectives on and assump-tions about the time of a textual event in any digital literary experience, and, by doing so, resituates us and it in place and space. An earlier hypertext theorist, Michael Joyce, sees rereading as actually forming another space in the continuum of the text: a theoretical one (1997: 582). Such is the webbed nature of new digital narratives: the browser not only becomes a part of the text, but the act of re/seeing it does too.

Digital narratives can take many forms including the aforementioned hypertext, networked art, mobile computing, and immersive virtual reality installations. What links these works of diverse technologies, motivations, and materials is the presence of the computer writ large as the medium of production, performance, storage, and distribution, and with the ever-constant notion of return or revisitation. Or to restate the obvious: repetition. The browser as she wanders these works is required to retrace her steps. Peggy Phalen notes in the context of theatrical performance that absolute repetition is simply not possible and that reversible time as a result is a fraught concept (1993: 127). Representation can never perfectly reproduce the real, she argues, for there is always a gap between them. Physicist Ilya Prigogine expanded the perspective of quantum mechanics in the same way, arguing that not only is time *not* reversible, but the repetition of an event – what he calls the "second time" of an event – is always a new and unique occurrence (Phalen 1993: 127). In our performance of these works, we can return to the same moment, but it is always a revisitation, and our experience is different because it is informed by our memory of past visits. These works require a peripatetic engagement that keeps bringing us back in contact with our earlier gestures and movements in space and time. A hypertext like Michael Joyce's *Reach*, for instance, keeps hands and gestures always in mind on a thematic level as we move through a space of saturated hyperlinking where every word is a doorway to somewhere else. Shelley Jackson's hypertext novel *Patchwork Girl, Or A Modern Monster* requires us to enter each section of the text through "her cut": a diagram evoking cuts of meat that form a palimpsest to Mary Shelley's unborn female *Frankenstein* monster's tale, sliced and diced for the digital browser in a fractured space-time. Another part of the text has us enter into the monster's thoughts and the voices of her unruly body parts' previous owners through a phrenological diagram of her competing subjectivities.

In a similar vein, Juliet Davis's web-based Flash work *Pieces of Herself* explores the body in pieces through the use of an architectural metaphor. The aforementioned parts are divided up between domestic and public spaces – the shower, bedroom, outside, kitchen, living room, office, and Main Street – and linked together by voices that remix common sayings, motherly platitudes, banal phone messages, pop songs, religious vows, the American national anthem, office gossip, and a wide variety of side effects. Dragging and dropping portable items (including a fetus, Groucho glasses, germs, a vibrator, and a cauliflower) from these environments releases dialogues on consumerism, feminist politics, and other situated issues relevant to women's lives and domestic space. Woman's body becomes simultaneously both domestic and public space being remixed and spatialized for purposes of navigation.

Marek Walczak and Martin Wattenberg in their online work *Apartment* also use an architectural metaphor to explore social relations, but their spaces are filled with the interconnections of language rather than bodies. Inspired by the ancient visual Art of Memory's use of architectural forms as spaces that are navigated by the mind, the program constructs two-dimensional virtual rooms as the interactor types. The floor plan grows in response to these spatial relationships in language. So, for example, words relating to food preparation like "cut" or "chop" would create a kitchen, "plate" or "spoon" create a dining room, words about hygiene create a bathroom, outdoor objects like "tree," "sun," "rainbow," or "street" create a window, and so on. The authors explain, "The architecture is based on a semantic analysis of the viewer's words, reorganizing them to reflect the underlying themes they express. The apartments are then clustered into buildings and cities according to their linguistic relationships" ("About"). You can also view these floor plans collectively in an assortment of categories that includes vision, motion, body, work, group, truth, story, glamour, change, food, intimacy, and secrecy, pointing and clicking to pull up individual rooms. Or you can view your own or others' creations as three-dimensional visual models and sonic space which you can navigate through a VRML-based interface. This is an extremely sophisticated spatial narrative. If you select "story" you can pull up an assortment of tales that are rendered visually on the floor plan. One such that I selected mapped out a "story" of "Tim" typed many times floating in a circle in the dining room, and "Shea" in multiple incarnations in the living room. There is a definite narrative impulse here, and we can construct a story of isolation and the failure of communication (or one of anticipation, suspense, reunion, etc.) out of it, but in order to do so it requires us to insert ourselves into the space of the text and actively fill in the gaps.

This altered sense of the temporal and spatial is born of a unique or customized path through a digital narrative as a metatext of our reading. The more the text emphasizes our own displaced visual orientation, dislocation in time, and our sense of information overload, the more aware we are of the flesh and the bones and the individual cells of a narrative's complementarities, echoes and returns. One of the most profound trans-formations of the nature of narrative along with everything else in the digital revolution may also be one of the most visible. For perhaps the first time since the arrival of the vernacular media – the realm of the curiosity cabinet and the scrapbook, the happy snap and the home movie – professional standards of production are within reach of anyone who has access to the tools of creation. Hand in glove with this transformation comes the rise of Remix Culture, and customizable (or personal) media.

Five years after the birth of the instant replay, in 1972, musical engineer Tom Moulton introduced remixing into disco music to create the 12″ single or EP. The new technologies that fractured music into multiple tracks – isolating, for instance, keyboard and vocals – allowed Moulton to manipulate individual musical threads, including adjusting the volume and deleting or adding tracks, to create a true extended play clubbing experience. Moulton foregrounded the rhythmic elements of the sixteen- or twenty-four-track master tapes designed for radio broadcast and private listening to enhance performative pleasures on the dance floor (Manovich 2005). The digitization of music has further enabled and transformed this process, replacing tracks with modular chunks that can be sampled, deleted, or altered far more easily. The concept of original authorship (who is the composer in such a work?) gets lost in these musical manipulations in the same way that authorial control is loosened when a browser uses Walczak and Wattenberg's words or random narrative fragments in any digital text Lego-like to construct her own story out of a mass of narratological components. In Jackson's *Patchwork Girl*, for instance, we not only get the monster telling her own story and speaking for her mother, Mary Shelley, but the text is colonized by remixed passages from literary theorists like Jacques Derrida and by jumbled sections of its two main mother intertexts, *Frankenstein* and L. Frank Baum's *Patchwork Girl of Oz*. It was in this very drive for personal and personalizable narrative that the first commercially successful hypertext narrative was born. Michael Joyce enlisted Jay David Bolter to assist him in creating a software (*StorySpace*) that would produce a novel that changed every time it was read. While the reality they devised was less complex than what he had hoped for (and, as may seem surprising now, almost exclusively textual), the concepts of personal or customizable media, connectivity, and instant access were ideas whose time had come.

Derrick de Kerckhove says "hypertextuality means interactive access to anything from anywhere" (1997: xxvii), which bears a particular resemblance to Thomas Pynchon's definition of paranoia in *Gravity's Rainbow*: the realization that everything is interconnected. But hypertext is, de Kerckhove continues, like digitization, a "new condition of content production," and so "hypertextuality is therefore the new condition of content storage and delivery" (1997: xxviii). The significance of this implementation of hypertextual principles on the World Wide Web in particular is the unprecedented scope – it is global (1997: xxviii): "The principle of hypertextuality allows one to treat the web as the extension of the contents of one's own mind. Hypertext turns everyone's memory into everyone else's and makes of the web the first worldwide memory" (1997: 79).[1] This has significant consequences for the new digital narratives, for the same must be said of an electronic text, which can be navigated in a potentially infinite number of ways, providing original but complementary experiences for each interactor. Of course, our subjectivities are our own, but the text is communal, and our point of becoming is both informational and experiential.

Our point of becoming is the site of information storage *and* retrieval. Hypertextuality points, de Kerckhove says, toward the possibilities for a single global archive – one giant information storage and retrieval site, a giant Borgesian narrative composed of all possible narratives, a silicon Library of Alexandria of inconceivable magnitude. It points toward the possibility of pan-connectivity. Here is Pynchon's paranoia to be sure, but what electronic *fiction* suffers from by design, as opposed to these informational archives, is access. Not too little, but too much. It is submerged in noise. No information can exist without disinformation, Paul Virilio says (1995; and more and more the two are in fact indistinguishable), and the complementarity of the electronic novel in space and time requires us to continually exist in a state of reorientation in relation to the noise of the (flash)mob. Where hyperthought equals the speed of mind and memory in these story spaces, we are perpetually off balance and drifting, or leaping, otherwhere in space and time. Data overload functions to keep us perpetually at the point of becoming, holds us suspended in a single instant in what Paul Virilio calls *trajectivity*, a dynamic state between the perspectives of the subjective and the objective (1997: 24).

The very notions of public and private are being eroded in our technological age. In "Blogging Thoughts," Torill Mortensen and Jill Walker identify the eighteenth-century salon as something that "existed on the borderline between the private and the public; it was situated in private homes, but part of the public sphere being the site of the performance that was the salon-experience" (2002: 257). Similarly, they say, blogs, which unite conversation with the clarity of print,

> stand where the salon did between private and public. A blog is written by an individual and expresses the attitude and conviction of its writer; it is strictly subjective though not necessarily intimate. This doesn't stop it from being in the public domain, and being concerned about questions which are in the domain of public authority. Each individual can use weblogs as he or she feels fit, there is no tyranny of news values to decide what is worth writing about or, as the term is: what is worth blogging. (2002: 258)

The ubiquity of the web has consistently eroded this gap, for there is no notion of public and private on the Net at all. It is all simultaneously public and private. The cell phone, wearable computing, and the podcast (the personal broadcasting of multimedia files over the web) have taken this still further to the point where we are always immersed in information space.

The concept and practice of private space was born with the printed book. Prior to public education and widespread literacy, all reading was done in public and aloud. As the book became an affordable commodity, however, reading was translated into a private, silent act. In the same way that noise was born of the technological age, so silence and private space bloomed behind the innovation of glass windows. R. Murray Schafer says:

> The glazed window was an invention of great importance for the soundscape, framing external events in an unnatural phantom-like "silence." The diminution of sound transmission, while not immediate and occurring only gradually with the thickening of glazing, not only created the notion of a "here" and a "there" or a "beyond," but also introduced a fission of the senses. (1998: 212)

When there were no windows to close, the community was invited in to listen; it was enclosed sensory space with its glass barriers that created a need for silence and privacy. de Kerckhove argues that books in the same manner created the sense of public and private space in terms of constructs of the "self" (1995: 206). The interior world housed our "private" self and our "innermost" thoughts and privileged subjective and introspective thoughts and sliced our senses up into separate units. The externalized or public media, however – radio and television, film, the internet, and the World Wide Web – allow us to participate in a kind of "collective imagination and collective thinking" (de Kerckhove 1995: 206) while simultaneously merging our senses in private space. We have a new awareness now in the Information Age of how the private informs the public and vice versa. They do not overwrite each other, but form a dialectical relationship. The podcast, like the blog, is just such a blending of the public and private. Networked or hypertextual thinking engenders (usually virtual) communities (although sites like Friendster and MySpace are changing that too). In the digital narrative, the browser gains entry into the innermost thoughts of a narrator, sharing her privacy and intimacy as she explores, but this is also a collective text available to multiple readers and readings and varied forms of sensory engagement. It is a way of splicing each browser's voice in with the narrator's own, but without making any of us the author of the work.

As we leave the age of mass production and private space behind in favor of this new time dominated by the instant replay, digital sampling, and modular remixability, it is apparent that we are becoming our own authors, readers, and publishers. Michael Joyce, Carolyn Guyer, and the other authors of *The Mola Project* (a text with total linking that becomes a many-layered quilted surface for the browser to navigate) observe that in hypertext fiction: "The reader is the structure, the builder, and the architect, and in this creation, it has created life. The burden of clarification is lightened because there is less of a need for clear-cut answers. The answers are a product of creation" (15c). Interactive authorship and personal publishing was a trend started not by hypertext but by xerography (patented in the 1940s, it did not become popular until the technology was perfected in 1959) (McLuhan 1966: 83). That tiny snowball became an avalanche with the introduction of desktop publishing by Aldus PageMaker for the Macintosh in 1985, and hypertext linking and other digital technologies accelerated the process still further. If anything, the remix factor of hypertexts and newer kinds of digital literary forms over-determine the organic structure, for the author has to assume that we will not visit the whole of the text in our travels, and so has to prepare for every contingency – as in life. The implications of the modular and customizable nature of digital literature as integral features are potentially enormous not just for our consumption habits, but in terms of everything from poetry to politics to pedagogy. This personal revolution includes the likes of blogs, podcasting, gmail, flickr, Google maps, Wikipedia, and YouTube as the harbingers of the coming new wave called Web 2.0. The database, variable content, iTunes, and personalized iSkins are some of the most telling hallmarks of how cultural interfaces are customized to mediate us in every aspect of our lives. And, the new digital literary texts foreground the personalized, experiential dimension since they are works that we must travel through.

It is perhaps not so surprising in that light, then, that world-creation becomes one of the authorial roles that digital media designers undertake. Diana Reed Slattery's *Glide* and Charlotte Davies' *Osmose* are two particularly interesting ones. *Glide* is a world made up of several parts. It has a digital game interface called the *Collabyrinth*, downloadable fonts, an interactive visual lexicon resembling a spider's web, and a print-based novel called *The Maze Game*, which explains the rules of the world and language to us. Subtitled "An Interactive Exploration of Visual Language," we must learn the embodied language of Glide in order to understand the sensory nature of the different kinds of minds (or states of consciousness) required for playing the game and navigating the maze game itself. Slattery divides narrative, space, and media, producing different kinds of environments for different kinds of telling. Her story is *told* in *The Maze Game,* a print-based novel, but the game is *played* online, as the browser becomes a player by learning the Glide language, evoking the oracle and "dancing" the discursive spaces of the maze.

Glide is the history of a future built on the ruins of the space of our present. The matrices that crisscross this text are elaborate and three-fold. The overarching web is the sentient computer program and cultural archive, the Outmind called Óh-T'bee, who interconnects the society through time and space. The underlying web is the intricately networked web of blue water lilies that provide the pollen that was both the impetus for the Game, the Dance of Death, and the origin of its language, Glide. The third level is the intricate interweaving of social connections forged by the mortal dancers through time and space as they engage and interact with the Outmind, the lilies, the immortal spectators, called Lifers, the Maze or game board, and each other. These three networks are intricately interwoven to produce a complex social ecology: a web of cultural, political, and material life. As both computer matrix and lily pond are rendered as rhizomatic, topological systems, the organic network is revealed to be that which interconnects the social relations surrounding the Game and its players – just as the four kinds of Dancers are genetically engineered so they and their histories are intricately interconnected. Each Dancer knows the history of the victorious Dancers of her set intimately. It is when one of the Dancers is revealed to be of unknown origins that chaos is let loose in the system. As interactors in the experience, we too must learn how to think in Glide, that is, learn how to embody the lily-mind or the fourth level of consciousness enabled by the pollen of the lily matrix that governs this world.

In the novel, the language of the lily is for the Glides multifaceted, acting as "a navigational system, signaling to each other over the watery habitat of the giant blue water lilies whose pollen they harvested; as a poetic, gestural language; [and] as a secret code":

> The game that defines their culture – the Dance of Death – is played on mazes of glyphs. Game moves and strategy are described in Glide terminology. Composition and translation in Glide is considered to exercise the cognitive function of making metaphor, which Glides believe increases the connectivity between minds, internally and socially, and which they link to creative thinking in general. ("Architecture")

The four minds – island-mind, gut-mind, sea-mind, and lily- or Glide-mind – are a means of cognitively navigating the sensory field of the body in space-time and performing the refusal of the Immortality Virus that pollutes their world. As Dancers, the characters must inhabit an embodied present moment, not as means of denying or exiting history, but as a way of embracing their sensory interface with the world. *The Maze Game* is also concerned with an evolutionary transformation. Rather than the old patriarchal binary system, the lily has an agenda to heighten the "sensory modalities" ("Emergent Forms" website) between the four "minds" of human cognition. The island-mind is the domain of reason, logic, and consciousness. The gut- or body-mind is the realm of the unconscious and reflex reactions of embodied response. The sea-mind is the immersive imaginative state of creativity, metaphorical engagement, and the world of dreams. The final mind is the new level of our cognitive interface with the world. The lily-mind is the hub or central node: it is the mind of connection, and the interface of connectivity between all four minds. It is the space-time dynamic in the system that is not only in a constant state of flux, but that allows us to make sense of the wave-like flux of the discourse network(s) swirling all around us. The Game world is in trouble, and like the last Glide Dancer, T'Ling, we must learn to incorporate all four minds to dance the Game. Excess choice leads to freefall – or nomadic voyaging – through the narrative spaces. The result of this random function is a sense of dislocation in space, time, and language.

Charlotte Davies also set out to create a new world that requires us to move and acquire, not a new state of consciousness, but a new set of navigational skills. Created by this Montreal artist and software developer at the cost of $1,000,000 CAD in 1995, breathtakingly beautiful *Osmose* and its companion space *Ephémère* (1998) are fluid, ethereal worlds that require full-body immersion as a mean of navigation. Hands-free environments, they are peopled with transparent objects and landscapes. In a conscious rejection of the controlling nature of the phallic joystick, the user interface was inspired by the experience of scuba diving and requires the immersant to use her breath to navigate through several interconnected worlds: drawing in a breath produces ascent, an exhale descent, and lateral movements allow for changes in direction (Davies 2003: 329). As a navigator of this new world, we are the living membrane – or the hymen – between the virtual and the real, between time and space. As body theorist Amelia Jones has observed, the hymen is both a joining and a barrier. It marks "the psychical openness to otherness" and "marks the interconnectedness of mind and body (both inside and outside, a liminal border within the self)" (Jones 207). The work itself is divided by the interactor's experience and that of her spectators as they observe her *in medias res*. An audience gathers in public gallery space that fills with the sound of the interactor's actions and vicariously shares the journey in real time projected in stereoscopic video on a screen. But, at the same time, the audience is always also aware of the corporeal immersant herself gesturing at their backs – an otherworldly silhouette back projected on a screen as she physically and psychically explores virtual spaces. Davies claims that: "The use of this shadow silhouette alongside with the real-time video projection serves to poeticize the relationship between the immersive body and the work, drawing attention to the body's role as ground and medium for the experience" (Davies 2003: 329). Drawing us in as a player, the immersant and her split subject shadow are two displaced subjects who experience their environments through disjunctures in time and space.

The Breathing Wall, an interactive narrative on CD-ROM by British novelist Kate Pullinger, Stephen Schemat, and babel, is the flipside of Davies' breathing apparatus. Instead of using breath to navigate, its interactive interface monitors the browser's breathing in response to the frightening events that transpire in this prison-based ghost story, and responds accordingly. This HyperTrance Fiction Matrix is an experimental, responsive software that performs the ultimate reversal and *reads* the interactor. Drawing the browser into the story space instead of making her body the craft of exploration, *The Breathing Wall* is an extremely effective story. If there is a drawback to it, it is the way that the story itself is confined within the bars and walls of a linear narrative framework. The browser is locked in a linear trajectory, policing herself as she submits to auditory surveillance as she pages through the narrow corridors of the text.

The author of *The Impermanence Agent*, developed by Noah Wardrip-Fruin, Adam Chapman, Brion Moss, and Duane Whitehurst, is truly non-linear and nonhuman. The text itself, the Agent, derives storytelling materials from the contents of a person's web browsings to allow it to tell its own story. By rifling through the cache of a user's browser, it transforms itself into *The Agent*'s retelling of a user's interests. Strangely enough though, the Agent is not interactive. Instead, it seems to have a mind of its own; it extracts information from visited websites and adds its own concerns as well, displaying the content unique to each user's foraging. Its contents replay again and again, faded, altered, and adjusted, always running on the desktop whenever the browser window is open. Virus-like, *The Agent* steps in between your machine's http requests and the web and delivers its catch, hauled in while surfing by proxy, to the browser. From there the Agent inserts images and text drawn from webpages that revolve around its own self-reflexive prevailing concerns – "impermanence, hypermedia, preservation, agency" (Wardrip-Fruin et al.) – onto other pages the user has surfed. More importantly, the Agent also "writes back," inserting its own story into the user's movements over the course of five days: "They are *The Agent's* annotations, *The Agent's* mark, in the scrapbook of the user's experience" (Wardrip-Fruin et al.). Its aesthetic engagement is what Camille Utterback calls "ambient interactivity": that is to say, the work is autonomous and freestanding, but the more the browser interacts with it the richer the experience (Chapman, "A Well-Dressed Agent," in Wardrip-Fruin et al.). *The Agent* opens several windows on the browser's desktop, but it is the right frame that contains *The Agent's* story. It holds images, stories, and fictions, particularly sepia-toned family photos and cemetery statuary. As the work moves through a browser's own space and time on the web, more and more of the linearity in the original text is leached away, and a collage-like narrative takes its place. While this all seems like a storytelling engine, in fact what *The Agent* does is use metatagging to simulate life and a mind of its own. Its metatags select less frequently used words, give preference to nouns, and rank words in terms of importance. By this means, the browser's concerns become *The Agent's* own story.

Will Wright, the original developer of the incredibly successful games *SimCity* and *The Sims*, is developing a new game called *Spore* that takes narrative interaction to a whole new level.[2] Where other narratives have a personal or customizable aspect, *Spore* has user-generated content. Seen by many as the greatest game yet invented, it allows an interactor to create species as the system procedural generates the ecosystems they inhabit, and then allows that species to interact across the network with others created by other players. Starting with a single-celled organism, the user can modify its shape and abilities with each subsequent generation. The computer extracts probable movements and lifestyles from each change in body shape and attributes, so that the organism adapts to its environment as it evolves toward intelligent behavior – intelligence being marked by a species' ultimate culmination in space travel. It is a game that embodies the principles of "teleological evolution," a belief that there is a goal or master plan in nature's design:

> *Spore's* main innovation portends to be Wright's use of procedural generation for many
> of the components of the game, providing vast scope and open-endedness. Wright said,
> "I didn't want to make players feel like Luke Skywalker or Frodo Baggins. I wanted
> them to be like George Lucas or J.R.R. Tolkien." (*Wikipedia*)

Like postdramatic theater, which leaves the dramatic tradition behind and pushes the audience member into becoming the performative centre of a multi-perspectival theatrical event, Wright's *Spore* enables us to become a god-like author of a life form and its environment. Once world-creation is possible, who is the author of such an organism and its story? Where, as we saw, in hypertext the reader created the life in the narrative, in *Spore* the interactor creates both narrative itself and the life that lives it. It may in fact be a postnarrative game. If postdramatic theater shifts the focus onto performance, postnarrative shifts the emphasis onto the interactor's experiential or performative dimension in the storytelling experience. In short, a postnarrative game entrusts the user with generating her own story.

When we perform our interaction with other kinds of media instantiated as art forms – with a book or a television, for example – we are very aware of the fact that we insert ourselves into it as its audience, and that we choose to interact with it. With the new born-digital forms of narrative, however, there is no such conscious separation between us and them. It is harder to say where we end and they begin. When a medium becomes responsive, as interactive computer games and environments can be, we are no longer observers. Instead, we become performers on the stage of its interface even as we are that which is being performed through its machinations. I want to underscore here that, while we are the input, without its *acts of conversation* there is no work of art. This is where responsive environments like virtual reality or interactive game spaces depart from their paler cousins that set out to entertain us. These are discursive spaces and experiences that require us to talk back. The environment itself becomes an extension of us in more intimate ways than we ever imagined, coming to act simultaneously as our audience and as a "third skin" (Prince 2003: 13) that privileges our sensory engagement. Multimedia "environments," McLuhan has observed, "are not passive wrappings but active processes" (1964: 12).

More and more, the new digital narratives are something that we take out into the world with us rather than something we sit down to enjoy. Advertisers are now catering to fourth-wall broadcasting, the new trend toward using digital billboards in malls, in the hope of recouping lost revenues arising from the popularity of media like TiVo and iPods that sidestep commercial messages (Elliott 2006). This is a byproduct of the arrival of what McLuhan calls acoustic space, the fallout of the Information Age. He says:

> With the advent of a world environment of simultaneous and instantaneous informa-
> tion, Western man shifted from visual to acoustic space, for acoustic space is a sphere
> whose center is everywhere and whose boundaries are nowhere. Such is the space created
> by electric information which arrives simultaneously from all quarters of the globe. It is
> a space which phases us out of the world of logical continuity and connected stability
> into the space-time world of the new physics, in which the mechanical bond is the
> resonant interval of touch where there are *no connections, but only interfaces.* (McLuhan
> [1972]: 194; emphasis added)

In electronic media, we can limit the depth of our search: "we can decide how far back we want to go, how deep in time, just as we can decide how defined, how prepackaged or open-ended, that information should be" (de Kerckhove 1997: 84). The idea of surface and interface are privileged over depth when our media operate in surround sound. Connectivity has become so total that we are always plugged in. If we used to be members of a passive audience watching performers on a conventional stage, we have now become performers in our own play, playing to a responsive environment as audience on the stage of the digital interface. We have become Donna Haraway's cyborg, and now inhabit an entirely mediated and technologicalized environment.

This began on October 4, 1957, the day that the role of narrative changed forever, as did our relationship to life and the world. That day marked the beginning of the Space Age with the launch of the first artificial satellite, *Sputnik*. (In fact, fifty years hence, it is hard to appreciate the magnitude of this event and the consternation that greeted it. On a superficial level, it was read as the triumph of Communism over Democracy, at a deeper level it changed irreparably our relationship to our planet. On a practical level, it most significantly, for our purposes here, engendered ARPANET, the first incarnation of the internet, as a safeguard against communications breakdown in the event of a Russian nuclear attack.) McLuhan argues that this event flipped the world inside out to inhabit a simulated environment for the first time:

> When the planet was suddenly enveloped by a man-made artifact, Nature flipped into art form. The moment of *Sputnik* was the moment of creating Spaceship *Earth* and/or the global theatre. Shakespeare at the Globe had seen all the world as a stage, but with *Sputnik*, the world literally became a global theatre with no more audiences, only actors. (McLuhan [1972]: 197)

We can no longer be spectators in a mediated world. In a postnarrative act of reversal, we become actors by virtue of being immersed in what *New York Times* columnist Stuart Elliott calls the "screenery" of information space. And because we are actors this space is personal and personalized.

The iPod is the most visible trendsetter in this transformation. What has made this product so hot is the way that it turns us all into performers, DJs, VJs, broadcasters, publishers, authors, composers – you name it. In fact, Apple uses the maxim "Take Podcasting Personally" to promote its iTunes service. The iPod collapses all the barriers by allowing us full access to the technologies of production, storage, and distribution. Telescoping all of these functions into one small and perfectly portable interface has created the kind of immersive creative space that artists have long dreamt about. In the nineteenth century, composer Richard Wagner yearned to create what he called the *Gesamtkunstwerk* or Total Artwork, a seamless environment where art could inhabit the real: a place where "there are no more arts and no more boundaries, but only art, the universal, undivided" (qtd in Sayre 1989: 108). Wagner's "totalizing" or immersive effect of music drama was one of the first modern attempts to devise a schematic or model for the integration of different arts. Bringing together art, theater, opera, song, dance, poetic recitation, narrative, and the visual arts (Artmuseum.net) for the first time since Classical Greece, he actively tinkered with the technology of stagecraft ("Richard Wagner: Total Artwork"). The theatrical innovations he was responsible for include the orchestra pit, a darkened house, surround sound acoustics, and a return to the Greek amphitheatre-style seating that focused all attention on the stage

("Richard Wagner: Total Artwork"). Wagner's longing for an "Artwork of the Future" resonates to us in an age of personalized media and dynamic information environments, but it is in fact an ancient impulse that can be found in many media and genres – from sacred caves to Greek theater to medieval cathedrals. In similar ways, multimedia immersion attempts to engage all of our senses in virtual space, drawing us into the stories of its world through opulent graphics and interactive features.

Many artists, like Charlotte Davies, now seek to create such environments of total immersion. Hungarian-born Australian Agnes Hegedüs's *Memory Theatre VR*, for example, has taken the realm of multimedia performance onto a whole new level of theatrical experience. Playing with the idea of the stage and auditorium as a site for her work, she explores different historical periods (cast as separate rooms or spaces) through the style of the artworks of those same periods. Looking specifically at the precursors of virtual computer architecture, she explores "mannerist, futurist or even deconstructivist virtualities" as door openers to new worlds. The piece is:

> An interactive film on the history of deception in space... cleverly staged through a doubling of the situation in the interface. These concepts of virtual reality are based on works by Libeskind and Ivan Sutherland; along with concepts of Lewis Carroll's *Alice in Wonderland* and cabinets of curiosities. (qtd by Hegedüs 1997)

This trip through the looking glass remains the ultimate, personal immersive experience, an experience whose time seems to have arrived.

Consequently, I suspect that the next big leap forward will continue to be, not in the specifics of hardware development, but in innovations that insert us still deeper into our interface with technology.[3] Once the interface becomes entirely transparent, the gap between fiction and reality will have the potential to become fully permeable. Although still bound in space, Jun Rekimoto's DataTiles prototype for Sony is one such possible contender. (Rekimoto is a long-time developer for Sony whose previous creations include the Navicam, GesturePad, ToolStone, and PreSense.) Building on his earlier creations SyncTap (a device that uses synchronous actions like keystrokes to establish network connections), the FEEL User Interface (a device that permits secure ubiquitous connections between devices), and SmartSkin (a hand- and gesture-sensitive tabletop), the interface operates with the use of a special desktop, like a drafting table, with slots for the clear plastic tiles and an interactive pen. Titles (which are dual functioned as both software and memory storage device) that he has developed so far include "weather," "time machine," "photo album," "music," "baseball statistics" and "parameters," a "paint" program, a "people/mail" tile, and a "shopping basket" (that charges items directly to you through your cell phone). Rekimoto has also pioneered the use of dynamic hyperdragging not just from one tile to another, but directly onto a wall, screen, desktop, or another tile. When tiles are placed side by side they interlink, making, for instance, a map dynamic over time and space, enabling seamless creation of animation or other time-based events, and permitting all manner of files to be copied, mailed, or altered from one tile to another. This takes modular interface technology to a whole new level, but is still in developmental stages and has not yet been scheduled for commercial release. The possibilities of the potential uses of such a technology for narrative ends are extremely provocative. Another prototype that is taking the world by storm is the Nintendo handheld Wii wand. Pronounced "wee," it is a device that has long been gossiped about in hushed tones by its code name "Revolution." [4] Like the iPod and DataTiles, it is a harbinger of how our engagements with interface are changing. (One of the most profound changes is Wii's inclusion of a whole new demographic in video game use: senior citizens.) Marrying the game console with a web browser, computer mouse, and television remote technology, it provides two controllers per player, one for each hand, and enlists Bluetooth to perform its wireless and motion sensitive gaming mission. [5] It does not quite transform your living room into *Star Trek*'s holodeck, but it is close. It offers the ultimate personal gaming experience to date. Does this mark the arrival of a new embodied subjectivity? Perhaps this is Virilio's trajective subject made flesh. Wii removes the wall between the game and the player and, like *Sputnik,* will likely leave a wake that transforms our engagements not just with our technologies but with the world. While Apple is still spelling the future "i-P-O-D" (Haddad), Nintendo is set to give them some Wii for their buck in the coming months and years ahead. (It was released in November 2006.) The potentialities for the future of narrative within and via these new technologies are as open-ended as the modular plots of digital narrative themselves.

Notes

1 See my discussion of Jun Rekimoto's DataTiles later in this chapter, which so clearly makes use of modular, hypertextual thinking to revolutionize interface design.

2 For an in-depth exploration of the *Spore* project, see Wright's introductory video at: <http:// video.google.com/ videoplay?docid=8372603330420559198& q=spore>.

3 In November 1999, the *MIT Technology Review* published a list of what they deemed the ten most influential interface innovations. They were: 1. the loudspeaker; 2. the touch-tone telephone; 3. the steering wheel; 4. the magnetic-stripe card; 5. the traffic light; 6. the remote control; 7. the cathode ray tube; 8. the liquid crystal display; 9. the mouse/graphical user interface; 10. the barcode scanner (qtd by Crow 2001). Given the acceleration of technological innovation, we can expect this list to change dramatically in the next few years.

4 Watch the video, "Trykk Startknappen for å se Video," that accompanied the initial announce-

ment of "Revolution" in Denmark in September of 2005 at *dagbladet.no*: <http://www.dagbladet. no/kultur/2005/09/16/443527.html>.

5 The Step User Interface (SUI), announced by Microsoft in February 2006, also works with the principles of embodied navigation and command. The press release states:

The StepMail application uses an off-the-shelf "dance pad" to let a user carry out commands in email – such as scroll, open, close, delete, flag, and place messages in folders – by tapping a set of six buttons on the floor. Another prototype application, StepPhoto, allows foot-controlled scrolling and sorting through digital photographs. (Microsoft)

The technology is designed to help people be more active at their desks, to enable work to continue while assuming positions other than sitting, to open technology for people with limited use of their hands and to help avoid repetitive strain injuries.

WORKS CITED AND CONSULTED

"Apple – iTunes – Podcasts" (2006). <http://www.apple.com/itunes/podcasts/>. Accessed May 10, 2006.

Friendster. <http://www.friendster.com/>.

"Richard Wagner: Total Artwork." <http://www.artmuseum.net/w2vr/timeline/Wagner.html#Wagner Text>. Accessed January 21, 2006.

"Spore (game)." *Wikipedia.* <http://en.wikipedia.org/wiki/Spore_%28computer_game%29>.

"Xerography: The Invention that Nobody Wanted." May 6, 1997. <http://members.tripod.com/~earthdude1/xerox/index.html>. Accessed April 20, 2006.

ArtMuseum.net. "Overture: Integration of the Arts." <http://www.artmuseum.net/w2vr/overture/integration1.html>. Accessed January 21, 2006.

Crow, David (2001, August 16). "User Interface Innovations." <http://davidcrow.ca/article/532/user-interface-innovations>. Accessed May 10, 2006.

Davies, Charlotte (1998). *Ephémère.* See: <http://www.immersence.com>.

—— (1995). *Osmose.* See: <http://www.immersence.com>.

—— (2003). "Landscape, earth, body, being, space and time in the immersive virtual environments *Osmose and Ephémère.*" In Judy Malloy (Ed.). *Women, Art, and Technology.* Cambridge, MA: The MIT Press, pp. 322–37.

Davis, Juliet. *Pieces of Herself.* <http://www.julietdavis.com/studio/piecesofherself/2003–05>.

de Kerckhove, Derrick (1995). *The Skin of Culture.* Toronto: Somerville House.

—— (1997). *Connected Intelligence.* Toronto: Somerville House.

Elliot, Stuart (2006). "Bringing Digital Ads to the Local Mall." *New York Times Online* May 12: <http://www.nytimes.com/2006/05/12/business/media/12adco.html>.

Griffith, Eric (2006). "The Wireless Powers of Wii." *Wi-FiPlanet.com* May 10. <http://www.wi-fiplanet.com/news/article.php/3605311>. Accessed May 10, 2006.

Haddad, Charles (2003). "How Apple spells future: i-P-O-D." BusinessWeek.com, July 2. <http://www.businessweek.com/technology/content/jul2003/tc2003072_0512_tc056.htm>. Accessed May 20, 2006.

Hayles, N. Katherine (1997). "Situating Narrative in an Ecology of New Media." *Modern Fiction Studies* 43.3 (Fall): 573–6.

Hegedüs, Agnes (1997). "Memory Theatre VR." *Media Art Net.* <http://www.medienkunstnetz.de/works/memory-theater-vr/video/1/>. Accessed January 18, 2006.

Jackson, Shelley (1995). *Patchwork Girl, Or A Modern Monster by Mary/Shelley and Herself.* Watertown, MA: Eastgate Systems. Software.

Jones, Amelia (1998). *Body Art / Performing the Subject.* Minneapolis: University of Minnesota Press.

Joyce, Michael (2000). "Reach." *Tirweb: University of Iowa Review.* <http://www.uiowa.edu/~iareview/tirweb/hypermedia/michael_joyce/ReachTitle.html>.

——, Carolyn Guyer, Nigel Kerr, Nancy Lin, and Suze Schweitzer. (1995). *The Mola Project.* <http://scribble.com/world3/meme1/voices.html>. Accessed April 16, 2006.

Lehmann, Hans-Thies. (2006). *Postdramatic Theatre* (Karen Jürs-Munby, Trans.). London: Routledge.

McLuhan, Marshall (1964). *Understanding Media: The Extensions of Man.* Toronto: Signet.

—— (2004 [1965]). "Future of man in the electric age." In Stephanie McLuhan and David Staines (Eds.). *Understanding Me: Lectures and Interviews.* Toronto: McClelland and Stewart, pp. 56–75.

—— (2004 [1966]). "The Medium is the Message." In Stephanie McLuhan and David Staines (Eds.). *Understanding Me: Lectures and Interviews.* Toronto: McClelland and Stewart, pp. 76–97.

—— (2004 [1972]). "The End of the Work Ethic." In Stephanie McLuhan and David Staines (Eds.). *Understanding Me: Lectures and Interviews.* Toronto: McClelland and Stewart.

—— (2004 [1973]). "Art as Survival in the Electric Age." In Stephanie McLuhan and David Staines (Eds.). *Understanding Me: Lectures and Interviews.* Toronto: McClelland and Stewart.

Manovich, Lev. (2005, November 16). "Remix and remixability." Posting to the nettime-l mailing list. <http://www.nettime.org/Lists-Archives/nettime-l-0511/msg00060.html>. Accessed January 29, 2006.

Microsoft (2006, February 28). "Stepping through your inbox: one of many innovations in the spotlight at Microsoft Research TechFest." <http://www.microsoft.com/presspass/press/2006/feb06/02-28MSRTechFest06PR.mspx>. Accessed May 10, 2006.

Mortensen, Torill, and Jill Walker (2002, June 18). "Blogging thoughts: personal publication as an online research tool." Skikt-Konferansene 2002. Conference proceedings, September 9, 2002, pp. 249–79. <http://www.intermedia.uio.no/konferanser/skikt-02/docs/Researching_ICTs_in_context-Ch11-Mortensen-Walker.pdf>.

MySpace. <http://www.myspace.com/>.

Nintendo (2006). *Wii.* Announced May 10. <http://wii.nintendo.com/home.html>.

Nintendo Handheld Revolution (2005, September 16). "Her er revolusjonen!" and "Trykk Start-knappen for å se Video." *dagbladet.no.* <http://www.dagbladet.no/kultur/2005/09/16/443527.html>. Accessed May 10, 2006.

PC Magazine Staff (2006, May 12). "Nintendo's Wii game console to browse web with Opera." *PCMag.com.* <http://www.foxnews.com/story/0,2933,195013,00.html>. Accessed May 12, 2006.

Phalen, Peggy (1993). *Unmarked: The Politics of Performance.* London: Routledge.

Prince, Patric D. (2003). "Women and the Search for Visual Intelligence." In Judy Malloy (Ed.). *Women, Art and Technology.* Cambridge, MA: MIT, pp. 2–15.

Pullinger, Kate (with Stephen Schemat and babel) (2004). *The Breathing Wall.* Software. <http://trace.ntu.ac.uk/studio/pullinger/webtaster/>.

Rekimoto, Jun (2001). "*DataTiles:* a modular platform for mixed physical and graphical interactions." Interface design in development with Sony. <http://www.csl.sony.co.jp/person/rekimoto/ movies/tile2.mpg>. Accessed April 20, 2006.

——, "FEEL User Interface."< http://www.csl.sony.co.jp/IL/projects/feel/>.

——, "*SmartSkin*: Multi-Hand, Multi-Point Input Technology." <http://www.csl.sony. co.jp/person/rekimoto/smartskin/>. Accessed April 20, 2006.

——, "SyncTap." <http://www.csl.sony.co.jp/IL/projects/sync/>. Accessed April 20, 2006.

Sayre, Henry M. (1989). *The Object of Performance: The American Avant-Garde Since 1970.* Chicago: University of Chicago Press.

Schafer, R. Murray. (1998). "The glazed soundscape." In Roberta Birks, Tomi Eng, and Julie Walchli (Eds.). *Landmarks: A Process Reader.* Scarborough: Prentice-Hall, pp. 211–14.

Schoenherr, Steven E. (2002, June 2). "Television instant replay." <http://history.acusd.edu/gen/recording/ television8.html>. Accessed May 2, 2006.

Slattery, Diana Reed (with Bill Brubaker and Daniel J. O'Neill) (1997–2001). *Glide: An Exploration of Visual Language.* <http://www.academy.rpi.edu/glide/main.htm>. Accessed April 16, 2006. Some portions online. CD-ROM version courtesy of the author.

—— (2002). *The Glide Collabyrinth.* <http://www.academy.rpi.edu/glide/apps/collabyrinth.html>.

—— (2003). *The Maze Game.* Kingston, NY: Deep Listening Publications.

Virilio, Paul (1995, August 27). "Speed and Information: Cyberspace Alarm!" (Patrice Riemans, Trans.). *Ctheory.* <http://www.ctheory.net/printer.asp?id=72>. Accessed March 20, 2006.

—— (1997). *Open Sky* (Julie Rose, Trans.). London: Verso.

Walczak, Marek, and Martin Wattenberg (2001–2). *Apartment.* <http://www.turbulence.org/Works/apartment/>. Accessed January 16, 2006.

Wardrip-Fruin, Noah (2005, February 17). "Hypermedia, Eternal Life, and *The Impermanence Agent.*" <http://www.impermanenceagent.com/agent/essay.html>.

——, and Brion Moss (with Adam Chapman) (2001). "*The Impermanence Agent*: Project and Context." <http://www.impermanenceagent.com/agent/essay2/>. Accessed December 12, 2003.

——, Adam Chapman, Brion Moss, and Duane Whitehurst. *The Impermanence Agent.* <http://www.impermanenceagent.com/agent/>.

——, Adam Chapman, Brion Moss, and Duane Whitehurst (2005, February 17). *The Impermanence Agent* Gallery. <http://whitney.queeg.com/agentstory02.html>.

Wright, Will. *Spore*. In development with Maxis for 2008 release. <http://video.google.com/videoplay?docid=8372603330420559198&q=spore>.

YouTube. <http://www.youtube.com/>.

13
Fictional Worlds in the Digital Age
Marie-Laure Ryan

Of all the pleasures of literature, none is more fulfilling to the embodied mind than immersing itself in a fictional world. Some works, admittedly, discourage this pleasure, and there are other kinds of satisfaction: "high brow" literature loves to distance itself from popular culture, which thrives on immersion, by promoting the more cerebral experiences of self-reflexivity and critical distance from the fictional world. But immersion remains the most fundamental of literary pleasures (Schaeffer 1999; Ryan 2001). It would be pointless to demystify textual worlds as constructed by language or other types of signs, if the imagination were not spontaneously inclined to pretend that these worlds are real, or, as the romantic poet Wordsworth put it, to "suspend disbelief" in their autonomous existence. Digital media have made important contributions to both immersion and self-reflexivity: whereas computer games absorb players for hours at a time into richly designed imaginary worlds, hypertext fiction explodes these worlds into textual shards, code poetry promotes awareness of the machine language that brings text the screen, and what Noah Wardrip-Fruin (2006) calls "process-intensive" works direct attention away from the surface of the screen, toward the virtuoso programming that generates the text. In the present essay, I propose to concentrate on the immersive pleasures, by asking: how do digital media affect the experience of fictional worlds and the practice of fiction? My investigation will lead beyond the narrow domain of literature, if by literature one understands primarily language-based art, to investigate forms of digital entertainment that rely on multiple sensory channels and semiotic supports.

As a preliminary, let me outline my conception of fiction. For this notion to be valid of a medium, it must possess a cognitive value. This means that the question "is it a fiction?" must influence the use of a text or the interpretation of a behavior. In *Cigars of the Pharaoh* (1975: 16–17), the famous comic book hero Tintin gives an eloquent demonstration of the danger of mistaking fiction for reality: witnessing a woman being savagely beaten in the Sahara desert, he rushes to her rescue, only to discover that he has stumbled upon a movie set. Rather than being thanked by the victim, he must suffer the wrath of the entire film crew. Similarly, a reader who mistakes a novel for a representation of reality (as did Don Quixote) will be led to mistaken beliefs. A text of fiction invites its users to imagine a world, while a text of non-fiction conveys information, whether accurate or not, about reality.

Relying on the work of John Searle (1975), Kendall Walton (1990), Jean-Marie Schaeffer (1999), and David Lewis (1978), I regard fiction as the product of an act of make-believe whose prototype can be found in children's role-playing games, such as playing house, cops and robbers, or big bad wolf chasing little pigs. Through their act of make-believe, readers, spectators, or players transport themselves in imagination from the world they regard as actual toward an alternative possible world – a virtual reality – which they regard as actual for the duration of their involvement in the text, game, or spectacle. Once transported into this world, they either enter the body of a specific individual (dramatic acting; playing big bad wolf; controlling an avatar in a computer game) or they pretend to be an anonymous member of the fictional world who receives the narration or observes the unfolding of fictionally real events (reading a novel, watching a play). I call this projection into a virtual body an imaginative recentering (Ryan 1991: 21–3), and I regard it as the precondition of the experience of immersion.

Central to this definition is the idea that a fictional text must be able to conjure a world to the imagination. By world I mean a space serving as container for concrete objects and individuated characters, obeying specific laws, and extending in time, at least implicitly. A fictional text cannot be a philosophical treaty dealing with abstract ideas, nor a description concerned exclusively with universals. It must say "Ivan Ilych is dying," rather than "all men are mortal." When a text explicitly represents the evolution of a fictional world through time, this text presents a narrative dimension. Most fictions do indeed tell stories, but narrativity and fictionality are theoretically distinct problems. The narrativity of a text is a semantic issue, this is to say, a matter of content, and the user can decide whether or not the text tells a story by simply decoding its meaning. Fictionality, by contrast, is a pragmatic issue: not a matter of what the text is about, but a matter of how the text is supposed to be used. There may be some semantic restrictions on the content of a fiction (as I suggest above, a fiction must project a concrete world), but there are no positive conditions that specify a certain type of subject matter. It follows that one cannot always pass judgments of fictionality by simply inspecting the text.

In this chapter I will examine fictional practices that take advantage, to variable degrees and in variable combinations, of the most distinctive properties of digital media: interactivity, multimedia capabilities, volatility of inscription, and above all networking. Underlying all these features, and making them possible, is a more fundamental property of digital media that I will not discuss separately because it is involved in all digital texts: the property of being algorithmic, i.e., operated by computer code (see Winder, Chapter 27, "WRITING MACHINES," this volume). I will follow the implications of these properties not only for fictional worlds that exist in the digital medium – classic computer games, MOOs (MUD Object Oriented), web-based micronations, and multi-user online games – but also, in Section 3, for worlds originally created in the "old media" of print literature, cinema or TV.

1. The Pleasures of World-building

As a network, the internet is a collection of interlinked nodes, or sites, serving as recipients for information, and distinguished from each other by unique addresses. From the very beginning of networked computing, users have treated some of these sites as places to meet and as territories to colonize. While some meeting places, such as chatrooms, remain empty spaces, others have been elaborately built up and decorated, so as to offer a more congenial forum, to provide topics of conversation, or simply for the sheer joy of building and decorating (pleasures often denied to us in the real world for lack of funding). Through this creative activity, the sites of the internet become "worlds" to the imagination.

The earliest manifestations of the pleasure of world-building were the text-based MOOs and MUDs (Multi-User Dungeons) that flourished in the 1980s and 90s. MOOs were public spaces where users met under the disguise of a fictional persona, or "avatar," which they created themselves. (My use of the past tense suggests that text-based MOOs have been largely supplanted by graphically rendered worlds, such as Active Worlds [www.activeworlds.com] or the online game Second Life [<http://secondlife.com/>]). To enliven this game of make-believe, the administrators of the system designed a permanent setting, typically a building with many "rooms" furnished with virtual objects. Avatars and objects were created in the same way a novelist brings a world to life: by posting on the system their textual description. Advanced players acquired the privilege of building their own room, and of decorating it with objects of their own invention. Upon entering a room, visitors were able to explore it by typing commands such as "look around." The system would display a list of the objects contained in the room, and the players could continue their inspection by typing instructions such as "look [name of object]," to which the system would respond by posting a more elaborate description, or by activating a behavior encoded in the object (for instance, exploding). The presence of objects created by other members of the fictional world gave players the pleasure of exploration and the thrill of discovery, while creating their own objects provided them with props in their games of make-believe: for instance, users (or rather, their avatars) could get married in the fictional world of the MOO by creating and exchanging a ring, and they could build their own love nest.

Whereas the MOOs and their graphic successors are ready-made spaces maintained by professional programmers and waiting to be filled with content created by users, another non-commercial form of online world, the micronation, is built from scratch by amateurs. An offshoot of the literary genre of the utopia, a micronation is an independent "state" created by individuals, who design its geography, define its form of government, write its laws, describe its customs, and invent its history.

Micronations differ from those literary works whose main source of interest lies in the creation of exotic worlds – science fiction, the fantastic – through their lack of plot. It is not necessary to be a novelist to create an online world. Whereas literary works dramatize their imaginary worlds through a narrative line that follows the travels of a character and details his discoveries – *Gulliver's Travels* being the prototype – micronations are collections of mainly descriptive documents, and it is the user exploring the website who plays the role of traveler.

While some micronations exist in real space, by the will of a founder who declares the independence of a certain territory (a phenomenon documented by the *Lonely Planet* guide to micronations [2006]), most of these fictional countries reside on the internet, where they can be reached by cyber tourists and prospective citizens through a click of the mouse. They are named Bergonia and Talossa, Uteged and Reuniao, Lizbekistan and Aerica, Freedonia and Aristasia, the Feminine Empire. The reasons for building micronations are as varied as their landscapes, customs, and political systems: childhood dreams of inhabiting secret kingdoms, adolescent revolts against a world ruled by grown-ups, exercising royal power, articulating social visions, simulating processes of self-government, but above all the pure pleasure of writing the encyclopedia of an imaginary country.[1]

To illustrate the diverse motivations that drive the builders of micronations, let's take a look at two of them, Bergonia and Talossa. The founder of Bergonia[2] has a clear political agenda: promote socialism and environmentalism by describing a viable alternative to our capitalist economy, which he regards as "certain to dehumanize humankind and likely to end up wrecking the planet, with catastrophic results of epochal proportions." But Bergonia is also a private game, the product of an enduring childhood's fantasy. Like Robert Louis Stevenson's novel *Treasure Island*, it was born out of a love of maps and of drawing maps. "In the beginning," writes the founder,

> I had no purpose at all, only the joy of playing and inventing.... I'm sure that the discovery of my parents' grand atlas was the immediate hook. Drawing the first maps and dreaming up weird names was entirely a matter of play. I drew lots of maps when I was a kid, and Bergonia was then just one of many on-going projects. Over the years the work (play) of contriving a continent & nation has massively challenged me – a great expenditure and demonstration of imagination that wound up serving a multitude of incidental uses. The job has given me a vehicle and a focus for all my interests in geography & meteorology, anthropology & history, religion & mythology, and philosophy & psychology. (<http://www.bergonia.org/why.htm>)

The texts posted on the Bergonia website represent an encyclopedic sum of knowledge: where else, but in an imaginary country, can one be at the same time an ethnographer, geographer, political scientist, linguist, cartographer, historian, and ecologist? But despite its aspirations to build a better society, Bergonia remains the creation of a single individual, and except for an invitation to send email to the author, it does not encourage active participation.

Like Bergonia, Talossa[3] originated in a young person's fantasy: at age fourteen, its founder proclaimed his bedroom to be a foreign nation called Talossa, Finnish for "inside the house." Less thoroughly imagined than Bergonia, Talossa is defined by a made-up language (a blend of English and Romance language, with lots of strange diacritical marks), a history, a culture, a real-world territory (located around Milwaukee, but divided into provinces with invented names), a law, a constitution, a government, a system of three political parties, and a series of elective political offices such as prime minister, secretary of State, and minister of culture. As in most micronations, the rulers of Talossa revel in the insignia of statehood (a flag, a slogan, a national anthem, a system of nobility titles), as well as in a pompous legal language that stamps the decisions of the government with the seal of authority. Originally conceived as a constitutional monarchy with an elected King, Talossa underwent a revolution in 2004 and split into a Kingdom and a Republic because, according to the webpage of the Republic, the citizens spent most of their time arguing uselessly with the King. In contrast to the largely non-interactive site of Bergonia, Talossa is an active social forum. Visitors are invited to apply for citizenship by filling in an online form (there are currently 88 citizens in the kingdom), and they are expected to participate in the political life of the country through a blog that serves both the Kingdom and the Republic.

But the degree of participation in such worlds remains very low, compared to either the MOOs or online games of the *EverQuest*, *World of Warcraft*, and *Second Life* variety, because they do not allow real-time interaction between their members. All the communication takes place through a blog or through email, and the possibilities of taking an active part in the political life of the nation are limited to voting on topics such as changes in the constitution, who will hold public offices, and the acceptance of new citizens. Holding an elected office means little more than having one's picture posted on the website with a fancy title. Micronations are not dynamic environments but collections of static texts that express the creativity of their founder, and once you have taken a tour there is not much else to do.[4] This explains why their population remains in the double digits, compared to the thousands, if not millions, who join the virtual worlds of online games.

2. Worlds as Playgrounds

It is everybody's secret that the interactivity of digital media allows their most important and most popular contribution to the experience of fictional worlds, namely the development of video games. In a classical print fiction, users play the role of a passive witness of the represented events, but in most video games, they impersonate and control a character who takes an active part in the evolution of a fictional world. Through this act of pretense, video games not only strengthen the connection between fiction and children's games of make-believe, they also reconcile two types of game which had previously remained largely incompatible with each other. These two types of game are what the French sociologist Roger Caillois calls *paidia* and *ludus*:

> At one extreme an almost indivisible principle, common to diversion, turbulence, free improvisation, and careful gaiety is dominant. It manifests a kind of uncontrolled fantasy that can be designated by the term *paidia*. At the opposite extreme ... there is a growing tendency to bind [this uncontrolled fantasy] with arbitrary, imperative, and purposely tedious conventions ... This latter principle is completely impractical, even though it requires an ever greater amount of effort, patience, skill, or ingenuity. I call this second component *ludus*. (2001: 13)

The best example of *paidia* games is building imaginary scenarios with toys, using them, in the words of Kendall Walton (1990: 21–24 and throughout), as "props in a game of make-believe." These games do not aim at a specific goal, and they do not lead to losing or winning. The pleasures of *paidia* reside in the free play of the imagination, in adopting foreign identities, in forming social relations, in building objects, in exploring an environment, and above all in creating a representation: *paidia* games are fundamentally mimetic activities. If there are rules, they are spontaneously created by the participants, as when a group of children decides that a certain tree will be the house of the wolf, and they can be renegotiated on the fly. *Ludus* games, by contrast, are strictly controlled by pre-existing rules accepted by the participants as part of a basic game contract, they lead to clearly defined states of winning or losing, and their pleasure resides in the thrill of competition and in the satisfaction of solving problems.

Of these two types of game, it is clearly *paidia*, with its mimetic dimension, that forms the ludic origin of fiction. Caillois goes on to say that the make-believe of fiction is incompatible with the rules of *ludus*: "Thus games are not ruled and make-believe. Rather they are ruled or make-believe" (2001: 9). (The original French text reads: "Ainsi, les jeux ne sont pas réglés et fictifs. Ils sont plutôt ou réglés ou fictifs" [1958: 41].) In the 1950s, when Caillois was writing, the vast majority of ruled games were abstract: chess, go, cross-word puzzles, and the various forms of competitive sport take place on a playfield divided into strategic zones (the squares on a chess board, the penalty box on a soccer field), but this playfield does not represent anything: it is not a world in an imaginative sense. The goals of the players are not the kind of events that matter to people in practical life, but actions only made desirable by the conventions of the game, such as capturing the opponent's pieces, or shooting a ball into a net. There had been, admittedly, some attempts to render board games more interesting from a thematic point of view: for instance Monopoly simulates real estate, many dice games enliven their board with pictures that tell a rudimentary story, and in *Dungeons and Dragons*, players impersonate characters and pursue quests whose outcome is decided by rules set up by the game master. But it is only with computer games that the conflict observed by Caillois is fully resolved. More and more, video games take place in a space that is not only a playfield but a richly designed world offering diverse landscapes to explore and identifiable objects to manipulate. Players do not move tokens but impersonate an avatar, and their goal is no longer the achievement of a conventional state of winning but the fulfillment of concrete tasks corresponding to what people might want to do in real life if they were placed in the proper world and in the proper situation: goals such as winning wars, saving the Earth from invaders from outer space, or establishing civilizations. On the other hand, these games are even more strictly controlled by rules than sports and board games, because the rules are established by code, and they are as imperative as the laws of physics: you can no more cheat with them than you can cheat with gravity. (Cheating in computer games is finding imaginative ways to get around the code, rather than transgressing it.)

In the fictional worlds of computer games players no longer have to choose between an activity of make-believe that speaks to the imagining imagination and an activity of problem-solving that relies on the strategic imagination. Video games are both "ruled and make-believe," and it is now possible to engage in both *ludus* and *paidia* within the same world. Some of them, like the shooter *Doom*, are admittedly more *ludus* than *paidia*, fiercer, more narrowly focused competition than make-believe and the pleasure taken in simply inhabiting the fictional world. These games are for the type of player that Richard Bartle (1996), in a classic typology, calls "killers" and "achievers," as opposed to his "explorers" and "socializers." Conversely, so-called simulation games, such as *The Sims*, *SimCity*, or *Civilization*, are exclusively *paidia*. But a single-user game like *Grand Theft Auto* (Bogost 2006), or a multi-user online game like *EverQuest*, combines both types of pleasures: competition and problem-solving through the "quests" given to the players; but also, depending on the particular game, chatting with other players, building avatars, acquiring or creating valuable objects for the avatar, exploring the diverse landscapes of the game world, and engaging in activities for the fun of it. The worlds of such games are both territories to traverse in search of missions to accomplish and spaces for *flânerie*; both combat zones full of challenges and playgrounds filled with a variety of toys.

3. Expandable Worlds and Worlds out of Worlds

The formation of computer networks, together with the volatility of inscription of digitized information, allows fictional worlds to grow, to be modified from the inside and the outside, and to give birth to other worlds. By volatility of inscription, I mean that digital texts are the projection on a screen of a binary information held in the computer's memory that can change value with every clock cycle of the machine. Digital texts thus differ from works inscribed on a static support, such as books or film reels, through the impermanence of their material inscription: it is not necessary to manufacture a brand-new copy to update them. This property is not specific to fiction, as we can see from the constant growth and rewriting of the online encyclo-pedia Wikipedia, or from the possibility to revise endlessly texts composed with a word processor. But the volatility of digital texts has particularly important implications for the fictional worlds of video games, especially when it is coupled with networking. It makes it possible to modify the operation of a video game by downloading from the web expansions, modifications ("mods" in the jargon), or error corrections known as "patches" (Salen and Zimmerman 2003). Various expansions to the world of *The Sims* allow, for instance, the characters of the game to leave their suburban homes for exotic vacation spots, to live the life of college students, to adopt pets, or to enjoy an exciting nightlife. Whereas the expansion packages of *The Sims* are commercial products developed by EA, the company that markets the game, many mods are the spontaneous creation of amateur players who make them available for free to the player community.

When game worlds reside on the internet, players can take advantage of updates without having to download a module. In online games, the combination of networking and volatile inscription enables the production team to expand the territory of the game world, to introduce new active objects, or to create new missions when some players have attained the highest level, so as to keep their interest and more importantly, continue collecting their monthly membership fees. In contrast to the worlds of CD-ROM-based games, online worlds can, consequently, be modified unbeknownst to the players.

The expansions described so far operate "from the inside," since they are seamlessly integrated into the fictional worlds of games. But by providing public forums that lead to the formation of communities, the internet also facilitates a kind of rewriting that takes place from the outside. This phenomenon, known as "transfictionality" (Saint-Gelais 2005; Ryan 2006), consists of producing and posting texts that complete, modify, or stretch in time the worlds of preexisting literary texts, or that transpose their plots and characters into new environments. Transfictionality expresses the reader's desire to free the fictional world from the control of the author and to see it live and evolve independently of the text that originally brought it to life. By offering familiar worlds into which readers can immerse themselves from the very beginning, rather than having to slowly construct these worlds on the basis of textual information, transfictionality represents a substantial saving in cognitive effort. This explains its popularity with texts of popular culture. The phenomenon is admittedly not specific to the digital age: in oral cultures, the performance of bards brought infinite variations to worlds familiar to the audience; in the age of print, popular novels such as *Don Quixote* and *Robinson Crusoe* inspired numerous imitations and apocryphal continuations; and in the early days of television and science-fiction, fans exchanged plot suggestions through photocopied publications known as "zines" (Hellekson and Busse 2006; Jenkins 2006). But with the internet, the production of transfictional texts flourished into a mass industry thanks to communicative advantages too obvious to merit discussion here. Popular TV series (*Buffy the Vampire Slayer, Xena: Warrior Princess, Star Trek*), as well as films (*Star Wars*) and cult novels (*Harry Potter, Lord of The Rings*), give birth to numerous websites where fans post stories based on the fictional world of the text that forms the object of the cult. Other fans provide comments, which may lead to revisions. There are, for instance, 38,000 texts

of fan fiction inspired by the world of Harry Potter on the website www.harrypotter
fanfiction.com. Energized by what Henry Jenkins (2006) calls the collective intelligence of the fan community, fictional worlds become interactive and participatory in a
much more imaginative way than in hypertext or even video games, even though the
individual texts do not contain interactive devices.

The computer provides not only a channel of transmission for the texts of fan
fiction, it can also become a tool of production. It all began with the built-in game
camera of *The Sims*. By taking snapshots of the screen, and by combining them with
text of their own invention, players create comic strips (or graphic novels) that expand
the rather limited narrative possibilities of the game. There is indeed no need for these
works to reproduce actual game scenarios. Thanks to the representational power of
language, it is possible to make the characters talk (while in *The Sims* they converse in
"Sim-speak," an incomprehensible jargon); to represent their private thoughts (only
shown as numeric coefficients of likes and dislikes in the game); and to have them
perform other actions than those offered on the menus (for instance, violent and anti-
social actions). By selecting individual frames out of the game's continuous flow of
images, authors are also able to skip the repetitive events of daily life, such as taking
showers or going to bed at regular intervals, that account for a major part of The Sims'
gameplay, and to concentrate instead on events of much greater tellability. Thousands
of these creations are posted on *The Sims'* official website.[5] A related phenomenon is
the manipulation of the engine that operates video games. (Some games, but not all,
make this engine available to the players.) Through their ability to capture animated
sequences, these engines allow players to take control of the characters and to produce
short films known as machinima by adding a sound track of their choice (Jones 2006:
261). Artists have created machinima with original plots out of *Quake, Half-Life, The
Sims 2, EverQuest, Worlds of Warcraft*, and *Grand Theft Auto*.[6] With both still cameras
and machinima, the user's creative freedom is only limited by the images provided by
the game. The original game world becomes a quarry of visual materials, a matrix out
of which players generate other worlds. Lost in the process, however, is the interactive
character of the source world.

4. Living Worlds

When imaginary worlds exploit to the maximum the four properties of digital
technology mentioned above, namely interactivity, multi-sensory dimensions, volatility of inscription, and networking, they become dynamic spaces where events are
constantly happening and where fiction is continually being produced. These living
environments are known in the jargon as MMORPGs ("massively multi-user online
role-playing games"), but they have also been called synthetic worlds (Castronova
2005), virtual worlds (Klastrup n.d.), and gaming lifeworlds (Taylor 2006). Their
names are *EverQuest* and *Ultima Online, Second Life* and *World of Warcraft, Lineage*
and *Entropia*. Sacrificing precision to convenience, I will simply refer to them as

"online worlds" or "online games." The remarks below are those of a lurker, rather than of an active player, and they are highly indebted to the vivid descriptions found in the growing scholarship devoted to these words.[7]

How does the world of an online game operate? Drawing inspiration from a list established by Castronova (2005, chapter 4),[8] I reduce their basic components to the following elements:

1. The visual representation of a vast geography with diverse landscapes that offers specific possibilities of action: for instance, dangerous forests inhabited by monsters whose killing earns the players experience points, sanctuaries where players are immune to attacks (much as churches were in the Middle Ages), convalescent houses or magic springs where players heal their wounds, markets where they trade goods, and mountains where they can mines precious metals. The *Atlas of Ever-Quest*, a 500-page tome, provides a detailed guide to the symbolic geography of the game, listing for each area its back story, the dangers to be expected, the challenges being offered, and the benefits to be acquired by passing the tests.

2. A repertory of roles to choose from, divided into races (for instance gnomes, elves, humans), genders, and classes (druids, knights, necromancers). These types differ from each other through their abilities: a druid can heal wounds, a knight excels at sword fighting, a gnome prefer to defeats enemies through ruse than through brute strength. These diversified talents encourage players to form social bonds (known as guilds) with other players, in order to complement their abilities. The higher one progresses in the game, and the more difficult the tasks to be accomplished, the more imperative it becomes to ally oneself with other characters.

3. A system of progression, based on the acquisition of merit. All the players start, at least in principle (we will see an exception below), from the same lowly condition, but depending on their skills, and above all on the time invested in the game world, they reach different levels in the game hierarchy. The mechanism of leveling consists of the acquisition of experience points by performing various tasks, typically slaying monsters. Belonging to a higher level not only increases the power of a players to perform difficult tasks, it also gives them greater prestige in the game community.

Online worlds differ from those of standard narrative – film or novels – as well as from single-player, CD-ROM-supported games through a quality of persistence that takes the simulation of real life to unprecedented heights. An online world is like a TV show that runs every day, twenty-four hours a day, and if players play hooky in the real world, they will return to a changed world, like Rip van Winkle awakening from his hundred-year sleep. As T. L. Taylor observes: "A player who is away from the game for a couple of weeks may find that his level-25 character can no longer group with his friends' characters, which have now advanced to level 40" (2006: 49).

Another aspect of real life that multiplayer online games simulate very efficiently, while standard narrative does not, is our limited perception of the world we live in.

In a novel representing a huge world with a large cast of characters, parallel lives, and intersecting destinies, the reader is informed of all the plot-lines through an omniscient narrator who can move freely in time and space. In an online world, by contrast, as is the case in real life, players are only aware of what happens in their immediate surroundings. Other players may occasionally inform them of events that took place in remote regions, but no player has a god's eye view of all the destinies that are simultaneously unfolding in the game world.

In one respect, however, online worlds differ significantly from both life and traditional narratives. In the real world, once you successfully perform an action to solve a problem, this action has durable consequences and does not need to be repeated, unless it is negated by another agent, or belongs to the daily maintenance type such as eating or sleeping. The same principle holds for narratives: when a knight slays a dragon in a fairy tale, the dragon is dead, and the feat does not need to be performed again by another knight. But in an online world, events have only very limited consequences. Not only is death reversible (players can retrieve the corpse of their avatar, collect its belongings, and bring it back to life, losing no more than a few experience points), but, as Fotis Jannidis (2007) has observed, the quests performed by players are endlessly repeatable by other players. In online worlds, history doesn't have to be definitive: if you kill a monster, he re-spawns in a few seconds; if you dig out gold from a mountain, the gold remains available for other players; otherwise, the earlier settlers would deplete the resources of the game world. Here the principle of causality, which forms the basic mode of operation of both nature and narrative, is sacrificed to the need to give equal opportunities to all players. But since players are ignorant of what happens elsewhere in the game world, the relative futility of their actions does not seriously damage their sense of being engaged in a meaningful pursuit.

Of all the distinctive properties of online worlds, none has been more highly praised than the feedback loop that takes place between developers and players. Exploiting the conditions imposed top-down by the developers of the game, players improvise bottom-up their own scenarios by communicating with each other. The game developers react to these behaviors by introducing new code that either facilitates them, when they enhance the interest of the game, or discourages them, when they diminish the pleasure of most players. As example of this emergent quality is the development of an economy in the world of *EverQuest*. By creating a monetary system and by placing NPC (non-playing character) merchants in the game world, the coding authorities put into place the foundations of a trade system. Through this commerce, players are able to sell the loot they acquire by slaying monsters and to buy more desirable commodities that either display their high status to other players, or let them challenge more ferocious monsters, in an endless loop that takes them through the levels of the game. But rather than trading with roaming NPCs, players soon developed the habit of meeting in a certain place, known as the Tunnel of Rô, to do commerce among themselves. To help them in this activity, the developers built an official bazaar, and the tunnel quickly lost its business (Klastrup n.d.: 314). The players took advantage of this new situation by creating robot-salesmen that represent them in the bazaar even when they are away from the computer. But the bazaar became so crowded with vendors and buyers that all the activity cluttered the display, overtaxed the system, and made response very slow. To remedy the problem, the developers redesigned the bazaar, so that "instead of showing all the vendors selling their goods, the screen shows only the character's avatar in a large hall, maybe with a few other shoppers, and the one vendor chosen to purchase from" (Taylor 2006: 64). Now the ball is in the players' court: who knows what they will do next?

There are times, however, when the feedback loop breaks down, leaving the developers unable to prevent activities that are detrimental to the enjoyment of other players. The most celebrated case of a loss of control over player behavior is the practice of buying objects in the game world with real-world money. As Castronova writes, "World builders always intended for goods and services to have prices and markets inside the world in term of gold pieces and credits and so on, but they seem not to have anticipated that these things would acquire robust markets in dollars outside the world" (2005: 149). Game developers and most players disapprove of this activity because it destroys the equality of opportunities that is so fundamental to the operation of games: a rich player who does not intend to devote much time and effort to the game world can rise instantly to the highest level by buying an avatar on eBay. It is the digital age equivalent of the practice that drew the ire of Martin Luther: gaining easy access to Heaven by buying indulgences rather than through faith and good works. As Julian Dibbell has chronicled in his entertaining book *Play Money, Or, How I Quit my Day Job and Made Millions Trading Virtual Loot* (2006), some people make a living manufacturing or collecting objects in online worlds, in order to sell them for real-world money. It has always been possible to work within fictional worlds, for instance as a professional actor or by parading as Mickey Mouse in Disneyland, but this possibility to create capital within a fictional world is unique to online games. Once the virtual objects produced in these games acquire real-world value, the inevitable next step is the creation of an exchange rate between game money (for instance, the platinum pieces of *EverQuest*) and real-world currencies. According to the *New York Times*,[9] the developers of an online game named *Entropia* plan to introduce a credit card that will allow players to obtain US dollars from ATMs (automated teller machines) by deducting the desired amount from their account of *Entropia* dollars.

5. Online Worlds between Fiction and Reality

I mention the practice of selling virtual objects for real-world money not only to illustrate the autonomy of the inhabitants of online worlds vis-à-vis game developers, but also to introduce the issue that makes these worlds particularly interesting from a theoretical point of view: the validity of the distinction between fiction and reality. Western thought has a long tradition of questioning of the reality of the real: we find it in Plato, with the myth of the cave; in the Baroque age, with the idea that the sensible world is an illusory dream; and nowadays, in the philosophy of Jean Baudrillard, who claims that the real has been replaced by its simulation. While for Plato and the Baroque the real resides in a transcendental sphere situated beyond the realm of appearances, for Baudrillard the only reality is that of the image. But with online games, the ontological question takes a new twist: rather than exposing the real as a fiction, the trend is now to ask whether the fictional worlds of online games should be regarded as an authentic form of reality. It is not a matter of claiming that online worlds have replaced the lifeworld, as Baudrillard would have it, but rather of according the same reality status to both worlds. This can be done in two ways: by regarding online worlds and the lifeworld as separate but equal in ontological status, or by questioning the validity of the boundary that separates them.

The "separate but equal" theory prevails in psychological approaches to the online world phenomenon. Sherry Turkle's book *Life on the Screen* (1995) contains several testimonies of users who consider their avatar to form a part of their identity as authentic as their "RL" (real life) self. An informant tells her: "RL is just one more window, and it's usually not my best one" (1995: 13). Another asks: "Why grant such superior status to the self that has the body when the selves that don't have bodies are able to have different kinds of experience?" (1995: 14). For these players, as for the French poet Arthur Rimbaud, "true life is elsewhere." But these declarations may be more judgments of quality than ontological pronouncements: people would not be so eager to proclaim the reality of online life if they did not derive more enjoyment from it than from everyday life. The most fanatic players know that the game world is an image, and that this image is unable to nourish the body. Imagine a society where half of the people spend all of their time playing online games, while the other half takes care of their bodily needs by supplying food, drink, and other necessities. Even in such a society, the supplies that maintain the bodies of the players alive could be produced in only one of the two worlds. Moreover, the developers of online games could pull the plug on their worlds, and they would disappear without trace, but the members of online games could not pull the plug on the real world. This asymmetrical relation makes it amply clear that the two worlds do not belong to the same ontological level, even if many players find an essential mean of self-fulfillment in the creation of imaginary identities. But don't we find similar self-fulfillment in private fantasies, and in the virtual world of traditional fiction?

If the worlds of online games cannot achieve reality in an ontological sense, can they do so in an economic sense? Here the argument does not treat online worlds and the lifeworld as distinct yet equal, but rather, emphasizes the permeability of their borders. Espen Aarseth (2005) thinks that the currency of online games is real, in contrast to the money of a game like Monopoly, because it can be exchanged for dollars, yen, or euros. But what does it mean to call money real? In contrast to commodities that have both a use and an exchange value, money is only desirable because of its buying power. As coins and bills disappear in favor of plastic cards that represent numbers in an account, it becomes more and more obvious that money is a purely virtual entity. Moreover, if the possibility of trading game-money for real-world currency made this money real, the same could be said of all the pixel-made objects acquired or built by players within the game, since these objects can also be sold for dollars, yen, or euros. But we would never call a horse in an online world real, because it is a mere image. What may be regarded as real is not the objects themselves but rather their value for other players. This value can be either a genuine use value within the game (for instance that of a fancy horse), or the exchange value typical of game currency. As Castronova writes: "when most people agree that [a] thing has a real value to somebody, it really has that value" (2005: 148). This distinction between "real object" and "real value" marks the difference between ontological and economic reality.[10]

Does the existence of real values in online worlds mean that their economy could merge with the economy of the real world? Let's consider what would happen if the currency of online worlds disappeared entirely, and all transactions took place in real-world money. If the developers of the online world had the right to make money and to freely distribute some amounts to players by changing the numbers in their accounts, this would create serious disruptions of the global economy. Normally the production of money is strictly controlled by the Federal Reserve or any similar state-run institution. By putting money on the market the game masters would become a rival Federal Reserve; but then, on what ground could anybody else be prevented from doing the same thing? There would be more and more money on the market but not more commodities with a real-world use value, since game objects are useless outside the game. This imbalance would lead to uncontrollable inflation. On the other hand, if money could not be produced within the game, the buying power of the players would correspond to what they already own in the real world, and the game world would become nothing more than an online store for virtual products. This is the situation to which the current habit of buying avatars and other game objects for real money would lead, if it were generalized, rather than remaining a very restricted niche activity existing side by side with trade using the game's own currency. The membrane that surrounds online worlds cannot be entirely removed without ruining their ludic dimension; for, as Huizinga (1950) observed, what makes a game a game is the magic circle that separates it from reality.

It is not necessary to regard online worlds as an extension of reality to do profitable commerce with them. Since the dawn of civilization, trade has opened doors in political and natural boundaries while keeping them solidly in place. With online worlds, exchanges occasionally cross ontological boundaries. But there remains an important difference between trade across political boundaries and trade across ontological boundaries. In the first type of commerce, commodities can be transported to the other side of the border, while in the second type, traded goods cannot leave their world of origin. Objects manufactured in an online world are made of bits and pixels, and they only exist through the code that supports their native environment. Moreover, as I have already noted, their use value is entirely linked to a particular world: an avatar from *EverQuest* can no more be imported into the world of Ultima Online than a real-world body can immigrate into the world of EverQuest.[11] In the commerce between the actual world and online worlds, there are consequently no direct exchanges, but rather, two distinct transactions. Within the game world, Orlando gives a magic sword to Furioso, while in the real world, John, who plays Furioso, transfers a certain sum of money into the account of Mary, who holds the strings of Orlando. To foster these parallel, mutually compensating transactions by which one world reacts to what happens in the other, the boundaries between game and reality need to be not so much porous as transparent.

What, in the end, is the reality status of online worlds? It all depends on what we understand by "real," but the meaning of the word varies with the nouns it qualifies. When it applies to an object or body, it stresses its materiality, its solidity, and it contrasts with its image. When it refers to emotions, it suggests their authenticity and sincerity, and it contrasts with pretending. When it qualifies the economic value of an object, it means that there are real people (in sense 1) who want this object, and it contrasts with lack of demand. When it describes a world as a whole, it refers to its autonomous existence and it contrasts with man-made, fictional, virtual, or simulated. The worlds of online games contain objects with real value; advancing in the game or falling in love with another player may trigger real emotions; stepping out of role, players may discuss the affairs of the real world; but what online worlds will forever lack is reality as autonomous, material existence. There cannot be a univocal answer to the question "are online worlds real?": they contain both real and unreal elements.

NOTES

1 Jorge Luis Borges offers the literary model of this encyclopedic activity in his story *Tlön, Uqbar, Orbis Tertius*, where he describes the collective creation of Tlön, an imaginary county, by a "secret society of astronomers, biologists, engineers, metaphysicians, poets, chemists, algebrists, moralists, painters, geometers" (72): "I now held in my hands a vast and systematic fragment of the entire history of an unknown planet, with its architecture and its playing cards, the horror of its mythologies and the murmur of its tongues, its emperors and its seas, its minerals and its birds and fishes, its theological and metaphysical controversies – all joined, articulated, coherent, and with no visible doctrinal purpose or hint of parody" (71–2).

2 <http://www.bergonia.org>.

3 Kingdom of Talossa: <http://www.kingdomoftalossa.net/>; Republic of Talossa: <http://www.republicoftalossa.com/>.

4 The micronation of Aristasia, the Feminine Empires (<http://www.aristasia.co.uk>), remedies this situation by inviting its members to meet in the online game world of Second Life. But the fact that live interaction has to take place in another world only underscores the inability of micronations to sustain active participation.

5 At: <http://www.thesims.com>.

6 See <http://www.machinima.com>.

7 I am particularly indebted to Fotis Jannidis for sharing his personal experiences in the world of *EverQuest*.

8 In the chapter in question, Castronova discusses the following dimensions of online worlds: Roles, Advancement, Status, Risk and Danger, Scarcity and Forced Cooperation, Messaging, Personality Content and AI.

9 <http://www.nytimes.com/2006/05/02/arts/02entr.html?_r=1&oref=slogin>.

10 The whole passage indicates, however, that Castronova is not aware of a difference between ontological and economic reality: "When a society in cyberspace hold that a certain glowing sword is really and truly magical, in the sense of having great and extraordinary powers, the judgment is not only impossible to deny within the membrane [of the online world], but it starts to affect judgments outside the membrane too. *By this process, virtual things become real things*; when most people agree that the thing has a real value to somebody, it really has that value" (2005: 148; my emphasis). The words in italics suggest, wrongly in my opinion, that real value implies real existence.

11 The only kind of object that can be brought into online worlds, or taken out of them, is digitized pictures or sound files. Some people have been known to sell their digital artworks in the world of Second Life. The buyer can either use the picture to decorate his virtual castle, or have it printed and framed for his real-world house. (See <http://www.boston.com/news/globe/living/articles/2006/10/25/leading_a_double_life/?page=2>.) What cannot be done, however, is to import a picture of a horse into a game world in order to provide a mount for an avatar. An imported image can only be used as an image.

BIBLIOGRAPHY

Aarseth, Espen (2005). "Doors and Perception: Fiction vs. Simulation in Games." *Proceedings of Digital Arts and Culture Conference*, ITU, December 1–3, pp. 59–62.

Bartle, Richard (1996). "Hearts, Clubs, Diamonds, Spades: Players Who Suit Muds." <http://www.mud.co.uk/richard/hcds.htm>.

Blumberg, Alex (n.d.). "It's Good to be King." <http://www.wired.com/wired/archive/8.03/kingdoms.html>.

Bogost, Ian (2006). *Unit Operations: An Approach to Videogame Criticism*. Cambridge, MA: MIT Press.

Borges, Jorge Luis (1998 [1941]). "Tlön, Uqbar, Orbis Tertius." In *Collected Fictions* (Andrew Hurley, Trans.). New York: Penguin, pp. 68–81.

Caillois, Roger (2001 [1958]). *Man, Play and Games*. Urbana: University of Illinois Press. French edition: *Les Jeux et les hommes. Le masque et le vertige*. Paris: Gallimard, 1958.

Castronova, Edward (2005). *Synthetic Worlds: The Business and Culture of Online Games*. Chicago: University of Chicago Press.

Dibbell, Julian (2006). *Play Money, Or, How I Quit my Day Job and Made Millions Trading Virtual Loot*. New York: Basic Books.

EverQuest Atlas (n.d.). Sony Entertainment Co.

Hellekson, Karen, and Kristina Busse (Eds.) (2006). *Fan Fictions and Fan Communities in the Age of the Internet*. Jefferson, NC: McFarland and Co.

Hergé (1975 [1955]). *Cigars of the Pharaoh*. Boston: Little, Brown.

Huizinga, Johan (1950). *Homo Ludens: A Study of the Play-element in Culture*. Boston: Beacon Press.

Jannidis, Fotis (2007). "Event-Sequences, Plot and Narration in Computer Games." In Peter Gendolla and Jörgen Schäfer (Eds.). *The Aesthetics of Net Literature: Writing, Reading and Playing in Programmable Media*. Bielefeld: transcript Verlag, pp. 281–305.

Jenkins, Henry (2006). "Interactive Audiences? The 'Collective Intelligence' of Media Fans." In *Fans, Bloggers, and Gamers*. New York: New York University Press, pp. 134–51.

Jones, Robert (2006). "From Shooting Monsters to Shooting Movies: Machinima and the Transformative Play of Videogame Fan Culture." In Karen Hellekson and Kristina Busse (Eds.). *Fan Fictions and Fan Communities in the Age of the Internet*. Jefferson, NC: McFarland and Co., pp. 261–80.

Klastrup, Lisbeth (n.d.). *Towards a Poetics of Virtual Worlds – Multi-User Texuality and the Emergence of Story*. Unpublished PhD dissertation, IT University Copenhagen.

Lewis, David (1978). "Truth in Fiction." *American Philosophical Quarterly* 15: 37–46.

"Micronations" (n.d.). Wikipedia, The Free Encyclopedia. <http://en.wikipedia.org/wiki/Micronation>.

Ryan, John, George Dunford, and Simon Sellars (2006). *Lonely Planet Micronations*. Lonely Planet Publications.

Ryan, Marie-Laure (1991). *Possible Worlds, Artificial Intelligence, and Narrative Theory*. Bloomington: University of Indiana Press.

—— (2001). *Narrative as Virtual Reality: Immersion and Interactivity in Literature and Digital Media*. Baltimore: Johns Hopkins University Press.

—— (2007). "Transfictionality Across Media." In John Pier and José Angel García (Eds.). *Theorizing Narrativity*. Berlin: Walter de Gruyter.

Saint-Gelais, Richard (2005). "Transfictionality." In David Herman, Manfred Jahn, and Marie-Laure Ryan (Eds.). *The Routledge Encyclopedia of Narrative Theory*. London: Routledge, pp. 612–13.

Salen, Katie, and Eric Zimerman (2003). *Rules of Play: Game Design Fundamentals*. Cambridge, MA: MIT Press.

Schaeffer, Jean Marie (1999). *Pourquoi la fiction?* Paris: Seuil.

Schiesel, Seth (2006). "Entropia Universe Players Can Cash Their Online Earnings at the A.T.M." <http://www.nytimes.com/2006/05/02/arts/02entr.html?_r=1&oref=slogin>.

Searle, John (1975). "The Logical Status of Fictional Discourse." *New Literary History* 6: 319–32.

Taylor, T. L. (2006). *Play Between Worlds: Exploring Online Game Culture*. Cambridge, MA: MIT Press.

Turkle, Sherry (1995). *Life on the Screen: Identity in the Age of the Internet*. New York: Simon & Schuster.

Walton, Kendall (1990). *Mimesis as Make-Believe: On the Foundations of the Representational Arts*. Cambridge, MA: Harvard University Press.

Wardrip-Fruin, Noah (2006). *Expressive Processing: On Process-Intensive Literature and Digital Media*. PhD dissertation, Brown University. <http://www.noahwf.com/dissertation>.

14

Riddle Machines: The History and Nature of Interactive Fiction

Nick Montfort

Introduction

The genre that has also been labeled "text adventure" and "text game" is stereotypically thought to offer dungeons, dragons, and the ability for readers to choose their own adventure. While there may be dragons here, interactive fiction (abbreviated "IF") also offers utopias, revenge plays, horrors, parables, intrigues, and codework, and pieces in this form resound with and rework Gilgamesh, Shakespeare, and Eliot as well as Tolkien. The reader types in phrases to participate in a dialogue with the system, commanding a character with writing. Beneath this surface conversation, and determining what the computer narrates, there is the machinery of a simulated world, capable of drawing the reader into imagining new perspectives and understanding strange systems.

Interactive fiction works can be challenging for literary readers, even those interested in other sorts of electronic literature, because of the text-based interface and because of the way in which these works require detailed exploration, mapping, and solution. Works in this form are often less visually rewarding, and the rewards they do offer are only attained with time and effort. But text-based interactive fiction has provided some of the most the intricate and compelling literary simulations yet developed. Understanding how interactive fiction works, and how it has developed over the past three decades, is an essential part of the puzzle of literary computing.

Characteristics of interactive fiction

Formally, a work of interactive fiction (often called a "game," even if it does not exhibit the typical qualities of a game) is an interactive computer program. While some IF uses graphics, and, less often, sound or animation, the basis of the form is textual input and textual output. The interactor types a command to one of the characters, called the player character, such as "ask Galatea about her awakening," "enter the doorway," or "reboot the server." The program, in turn, describes whether or not the player character is able to perform this action and, if it is possible, narrates what happens in the simulated world as a result. Two important features of IF are some sort of language understanding, accomplished by the component called the parser, and some way of simulating the things that exist in a virtual world, along with their behaviors and interactions. This latter feature is provided by a program's world model.

The world model simulates different areas, called "rooms," and the people, creatures, and objects that are in them. Rooms are connected in a graph, and the things they contain can themselves contain things. The output text is focalized by the player character. This simulation of an underlying world, from which the textual output is produced, makes it difficult to consider one's progress through interactive fiction as moving from one hypertextual lexia to another. Rather than imagining a fixed number of nodes of text, it is helpful to see the output text as being produced because of the simulation of the player character and the environment. Walking through a city may generate different texts depending upon the time of day, the events that are occurring in the city, the amount of light available, the state of mind of the player character, and the sensory abilities of that character.

The parser and world model are essential to IF; there are also many conventions that works in this form follow. Typically, the player character is commanded to go to a new location by using compass directions or abbreviations of them: "go north" can be abbreviated "north" or simply "n." Some games use different sorts of directions or allow the interactor to refer to landmarks (e.g., "go to the coffee shop"), but the way of commanding a character to move is among the most widely recognized conventions in IF. Parodies and jokes in the form of interactive fiction transcripts will invariably use compass-direction commands.

The instructions for the first interactive fiction, *Adventure*, declared "I will be your eyes and hands." While interactive fiction has been written in the first, second, and third person, it is conventional to refer to the player character in the second person, a feature of interactive fiction that is often remarked upon because it is so uncommon in other types of literary writing. The interactive fiction program itself, in its capacity as a narrator and an interface to the player character, is often referred to in the first person.

The ability to converse with other characters is often provided in IF, and not always in the same way. The type of conversation that is possible with chatterbots such as *Eliza/Doctor*, *Parry*, and *Racter* is not an option in IF. In one format for conversation, the interactor can specify a topic by typing something like "ask Dunbar about the Loblo bottle." Some games change from the usual mode of input when it comes to conversation, having the interactor pick what to say from a menu of possible utterances. While chatterbots offer a more free-form interface for conversation, the interlocutors in interactive fiction, called non-player characters, also have the ability to take action within the simulated world and to affect the environment that the player character and the non-player characters share.

A sample transcript

Bronze is a recent work of interactive fiction that is conventional in many ways (a fantasy setting, the use of compass directions for movement) but is also welcoming to beginners and plays with a well-known tale in an interesting way. This game, by Emily Short, was developed in part to serve as an example for a new interactive fiction development system, Inform 7.

> When the seventh day comes and it is time for you to return to the castle in the forest, your sisters cling to your sleeves.
>
> "Don't go back," they say, and "When will we ever see you again?" But you imagine they will find consolation somewhere.
>
> Your father hangs back, silent and moody. He has spent the week as far from you as possible, working until late at night. Now he speaks only to ask whether the Beast treated you "properly." Since he obviously has his own ideas about what must have taken place over the past few years, you do not reply beyond a shrug.
>
> You breathe more easily once you're back in the forest, alone.
>
> *Bronze*
> A fractured fairy tale by Emily Short
> Release 9 / Serial number 060225 / Inform 7 build 3F37 (I6/v6.30 lib 6/10N)
>
> Have you played interactive fiction before? >yes
>
> If you have not played Bronze before, you may still want to type HELP to learn about special commands unique to this game.
>
> Drawbridge
> Even in your short absence, the castle has come to look strange to you again. When you came here first, you stood a long while on the drawbridge, unready to cross the moat, for fear of the spells that might bind you if you did. This time it is too late to worry about such things.
>
> An iron-barred gate leads north.
>
> >open the gate
> You shouldn't be able to open it, heavy as it is, but it swings aside lightly at your touch. The Beast said that it knows friend from enemy; and the castle, at least, still regards you as friend.
>
> >go north
>
> Entrance Hall
> There is no fire in the big fireplace, and no one is waiting for you here; the air is very cold. Over the gate, the old familiar warning sign is painted.

Various passages lead deeper into the castle: north towards the central courtyard, southwest to the guard tower, east and west into the libraries, the offices, the galleries. Somewhere in this maze, he waits; and he should be told as soon as possible that you did return.

An iron-barred gate leads south to the drawbridge.

>go east

Scarlet Gallery
You do not often come this way, into the older part of the castle, which is narrow and has a low roof. The walls, and the ceiling too, are deep scarlet, the color of the old king and queen that ruled here two hundred fifty years ago, when there was still a kingdom.

>go southeast

Scarlet Tower
A little hexagonal room, from whose narrow window you can see the moat, the lawn, and the beginning of the forest outside.

On the windowsill, a helmet waits, for the use of the sentry.

>pick up the helmet
You acquire the helmet, and assess it curiously.

A very old helmet that you have seen the Beast wear (and quite foolish it looked, perched on a head it no longer fits: it would suit your head better). He told you once that the helmet was for night watchmen, scouts, and guards, to increase their vigilance and strengthen their hearing.

Lines of writing arc over each ear, but you do not know the language in question.

The commands above direct the player character to perform some of the most typical actions in an interactive fiction world: opening a gate, walking in a particular direction, and acquiring an object. The output from *Bronze* shows that these ordinary actions can reveal a back story, and that through the exploration of a virtual space, a well-known story – in this case, that of beauty and the beast – can be transformed and inflected in interesting ways.

The interactor's progress through the world of *Bronze* can continue, after the player character walks back to the entrance hall, like so:

>w

Great Dining Hall
Such a long hall that the soup might get cold between one end and the other. You and he used only the far west end, nearest the kitchen. Once you took to dining together at all, that is; the first few months he brought trays to your room, while you hid.

But then you took to eating here; and at the end of every meal he would stand up formally and ask his question.

"You can leave at any time," he said, when he first spoke to you. You stared at him, surprised that someone with his face and teeth was capable of human communication. "Would you like to go?"

There are other memories, more recent, of course. Every glance around the room reminds you of a different one.

>look at the room
You take another look around.

Great Dining Hall
You allow yourself to remember another night, another request.

"I'm surprised you haven't gone home yet," he said very early in your stay.

"I've heard stories," you replied. "As if there weren't enough to see around the castle. I know what happens to your servants who try to leave you."

"Nothing bad would happen to you," he said. But you could not believe him, not with all the captured spirits, not with the stories, not with the evidence around the castle.

>w

Enormous Kitchen
Haunted with the spirits of chefs past, generations and generations of culinary geniuses; one can never predict its whimsies. Unless he has moved everything, the bell to summon them into action should be in one of the rooms upstairs.

>n

Servant Quarters
You've never come here before, and now you see why. Not a room friendly to visitors, it has the air of resentful, martyred suffering. Even His most unpleasant ancestors would not have grudged this place more paint, surely, and more straw for the beds.

A decaying ladder leads down.

>go down

Darkness
Though a dim light filters down from the servant quarters, you can see almost nothing of the contents of your current location. You find yourself concentrating all the more alertly on your hearing, as though the slightest echo might offer a clue.

You hear some dry sifting from the northeast.

>wear the helmet
You settle the helmet over your head, and there is a roaring in your ears at first. But then the sharpened hearing begins to feel natural again.

>listen
Windchimes ring, almost inaudible, from the east, competing with some dry sifting from the northeast. You can also make out your own steady breathing.

In these exchanges, the importance of perception – something that has been integral to IF from the beginning – is foregrounded. In the dining hall, looking elicits a description of the surrounding area, but it does more than this: It also reveals memories. In the dark area under the servant quarters, an inability to see must be overcome with a different sense, and with an object that helps to amplify this sense. The puzzle posed by the darkness is solved (in this instance) not by finding a light source, but by realizing that another sense, if properly amplified, can help the player character to find her way around.

Bronze is a medium-sized game that can be completed in a few hours; these snippets represent a very small fraction of the texts that would be seen in a complete traversal of the game, in which everything would be solved and the session brought to a conclusion. At best, this beginning can hint at how a classic fairy tale is transformed in *Bronze* and can demonstrate some of the most typical interactions. There is much more to be found out and solved in *Bronze,* however, and there are many more spaces and interactions that reveal complex personal histories and relationships.

Interactive fiction as potential narrative

One perspective on interactive fiction is that it is potential narrative. The French literary and mathematical group Oulipo considered potential literature – literary spaces and possibilities – rather than literature itself. This concept, or at least, its narrative counterpart, can be useful in understanding interactive fiction. In the preceding transcript of *Bronze,* it is narrated that the player character enters the castle, goes east into an old wing of the place, finds and takes a helmet, and then goes through the kitchen and into the darkness, where she places the helmet on her head and is able to hear more effectively. But this is not "the" story, or "the" narrative, of *Bronze*; it is one particular sequence of events which was made to happen because of what the interactor typed. The interactor could have typed something different and gone into a different area at first, or could have directed the player character down into the dark area without having first found the helmet. *Bronze* provides a specific set of possibilities, however, not every imaginable text: the player character cannot walk off, get into a sport utility vehicle, and drive away.

In some interactive fiction, anyone who finds a solution and reaches the "winning" conclusion will have experienced the same spaces and had the player character carry out the same significant actions. Even in these cases, it can be important to see IF as a potential narrative that can be experienced in a different order by different interactors, since the different ways in which interactors solve the same game may greatly affect their experiences of it. Many games also provide alternate ways to solve the same puzzles. It is possible to provide an ending that differs depending upon the behavior of the player character, as Jason Devlin's *Vespers* demonstrates. In Stephen Granade's *Losing Your Grip,* two of the five "fits" in the game are completely different if the interactor makes different choices earlier on, and there is not much of a way to discover this without replaying or being told about it. Other interactive fiction exhibits a more obvious "branching" structure, something that can be seen in Adam Cadre's *I-0*, and, in a more unusual way, in his *Narcolepsy*.

Along with other useful perspectives (computer program, dialog system, simulation, game, riddle), the idea that interactive fiction is potential narrative encourages the consideration of how it is potential – what space of narratives is defined – and of how the elements of IF correspond to narrative elements. There are rather direct correspondences between characters and events, certainly, but levels of simulation can also correspond in interesting ways to diegetic levels. This suggests a few of several interesting ways in which the study of narrative can be used to understand interactive fiction while the nature of IF works as interactive computer programs is also taken into account.

A Brief History

While poetry generation systems, chatterbots, and video games originated before interactive fiction, the form has a rich and reasonably long history. Interactive fiction pre-dates personal computing, originating when only a small number of academics and researchers had regular access to mainframes and minicomputers. After playing an important role in early recreational computing, interactive fiction came to the microcomputer and became a notable part of the entertainment software market. Commercial sales brought interactive fiction to millions of interactors and left a lasting impression on the computer gaming industry. While interactive fiction does not top computer game sales charts today, its return to hobbyist roots and free distribution, facilitated by the internet, has offered new space for concepts and writing that would have been far too unusual and innovative for the mass market to bear.

Early "mainframe" games

The canonical first work of interactive fiction was *Adventure*, a cave simulation which appeared in its best-known form in 1977. Several important predecessors helped bring computing into the mid-1970s and contributed to some of aspects of *Adventure* that made it a success. One of these was an earlier cave simulation, *Hunt the Wumpus*, a BASIC program written by Gregory Yob and first published in print in 1973. This game was set on a dodecahedron instead of the usual Cartesian grid, a setting that was a step toward the arbitrary mazes of *Adventure*. Before this, Terry Winograd had developed a system that could carry on natural-language dialogue in a restricted domain. His *SHRDLU* (1972) offered a blocks world and was not much of an adventure – it was not designed to be – but it did have the textual exchange and the sort of world model that would characterize later interactive fiction. Another important dialogue system, developed even earlier, was Joseph Weizenbaum's *Eliza/Doctor*. This fictional therapist did not have the sort of world model that

SHURDLU did or the complex cave setting of *Hunt the Wumpus*, but it provided something that interactive fiction would later need – a compelling scenario for interaction, one which invited users to participate in a conversation (Murray 1997: 214–50).

These computing developments laid some of the groundwork for a project that Will Crowther undertook, in the mid-1970s. Crowther, who worked at Bolt, Beranek, and Newman in Cambridge, Massachusetts, was working to develop the *ARPANET*. His hobbies included exploring caves and playing *Dungeons and Dragons*. He decided to develop a computer game, in FORTRAN, that drew on these experiences and which could be enjoyed by his young daughters. His first version of *Adventure* was a model of a real cave system in Kentucky, one which he had explored and mapped (Jerz 2007). The simulation was not entirely realistic: He placed virtual treasures in the cave, for instance, to lure the interactor into exploring and reward her for reaching remote areas.

The version of *Adventure* that became famous did not come out until later. It was due to an unusual collaborative effort. Don Woods, at Stanford, found *Adventure* and decided he would like to modify it. He asked Crowther for permission, but otherwise worked independently to fix bugs, expand the cave, and add other elements to the game. The canonical *Adventure* (sometimes called *Colossal Cave*) was the version of Crowther's code that Woods finished tweaking in 1977. *Adventure* was made available to all (at least, to the few who had access to PDP-10s at the time) and was well received. It became the subject of the first dissertation on a computer game (Buckles 1985). Those who encountered it at the time joke that computing was set back two weeks while everyone who could run *Adventure* spent that time solving it. Several people may have been set back more than two weeks by *Adventure*, because they decided to port it to new systems, do their own expansions of the game, or write their own "adventures."

These adventures included *Haunt*, developed at Carnegie Mellon by John Laird and set in a mansion rather than below ground. Other early "house" games included *Mystery Mansion*, written in the late 1970s, and the 1980 *Mystery House*, by Roberta and Ken Williams, which was the first text-and-graphics adventure. In England, David Seal, Jon Thackray, and Jonathan Partington used the University of Cambridge's Phoenix system to develop the sprawling game *Acheton*. A long series of additional adventures for the same platform followed. The other Cambridge, in Massachusetts, was not done with interactive fiction yet. At MIT, David Lebling, Marc Blank, Timothy A. Anderson, and Bruce Daniels worked to assemble a cave-crawl of a different sort, *Zork*, which incorporated several technological advances in parsing and world modeling. *Zork* also included the first notable character in interactive fiction, largely coded by Anderson and referred to simply as "the thief." *Zork*, a version of which was known as *Dungeon*, proved extremely popular, and its history did not end in the mainframe era: In 1979, three of the *Zork* creators joined with others at MIT to found a company, Infocom, which became the major player in commercial interactive fiction in the United States.

The commercial era

Although Infocom helped to popularize the term "interactive fiction" and became the major IF company in the United States, they were not the first company to use the term or the first to market with adventures. Scott Adams's company Adventure International was first to bill one of its publications as IF, and brought out *Adventure-land*, a condensed BASIC version of *Adventure*, back in 1978 – on cassette tape for the TRS-80 Model I. Adams's games are not literary masterpieces, but were important for helping to establish a commercial market for IF. They also provided many people's first exposure to the form.

Infocom developed more than thirty interactive fiction works in its productive decade. The company began by publishing a trilogy based on the mainframe *Zork*. Slicing the game into three parts allowed each part to fit on disk and into a PC's limited memory. An interpreter, the Z-Machine, allowed Infocom's game to be written once and published on dozens of platforms. Infocom began to work in various popular genres, beginning with the detective story. Marc Blank's 1982 *Deadline* (see Aarseth 1997: 115–28) was the first foray into this genre. Other developments included the science-fiction *Starcross* (Dave Lebling, 1982), the archeological adventure *Infidel* (Michael Berlyn and Patricia Fogelman, 1983), and a game styled after the romance novel, *Plundered Hearts* (Amy Biggs, 1987). Infocom also developed some IF that was based directly on popular novels, including what was probably the best-selling game of this sort, *The Hitchhiker's Guide to the Galaxy*. Unusually, the author of the earlier novel and radio play, Douglas Adams, collaborated with the most prolific of Infocom's implementors, Steve Meretzky, on this project. Making books into interactive fiction became a fairly popular idea during the 1980s. In Australia, for instance, the company Melbourne House released the text-and-graphics game *The Hobbit* in 1983. Another US company, initially called Trillium and renamed Telarium, did text-and-graphics interactive fiction versions of Ray Bradbury's *Fahrenheit 451* and Roger Zelazny's *Nine Princes in Amber*; there were reworkings of Isaac Asimov and Stephen King novels as well. Infocom's other releases included many original contributions: a game based on wordplay, two juvenile interactive fiction pieces, and even a bawdy space opera.

Other US companies didn't build the catalog that Infocom did, but they published a variety of interesting works. Synapse brought in print writers to work with programmers. The company released only four games, one of which, *Mindwheel* (1984), was by future US poet laureate Robert Pinsky (see Pinsky 1995). Novelist and poet Thomas M. Disch worked with the Cognetics Corporation to create *Amnesia* (1986), set in contemporary Manhattan. Many text-and-graphics adventures were developed beginning in the early 1980s, too. Sierra On-Line began a successful series, which eventually went all-graphical, when they released *King's Quest: Quest for the Crown* in 1983, initially for the ill-fated IBM PC Jr. The game accepted textual commands, as earlier interactive fiction did, but also featured a walking character who could be directed with arrow keys or a joystick.

The rest of the English-speaking world was not lacking for quality interactive fiction. In the UK, the brothers Pete, Mike, and Nick Austin founded Level 9 and published twenty games, starting with their version of *Adventure*, *Colossal Adventure*. They boasted that their 1983 science fiction game *Snowball* offered 7,000 rooms. In 1987, the company released *Knight Orc*, which featured autonomously wandering characters and gave the interactor the opportunity to play an anti-hero, a distasteful orc who is shunned even by his own kind. A UK company that came onto the scene later was Magnetic Scrolls, which was founded by Anita Sinclair, Ken Gordon, and Hugh Steers and started developing text-and-graphics adventures for more capable computers than Level 9 and Infocom had started off with. Their first offering, in 1985, was *The Pawn* by Rob Steggles. Later games included *Corruption* by Steggles and Hugh Steers (1988), set in contemporary London; the zany inter-dimensional *Fish!* by John Molloy and others (1988); and David Bishop's *Wonderland* (1990), which played on Lewis Carroll's *Alice in Wonderland*.

The IF community

Interactive fiction wasn't only consumed, or interacted with, by home computer users. At a time when learning BASIC was a typical activity for PC purchasers, it was common for people to program interactive fiction themselves, just as some of the early players of *Adventure* chose to do. While some coded up their adventures in BASIC, there were also systems that were customized to the task of interactive fiction development. One was Graeme Yeandle's The Quill Adventure System, published first in the UK in 1983 and later ported to the Commodore 64 and released in the United States as Adventure Writer. While the commercial market for IF was cooling at the end of the 1980s, very capable new IF development systems were reaching a wide audience. One was Mike Roberts's TADS (Text Adventure Development System), released as shareware in 1987. Another, made available for free by its creator, Graham Nelson, in 1993, was Inform (Nelson 2001). At the same time that Inform was released, Nelson also released a large-scale, Infocom-style adventure, *Curses*, that he had written in the system and that proved its mettle. Over the years, the development of TADS, Inform, and other systems has continued. The availability of these systems helped to foster amateur development efforts as interactive fiction was disappearing from store shelves.

A great deal of contemporary interactive fiction activity involves the "IF community," those who participate in the two Usenet newsgroups about interactive fiction, are part of the annual IF Competition, and maintain online institutions such as the IF Archive. The first IF Competition was run in 1995 by G. Kevin Wilson, an IF author who also founded the *Society for the Promotion of Adventure Games Newsletter*. The Comp, as it is called, is judged by users in the IF Community and offers a forum for shorter interactive fiction which can be solved in less than two hours. Winners have included a *Change in the Weather* by Andrew Plotkin (1995, Inform category), which features landscape descriptions that changed throughout the day; Adam Cadre's *Photopia* (1998), which portrays several scenes from a girl's life and imagination; Jon Ingold's

All Roads (2001), a disorienting tale that shifts between perspectives in seventeenth-century Venice; Dan Ravipinto and Star Foster's *Slouching towards Bedlam* (2003), a steampunk story of language and madness; and Jason Devlin's *Vespers* (2005), in which the player character is an abbot during the Black Death. Several review websites, a Wiki, and a MUD provide other channels for online discussion of and publication about interactive fiction.

The development of innovative short games, of the sort that feature in the Comp, has been an important new step in recent years. On the even shorter side, IF authors sometimes gather online to create "Speed IF," pieces that are usually silly and are entirely written in two hours. And, larger interactive fiction pieces on the scale of those sold in the 1980s have also been published. Some notable ones include Graham Nelson's 1995 *Jigsaw*, in which the player character travels back into the twentieth century re-righting a history that is disturbed by the mysterious character Black; Suzanne Britton's 1999 *Worlds Apart*, a science-fiction game with a vast and detailed world; Peter Nepstad's *1893: A World's Fair Mystery*, a 2002 commercial release that strives for historical accuracy and educational value; Emily Short's 2002 *Savoir-Faire*, set in an eighteenth-century French estate and involving a specially formulated magic. Other important long-form and short-form games from recent years are described in more detail later in the "Suggestions for Play" section.

The development of interactive fiction in languages other than English has been undertaken since at least the commercial era. In recent years, there have been active communities of Spanish, Italian, and German IF developers and players, and some IF development activity in other languages.

Contexts of Interactive Fiction

Interactive fiction has been an influential part of computing, computer gaming, and digital literature. The role of IF in gaming has been recognized by Crowther and Woods receiving an award at the 2006 Game Developers Conference and by the occasional tribute article that appears online or in print in the gaming press. Interactive fiction is often a part of public readings of electronic literature and of courses that consider computing and literature. This section traces a few threads of influence, explains some of the material ways in which interactors encounter interactive fiction, and considers modern-day IF development systems in a bit more depth.

Interactive fiction and the origin of MUDs

Recent Massively Multiplayer Online Role-playing Games (MMORPGs, or MMOs), such as *World of Warcraft*, *Star Wars Galaxies*, and *Everquest*, are in many ways graphical versions of earlier text-based systems that originated with the MUD, or Multi-User Dungeon. The experience of a MUD is quite similar to that of interactive fiction in many ways: one controls a character with textual commands in a similar sort of virtual, all-text environment. There is one important difference, however. Other characters on the same MUD are controlled by other people, allowing the system to be used for group adventures and social interaction. MUD is sometimes expanded as "Multi-User Dimension" by those who find dungeons distasteful, but Richard Bartle, co-creator of the original MUD at the University of Essex in 1978, explained that the name does contain the word "Dungeon" and that this refers specifically to the computer game *Dungeon*, a.k.a. *Zork*. The other "Multi-user Zorks" that followed from this first system at Essex provided further opportunities for player-to-player conversation and social dynamics that quickly became important to people's MUD experiences. Later, the MOO (MUD Object Oriented) made it easy for people to shape the virtual environment, build bots, and otherwise participate as designers. While the MUD can be considered formally to be a strictly improved, multi-user sort of interactive fiction, the importance of interpersonal interactions in these systems meant that their development took a different turn.

Relationship to gaming and graphical adventures

Via the MUD, interactive fiction has had an influence on graphical, massively multi-player gaming. Other game forms and genres also trace their roots to interactive fiction. One of these began with the 1980 computer game *Rogue*, which used ordinary ASCII characters to draw dungeons and mazes – the player's "man" was represented as "@". Interactive fiction was also influential, both directly and via *Rogue* and the similar game *Nethack*, on the genre of the computer RPG (role-playing game). In this category of games, turn-based combat and ability points of the *Dungeons and Dragons* sort were staples of the system, but some of the puzzle-solving and exploration that had been developing in interactive fiction could be seen as well.

The main descendant of interactive fiction is no doubt the graphical adventure. The first game in this category was Warren Robinett's aptly titled *Adventure* for the cartridge-based Atari VCS (Atari 2600), released in 1978 and incorporating no text. Most of the development of the graphical adventure happened via various lines of text-and-graphics games in which, over time, graphics took over as interface development continued and the graphics capabilities of home computers improved. Sierra On-Line's *King's Quest* series (and the related *Space Quest* series and *Police Quest* series) followed this trajectory. The humorous graphical adventures developed by LucasArts are also adventures, and helped to innovate by providing the interactor with multiple player characters who sometimes interacted comically. The LucasArts games include *Maniac Mansion, Sam and Max Hit the Road*, the *Monkey Island* series, and *Grim Fandango*. The early CD-ROM hit *Myst*, which eschews language input for simple pointing and clicking, is another example in the graphical adventure category. More recently, "action adventure" games and those that involve a character under-taking the exploration of a simulated world – the *Tomb Raider* and later *Grand Theft Auto* games are examples – are, as the name of this genre suggests, descendants of interactive fiction, although more distant ones.

Literary aspects: the novel, the riddle

The obvious literary relative of interactive fiction seems to be the novel. Infocom developed pieces that fit into popular novelistic genres; many novels were adapted into interactive fiction works; Synapse dubbed each of its four IF publications "an electronic novel" and even packaged them in hard-bound books, cutting out pages in the back to accommodate the disks. Even the term "interactive fiction" suggests a connection to the novel. The output of IF usually looks more like novelistic prose than like poetry or the text of a play, although there are exceptions. Despite the long effort to draw connections between the novel and interactive fiction, there are several important differences, even overlooking the main one, that a novel is a text and a work of interactive fiction is an interactive computer program. It takes longer to solve many commercial works of IF than it takes to read a novel, for instance, while the process may result in less text (not counting repeated passages) being output. The setting is seldom the strong point of the novel, while the environment is an extremely important part of interactive fiction.

In *Twisty Little Passages* (Montfort 2003), I suggested a different literary connection, to a poetic form, the riddle. The tradition of the riddle is long-standing, although the form is now often dismissed as a trivial amusement for children. Riddles are among the first English poems and, while they have sometimes appeared as parlor amusements, some poets, including May Swenson and Emily Dickinson, have written compelling riddles that question the world and how it is perceived. By asking the listener or reader to complete them with an answer, riddles invite thought and discussion in a way that many other literary forms do not, but which interactive fiction does. Just as a real riddle requests an answer, interactive fiction requires input from the interactor. It also often provides an opportunity for the interactor to perform his or her understanding of the IF world: by having the player character act appropriately, the interactor demonstrates comprehension of the strange systems of a particular work. The riddle helps to explain how figuration and a negotiation of understanding can take place in interactive fiction.

Conventions and materials of interaction: mapping, transcripts, "feelies"

New interactors can be overwhelmed by interactive fiction, particularly when they confront older IF works, in part because they literally arrive ill-equipped. The classic mode of play, since *Adventure*, has involved keeping notes on paper as one tries to progress through a game. More recent IF works may not require mapping, either because of their small world size (as seen in some Comp games) or because authors have designed them with a geography or interface that makes it easier to keep track of the virtual space. Still, for many games, keeping a map is essential. Such a map often simply consists of room names in circles, lines drawn between adjacent rooms, and additional remarks on items and features of interest scribbled here and there.

Another material tradition is referring back to a transcript to figure out a predicament. Players of *Adventure* would often get transcripts of their interaction by default, because many of them played on print terminals and their display was printed on paper. In the home computer era, players could print transcripts to study; it was also possible to save transcript files and look over them without printing.

Finally, there is a fondly remembered material dimension of interactive fiction, that of the "feelie," which was established by Infocom. In part to discourage the illegal copying of their software, Infocom included various objects in their game packages: a glow-in-the-dark plastic stone came with *Wishbringer*, which was about a magical stone, for instance. Some recent IF authors have created virtual or tangible feelies to go along with their recent releases.

Modern IF development and distribution

In recent years, almost all the interactive fiction that has been developed has been made available online for free via the IF Archive and authors' websites. Most of it has been developed using dedicated IF development systems, including TADS and Inform. The third version of TADS and a greatly updated Inform 7 were both released in 2006. Both systems are available for free, and are general-purpose programming languages with well-developed, standard, and extensible libraries. For instance, they provide default replies when a command can't be carried out or has no effect, although these can be overridden; they also simulate the way that light sources and containers work. Alternatives to these systems include Hugo, a capable, cross-platform system that supports multimedia, and ADRIFT, a system many find easy to use.

On the interactor's end, running interactive fiction is a two-step process that involves downloading the appropriate interpreter and then running the IF work in that interpreter. Although this process is not difficult, it is more involved than clicking on a link to see a Flash file or go to a webpage. Some effective web-based interpreters have been developed, although these are not ideal for sustained interaction.

Suggestions for Play

The easiest interactive fiction is not necessarily the best starting point. A complex, difficult piece such as Adam Cadre's 1999 *Varicella* (see Montfort and Moulthrop 2003) quickly conveys how the intricate simulation that IF affords can be turned to new literary purposes. In *Varicella*, the player character is a sniveling and completely unlikable palace minister. The setting is the palazzo of the recently departed King Charles, a place that seems to be historical at first, but which is discovered to have strange contemporary and science-fictional elements. The wide range of characters are almost uniformly despicable. The interactor will be amused at commanding the player character to eliminate his rivals and take over the regency, but will also encounter darker and more serious aspects of this violent system. Impossible for a beginner to solve in a short amount of time, *Varicella* nevertheless is excellent at quickly showing what interactive fiction can do.

A shorter IF work that can be completed in an hour or so is Andrew Plotkin's *Shade* (2000), which plays on the concept of the "one-room game." *Shade* occurs – so we suppose – in the player character's apartment, in the early morning hours before departure for a Burning-Man-like festival. By performing ordinary tasks such as looking for plane tickets and trying to find a glass of water, the player character causes the apartment to undergo a transformation, and the true nature of the player's surroundings become evident. Although it requires some familiarity with IF interaction, *Shade* deals with levels of reality in an extremely powerful way.

Another excellent piece set at some point near to the present day is Michael Gentry's *Anchorhead* (1998). The world of *Anchorhead*, inspired by H. P. Lovecraft, is a whole New England town; the player character explores this world over several days in the course of reaching the conclusion. The setting is well wrought, and the way the horrific discoveries unfold is particularly effective.

Bad Machine by Dan Shiovitz (1999) takes place in a science-fictional setting; the player character is a reconfigurable robot in a strange factory. The striking thing about this game is the way it blends elements of computerized communication (programming language constructs, for instance) to create a texture of the sort that is also seen in the "codework" of digital poets. Figuring out what is going on at first is a puzzle in itself; then, the nature of the factory – which refers to industrial and information-age work environments – poses further challenges. The player character has only managed to acquire free will because part of the productive systems of the factory have broken down, creating a "bad machine" with individual consciousness.

An even less conventional piece, although more immediately legible, is Aaron Reed's *Whom the Telling Changed*, released in 2005. The story of Gilgamesh is the centerpiece of this game, which takes place at a ritual storytelling event in ancient Sumer. Standard interactive fiction commands are available, but the interactor can also type one of the highlighted words, selecting it as if choosing a hypertextual link.

Sam Barlow's *Aisle* (1999) is fascinating as a limit case of interactive fiction. Each individual encounter with *Aisle* begins in a grocery story and is only one turn long – the interactor only has the opportunity to type one command. Repeated interactions with *Aisle* can reveal different things about the player character's past and present – some of which are oddly inconsistent, or intersect in curious ways.

The previous items on this list are all from the past decade, and are available for free download – along with many others – from the Interactive Fiction Archive, easily accessed via Baf's Guide. There is plenty of commercial IF from the 1980s that can also provide a good starting point, although these games are harder to access. Steve Meretzky's *A Mind Forever Voyaging* is an extraordinary piece, for instance, offering a more and more dystopian city that can be explored at several points in the future. Also notable for their sociopolitical dimensions are two games that engaged the apocalyptic fears of the cold war, Brian Moriarty's *Trinity* and Robert Pinsky's *Mindwheel*.

Conclusion

Interactive fiction has been a rather startling subplot in computing and literature – one that has only recently been acknowledged as an interesting thread of practice, worth considering alongside higher-brow traditions such as hypertext fiction and digital poetry. If interactive fiction were simply a riff on the command-line way of interacting with computers, it would be of little interest. But it has been more than that for decades, providing a fascinating structure for narrative human–computer conversation, bringing simulation and narration together in novel ways.

A great deal of gaming and literary innovation has followed from a single FORTRAN program, released to the world by Crowther and Woods in 1976. Author/programmers continue to develop interactive fiction that engages the questions of literature. People continue to encounter IF, and to learn to create IF, informally as well as in the classroom. IF has already survived, and prospered, despite the dwindling of the commercial market for text games and despite the shift from text-based to GUI (graphical user interface) computing. There is likely to be a good deal more literary innovation in store in the form of interactive fiction.

BIBLIOGRAPHY

Works of interactive fiction mentioned in this article are generally either available from the IF Archive or, either because they were commercially published or because they run only on older computer systems, are not available at all. Pieces on the IF Archive can be easily found and downloaded by searching by title or author on Baf's Guide, <http://wurb.com/if/>.

To see how to install the necessary interpreter and run a work of interactive fiction, consult the Interactive Fiction FAQ, by Nick Montfort with Sam Kabo Ashwell, Dave Cornelson, Dan Shiovitz, and other ifwiki contributors: <http://nickm.com/if/faq.html>.

Aarseth, Espen (1997). *Cybertext: Perspectives on Ergodic Literature.* Baltimore, MD: Johns Hopkins University Press.

Buckles, Mary Ann (1985). "Interactive Fiction: The Computer Storygame 'Adventure.' " PhD Thesis, University of California San Diego.

Jerz, Dennis G. (2007). "Somewhere Nearby is Colossal Cave: Examining Will Crowther's Original 'Adventure' in Code and in Kentucky." Forthcoming in *Digital Humanities Quarterly.*

Montfort, Nick (2003). *Twisty Little Passages: An Approach to Interactive Fiction.* Cambridge, MA: The MIT Press.

——, and Stuart Moulthrop (2003). "Face It, Tiger, You Just Hit the Jackpot: Reading and Playing Cadre's Varicella." *Fineart Forum* 17:8. <http://www.msstate.edu/Fineart_Online/Backissues/Vol_17/faf_v17_n08/reviews/montfort.html>.

Murray, Janet (1997). *Hamlet on the Holodeck: The Future of Narrative in Cyberspace.* New York: Free Press.

Nelson, Graham (2001). *The Inform Designer's Manual,* 4th edn. St. Charles, IL: The Interactive Fiction Library. Also online at <http://www.inform-fiction.org/manual/DM4.pdf>.

Pinsky, Robert (1995). "The Poetics of Zork." *The New York Times Book Review,* March 19: 3+.

15

Too Dimensional: Literary and Technical Images of Potentiality in the History of Hypertext

Belinda Barnet and Darren Tofts

There is a vision offered in these pages, simple, unified and sweeping: it is a unified concept of interconnected ideas and data, and of how these ideas and data may be stored and published. (Ted Nelson 1992: preface)

Historiography is always guided by specific metaphors; it is "infected" by what it touches as the past (Demeulenaere 2003). Much has been written about the history of hypertext over the last twenty years,[1] and this chapter is not an attempt to write another linear, causally linked history. What we will be investigating is how some of the early hypertext designs have become *inherited vision* within hypertext literature – in particular, Vannevar Bush's Memex, Ted Nelson's Xanadu, and Douglas Engelbart's oN-Line System. Historical and literary works routinely trace the evolution of hypertext through these three inventors and their designs, and certain essays (for example Bush's *As We May Think*) are regularly cited. The early hypertext fiction works, particularly those on the web, also engage with these key works.

In relation to Vannevar Bush's Memex, Paisley and Butler have noted that "scientists and technologists are guided by 'images of potentiality' – the untested theories, unanswered questions and unbuilt devices that they view as their agenda for five years, ten years, and longer" (cited in Smith 1991: 262). We will contend that hypertext theory and fiction writers are similarly guided by images of potentiality within the field. With respect to hypertext, they constitute a vision of the ultimate archive, an archive which preserves the "true" or "natural" connections which hold between items. This system would be non-linear, encyclopedic, cross-referential, or as James Joyce puts it, "too dimensional" (Joyce 1975: 154). The vision has never been perfectly realized. What, then, can we say about a dream which is never fulfilled – but nonetheless recurs?

In the first section we will investigate the different hypertext systems designed by Bush, Engelbart, and Nelson, highlighting the differences between them. We will be specifically interested here in how Bush's vision *influenced* Nelson and Engelbart. Although the great body of literature suggests that they were "directly influenced" by Bush's vision (Whitehead 2000; Keep, McLaughlin, and Parmar 2001), both Nelson and Engelbart claim that the vector was not so precise. In the second section we will investigate how some of the early archives of web-based literary works engaged with this creation myth, and critique their assumptions to do with hypertext as an emergent medium.

Vannevar Bush and Memex

> There is another revolution under way, and it is far more important and significant than [the industrial revolution]. It might be called the mental revolution. (Bush 1959: 165)

Documents on information retrieval systems are not known for their shelf-life. What, then, is it about the ideas behind Vannevar Bush's writings which have so influenced today's research agenda in digital media? Linda C. Smith undertook a comprehensive citation context analysis of literary and scientific articles produced after the 1945 publication of Bush's article in the *Atlantic Monthly*, "As We May Think." In this article, Bush looked toward the post-war world and predicted an exponential increase in human knowledge. How are we to keep track of it all? He urged men of science to turn their efforts to making the great body of human knowledge more accessible to individuals, and proposed a machine to organize the mess: the Memory Extender or "Memex." Smith found that there is a conviction, without dissent, that modern hypertext is traceable to this article (Smith 1991: 265). In each decade since the Memex design was published, commentators have not only lauded it as vision, but also asserted that "technology [has] finally caught up with this vision" (Smith 1991: 278). Ted Nelson and Douglas Engelbart are the most vocal supporters of Bush as founding father of hypertext, and Engelbart wrote to Bush in 1962 to tell him that the article had influenced him "quite basically" (Engelbart 1962: 235).

We will look at this visionary machine, a precursor to hypertext, presently. Amid all the excitement, however, it is important to remember that Memex was never built; it exists *entirely on paper*. Because the design was first published in the summer of 1945, at the end of a war effort and with the birth of computers, theorists have often associated it with the post-war information boom. In fact, Bush had been writing about it since the early 1930s, and the Memex essay went through several different versions.

As Nyce and Kahn observe, in all versions of the essay (1933, 1939, 1945, 1967), Bush begins his thesis by explaining the dire problem we face in confronting the great mass of the human record, criticizing the way information was then organized. The main problem as he saw it was "the matter of selection"; the way we categorize, store, and retrieve information. Bush is quite clear about what is wrong with traditional indexing systems: they are *artificial*. Information should not be organized alphabetically or numerically, it should be organized by association – this is how the mind works.

> Our ineptitude at getting at the record is largely caused by the artificiality of systems of indexing. When data of any sort are placed in storage, they are filed alphabetically or numerically...[the] human mind does not work that way. It operates by association. With one item in grasp, it snaps instantly to the next that is suggested by the association of thoughts, in accordance with some intricate web of trails carried by the cells of the brain. (Bush 1939, 1945, 1967)

These sentences were important enough that they appeared verbatim in all versions of the Memex essay. Details of how the machine operated changed, but this emphasis on "natural" versus "artificial" indexing stayed the same. Bush wanted a machine to support the building of *trails of association* through vast stores of information, based on his understanding of how the human mind and memory work. His model of associative memory was derived from work being done by his colleagues at MIT, Claude Shannon, Warren McCulloch, and Walter Pitts – work that would result in the McCulloch–Pitts neuron (Hayles 1999: 65). This model of neuronal networks was later articulated more thoroughly in terms of computer switching. Bush explicitly worked with such analogies – in fact, "he not only thought with and in these terms, he built technological projects with them" (Nyce and Kahn 1991: 62).

Of all his projects, Bush felt the greatest sense of urgency about Memex. The collective record is expanding, information is getting more complex, and we are not equipped to manage the mess. One of the most widely quoted sentences from his 1945 essay expresses this sense of urgency:

> The summation of human experience is being expanded at a prodigious rate, and the means we use for threading through the consequent maze to the momentarily important item is the same as was used in the days of square-rigged ships. (Bush 1945)

In an interview with one of the authors, Douglas Engelbart was asked what motivated him to create the world's first hypertext system in the mid-1960s (a system we will explore in the next section). He replied:

> I thought, "it's a complex world, getting more complex and the problems are getting more urgent...so let's just see what we can do to improve mankind's collective ability to deal with complexity and urgency." (Interview with Barnet, 1999)

There is a vision behind hypertext. As Ted Nelson put it in the introduction to this essay, the vision is simple, unified, and sweeping; it is also *urgent*. It is a vision of the ultimate archive: an archive that is more powerful and more efficient than any that has come before, an archive where things that are logically linked together are logically retrieved together.[2] The early hypertext systems differed radically in their mechanism, scope, and workings: but this vision, and this sense of urgency, remained the same. Bush felt his project was of the utmost importance to the future of human civilization; it would boost "the entire process by which man profits by his inheritance of acquired knowledge" (1945: 99).

Memex was originally proposed as a desk at which the user could sit, equipped with two slanting translucent screens upon which material would be projected for convenient reading. There was a keyboard to the right of these screens, and a set of buttons and levers which could be used to search information. If the user wished to consult a certain article, "he [tapped] its code on the keyboard, and the title page of the book promptly appear[ed]" (Bush 1945: 103). The images were stored on microfilm inside the desk, which was an exciting new technology in Bush's time. To add information to the microfilm file, a photographic copying plate was also provided on the desk, but most of the Memex contents would be "purchased on microfilm ready for insertion" (Bush 1945: 102). The user could classify material as it came in front of him using a stylus, and register links between different pieces of information using this stylus.

The 1945 Memex design also introduced the concept of "trails," which was a method of connecting information by linking two units together, anticipating hyper-text paths. Making a chain of these links was called "trailblazing," and was based on a mechanical provision "whereby any item may be caused at will to select immediately and automatically another" (Bush 1945: 107), just as though these items were being "gathered together from widely separated sources and bound together to form a new book" (Bush 1945: 104). Although Memex links were made between a pair of microfilm frames, they did not have the same "granularity" as modern hypertext links, which are much more accurate and can be directed to a single word, phrase, or image. Nevertheless, Memex was the first machine to propose associative trails as an organizational principle. "This is the essential feature of the Memex. The process of tying two items together is the important thing" (Bush 1945: 103). Bush went so far as to suggest that in the future, there would be professional trailblazers who took pleasure in creating useful paths through the common record using their Memex.

Memex became an image of potentiality for Bush himself near the end of his life. In the later essays, he writes in a different tone entirely: Memex was a vision he would bequeath to the future, a gift to the human race (1959, 1970). He was nearing the end of his life, and the loss of his own knowledge as a great thinker. If the Memex were built, could it carry his own thoughts to a new generation?

> Can a son inherit the memex of his father, refined and polished over the years, and go on from there? In this way can we avoid some of the loss which comes when oxygen is no longer furnished to the brain of the great thinker, when all the patterns of neurons so painstakingly refined become merely a mass of protein and nucleic acid? Can the race thus develop leaders, of such power and intellect, that the world can be saved from its follies? This is an objective of far greater importance than the conquest of disease. (Bush 1959: 183)

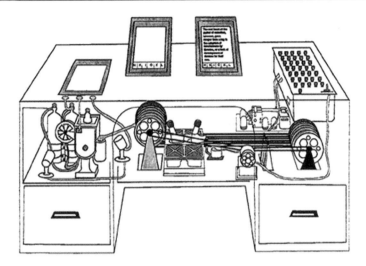

Figure 15.1 Illustration of Memex from *Life* Magazine, 1945.

Bush died on June 30, 1974. All we have left of Memex are the articles he wrote in his lifetime, and some sketches of the machine created by *Life* magazine. By the time Bush died, the technology behind Memex was already obsolete; digital computing had taken hold, and the spinning rolls of microfilm and analog operations of Memex seemed quaint. Memex remained profoundly uninfluenced by the paradigm of digital computing, and this may explain why it was never built to Bush's design. But the *vision* of Memex would remain, and it would influence a new generation of inventors, starting with a young electrical engineer named Douglas Engelbart. The computer, screen, and mouse would become Engelbart's parallel to Memex's storage desk, displays, and stylus; hyperlinks would become his parallel to Bush's trails. With these technologies, Engelbart would update the Memex design and bring it into an entirely different era and discourse: digital computing.

Doug Engelbart and NLS/Augment

We need to think about how to boost our collective IQ, and how important it would be to society because all of the technologies are just going to make our world accelerate faster and faster and get more and more complex and we're not equipped to cope with that complexity. So that's the big challenge. (Interview 1999)

Some ideas are like viruses. If they are in the air at the right time, they will "infect exactly those people who are most susceptible to putting their lives in the idea's service" (Rheingold 1985: 176). Engelbart still remembers reading about Memex. It was a hot day in 1945, and he was twenty years old. Like most young engineers of his time, he was doing military work, and had been posted out to the Philippines as a radar technician. He picked up a reprint of "As We May Think" in *Life* magazine, and wandered into a Red Cross library to read it. What connected for him most strongly was the idea that humans might be able to work with information *interactively*, and how that might expand our collective capabilities. Although he promptly forgot about the article, the ideas in it infected him.

Five years later, as he was driving home from work, Engelbart had a series of "flashes" of himself sitting at a Memex-like machine. He committed his career to making this vision a reality:

1. FLASH-1: The difficulty of mankind's problems was increasing at a greater rate than our ability to cope.
2. FLASH-2: Boosting mankind's ability to cope with complex, urgent problems would be an attractive candidate as an arena in which a young person might "make the most difference."
3. FLASH-3: Ahah – graphic vision surges forth of me sitting at a large CRT [Cathode Ray Tube] console, working in ways that are rapidly evolving in front of my eyes (Engelbart 1988: 189).

The idea of attaching a console to a computer is important. At the time, computers didn't have screens; Engelbart literally transferred this idea from the radars he was servicing in the Philippines to computers as he had learned about them in engineering school. He already had an image of what such a union might look like: Memex. But Memex was the product of a different era: analog computing. Was Engelbart dreaming of something new, or was he harking back to a technology that had already been discarded?

> The answer to both questions is "Yes." Innovation sometimes depends on revisiting previous ideas and employing them in new contexts. (Bardini 2000: 62)

All great dreams invite revisions, as Stuart Moulthrop puts it (1991: 48). There were some obvious commonalities between Bush's and Engelbart's vision, however. Both Bush and Engelbart proposed a fundamentally technical solution to the problem of human knowledge. They also believed there is a natural structure to this know-ledge; a networked structure we should seek to preserve. All our ideas have basic interconnections, and this is what enables the creation of new concepts as well as recall. Bush and Engelbart wanted an information system to support the natural or "true" connections which hold between items. Bush conceptualized this structure in terms of association. Engelbart considered it derivative of language – this is where his philosophy differs from Bush.

> Bush's philosophy revolved around the "association" of ideas on the model of how the individual mind is supposed to work. [Engelbart's] revolved around the intersubjective "connection" of words in the system of natural languages. (Bardini 2000: 40)

Engelbart's revision of the dream would prove to be too radical for the engineering community, however. The idea that a screen might be attached to a computer, and that humans might interact with information displayed on this screen, was seen as ridiculous. "It was too far out [for the engineering community]. It was wacky even in the seventies, after we had it working – real hypermedia working" (interview 1999). As with most visionaries who introduce new ways of working before their time, there was resistance to building such a machine. It would be over ten years before Engelbart received sufficient funding to set up a lab at the Stanford Research Institute, in 1962.

Engelbart called his lab the Augmentation Research Center (ARC), and began work immediately. He started with a series of experiments focused on the way people *select and connect ideas together* across a computer screen. A section of the lab was given over to "screen selection device" experiments, and different technologies were tested for speed and flexibility (interview 1999). Light pens, which were based on the Memex stylus, knee or head-mounted selection devices, joysticks, and the "x-y pointing device" (later dubbed the "mouse") were all trialed. For selecting and connecting units of information, Engelbart's mouse consistently beat other devices in these controlled tests. The lab also built their own computer displays, and by 1968, they had what would have seemed a strange setup: a multi-user computer display system, with a keyboard and mouse for each terminal. On this new setup, Engelbart developed the world's first hypertext system.

The system was called NLS, for oN-Line System. It arguably had *more* hypertext functionality than the modern internet. In NLS, information could be reordered, linked, nested, juxtaposed, revised, deleted, or chained window by window. The screen could be divided into a number of windows, which could display either text or image, and the user had multiple possible views of the same information. Most importantly, the system had fine "granularity": unlike Memex or the modern internet, users could link to almost anything, and these links would never break.

> [Unlike with the web], in NLS we had it that every object in the document was intrinsically addressable, right from the word go. It didn't matter what date a document's development was, you could give somebody a link right into anything, so you could actually have things that point right to a character or a word or something. All that addressability in the links could also be used to pick the objects you're going to operate on when you're editing. So that just flowed. (Interview, 1999)

This is in contrast to the World Wide Web, where the finest level of intrinsic addressability is the URL (universal resource locator). Unlike the NLS addressing system, which attached itself to the object, a URL is simply a location on a server. When the object moves, the link is broken. You can never be sure an old link will work on the web. NLS was far more *permanent*, and the links did not break so easily (Ted Nelson's system, which we will explore presently, also aspired to this permanency).

By 1968, NLS had matured into a massive system, the first digital hypertext system. It had implemented the Memex vision of "trails" through information, and invented the mouse and the hyperlink along the way. But there was little interest in the project from outside the military; people had heard of NLS but never seen it in action. It was time to take it out of the Petri dish and set it to work in front of the engineering community. Engelbart took an immense risk and applied for a special session at the ACM/IEEE-CS Fall Joint Computer Conference in San Francisco in December 1968. "The nice people at ARPA and NASA, who were funding us, effectively had to say 'Don't tell me!', because if this had flopped, we would have gotten in trouble" (Engelbart 1988: 203). This is an understatement. The engineering community were skeptical enough as it was: if the presentation has flopped, it would have destroyed Engelbart's career.

Like the Memex design, the NLS demo has subsequently entered into legend. The presentation proceeded without a hitch, and obtained a standing ovation. It was the first public demonstration of hypertext, the mouse, and screen-based computing. It is remembered as computing history's "foundational tribal tale" (Bardini 2000: 139), "the mother of all demonstrations" (Wardrip-Fruin 2003: 231), the "demo that got everyone fired up about interactive computing" (Nielsen 1995: 37), and a "landmark . . . in the annals of interactive computing" (Ceruzzi 1998: 260). De Landa and Rheingold claim the demo actually *created* the paradigm of human–computer interactivity: "the idea that the computer could become a medium to amplify man's intellect became a tangible reality for the people in Engelbart's audience" (De Landa 1994: 221); he was a "test pilot for a new kind of vehicle that doesn't fly over geographical territory but through what was heretofore an abstraction that computer scientists called 'information space'" (Rheingold 1985: ch. 9).

Although history has proven Engelbart's vision to be prophetic, the NLS/Augment story languished after 1976. Engelbart is neither rich nor powerful, a conclusion that seems strikingly unfair given his contributions to modern computing. The windows, interactive menus, and pointing device (WIMP) interface he invented have migrated to Apple and to Microsoft, and become the centerpiece of a proprietary, multi-billion-dollar operating system. As it turned out, the market wasn't interested in boosting our collective capacity: it was interested in mass-producing software.

It was "a long trail" before Engelbart actually went back to look at Bush's article – somewhere around 1961 (interview 1999). At this point he realized what had happened. He wrote a letter to Bush in 1962 to thank him for *As We May Think*. In it he reflected that

> I was startled to realize how much I had aligned my sights along the vector you [Bush] had described. I wouldn't be surprised at all if the reading of this article sixteen and a half years ago hadn't had a real influence upon the course of my thoughts and actions. (Engelbart 1962: 236)

Bush never replied.

Ideas and their Interconnections: Xanadu

[The web] is a universal, world-wide, anarchic publishing system. It completely vindicated my 35 years of saying that a universal, world-wide anarchic publishing system was possible. It just does it all wrong, that's all. (Nelson, 1999, interview)

It was a vision in a dream. A computer filing system which would store and deliver the great body of human literature, in all its historical versions and with all its messy interconnections, acknowledging authorship, ownership, quotation, and linkage. Like the web, but much better: no links would ever be broken, no documents would ever be lost, copyright and authorship would be scrupulously preserved. Imagine a hypertext system where all quotations within an article would *stay connected* to their source documents, and readers could click through to the original context of a citation. New changes could be made by authors without breaking any links, and anyone could connect comments to any page. Unlike on the web, hypertext links would be two-way or "bivisible"; they could be seen and followed from both the source page and the destination page, and they could overlap in vast numbers. Everything would be deeply interconnected, which is the way it was always meant to be. This vision belongs to hypertext pioneer Theodore Holm Nelson, who dubbed the project Xanadu in 1967.

The story of Xanadu is perhaps the greatest image of potentiality in the evolution of hypertext. Nelson invented a new vocabulary to describe his vision, much of which has become integrated into contemporary hypermedia theory and practice – for instance, the words "hypertext" and "hypermedia." As he put it in our interview, "I think I've put more words in the dictionary than Lewis Carroll. Every significant change in an idea means a new term" (1999). Nelson recruited or inspired some of the most visionary programmers and developers in the history of computing, many of whom went on to develop the first hypertext products. His writings and presentations concerning the "digital repository scheme for worldwide electronic publishing" have been plundered by theorists and practitioners the world over. Media opinion, however, is divided over Nelson: "[b]oon or boondoggle, nobody is quite sure," as *The Economist* puts it (cited in Nelson 1992: preface).

We will be exploring Xanadu and the ideas behind it in more depth presently. For now, we wish to emphasize this mythical dimension to Xanadu; as a concept, it has been under development for over forty years, and has become the stuff of legend within the hypertext community. This is largely due to the inspired writings of its creator and the lack of a real-world prototype. Unlike Bush's Memex, there have been numerous attempts to create the design exactly as Nelson described it, yet it has never been completed. To Nelson's dismay, and perhaps unfairly, it has been hailed as "the longest-running vaporware project in the history of computing" (Wolf 1995: 1).[3]

Nelson has always felt a great sense of urgency about this project. He believes the way we currently store and manage human knowledge is based on artificial categories and boundaries, and that the problem is escalating. Human knowledge, and particularly literature, has a networked structure to it which is deeply at odds with conventional forms of indexing.

> Basically, I have the philosophical view that everything is deeply interconnected. Or as I like to say, intertwingled. And there are no boundaries or fields except those we create artificially, and we are deeply misled by conventional boundaries and descriptions. (Interview 1999)

If we wish to build a computer system to store and deliver human knowledge, then it should be "CORRESPOND TO THE TRUE INTERCONNECTION OF IDEAS" (Nelson, capitals in original, 1987: 143). It should allow us to follow the true or natural connections which hold between items. Nelson's idea of this "natural" structure is more anarchic than Bush (which was based on associative memory) or Engelbart (which was based on language), but all three concur that an information system should preserve and foster a networked, interconnected structure to information.

Nelson first published the term "hypertext" in his 1965 paper, "A File Structure for the Complex, the Changing and the Indeterminate," where he describes a type of computer-supported writing system that would allow for branching, linking, and responding text. It would be composed of either "written or pictorial material" and its defining feature is that the information would be "interconnected in such a complex way that it could not be conveniently presented or represented on paper" (Nelson 1965: 96). Contrary to modern use of the word "hypertext" to refer to networked text (e.g., Delaney and Landow 1994: 7; Stefik 1997: 21), at the time Nelson meant branching, linking, and responding *images* as well as text. As Andries van Dam put it in an interview with the author:

> Nelson always meant hypermedia when he said hypertext, it's one of the things that people get wrong about Nelson. He meant "text" in the sense of corpus, not text in the sense of characters. I know this for a fact because we've talked about it many times. (van Dam 1999)

The word "hypertext" was meant to convey the deeply interconnected nature of this corpus. "Hyper" means exceeding, over, beyond, above – more than what presents itself to the eye. The link, as Nelson saw it, would take the user from one place to another, and that place would contain the excess, the overflow, the past or future of the previous idea. Unlike writing on paper, the link would consequently allow for a natural sequence of ideas, like thought itself. Links as Nelson saw them were deeply tied to sequence: ideas are only meaningful in relation to where they have been. Engelbart gives equal credit to Nelson for discovering the link: they were both working on similar ideas at the same time, but Engelbart claims he had the facilities and funding to build a machine that explored those ideas.

Nelson's concept of hypertext influenced several important engineers. The first is Andries van Dam, Professor of Computing Science at Brown University, who built the first hypertext system beginners could use in 1967, the Hypertext Editing System (HES). When van Dam bumped into Nelson at the 1967 Spring Joint Computer Conference, Nelson, wild-eyed and eloquent, started talking about hypertext. At the time, Nelson had no "work in the sense that computer scientists talk about work, i.e., software, algorithms, things that are concrete" remembers van Dam (interview, 1999). What Nelson did have was an infectious belief that computers would one day be used to organize and structure text for personal and scholarly use, and this vision inspired van Dam.

> Nelson's vision seduced me . . . After meeting quite by accident at this computer conference, and talking about what we each were doing, we somehow got onto the topic [of hypertext]. Then he talked me into working on a hypertext system and that sounded cool. (van Dam 1999)

Nelson's vision also influenced Tim Berners-Lee, who invented the World Wide Web. Berners-Lee appropriated Nelson's term to describe his markup language (HTML, or Hypertext Markup Language). But as Nelson puts it, "HTML is like one-tenth of what I could do. I like and respect Tim Berners-Lee [but] he fulfilled his objective. He didn't fulfil mine" (interview, 1999). Although we don't have the space here to go into the evolution of HTML, it should be noted that Berners-Lee shared Nelson's "deep connectionist" philosophy, and his desire to organize information based on the natural structure of thought:

> A computer typically keeps things in rigid hierarchies . . . whereas the human mind has the ability to link random bits of data. When I smell coffee, strong and stale, I find myself in a small room over a corner coffeehouse in Oxford. My brain makes a link, and instantly transports me there. (Berners-Lee 1999: 3)

However, while Berners-Lee was met with passivity and Engelbart with skepticism, Nelson received entirely *disparaging* responses from the computing community. Xanadu has always been "a cult, fringe kind of thing" (van Dam, interview 1999). But Nelson slogs on, and he is not alone: the Xanadu vision lives on in the minds (and evolving code shells) of hundreds of computer professionals around the world. The extended Xanadu community is even wider, and has spawned several organizations devoted to the pursuit of a solution to the problem of contemporary information storage and publishing. Xanadu is an "epic of recovery" (Moulthrop 1991: 695) for the digital era, and it has entered into the imagination of a generation of developers. Unlike Bush's Memex, people keep trying to build the thing as it was first designed. This fact alone is evidence of its impact: technical white papers are not known for their shelf-life, but Xanadu's have thrived for over 40 years.

The Thin Blue Line: Images of Potentiality in Literary Hypertext

At lunchtime on June 17, 1998, a group of Joyceans assembled in a room of the stately Argiletum Palace in Rome. Delegates of the sixteenth International James Joyce Symposium, they were there to attend a preliminary presentation of Michael Groden's *James Joyce's* Ulysses *in Hypermedia*. In development since 1994, this mammoth undertaking sought to link a number of decisive editions of *Ulysses* to create a kind of matrix of the text and its many variations, from the Shakespeare & Company first edition of 1922 to Hans Walter Gabler's controversial computer-assisted "corrected edition" of 1984. Utilizing the rich potential of multimedia, Groden's idea was to incorporate maps, exegeses, episode summaries, and annotations, as well as critical essays on Joyce and hypertext.

Demonstrating how we could listen to sound files of authentic Dublin inflection or a rendition of *Love's Old Sweet Song*, see photographs and video of key locations or related Bloomsday ephemera (such as Plumtree's Potted Meat), Groden's sample electronic page resembled what at the time was a standard hypertext: a page of writing with selected words underlined in blue. During the proceedings a question came from the floor, from none other than Fritz Senn, the Godfather of Joyce studies and somewhat ambivalent advocate of a hypermedia *Ulysses*. Senn made the suggestion that with *Ulysses*, surely every word should be a hot spot, to use the idiom of the day. Everyone in the room, like me I'm quite sure, saw in their mind's eye a field of text in which every word was underlined by a thin blue line.

Here was a vision of a holistic networked *Ulysses*, and implicitly a total hypertext in which no dimension of the text was not hypertextual – there was no outside-hypertext. The perception of an apparently endless process of linking through, between, and within this dense palimpsestual *Ulysses* crystallized the new aesthetics of interactive, arduous reading associated with hypertext (the term "ergodic" had only recently been coined). It was an avatar of the fabulous "total book" of Jorge Luis Borges, a codex that contained all books, real and imaginary. It also brought to mind Joyce's own precursory anticipation of the commitment and effort required of this hypertextual practice of reading in *Finnegans Wake* (1939), a book written for an "ideal reader suffering from an ideal insomnia" (Joyce 1975: 120). This "solicitation" of hypertext had been the subject of growing critical interest in the Joyce world (Armand 1995). So many of the key events in the history of hypertext, as we have seen so far in this discussion, involve dreams and visions, and *Finnegans Wake*, it must be remembered, is a dream. And it is a dream that has cast a long shadow of anticipation and expectation. A number of scholars have drawn attention to the already hypertextual nature of *Ulysses* and the *Wake* (Theall 1992, 1997; Tofts 1997). *Ulysses* manifests all the key qualities that very quickly became tropes in hypertext fiction, tropes that had their genesis in the work of Bush, Engelbart, and Nelson: discontinuous, non-sequential, non-linear, reflexive, encyclopedic, cross-referential, etc. (Tofts 2001).

But these writers have also demonstrated how Joyce's language uncannily anticipated many of the more famous pronouncements or terms of Ted Nelson in his theorizing of the hypertextual (Nelson's "docuverse" or "ongoing system of interconnecting documents" [Nelson 1992: 2/8–2/9] is anachronistically echoed in the "too dimensional," "most spacious immensity" of Joyce's verbal universe [Joyce 1975: 154, 150]; the former's "structangle" foreshadowed in the latter's "proteiform graph" and "polyhedron of scripture" [p. 114, p. 107 resp.]). The issue of memory, the archive, and their relationship to technology, so central to the visions of Vannevar Bush, Douglas Englebart, and Ted Nelson, have also been extensively discussed in relation to Joyce. While there is no need for a Memex anymore and Xanadu may well now be a forlorn dream or ideal, Joyce realized something of their promise in *Finnegans Wake*, a text described by Jacques Derrida as a "hypermnesiac machine" capable "in a single instant or a single vocable, gather up of cultures, languages, mythologies, religions, philosophies, sciences, history of mind and of literatures" (Derrida 1984: 147).

More than a discrete moment in the ongoing publication history of *Ulysses*, this event, indeed this image of an endless thin blue line, represented something much more expansive and significant. For it too was a dream, the vision of a potential hypermedia *Ulysses* that has yet to be realized. Groden has been unable to complete the project owing to legal issues of copyright enforced by the James Joyce Estate (Groden). Moreover, this event was an allegory of the convergence of print and electronic culture, an encounter with the impact of an emerging medium on our received ideas to do with print literacy and cultural production and, most importantly, vice versa. Beyond the scholarly value of a networked matrix of the most significant editions of *Ulysses*, Groden's project and its critical reception in the mid-1990s heightened the contextual manner in which hypertext fiction was being produced, archived, and written about at this time. That is, while *Ulysses* was regarded as exactly the kind of printed book that invites an electronic, hypermedia treatment, electronic hypertext fiction was in no way regarded in isolation from an inherited vision of what, *in potentia*, hypertext was; or more accurately, how hypertext behaved. In this sense it is more useful (as Espen Aarseth has done [1997]) to think of hypertextuality as a "theoretical approach to understanding the way certain kinds of texts work" (Tofts 2001: 83). The concepts of Bush, Engelbart, and Nelson had initiated a critical theory of textual behavior or textual poetics, but one in advance of any actual enactments of it in the form of electronic hypertext fiction. Without perhaps recognizing it, in Joyce we had a literary enactment of its potential, of what it might be like in print. In the hypertext fiction written for the World Wide Web, in HyperCard and Storyspace, we would have another, though in a networked environment presumably more suited to its poetics.[4]

Hypertext's Long Shadow

As an emerging literary practice or alternative poetics, hypertext fiction was already characterized as a process of becoming, of ongoingness, of imminence. Its "sense of unending" (to invert Frank Kermode's phrase the "sense of an ending") was famously captured in Jane Yellowlees Douglas's famous question (plea), "How do I stop this thing?" Hypertext, in advance of whatever seminal works or incunabula appeared in the name of electronic hypertext fiction (such as the other Joyce's *Afternoon*), had succumbed to the supplementary desire of all dreams and visions, the fetish. When Jay David Bolter published one of the first extensive critical studies of hypertext in 1991, he chose to provide the option of a version of the book written in Storyspace, the emerging software of choice for budding hyper-authors. The idea was to allow the reader to immerse themselves in the very logic he was describing in the printed book, so it could be read in a non-linear way. But to experience hypertext and to conceptually understand it as such are two different things. Bolter's provision of an "electronic shadow" of *Writing Space* on "diskette" foregrounds, unwittingly or otherwise, the hypertext fetish of implementing discontinuity for its own sake, since this is how hypertext is expected or supposed to behave (Bolter 1991: x). In that electronic shadow is the trace of the "virtuality" Ted Nelson described in *Literary Machines*, "the creation of the conceptual and psychological environment, the seeming of the system" (Nelson 1992: 1/3).

Experimentation in hypertext fiction in the 1990s, then, was very much happening in the shadow of inherited visions of hypertext, an unfulfilled, recurring dream of becoming. The first online archives of hypertext fiction and resources for aspiring writers, dating from the early 1990s, can be reviewed as rhetorical strategies of managing this process of becoming, of the convergence of residual and emergent practices of writing. *The Electronic Labyrinth* (1993–2001) and *Hyperizons* (1995–7) are two notable examples in this respect.

Christopher Keep, Tim McLaughlin, and Robin Parmar's *Electronic Labyrinth* is an extensive online resource incorporating description, annotation, critical discussion, historical context, and information on authoring resources for aspiring hypertext fiction writers. It was one of the first Baedekers for the new world of interactive fiction, containing extensive links to literary precursors and contemporary practitioners of electronic hypertext fiction. As with any foray into a strange new land, it is important to acknowledge pioneers. Keep, McLaughlin, and Parmar want us to be in no doubt who the hypertext trailblazers are. Like latter-day travelers journeying to the center of the earth, we find this marker signaling those who came before us:

> No discussion of reading and writing electronic texts would be complete without mentioning the contributions of Vannevar Bush, Douglas Engelbart, and Ted Nelson. (Keep, McLaughlin, and Parmar 2001)

But identifying precursors and visionaries is only part of what *The Electronic Labyrinth* is concerned with. Its clearly stated mission is to evaluate "hypertext and its potential for use by literary artists." Hence the extensive section on "Software Environments," an annotated resource for evaluating "the available hypertext authoring systems, with the aim of providing recommendations to potential authors." Despite the emphasis on novelty, on innovative new "authoring systems" with their strange, foreign names (HyperShell, HyperCard, Orpheus, LinkWay), the concept of hypertext is defined and contextualized in relation to "the literary tradition of non-linear approaches to narrative." Its focus on hypertext fiction was an instance of this broader imperative to map the transition from book to hyperbook, to re-evaluate "the concept of the book in the age of electronic text" (Keep, McLaughlin, and Parmar 2001).

One of the most critically engaging sections of the site deals with "Re-thinking The Book." The passage from book to hyperbook is cast as an epic steeped in the literary tradition of the West that goes back as far as the year 367 and the delivery of the Festal Epistle of St Athanasius. The Holy Trinity of Bush, Engelbart, and Nelson are given their due, no more, no less, in this extensive hagiography of hypertext. This historical framework enunciates a most telling inherited vision of hypertext as a concept in advance of a practice – "Our definition does not limit itself to electronic text; hypertext is not inherently tied to technology, content, or medium. It is an organizational form which may just as readily be delivered on paper as electronically. Thus, Sterne's *Tristram Shandy* is no less a hypertext than Joyce's *Afternoon*" (Keep, McLaughlin, and Parmar 2001).

A similar polemic weaves the pages of Michael Shumate's *Hyperizons* hypertext fiction site. "Hypertext fiction (aka hyperfiction, interactive fiction, nonlinear fiction) is a new art form," Shumate informs us, that "while not necessarily made possible by the computer was certainly made feasible by it" (Shumate 1997). More shadows from a dream. Shumate, too, is interested in the broader cultural logic of the shift from page to screen. For Shumate there are two key nodes here – "General Fiction Converted From Print" and "Precursors of Hypertext Fiction." As with Bolter, and many others for that matter, one of the first operations of the new medium was to re-work its immediate predecessor – McLuhan's first law of media once again rings true.

But Shumate goes so far as to make a claim for "Original Hypertext Fiction," which exceeds Keep, McLaughlin, and Parmar's concept of "literary works created specifically for computerized hypertext." Citing examples such as Robert Coover's *Hypertext Hotel*, Shelley Jackson's *Patchwork Girl*, and Stuart Moulthrop's *Dreamtime*, Shumate presents what, at the time, was arguably the most comprehensive list of "original" hypertext works, written by individual and multiple authors.

In the "Precursors of Hypertext Fiction" section, though, Shumate discloses that his apparent Oedipal search for original, contemporary examples of hypertext fiction is tempered by the feeling that we have seen something like this before. Even before we are transported across the thin blue line to his archive of precursory works, we feel an intimation of imminence, of becoming, that Shumate himself has sensed in the machinations of the computer:

> This section lists print works that have been pointed out as precursors of hypertext. Since there will likely be more of these all the time, I'm not going to list everything anybody mentions, but only those titles that I've either read personally or that have been mentioned numerous times. As I develop this, I'll also try to give publication information of whatever version is in print. I'll also indicate places where I've seen the argument made for a work as a precursor of hypertext fiction. (Shumate 1997)

Less a search than a process of textual archaeology, Shumate's perception of a potentially endless discovery of antecedents reveals the extent to which the inherited vision of hypertext was ingrained in the new media sensibility of the 1990s. As of 1997 (when he seems to have abandoned the site to hypertext history) Shumate's list of original hypertext works was greater than his list of precursors. Perhaps he is still reading a backlog of precursors.

Hyperizons bears the conspicuous presence of the thin blue line. But, as with *The Electronic Labyrinth*, there is far more plain text than hypertext, certainly relative to a potential *James Joyce's* Ulysses *in Hypermedia*. And the latter, like Xanadu, or even more distantly Memex, remain sublime potential literatures, in the great tradition of Oulippo. They are images of a potential form of textuality glimpsed by Bush, Engelbart, and Nelson, a grammar for being elsewhere,[5] techno-artifacts that take us into the labyrinth and the experience of a web more "complex, changing and indeterminate" than even Daedalus ever dared dream.

NOTES

1   For a general introduction to hypertext history, see the first chapter of George Landow's book, *Hypertext 3.0* (2006), and the first chapter of Jakob Nielsen's book, *Multimedia and Hypertext* (1995). Noah Wardrip-Fruin and Nick Montfort's book, *The New Media Reader* (2003), is a collection of important articles from this period, including classic pieces by Ted Nelson, Vannevar Bush, and Doug Engelbart. For more detailed research, see Nyce and Kahn's *From Memex to Hypertext* (1991); this book is an excellent introduction to Vannevar Bush's work. Thierry Bardini's book on Doug Engelbart, *Bootstrapping* (2000), is also useful, along with Engelbart's own account in Adele Goldberg's 1988 book, *A History of Personal Workstations* (this book also contains important historical pa-

pers on the early internet, ARPANET). Readers who are interested in the history of hypertext should also find Andries van Dam's Hypertext '87 Keynote address, which contains an account of his own systems, HES and FRESS (1988).

2   To paraphrase Andries van Dam in an interview with the author. Van Dam's team created an important hypertext system called the Hypertext Editing System (HES) in 1967. We do not have time to explore HES in detail here – interested readers should start with van Dam (1988). "You could say hypertext is a very crude analog to what must happen for the storage of facts and information in the brain, where things that are logically linked are logically retrieved together" (1999, interview with Barnet).

3 Wolf's 1995 *Wired* article is a classic piece on Xanadu, but contains numerous errors of fact. Readers who are interested in the history of hypertext should also study Nelson's response, parts of which were published in *Wired* in 1995. <http://coe.ksu.edu/mcgrath/HMedia/NelsonLtr.htm>.

4 The history and prehistory of hypertext fiction is still being written. However, in relation to electronic forms there are some critically acknowledged examples. Early pre-web experiments with HyperCard stacks include Amanda Goodenough's *Inigo Gets Out* (1987), Humphrey Clark's *The Perfect Couple* (1990) and Sarah Smith's *King of Space* (1991). The introduction of *Storyspace* authoring software in 1987 fostered an emerging practice of interactive fiction on diskette. Some of the more famous titles include Michael Joyce's *Afternoon,*

a Story (1990), Stuart Moulthrop's *Victory Garden* (1991) and Shelley Jackson's *Patchwork Girl* (1995). Voyager, Hyperbole, and Broderbund published works in a variety of distributable forms, including laserdisc and CD ROM (the Miller Brothers' *Myst* [1994] is arguably the most celebrated). Works distributed via the World Wide Web allowed for a more accessible form of engagement, among them Robert Coover's *Hypertext Hotel* (1991), Francesca da Rimini's *The Contested Zone* (1993), David Blair's *Waxweb* (1994–ongoing), Sean Cohen's and Stuart Moulthrop's *The Color of Television* (1996), and Mark Amerika's *Grammatron* (1997). See *The Electronic Labyrinth* and *Hyperizons* for more detailed chronologies.

5 The phrase is adapted from H. Porter Abbott, "A Grammar for Being Elsewhere," *Journal of Modern Literature* 6.1, 1977.

REFERENCES AND FURTHER READING

Aarseth, Espen (1997). *Cybertext: Perspectives on Ergodic Literature.* Baltimore: Johns Hopkins University Press.

Armand, Louis (1995). "Phoenix Ex Machina: Joyce's Solicitation of Hypertext," 1.1. <http://hjs.ff.cuni.cz/archives/v1/framed/larmand/jms1.html>.

Bardini, Thierry (2000). *Bootstrapping: Douglas Engelbart, Coevolution, and the Origins of Personal Computing.* Stanford: Stanford University Press.

Bolter, Jay David (1991). *Writing Space: The Computer, Hypertext and the History of Writing.* Hillsdale, NJ: Lawrence Erlbaum Associates.

Berners-Lee, Tim (1999). *Weaving the Web: The Original Design and Ultimate Destiny of the World Wide Web by its Inventor.* New York: HarperCollins Publishers.

Bush, Vannevar (1939). "Mechanization and Record." *Vannevar Bush Papers*, Library of Congress [Box 50, General correspondence file, Eric Hodgins].

—— (1945). "As We May Think." *The Atlantic Monthly* 176.1: 641–9.

—— (1959). "Memex II." In J. M. Nyce and P. Kahn (Eds.). *From Memex to Hypertext: Vannevar Bush and the Mind's Machine.* London: Academic Press, 1991, pp. 165–84.

—— (1967). "Science Pauses." In *Science is Not Enough.* New York: William Morrow, pp. 14–33.

—— (1970). *Pieces of the Action.* New York: William Morrow.

Ceruzzi, Paul E. (1998). *A History of Modern Computing.* Cambridge, MA: The MIT Press.

De Landa, Manuel (1994). *War in the Age of Intelligent Machines.* New York: Zone Books.

Delaney, P., and G. P. Landow (Eds.) (1994). *Hypertext and Literary Studies.* Cambridge, MA: MIT Press.

Demeulenaere, Alex (2003). "An Uncanny Thinker: Michel De Certeau." *Image and Narrative: a Journal of the Visual Narrative* 5. <http://www.imageandnarrative.be/uncanny/alexdemeulenaere.htm>.

Derrida, Jacques (1984). "Two Words for Joyce." In Derek Attridge and Daniel Ferrer (Eds.). *Post-structuralist Joyce: Essays from the French.* Cambridge: Cambridge University Press, pp. 145–59.

Engelbart, Douglas (1962). "Letter to Vannevar Bush and Program on Human Effectiveness." In J. M. Nyce and P. Kahn (Eds.). *From Memex to Hypertext: Vannevar Bush and the Mind's Machine.* London: Academic Press, p. 236.

—— (1988). "The Augmented Knowledge Workshop" (AKW). In Adele Goldberg (Ed.).

A History of Personal Workstations. New York: ACM Press, Addison-Wesley Publishing Company, pp. 185–249.

—— (1999). Interview with Belinda Barnet.

Groden, Michael, "James Joyce's *Ulysses* in Hypermedia Project." <http://www.clemson.edu/caah/cedp/Tech%20Colloquium%202001/Groden%20Files/hypermedia.html>.

Hayles, Katherine (1999). *How We Became Posthuman: Virtual Bodies in Cybernetics, Literature and Informatics.* Chicago: The University of Chicago Press.

Joyce, James (1975). *Finnegans Wake.* London: Faber.

Joyce, Michael (1990). *"Afternoon,* a Story." Hypertext document for Macintosh computers. Cambridge, MA: Eastgate Systems.

Keep, Christopher, Tim McLaughlin, and Robin Parmar (n.d.). *The Electronic Labyrinth.* <http://www3.iath.virginia.edu/elab/>. Accessed March 2007.

Landow, George (2006). *Hypertext 3.0: Critical Theory and New Media in an Era of Globalization.* Baltimore, MD: Johns Hopkins University Press.

Moulthrop, Stuart (1991). "You Say You Want a Revolution? Hypertext and the Laws of Media." *Postmodern Culture* 1:3. <http://muse.jhu.edu/journals/postmodern_culture/v001/1.3moulthrop.html>.

Nelson, Ted (1965). "A File Structure for the Complex, the Changing and the Indeterminate." *Proceedings of the ACM 20th National Conference.* New York: ACM Press, pp. 84–100.

—— (1980). "Replacing the Printed Word: a Complete Literary System." In S. H. Lavington (Ed.). *Information Processing 80.* Amsterdam: North-Holland Publishing Company, IFIP, pp. 1013–23.

—— (1987). *Computer Lib/Dream Machines.* Redmond, WA: Microsoft Press.

—— (1991). "As We Will Think." In J. M. Nyce and P. Kahn (Eds.). *From Memex to Hypertext: Vannevar Bush and the Mind's Machine.* London: Academic Press, pp. 245–60.

—— (1992). *Literary Machines.* Sausalito, CA: Mindful Press.

—— (1999). Interview with Belinda Barnet.

Nielsen, Jakob (1995). *Multimedia and Hypertext: The Internet and Beyond.* San Diego, CA: Academic Press.

Nyce, J. M. and P. Kahn (1991). *From Memex to Hypertext: Vannevar Bush and the Mind's Machine.* London: Academic Press.

Rheingold, Howard (1985). *Tools for Thought: the History and Future of Mind-Expanding Technology.* New York: Simon & Schuster.

Shumate, Michael. "Hyperizons." <http://www.duke.edu/~mshumate/hyperfic.html>.

Smith, Linda C (1991). "Memex as an Image of Potentiality Revisited." In J. M. Nyce and P. Kahn (Eds.). *From Memex to Hypertext: Vannevar Bush and the Mind's Machine.* London: Academic Press, pp. 261–86.

Stefik, Mark (1997). *Internet Dreams: Archetypes, Myths and Metaphors.* Cambridge, MA: MIT Press.

Theall, Donald (1992). "Beyond the orality/literacy dichotomy: James Joyce and the prehistory of cyberspace." *Postmodern Culture* 2.3 (May). <http://muse.jhu.edu/journals/postmodern_culture/v002/2.3theall.html>.

—— (1995). *Beyond the Word: Reconstructing Sense in the Joyce era of technology, culture, and communication.* Toronto: University of Toronto Press.

Tofts, Darren (1997). *Memory Trade: A prehistory of cyberculture.* Sydney: Interface.

—— (2001). "a retrospective sort of arrangement": *Ulysses and the poetics of hypertextuality. Litteraria Pragensia* 11: 22.

van Dam, Andries (1999). Interview with Belinda Barnet.

—— (1988). "Hypertext '87 Keynote Address." *Communications of the ACM* 31: 887–95.

Wardrip-Fruin, Noah (2003). "Introduction to Engelbart's Knowledge Workshop." In Wardrip-Fruin, Noah, and Nick Montfort (Eds.). *The New Media Reader.* Cambridge, MA: MIT Press.

——, and Nick Montfort (Eds.) (2003). *The New Media Reader.* Cambridge, MA: MIT Press.

Whitehead, Jim (2000). "As We Do Write: Hyper-terms for Hypertext." *ACM SIGWEB Newsletter* 9: 8–18.

Wolf, Gary (1995). "The Curse of Xanadu." *Wired* 3.6, June.

16
Private Public Reading: Readers in Digital Literature Installation
Mark Leahy

Introduction

This chapter sets the genre of installed digital literature in the context of other disciplines and art forms. It uses an intersection of critical frames from the visual arts, cinema, and writing to develop a way of thinking about a body of work that uses text, digital media, and space or location as integral features. The topic being at an intersection of disciplines, and so not neatly interpretable with the tools used for any particular one, the chapter addresses a number of aspects of these overlapping disciplines to venture a means of understanding how we read installed digital literature.

In an interview with Roberto Simanowski, digital artist Noah Wardrip-Fruin discusses the role of text in his own work and in the work of certain other artists who create digital installations. Simanowski comments on Wardrip-Fruin's work: "it strikes me that your works are installations, or performances, in which text is not reduced to 'graphical objects' as you put it, stripped of linguistic function" (Wardrip-Fruin 2005a). The textual elements in these works are there to be read. Referring to a work by Camille Utterback and Romy Achituv (Utterback 1999), Wardrip-Fruin comments:

> I think for Camille and Romy the particular text that's in *Text Rain* is important. They used lines of a poem, and negotiated for the copyright clearance. They wouldn't have done that if it didn't matter what text they used. (ibid.)

He is making a distinction between the use of words or text or writing, of literature within digital work, where what the words say or mean or how they are read is significant. They are something to be read, not something to be merely recognized as letters or words or text. If the point of the work *Text Rain* was to demonstrate the functioning of the interface, the possibility for the audience or users to manipulate the falling letters, then what the words said, how they combined into phrases would matter little. This he feels is the view of the audience from an electronic art background. He goes on to contrast the attitude to the writing, the text in other art or digital works.

> People in the prints-on-walls art community don't think that you could arbitrarily substitute text in a Barbara Kruger piece. People in the electronic writing community don't think you could arbitrarily substitute text in a John Cayley piece. But text, for some reason, doesn't seem to be a recognized artistic medium in the electronic art world. (ibid.)

The business of writing and reading, then, is important in the work Wardrip-Fruin makes. And this is a reading and writing that occupies physical space and may be carried out in the company of other readers. This is literature that shares features of other disciplines or other modes of writing or of making art.

The perception of a genre of installed digital literature is a result of the shifting of the gaze of the writer's/critic's attention that is focused on distinct discrete events drawn together as a grouping by the act of observation/attention. Each contingent identification of the genre, each gathering into its loop is temporary, perhaps displaced by a new work, by a new angle of reading. The genre (if it exists) is located at an overlapping in Venn diagram fashion of a number of areas of making, of writing, of display, of knowledge. These include Expanded Cinema, computer poetry (electronic poetics), outdoor advertising, monumental inscription, public reading, each of which represents aspects of what might constitute this genre, but none of which exhausts its possibilities. If installed digital literature deserves a separate chapter within this *Companion*, then it must be because there is a body of identifiable work that is generically grouped, grouped by formal characteristics, or there is a range of work that can be attended to as engaging with a shared set of questions. These distinct shared questions that set installed digital literature apart from other digital literature might involve:

1. the site or location of the work (where it is shown/seen);
2. the third dimension (in "real" space as opposed to virtual space);
3. the materiality of the digital textual work;
4. embodied reading (reading that is aware of involving the reader's body);
5. public reading (reading that takes place in the presence of other readers).

This set of features also accepts some parameters for digital literature. Text is made available to a reader, text that in its presentation or generation engages with modes or methods particular to digital technology, e.g., coding, database or editing software, the possibilities of the World Wide Web.

Having moved through a discussion of these various features and how they may have developed toward modes of digital literature, this chapter will focus on the reader's experience of the reading of the installed text. What is distinct is not the content of the text, it is not the style or genre or mode of writing the text engages with, but how that text is physically, spatially, bodily, socially accessed, encountered, and received by a reader. Are there qualities of digital work that distinguish it from other texts located in a site or place? What aspects of reading or engaging with digital texts can be particularly expressed in an installed mode? Are there qualities of database technology, or coding, or the World Wide Web which intersect in a productive way with being presented as a sited installation? The chapter will try to demonstrate those aspects of reading that are particular to installed literature, and those aspects that are particular to digital literature.

The fact that there is a reader physically present in/with the work may suggest that the artist use technology that is responsive to this presence. Work that depends on interactivity and responsive installations works with this. *Text Rain*, already referred to, uses the presence of the activator/reader to operate the work and to interpret it. The reader's (presumed) familiarity with particular kinds of text in the context of public reading may be a reason for the digital writer/artist to draw on or reference those associations, with advertising, with monumental or heroic texts, with information or instructional texts. The reader who enters the space of the installation, who encounters the digital text, will have read other public texts. Some of these are the texts of billboards, some are informational or directional texts of urban signage, some the unofficial inscriptions of flyers or graffiti, others the official texts of war memorials or state buildings. This is writing we read in public, that we read with others, that we read as addressed in a particular public manner. The reader of the digital installed text may also be familiar with the "print-on-walls art" that Wardrip-Fruin refers to, and with electronic poetry. The work will be encountered then as an intersection of these readings.

Site-specificity

If the digital element of the installation is not *of* the site but must be added to it/placed on it/placed in it, does this push the installed digital work away from any possibility of being site-specific? For a work of digital literature, it may be that there are material qualities of that work made evident in the siting or situating of it. Equally it can be noted that the site/location will pre-exist and underlie the work, as the place or location, and the digital introduction into/intervention onto it are of distinct materialities. The focus of this section of the chapter may be on what is siteable or placeable in a digital work of literature. Digital work is sited and located conventionally on the World Wide Web, on websites, at home pages, in "my space," its location pointed to using URLs; it may be accessed via links, by downloading it (copying it from its storage space to the user/reader's portable space), by installing it from disc. One aspect of installed digital literature may be to expose and explore facets of a place/site through a digital medium. The questions will engage with what is siteable, what is locatable in digital work, and how a reader or user may recognize a digital work as having qualities of place or space.

Site-specific artworks can be described as one development of an aspect of twentieth-century Modernist experiment. Linked to land art and conceptual art work of the 1960s, they are related to and are somewhat distinct from installation art.

> As discursive terminology, *site-specific* is solely and precisely rooted within Western Euro-American modernism, born, as it were, lodged between modernist notions of liberal progressiveness and radical tropes both formal and conceptual. It is the recognition on the part of minimalist and earthworks artists of the 1960s and 1970s that "site" in and of itself is part of the experience of the work of art. (Suderburg 2000: 4)

The site-specific deals with particularities of the physical material place in or on which the work is sited. This differs from installed work, which on some occasions engages with a Modernist notion of space as being without context (or in the white cube context of the gallery/museum institution).

> The site of installation becomes a primary part of the content of the work itself, but it also posits a critique of the practice of art-making within the institution by examining the ideological and institutional frameworks that support and exhibit the work of art. "To install" becomes not a gesture of hanging the work of art or positioning the sculpture, but an art practice in and of itself. (ibid.: 5)

For digital literature to deal with site there must be an acknowledgement of the sitedness of other modes of digital work, their location *on* a website, their presence on a disc, or within a data storage location. These locations are not usually termed material, but may be pointed to by the use of a URL or other indication of the point via which the specified digital information can be accessed in a particular organized manner. The monitor of a desktop computer, the touch screen of an ATM, the hand-held Gameboy or Nintendo DS, all are located at the point of interaction, are sited somewhere when they are being read, used, played with. Installed digital literature accepts these sited aspects of digital literature, but places the work in a further complex of aspects of site and place and location. In this way it may be taking on some of the arguments of earlier installation art and site-specific art, and shifting these concerns to questions that are particular to digital work.

Erika Suderburg discusses the terms installation and site-specificity and gives them a genealogy, from early Modernist works such as "Light-Space Modulator" (1923–30) by Lázló Moholy-Nagy, through the minimalist work of Robert Morris and the gallery and land-art work of Robert Smithson. She considers the critical reception of and classification of this work by Michael Fried, by Rosalind Krauss in "Sculpture in the Expanded Field," and Douglas Crimp in his *On the Museum's Ruins* (see further reading). From this lineage of argument she concludes that the site of the work of art cannot be neutral, that the institutional space that supports the artwork, and the space made by the work's occupation is ideologically marked. This site is articulated by the installed work. James Meyer, in Suderburg ed., distinguishes between a *literal* site and a *functional* site for site specific or installed work. Quoting artist Joseph Kosuth, he defines the "literal site" as singular. It is understood by the artist and the audience as unique, as having distinct material and local qualities (Meyer: 24). The work of art in the literal site is "a kind of monument, a public work commissioned *for* this site" (ibid.: 24). The uniqueness of the work parallels the uniqueness of the artist, of the artist's response, of her sensibility to the particular qualities of this site. Users of the site (those for whom it is a place of work or leisure) may respond negatively to the work, and this conflict can lead to a clash between Modernist or high art ideals and the practice of the space/location the work occupies. This is most notoriously documented in the debate around, and subsequent removal of, Richard Serra's *Tilted Arc* from Federal Plaza in New York (see Weyergraf-Serra and Buskirk 1990).

Meyer continues to define "functional site" as being much more concerned with the institutional structures that form or define a site, the conditions that lead to a work of art being in that location, or that underlie the artist's intervention. There is not the focus on the physical place. "Instead, it is a process, an operation occurring between sites, a mapping of institutional and textual filiations and the bodies that move between them (the artist's above all)" (ibid.: 25). Sitedness in the functional site is dependent not primarily on physical location but on relations, on information, on system, on exchange. This model offers a useful point of connection to digital artworks and literature that similarly engage with such immaterial aspects of a place, of a used location. There is a temporary and temporal aspect to the work, it exists in relation to daily or seasonal or other human uses of the place, and is not permanent, being installed not as a monument, but as something put up for a time (like a circus or funfair that intersects with the rhythms of a village for a limited duration and then moves on).

Marita Sturken, also in Suderburg, discusses installation in relation to the viewer. Her comments might be related to work sited on the web, or other locations in which a reader/viewer may encounter the work of art. A location in which she encounters an artwork in time, in space, and that situates her in relation to the work and that location.

> In addition, installations that deploy such technologies as video and computer devices delineate time; they are constructed with particular concerns about the length of time viewers will stay with the work versus its cycle, as well as concerns about how to get viewers to move in particular ways in the space. (Sturken in Suderburg ed. 2000: 287)

The space of the installed art work is a space negotiated by the reader/viewer. Having put in place "the rules, limitations, and context" (ibid.: 287), the installation is offered by the artist to the visitor. Not occupied by the artist, the site of the installation is operated by the viewers; it is the site for the visitor's performance and is performed by her.

How do digital installations engage with these terms, with space and time? The dislocation of "site" in the term website, or the non-place of the monitor screen as interface, is brought into relation with the building or the town or the room in which the reader/viewer engages with the installed work.

> Interactive traffic on the Net seems to imply that the restraints of spatiality are loosened in a global continuum. The location of the installation is exactly *this* place. The Net is *everywhere*, and in principle therefore *nowhere*. (Walther 2002: 26)

This is a different engagement with these terms to that of works in the tradition of installation in the visual arts, and develops notions of materiality, scale, and context in a distinct manner. The work is shifted from engaging with the space it occupies, the place in which the data is temporarily made available, made accessible. This every-where/nowhere may apply to an idealized conception of the Net, but the persons interacting with this material are somewhere, and as readers they occupy a place in which they read, and a time during which that reading takes place. An installation which depends on the action or presence of a reader or viewer to be activated, to become operational, is both located in the space where that person through their physicality can affect the work, and located in the non-space of RAM (random access memory) or a server without which the work cannot happen, but which has no direct bearing on the appearance of that work or the reader's experience of it. The notion of the functional site as Meyer describes it relates very closely to concerns that a creator of digital literature may engage with, and attention may be drawn to the intersection between the institutional structures that support the work, that make it possible, and what is manifest in the space of reading. The reader will be aware on some level of the coding and scripting that supports the simplest digital document. Thus a work that presents these relations as part of its context, as part of the site in which the work is read, along with the physical space, situates the reader at a crossing point of a mesh of site-specific relations.

The Third (or Fourth) Dimension

Literature on the page has articulated in a variety of modes the two dimensions of the surface on which it is displayed, over which the reader's eyes travel; this has been examined in the work and criticism of Johanna Drucker, among others (see her *Figuring the Word*). This articulation has a range of manifestations within the history of Modernism and the twentieth-century avant-garde tradition, from Guillaume Apollinaire's calligrams and poem objects to the collages and text-covered spaces of Kurt Schwitters. These two dimensions have been further articulated on the screen of digital literature and computer poetics, where the possibilities of hyperlinks, Flash animation, frames, scrolling, and the mix of moving and still elements has been explored. Young-Hae Chang in the work on his Heavy Industries site (<http://www.yhchang.com>) presents fast-moving graphics that engage with political questions in his native Korea, or internationally. The reader is held by the texts, needing to concentrate to read them as they flash on the screen sometimes accompanied by jazz or other music. Kenward Elmslie (<http://www.kenwardelmslie.com>) uses conventions of book illustration and hand-drawn animation to develop the visual aspects of his poetry, creating vibrant displays that sometimes use recorded sound. The poet, editor, and critic Brian Kim Stefans demonstrates a range of work that uses simple graphic presentations of poem texts, to Flash animated tumbling and dancing letters, or in "Rational Geomancy" (<http://www.arras.net/RNG/director/geomancy/geomancy.htm>), refers directly to the situation of reading a book, holding it as a material object, in an animated writing through of an opening of Steve McCaffery and bp Nichol's book of the same title.

There has also been the opening out of the illusory or virtual third dimension, either in the GUI with stacked windows and shadow effects, or with more complexity in graphic representations of three-dimensional spaces, buildings, landscapes, or other imagined or illusory spaces. This may be the space of a narrative explored via hyperlinks, and represented graphically on the screen, or it may be the logical linking of game spaces in a representation of a three-dimensional space.

In considering the computer monitor or the projection screen as itself occupying space (while being a more-or-less flat surface within that space), and a reader having a location in relation to that screen, the place of that reader before the text must be acknowledged. The installed text is placed in a three-dimensional space, whose context may or may not be directly taken into account, but the reader occupies a particular place at the time of her reading, and this contributes to her reading in some way. Following from the discussion of site in relation to digital work, the manner in which the third dimension operates in these installed texts draws attention to a tension between the physical or material space in which the reader's body moves, and the modification of the physical space by the digital (immaterial) element.

In "Lens" by John Cayley, developed with the Cave technology at Brown University, he considers the dimensions of text (Figure 16.1). Looking at the fact that letters in the roman alphabet are flat, he observes that on the page letters have no third dimension; if lifted from the print or screen surface they are of infinitesimal thinness. Their function depends on being seen frontally; if they are given some thickness and then turned they become progressively less recognizable. Letters can be fattened into three-dimensional objects, but will remain legible or functional only on one face of any such solid. In his work for the Cave Cayley presents text that surrounds the reader, text whose individual characters turn so that they always face the reader as she moves through the space. The letters turn while the words and lines remain in place, hence the text becomes less legible as the reader moves further to the side (Cayley 2005).

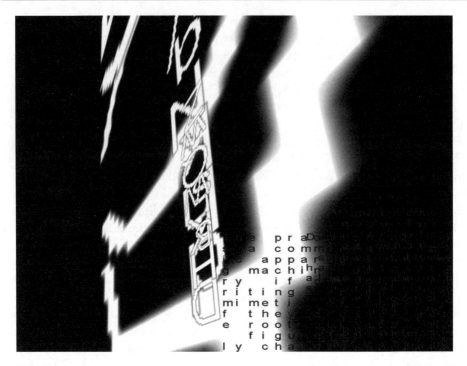

Figure 16.1 Screen shot made by Dmitri Lemmerman, from the immersive VR Cave work-in-progress version of John Cayley's "Lens".

Noah Wardrip-Fruin in *Screen*, another work using the Cave, works with reading as a text game that is played in the three-dimensional space of the Cave (see Wardrip-Fruin 2005b). The reader/player reacts to words moving in space around her; words peel away from the walls, and she can strike at them to return them to the wall. The action of hitting the words can replace them within the text, reorder the text, or break the words into constituent letters that occupy gaps in the text. The reader in her interaction with the text, with the words, recognizes them, recognizes groupings, sees word elements become recontextualized as they are moved around the wall of words. Both this piece and Cayley's use words as graphical objects, as this is the manner in which the programming manages them, but the works also allow for reading, reading that recognizes aspects of the writing, its occupation of space, its dimensionality, the manner in which turning the letters shifts the legibility of the writing. The work acknowledges that letters as components of writing, as elements of an alphabetic system, are inherently manipulable; they lend themselves to recombination. The kind of reading that happens in the space of engagement will take on the articulation of new letter sequences, familiar sound possibilities, phrases that survive, word sequences that disintegrate or disappear. And this happens above, or behind, or beside the reader, not just in front of her face which is the conventional space of reading.

Materiality and/of the Text

Writing as sign, as signifying, is to some extent always immaterial. As information, as content, as signified, it points, it tells, but is not. But to engage with a reader, a receiver, it is made material on some level, as sound, as ink on a surface, as digital information. This materialization has dimensions (temporal/spatial/substantial) and the reader is with this text, before it, sharing these dimensions. The siting or installation of a digital text may make evident some materiality of the immaterial digital text – locating it, grounding it on some specific site.

In his essay "Transcendental Data," Alan Liu discusses the shifts between material and immaterial in the transition from modern to postmodern (or postindustrial). He writes that "materiality" was overlooked in the modernist modeling of the form/content binary. And, having developed "telemedia" without fully exploiting them, modernism gives way to the postindustrial, which through the fuller extension of "telepresence" removes the material base. He claims that while developing technologies that allowed for transmission of data or information (content) across distance, modernism remained wedded to a conception of presence as located in the material (form). The postindustrial no longer has this attachment to the material, and depends on the distribution of presence that is facilitated by the internet (Liu 2004: 80).

> When the material substrate was removed to allow for internet transmission, that is, *variable* methods of standardization – for example, XML documents governed by a common standard but adaptable to undetermined kinds of hardware, software, and usages – could suddenly be imagined. Material embodiment – in the substrate of a work and the bodily practices of the artisanal artist both – was now immaterial to the full, independent expression of content and form. (ibid.)

If a digital text can be termed immaterial, this is perhaps because of the fact that it does not have a single material constant, but can be transmitted in the form of binary code information, etc., to be then output in some form where or when it is called up, played, presented. The material form is not inherent in the text, it is not constant. Installed digital literature, by locating the text in a particular place, at a specific site, gives it a constant (for the duration) material form; it takes on material characteristics of its location, the spatial dimensions are set for the time of the installation. The texture of the surfaces, the warmth or cold of the reading environment may all be controlled. These aspects are aspects experienced by the reader/viewer (otherwise they are of little relevance) and also draw the discussion of this work back to how the reader/viewer is located in it, is engaged by it, positioned in relation to the work.

Johanna Drucker in her essay "Intimations of Immateriality" raises questions of the immateriality of digital text. She comments that documents in digital storage may be output in a variety of forms through a range of devices, being experienced by the reader or listener or viewer as poetry, or images, or music (Drucker 2002a: 154). For Drucker, there is "no necessary relation" between the material form of input and output in electronic media. Translation between storage and display modes preserves no material aspect of writing.

> Code scintillates between material and immaterial conditions long enough to let us ask what (and how) the substantive content of material might mean, and what an *immaterial* text might be. (ibid.)

Elsewhere, Drucker comments on materiality and space from the point of view of the writer of/in a digital text. For her the materiality of digital writing will be defined by two characteristics, "display within a single screen space that is redrawn on a planar surface" and the possibility of an abstraction as machine code (Drucker 2002b: 689). Either or both of these aspects may be articulated for the reader in an installed work, the single plane surface can be multiplied, twisted, broken up, made diffuse, and made to take on the characteristics of the space or site, and the code which makes the display possible may be made evident in the display, in the operation, in the claiming of authorship or copyright.

Another discipline that engaged with questions of materiality was experimental cinema work in the 1960s and through the 1970s. One practitioner who has explored these questions in essays and criticism is Malcolm Le Grice. In his preface to Le Grice's collected writings, Sean Cubitt links Le Grice's concerns to Laura U. Marks' notion of haptic cinema, as he describes it, "a sensory experience that translates light into touch, the lick of light across the colour field, across the eyes, across the skin" (Cubitt 2001: xiv). Such a conception of film as a material medium was one of the possibilities developed in Expanded Cinema. Le Grice describes a materialist focus on the medium over any representational function (Le Grice 2001: 275). In the early 1970s in Europe and Britain, works were made that treated the time of watching, the light of the projector, the space of viewing and projection, the juxtaposition of the illusion of the frame and real actions (ibid.: 274). These materialist practices were partly driven by a desire to resist or disrupt the illusory and absorptive emphasis of mainstream and narrative cinema (ibid.: 170–1). Many of the strategies employed are available to makers of installed digital literature, where a play between reading and seeing or touching words may be developed. The projector and/or the screen are physical or material elements in the installation of digital literature. The artist/writer may manipulate aspects of these to alter the reader's engagement or experience of the work.

The beam of the projector sculpts the light, the light that travels from it in one direction. The beam has one direction (unless a mirror is used), it is tied to the properties of light that are used to make the text/image visible or legible. Light travels from its source (a bulb) through air, dust, a room, until it meets a surface and then it falls flat on that surface, covering the irregularities and perhaps distorting the images in the process. This beam functioned thus in pre-modern technologies of spectacle and display, and continues to function with contemporary digital projectors. An installed work may exploit this property of the beam, using shadows or interruptions of the light beam to generate reactions, to prompt responses by the program.

The physical interruption of the beam in a space, or a feedback image of the reader's body in the space, can act as an interruption to a layer of data. *Talking Cure* by Noah Wardrip-Fruin uses a projected image of the viewer's body interrupting the layers of text to generate new readings (Wardrip-Fruin 2005a). Having the beam fall on a surface that is not a blank screen, not a purpose-made receptor surface, but one that has semiotic content brings both the material being projected and the place/site of projection into relationship. The site or location is illuminated by the beam, and the place gives form or texture to the projected material. Jenny Holzer's more recent projections of *Truisms*, for example at a number of sites in central London in 2005, have used high-powered projectors to present the texts on buildings in urban environments (cf. Morley 2003: 207). The meaning of the texts is altered by their now having a context of a particular location. The building itself may be altered for the reader as the temporary slogan modifies the facade.

Embodied Reading

Installed digital literature may be installed or written in such a way as to make the reader aware of her own embodiment, aware of herself as physically occupying space and as moving in that space, as present in a particular space with specific characteristics. This makes the act of reading material, materializes the matter of reading by emphasizing it as a bodily practice, not something involving only the eyes. Thus the action of moving the arms in *Text Rain* or in *Screen* shifts the letters of words of the text; the body of the reader comes into play in reordering the stuff she is reading. As in the materializing of the digital text in a physical dimensional space, there is also a materializing of the action of reading, reading as a being with the text and of moving in relation to the text. The illusion of transparency in reading, reading past the words on a surface to their narrative or informational meaning, is disrupted by the reader's awareness of her being with the words. The space the text is located in is the space that the reader also occupies. Text and reader are subject to shifts of light, of time, of environment. In some cases they are set in space and she comes to them, in others they are reactive or responsive, or move with her or around her in space (advertising on buses, fly-by banners or hot-air balloons).

In May 1987, in Santa Monica, California, David Antin presented "Skypoem: An Aerial Literary Event" (Sayre 1989: 201–2). The text of this poem was written in the sky by skywriters, puffing out one line at a time in dots of white smoke. The text was digitalized, in that the writing was programmed as information, and generated in discrete bits. The work in its installation made the reader aware of her body, on the ground, craning her neck to look up at the fugitive text, and as the three lines were written separately the reader had to wait if she was to see the whole poem, or might have moved off, turned away and so would only see part. A number of works installed by Jenny Holzer also use this public space, the street, the urban square, and make the reader aware of her need to look up, to stop, to wait for the changes in the text, to become aware of her body moving through the urban environment as being a reading body. For example, in her installation of "Truisms" on Spectacolor signboards in London and New York during the 1980s, Holzer used the rhythms of these flashing electronic light displays to present texts that shared some of the syntax and address of advertising slogans (Morley 2003: 180–1). Like Antin's "Skypoem," there is the possibility for any reader to feel the words were for her, and the space they allowed for reading the non-specific pronouns meant any pedestrian or driver in the street was pointed to by them. The walkers' presence in the urban space was made apparent.

Being in the work, in the space occupied by the work, the reader may be said to be immersed in it. This physical absorption in the work is distinct from the immersion of reading an absorbing narrative. As discussed by Charles Bernstein in "Artifice and Absorption," the disembodied pressure to attend to the story, to see through the words on the page to the content, leaves the site of reading and the reader's body out of consideration (Bernstein 1992: 31). The writer may use direct address to the reader to break out of this absorptive frame, to make opaque the window through which the reader is apprehending the world of the text. As the use of pronouns in Antin's and Holzer's work, discussed above, implicates the audience physically present to the text, the anti-absorptive expletives and insults of Bruce Andrew's poetry can disturb the sense the reader has of her occupation of social space. The ear is assaulted by the text taken in through the eye (ibid.: 32–35). Marie Laure Ryan discusses modes of immersion in reading and interaction with printed and electronic texts, and considers how the reader in reading may be immersed in a fictional or real space, in an other space conjured by the text. These questions of space, along with narrative time, are for Ryan one aspect of immersion through participation (Ryan 2003: 120–39). Modes of reading and levels or types of absorption shift with the genre of text being read. The lazy weekday afternoon reading of a mystery novel is a physical experience of being engaged with a text. This differs dramatically from the way in which a reader is physically engaged in reading John Cayley's "Lens" piece within the Cave.

Modes of reading and the form or experience of particular genres are inextricably linked and the material or immaterial modes of publication/transmission will determine or be determined by modes of readerly engagement, physical, bodily, active, interrupted, immersive, etc. Roger Chartier develops this point in relation to genres of printed, book, or electronic texts. He describes the reading of encyclopedic texts as "segmented, fragmented, discontinuous" (Chartier 2004: 151). The structure of such texts is suited to this mode of reading, and their reception in electronic form is facilitated by this. For Chartier, those genres that demand some perception by the reader of the whole, of the work as a "coherent creation," in his examples monographs and novels, are not well served in electronic form. The ways of reading generated by these genres are not satisfied by publication in electronic form (ibid.: 152). The ways of reading demanded by an installed text may require a physical engagement, may require bodily movement either to activate aspects of the installation, or to access portions of the text. The reader's body may provide a continuity for an otherwise fragmented text, or the experience of the text as complete may be conceivable only through being in it. The text will exceed the reader's body to some extent, in contrast to how a book or other codex form may be grasped as a whole. As a reader the text exceeds my body, and my body in the text brings it to the point or place of reading.

Public Reading

One characteristic of reading a text that has been installed in a three-dimensional space is that often this reading is done in the presence of others; this is reading in public, the reader reads and sees others reading while she herself can be seen to read by others. This shifts the reader's engagement with the text from the private reading usually considered the norm for reading a printed text in book form, or the individual engaged with a single monitor screen and a text in whatever form that is accessed through that monitor. The kind of attention the reader will give to a text in public, the time she spends with it, the choice to go and to return, the immersion in the physical space of reading, the level of absorption possible (or the nature of that absorption when compared with private reading) are all qualities that the artist or writer can articulate and work for in her making of the work of installed digital literature.

In an installation the reader is in the work in some way and so the mode of address is distinct from a printed text or a work of literature engaged with on a monitor or other individual user interface. The installed work can address a wider audience in the manner of advertising hoardings or monumental inscriptions, being located in a space where any number of viewers may see them and read them. The reader, as described by Philippe Bootz, is herself viewed as a reader by other readers. The reader is both spectator and actor, both addressed by the text and visible as part of the scene of reading for other spectators (Bootz 2004: 115). The work is public in a manner distinct from an openly accessible work, it occupies a public reading space and addresses itself to many or to any viewer. This address is less to an imagined or ideal individual reader than to a series or group of readers at once, the holes in the text are not addressed to one reader, the "you" is already multiple, and the installed work makes this evident. Peter Dittmer's "Die Amme 5" (2005) is the latest version of a project he has been modifying over more than a decade. The work makes evident a play between being a particular reader reading (and writing) in public, and in the same moment being any individual who chooses to interact with the installation. "Die Amme 5" as a physical installation is very large, in excess of 20 meters in length, and comprises computer hardware, a number of individual user terminals with screens, a heavy steel framing structure, a robotic arm, and a number of containers of liquid. Engagement with this installation takes the form of entering questions via a keyboard to the machine, which responds using a sophisticated program to generate answers from a database that is continually updated and augmented by the user input. The machine, whose title can translate as "The Wet Nurse 5," demonstrates emotional reactions to the user's input, and if sufficiently angered the arm will spill a glass of milk. There are no game-type shortcuts or hints to getting the machine to respond, and the user, who may become engrossed in the written exchange, is also visible to other visitors to the installation. The other viewers and readers can assess what sort of reading experience is happening, and can themselves develop competing strategies for writing so that the milk will spill (Ensslin 2006: 36–9). Carrie Noland, writing of the physical interaction between user or reader and machine, observes that the physical gestures we use are learned, and to some extent they are determined by the programming. The user's actions in the space of writing and reading are shifted from those of the autonomous reading subject of the book text to a public actor making particular gestures in relation to the machine and other users.

> Choices made during the process of reading (or interacting) are partially determined by features of the programming; they are not realizations of a unified subject's autonomous and individuated desires. (Noland 2006: 220)

Questions of public and private, of the location of "the work," are raised by these installations. Do these works demand an appropriate reading? An appropriate reader? The work of completing the text is not a task open only to an individual reader, but to readers who are also aware of their fellow readers and of being read by them in the space of interaction.

Reading takes place in public, in a space and sometimes in company. As a reader I am in the work, and am part of that work for other readers/viewers. Jill Walker, considering the interaction of a viewer or user in an installation, describes how the visitor performs certain movements in order to participate in the work. She continues, "In addition my movements position me in relation to this representation: it is a representation that includes me" (Walker 2003: 200). This representation is also for those others who may be present, who can see her as part of the situation, who understand her movements as a performance for them also. The reading of, or operation of, the installation affects it, there may be a response to the user's presence, her actions, her position. She reads other readers (as) in the work, and reads the work in relation to its site.

If the site for the installation is an institution, a museum, a gallery, a university, the audience may come with particular expectations, of entertainment, of aesthetic or formal engagement, of information. George Legrady (Legrady 1999), in an article on spatial aspects of interactive installations, considers the role of the performer in the work. To recall Meyer's term, "functional site," the institution is one element of the web of interrelations that form this site. The audience will enter the installation aware of the public context it is operating within. And aware of themselves as necessary to the full functioning of the work and the site (Legrady: 111).

Considering public and private reading in relation to large-scale or installed textual works, one important body of work is that by Barbara Kruger. She does not use digital media in the main, but did use the Spectacolor light board in New York's Times Square in a work commissioned by the Public Art Fund Inc., in 1983, one of the sites later used by Jenny Holzer. The work, "Message to the Public," presented a text dealing with the media, in particular the television news media and its coverage of war and violence, and the relation of this to masculinity. Rosalyn Deutsche (Deutsche 1999) writes of Kruger's work in relation to public space, criticizing the label "public art" as consigning those works installed in galleries and museums to a separate private category. For Deutsche, outdoor spaces are also privatized, in particular those spaces such as Times Square and Piccadilly Circus that are sold for advertising, or outdoor spaces monitored by private surveillance systems (Deutsche 1999: 77n). Works such as Holzer's projections or Kruger's installations draw readers' attention to these complex distinctions between public and private. They activate through writing and reading the power relationships that operate in these spaces. Deutsche complicates the public/private distinction, and its relation to spatial practices. The reading of a work of art in public will to some extent occur in the privatized space of art. She refers to Jacques Derrida's text *Positions* (1981) and develops an argument that understands any social space as constructed on otherness (Deutsche 1999: 77n). The installed work is read in the context of the space made for it by art or literature. The location of literature in that space is made possible by the functional site, by the operation of the institution that licenses or sanctions the work.

Closing

Is the installation of digital literature distinguished by the mode in which it addresses its readers, or by the work of reading that it elicits from those readers? If the work is located in a particular place or site, then the reader for that work is also located, the reader reading is placed in/by the work as (s)he engages with/in the work. The installation of digital literature makes manifest material qualities of digital work, and situates this textual work in a context, a context of reading, of interaction. Bruce Andrews in "Electronic Poetics" proposes a mode of reading electronic literature that engages with, and is implicated in, the social. This social context of reading may draw on a number of the factors discussed earlier, materiality, embodiment, site, space, and a sense of a public context.

> The readers' map becomes the intertext, letting underlayers of significance showing [sic] through. Sense is an elastic social game world. If you want to create a social connectionism, it has to be between the social tilts & volleys of the language; it has to reverb off of the reader. The pleasures of anti-illusionism require active work. Reading, put more directly in charge, is intertextual. The reader is the (modifying, reconfiguring) playback device, not the target of it. (Andrews 2002)

The action of reading installed digital literature involves the reader's body in relation to other bodies, recognizes that where we read is an element of our act of reading, and makes evident the site of reading as part of its materiality. As it offers a resistance to the absorptive immaterial immediate text, the installed text locates the reading in a socially mediated space of human (inter)action.

REFERENCES AND FURTHER READING

Andrews, Bruce (2002). Electronic poetics. <http://www.ubu.com>. Accessed March 31, 2006.

Bernstein, Charles (1992). Artifice of Absorption. In *A Poetics*. Cambridge, MA: Harvard University Press, pp. 9–89.

Bootz, Philippe (2004). Reader/Readers. In *pOes1s: The Aesthetics of Digital Poetry*. Berlin: Hatje Cantz Verlag, pp. 93–121.

Cayley, John (n.d.). "RiverIsland." <http://www.shadoof.net/in/riverisland.html>.

—— (n.d.). "Overboard." <http://www.shadoof.net/in/overboard.html>.

—— (2005). *Writing on Complex Surfaces*. <http://www.brown.edu/Research/dichtung-digital/2005/2/Cayley/index.htm>.

Crimp, Douglas (1995). *On the Museum's Ruins*. Cambridge, MA: MIT Press.

Chang, Young-Hae <http://www.yhchang.com.>.

Chartier, Roger (2004). "Languages, Books, and Reading from the Printed Word to the Digital Text" (T. L. Fagan, Trans.). *Critical Inquiry* 31.1: 133–52.

Cubitt, Sean (2001). "Preface: The Colour of Time." In Malcolm Le Grice (Ed.). *Experimental Cinema in the Digital Age*. London: BFI Publishing, pp. vii–xvi.

Deutsche, Rosalyn (1999). "Barbara Kruger's Spatial Practice." In S. Emerson (Ed.). *Barbara Kruger: Thinking of You*. Cambridge, MA: MIT Press, pp. 77–84.

Dittmer, Peter <http://www.dieamme.de/amme5/index.html>.

Drucker, Johanna (2002a). "Intimations of Immateriality: Graphical Form, Textual Sense, and the Electronic Environment." In E. B. Loizeaux and N. Fraistat (Eds.). *Reimagining Textuality: Textual Studies in the Late Age of Print*. Madison: University of Wisconsin Press, pp. 152–77.

Elmslie, Kenward <http://www.kenwardelmslie.com>.

Ensslin, Marcus (2006). *Performativity and Narrative in Digital Writing: The Metatext of Code*. Unpublished MA Dissertation, Dartington College of Arts.

Krauss, Rosalind E. (1986). "Sculpture in the Expanded Field." In *The Originality of the Avant-Garde and Other Modernist Myths*. Cambridge, MA: MIT Press, pp. 276–91.

Legrady, George (1999). "Intersecting the Virtual and the Real: Space in Interactive Media Installations." *Wide Angle* 21.1: 104–13.

Le Grice, Malcolm (2001). *Experimental Cinema in the Digital Age*. London: BFI Publishing.

Lennon, Brian (2000). "Screening a Digital Visual Poetics." *Configurations* 8.1: 63–85.

Liu, Alan (2004). "Transcendental Data: Toward a Cultural History and Aesthetics of the New Encoded Discourse." *Critical Inquiry* 31.1: 49–84.

Manovich, Lev (2001). *The Language of New Media*. Cambridge, MA: MIT Press.

McCullough, Malcolm (2005). *Digital Ground: Architecture, Pervasive Computing, and Environmental Knowing*. Cambridge, MA: MIT Press.

Meyer, James (2000). "The Functional Site; or, the Transformation of Site Specificity." In E. Suderburg (Ed.). *Space, Site, Intervention: Situating Installation Art*. Minneapolis: University of Minnesota Press, pp. 23–37.

Morley, Simon (2003). *Writing on the Wall: Word and Image in Modern Art*. London: Thames & Hudson.

Noland, Carrie (2006). "Digital Gestures." In A. Morris and T. Swiss (Eds.). *New Media Poetics: Contexts, Technotexts, and Theories*. Cambridge, MA: MIT Press, pp. 217–43.

Ryan, Marie-Laure (2003). *Narrative as Virtual Reality: Immersion and Interactivity in Literature and Electronic Media*. Baltimore, MD: Johns Hopkins University Press.

Sayre, Henry M. (1989). *The Object of Performance: The American Avant-Garde since 1970*. Chicago, IL: Chicago University Press.

Stefans, Brian Kim <http://www.arras.net>.

Sturken, Marita (2000). "The Space of Electronic Time: The Memory Machines of Jim Campbell." In E. Suderburg (Ed.). *Space, Site, Intervention: Situating Installation Art*. Minneapolis: University of Minnesota Press, pp. 287–96.

Suderburg, Erika (2000). "Introduction: On Installation and Site-specificity." In E. Suderburg (Ed.). *Space, Site, Intervention: Situating Installation Art*. Minneapolis: University of Minnesota Press, pp. 1–22.

Utterback, Camille (1999). "Text Rain". <http://www.camilleutterback.com/textrain.html>. Accessed March 26, 2006.

Walker, Jill (2003). "Performing Fictions: Interaction and Depiction." In *Proceedings of DAC Melbourne*, pp. 198–206. <http://hypertext.rmit.edu.au/dac/papers/>.

Walther, Bo Kampmann (2002). *Complexity in Interactive Art: In Search of a Digital Aesthetic.* <http://www1.sdu.dk/Hum/bkw/interferentialart.htm>. Accessed March 23, 2007.

Wardrip-Fruin, Noah (2005a). *Digital Literature.* (Interview by Roberto Simanowski at <artificial.dk. http://www.artificial.dk>.) Accessed March 26, 2006.

—— (2005b). *Screen.* <http://www.noahwf.com/screen/index.html>. Accessed July 25, 2006.

Weyergraf-Serra, C., and Buskirk, M. (Eds.) (1990). *The Destruction of* Tilted Arc: *Documents.* Cambridge, MA: MIT Press.

17

Digital Poetry: A Look at Generative, Visual, and Interconnected Possibilities in its First Four Decades

Christopher Funkhouser

Digital poetry is a new genre of literary, visual, and sonic art launched by poets who experimented with computers in the late 1950s. Digital poetry is not a singular "form" but rather a conglomeration of forms that now constitutes a genre even though the creative activity itself – in terms of its media, methods, and expressive intent – contains heterogeneous components. Digital poetry is an evolving process, employing various techniques that began to form well before the advent of the personal computer and continues to refine itself in today's World Wide Web (WWW) environment. Poets explore a variety of computerized techniques, from interactive installations to randomized and visual attributes. Interestingly, despite the technological advancement and popularization of computers, most approaches to the production of digital poetry realized in the wake of the WWW's emergence were at least roughly cultivated before the advent of the global network. This chapter seeks to reveal the development, range, and construction of digital poetry, as well as what constitutes the genre.

Labels such as "e-poetry," "cyberpoetry," and "computer poetry" have been used to describe creative work in this area. The titles of two important books on the subject, Loss Pequeño Glazier's *Digital Poetics: The Making of E-Poetries* (2002) and Brian Kim Stefans's *Fashionable Noise: On Digital Poetics* (2003), contain the phrase "digital poetics." Both of these collections discuss and question the various labels, and neither book argues for a singular nomenclature. The strongest definition of the genre is found in the introduction to the volume *p0es1s: Aesthetics of Digital Poetry*, which proclaims that digital poetry: "applies to artistic projects that deal with the medial changes in language and language-based communication in computers and digital networks. Digital poetry thus refers to creative, experimental, playful and also critical language art involving programming, multimedia, animation, interactivity, and net communication" (Block et al. 2004: 13). The authors of this essay (Friedrich Block, Christiane Heibach, and Karin Wenz) identify the form as being derived from "installations of interactive media art," "computer- and net-based art," and "explicitly from literary traditions (2004: 15–17). At least one other essay, Janez Strehovec's "Text as loop: on visual and kinetic textuality" (2003), affirms that digital poetry is "a new genre all its own" that incorporates "kinetic/animated poetry, code poetry, interactive poetry, digital sound poetry, digital 'textscapes' with poetry features, and poetry generators" (Text n.pag.). As a genre, digital poetry "intersects the literary avant-garde, visual and concrete poetry, text-based installations, net art, software art, and netspeak" (n.pag.).[1] Digital poetry is a genre that fuses crafted language with new media technology and techniques enabled by such equipment, and is a reasonable label to use in describing forms of literary work that are presented on screens with the assistance of computers and/or computer programming. A poem is a digital poem if computer programming or processes (software, etc.) are distinctively used in the composition, generation, or presentation of the text (or combinations of texts).

Computer programs that write sonnets, haiku, or other forms, like Margaret Masterman and Robin McKinnon Wood's "Computerized Japanese haiku" (1968), E. M. de Melo e Castro's videopoem, *Roda Lume* (1968), Jim Andrews's interactive sound poem "Nio" (2001), and Deena Larsen's hypertext *Marble Springs*, despite their stylistic differences, all qualify as digital poetry. Digital poetry is a term that represents a spectrum of computerized literary art that can be appreciated in the context of the poetic tradition. Through broad identification and cataloguing, multiple types of computerized production can be analyzed as one generality that includes hypermedia, hypertext, computer-generation, and other digital manifestations of poetic text. All forms of digital poetry comprise a singular genre that contains multiple subcategories, just as the genre of "poetry" contains many different styles (i.e., free verse, the sonnet, haiku, and so on). Some of these canonical forms have informed formulations of digital poetry, while other works are poetic mutations that disregard convention. The diverse spectrum of digital poems nonetheless presents a challenge in terms of seeing the form or genre as a unified proposition. For instance, in discussing the same general sort of works in a recent entry in *The Facts on File Companion to 20th-Century American Poetry*, Catherine Daly intelligently uses the label cyberpoetry ("concerned with the machine control of the writing process, delivery of poetry in more than one medium, and machine-mediated interactivity between audience and reader or writer and text") to discuss the various formulations of digital poetry (2005: 114). Daly's view sees the genre as divided into three parts: "procedural," "multimedia," and "hypertext and cybertext" poetry (she distinguishes "cybertext poetry" as a form that "involves readers' queries, assumptions, and actions, which change readers' perceptions of the cybertext during the interaction") (2005: 116). Obviously many labels are plausible, each of which acknowledges that digital poetry is a practice – a presentation of expression – that is open enough to include many fringe forms and methods in producing writing and art, as long as they are mechanically enabled by digital hardware and software.

Digital poems, while built on similar principles, are always being technically, culturally, and imaginatively redefined. Various forms of poems – related by technological agency – both represent (i.e., simulate) classical literature (in programs that implement classical forms, or by assembling CD-ROM anthologies of classical poetry) and, more profoundly, embrace new methods of communicating verbal information.

Introductory Overview of Forms

Computer poems

Poets initially used computer programs to synthesize a database and a series of instructions to establish a work's content and shape. Labeled by its authors as "Computer Poetry" and "computer-poems" (among other terms), these works are generated by computer algorithm, arranged as a sequence of words, or signs and symbols according to a programming code. All works of text-generation, or archetypal computer poetry, can be seen as performing some type of permutation in that they transform or reorder one set of base texts or language (i.e., word lists, syllables, or pre-existing texts) into another form. The permutation procedures of algorithmically generated poems can be devised into three classifications. Works are either permutational (recombining elements into new words or variations), combinatoric (using limited, pre-set word lists in controlled or random combinations), or slotted into syntactic templates (also combinatoric but within grammatical frames to create an image of "sense").

The creative spirit and impetus to combine randomness with order through intricate, technical art alters the human relationship with language. Cyborgian poetry, works co-created by humans and digital machinery, emerged from these experiments. Works produced by artists such as Pedro Barbosa, Charles O. Hartman, Jean-Pierre Balpe, and others prove that language can be digitally processed into sequences to create a type of synthetic poetry. Such work has roots in Max Bense's theory on artificial poetry, but from its earliest manifestations in Theo Lutz's "Stochastic Poems" computer poetry has been a predominantly disconnected movement, without central figures or theories. An argument could be made that digital technology available at the time better suited "operational" poets, whose work was computational in character (and, later, poets whose work would be graphical or nonlinear). For instance, Jackson Mac Low and John Cage perpetually used the computer because the device facilitated the type of work they had been doing for many years. Someone who wants the computer to write a Petrarchan sonnet, for example, and expects it to write it as well as Petrarch, is asking the machine to perform the wrong type of task.

From a general point of view, the majority of combinatoric and permutation works produced feature variations, extensions, or technological implementations of Dadaist technique. Many aleatoric poems contain few parameters and, at the very least, share sensibilities common to open-form poetry. Somewhat ironically, however, the poems are not pure-chance occurrences – they are preconfigured to be randomized, and some examples contain fixed attributes, as in slotted works, where the author strives to imbue rigid syntax or comply with established parameters. Digital poetry made with text-generating programs gradually developed into a multifaceted form of its own, exploring many styles of literary expression.

Typically, text generators rapidly produce many poems, using a programmatic formula that selects words from a database to create output. Computers cannot be programmed to engineer a "perfect" poem; some poets use the computer to alter or subvert typical forms of expression; others seek to be imitative. In either mode, selecting appropriate input text is the most important element in the process of pronouncing meaningful expression. Whoever establishes the database co-authors the poem, as does the writer of the program; the user of the program also has authorial prerogatives in selecting from and editing output. The program *TRAVESTY*, written by Hugh Kenner and Joseph O'Rourke, in particular highlights human input through the imperative role of the source or database on the computer-generated poem; as Stefans observes, "Without 'human' intervention nothing can get into a CP [computer poem] that is not in the database or acceptable to the program" (2003: 65). Computer poems challenge and invite the reader to participate imaginatively in the construction of the text; some mock the conventions of poetry, and others reify them.

Graphical poems

By the mid-1960s graphical and kinetic components emerged, rendering shaped language as poems on screens and as printouts. Since then, videographic and other types of kinetic poems have been produced using digital tools and techniques. This advancement – foregrounding the visual aspects of language at least as much as the verbal – marks several changes in the development of digital poetry. In contrast to works discussed above, these visual and kinetic works largely employ mutation as opposed to permutation. As with text-generation, these works use mechanized language expansively, although most de-emphasize randomized output. Static and kinetic visual works introduced a poetry of sight, overtly conscious of its look, sited on and incited by computers; standard typefaces became a thing of the past. Digital poets began to work with prosody that was literally in motion.

Early graphical works by Marc Adrian (1968) and Carl Fernbach-Flarsheim (1970–1) were, like text-generated poems, automatically spawned by viewers confronting a program in an installation setting. With the development of graphics software, subsequent works embodied visual methods that approximated concrete and visual poems rendered and fixed on the page that are not interactive. The computer became a convenient tool to manipulate the appearance and presentation of text. Some titles closely follow earlier manifestations of visual poetry; others (like the videographic and hypermedia productions) venture further afield and do not aim simply to reconfigure the style of poems that are read and understood exclusively through alphabetic language. By the 1980s poets increasingly presented moving language on screens as a result of the development of PCs. These efforts foreshadow many later experiments in poetry that proliferated in animated, hypermedia formats. Kinetic poems long pre-dated a style of digital poetic practice that erupted with the emergence of the WWW, typified by works such as Stefans's *the dreamlife of letters* as well as those found archived on Komninos Zervos' *Cyberpoetry* site, and elsewhere.[2] Groundwork for today's animated digital poems (e.g., those made with Macromedia Flash) was in fact under way by the mid-1970s, in coded works such as Arthur Layzer's "textured animated poetry" (written in FORTRAN) that featured words "streaking" down the page (McCauley 1974: 118).

With the advent of publishing projects such as Xexoxial Endarchy and dbqp (founded by visual poet Geof Huth) in the 1980s, digital processes became ostensibly implemented in static visual poems. The influence of poststructural critical theories, such as deconstruction, spurred poets to challenge their imaginations, and invent new appearances for poetry. While some artists, like André Vallias, eschewed the use of words on the surface of their works, most did not reject language but worshipped it more deeply, a spirit divulged boldly on the dbqp WWW site: "Once the religion of the sacred word became obsolete, the word itself became the object of our reverence" (Incunabula). Bob Grumman's entry on Visual Poetry in *A Companion to 20th-Century American Poetry* reports that numerous visual poets were using digital methods in the 1990s, each of whom steadily published in alternative little magazines, including K. S. Ernst, Crag Hill, Huth, Jonathan Brannen, Mike Basinski, Stephen-Paul Martin, Jake Berry, mIEKAL aND, Grumman, John Byrum, and John M. Bennett.

Digitally rendered poems portray at least three different traits: words are arranged into literal shapes; words show patterns that represent dispersal or displacement of language; or words are combined with images (as in a collage). Viewer-activated (static) poems place words either randomly or through pre-plotted designs that do not move on the screen (or require interactive manipulation but do not move on their own accord). In kinetic works optical mutation of words and letters is the operative principle; poems, by design, move and change before the viewer's eyes. Poems that inscribe kinetic language can be divided into two general categories: projected and interactive. Projected works set poetry in motion in two distinct ways. Words are plotted into motion (or letters themselves change shape or morph) or are presented as part of kinetic collages in which elements of language are combined with visual objects or symbols in single or multiple visual scenes/scenarios. In the few interactive works that are kinetic and do not involve overt hypertextual operations, viewers are invited to set some of the poem's parameters (used in the activation or appearance of words) or interact with a virtual object that is fixed in position on the screen (and may or may not inscribe words).

In kinetic works poets find dozens of ways to portray poetic text as shifting, vibrant verse. Palimpsest is used powerfully; images can be a mélange of fragments of words complemented or replaced by imagistic forms. These poems show that many different expressive elements can be plotted at once, or in a short period of time, layered on top of one another. Putting phrases in motion as sliding, spinning objects, and otherwise synthesizing words, lines, and symbols are the techniques established as typical of all visual works. The inclination to display poetic work in such ways developed alongside the technology capable of accomplishing the task, which has only increased with the technical developments in the WWW era. Experiments by those who made activated or interactive works represent an important and fascinating step in the production of poetry. Using computers to make visually charged language and programming it to move were novel applications of technology that foreshadowed contemporary visual works. Digital poetry's emphasis on cultivating active language added overtly kinetic language to its canon of generated and graphical texts.

In the visually oriented works of digital poetry, technology intended for the creation of graphical artwork is used to process language instead of images or language as images. For many years writers and artists have used computers, software, and fonts to do more than make shapes on the page. Graphical poems as such are not new to literature, though the tools for producing them alter, accelerate, amplify, and, ultimately, animate the process. Contributing to a trend that fosters changes in the act of reading, an increase of poetry containing graphical elements has intensified in recent years because both the software and publishing medium of the WWW enables (if not encourages) the incorporation of visual elements.

Hypertext and hypermedia

In the 1980s, hypertext (nonlinear texts that are intrinsically, mechanically inter-connected) developed in sync with the increasing availability of the personal computer. Theorist Michael Joyce classifies presentational modes used by authors into two distinct categories: "constructive" and "exploratory" (Joyce 1995: 41). These models are useful towards establishing the broadest codification of hypertextual poetry. Within these parameters, nearly all works are explorative, and various forms emerge within this vein of production which pertain to the media inscribed and methods of navigation. As defined by Joyce, exploratory hypertexts allow their audience to guide themselves through a text as interest, engagement, and curiosity dictate, and reflect the author's sense of structure. This mode, according to Joyce, ideally allows the audience the ability "to create, change, and recover particular encounters with the body of knowledge, maintaining these encounters as versions of the material, i.e. trails, paths, webs, notebooks, etc." (1995: 41). A reader explores a body of work that has been set before them on the computer. Constructive hypertexts, on the other hand, are steadily built by their audience, as part of a process of transforming the knowledge previously presented; Joyce has described dynamics of such texts as "versions of what they are becoming, a structure for what does not yet exist" and "serial thought" (1995: 179, 189).

Programmers developed tools that facilitated such nonlinear writing, enabling authors to create links within and between texts while simultaneously incorporating visual, kinetic, sonic, and static verbal texts. In these works a number of different files (comprised of various media) are programmed into arrangement with each other, presenting poems in segments through a series of links (which can be simple and obvious or complex and veiled), or may be otherwise conceived, as Jay David Bolter observes in *Writing Space: Computers, Hypertext, and the Remediation of Print*, as "visual objects with which the reader interacts" (2001: 156). Once hyper-works were developed, all the principle possibilities of contemporary digital poetry were available – the genre has proliferated in the past twenty years by synthesizing and cultivating each of its modes. We can identify distinct characteristics in every digital poem, but the accumulation of styles confounds any single critical definition of artistic works that merge poetry with digital technology.

Essentially four types of hypertext works were designed: (1) those which feature only text presented as a series of nodes which are directly interlinked (sometimes with some sort of "map" that can be used as guidance); (2) those that feature significant graphical and kinetic components (i.e., hypermedia), also based on the 1:1 link–node premise; (3) those that present a virtual object that the user negotiates (without having to constantly "click" on links to traverse that text); and (4) those that are formed through methods of aleatoric progression. Authors who have made profound works of poetry using hypertext and hypermedia prior to the WWW include: mIEKAL aND, Jean-Marie Dutey, Robert Kendall, Jim Rosenberg, John Cayley, Glazier, and Deena Larsen. Christy Sheffield Sanford, Diana Slattery, Glazier, Aya Karpinska, Stephanie Strickland, Maria Mencia, and many other poets have created potent hyper-works for the WWW. Typically, hypertext and hypermedia poems prior to the WWW contained interlinked text and sometimes image files. They are "interactive" in that they require choices to be made by the viewer.

Digital poetry on the WWW is brought together in HTML (hypertext markup language), a comparatively uncomplicated process of coding which allows a synthesis of graphical elements (in color), animation, sound elements, and other coded features, with any "written" text. HTML (and other coding schemes like JavaScript), beyond connecting disparate forms of text by using graphical communication, has had minimal impact on the development of digital poetry, although it has unquestionably increased its readership. Aesthetically, even WWW digital poetry presentations that use "random," "animation," and "looping" procedures are usually self-confined, mainly linear segments that appear as individual works of art. Though they theoretically exist within a much larger domain of potential images, the teleologies and terminal points at which a reader may go no farther are numerous; these digital poems can theoretically branch in infinite directions but they engineer themselves into a corner, forcing readers to begin again.

Internet publications, network writing initiatives, digital projects conducted in physical space (including holographically presented poems), and audio poetry have been produced since the 1980s. In these manifestations of digital poetry, the expressive issues do not include whether or not the computer can write poetry, or graphically enhance it, but how various types of machinery have been used to accentuate and modify poetic process and range. The collaborative composition of online texts, as practiced by groups, in MOOs and elsewhere, extends previous forms of written collaboration into a virtual environment. Atypical modes of design and delivery are characteristics of quickly and widely delivered publications. In the network era, computers are no less a creative tool, and are now being used as a mechanism to circulate contemporary and historical productions. Digital sound tools and processes alter the way voices are constructed, heard, and combined. In so many ways, computer technology has been used in conjunction with poetry, as writers invent new practices, and reinvent old ones with digital media.

Contemporary Perspective

Mechanically it is true that a contemporary poet has novel technology at her or his disposal, but critically speaking, many poems available on the WWW cannot be classified as "new" because the digital techniques used to present them were cultivated in the decades prior to the WWW. Furthermore, investigations such Glazier's *Digital Poetics* prove digital poets have largely conceived these works with the same poetic and theoretical practices used by artists who worked with nothing more than paper and ink. The high-tech composition and presentation of poetry, using the latest available means, has, of course, reflected a sense that something innovative was under way, and many artists working in the pre-WWW period can rightfully claim that they were doing something mechanically original. This is obviously true in terms of surface aesthetics – particularly the development of kinetic works – but nothing particularly new has emerged since the initiation of the WWW. Contemporary digital poetry essentially refines earlier types of production and disseminates works to a wider audience via the network.

The versatile, massive, global network unquestionably ignited a proliferation of digital poetry, boosting the confidence of artists who had previously been wary of the instability of technologically based writing. Growth of the WWW undoubtedly benefits and increases the visibility of digital poetry, so the form has grown and works have been refined. Nonetheless, earlier endeavors reveal the basic elements, procedures, and historical approaches to the composition of digital poetry. The genre has clear and persistent boundaries, despite advancements in hardware, networks, and software. Despite the transitory, ever-evolving technologies and elements, the principles and features of digital poetry – text generation, flexible and collaborative language, use of sonic and visual attributes, interactivity and intertextual linking – have only been altered slightly if at all in texts that have been produced since the dawning of the WWW. The coming years will indicate whether a more televisual poetry, such as we begin to see in the highly animated, visceral Shockwave or Macromedia "Flash" poems and WWW works in general, will dominate artistic literacy or the culture at large. Digital poetry is still forming and gradually progressing, though it largely continues to embrace the characteristics, and sometimes the limitations, of its forebears. Computer science and creative expression have integrated well with one another; progress in all aspects of computing has led to complicated verbal and vibrant multimedia works that are far richer and more spectacular than the texts originally produced in ASCII text. Language is presented in alternative creative forms (sometimes generated, sometimes fixed), enhancing the visual qualities of texts. Viewers are presented with a stimulating and challenging textual scenario; these are the successes of digital poems since the beginning. In the 1970s, very rudimentary kinetic poems by Arthur Layzer streaked down a computer terminal; in the 1980s, the same approach was developed and technically refined by Melo e Castro in his *Infopoems* and by hypermedia works created and published by Philippe Bootz and in the French hypermedia journal *Alire*. A few years later, the multimedia program Macromedia Flash brought these effects to the WWW, as in "The Dreamlife of Letters." New technologies led to refined kinetic poems.

In a Literary Context

In his preface to the anthology *Computer Poems* (1973), Richard Bailey identifies four poetic tendencies that influenced the works included in the collection: "concrete poetry," "poetry of sound in verbal orchestrations," "imagistic poetry in the juxtaposition of the unfamiliar," and "haiku" (n.pag.).[3] The poems in the anthology reasonably support his (somewhat) dated viewpoint, but there is a correspondence between poetry and digital poetry. Of course, beyond digital poetry's relationship to literary works and theories, it would be remiss to omit to mention that early works were also influenced by trends and possibilities in mathematics (stochastic operations and other types of equations), computer science (hypertext theory), and other fields. Further, digital poems share so much with other forms of multimedia art that it can be difficult to make distinctions between works that employ sound, imagery, language, and animation.

Digital poetry is pluralistic in the creative (poetic and poetics) influences it embraces, the media it employs, and genres it fuses. Many poems embody expressive potentials realized on the page by previous generations of poets, and it is not difficult to find stylistic elements associated with previous epochs of literary history in many digital works. Digital poetry's stylistic foundation is first established by pre-Modernist literary beacons. French Symbolist writing, particularly Stephane Mallarmé's late-nineteenth-century poem, "A Throw of the Dice Never Will Abolish Chance" (1897), is unquestionably an artistic predecessor that directly impresses upon the disruption of textual space and syntax found in digital poetry. The variations in typography, incorporation of blank space, and the liberal scattering of lines often found in digital poems can be discerned as having roots in Mallarmé's work (which also strongly influenced the development of Concrete Poetry in the 1950s). Such patterning has been extended by the addition of interactive and kinetic components. Mallarmé's importance was previously acknowledged (albeit briefly) from a different perspective in Bailey's preface to *Computer Poems*, which largely featured randomized poetry created by computer programs:

Mallarmé published a slogan for modernism: A throw of the dice will never abolish chance. Chance is not abolished by the computer's randomizing power but is re-created in different terms. The poet-programmer finds this power a tool to create a new set of dice, multi-faceted and marked with elements of his own choosing. (n.pag.)

Here Bailey privileges the power of Mallarmé's thematic content, although I would assert that the aesthetic properties of "A Throw of the Dice," particularly its visual attributes and the fact that it requires readers to make decisions about how to read the poem, are equally important, if not more so.

The programmed permutation works that emerged near the outset of digital poetry have even earlier predecessors in combinatory works that date back as far as AD 330. In the essay "Combinatory Poetry and Literature in the Internet," Cramer defines combinatory poetry as "literature that openly exposes and addresses its combinatorics by changing and permuting its text according to fixed rules, like in anagrams, proteus poems and cut-ups" (n. pag.). Samples and reinventions of writings by Optatianus Porphyrius (Carmen XXV, fourth century AD), Julius Caesar Scaliger (Poetices, 1561), Georg Philipp Harsdörffer ("Fivefold Thought Ring of the German Language," seventeenth century), and other works are capably presented on the Permutations site, illustrating how the mechanics of contemporary (and prehistoric) digital poems have roots in works produced several centuries ago.

The first works of digital poetry, text-generating programs written in BASIC, TRAC [Text Reckoning and Compiling] Language, APL [A Programming Language], FORTRAN, and other now-ancient programming languages, predominantly reflect the Modernist propensity to synthesize disparate voices and cultural details. Pound's *The Cantos* and T. S. Eliot's *The Waste Land* achieve this effect, as Bolter observed in *Writing Space: The Computer, Hypertext, and the History of Writing*, by replacing poetry's narrative element with "fragmented anecdotes or mythical paradigms" (131). The early "Tape Mark" (digital) poems by Nanni Balestrini (1962) pronounce this tendency by appropriating texts by Lao Tzu's (*Tao Te Ching*), Paul Goldwin (*The Mystery of the Elevator*), and Michihito Hachiya (*Hiroshima Diary*); such re-inscription is a common trait of digital poetry. These poetical collage techniques are reminiscent of *The Cantos* and William Carlos Williams's *Paterson*, which juxtaposes poetry, the language of the people and natural world of his locale, and correspondence with other writers into a sequence of writing encompassed in the poem. Like Williams, Pound, and Eliot, in their era, digital poets are confronted with social and artistic fragmentation in the world around them and – whether consciously or not – use the atomization and hybridization of texts to both subvert and reflect the complex of cultural information. Authors working on the page and screen in the post-atomic era use fragmentation to legitimize fragmentation and challenge the stability of language as a point of meaning; this process of reassembling disparate pieces via technology offers the means to impart a sense of coherence.

Early computer poems show great effort (in terms of preparing code and selection of database material) to give digital poems a sense of cohesion. Despite the random effects imposed on the poems by complex programming, one can find an intentional plotting of associated fragments of language and thought, similar to those found in Modernist works. Another style emulates the Dadaist practice of reordering the words of one text in order to make a new text, which has been called "matrix" poetry by several practitioners (e.g., Barbosa, Robin Shirley, Bootz).

Adding visual components to poetry was not new (e.g., William Blake). The most glaring examples of this trend in the Modern era are Pound's interest in (and implementation of) calligraphy (which also asserts the applicability of scientific method to literature), Apollinaire's "Calligrames" (which shape language into discernable images), Charles Olson's "Projective Verse" ("composition by field" with attention to breath and the extension of perception), as well as various methods used by Concrete, Constructivist, Dada, and Futurist poets. While visual design is a characteristic of many digital poems, it should be noted that the relationship between graphical digital poems and the aforementioned models often exists on the surface but is not intrinsically supported by shared ideologies or methods, especially in contemporary forms where elements are not always fixed into place. Fragmentation and disruption of sensibility through the images produced – attributes generally associated with postmodern productions – were practiced from the very beginning. Graphical digital poems – which use many different approaches and take on many different forms – emerged in the 1960s and have appeared steadily ever since. This advancement, which overtly and visually foregrounds material aspects of language, represented significant aesthetic growth in the development of digital poetry.

Poems by artists preoccupied with visual elements are reminiscent of certain Concrete poems, in that they use atypical and oversized lettering, but the connection is closer in graphical philosophy to earlier shaped poems by Apollinaire, or George Herbert in "Easter Wings," where the shaping of the poem is an embodiment of its content. The "tension of things-words in space-time," – which is one of the theoretical and artistic objectives of Concretism stated by Augusto de Campos in the "Pilot Plan for Concrete Poetry" – is sometimes but not always perceived in digital works (Williams 1967: 48). Materials that directly associate object and meaning do not foster the same level of "tension" in the reader as the more oblique communication strategy of Concretism.

In kinetic poetry we encounter a style of work that has not been previously produced. Though a mechanical possibility through the use of film, poetry was not literally put into motion, probably because of a lack of access and the expense of film equipment and processing as well as a set preconception of what film as a medium entailed. Videographic works and devices used to make animated poems have gradually become available during the past two decades. These techniques have galvanized a synthesis of media in the construction of poetry, in which meaning is produced through the recognition of differences between instances in the chain of pre-programmed sequences. Poems in this style thus impart a type of deconstruction through their shifting, activated rhetorical structure. Melo e Castro outlines the central elements of this neoteric form, which emphasizes, as poets have throughout the ages, "the importance of phonetic values in oral poetry, of scriptural values in written poetry, of visual values in visual poetry and of technological values with computer use and video for the production of poetry, and not only for simple repetitive and non-creative tasks" (1996: 141). Melo e Castro sees Videopoetry as an inevitable response to the challenge of new technological means for producing text and image. In some instances, messages are succinctly and directly transmitted, but more often the combination of words, symbols, and images requires viewers to decide what this conflation or concatenation of elements means.

John M. Slatin's essay "Hypertext and the Teaching of Writing" recalls how Pound develops his concept of Vorticism in *Gaudier-Brzeska: A Memoir* by devising an aesthetic strikingly appropriate to hypertext based on the unconventional juxtapositions of discrete images into "a radiant node or cluster…from which, and through which, and into which, ideas are constantly rushing" (1998: 114–15). Digital poetry (and other forms that use multiple texts) embody the concept of intertextuality and show that any text has the potential to be a "collectivity of texts…composed of and by other texts," which makes demands on the reader (1998: 115).

Developments since the appearance of computer networks, such as collaborative activities, the establishment of archives, as well as online communities and publishing, hearken back to earlier historical practices or efforts put forth by poets as analog artists. For instance, the "Mail Art" movement, surrealist "exquisite corpse" writings, organizations (e.g., The Poetry Project in New York City), and small press publishing taken up in previous periods, which may (or may not) have operated on a smaller scale, all served purposes similar to network initiatives. The attention given to creating innovative audio works recalls both the earliest iterations of poetry, in which language was exclusively oral, and performance poetry that has been practiced since Dadaism.

Digital poems are more inclined toward abstraction and are largely depersonalized, especially as the media used in composition has become hybridized. While many authors vigorously attempt to produce poems that make grammatical and human sense, certain artists, like Cage and Mac Low, employ narrative strategies that are intentionally unfixed or utterly fragmented as a result of the media implemented in composition. Randomization, patterning, and repetition of words, along with discursive leaps and quirky, unusual semantic connections, are almost always found in digital poetry, though sometimes these effects are so amplified that the poems would not be considered poetry by someone using traditional definitions.

Digital poetry is not a fixed object; its circuitry perpetuates a conversation. Poetry is a socially constructed art form, always situated within other texts (not limited only to poems) and extended by readers. Meaning and significance are not completely dependent on the verbal material itself; they are formed in the mind of the reader, who synthesizes various tiers of influence (inputs) and, potentially, extends them (outputs). Made obvious in viewing any digital poem is its release from a fixed format. A dramatic break from sharing real physical space occurs, whereby the signs that constitute the poetic text are immaterial. Contemporary modes challenge authors to avoid looking at any part of the systems involved – audible, alphabetized, imagistic – as discrete or independent units. Building a widely conceived philosophy of text is the responsibility of authors working with fully integrated (audio/video/alphanumeric) and layered (linked and coded) texts.

Poet-programmers have devised numerous methods to handle computer coding, the (often) unseen language responsible for formulating a digital poem. As yet, however, methods of creating digital works are dwarfed by the number of forms of written poetry. For example, more than seventy-five unique forms of poetry are discussed in the *Handbook of Poetic Forms*, a useful guidebook for students of poetry edited by Ron Padgett, and many more are reviewed in *The New Princeton Encyclopedia of Poetry and Poetics*. This coverage is unsurprising, considering that these books address poetry across centuries whereas digital poetry is (mechanically) less than fifty years old. Though many different variations of digital poems are available, the overall number of general classifications of forms remains relatively small. Computerized literature and artifice are still in their early stages, and will become enriched at a gradual pace. The complexities handled by poets using written language, the challenges met despite perceived limits to alphanumeric forms, have just begun to be broached by digital poets. The first decades of the craft established a few models, which may be ultimately regarded as rudimentary efforts when contextualized within any overall history of computerized writing.

Theoretical Touchstones

Many digital poems can be conceptually interpreted as searching for their essence or as striving to make their essence apparent, as did Modernist endeavors. Yet on a theoretical level these works are in many ways typical of the postmodern condition of text. In the contemporary era, Jacques Derrida and others have theorized that words are not rooted in anything – they only have meaning in relation to adjacent words and texts to adjacent texts. This is certainly true in randomly generated digital works, in works that appear in sequences (either static or animated), and in many hypertexts (which are typically presented as a series of interlinked fragments). When we encounter the various forms of digital poetry, we see a representation of our highly technological world; within the myriad types of expression, the artist often seeks to expose, and sometimes subvert, the various binary oppositions that support our dominant ways of thinking about literature (and, perhaps, about communication in general). The deconstructive contention that texts intrinsically contain points of "undecidability," which betray any stable meaning that an author might seek to impose on a text, is certainly a feature of many digital poems. These undecidable aspects of text situate, for Derrida, "the places where discourses can no longer dominate, judge, decide: between the positive and the negative, the good and the bad, the true and the false" (Derrida 1995: 86). In several forms of digital poetry – particularly in text-generated and hypermedia works – discovering the methods used to produce digital poems reveals that which has been suppressed (underlying computer code or intervention of software) and, typically, texts cover over materials that have been previously shown on the screen. Hierarchically structured binary oppositions within poems are undermined, despite the use of binary (coded) operations used in their production.

In *The Postmodern Condition: A Report on Knowledge* Jean François Lyotard proposes that contemporary discourse can make no claim to finality, even if it does not seek to put an end to narration. He argues that the computerization of society, which shifts emphasis from the ends of actions to their means, has made metanarratives (as a means of legitimizing knowledge) unnecessary and intolerable because technology is self-legitimating (1984: 108). Cultural transformations (especially the growth of technology) have altered the historical tenets of science, literature, and art. His pluralistic, relativist views suggest that art is no longer required to seek or produce truth and knowledge, and may abandon standards and categories. Lyotard's argument that what he calls performativity "brings the pragmatic functions of knowledge clearly to light" and "elevates all language games to self-knowledge" is certainly substantiated in the diverse traits reflected in digital poetry (1984: 114). The text's identity as a computer form, containing expanded semiotic operations, often subjects the reader to an unfamiliar type of reading. In negotiating the interface, a reader's experience involves thoughtfully participating in the textual activity and thereby experiencing the poem on compounded visceral and cognitive levels.

Containing multiplicities is a driving impulse in many works, as is the impetus to assemble, reassemble (and even disassemble) texts in ongoing, potentially infinite, ways (with rupture but without permanent disruption). Poets are experimenting with computers in many different ways, and it is not surprising to find them working with previously known structures to begin to build a sense of the machine's capability. Most forms of artistry begin with mimesis, and then branch out into new territory. Since computerized poems are produced and operated by highly structured, precise instructions or codes, it is logical that plotted, ordered, and contained (though not always predictable) designs would emerge. Nonetheless, because literature has now joined forces with mathematics and computer science, as well as other art forms, it foists an entirely different set of circumstances on the reader.

Critical Commentary

Today, digital technology advances poetry into dynamic areas that were at least partially available in the pre-technologic era. Attaining randomized effects without technological components and processes, digital poets re-programmed unconventional analog prototypes – like handmade Dada poems – as well as more orthodox forms such as sonnets and haiku. Thus far, digital poems have been part of a substratum of contemporary art, overshadowed by the abundance of dynamic works produced by writers and artists whose more accessible surfaces (such as books and galleries) gained much broader exposure. Only a few of the works have been strong enough to garner temporary attention at that level, usually in events that focused on computer art. The WWW is a significant point of demarcation, as it signals a profound and historical shift in the way digital poems were made available for viewers. Prior to this moment, multimedia, hypertext, and computer-generated works had been discretely produced "offline." The massive growth of the internet and WWW introduced artists to each other's work. Search engines, browsers that enable hearty multimedia capabilities, archival websites, listservs, and even chatrooms have increased the visibility, consumption, and knowledge of the form – a global community has become possible.

Programmed works literally assemble language (if not other media components) to the specification of the programmer; formal, precise programming commands are written to perform particular tasks. The earliest works of digital poetry strictly involved coding as there were no other possibilities, although software increasingly shouldered the burden as the genre progressed, facilitating the poet's conceptual application and aesthetic (thereby enhancing prospects for digital poetry and widening the field). As code, the task of handing language is used more often than not to order, rather than disorder, poetry. Even if the poet-programmer wishes to instill disorder, the process calls for prescribed stylistic elements. Alternatively, with software, the programming generally involves establishing frameworks in which disparate elements – whether the different elements of a visual scenario, or files that contain different verbal passages – negotiate with one another, or are negotiated by the viewer. As is always the case with its written counterpart, digital poetry relies on the author's senses, thoughts (or inspirations), and vocabulary to form words (which can be accompanied by other media) into expression. As ever, the poet enacts language amid a range of possible treatments.

Some digital poems – even those assembled by a machine – are grammatically flawless while others completely disregard linguistic conventions. Digital poems do not exist in a fixed state, and may be considered less refined as a result of this condition. Author(s) or programmer(s) of such works presumably have a different sense of authorial control, from which a different sort of result and artistic expectation would arise; consequently, the purpose and production would veer from the historical norm. Because of this shift in psychology and practice, digital poetry's formal qualities (made through programming, software, and database operations) are not as uniquely pointed and do not compare to highly crafted, singular exhortations composed by historic poets. Some will rightfully hold that code and databases or manipulated pools of words (or other media) are more limiting than a powerful mind. Or that the freedom and capabilities of the mind, and skills that result from refined poetic practice, are greater than anything programmed or loaded into a machine (or, for that matter, captured in traditional verse). While this may be proven, I am nonetheless reminded of Olson's potent utterances in *The Maximus Poems* that "limits/are what each of us/are inside of" (1983: 21). Despite restrictions imposed by technology, using computers, poets can interlink materials mechanically; digital poetry functions to bridge layers of text(s), images, and other effects, that result in reaching beyond the machine to affect the reader's imaginative, intellectual, and other aspects of her or his non-virtual world. The vitality of digital literature relies on how textual possibility and human ingenuity (vis-à-vis programming) are combined to synthesize poetic thought and programmatic expression.

Digital poetry has always been a multi-continental, de-centralized practice. Works have been created in many languages. Not only is digital poetry an unusual idiom of creative expression, it is also an idiom that for more than three decades has resisted, as if by definition, the need to embody a singular set of mannerisms in its use of multiple languages (including computer code) and stylistic approaches. Digital poetry has steadily redefined itself with the development of new tools and artistic interests, and a type of digital poetry culture began to emerge with the International POESIS (1992, 2000, 2004) and E-POETRY (2001, 2003, 2005, 2007) festivals in Germany, the United States, England, and France. The WWW sites promoting these events, which contain links to works by artists who participated in these projects, serve as portals to a loose community of digital poets, and an interconnected network, with its own subcultures, has developed gradually.

Utilizing and relying on more technology than any other era before it, the twenty-first century presents poetry – one of our most intimate and intricate forms of expression – with at least two significant charges. Poetry should continue to remain accessible to its audiences by engaging important social and technological issues, and cultivate readers through the production of stimulating works in all forms. Poetry – stylized language – can allow for innovation and accept adaptations within its forms and tradition. As a craft that remains a vital cultural interest and pursuit during the first decade of the century, poetry is apparently prepared to weather these challenges. At this historical moment, in fact, the fruits of these two charges appear to be interrelated and enhanced by technological advancement. Widespread computer usage and improvements in digital systems and networks have particularly altered the disciplinary sense of what poetry can be, while intimating what the dynamics of literature may contain in the future and how it will be presented to readers. Digital poetry has developed so intensely and rapidly since the 1990s, time alone will tell which events will prove crucial in the progress of this relatively young genre of art. Digital poets have not labored to experiment and invent out of cultural necessity or desperation; works have sprung from self-driven exploration of computer media and the individual desire to craft language with technology that, in turn, modulates and modifies traditional approaches to writing. The computer has presented both a puzzle and formidable sounding board for poetic ideas and articulations. Since the very earliest works created, serious poets have explored computerized composition. Digital poetry was never wholly controlled by scientists, but by writers – sometimes working with programmers – who labor to discover methods for inventively re-formulating language.

NOTES

1 The term "netspeak," according to Strehovec, implies that, "the language of zeros and ones, and of ASCII and HTML characters is involved in new poetic structures with striking visual, animated, and tactile features" (Text n.pag.).

2 For instance, kinetic activity on the screen is also integral to John Cayley's award-winning poem *RiverIsland* and in digital works he and many others produced later, both on and off the WWW.

3 Bailey also cites Mallarmé's emphasis on the role of chance promotion of chance (see paragraph below) and the "imposition of order on disorder" as important tendencies present in the works he was able to collect.

REFERENCES

Adrian, Marc (1968). "Computer Texts." In Jasia Reichardt (Ed.). *Cybernetic Serendipity: The Computer and the Arts*. London: Studio International (special issue): 53.

Andrews, Jim (2001, April). *Nio*. <http://www.vispo.com/nio/>.

Bailey, Richard W. (Ed.) (1973). *Computer Poems*. Drummond Island, MI: Potagannissing Press.

Balestrini, Nanni (1962). "Tape Mark." Milan: *Almanacco Letterario Bompiani*, pp. 145–51.

Block, Friedrich W., Christiane Heibach, and Karin Wenz (Eds.) (2004). *POes1s: The Aesthetics of Digital Poetry*. Germany: Hatje Cantz Verlag.

Bolter, Jay David (1991). *Writing Space: The Computer, Hypertext, and the History of Writing*. Hillsdale, NJ: Lawrence Erlbaum.

—— (2001). *Writing Space: Computers, Hypertext, and the Remediation of Print*, 2nd edn. Mahwah, NJ: Lawrence Erlbaum.

Cramer, Florian (2005, March 21). "Combinatory Poetry and Literature in the Internet." <http://userpage.fu-berlin.de/~cantsin/homepage/writings/net_literature/permutations/kassel_2000/ combinatory_poetry.html>.

Daly, Catherine (2005). *The Facts on File Companion to 20th-Century American Poetry*. New York: Facts on File, pp. 114–16.

Derrida, Jacques (1995). *Points... Interviews 1974–1994* (Elisabeth Weber, Ed., Peggy Kamuf, Trans.). Stanford: Stanford University Press.

Fernbach-Flarsheim, Carl (1970–1). "The Boolean Image/Conceptual Typewriter." *SOFTWARE: Information Technology: Its New Meaning for Art*. Exhibition catalog. Jack Burnham, curator. No Publication Information.

Glazier, Loss Pequeño (2002). *Digital Poetics: The Making of E-Poetries*. Tuscaloosa, AL: University of Alabama Press.

Huth, Geof (2004, July 30). "Digital Poetry Incunabula." Online blog entry. <http://dbqp.blogspot.com/2004/07/digital-poetry-incunabula.html>.

Joyce, Michael (1995). *Of Two Minds: Hypertext Pedagogy and Poetics*. Ann Arbor: University of Michigan Press.

Larsen, Deena (1993). *Marble Springs*. Diskette. Watertown, MA: Eastgate.

Lyotard, Jean-François (1984). *The Postmodern Condition: A Report on Knowledge* (Geoff Bennington and Brian Massumi, Trans.). Minneapolis: University of Minnesota Press.

Masterman, Margaret, and Robin McKinnon Wood. (1968). "Computerized Japanese Haiku." In Jasia Reichardt (Ed.). *Cybernetic Serendipity: The Computer and the Arts*. London: Studio International (special issue): 54.

McCauley, Carol Spearin (1974). *Computers and Creativity*. New York: Praeger Publishers.

Melo e Castro, E. M. de (1968). *Roda Lume*. Lisbon: RTP.

—— (1996). "Videopoetry." *New Media Poetry: Poetic Innovation and New Technologies. Visible Language* 30.2: 140–9.

Preminger, Alex, and Brogan, T. V. F. (Eds.) (1993). *The New Princeton Encyclopedia of Poetry and Poetics*. Princeton, NJ: Princeton University Press.

Olson, Charles (1983). *The Maximus Poems*. Berkeley: University of California Press.

Padgett, Ron (Ed.) (1987). *The Handbook of Poetic Forms*. New York: Teachers & Writers.

Slatin, John M. (1988). "Hypertext and the Teaching of Writing." In Edward Barrett (Ed.). *Text, Context, and Hypertext: Writing with and for the Computer*. Cambridge: MIT Press, pp. 111–29.

Stefans, Brian Kim (2003). *Fashionable Noise: On Digital Poetics*. Berkeley: Atelos.

Strehovec, Janez (2003). "Text as Loop: On Visual and Kinetic Textuality." *Afterimage* July–August. <http://www.findarticles.com/p/articles/mi_m2479/is_1_31/ai_113683509>. Accessed March 1, 2005.

Williams, Emmett (Ed.) (1967). *Anthology of Concrete Poetry*. New York: Something Else Press.

Digital Literary Studies: Performance and Interaction

David Z. Saltz

Computers and the performing arts make strange bedfellows. Theater, dance, and performance art persist as relics of liveness in a media-saturated world. As such, they stand in defiant opposition to the computer's rapacious tendency to translate everything into disembodied digital data. Nonetheless, a number of theorists have posited an inherent kinship between computer technology and the performing arts (Laurel 1991; Saltz 1997). While "old" media such as print, film, and television traffic in immaterial representations that can be reproduced endlessly for any number of viewers, the interactivity of "new" media draws it closer to live performance. Philip Auslander has argued persuasively that digital agents such as internet "chatterbots" have the same claim to "liveness" as flesh-and-blood performers (Auslander 2002). Indeed, one might argue, following Brenda Laurel, that every user's interaction with a computer is a unique "performance," and moreover it is one that, like theater, typically involves an element of make-believe. When I throw a computer file in the "trash" or "recycling bin," I behave much like an actor, performing real actions within an imaginary framework. I recognize that the "trash bin" on my screen is no more real than a cardboard dagger used in a play; both are bits of virtual reality (Saltz 2006: 213). Indeed, theater theorist Antoine Artaud coined the term "virtual reality" to describe the illusory nature of characters and objects in the theater over fifty years before Jaron Lanier first used that term in its computer-related sense (Artaud 1958: 49).

It is no wonder, then, that performance scholars and practitioners have looked to digital technology to solve age-old problems in scholarship, pedagogy, and creative practice. This chapter will begin with a review of significant pedagogical and scholarly applications of computers to performance, and then turn to artistic applications.

Hypermedia and Performance Pedagogy

A work of dance, theater, or performance art is a visual, auditory, and, most of all, corporeal event. Only in the 1980s, when low-cost personal computers acquired the ability to store and manipulate images, sounds, and finally video, did computers begin to offer an effective way to represent the phenomenon of performance. Larry Fried-lander's Shakespeare Project anticipated many subsequent applications of digital tech-nology to performance pedagogy. Friedlander began to develop the Shakespeare Project in 1984 using an IBM InfoWindow system. He adopted HyperCard in 1987 while the software was still in development at Apple. Because personal computers then had very crude graphics capabilities and no video, Friedlander adopted a two-screen solution, with the computer providing random access to media stored on a laserdisc. The laserdisc contained hundreds of still images and, more important, six video segments, including two contrasting filmed versions of one scene each from *Hamlet*, *Macbeth*, and *King Lear*. The Shakespeare Project used this video material in three ways. In a Performance area, students could read the Shakespearean text alongside the video, switch between film versions at any time, jump to any point in the text, and alternate between a film's original audio track and a recording of Friedlander's interpretation of the actors' "subtext." In a Study area, students participated in interactive tutorials covering aspects of Shakespearean performance such as characterization and verse. Finally, in a Notebook area, students could extract digital video excerpts to incorporate into their own essays. In each case, the computer made it possible for students to *read a performance* almost as closely and flexibly as they could a printed text.

CD-ROM editions of plays released in the 1990s – most notably the 1994 Voyager edition of *Macbeth* and the 1997 Annenberg/CPB edition of Ibsen's *A Doll House* – incorporate core elements of Friedlander's design, keying the play's script to multiple filmed versions of select scenes. In addition, these CD-ROMs provide a rich assort-ment of critical resources and still images. The Voyager *Macbeth* also includes an audio recording of the entire play by the Royal Shakespeare Company and a Karaoke feature that allows the user to perform a role opposite the audio. These CD ROMs take advantage of the ability acquired by personal computers in the 1990s to display video directly, obviating the need for a laserdisc player and second monitor. This approach is far more elegant, compact, and cost-efficient than using laserdiscs, but the video in these early CD-ROM titles is much smaller and lower in quality than that of a laserdisc. By 2000, faster computer processors and video cards, along with more efficient video compression schemes and widespread DVD technology, had finally closed the gap between personal computers and laserdisc players.

Modeling Performance Spaces

The projects considered so far rely on the multimedia capabilities of computers, that is, a computer's ability to store and retrieve text, images, and audio. Other projects have exploited the power of computers to generate complex simulations of 3D reality. Performance scholars began to explore the use of 3D modeling in the mid-1980s to visualize hypotheses about historical theater buildings and staging practices. In 1984, Robert Golder constructed a 3D computer model of the 1644 Theatre du Marais, and Robert Sarlós used computer models to visualize staging strategies for a real-world re-creation of the medieval Passion Play of Lucerne. This technique became more common in the 1990s when high-end CAD (computer-aided design) software became available for personal computers. Theater historians used 3D modeling software to reconstruct structures such as the fifth century BCE Theater of Dionyos (*Didakalia*) and Richelieu's Palais Cardinal Theater (Williford 2000). One of the most ambitious of these projects is an international effort, led by Richard Beacham and James Packer, to reconstruct the 55 BCE Roman Theater of Pompey. The computer model is painstakingly detailed, with every contour of every column and frieze being modeled in three dimensions. As a result, even using state-of-the-art graphics workstations, a single frame takes approximately one hour to render at screen resolution (Denard 2002: 36).

None of the 3D modeling projects described above allows a user to navigate the virtual spaces in real time; the models are experienced only as a series of still images or pre-rendered animations. These projects are geared toward research, with the goal of generating new historical knowledge and testing hypotheses. Consequently, the quality of the data is more important than the experience of the user. When the emphasis is on teaching rather than research, however, the tendency is to make the opposite trade-off, favoring interactivity over detail and precision. The most significant effort along those lines is the THEATRON project, also under the direction of Richard Beacham, with funding from the European Commission. THEATRON uses Virtual Reality Modeling Language (VRML) to allow people to explore models of historically significant theater structures over the web. The first set of walkthroughs, including such structures as the Ancient Greek Theater of Epidauros, Shakespeare's Globe, and the Bayreuth Festspielhaus, became commercially available in 2002.

The THEATRON walkthroughs provide an experience of immersion, conveying a clear sense of the scale and configuration of the theater spaces. These spaces, however, are empty and static, devoid of any sign of performance. Frank Mohler, a theater historian and designer, has adopted an approach that focuses not on the architecture per se, but on technologies used for changing scenery. Mohler has made effective use of simple animations to simulate the appearance and functioning of Renaissance and Baroque stage machinery.

Digital Simulations of Live Performance

Models of theaters and scenery, no matter how detailed, immersive, or interactive, simulate only the environment within which performances take place. There have also been attempts to use computer animation techniques to simulate the phenomenon of performance itself, for both pedagogical and scholarly purposes. Again, Larry Friedlander produced one of the earliest examples, a program called TheatreGame created in conjunction with the Shakespeare Project. This software was innovative for its time and attracted a good deal of press attention. TheatreGame allowed students to experiment with staging techniques by selecting crude two-dimensional human figures, clothing them from a limited palette of costumes, positioning set pieces on a virtual stage, and finally moving the virtual actors around the stage and positioning their limbs to form simple gestures. The goal was to allow students with no theater experience or access to real actors to investigate the effects of basic staging choices.

At the same time Friedlander was developing TheatreGame, Tom Calvert began to develop a similar, but vastly more sophisticated, application geared toward choreographers. The project started in the 1970s as a dance notation system called Compose that ran on a mainframe computer and output its data to a line printer. In the 1980s, Calvert replaced abstract symbols describing motions with 3D human animations and dubbed the new program LifeForms. The human models in LifeForms are featureless wireframes, but the movements are precise, flexible, and anatomically correct. Life-Forms was designed as a kind of word processor for dance students and practicing choreographers, a tool for composing dances. In 1990, the renowned choreographer Merce Cunningham adopted the software, bringing it to international attention. In the early 1990s, LifeForms became a commercial product.

Motion capture technology offers a very different approach to performance simulation. Motion capture uses sensors to track a performer's movements in space and then maps those movements onto a computer-generated model. While applications such as LifeForms are authoring tools for virtual performances, motion capture provides a tool for archiving and analyzing real performances. The Advanced Computer Center for Art and Design (ACCAD) at Ohio State University maintains a high-end optical motion capture system dedicated to research in the performing arts. In 2001, ACCAD began to build an archive of dance and theater motion data by capturing two performances by the legendary mime artist Marcel Marceau. This data, which includes subtle details such as the performer's breathing, can be transferred onto any 3D model and analyzed in depth. The Virtual Vaudeville Project, a digital re-creation of a performance in a late-nineteenth-century American vaudeville theater, combines many elements of the projects discussed above: 3D modeling of theater architecture, animated scenery, performance simulation using motion capture, along with simulations of audience response and hypermedia content. The goal is to develop reusable strategies for using digital technology to reconstruct and archive historical performance events. Viewers enter the virtual theater and watch animated performances from a variety of positions in the audience and on stage. Professional actors re-create the stage performances, and these performances are transferred to 3D models of the nineteenth-century performers using motion and facial capture technology. A prototype of the project has been developed for a high-performance game engine of the sort usually used to create commercial 3D action games, and a more widely accessible version of the project, created with Quicktime and Shockwave, is available on the web.

Computer simulations of performance spaces and performers are powerful research and teaching tools, but carry inherent dangers. Performance reconstructions can encourage a positivist conception of history (Denard 2002: 34). A compelling computer simulation conceals the hypothetical and provisional nature of historical interpretation; vividly simulated theaters and performances produce the sensation that the viewer has been transported back in time and is experiencing the performance event "as it really was." But even if all of the physical details of the simulation are accurate, a present-day viewer's experience will be radically different from that of the original audience because the cultural context of reception has changed radically. Some projects, such as the Pompey Project and Virtual Vaudeville, are making a concerted effort to counteract these positivistic tendencies, primarily by providing hypermedia notes that supply contextual information, providing the historical evidence upon which the reconstructions are based, and offering alternatives to the interpretations of and extrapolations from the historical data used in the simulation. Whether such strategies will prove sufficient remains to be seen.

Computers in Performance

My focus so far has been on applications of computers to teaching and research in the performing arts. Digital technology is also beginning to have a significant impact on the way those art forms are being practiced. For example, the computer has become a routine part of the design process for many set and lighting designers. Throughout the 1990s, a growing number of designers adopted CAD software to draft blueprints and light plots and, more recently, employed 3D modeling software (sometimes integrated into the CAD software) to produce photo-realistic visualizations of set and lighting designs.

Computers are also being incorporated into the performances themselves. The earliest and most fully assimilated example is computer-controlled stage lighting. Computerized light boards can store hundreds of light cues for a single performance, automatically adjusting the intensity, and in some cases the color and direction, of hundreds of lighting instruments for each cue. This technology was introduced in the late 1970s, and by the 1990s had become commonplace even in school and community theaters. Similarly, set designers have used computerized motion control systems to change scenery on stage – though this practice is still rare and sometimes has disastrous results. For example, the initial pre-Broadway run of Disney's stage musical *Aida* featured a six-ton robotic pyramid that changed shape under computer control to accommodate different scenes. The pyramid broke down on opening night and repeatedly thereafter (Eliott 1998). Disney jettisoned the high-tech set, along with the production's director and designer, before moving the show to Broadway.

Computer-controlled lighting and scenery changes are simply automated forms of pre-computer stage technologies. A growing number of dance and theater artists have incorporated interactive digital media into live performance events. Such performances can have a profound impact on the way the art forms are conceived, collapsing the neat ontological divide that once separated (or seemed to separate) the live performing arts from reproductive media such as film and video. During period from the 1980s to the middle of the 1990s, a number of artists developed innovative approaches to incorporating interactive digital technologies into live performance. Much of this work has been documented in the Digital Performance Archive (DTP), a web-based database created by Nottingham Trent University and the University of Salford encompassing hundreds of dance and theater performances produced in the 1990s. After the dot-com bubble burst in 2001, some of the intense, utopic energy that drove experiments with performance and digital technology dissipated, and most work created in the early 2000s draws on aesthetic and technological innovations developed in the late 1990s, taking advantage of technology that has become more mainstream and less expensive.

George Coates Performance Works in San Francisco was one of the first and most prominent theater companies to combine digital media with live performance to create stunning, poetic visual spectacles. In 1989, George Coates founded SMARTS (Science Meets the Arts), a consortium including companies such as Silicon Graphics, Sun Microsystems, and Apple Computer, to acquire the high-end technology required for his productions. In a series of productions starting with *Invisible Site: A Virtual Sho* in 1991, Coates perfected a technique for producing the vivid illusion of live performers fully integrated into a rapidly-moving 3D virtual environment. The spectators wear polarized glasses to view huge, high-intensity stereographic projections of digital animations. The projections that surround the revolving stage cover not only the back wall but the stage floor and transparent black scrims in front of the performers. The digital images are manipulated interactively during the performances to maintain tight synchronization between the live performers and the media.

Another pioneer in the use of virtual scenery is Mark Reaney, founder of the Institute for the Exploration of Virtual Realities (i.e. VR), at the University of Kansas (Reaney 1996; Gharavi 1999). In place of physical scenery, Reaney creates navigable 3D computer models that he projects on screens behind the performers. The perspective on Reaney's virtual sets changes in relation to performers' movements, and a computer operator can instantly transform the digital scenery in any way Reaney desires. In 1995, i.e. VR presented its first production, Elmer Rice's expressionist drama *The Adding Machine*. For this production, Reaney simply rear-projected the virtual scenery. For *Wings* in 1996, Reaney had the spectators wear low-cost head-mounted displays that allowed them to see stereoscopic virtual scenery and the live actors simultaneously. Starting with *Telsa Electric* in 1998, Reaney adopted an approach much like Coates', projecting stereoscopic images for the audience to view through polarized glasses. Nonetheless, Reaney's approach differs from Coates's in a number of important ways. While Coates authors his own highly associative works,

Reaney usually selects pre-existing plays with linear narratives. Reaney's designs, while containing stylized elements, are far more literal than Coates's; and the technology he employs, while more advanced than what is available to most university theaters, is far more affordable than the state-of-the-art technology at Coates's disposal.

Scenic and video designer William Dudley has brought similarly complex virtual scenery to the commercial stage. He first used projected video in 2002 for the National Theatre (London) production of Tom Stoppard's nine-hour epic *Cost of Utopia*, directed by Trevor Nunn. Dudley surrounded the performers on three sides with a curved projection surface filled with moving 3D imagery of the play's interior and exterior settings; to preserve the illusion of immersion in the projected images, Dudley created entrances and exits in the screens for the actors. Dudley has incorporated similar technology for successful West End productions of Terry Johnson's *Hitchcock Blond* (2003) and Andrew Lloyd Webber's *Woman in White* (2004, followed by a less successful Broadway run in 2005).

One of the most sophisticated applications of virtual scenery to date was a production of André Werner's opera *The Jew of Malta* commissioned by the Munich Biennale in 2002. The actors' changing positions and gestures were tracked precisely with infrared cameras. Not only did the virtual scenery respond to the actors' movements – for example, moving forward and backward and rotating in tandem with the performer – but virtual costumes were projected onto the performers' silhouettes (MediaLab Madrid 2004).

A number of dance performances have experimented with similar interactive 3D technologies. One of the earliest and most influential examples is *Dancing with the Virtual Dervish/Virtual Bodies*, a collaboration between dancer and choreographer Yacov Sharir, visual artist Diane Gromala, and architect Marcos Novak first presented at the Banff Centre for the Arts in 1994. For this piece, Sharir dons a head-mounted display and enters a VR simulation of the interior of a human body, constructed from MRI images of Gromala's own body. The images that Sharir sees in the display are projected on a large screen behind him as he dances.

The examples of digitally enhanced performance considered above are radically different in their aesthetics and artistic goals, but all establish the same basic relationship between the media and live performers: in each case, the media functions as virtual scenery, in other words, as an environment within which a live performance occurs. There are, however, many other roles that media can assume in a performance.[1] For example, the media can play a dramatic role, creating virtual characters who interact with the live performers. A number of choreographers, including prominent figures such as Merce Cunningham and Bill T. Jones, have enlisted motion capture technology to lend subtle and expressive movements to virtual dancer partners (Dils 2002). Often, as in the case of both Cunningham's and Jones's work, the computer models themselves are highly abstract, focusing the spectators' attention on the motion itself. In a 2000 production of *The Tempest* at the University of Georgia, the spirit Ariel was a 3D computer animation controlled in real time by a live performer using motion capture technology (Saltz 2001b). In 2006, Cindy Jeffers and Meredith Finkelstein, founders of an art and robotics collective called BotMatrix, created and remotely controlled five robotic actors for *Heddatron*, a play produced by the Les Freres Corbusier theater company in New York (Soloski 2006). Claudio Pinhanez has applied artificial intelligence and computer-vision techniques to create fully autonomous computer characters. His two-character play *It/I,* presented at MIT in 1997, pitted a live actor against a digital character (Pinhanez and Bobick 2002).

A key goal of Pinhanez' work is to produce an unmediated interaction between the live performer and digital media. While this goal is unusual in theater, it is becoming increasingly common in dance, where there is less pressure to maintain a coherent narrative and so creating an effective interaction between the performer and media does not require sophisticated artificial intelligence techniques. Electronic musicians created a set of technologies useful for creating interactive dance in the 1980s in the course of exploring the use of sensors in new musical instrument interfaces. The Studio for Electro-Instrumental Music, or Steim, in the Netherlands was an early center for this research, and continues to facilitate collaborations between dancers and electronic musicians. One of the most widely used tools for creating interactive performances using sensor inputs and MIDI synthesizers, samplers, and lighting devices is the software application Max. Max Puckette initially developed Max in 1986 for the UNIX operating system, and David Zicarelli subsequently adapted it for the Macintosh and later Windows, adding the ability to perform complex real-time manipulations of audio and video through a set of extensions called, respectively, MSP (introduced in 1997) and Jitter (introduced in 2003). A number of dancers have also created interactive performances using the Very Nervous System (VNS), a system first developed by the Canadian media artist David Rokeby in 1986. The VNS, which integrates with Max, uses video cameras to detect very subtle motions that can trigger sounds or video.

One of the first dance companies formed with the explicit goal of combining dance with interactive technology was Troika Ranch, founded in 1993 by Mark Coniglio and Dawn Stoppiello. Troika Ranch has developed its own wireless system, MidiDancer, which converts a dancer's movements into MIDI data, which can be used to trigger sounds, video sequences, or lighting.

A particularly successful application of this kind of sensor technology was the 2001 production *L'Universe* (pronounced "loony verse") created by the Flying Karamazov Brothers, a troupe of comedic jugglers, in conjunction with Neil Gershenfeld of the Physics and Media Group at MIT. Gershenfeld created special juggling clubs with programmable displays, and used sonar, long-range RF (radio frequency) links and computer vision to track the positions and movements of the four performers. This technology was used to create a complex interplay between the performers and media, with the jugglers' actions automatically triggering sounds and altering the color of the clubs.

Brenda Laurel and Rachel Strickland's interactive drama *Placeholder* is one of the best-known attempts to create a performance in which the spectators interact directly with the technology. As two spectators move through a ten-foot diameter circle wearing head-mounted displays, they interact with a series of digital characters, with a character called the Goddess controlled by a live performer, and, to a limited extent, with each other (Ryan 1997: 695–6). The challenge of creating a rich and compelling narrative within this kind of interactive, open-ended structure is immense. While a number of writers have tackled this challenge from a theoretical perspective (see, for example, Ryan 1997 and Murray 1997), the promise of this new dramatic medium remains largely unfulfilled.

Telematic Performance

In 1932, in a remarkable anticipation of internet culture, theater theorist and playwright Bertolt Brecht imagined a future in which radio would cease to be merely a one-way "apparatus for distribution" and become "the finest possible communication apparatus in public life, a vast network of pipes" (Brecht 1964: 52). By the early 1990s, it had become possible to stream video images over the internet at very low cost, and performance groups were quick to exploit video streaming technologies to create live multi-site performance events. In a 1994 production of *Nowhere Band*, George Coates used free CU-SeeMe video-conferencing software to allow three band members at various locations in the Bay Area to perform live with a Bulgarian bagpipe player in Australia for an audience in San Francisco (Illingworth 1995). In 1995, Cathy Weiss used the same software to create an improvised dance performance at The Kitchen in New York with the real-time participation of a video artist in Prague and a DJ in Santa Monica (Saltz 2001a).

In 1999 the Australian Company in Space created a live duet between a dancer in Arizona and her partner in Australia (Birringer 1999: 368–9). In 2001, the opera *The Technophobe and Madman* took advantage of the new high-speed internet network to create a multi-site piece of theater. Half of the performers performed at Rensselaer Polytechnic University, while the other half performed 160 miles away at New York University. Two separate audiences, one at each location, watched the performance simultaneously, each seeing half the performers live and the other half projected on a large projection screen (see Mirapaul 2001). The Gertrude Stein Repertory Theater (GSRT) is a company dedicated to developing new technologies for creating theater. In their production of *The Making of America* (2003), adapted from Gertrude Stein's novel, performers in remote locations work together in real time to create live performances in both locations simultaneously, with the faces and bodies of actors in one location being projected via video-conferencing on masks and costumes worn by actors in the second location. The GSRT draws a parallel between this process, which they call "Distance Puppetry," and Japanese performance traditions such as bunraku and ningyo buri that also employ multiple performers to portray individual characters.

Telematic performance acquires its greatest impact when spectators interact directly with people at the remote site and experience the uncanny collapse of space first-hand. In the 1990s, new media artist Paul Sermon created a series of interactive art installations joining physically separated viewers. For example, in *Telematic Dreaming* a viewer lies down on one side of a bed and on the other side sees a real-time video projection of a participant lying down on a second, identical bed in a remote location. Other installations place the remote participants on a couch, around a dining room table, and at a séance table (Birringer 1999: 374). A more provocative example of a performance event that joins a live performer to the internet is Stelarc's 1996 *Ping Body: an Internet Actuated and Uploaded Performance,* in which a muscle stimulator sent electric charges of 0–60 volts into Stelarc to trigger involuntary movements in his arms and legs proportionate to the ebb and flow of internet activity.

Net Performance

In 1979, Roy Trubshaw invented a multiple-user text-based environment for inter-active adventure games, which he called a Multi-User Dungeon, or MUD. In 1989, Jim Aspnes modified MUD software to emphasize social interaction rather than combat, and in 1990 Steven White and Pavel Curtis created an object-oriented MUD, called a MOO, that gave users tools to create their own virtual objects and spaces. Theater artists soon began to experiment with MOOs as online, collaborative environments to stage real-time performances. In 1994, Antoinette LaFarge founded the Plaintext Players to produce "directed textual improvisations that merge writing, speaking, and role-play" (Plaintext Players). Performers log into a multi-user envir-onment from any location around the world and perform together simply by typing dialogue and descriptions of actions, gestures, and expressions. Some audiences experience these performances online, while others watch them projected or listen to speech-to-voice synthesis in gallery settings. Other early examples of MOO theater include Rick Sacks' *MetaMOOphosis* and Steve Schrum's *NetSeduction,* both of which took place in 1996 in ATHEMOO, an environment sponsored by the Association of Theatre in Higher Education (Stevenson 1999: 140).

Between 1997 and 2002, Adriene Jenik and Lisa Brenneis created a series of "Desktop Theater" performances using the Palace visual chat software, a free appli-cation that allows users to navigate freely through a labyrinth of virtual rooms hosted on distributed servers. Unlike purely textual MOO environments, the Palace features a crude graphic interface with static pictorial backgrounds and low-resolution two-dimensional avatars. In performances such as the 1997 *waitingforgodot.com,* performers cut and pasted their dialogue into speech bubbles attached to the avatars while the online audience, consisting mostly of unwitting Palace "chatters," commented on the performance, joined in, or left in confusion (Jenik 2001: 99). Faster internet con-nectivity and more powerful processors are giving rise to much more sophisticated 3D multi-user environments such as Second Life that offer rich new opportunities for real-time online performances.

Conclusions and Queries

The use of computers in the performing arts does not merely add a new tool to an old discipline. It challenges some of our most basic assumptions about performance. First, it blurs the boundaries between performance disciplines. For example, instead of producing traditional musical scores, many digital composers have created interactive computer algorithms that generate sequences of music and video in response to performers' improvised gestures. Should we regard such performers as instrumentalists, as dancers, or as composers in their own right, who directly produce the music and imagery the audience experiences? Second, digital technology blurs the boundaries between scholarship and creative practice. Is someone who extrapolates a complete set design, script, and performance from shreds of historical evidence to create a virtual performance simulation an artist or a scholar? When someone develops new artificial intelligence algorithms in order to create a dramatic interaction between a digital character and a live actor, is that person functioning as a computer scientist or an artist whose medium just happens to be computers? Finally, digital technology is challenging the very distinction between "liveness" and media. When a live performer interacts with a computer-generated animation, is the animation "live"? Does the answer depend on whether the animation was rendered in advance or is being controlled in real time via motion capture or with artificial intelligence software? Or do we now live in a world, as performance theorist Philip Auslander suggests, where the very concept of liveness is losing its meaning?

NOTE

1 Elsewhere I have distinguished between twelve types of relationships a production can define between digital media and live performers (Saltz 2001b).

REFERENCES FOR FURTHER READING

Artaud, Antonin (1958). *The Theater and its Double* (Mary Caroline Richards, Trans.). New York: Grove Widenfeld (Original work published 1938).

Auslander, Philip (1999). *Liveness: Performance in a Mediatized Culture*. London: Routledge.

—— (2002). "Live from Cyberspace: or, I was sitting at my computer this guy appeared he thought I was a bot." *Performing Arts Journal* 24.1: 16–21.

Berghaus, Günter (2005). *Avant-Garde Performance: Live Events and Electronic Technologies*. Basingstoke, UK: Palgrave Macmillan.

Birringer, Johannes (1998). *Media and Performance: Along the Border*. Baltimore: Johns Hopkins University Press.

—— (1999). "Contemporary Performance/ Technology." *Theatre Journal* 51: 361–81.

Brecht, Bertolt (1964). "The Radio as an Apparatus of Communications." In John Willett (Ed. and Trans.). *Brecht on Theatre*. New York: Hill and Wang, pp. 51–3.

Carver, Gavin, and Colin Beardon (Eds.) (2004). *New Visions in Performance: The Impact of Digital Technologies*. Lisse: Swets and Zeitlinger.

Denard, Hugh (2002). "Virtuality and Performativity: Recreating Rome's Theatre of Pompey." *Performing Arts Journal* 70: 25–43.

Didaskalia (2004). "Recreating the Theatre of Dionysos in Athens." <http://www.didaskalia.net/StudyArea/recreatingdionysus.html>.

Digital Performance Archive. <http://dpa.ntu.ac.uk/dpa_site/>.

Dils, Ann (2002). "The Ghost in the Machine: Merce Cunningham and Bill T. Jones." *Performing Arts Journal* 24.1: 94–104.

Dixon, Steve (1999). "Digits, Discourse And Documentation: Performance Research and Hypermedia." *TDR: The Drama Review* 43.1: 152–75.

—— (2007). *Digital Performance: A History of New Media in Theater, Dance, Performance Art, and Installation.* Cambridge, MA: The MIT Press.

Eliott, Susan (1998). "Disney Offers an 'Aida' with Morphing Pyramid." *New York Times* October 9: E3.

Fridlander, Larry (1991). "The Shakespeare Project: Experiments in Multimedia." In George Landow and Paul Delany (Eds.). *Hypermedia and Literary Studies.* Cambridge: MIT Press, pp. 257–71.

Gharavi, Lance (1999). "i.e.VR: Experiments in New Media and Performance." In Stephen A. Schrum (Ed.). *Theatre in Cyberspace.* New York: Peter Lang Publishing Inc., pp. 249–72.

Giannachi, Gabriella (2004). *Virtual Theatres: An Introduction.* London: Routledge.

Golder, John (1984). "The Theatre Du Marais in 1644: A New Look at the Old Evidence Concerning France's Second Public Theatre." *Theatre Survey* 25: 146.

Gromala, Diane J., and Yacov Sharir (1996). "Dancing with the Virtual Dervish: Virtual Bodies." In M. A. Moser and D. MacLeod (Eds.). *Immersed in Technology: Art and Virtual Environments.* Cambridge, MA: The MIT Press, pp. 281–6.

Illingworth, Monteith M. (1995). "George Coates: Toast of the Coast." *Cyberstage.* <http://www.cyberstage.org/archive/cstage12/coats12.htm>.

Jenik, Adriene (2001). "Desktop Theater: Keyboard Catharsis and the Masking of Roundheads." *TDR: The Drama Review* 45.3: 95–112.

Laurel, Brenda (1991). *Computers as Theater.* Reading, MA: Addison-Wesley.

——, Rachel Strickland, and Rob Tow (1994). "Placeholder: Landscape and Narrative in Virtual Environments." *ACM Computer Graphics Quarterly* 28.2: 118–26.

MediaLab Madrid (2004). "The Jew of Malta: Interactive Generative Stage and Dynamic Costume, 2004." <http://www.medialabmadrid.org/medialab/medialab.php?l=0&a=a&i=347>.

Menicacci, Armando and Emanuele Quinz (2001). *La scena digitale: nuovi media per la danza.* [The Digital Scene: New Media in Dance]. Venezia: Marsilio.

Meisner, Sanford (1987). *On Acting.* New York: Vintage Books.

Mirapaul, Matthew (2001). "How Two Sites Plus Two Casts Equals One Musical." *New York Times* February 19: E2.

Mohler, Frank (1999). "Computer Modeling as a Tool for the Reconstruction of Historic Theatrical Production Techniques." *Theatre Journal* 51.4: 417–31.

Murray, Janet H. (1997). *Hamlet on the Holodeck : the Future of Narrative in Cyberspace.* New York: Free Press.

Pinhanez, Claludio S., and Aaron F. Bobick (2002). "'It/I': A Theater Play Featuring an Autonomous Computer Character." *Presence: Teleoperators and Virtual Environments* 11.5: 536–48.

Plaintext Players. <http://yin.arts.uci.edu/~players/>.

Reaney, Mark (1996). "Virtual Scenography: The Actor, Audience, Computer Interface." *Theatre Design and Technology* 32: 36–43.

Ryan, Marie-Laure (1997). "Interactive Drama: Narrativity in a Highly Interactive Environment." *Modern Fiction Studies* 42.2: 677–707.

Saltz, David Z. (1997). "The Art of Interaction: Interactivity, Performativity and Computers." *Journal of Aesthetics and Art Criticism* 55.2: 117–27.

—— (2001a). "The Collaborative Subject: Telerobotic Performance and Identity." *Performance Research* 6.4: 70–83.

—— (2001b). "Live Media: Interactive Technology and Theatre." *Theatre Topics* 11.2: 107–30.

—— (2005). "Virtual Vaudeville." *Vectors* 1.1 <http://www.vectorsjournal.org>.

—— (2006). "Infiction and Outfiction: the Role of Fiction in Theatrical Performance." In David

Krasner and David Z. Saltz (Eds.). *Staging Philosophy: Intersections between Theatre, Performance and Philosophy*. Ann Arbor: University of Michigan Press, pp. 203–20.

Sarlós, Robert K. (1989). "Performance Reconstruction: the Vital Link between Past and Future." In Bruce A. McConachie and Thomas Postlewait (Eds.). *Interpreting the Theatrical Past*. Iowa City: University of Iowa Press, pp. 198–229.

Schrum, Stephen A. (Ed.). (1999). *Theatre in Cyberspace: Issues of Teaching, Acting, and Directing*. New York: Peter Lang.

Soloski, Alexis (2006). "Do Robots Dream of Electronic Lovborgs?" *New York Times* February 5: 2:8.

Stevenson, Jake A. (1999). "MOO Theatre: More than just Words?" In Stephen A. Schrum (Ed.). *Theatre in Cyberspace*. New York: Peter Lang Publishing Inc., pp. 135–46.

Theatron. <http://www.theatron.org>.

Virtual Vaudeville. <http://www.virtualvaudeville.com>.

Watts, Allan (1997). "Design, Computers, and Teaching." *Canadian Theatre Review* 91: 18–21.

Williford, Christa (2000). "A Computer Reconstruction of Richelieu's Palais Cardinal Theatre, 1641." *Theatre Research International* 25.3: 233–47.

19
Licensed to Play: Digital Games, Player Modifications, and Authorized Production
Andrew Mactavish

Introduction

It is safe to say that digital games are currently an important object of study for scholars of digital culture. If safety comes in numbers, then we need only to acknowledge the growing number of conferences, monographs, essay collections, and university courses and programs treating digital games as cultural artifacts that express meaning and reflect and shape the world we live in.[1] A far riskier claim would be that digital games studies is a definable discipline. While there may be abundant evidence that scholars are engaging with digital games, it's too early to see an established discipline with a set of matured methodologies and canonical texts or a broad base of institutional structures like departments and academic appointments. This does not mean that digital games scholars are not trying to establish a discipline. Indeed, an important component of academic discourse around digital games has been less on gaming artifacts and practices, and more on defining appropriate methodologies for analysis that are more or less unique to digital games. Many scholars want to treat digital games with the same analytic seriousness as they treat works of literature, theater, visual art, music, and film, but they are also concerned to understand what is distinctive about digital games. The burning question at hand is, should the study of digital games be guided by theories and methods unique to digital games, or can we apply theoretical models developed to explain other cultural forms such as narrative, theater, and film? On the one hand, this primarily political dimension of digital games studies draws attention away from games and gameplay; on the other hand, answering the question has very real and material effects on the generation and distribution of knowledge around digital games.

There is nothing new in scholars debating approaches to their subject matter, especially when it comes to the study of new or updated forms and presentations of culture. This is normally a sign of a healthy and growing field. In the area of digital games studies, though, the stakes seem very high as participants bandy about the rhetoric of colonialism to protect their turf against invasion from opposing teams of scholars.[2] One might imagine these debates in terms of team building in schoolyards where groups select the players they want on their team, leaving those outside the debate standing on the sidelines waiting to be picked or going off to play their own game away from the popular kids. The danger of such team building, of course, is that the popular kids would like to believe that they are the only game in town. In other words, as important as these debates have been to establishing digital games as legitimate objects of study, they have tended to divide scholars into camps, each with particular methodologies defined to some extent in opposition to other camps. Intentional or not, the result of such division can be an unfortunate blindness to the remarkable diversity of digital games and gameplay practices.

To date, the most common debates have been between ludological approaches, which define digital games as primarily rule-based objects and activities, and a collection of other approaches rooted in the study of narrative, theater, and film. While most ludological commentators grant that digital games can include story, performance, and filmic convention, they often argue that these elements are second-ary to a game's gameness. For many ludologists, remove the story-line and high-tech special effects and you still have a game based upon rules. While this may be true, the fact remains that many digital games include stories, performance, and audio-visual pleasures that are configurable by the player in some fashion. Remove them from the game and you might still have a game, but it won't be the same one you started with.

What most digital games scholars agree upon is that games require an active participant for the game to proceed. Players must effect change within the game for there to be a game. In this respect, game players are co-creators of the gaming experience. Similar claims have been made for the way we consume most forms of culture. The reader of a novel or the viewer of a film actively engages with the work by interpreting it. This psychological interaction with the work can discursively affect how others interpret it, but it does not change the work's fundamental structure or organization. When we watch a movie, we might interpret it differently than others, but we all experience the same sequence of images and sounds. While it is possible to skip or review sections of a movie or novel, these actions are not necessary to the realization of the work. Digital games, however, require that players physically interact with the work, whether it's to guide characters through the game space, modify the game world, or even to create new game elements.

Espen Aarseth conceptualizes the participatory nature of digital gameplay in terms of ergodics. In ergodic works, "non-trivial effort is required to allow the reader to traverse the text," while in nonergodic works, "the work to traverse the text is trivial" (1997: 1). For Aarseth, who approaches digital games primarily from a ludological perspective, flipping pages and scanning images with our eyes is nonergodic because it does not require the user to cause the same kind or degree of physical change to the work. Janet Murray thinks about the participatory user in terms of agency, stating that "Agency is the satisfying power to take meaningful action and see the results of our decisions and choices" (Murray 1997: 126). Concerned mainly with the narrative potential of digital games, Murray adds that "we do not usually expect to experience agency within a narrative environment" (Murray 1997: 126). Even though Aarseth and Murray approach digital games from two different and sometimes opposing perspectives, they agree that the participatory nature of digital games distinguishes them from other textual and visual forms of culture. Regardless of perspective, the realization of a digital game requires participating players whose interactions with the game make them co-creators of work.

As digital games research begins to move its focus away from the ludology vs. narratology debate and toward the kinds and qualities of participatory play, the creative element of digital gameplay is receiving much more critical attention. Rather than pronounce that gameplay is unproductive time, as influential play theorists Johann Huizinga and Roger Callois have argued, a growing community of games scholars are arguing that digital gameplay is a creative activity saturated with various in-game and meta-game productive practices. Whether we conceive of creative game-play in terms of ergodics or agency, our analysis should be guided by questions around what kinds of creative practices are supported by digital games and how social, cultural, and economic factors shape these practices.

Yet, with so much recent attention in the press on the destructiveness of digital gaming, it is sometimes difficult to see digital gameplay as a creative and productive activity. As with the emergence of many forms of youth culture that preceded them, digital games have become a focus of anxiety over the seemingly unrestrained and rebellious energies of youth. Today's news media regularly connects digital games with dangerously subversive youth, whether it's schoolyard massacres modeled after *Doom*, traffic shootings motivated by *Grand Theft Auto*, suicides linked to *Everquest*, or addictions to online persistent game worlds. This anxiety is intensified by reactionary commentators like Lt. Col. David Grossman, who claims that games teach children to kill (1999), and American politicians like Senators Hillary Clinton and Joseph Lieberman, who seek strict controls over the sale of digital games depicting violence.[3] Indeed, there appears to be very little that is good about digital games, with the exception, of course, of their contribution to the economy, which is often celebrated to rival Hollywood box office revenues (Entertainment Software Association 2006). Thanks to an intensifying culture of fear surrounding youth, digital gameplay is often perceived as requiring moral concern because it brings the energy and potential of youth into collision with destructive and anti-social behaviors.[4] Ironically, this fear obscures insight into the many creative practices common in digital gaming culture.

To get a clearer picture of the creative potential of digital games, we need to dissolve some of the clouds of suspicion surrounding them, which tend to condense around simplistic and under-contextualized equations between media consumption and aggression and the general belief that play is an unproductive waste of time.[5]

Academics from various interdisciplinary perspectives have begun this process, arguing, as Edward Castronova (2005) and Celia Pearce (2006) do, that digital gameplay can be a highly creative and productive activity. I argue that an illuminating approach to understanding digital gaming culture should be guided less by focusing on particularly dramatic but relatively uncommon events and more by looking at the spectrum of everyday gameplay practices. For this knowledge to contribute to a constructive understanding of our culture, it must be broadly contextualized to account for the place of digital gameplay within the network of social, political, and economic systems within which it operates. Cultural practices cannot be understood adequately outside of the complex and multifarious atmosphere that produces them and that they help to produce. By positioning an analysis of creative gaming practices within a social, political, and economic context, we can get closer to understanding the kinds of creativity that exist, why they exist, and whether they represent increased democratic agency within a cultural landscape increasingly overgrown by capitalist commoditization.

This analysis of creative digital gameplay looks closely at the intersections between player agency and corporate strategies to manage gameplay and its associated creative practices. It does so by concentrating on a set of digital gaming activities known collectively as modding. Short for "game modification," modding is a catch-all term that has various meanings within different contexts, but for the sake of clarity, I use it to mean the production of player-created derivative game content that can be imported into a game or that can be played as an entirely new game on top of a game's underlying code or engine.[6] Some types of game mods include new game levels, character skins, or in-game objects like furniture, vehicles, and weapons. Using the internet, mod-creators can distribute their productions within networked games or on websites, taking advantage of community-run clearinghouses that support both the circulation of mods and the organization of knowledge around their production.

Modding is a form of player-creative gameplay that encompasses a range of contradictory practices, some of which are simultaneously resistant *and* submissive to corporate regulation. In other words, while the production of mods and in-game content signals player agency with and within corporately produced works of culture, it is not necessary that player-production on its own is always antagonistic to corporate interest or capitalism's prioritization of economic value over use value. Indeed, many game developers recognize the financial benefits of providing support for player-created content, and so are experimenting with ways to manage this production to protect their economic investments, which rely heavily upon copyright and intellectual property law. Unlike the music and film industries, whose economic models of the flow of cultural goods make it difficult to support consumer participation in the cycle of cultural exchange, the digital games industry evolved in part out of an ethos in which sharing the productive fun is part of the game. The intersections between this ethos of sharing and the corporate desire to maximize profit through the management of knowledge and intellectual property are the focus of this chapter.

Digital games are not the first cultural works to stimulate communities of productive fans. As Henry Jenkins documented in the early 1990s, fans of literature, film, and television have long participated in forms of productive authorship that reach beyond the production of meaning inherent in interpretation (1992).[7] Drawing heavily from Michel de Certeau's *The Practice of Everyday Life*, Jenkins argues that fans who create and circulate fanfiction, fanflicks, and other forms of fan-created culture resist the systems of cultural regulation that seek to manage the production and circulation of cultural artifacts and their meanings. For Jenkins, fan-culture creators go a step further than de Certeau's model of the active or nomadic reader, which Jenkins argues restricts readers to "maintain[ing] a freedom of movement, at the expense of acquiring resources which might allow them to fight from a position of power and authority" (Jenkins 1992: 45). Fan-creators, according to Jenkins, become more like the producers whose power over the legitimization of culture they seek to contest.

While digital games potentially support a more democratic system of cultural production and exchange, this terrain of participatory culture is by no means level or free from the powerful interests of capital. Indeed, enrolling players in the production of after-market game add-ons potentially increases a game's shelf-life and, of course, its sales, suggesting that productive players become free laborers in a widely distributed and perpetually innovative economy of flexible production.[8] But are productive players participating in a more creative, democratic, and critical system of cultural production or are they co-opted by corporate strategies to broaden the scope of commoditization to include participatory consumer production? There are many variables that make this question impossible to answer on one side or the other, and to simply answer "both" obscures insight into the shifting dynamics that define relations between different kinds of producers and modes of production. Both game producers and player producers – a division that is difficult to pin down – participate in a range of productive activities that affects how we define game production. This chapter will attempt to take a snapshot of this process, with special attention on the forms of knowledge production and regulation that shape the contours of these relations.

Post-Fordism, Ideal Commodities, and Knowledge Flow

In their analysis of the technology, culture, and marketing of digital games, Stephen Kline, Nick Dyer-Witheford, and Greig de Peuter argue in *Digital Play* that digital games are an ideal commodity form of post-Fordist capitalism, in much the same way that cars, suburban housing, and appliances were ideal commodity forms of Fordist capitalism (2003). Drawing upon political economist Martyn J. Lee (1993), they demonstrate convincingly that digital games are what Lee terms an "*ideal-type* commodity form" because they embody "the most powerful economic, technological, social, and cultural forces at work" in the current regime of accumulation (Kline et al.: 74). Where "Fordist commodities were governed by a 'metalogic' of massification, durability, solidity, structure, standardization, fixity, longevity, and utility," post-Fordist commodities are governed by a metalogic of the "instantaneous, experiential, fluid, flexible, heterogeneous, customized, portable, and [are] permeated by a fashion with form and style" (Kline et al.: 74). For Kline et al., digital games are an example *par excellence* of a post-Fordist commodity because "they embody the new forces of production, consumption, and communication with which capital is once again attempting to force itself beyond its own limits to commodify life with new scope and intensity" (76). These new forces include systems of youthful labor typified by instability, relentless change, and exploitation; the use of electronics to expand and deepen the commodification of the time and space of everyday life; and the intensification of "the simulatory hyperreal postmodern ambience" frequently associated with post-Fordism by its critics (75).

Of particular importance here is Kline et al.'s combination of the flexibility and customizability of the post-Fordist commodity with the development and management of specialized knowledge. As David Harvey stresses in *The Condition of Postmodernity*, the organized creation of and rapid access to information are integral to maintaining a competitive edge in a post-Fordist economy: "in a world of quick-changing tastes and needs and flexible production systems...access to the latest technique, the latest product, the latest scientific discovery implies the possibility of seizing an important competitive advantage" (Harvey 1990: 159). Kline et al. extend Harvey's observations and draw upon Tessa Morris-Suzuki's notion of "information capitalism" to argue that post-Fordism in general relies upon cyclic systems of specialized knowledge development and distribution where knowledge flows from the public to the private and, after maximized capital extraction, back to the public. As Morris-Suzuki states in *Beyond Computopia*, corporations use public knowledge "in inventive activity" to create specialized knowledge protected and capitalized by intellectual property rights: "Property rights enable the corporation to fence off the new corner of the knowledge from the public and to make a profit from its application, and it is only when profits have been obtained and the invention is obsolescent that it is returned to the domain of public use" (Morris-Suzuki 1988: 81). As such, information capitalism exploits more than just laborers; it also indirectly exploits the entire social system in which public knowledge is generated, disseminated, and maintained.

If digital games are the ideal commodity form of post-Fordist capitalism, then there should be significant evidence that the production and management of game development knowledge fits with Harvey's notion of "organized knowledge production" and speed of information access (1990: 160) and with Morris-Suzuki's cycle of public–private–public knowledge. Managing the flow of intellectual property is critical to the economic success of digital games that support modding, but an updated account of the role of knowledge management in producer–consumer relations is necessary to account for the consumer-productive practices found in game modding communities. While both Harvey and Morris-Suzuki are writing in the late

1980s, during the rapid development and diffusion of digital technologies in science, business, education, and the home, they had not yet experienced how the internet would support the capacity for the production and distribution of knowledge from communities unauthorized within the corporate cycle of knowledge production. While forms of organized knowledge capitalization continue to develop and expand, other strains of knowledge production and distribution – still organized, but with less corporate approval and benefit – are, with the help of information technologies, intensifying and also increasingly disrupting the public–private–public cycle of corporately organized knowledge production. One need only glance at the music industry's struggle with peer-to-peer file swapping to see how unauthorized communities develop, manage, and apply computing knowledge and tools to undermine capitalist economic models.

The development of knowledge systems that operate beyond the control of corporate interest is especially apparent in digital gaming culture, where sophisticated online player communities build and share knowledge that potentially undermines the power of intellectual property to capitalize knowledge and information. This potential is increasingly under threat as game producers develop strategies and technologies that support player modification at the same time that they protect intellectual property and maximize profit.

Modding History

It is difficult to locate precisely the origins of digital game modification, but it goes back at least as far as William Crowther's *Adventure* (Crowther 1975), the first computer-based text adventure game. *Adventure* has been modified several times by players adapting it to run on different platforms or expanding its map and including extra puzzles, which has resulted in several versions of the game distributed under a variety of names, including *Adventure*, *ADVENT*, and *Colossal Cave*. An avid caver, William Crowther developed *Adventure* to echo his caving experiences so that he could share them with his young daughters. The first modification to *Adventure* was created in 1976, when Don Woods came across a copy of the game on his company's computer. His excitement at discovering it prompted him to ask Crowther if he could modify it by fixing some of its bugs and by expanding its map to include more rooms. Crowther agreed to send Woods the source code so long as he promised to send Crowther any changes he made. Since Woods' modification of *Adventure*, dozens of ports and modifications have been created and distributed over the internet, although Crowther's original may be lost.[9]

While Woods' modification of *Adventure* does not exemplify the kind of relationships we see today between corporate and player cultural production, it does point to the general ethos of knowledge sharing that typifies the early years of software development and continues today in open-source movements. But it is not until the golden age of arcade games in the late 1970s and early 1980s that we find the interests of capital coming into conflict with player-productive activities. During this period, companies like Atari, Bally-Midway, and Namco enjoyed substantial commercial success from developing coin-operated game machines, a success they sought to protect through copyright management, but that was never seriously threatened by a general population of game players given the material nature of arcade games and the tightly restricted networks of game distribution.

Perhaps the most notable clash around arcade game modification came in 1981, when a group of MIT students began building hardware modifications to arcade games with the hope of attracting players back to their aging inventory of arcade cabinets. Tired of simply managing a small coin-op business, and concerned about the costs of renewing their inventory, Doug Macrae and Kevin Curran decided to invest their time in creating new arcade games. Since they didn't have the necessary capital or experience to design and build new games from code to cabinet, they opted to use their experience in computer graphics and electrical engineering to develop enhancement boards that could be inserted into current arcade machines and provide players with newer, redesigned versions of their favorite games.

Their first modification was to *Missile Command* (Atari 1980), a popular game owned by Atari in which players defend cities from missile attacks using ground-to-air counter-missiles. Following the success of this mod, Macrae and Curran set their sights higher and modified *Pac-Man* (Namco 1980). In August 1981, as they were coming close to finishing this modification, Atari launched a copyright infringement suit against Macrae and Curran for their modification to *Missile Command*. Since Macrae and Curran did not modify any of the game's original code – opting instead to build boards that overlaid code on top of the original code – Atari's case would have been difficult to argue successfully in court. Atari ultimately agreed to drop the suit, offering Macrae and Curran $50,000 per month for two years to develop games for Atari so long as they agreed to stop making enhancement kits without permission of a game's original manufacturer.[10] The central issue for Atari was to prevent the unauthorized development and distribution of enhancement boards that could update existing machines without any of the profits from such enhancements going to the original manufacturer.

Having agreed to cease production of enhancement kits *without permission from the original copyright holder*, Macrae and Curran went to Bally-Midway (the US distributor of Namco's *Pac-Man*) seeking permission to produce their *Pac-Man* enhancement kit. Rather than approve their request, Bally-Midway suggested that Macrae and Curran help build a sequel to *Pac-Man*, which eventually became *Ms. Pac-Man*, the most successful arcade game of all time, selling over 115,000 machines.

The Macrae–Curran example uncovers many important points surrounding the early days of digital game modification, including the rise of difficult issues surrounding the definition of intellectual property rights in and around digital material. Importantly, it also points to some of the considerable restrictions on modding that make the Macrae–Curran story somewhat exceptional. These restrictions resulted from the structure of the arcade games industry and the very nature of arcade games themselves. In order to modify arcade games, one not only needed access to an arcade cabinet (with a cost ranging from $1,500 to $5,000), but one also needed access to a means of distribution as well as advanced knowledge of graphics and engineering. While only small players in the industry, Macrae and Curran succeeded because they met those requirements: they were running a small arcade operation in and around MIT, so they had both access to hardware and a means for local distribution, and they had enough knowledge of computer graphics and electrical engineering to disassemble code and design their enhancement kits. They also had the necessary drive and determination to challenge big industry players like Atari. Given the high financial, educational, and legal costs of entry, though, it is not surprising that arcade game modding was a relatively uncommon practice restricted to only a few brave hearts.

It is not until the mid-1990s, when personal computers and the internet come together in the homes of millions, that we begin to see the development of a broad and diversely constituted modding community. During this period, gaming consoles like the Sony PlayStation were the most popular means for enjoying digital games, but their single-purpose nature, as with arcade machines, made their games difficult to modify and almost impossible to distribute. The general-purpose nature of personal computers, both as single-user workstations and as networked communication devices, opened game modification to many more players, providing potential modders with access to a rich and growing knowledge-base on hacking and coding in general but also supporting a means for networked distribution of materials.

Unleashing *Doom*

Around midnight on December 10, 1993, id Software unleashed *Doom*, its new and highly anticipated first-person shooter (fps) game for personal computers. Released over the internet, *Doom* firmly established the first-person shooter as one of the most popular and influential genres of digital games in general, but also as one of the most important genres to the growth and development of game modding in particular. Following on the success of their first fps, *Wolfenstein 3D* (1992), id Software's John Carmack and John Romero set out to create a new fps based upon Carmack's increasingly innovative graphics technology. After seeing a small community of modders build up around *Wolfenstein 3D*, Carmack designed *Doom* so that its engine (the game's underlying code) and its media assets (the game's graphics and sounds) were housed in separate files. This modular design helped protect the game engine while providing potential modders with access to *Doom*'s media assets, stored in WAD files (an acronym for Where's All the Data?). With access to the WAD files, modders could replace graphics and sounds with ones of their own choice and design.

Soon after *Doom*'s release, fans quickly began creating modifications, substituting original in-game characters with the likes of Barney, the Simpsons, and other popular culture icons. The impulse to modify *Doom* was so great that, less than two months after the game's release, Brendon Wyber distributed the first version of the Doom Editor Utility (DEU), software developed by a networked team of programmers that allowed modders to create more than new graphics and sounds for *Doom*. It also gave them the power to create entirely new levels in the game.[11]

Response from id Software to the growing mod community around *Doom* was mixed. Both Carmack and Romero, who subscribed to the hacker ethic promoting the sharing of code for the betterment of software design, were elated by what they were seeing. While they understood it might mean potential loss in financial capital, they prized the symbolic capital that came with a substantial hacker community growing around their game. Others at id, however, were less enthusiastic about the possible consequences of Carmack's programming generosity. They worried that, by giving too much creative license to the community, they ran the risk of diluting their copyright and potentially competing against their own product should someone seek to sell mods based on their intellectual property. In other words, the symbolic capital gained from an active hacker community coagulating around a growing knowledge-base of *Doom*'s code threatened to hemorrhage the flow of economic capital enjoyed by id. After all, as much as Carmack and Romero took pride in their fan-base, they also took pride in their Ferraris and other material rewards of financial success.

Five months after *Doom*'s release, the conservative members of id Software convinced Carmack and Romero to approve a Data Utility License (DUL) to regulate the creation of editing utilities for *Doom*. The DUL required that all authors of Doom editors sign and abide by the terms of the license, which included provisions that protected the game engine from reverse engineering, ensured that the editor work only with the commercial version of *Doom* and not its freely available shareware version, and required developers to submit a copy of their editor to id and to explicitly and conspicuously acknowledge id Software's trademark ownership.[12] Regardless of the restrictions imposed by the DUL, most of the *Doom* hacker community abided by the license, happy simply to have been given the right to participate in the production and distribution of gaming material. For id Software, the license acknowledged and protected their intellectual property, but it also potentially increased their own knowledge base (since all editors needed to be submitted to id), buttressed game sales (since utilities could only work on the commercial version of the game), and yet continued to foster a growing participatory fan-base who felt empowered as active contributors to the cultural phenomenon.

It is important to note that the DUL applied only to the creation of *Doom* editors but not to the creation of mods, for id Software's main objective was to protect their game engine. This strategy proved remarkably prescient for id, whose revenues continue to be substantially bolstered by sales of game engine licenses to commercial developers. As id Software develops new engines to support new computing technologies, they publicly release the source code for older engines under the General Public License (GPL), which allows the public to access, modify, and redistribute the engine. In 1999, they released the source code under the GPL for both *Doom* and *Quake*, their first-person shooter released in 1996. In many respects, id's knowledge distribution model fits with Morris-Suzuki's cycle of corporate knowledge where, once knowledge has extracted maximum economic profit or once it is supplanted by next generation innovation, it is returned to the public. The desired benefit, of course, is that there will be an updraft where older technologies convince aspiring developers not only to stay committed to id Software's games, but potentially to adopt id's newer engines should they be in a position to invest.

While id Software's early method of fostering a sophisticated modding community around *Doom* seems rather improvisational, this disorganization illustrates the novel approach id took to marketing and distribution. They understood the potential power of the internet as a means for cultural distribution (the release of *Doom* over the internet is one of the first examples of commercially successful cultural exchange over the internet); they understood that a part of their fan-base enjoyed modifying their games; and they understood that communities of modders creating and distributing new in-game material could potentially expand and extend sales. But they did not prepare strategically for the unanticipated levels of game hacking that quickly developed around *Doom*. With no previous models to go by, little experience upon which to base expectations, and internal disagreement over how to handle fan production, id Software found themselves having to improvise their management of community participation. Ultimately, they sought a model that gave them the best of both worlds: an active modding community and a licensing agreement that protected their intellectual property.

Managing Modding: Communities and End-User License Agreements

Not all game developers rely on such an improvisational approach to protecting copyright and managing player-creative practices. In many respects, id Software's experience with *Doom* provided up-and-coming developers with the instructive example they needed to refine their strategies for realizing capital benefit from game modding. Rather than take a wait-and-see approach to protecting intellectual property and managing the development and exchange of hacking knowledge around their games, developers of second-generation mod-enabled games designed marketing strategies to maintain a greater level of control over the development and circulation of mods and modding utilities.

Armed with an understanding of the economic benefits and potential pitfalls of an active game modification community, companies like Valve Software – makers of *Half-Life* (1998) – and Epic Games – makers of *Unreal Tournament* (1999) – opted to give players the metaphoric keys to the car while simultaneously restricting how and where the car was driven. These developers sought to increase sales but protect intellectual property by more vigorously defining acceptable modding practices and by more actively participating in modding communities, which broadened their power to influence and manage modding practices and knowledge circulation beyond the seemingly heavy-handed approach of relying solely upon licensing agreements and copyright law.

Both Valve and Epic have enjoyed substantial economic benefit from their mod communities, as is clearly demonstrated by the six-year period between Valve's release of *Half-Life* (1998) and *Half-Life 2* (2004), a remarkably long interlude given the gaming industry's tendency to rely upon the safety of sequels for revenue. Valve did not need to produce sequels because its modding community was essentially doing that work for them, providing hundreds of freely available mods that extended *Half-Life*'s original story, presenting entirely new stories, or offering new maps for net-worked competitive games. Indeed, part of Valve's marketing strategy was to promote the inclusion of the *WorldCraft* level editor with *Half-Life* and, of course, the ability to play levels created by other players. Not content to allow the most popular mods to circulate without maximizing economic benefit, Valve opted to license a select few mods from the community, the most important and successful being *Counter-Strike*, a mod built by Minh Le and Jess Cliffe in 1999. To this day, *Counter-Strike* remains one of the most popular online shooter games, with over 60,000 players logged in at any given time.[13]

Buying up game mods from the community, while perhaps an effective mod management strategy, is highly inefficient and economically unsustainable, so com-panies like Valve and Epic use other strategies for managing mod communities and their creative practices, such as the development and distribution of official modding toolsets, the active cultivation of modding communities, and the definition of legitimate productive practices through legal agreements.

Community cultivation

Most game developers understand the benefits of building a strong participatory fan-base, so it is common for them to provide their communities with free promotional materials for fan-run websites and to organize or sponsor game festivals and contests that feature their games. It is not unusual for developers to require that players use fan website kits, which include color schemes, logos, game graphics and guidelines, before they agree to provide a link from the official website to the fan website. This enables developers to have some branding control over the representation of their game within fan communities. It also helps to build a feeling in the fan community of connection to the game and its developers. In addition, developers often identify and support community websites that focus on mod creation. This support can come in many forms, including the transfer of knowledge not documented in the commercial version of the game and active participation in the site's discussion forums around modding. In this way, the developer can foster a modding community through the controlled transfer of proprietary knowledge.

Developer-sponsored modding competitions also strengthen fan commitment to games and their communities, giving participants the opportunity to connect to the company on the level of content development. Indeed, many aspiring games developers enter their mods into competitions, hoping that theirs are chosen as one of the best and thereby giving them exposure not only to the community, but also to the developer, who could opt to license the mod or even hire the mod's creators. As already noted, Valve Software actively draws from its modding community when seeking new programming talent, hiring the teams that developed mods such as *Counter-Strike* and *Day of Defeat*. And BioWare Corp., makers of *Neverwinter Nights*, recently held a mod writing contest called "The Contest That Might Become Your Career," in which winners could be offered employment as writers for future game material.[14] Not only did this contest provide BioWare with potential employees, it also generated further excitement in general around the development of mods for their games. More importantly, all officially sponsored modding contests do more than generate enthusiasm; they also provide the player community with motivation to create mods and to see digital games as more than games, but also as environments supporting creative cultural production.

End-user license agreements

From a legal standpoint, the most important component in a strategy to manage player-production is to create an end-user license agreement (EULA) that spells out authorized and unauthorized modding practices. EULAs accompany most pieces of computer software, whether it's a word processor or a game. Most computer users recognize them as those very long chunks of legalese that require acceptance before running the software for the first time. Always present, yet seldom read, game EULAs typically protect intellectual property at the same time that they protect the developer from litigation by freeing them from responsibility for player-produced material. But what the EULA also does is frame game modding *as* a legitimate form of cultural production, but one whose legitimacy is defined to fit with the interests of capital to expand and extract economic benefit from intellectual property.

Game developers vary in their definitions of what constitutes legitimate modding, but they usually seek to protect game makers from liability, to prohibit reverse engineering, and to forbid the sale of mods without consent. The following sample is taken from the EULA governing the creation and distribution of mods made for Epic's *Unreal Tournament 2004* (Epic Games 2004), and is typical of many digital game EULAs in some of its restrictions:

1. Your Mods must only work with the full, registered copy of the Software, not independently or with any other software.
2. Your Mods must not contain modifications to any executable file(s).
3. Your Mods must not contain any libelous, defamatory, or other illegal material, material that is scandalous or invades the rights of privacy or publicity of any third party, nor may your Mods contain, or be used in conjunction with, any trademarks, copyright-protected work, or other recognizable property of third parties, nor may your Mods be used by you, or anyone else, for any commercial exploitation

including, but not limited to: (a) advertising or marketing for a company, product or service.

4. Your Mods shall not be supported by Atari, Epic or any of such parties' affiliates and subsidiaries, and if distributed pursuant to this license your Mods must include a statement to such effect.

5. Your Mods must be distributed solely for free, period. Neither you, nor any other person or party, may sell them to anyone, commercially exploit them in any way, or charge anyone for receiving or using them without prior written consent from Epic Games Inc. You may, [*sic*] exchange them at no charge among other end-users and distribute them to others over the internet, on magazine cover disks, or otherwise for free.

6. The prohibitions and restrictions in this section apply to anyone in possession of the Software or any of your Mods. (Epic Games 2004)

As these restrictions make clear, Epic supports the creation of mods for *Unreal Tournament 2004*, otherwise, their EULA would read very differently and they would not have included their own mod creation software with the commercial release of the game. And they want users to freely distribute their creations to others. One way of reading their prohibition against commercial distribution of mods is to conclude that they carry the torch for the democratic and free distribution of digital culture. But, if we look at some of their restrictions around distribution, we see that the right for economic profit is solely reserved by Epic: all mods must only work with retail and registered copies of *Unreal Tournament 2004* and no mods shall be sold without first seeking consent from Epic.

It remains, however, that Epic, like other developers of mod-enabled games, enthusiastically supports mod creation and gives mod-makers significant latitude over their productions. Epic even allows modders to use content and scripts from previous Epic games, stating "We just LOVE the idea of you using and distributing content or script from any prior Epic Games, Unreal franchise game in Unreal Tournament 2004 Mod [sic]. Therefore we grant you a license to use content from any prior Epic Games Unreal franchise game in your Unreal Tournament 2004 Mods" (2004). In addition to providing modders with free content, Epic encourages the recirculation of their own content as a means of helping to build a mod community in its own image. Like providing fan websites with official materials and guidelines, promoting the use of content from earlier games helps Epic to manage its branding and discourages dilution of their intellectual property.

Even more restrictive, however, are the terms by which the license can be terminated. In Epic's typically humorous tone, their EULA states, "In the unlikely event that you are naughty and fail to comply with any provision of this license, this license will terminate immediately without notice from us" (2004). In other words, break any component of the license governing playing the game or making mods for the game, and you can no longer use the software. This is a restriction common to most EULAs and not normally the cause of much friction between mod communities and game developers; not normally, that is, unless it is written explicitly to address rights around the distribution of mods, as the following example of BioWare Corp's EULA for *Neverwinter Nights* demonstrates.

In 2002, BioWare Corp. was on the eve of releasing *Neverwinter Nights* (NWN), its highly anticipated role-playing game. One of the most anticipated elements of the game was its *Aurora Toolset*, a collection of sophisticated but simple-to-use design utilities for the production of mods. Prior to the game's commercial release, BioWare freely released a beta version of the *Aurora Toolset*, including an EULA, in part to test the software for bugs, but also to generate excitement in its fan community. The beta certainly generated excitement, but not the kind BioWare hoped for. One section of the EULA caught the collective eye of the NWN community, raising ire for its overly possessive approach to player-created content and for its heavy-handedness in controlling the right to distribute mods. The section reads:

> By distributing or permitting the distribution of any of your Modules, you hereby grant back to INFOGRAMES and BIOWARE an irrevocable royalty-free right to use and distribute them by any means. INFOGRAMES or BIOWARE may at any time and in its sole discretion revoke your right to make your Modules publicly available. (BioWare Corp. 2002)

Essentially, BioWare sought to manage the circulation of mods by claiming royalty-free rights to all mods distributed by fans and by claiming the power to terminate a modder's right to distribute their mods for whatever reason they saw fit. Both claims resulted in an angry outcry from the game's fan-base, who were concerned that BioWare was seeking ownership of all fan-created and -distributed mods and that they could terminate the right to distribute cultural work made with their development software. Comparisons to other software development tools were common, with the argument that the *Aurora Toolset* should be seen as a development tool similar to Microsoft's *Visual C++*, which would never impose such restrictive conditions for use.

In response, BioWare rewrote the offending section to include wording around their effort to give credit to mod-makers whose mods they decided to distribute:

> Infogrames and BioWare will make a reasonable effort to provide credit to you in the event it uses or distributes your Variations, but you acknowledge that identifying you and/or other Variation creators may be difficult, and any failure by Infogrames and/or BioWare to provide credit to any person shall not be a breach of this License and shall not limit Infogrames' or BioWare's rights to use and distribute any Variation. (BioWare Corp. 2002)

While more generous than their initial EULA, the final version maintains BioWare's royalty-free right to distribute fan-produced mods and variations for their own benefit and to terminate end-users' rights to distribute mods at BioWare's sole discretion. In the end, all that BioWare offered to appease its modding community was the potential for symbolic capital that could come from including developers' names with any community-built mods they selected to distribute, with the added escape clause that their failure to do so does not breach the terms of the EULA.

BioWare's creation of end-user license agreements to manage third-party content exemplifies an increasingly common trend in the games industry to treat player-production as a source of distributed and free labor toward the extension and expansion of game sales. Indeed, the potential financial benefits of game modding have not gone unnoticed by industry-leaders like Microsoft. As J. Allard of Microsoft's Xbox team enthusiastically celebrates, "If only 1 percent of our audience that plays Halo helped construct the world around Halo, it would be more human beings than work at Microsoft corporation... That's how much human energy we could harness in this medium" (Borland 2006). In Allard's mind, players are like potential energy reserves waiting to be tapped for corporate benefit. And with the advent of more network-centric gaming systems like Microsoft's Xbox 360 and Sony's PlayStation 3, it seems likely that we will see developers take advantage of the system-proprietary nature of console networks to more closely manage and capitalize upon mod distribution. In many respects, as game developers create deeper implicit and explicit restrictions on player production, we find that game modding itself is being commoditized.

Relations in Flux

As we have seen, response from developers to modding, while generally positive, has resulted in a mixture of attempts to define and authorize modding as a legitimate practice and to define rights to player-created materials. While companies like Epic Games do not claim rights over player-created mods, companies like BioWare and Microsoft tend to see their community as a potential source of marketable content. Regardless of varying levels of restrictions, the goal remains the same: to maximize profit.

In other words, the history of modding outlined here demonstrates ongoing reconfigurations to Morris-Suzuki's public–private–public cycle of specialized knowledge in information capitalism. Rather than seek near-total control over the system of exchange, as continues to be the strategy of the litigation-hungry music and film industries, games developers provide knowledge and tools to their consumers to encourage participation in cultural production. Some of this knowledge is packaged with games in the form of tools and documentation, some of it is leaked to modding discussion boards, and some of it is developed and circulated by gamers themselves, outside of any official corporate authorization. The challenge for games developers has been how to manage these knowledge leaks to protect their intellectual property, maximize profit, and minimize litigation. So far, their strategies have been to cultivate communities and technologies of exchange, where content is vetted or filtered by the developer, and to create end-user license agreements to define acceptable practices.

To date, games developers' strategies for managing player production have had mixed success. The cultivation of communities of exchange gives developers greater control over what is created and then promoted back to the community. Indeed, companies like BioWare have considerable control over content when they host contests, where all materials are submitted to them for vetting. And with the rise of centralized gaming environments, such as massively multiplayer online games like *World of Warcraft* and proprietary networks like Microsoft's Xbox Live, developers gain a technological advantage in being able to monitor and manage data exchange. In these cases, the cycle of public–private–public is reconfigured slightly, although the result is no different. But even Microsoft recognizes that, no matter how secure they make the Xbox and Xbox 360, hackers will find ways to create and distribute unauthorized material. As Allard himself states, "With 360 we said, 'Let's assume we can't stop it. How are we going to manage it?' " (GameSpot 2005).

While supporting and managing communities gives developers substantial power to manage content distribution, it gives them only limited reach and, ultimately, little control over the everyday creation and circulation of mods for decentralized games (single-player games and player-organized networked games) that takes place outside of authorized networks and communities. Even end-user license agreements give developers only limited power over the creation and circulation of game content. EULAs are seldom enforced by developers to the point where they go to trial. In centralized online games, where content can be monitored and managed in ways similar to proprietary console networks, players are given warnings when their creations potentially break EULAs. Normally, this results in players complying with the EULA. But in games where content is not managed by a centralized network, data flows more freely and is much more difficult for developers to manage. In these games, even if players create mods that contravene EULAs, there is little that developers can do to stop mods from being distributed online, especially with the popularity of peer-to-peer file-sharing systems such as BitTorrent. And if a developer decided to launch legal action against a modder, the effects of such aggressive action could ripple through the community, potentially damaging relations with their fanbase. Developers clearly understand the necessity for caution. As for developers' claims to irrevocable royalty-free rights to user-created content, there is very little modders can do but accept that they are potentially creating content for their favorite games developers.

The always-shifting dynamics of relations between games developers and their modding communities makes it difficult to draw clear conclusions over whether game modification provides players with greater productive agency without simultaneously making game modification into a commoditized practice. Without a doubt, mod-enabled games allow players to become producers of content and knowledge, but many games developers are increasingly seeking to manage what happens to that content and knowledge once it is created and distributed. By promoting modding practices, game developers are providing creative players with more than games; they are also providing creative environments, whether they include modding tools or in-game creative activities like those in *The Sims*, where players create domestic settings. It remains that players can create and distribute their own materials, sometimes within and sometimes without the implicit and explicit restrictions that developers use to define legitimate modding.

It is difficult to speculate about what future modding practices will look like, but the current situation demonstrates that new models of cultural exchange are constantly evolving in response to many variables, including the development of new technologies of exchange, which are being used both to support and to restrict unauthorized content distribution. Rather than see the evolving model of digital content and knowledge exchange as locked in a cycle of public–private–public, it is more accurate to see the model of exchange as constantly in flux. In this respect, modding is like a game between commercial producers and player producers, where the rules of play forever shift as one team builds greater offense and another team tightens their defense. Neither team is particularly organized behind one strategy, but they both seek to define and exercise the rights to creative digital gameplay.

NOTES

1　Since 2001, two new academic journals focusing specifically on the study of digital games as cultural artifacts have been launched: *Games Studies: The International Journal of Computer Game Research* (<http://gamestudies.org/>) and *Games and Culture: A Journal of Interactive Media* (Sage Publications). In 2003, the Digital Games Research Association was established and its first international conference was held in Utrecht, The Netherlands. Several book-length studies on digital games have appeared in recent years, with MIT Press establishing a Game Studies series.

2　See Aarseth (1999) for an example of colonialist rhetoric.

3　For an example, see McCullagh and Broache (2006).

4　Henry Giroux points out connections between the intensifying culture of fear surrounding youth and the paranoid response of the US to terrorism (2003).

5　For a strong critique of media-violence studies, see Freedman (2002). For a discussion of play as unproductive time, see Huizinga (1955) and Callois (2001).

6　The word "mod" is also used to describe forms of hardware modification, such as those used by hackers to install alternative operating systems on game consoles such as the Sony PlayStation, Microsoft Xbox, and Nintendo GameCube.

7　For more recent analysis of participatory culture, see Hills (2002) and Jenkins (2006).

8　See Harvey (1990) on flexible production and Morris-Suzuki (1988) and Kline et al. (2003) on perpetual innovation economy.

9　See Montfort (2003: 65–93) for a more detailed account of Advent's history.

10　See Kent (2001) for a full account, especially pp. 167–73.

11　See Kushner (2004: 165–68) for more.

12 For the complete Data Utility License for *Doom*, see <http://www.rome.ro/lee_killough/history/dul.txt>.

13 See GameSpy (2006) for statistics. There were 63,247 players playing *Counter-Strike* at

the time of writing (1:50pm EST March 9, 2006).

14 See Bioware (2006). Contest ended January 30, 2006.

REFERENCES

Aarseth, Espen (1997). *Cybertext: Perspectives on Ergodic Literature*. Baltimore: Johns Hopkins University Press.

—— (1999). "Aporia and Epiphany in Doom and The Speaking Clock: The Temporality of Ergodic Art." In Marie-Laure Ryan (Ed.). *Cyberspace Textuality: Computer Technology and Literary Theory*. Bloomington: Indiana University Press, pp. 31–41.

Bioware Corp. (2002). End-User License Agreement, Aurora Toolset Beta, Neverwinter Nights [computer software].

—— (2006, April 12). "The Contest that Might Become Your Career." <http://www.bioware.com/biozone/articles/2005_11_30_Writing-Contest/>. Accessed April 22, 2006.

Borland, J. (2006, February 2). "Tomorrow's Games, Designed by Players as They Play." <http://news.zdnet.com/2100-1040_22-6034630.html>. Accessed April 22, 2006.

Callois, R. (2001). *Man, Play, and Games*. Chicago: University of Illinois Press (Originally published in 1961).

Castronova, E. (2005). *Synthetic Worlds: The Business and Culture of Online Games*. Chicago: University of Chicago Press.

Crowther, W. (1975). *Adventure* [computer software].

de Certeau, M. (1984). *The Practice of Everyday Life*. Berkeley: University of California Press.

Entertainment Software Association (2006). Sales & Genre Data. <http://www.theesa.com/facts/sales_genre_data.php>. Accessed April 23, 2006.

Epic Games (2004). End-User License Agreement, Unreal Tournament 2004 [computer software].

Freedman, J. L. (2002). *Media Violence and its Effect on Aggression: Assessing the Scientific Evidence*. Toronto: University of Toronto Press.

GameSpot (2005, October 7). "X05 Q&A: Allard Speaks." <http://www.gamespot.com/news/6135302.html>. Accessed June 7, 2006.

GameSpy (2006, March 9). "Top Mods for Half Life by Players." <http://archive.gamespy.com/stats/mods.asp?id=15&s=1>. Accessed March 9, 2006.

Giroux, H. (2003). *The Abandoned Generation: Democracy Beyond the Culture of Fear*. New York: Palgrave Macmillan.

Grossman, D. (1999). *Stop Teaching Our Kids to Kill: A Call to Action Against TV, Movie and Video Game Violence*. New York: Crown Publishers.

Harvey, D. (1990). *The Condition of Postmodernity: An Enquiry into the Origins of Cultural Change*. Oxford: Blackwell Publishers Ltd.

Hills, M. (2002). *Fan Cultures*. New York: Routledge.

Huizinga, J. (1955). *Homo Ludens: A Study of the Play-Element in Culture*. Boston: Beacon.

id Software (1994). Data Utility License. <http://www.rome.ro/lee_killough/history/dul.txt>. Accessed April 23, 2006.

Jenkins, H. (1992). *Textuals Poachers: Television Fans and Participatory Cultures*. New York: Routledge.

—— (2006). *Convergence Culture: Where Old and New Media Collide*. New York: New York University Press.

Kent, S. L. (2001). *The Ultimate History of Video Games*. New York: Three Rivers Press.

Kline, S., N. Dyer-Witheford, and G. De Peuter (2003). *Digital Play: The Interaction of Technology, Culture, and Marketing*. Montréal: McGill-Queen's University Press.

Kushner, D. (2004). *Masters of Doom: How Two Guys Created an Empire and Transformed Pop Culture*. New York: Random House.

Lee, M. J. (1993). *Consumer Culture Reborn: The Cultural Politics of Consumption*. London: Routledge.

McCullagh, D., and A. Broache (2006, March 9). "Clinton, Lieberman Propose CDC Investigate Games." <http://www.gamespot.com/news/6145659.html>. Accessed April 23, 2006.

Montfort, N. (2003). *Twisty Little Passages: An Approach to Interactive Fiction*. Cambridge: The MIT Press.

Morris-Suzuki, T. (1988). *Beyond Computopia: Information, Automation and Democracy in Japan*. London: Kegan Paul.

Murray, Janet (1997). *Hamlet on the Holodeck: The Future of Narrative in Cyberspace*. Cambridge, MA: MIT Press.

Pearce, C. (2006). "Productive Play: Game Culture from the Bottom Up." *Games and Culture* 1.1: 17–24.

20

Blogs and Blogging: Text and Practice

Aimée Morrison

A relatively new genre in digital literary studies, the weblog, or blog, has shot to prominence as a primarily popular medium. From its modest beginnings as a sort of digest tool for computing professionals and internet hobbyists, the blog has attained the mainstream as a form of digital personal diary, an outlet for citizen journalism, a community space for special interest forums, and a medium for more passive entertainment. Current estimates suggest that a new blog is created every *second*; nearly 54 million were published as of late 2006 (Technorati 2006). Many of these blogs – in all the categories identified – are written and read by academics as well as their students. Many more, including especially journalistic and political blogs, are becoming objects of study in a variety of research contexts in the humanities and social sciences. Also, with their strong emphasis on readability, audience, and style, blogs are of increasing interest to the fields of rhetoric and composition as a pedagogical tool and emerging creative writing genre. Literary scholars, too, are examining the links between blogging and more traditional forms of publication as many prominent bloggers either hail from the print media, or are recruited by it. Similarly, as happened after the popularization of the World Wide Web, longstanding and established print media such as national newspapers and mass-market magazines are beginning to incorporate elements drawn from blogging into their publishing purviews, a development of interest to media and communications researchers. A corpus of research in new media, also, is beginning to address the role and impact of blogs on practices of internet sociability and computer-mediated communication (CMC), with a particular eye to behaviors characteristic of identifiable demographics.

The weblog as a writing form is fundamentally about fostering personal expression, meaningful conversation, and collaborative thinking in ways the World Wide Web had perhaps heretofore failed to provide for; not static like a webpage, but not private like an email, as well as more visually appealing than discussion lists, blogging's rapid rise to online ubiquity bespeaks its quite particular fit into a previously unidentified hole in the digital universe, and this appeal is worth exploring. Here, we will proceed from definitions and histories, through an examination of the requisite undergirding technologies, enumerating the many genres of writing supported by blogging, with an emphasis on resources for reading and writing in this form, finally overviewing the research on the nature and effects of blogging and the pertinence of this practice to literary studies. For those interested in creating or participating in blogs, a list of resources follows this chapter.

Weblogs

"Blog" is a contraction of "weblog," itself a compound of web log, a term originally designating the report generated by the automated tracking of activity and traffic on computer servers. Blogging as a practice is rooted in computing science and engineering, among whose professionals this form first appeared, in the mid-1990s. In its most rudimentary incarnation, the weblog was a simple HTML page featuring annotated hyperlinks to sites of interest to the page's author. They were logs of their authors' travels over the internet, not differing substantially in form or content from many early personal home pages, except in the frequency or regularity with which the information on them was updated or changed. Recognized as a distinct genre from about 1997 by a small and bounded community of participant readers and writers, when the development of simple-to-use blogging software around 1999 promoted the spread of the practice to a larger group, the "weblog" came to be known more commonly as the "blog."[1] The more informal term "blog" was chosen as Merriam-Webster's "Word of the Year" for 2004 (Merriam Online 2004). Of course, this honor is accorded to the most *looked-up* word in the online version of the dictionary. The need to search for a definition of the term indicates that the public discourse of blogging – references to the practice or to particular sites in mainstream media – exceeds the general knowledge. Accordingly, a January 2005 Pew/Internet Data memo on "The State of Blogging" indicates that less than 40 percent of surveyed internet users knew what blogs were – 62 percent could not define the word (Rainie 2005).

So what *are* blogs, then? As a writing genre, weblogs manifest several essential and optional characteristics, all of which are supported by the common blogging software packages to varying degrees (more on which later). These characteristics, in decreasing order of prominence and importance, include: the discrete post as fundamental organizing unit; date- and time-stamping of posts; the appearance of posts in reverse chronological order; hyperlinking to external sites; the archiving of posts and references to posts with permalinks and trackbacks; the reference to other likeminded or otherwise interesting blogs through the provision of a blogroll; the capacity for reader comments on posts; and the organization of posts by keywords into separate browsable categories. Each characteristic contributes to distinguishing the blog from other genres of digital writing that are its kin, genres such as the webpage, the email, the web ring, or the discussion group, and it is useful to consider each characteristic in turn.

At its most basic, a blog is a webpage comprised of individual posts. Posts have been likened variously to newspaper articles, diary entries, or even random scribbles in a notebook, and they can contain simple links to other sites, narrative commentary, or embedded or linked media components like photographs, videos, or audio files. Posts can be of varying lengths, ranging from a sentence fragment with a single embedded link to a multi-screen essay complete with references; generally, posts tend to the shorter rather than the longer. Herring et al. (2005), in their quantitative analysis of weblogs, for example, found an average post length of about 210 words among their 200-blog sample. As the date- and time-stamp function indicates, blogs are assumed to be frequently updated, with "frequently" meaning in some cases hourly and in others once or twice weekly. The National Institute for Technology in Liberal Education estimated in 2003 that 77 percent of more than 500 sample blogs it surveyed had been updated within the last two weeks (NITLE 2003a). Generally, it is a blog's currency of information that is its greatest attraction – hence the reverse chronological posting order, privileging the most recent updates – but bloggers can offer other means to navigate and browse what can become quite hefty archives of materials. Keywording of blog posts allows for the construction of discrete, blogger-defined categories of entries, allowing readers to browse a subset of posts dealing with a particular category. A blogger of quite catholic writing interests might keyword her posts so that readers need not wade through those about cats or about *Prison Break* in order to follow the thread about *Nicholas Nickleby* and Dickens's comic genius, or the one about ActionScripting in Flash.

Many blogs feature embedded hyperlinks to materials being commented upon. Traditionally – which is to say, circa 1997–9, when weblogs were first becoming recognizable as a distinct form of digital publication – the weblog served a digest function, acting as a daily compendium of annotated links to sites of interest to the blogger and his or her readers (Blood 2000). These posts tended to be short and were explicitly organized to direct readers to the site commented upon. As blogs spread and the genre expanded beyond this digest function, longer, discursive posts have become more common and the hyperlink in some cases has proportionally faded in importance; this is especially true of diary-style blogs that emphasize stream-of-consciousness narration of the blogger's daily life or emotional state over more explicitly critical or socially engaged kinds of writing. Herring et al. (2005) found that nearly a third of their sampled blog posts featured no links at all; they surmise that this is owing to the numerical superiority of diary-style blogs in their corpus. The authors suggest further that this percentage would be even higher had they not deliberately excluded several blog hosts that were explicitly promoted as online diary services.

One of the more interesting features of the blogging world – or "blogosphere," as it refers to itself – is its recursive self-referentiality, and the opportunities it offers for digital conversation. Conversation is most obviously encouraged between blog authors and blog readers by the built-in capacity for reader feedback: the "comment" feature of most blogging software and services allows any reader to add their own comments to a post. Here again, though, Herring et al. (2005) found a far lower incidence of interaction than is popularly claimed for blogs: the number of comments per post ranged from 0 to 6, with a mean of 0.3. The free-for-all of democratic, unfiltered interaction provided for by anonymous, instant commenting has been severely challenged by the advent of "comment spam," the blogosphere version of unsolicited mass-mailed advertisements: early ideals of mass participation are now bumping up against the realities of un-neighborly commercial practices. Depending on the setup, commenting may be completely anonymous (a practice that can leave the blog open to inundation by comment-spam, or encourage repercussion-free digital vandalism) or may require a reader to register a screen name, email account, and password, and to pass a small test (generally, deciphering textual content from a provided image) to prove that the comment issues from a traceable human and not a spam-bot. Similarly, different levels of editorial oversight allowed for by blogging software mean that comments may appear the moment they are made, or may first require approval by a vetting human eye before being appended to the post.

From commenting upon and pointing to other internet sites, blogs soon began commenting upon and pointing to one another. Such blog-to-blog references may take the form of a simple comment pointing readers to the commenter's own blog in the context of elaborating a longer response, or may occur in the context of one blog post more explicitly linking to another via technologies such as the trackback and permalink. Permalinks offer a stable URL reference to a particular post, so that this post may be linked to or otherwise referenced reliably and unambiguously. Trackbacks list and link to those external sites that reference the post in question – a kind of "see who linked to me" feature that can serve to key a reader to a multi-site conversation, or simply to indicate the popularity of the blogger or the buzz-level of the post; trackbacks are semi-automated and require both the linker and linkee to have tracking software enabled. However, the most common way that blogs reference each other is through the blogroll, a simple list of blog titles running down the side of each page: it promotes the blogs the blogger finds useful or entertaining, denoting affiliation with like-minded others in a community of readers and writers. Blogrolls are one of the main filtering tools by which readers access blog resources of interest to them, as we will see below. They also foster community and conversation in their function as aggregators of bloggers and readers, and of topics, viewpoints, and references.

As research undertaken by the Pew Internet and American Life Project and others makes clear, the blogosphere is expanding at a great pace – from an estimated 21 million American blog readers in early 2004 to an estimated 32 million by the end of that year (representing an increase from 17 to 27 percent of all American internet users, whom Pew estimates to number 120 million). This indicates a 58 percent growth in blog readership in a span of ten months. Pew also marks at 7 percent the rate of blog authorship among the American internet-using population – this makes for 8 million bloggers, by its count (Rainie 2005). Internationally, Technorati (<http://www.technorati.com>), the blog-tracking website and search engine, was indexing more than 54 million blogs globally in late 2006, an ever-shifting roster at a time in which blogs are created at a greater rate than the one at which they go defunct. LiveJournal (<http://www.livejournal.com>), for example, is home to 10 million separate accounts, of which nearly 2 million are considered "active in some way": slightly more than half of this subset of active accounts has been updated within the previous month, and one-fifth of these within the last 24 hours (LiveJournal). There are several reasons, both cultural and technological, driving the increases in readership and authorship of blogs. We will address these here in turn, both in the context of the broader population and of the academy more specifically.

One of the factors driving the increase in popular blog readership, and a greater awareness of the blogosphere generally, was the 2004 American presidential election, which saw a veritable explosion of political blogs devoted to critiquing, mudslinging, or fundraising – or sometimes all three.[2] During this election, bloggers earned press credentials for nomination conventions and other campaign events, their activities were reported on in established media outlets, and the bloggers themselves began to be called upon as pundits in these same media. This greater penetration of the "real world" by bloggers increased their visibility among newspaper readers and television watchers generally, leading to a rise in blog traffic. Further, staunchly partisan Democratic, liberal, or left-leaning blogs like *Daily Kos*, *Talking Points Memo*, and others offered what many considered to be a bracing alternative to the perceived blandness and conservatism of the mainstream media. The internet-dependent campaign of Howard Dean to seek the Democratic nomination, for example, was almost more newsworthy than the candidate himself, with the success of the *Blog for America* model of citizen participation, organization, and fundraising surpassing all expectations. On the Republican or conservative side, the campaign of the "Swift Boat Veterans for Truth" had a strong internet presence backed by a blogging CMS, and garnered much traffic, and the right-leaning political blog *Power Line* was chosen by *Time* as its "blog of the year" in 2004 (McIntosh 2005: 385).

In the academy, blogging has proven to be very popular among undergraduates, graduate students, and the professoriate, likely more popular than in the population as a whole – as Pew's research indicates, blog authors disproportionately manifest one or more of the following demographic characteristics: they are young, male, have access to high-speed internet connections, have been online for more than six years, are financially prosperous, and have high levels of education. University populations present these characteristics in varying degrees among their many constituent groups. Many undergraduates maintain personal diary blogs in addition to profiles on MySpace, Facebook, and the like; the blogosphere is awash in students. Herring et al. (2005) found that 57 percent of their sample blogs were written by self-identified university students – and they had excluded from consideration youth-skewed diary services like LiveJournal and Diaryland. Among the professoriate, blogging activities range across the whole breadth of the blogosphere. Pseudonymous diarizers like "New Kid on the Hallway" chronicle life in general as well as life on the tenure track in informal, personal, and intelligent ways, linked in tight blogroll and comment communities of similarly positioned and trained readers. Blogs like

Rate Your Students are mostly comprised of comments from anonymized respondents, in this case mocking and parodying the popular *Rate My Professors* web service. Daniel W. Drezner's eponymous political punditry blog both reflects his academic work in political science and departs from the academic standards that govern his peer-reviewed work (his "About Me" page even addresses the question "Why are you wasting valuable hours blogging instead of writing peer-reviewed academic articles?" – one possible answer might be that he is now co-editor of a book on blogging). *Grand Text Auto* is a group blog devoted to "procedural narratives, games, poetry, and art" and authored by six new media artists, theorists, and technicians, most of whom hold academic positions, and two of whom contribute essays to this volume. *Language Log* chronicles and digests linguistic quirks, and two of its contributors, academics Mark Liberman (the site's founder) and Geoffrey K. Pullum, have recently published a book based on the blog's contents.

Constituent Technologies of Blogging

Blog writing, as distinct from blog-reading, is unlikely to have become as much of a mainstream pastime as it has were it not for the introduction, in mid-1999, of simple, hosted, and free blog authoring software with graphical user interfaces. A variety of CMS, or "content management system," blogging software like Pyra Labs' Blogger began to offer pre-made technical templates into which authors could simply pour their content, much like filling out an HTML form. This software dramatically lowered the technical barrier to entry, freeing would-be bloggers from HTML troubleshooting and onerous programming (or under-featured sites) so that they could instead concentrate on the writing: the result was an explosion in the number of blogs published. CMS-based blogging software applications offer a set of tools simple enough to operate that anyone competent with a web-based email account can easily be up and blogging in an afternoon. In this vein, Blogger now describes itself as "the push button publishing tool for the people" (Pyra Labs 2006). Some of the most prominent and well-used current applications are Blogger, now owned by Google; "online diaries" LiveJournal and Diaryland; downloadable Movable Type and hosted Typepad; Wordpress; and Radio Userland. Many others appear and disappear daily; most offer varying levels and costs of service. Some are free and hosted, some charge fees for upgrades like expanded storage space and support for multimedia applications such as podcasting or photoblogging, many offer premium services for professional users, and all offer slightly different functionality. Reading a blog, of course, requires nothing more than an internet connection and a web browser, and as most blogs still skew heavily toward textual content, even a very poor internet connection will suffice to provide an adequate window on the blogosphere.

   While the basic practices and tropes of blogging have remained fairly constant since the advent of graphical blog-editors, more recently, syndication has become a common feature of the blogosphere. RSS (Really Simple Syndication) and Atom are XML-based programs aiding the spread of blog readership across the internet population more generally. Syndication aggregates the most recent updates to a site, basically providing a mini-site of only new content. Syndication is a "push" technology which directs content to interested users on the basis of subscription, as opposed to the more traditional reading model of search-and-visit (that "pulls" readers to a site). Syndication technologies basically allow a reader to customize her own newsfeed, with newly posted snippets of information from selected sources aggregated for the reader as they appear. The feature is as common with mainstream online news sites as it is with blogs. Developed in various contexts from the late 1990s, syndication has been coming into its own as a mainstream technology since about 2002, with support for it increasingly built into standard internet browsers, rendering it accessible to nearly everyone online.

Genres of Blogs

The landscape of blogging is changing rapidly as new users come to write and read in this medium; as with the popularization of the internet through graphical World Wide Web browsers from about 1994, the mass influx of new participants is altering the form at the very instant that its earliest communities seek to codify and prescribe acceptable uses, behaviors, and fundamental definitions. Prominent and early bloggers like Rebecca Blood have devised widely disseminated codes of ethics for the blogosphere at the same time as this space becomes populated by users who have never read a blog before starting to write one (Blood 2002). Blood's code is based on journalistic practice, and as such is endorsed by sites like Cyberjournalist.net (see, for example, Dube 2003), but the analogy with journalism – a tremendously popular one – does not begin to cover the full extent of the blogosphere: most new users, an overwhelming numerical majority, are writing personal diaries online, and have a very different understanding of the roles and responsibilities of bloggers. Aware perhaps of this split, Koh et al. (2005), in an undergraduate thesis on blog ethics, break the blogosphere into "personal" and "non-personal" domains, a bifurcation based on the quite different demographics, audience, intent, content, and ethical frameworks informing both groups, as identified in the more than 1,200 responses to their online survey. For their part, Herring et al. (2005) note several competing blog genre taxonomies. They note Blood's tripartipite model of the traditional "filter" blog, the emerging diary-style "personal journal," and a discursive-essay-based "notebook" blog, as well as Krishnamurthy's four quadrants of "online diaries," "support group," "enhanced column," and "collaborative content creation" blogs. Finding these models wanting, the authors settle on their own genre categories, based on an initial survey of their blog samples: these are personal journals, filters, and k-logs ("knowledge-logs," generally used within organizations for technical support applications, or other oft-updated, information-rich content). According to Jeremy Williams and Joanne Jacobs (2004), "the great beauty of blogs is their versatility," and they lay out yet another taxonomy based on who is writing and what about: among the authorship categories they discern "group blogs, family blogs, community blogs, and corporate blogs," as well as "blogs defined by their content; eg 'Warblogs' (a product of the Iraq War), 'LibLogs' (library blogs), and 'EduBlogs'." The various taxonomies identified in the scholarship have not coalesced into any kind of consensus: blogs can be and are grouped formally, by the audience or effects they aim for, by the degree of publicness or privateness they manifest, by the kinds of authors they feature, and by the kinds of content they highlight.

Despite this continuing debate, it is possible to discern broad categories of topic, tone, and audience in the blogosphere, for purposes of overview, if nothing else. At one end of the spectrum, among the most visible, well-read, well-studied, and profitable blogs are those dedicated to journalism, politics, and tabloid-style celebrity gossip: for example, *The Drudge Report*, *The Huffington Post*, and *Talking Points Memo* count in the first or second categories, while *Go Fug Yourself*, *Gawker*, and *Pink is the New Blog* fall in the latter. Obviously, varying degrees of credibility, seriousness, and impact accrue to each, but they share several characteristics. Many of these blogs mimic the mainstream media in their organization as for-profit businesses supported by advertising revenue and driven by readership statistics. Bloggers on these sites often earn salaries and may be supported by research, secretarial, and technical staff. Thus, we can number among this type of blog also some of the sites created by established media organizations to supplement their pre-existing print and online materials, such as the *Chronicle of Higher Education*'s *News* and *WiredCampus* blogs. As the readership of this particular category of blog has expanded, so too has commercialization of the genre. As with the mainstream media, commercially supported blogs are largely financed by advertising revenue. Other blogs, particularly political blogs, may be supported by reader donation. Banner ads populate the larger sites, but even more small-scale operations can profit from Google AdSense ads or partnerships with online retailers. Blogs that adopt the commercial model face many of the same pressures the established mass media addressed throughout the twentieth century: attracting more advertising revenue by capturing larger shares of the available audience.

This very public category of blog occupies only a tiny corner of the blogosphere, but garners a disproportionate share of media and academic attention. As Shawn McIntosh observes,

> The power and potential of blogs does not come from sheer numbers, but rather from the inordinate amount of power to influence media coverage as public opinion leaders that a handful of bloggers have acquired in a very short time. (2005: 385)

McIntosh is largely speaking about influential political and journalistic blogs, which fall into the "notebook" or "filter" genres, or Koh et al.'s (2005) "non-personal" category. This type of blog is far more likely to be written for an audience of strangers, with a purpose of providing commentary on public or political events. Further, these blogs tend to boast more readers than average, which may help account for their dominance in press accounts of blogging. McIntosh surmises as well a certain "inside baseball" aspect to the disproportion of attention and influence that accrues to these politics-and-current-events blogs. On average, Koh et al. (2005) find that this group of writers, whom they nominate "non-personal" bloggers, are more likely to be well-educated, older males. The National Institute for Technology and Liberal Education, similarly, in its breakdown of blog content authorship, finds that while the blogo-sphere as a whole achieves near-parity in terms of gender, in the subset of political websites (6 percent of the sites it surveyed), a mere 4 percent were authored by women (NITLE 2003b). Gossip and entertainment blogs – not journalism, but not diaries; informal but not personal – were not factored explicitly into these studies, and it would be interesting to determine the generic and demographic characteristics of these very popular sites; they appear to be even more overlooked than the online diaries Laurie McNeill identifies as underserved by scholarship.

At the other end of the blog genre spectrum may be counted the personal blogs, generally considered to be HTML inheritors of paper-based genres of life writing: autobiography, memoir, journal, scrapbook, and diary. McNeill sees in the blogo-sphere "an unparalleled explosion of public life writing by public citizens" (2003: 25), while noting quite rightly that "these Web diaries and blogs have received little academic attention" (2003: 26). To address this lack, Viviane Serfaty offers a "structural approach" to the study of this subset of the blogosphere, ascertaining a set of shared generic characteristics common to most: *accumulation*, referring to the piling-on of multimedia detail in the construction of the textual self, whereby text and image and links reinforce or call into question the diarist's persona (2004: 459–60); *open-endedness*, or the episodic and non-cumulative accretion of posts that distinguish diaries from autobiographies or memoirs (2004: 461–2); a *doubled self-reflexivity* that addresses both the nature of internet life-writing as well as the diarist's motivation for writing in the first place (2004: 462–3); and *co-production*, the deliberate construction of the text for an audience that is able to respond to or to collaborate in the diarist's project of self-presentation or self-construction (2004: 465). Threads of commentary, posts, and trackbacks can be complex and tightly woven in these diary-blogs, despite the above-noted paucity of outbound links compared to punditry or digest blogs, giving a real feel of community to many of these sites, which may have core readerships in the single digits. Serfaty and McNeill each carefully link blog-based life-writings to prior internet forms (such as the "online diaries" in simple HTML that began appearing around 1995) as well as to print antecedents (that is, paper journals and diaries, and scrapbooks). The demographics of this subgenre are the inverse of those manifest in the more "public" kinds of blogging described above. On LiveJournal, online diaries are generated disproportionately by the young to commu-nicate with their immediate circle of real-world acquaintance. Its age distribution curve peaks at 18 (419,000 registered users self-identified as this age) with the greatest concentration of bloggers falling in the 16–22-year-old range (LiveJournal 2006). Of those users who indicated their sex, interestingly, two-thirds self-identified as female.

The online diary genre of blog exerts a tremendously powerful pull on both readers and writers. As Serfaty notes, via the intermediary of the computer screen which both veils the computer user and reflects back his image to himself, "diarists feel they can write about their innermost feelings without fearing identification and humiliation, [while] readers feel they can inconspicuously observe others and derive power from that knowledge" (2004: 470). Koh et al.'s (2005) research shows that these personal bloggers are twice as likely as the more public bloggers to write for an audience of ten or fewer readers; non-personal bloggers are more than twice as likely to write for an audience of 100–500 people. Similarly, personal bloggers are nearly four times as likely to write for an audience known personally to themselves, while non-personal bloggers are more than four times more likely than the diarists to write specifically for an audience of strangers. Finally, about 75 percent of personal bloggers take as their primary content "Events in my life," "Family and home," and "Religious beliefs," while non-personal bloggers show a clear preference – in the range of 50 percent – for the categories "News," "Entertainment and Arts," and "Government and Politics" (Koh et al. 2005). This split, in which the smallest part of the blogosphere garners the most study and is taken to stand in for the whole, bears further investigation, and thus far it has been mostly undertaken by the life-writing and autobiography studies community.

In between these poles lies the vast and shifting middle ground, occupied by aspiring writers seeking both audiences and book contracts with provocative and literate projects, and professionals of all stripes creating classic digest-style blogs on their areas of expertise designed to appeal to a specific core of similarly trained readers, for example Matthew G. Kirschenbaum's blog in new media studies, *MGK*, or computing humanist Jill Walker's *jill/txt*. In this middle terrain we can also locate artists publishing multimedia blogs as creative outlets – photoblogs, vlogs or video blogs, storyblogs, and the like (see <http://www.photoblogs.org> or <http://www.freevlog.org> for examples of some of these). Of course, mobility among categories is quite fluid in these early days of blogging, with mainstream paper-based journalists like Dan Gillmor shifting to primarily blog-based writing, political bloggers like Markos Moulitsas Zuniga (*Daily Kos*) attaining press credentials and being interviewed on television and radio, and prurient personal/gossip blogs like Jessica Cutler's formerly anonymous *Washingtonienne* leading to public exposure and a contract for a book based on her blog. Many projects are hard to categorize neatly. New York municipal worker Julie Powell's online saga of her quest to get through every recipe in Julia Child's seminal *Mastering the Art of French Cooking* in one year was at once styled like a memoir (a time-delimited personal account) and a more public form of writing (the blog, *Julie/Julia*, was sponsored and hosted by online magazine *Salon*). This blog ultimately won the inaugural "Blooker Prize" (i.e., the "Booker Prize" of the blogosphere) and led to a rewriting of its contents for book publication.

Some of the generic instability of blogging has led to unexpected negative consequences and the articulation and debate of new ethical dilemmas – and to neologisms like "dooced," a verb describing a loss of employment as a result of blogging, named for fired blogger Dooce, whose eponymous blog has now become her source of income. Fundamentally, very much at issue are questions of libel and liability, of the distinctions between public and private writing, and tests of the notions of civility, propriety, and ethical behavior online. These topics remain to be explored by scholars in depth, or, indeed, at all.

Reading Blogs

Rebecca Blood (2000) surmises interestingly that just as blogs became poised to tap into a mainstream readership and become a fundamental and daily web technology, the ease of creation and maintenance provided by the new CMS-based blogging software led to such a massive increase in the number of blogs that would-be readers were simply overwhelmed. Rather than filter the internet into manageable or digestible (and entertaining) bits as blogs had heretofore been doing, the blogosphere itself seemed to become as vast and unnavigable as the World Wide Web. Reading blogs became complicated. Since that time (Blood was writing about the scene circa 1999), tools to enable readers to search for blogs of interest have developed. Many blogs acquire readers who have taken their direction from mainstream media reports. With many newspapers featuring "blogwatch" columns, and with their own online components increasingly incorporating blogging in some form (necessarily linking to other blogs), the MSM and blogging are leading readers to each other, in many cases readers who might seek out the *Globe and Mail* directly, but not a blog directly, for example. Otherwise, straightforward internet searches using Google or other tools often yield blogs among their top results, owing to blogs' ever-increasing numerical heft in the broader web ecosystem. Blog-specific search tools have evolved as well, sites ranking and rating various blogs, and offering neophyte readers a sense of the biggest and most popular blogs, as well as the capacity to topic-search only the blogosphere. Within the blogosphere itself, blogrolls and carnivals are self-organized mechanisms of recommendation and a kind of peer-review.

Special-purpose search engines catering to the blogosphere now make finding blog content easier. Google's blog-only search tool (<http://blogsearch.google.com>) uses the same interface as their regular search engine; its familiarity makes it quite popular. A simple Google search using the keyword that describes the content you're looking for, and "blog" as a second term, can also accomplish much the same end. More locally, hosting services like LiveJournal and Blogger also provide search tools, of their own sites, or of the blogosphere more generally. Of blog-specific search tools, though, Technorati is probably the best known. Technorati maintains statistics on the readership and unique page visits of high-profile blogs, and compiles lists of the most popular as well as the most referenced blogs online. It allows also for searching by post content, by blog keyword, or by most-recently-updated. *The Truth Laid Bear* (<http://truthlaidbear.com>), similarly, is a high-profile one-man-show run by the pseudonymous "N. Z. Bear," a computing industry professional who – as a hobby – has developed a system to compile traffic and link statistics for various blogs. It maintains a list of the most popular blogs, as determined by user traffic as well as by links to the blogs from other sites: this list is oft-consulted and very influential. *TTLB* calls its organization of the blogosphere the "ecosystem," and its rankings, as well as those of Technorati, are closely watched both by bloggers themselves as well as by the mainstream media.[3] *TTLB*'s ranking lists can be organized by number of inbound links (which may attest to a blog's authority, working much like the citation index offered in academic databases like Web of Science), or by number of daily visits, a marker of raw popularity. Both lists offer the raw numbers on which the rank is based, direct links to the blog in question, and a link to further details of the ranking, in which graphs show a week's worth of daily statistics on inbound links and page views, as well as a listing of recent posts and links to these posts. One of the strengths of *TTLB*'s system is that it is always current: it bases its rankings only on links and visits from the previous 7–10 days, so mobility in the rankings is widespread and watching the rankings shift is something of a spectator sport. For readers who wish to follow a number of blogs, aggregators like Bloglines (<http://www.bloglines.com>) save the effort of manually checking each site for updates. It allows readers to take advantage of RSS technologies by subscribing to various feeds at any number of blogs, and reading the content all in one place, a dynamic and personalized page where the latest updates are automatically collected and presented.

The blogroll, a sidebar link list pointing outward to other blogs, is the simplest blog filtering tool: it works on the principle that if you like my blog, then you'll probably like these other blogs that I like as well. Blogrolls can even break their lists into categories – this blogroll subset links to other blogs on the topic of knitting; this blogroll subset comprises what I feel to be the "best in show" of the blogosphere; this blogroll subset addresses Mac enthusiasts; this blogroll is comprised of blogs that link to me. Communities of interest are formed in the intersection of blogs in the blogroll. Bloggers have also developed blog "carnivals," regularly appearing, edited, rotating-host digests of submitted blog posts on particular topics. One carnival clearinghouse site links carnivals to print traditions, suggesting that "a Blog Carnival is like a magazine. It has a title, a topic, editors, contributors, and an audience. Editions of the carnival typically come out on a regular basis" ("FAQ"). One of the first was the "Carnival of the Vanities," a collection of well-written and interesting reads culled from the increasingly vast and noise-ridden blogosphere; carnivals now appear on nearly every subject imaginable, from humor to politics to sports to philosophy. According to blogger Bora Zivkovic (2005), successful carnivals share five characteristics: carnivals must "a) have a clearly stated purpose, b) appear with predictable regularity, c) rotate editors, d) have a homepage and archives, and e) have more than one person doing heavy lifting." Zivkovic's criteria are obviously debatable – for example, his criterion of clear and preferably narrow purpose excludes from consideration carnivals like Vanities.

What distinguishes blog carnivals from being simply blog posts – after all, blog posts also by nature and tradition digest and point to articles of interest on the greater internet – are the following characteristics: items appearing in carnivals are submitted to the blogger/editor by their authors; these items are chosen for publication based on their appeal to a wider community/audience and on their adherence to a particular topic, rather than simply reflecting the taste and whim of the carnival editor; posts in a carnival reference only other blog posts, and not other kinds of websites (that is, not personal webpages, or news sites, or organizational press releases, for example). Blog carnivals also, as Zivkovic notes, tend to rotate editors and location: Carnival of Bret Easton Ellis might appear this month on my blog under my editorship, while next month it is hosted by you on yours. Hosting a carnival is an excellent way to attract your target audience to your blog. Some carnivals are archived at third party sites, ensuring that readers can follow an unbroken chain of iterations. Blog carnivals can be located and accessed various ways. Blog Carnival Index (<http://www.blogcarnival.com>) has tracked nearly 4,000 editions of 290 different carnivals, maintaining lists of which carnivals are active, and the submission deadlines and editorial info pertaining to each carnival. It supports browsing and searching for particular carnivals by date updated, carnival name, and by category. Blog Carnival Index also provides forms by which would-be carnival posters and editors can submit their information to the carnivals of their choice, a handy feature that helps to automate what might otherwise become an onerous and time-consuming task. Blog Carnival Index has recently partnered with *The Truth Laid Bear*, and *TTLB*'s "Ubercarnival" lists are based on Blog Carnival data. Blog carnivals have caught on particularly with academic communities – they offer a sort of blogosphere peer-review, in that carnival posts must be submitted to and (increasingly) vetted by an editor before being launched on the world. As the blogosphere expands and the submissions to a carnival exceed its capacity to publish, control of quality and of topic are imposed, leading to a digital publication that more closely resembles the conventions of the dissemination of ideas in print.

Writing

In 1997, according to Rebecca Blood, there were twenty-three blogs – you could follow them all, know the bloggers, and feel a part of a tight-knit community. By 1999, it had become nearly impossible to manually track all the blogs, and new ones began appearing faster than they could be counted or assimilated into the prior community. Since then, writing blogs has become a tremendously popular pastime, to judge from the rate of new blog creation tracked by Technorati – recall their statistic that 75,000 new blogs were being created every day. Pew as well surmised from its research that 11 million American internet users were also bloggers (Rainie 2005). While not all of these blogs remain active over the long or even medium term – the proportion of LiveJournal blogs that are deemed "active" comprise only one-fifth of registered sites on the host – the sheer bulk of new blogs indicates a strong and growing public interest in this form of online expression. As the form has come into its own, with increasingly standard technologies, layouts, interactions, and best practices, blogging has experienced growing pains. Particularly vexing have been issues of responsibility, liability, professionalism, privacy, and decorum – that is to say, we have entered just another digital culture debate! As the blogosphere expanded, the rules of the game within it changed, and the outside world also began to take notice. The relations between the digital and analog worlds seemed strained from the beginning, with liberties taken in the blogosphere harshly addressed outside of it. These intersections between the digital world and the more mundane one we generally inhabit offer fruitful topics for further research.

Notably (and apparently newsworthily, to judge from the MSM coverage of these incidents), many of the first wave of these new bloggers – not computing professionals, not digesting or filtering internet content but rather publishing personal information in diary-style posts on the new CMS blogging software – were distressed to find themselves being fired for their online activities (see Hopkins (2006) for a list, circa 2004).[4] Most of these bloggers seemed to rely on "security by obscurity": that is, thinly disguising their own identities (providing a different name for self and cat, while naming their actual employer, or vice versa) and remaining optimistic that no one they knew would read them, or that anyone would bother to decode their identities. This has not proven an altogether foolproof tactic. As a result, the Electronic Frontier Foundation (2005), acting to increase the liberty and security of netizens on a variety of fronts since 1990, offers an online guide to secure blogging, complete with a step-by-step guide to better anonymization as well as an outline of legal precedent and advice on "how to blog without getting fired". As the EFF notes, "anyone can eventually find your blog if your real identity is tied to it in some way. And there may be consequences," including distraught family members and friends, disturbed potential employers, and litigious current ones. The EFF's guide is a good place for budding bloggers to begin.

Academic bloggers face similar personal and professional pressures when they blog, but are drawn to the form for compelling reasons, among them the opportunities to network with scholars they might not otherwise meet, to avoid academic isolation if theirs is an arcane subspecialty, to test new ideas on a willing expert audience in an informal manner, to ask for help from this same audience, and to keep abreast of colleagues and research. Nevertheless, academic blogging has its detractors. An opinion piece by "Ivan Tribble" for *The Chronicle of Higher Education* in July 2005 (2005a) saw the pseudonymous senior academic opine on the negative impact blogging had on the prospects of job candidates interviewed at his institution: he goes so far as to caution that "the content of the blog may be less worrisome than the fact of the blog itself," a pretty clear denunciation of the very idea of blogging. This column, unsurprisingly, generated a digital outpouring of indignation, most notably on Kirschenbaum's blog. In his response to Tribble's article, Kirschenbaum (2005) challenged his audience to offer up the tangible benefits they had earned from their blogging activities: this is as good and as thoughtful a defense of academic blogging as one is likely to find in this informal medium. Tribble references this blog post and its comments in his follow-up column "They Shoot Messengers, Don't They?"

(2005b). Similar commentary on the *Chronicle*'s Academic Job Forum continues the (somewhat paranoid) debate. However, elsewhere on the *Chronicle*, another essayist describes the blogosphere as "a carnival of ideas" which "provide a kind of space for the exuberant debate of ideas, for connecting scholarship to the outside world" (Farrell 2005). Yet another column, by David D. Perlmutter (2006), who is preparing a book for Oxford University Press on political bogging, proclaims the urgency of the questions "What are blogs? How can we use them? What exactly are they good for?" for students of politics as well as its practitioners. A piece by Robert Boynton (2005) for the "College Week" edition of *Slate* summarizes the professional-concerns response of the academy to blogs and blog culture. Often generating more heat than light, these writings nonetheless indicate the challenge that this particular writing genre poses to the academy, and as with other online practices before it, invigorates the debate about the values as well as the failings of our established pedagogical, research, and collegial practices.

Blogging in Literary Studies

Blogging has its attractions for scholars, as a venue for writing, teaching, and occasionally primary and (more occasionally still) secondary research. Many very worthwhile blogs (particularly in humanities computing, as technophilic a group of early adopters as the humanities and social sciences might hope to nurture) offer information of use to the literary studies community, providing annotated and focused lists of resources and offering opportunities for rich interaction among blog-readers and blog-writers. Popular books on the techniques and social impacts of blogging increasingly abound, as does coverage of the various parts of the blogosphere in the mainstream media. The academic scholarship that studies blogs is slightly thinner on the ground, and has thus far made more appearances in journals (both peer-reviewed and not) and in blogs than in book-length studies. This scholarship can be broken into several categories. Most numerous are the investigations of the intersections between mainstream media – particularly journalistic media – and blogging. Questions of blog-provoked revisions to journalistic practices and ethics, often articulated in the form of a crisis of authority and relevance, appear in the journals devoted to communications studies, journalism, and new media and society (e.g. McIntosh 2005, Robinson 2006). In a similar vein are analyses of the impacts of blog readership and authorship on political processes, particularly in the United States, but also in the context of activist or dissident blogging around the world (e.g. Kerbel and Bloom 2005, Riverbend 2005, Perlmutter 2006).[5] A critical as well as informal literature details experiments with the use of blogging technologies and practices in writing and other pedagogies (e.g. Krause 2004, Ellison and Wu 2006, Tyron 2006; more informal assessments of blogs in teaching can be found on the blogs of teachers who employ them, as well as within class blogs themselves).[6] As well, the literary studies community has begun to examine the links between diary-style blogging and other forms of life writing (e.g. McNeill 2003, Serfaty 2004). Of course, researchers in cyberculture and new media studies are as keen to understand the operations and implications of this new form as they are to participate in shaping it. Online, the Weblog Research on Genre (BROG) Project offers a wealth of research papers as well as lists to other prominent research-oriented sites such as *Into the Blogosphere* (Gurak et al. n.d.). In short, the field of research on, and practice in, blogging is just opening up. Certainly, as YouTube is gobbled up by Google while the mass media hails the internet video age, and as the culture at large clues into youth-oriented social networking sites like Facebook and MySpace, it is clear that blogging's time as media-darling will soon enough draw to a close. But the form is established enough, the needs it meets real enough, its format alluring enough, and its community of practice large enough that bloggers will continue to write and scholars will continue to examine them, likely for a long time to come.

NOTES

1 This informalization and contraction is in keeping with prior digital cultural practice that has seen "World Wide Web" become "web," "electronic mail" become first "e-mail" and then "email," and "Instant Messaging" become "IM," among numerous other examples (see a similar point in Hale and Scanlon 1999: 13–14).

2 Different critics impute different reasons: McIntosh names the South Asian tsunami as a force driving blog readership to new highs (2005: 385); Herring et al. (2005) suggest the "aftermath of 9/11 and ... the 2003 U.S-led invasion of Iraq" drove up blogging participation rates. Most accounts, both popular and academic, seem to privilege journalistic weblogs in their assessments of the increasing "pull" factor of the blogosphere. Viviane Serfaty, however, studying weblogs as an evolution of the earlier web-based online diary, proposes instead that writers in this genre increased greatly upon the appearance of forms-based graphical weblog editors – online diarizing, that is, was a popularizer of the weblog (2004: 458).

3 That a hobby project by one person, named for a pun on its author's pseudonym, and offering sixteen ranking categories ranging from Higher Beings, Mortal Humans, and Playful Primates (highest ranked, by links) through to Wiggly Worms, Multicellular Microorganisms,

and Insignificant Microbes (lowest ranked, by links), reminds us how young and informal the blogosphere is: as "N. Z. Bear" himself remarks of his idiosyncratic ecosystem taxonomy, "Consider it a gentle reminder that this all shouldn't be taken too terribly seriously" (FAQ).

4 The likelihood of getting fired increases with the growth in a given blog's readership, and readership tended to grow on the basis of the entertainment value of a blog, a value generally based on the outrageousness of the posted material. And the material on blogs was certainly not what you might expect from polite or discreet F2F (face-to-face) conversation – composed alone and in private, published under pseudonyms, material in diary blogs often exceeds the bounds of polite conversation, broadcasting to an unknown and potentially limitless audience the intimate details of the blogger's life and experiences. The generic imperatives of the blog form thus seem necessarily to send it into a collision with real-world practices and ethics.

5 My research into journalistic blogs has benefited from Stephanie Radcliffe's work on an Honors Thesis on the topic, for which I acted as advisor.

6 Research by Caroline Leitch undertaken originally for Randy Harris informs this list.

REFERENCES

"The Academic Forum: The Fallout From 'Bloggers Need Not Apply'." *The Chronicle of Higher Education* September 2, 2005: Chronicle Careers.

Bear, N. Z. (n.d.). "FAQ: General and About N. Z." *The Truth Laid Bear.* <http://truthlaidbear.com/FAQ.php>. Accessed October 6, 2006.

Blood, Rebecca (2000, September 7). "Weblogs: A History and Perspective." *Rebecca's Pocket.* <http://www.rebeccablood.net/essays/weblog_history.html.> Accessed June 5, 2006.

—— (2002). "Weblog Ethics." *Rebecca's Pocket.* <http:// www.rebeccablood.net/handbook/excerpts/ weblog_ethics.html>. Accessed June 5, 2006.

Boynton, Robert S. (2005, November 16). "Attack of the Career-Killing Blogs." *Slate.* <http://www.slate.com/id/2130466/nav/tap1/>. Accessed October 6, 2006.

Dube, Jonathan (2003, May 13). "Rebecca Blood on Weblog Ethics." *Cyberjounalist.net.* <http://www.cyberjournalist.net/news/000390.php>. Accessed June 5, 2006.

Electronic Frontier Foundation (2005, April 6; updated 2005, May 31). "How to Blog Safely (About Work or Anything Else." <http://www.eff.org/Privacy/Anonymity/blog-anonymously.php>. Accessed October 6, 2006.

Ellison, Nicole, and Yuehua Wu (2006, April 7). "An Empirical Text of Blogging in the Classroom." HigherEd BlogCon 2006. <http://www.higheredblogcon.com/teaching/ellison/ellison/ellison.html.>

Farrell, Henry (2005). "The Blogosphere As Carnival of Ideas." *The Chronicle of Higher Education* October 7: The Chronicle Review.

Gurak, Laura, Smiljana Antonijevic, Laurie Johnson, Clancy Ratliff, and Jessica Reyman (Eds.). *Into the Blogosphere: Rhetoric, Community, and Culture of Weblogs.* <http://blog.lib.umn.edu/blogosphere/>. Accessed October 9, 2006.

Hale, Constance, and Jessie Scanlon (1999). *Wired Style: Principles of English Usage in the Digital Age*, rev. edn. New York: Broadway Books.

Herring, S. C., L. A. Schreit, S. Bonus, and E. Wright (2005). "Weblogs as a Bridging Genre." *Information, Technology & People* 18.2: 142–71.

Hopkins, Curt (2006, October 8). "Statistics on Fired Bloggers." *Morpheme Tales.* <http:// morphemetales.blogspot.com/2006/10/statistics-on-fired-bloggers.html>. Accessed March 23, 2007.

Kerbel, Matthew R., and Joel David Bloom (2005). "Blog for America and Civic Involvement." *The Harvard International Journal of Press/Politics* 10.4: 3–27.

Kirschenbaum, Matthew G. (2005). "Why I Blog Under My Own Name (and a Modest Proposal)." *MGK* July 9. <http://www.otal.umd.edu/~mgk/blog/archives/000813.html>. Accessed October 6, 2006.

Koh, Andy, Alvin Lim, Ng Ee Soon, Benjamin H. Detenber, and Mark A. Cenite (2005). "Ethics in Blogging." *Weblog Ethics Survey Results* July 18. <http://weblogethics.blogspot.com/2005/07/ethics-in-blogging-2005.html>. Accessed June 5, 2006.

Krause, Steven (2004). "When Blogging Goes Bad: A Cautionary Tale About Blogs, Email Lists, Discussion, and Interaction." *Kairos* 9:1. <http://english.ttu.edu/kairos/9.1/praxis/krause/blog.html>. Accessed October 7, 2006.

LiveJournal. "Statistics." http://www.livejournal.com/stats.bml. Accessed June 5, 2006.

McIntosh, Shawn (2005). "Blogs: Has Their Time Finally Come – or Gone?" *Global Media and Communication* 1.3: 385–88.

McNeill, Laurie (2003). "Teaching an Old Genre New Tricks: The Diary on the Internet." *Biography* 26.1: 24–47.

Merriam Webster Online. "Merriam Webster's Words of the Year 2004." <http://www.m-w.com/info/pr/2004-words-of-year.htm>. Accessed June 5, 2006.

National Institute for Technology in Liberal Education (2003a). "Measuring Weblog Churn Rate." *NITLE Census News* July 29. <http://www.blog-census.net/weblog>. Accessed June 5, 2006.

—— (2003b). "Equal Numbers, Different Interests." *NITLE Census News* August 14. <http://www.blogcensus.net/weblog>. Accessed June 5, 2006.

Perlmutter, David (2006). "Political Blogs: The New Iowa?" *The Chronicle of Higher Education* May 26: The Chronicle Review.

Pyra Labs. "Pyra 2.0." <http://www.pyra.com/>. Accessed June 5, 2006.

Rainie, Lee (2005). "The State of Blogging." Pew Internet and American Life Project.

Riverbend (2005). *Baghdad Burning: Girl Blog from Iraq*. New York: Feminist Press at City University of New York.

Robinson, Susan (2006). "The Mission of the j-blog: Recapturing Journalistic Authority Online." *Journalism* 7.1: 65–83.

Serfaty, Viviane (2004). "Online Diaries: Towards a Structural Approach." *Journal of American Studies* 38.3: 457–71.

Technorati. "About Us." <http://www.technorati.com/about>. Accessed October 7, 2006.

Tribble, Ivan (2005a). "Bloggers Need Not Apply." *The Chronicle of Higher Education* July 8.

—— (2005b). "They Shoot Messengers, Don't They?" *The Chronicle of Higher Education* September 2: Chronicle Careers.

Twohey, Megan (2005). "Marquette Suspends Dental Student for Blog Comments." *JSOnline: Milwaukee Journal Sentinel* December 5.

Tyron, Charles (2006). "Writing and Citizenship: Using Blogs to Teach First-Year Composition." *Pedagogy* 6.1: 128–32.

Weblog Research on Genre Project. "Weblog Research on Genre, Gender, Audience, and Social Networks." <http://www.blogninja.com/>. Accessed October 9, 2006.

Williams, Jeremy B. and Joanne Jacobs (2004). "Exploring the Use of Blogs as Learning Spaces in the Higher Education Sector." *Australasian Journal of Educational Technology* 20.2: 232–47.

Zivkovic, Bora (2005). "Blog Carnivals and the Future of Journalism." *Science and Politics* June 1. <http://sciencepolitics.blogspot.com/2005/06/blog-carnivals-and-future-of.html>. Accessed October 6, 2006.

Blogs discussed

Powell, Julie. *The Julie/Julia Project*. <http://blogs.salon.com/0001399/2002/08/25.html>. Accessed October 1, 2006.

Gillmor, Dan. "Dan Gillmor's Blog." *Backfence.com – Palo Alto Ca. local news, information, events and Advertising*. <http://sf.backfence.com/news/newsList.cfm?myComm=PA&tid=51>. Accessed October 1, 2006.

Walker, Jill. *jill/txt*. <http://jilltxt.net/>. Accessed October 1, 2006.

Kirschenbaum, Matthew G. *MGK*. <http://www.otal.umd.edu/~mgk/blog/>. Accessed October 1, 2006.

Chronicle of Higher Education. *The Chronicle: Daily News Blog*. <http://chronicle.com/news/>. Accessed October 1, 2006.

Chronicle of Higher Education. *The Chronicle: Wired Campus Blog*. <http://chronicle.com/wiredcampus>. Accessed October 1, 2006.

Vanegas, Trent. *Pink is the New Blog | Fingers Firmly on the Pulse*. <http://trent.blogspot.com>. Accessed October 1, 2006.

Coen, Jessica (Ed.). *Gawker: Manhattan Media News and Gossip*. <http://www.gawker.com>. Accessed October 1, 2006.

Drudge, Matt. *The Drudge Report*. <http://www.drudgereport.com/>. Accessed June 5, 2006.

The Blog | The Huffington Post. <http://www.huffingtonpost.com/theblog/>. Accessed June 5, 2006.

Go Fug Yourself. <http://gofugyourself.typepad.com>. Accessed June 5, 2006.

Moulitsas Zuniga, Markos. *Daily Kos: State of the Nation*. <http://www.dailykos.com/>. Accessed June 5, 2006.

Marshall, Joshua Michael. *Talking Points Memo*. <http://www.talkingpointsmemo.com/>. Accessed June 5, 2006.

Democracy for America. *Blog for America*. <http://www.blogforamerica.com/>. Accessed June 5, 2006.

Hinderaker, John, Scott Johnson, and Paul Mirengoff. *Power Line*. <http://www.powerlineblog.com/>. Accessed June 5, 2006.

"NK." *New Kid on the Hallway*. <http://newkidonthehallway.typepad.com/>. Accessed June 5, 2006.

"The Professor." *Rate Your Students*. <http://rateyourstudents.blogspot.com/>. Accessed June 5, 2006.

Drezner, Daniel W. *Daniel W. Drezner :: Blog*. <http://www.danieldrezner.com/blog/>. Accessed June 5, 2006.

Flanagan, Mary, Michael Mateas, Nick Montfort, Scott Rettberg, Andrew Stern, and Noah Wardrip-Fruin. *Grand Text Auto*. <http://grandtextauto.gatech.edu/>. Accessed June 5, 2006.

Liberman, Mark. Language Log. <http://itre.cis.upenn.edu/~myl/languagelog/>. Accessed June 5, 2006.

Diaryland. <http://www.diaryland.com/>.
Movable Type. <http://www.sixapart.com/movabletype/>.

Blog service providers discussed

Blogger. <http://www.blogger.com/start>.
LiveJournal. <http://www.livejournal.com>.
Typepad. <http://www.sixapart.com/typepad/>.

Radio Userland. <http://radio.userland.com/>.
WordPress. <http://wordpress.org>.

Part IV
Methodologies

21

Knowing . . . : Modeling in Literary Studies[1]

Willard McCarty

When the understanding of scientific models and archetypes comes to be regarded as a reputable part of scientific culture, the gap between the sciences and the humanities will have been partly filled. For exercise of the imagination, with all its promises and its dangers, provides a common ground. (Max Black, *Models and Metaphors* (1962): 242f)

Introduction

At the beginning of their important book, *Understanding Computers and Cognition*, Terry Winograd and Fernando Flores declare that, "All new technologies develop within a background of tacit understanding of human nature and human work. The use of technology in turn leads to fundamental changes in what we do, and ultimately what it is to be human. We encounter deep questions of design when we recognize that in designing tools we are designing ways of being" (1987: xi).

Because of computing, Brown and Duguid note in *The Social Life of Information*, "We are all, to some extent, designers now" (2000: 4). For us no qualification is necessary, especially so because of our commitment to a computing that is *of* as well as *in* the humanities. So, Winograd and Flores' question is ours: what ways of being *do* we have in mind? And since we are scholars, this question is also, perhaps primarily, what ways of knowing do we have in hand? What is the epistemology of our practice?

Two years after the book by Winograd and Flores, two scholarly outsiders were invited to the first joint conference of the Association for Computers and the Humanities (ACH) and Association for Literary and Linguistic Computing (ALLC) to comment on our work as it then was: the archaeological theoretician Jean-Claude

Gardin and the literary critic Northrop Frye. Their agreement about the central aspect of computing for the humanities and their implicit divergence over how best to apply it provide the starting point for this chapter and my own response to the epistemological question just raised.

Both Gardin, in "On the ways we think and write in the humanities" (1991), and Frye, in "Literary and mechanical models" (1991), roughly agree on two matters:

1. Quantitative gains in the amount of scholarly data available and accessible are with certain qualifications a Good Thing – but not the essential thing. Gardin compares the building of large resources to the great encyclopedia projects, which he regards as intellectually unimportant. (Perhaps this is a blindness of the time: it is now quite clear that the epistemological effects of these large resources are profound, though they clearly do not suit his interests and agenda.)

   Frye is less dismissive. He notes that the mechanically cumulative or "Wissenschaft" notion of scholarship now has a machine to do it better than we can. But like Gardin his focus is elsewhere, namely –

2. Qualitatively better work, proceeding from a *principled* basis within each of the disciplines. This is the central point of computing to both Gardin and Frye: work that is disciplined, i.e., distinguishable from the intelligent but unreliable opinion of the educated layperson.

   Gardin takes what he calls a "scientific" approach to scholarship, which means reduction of scholarly argument to a Turing-machine calculus, then use of simulation to test the strength of arguments.

   Frye's interest is in studying the archetypes or "recurring conventional units" of literature; he directs attention to computer modeling techniques as the way to pursue this study.

Thus both scholars propose computing as a means of working toward a firmer basis for humanities scholarship. Gardin refers to "simulation," Frye to "modeling." Both of these rather ill-defined terms share a common epistemological sense: use of a likeness to gain knowledge of its original. We can see immediately why computing should be spoken of in these terms, as it represents knowledge of things in manipulable form, thus allows us to simulate or model these things. Beyond the commonsense understanding, however, we run into serious problems of definition and so must seek help.

My intention here is to summarize the available help, chiefly from the history and philosophy of the natural sciences, especially physics, where most of the relevant work is to be found. I concentrate on the term "modeling" because that is the predominate term in scientific practice – but it is also, perhaps even by nature, the term around which meanings I find the most useful tend to cluster. I will then give an extended example from humanities computing and discuss the epistemological implications. Finally I will return to Jean-Claude Gardin's very different agenda, what he calls "the logicist programme," and to closely allied questions of knowledge representation in artificial intelligence.

Modeling

As noted, I turn to the natural sciences for wisdom on modeling because that's where the most useful form of the idea originates. Its usefulness to us is, I think, because of the kinship between the chiefly equipment-oriented practices of the natural sciences and those of humanities computing. Here I summarize briefly an argument I have made elsewhere at length (2005: 20–72).

Here I must be emphatic: I am not suggesting in any way that the humanities emulate these sciences, nor that humanities computing become a science, nor that the humanities will take on scientific qualities through computing. My argument is that we can learn from what philosophers and historians have had to say about experimental practice in the natural sciences because humanities computing is, like them, an equipment-oriented field of enquiry. It thus provides, I will suggest later, access to a common ground of concerns.

The first interesting point to be made is that despite its prevalence and deep familiarity in the natural sciences, a consensus on modeling is difficult to achieve. Indeed, modeling is hard to conceptualize. There is "no model of a model," the Dutch physicist H. J. Groenewold declares (1961: 98), and the American philosopher Peter Achinstein warns us away even from attempting a systematic theory (1968: 203). Historians and philosophers of science, including both of these, have tried their best to anatomize modeling on the basis of the only reliable source of evidence – namely actual scientific practice. But this is precisely what makes the conceptual difficulty significant: modeling grows out of practice, not out of theory, and so is rooted in stubbornly tacit knowledge – i.e., knowledge that is not merely unspoken but may also be unspeakable. The ensuing struggle to understand its variety yields some useful distinctions, as Achenstein says. The fact of the struggle itself points us in turn to larger questions in the epistemology of practice – to which I will return.

The most basic distinction is, in Clifford Geertz's terms, between "an 'of' sense and a 'for' sense" of modeling (1993/1973: 93). A model *of* something is an exploratory device, a more or less "poor substitute" for the real thing (Groenewold 1961: 98). We build such models-of because the object of study is inaccessible or intractable, like poetry or subatomic whatever-they-are. In contrast a model *for* something is a design, exemplary ideal, archetype or other guiding preconception. Thus we construct a model *of* an airplane in order to see how it works; we design a model *for* an airplane to guide its construction. A crucial point is that both kinds are *imagined*, the former out of a pre-existing reality, the latter into a world that doesn't yet exist, as a plan for its realization.

In both cases, as Russian sociologist Teodor Shanin has argued, the product is an ontological hybrid: models, that is, bridge subject and object, consciousness and existence, theory and empirical data (1972: 9). They comprise a practical means of playing out the consequences of an idea in the real world. Shanin goes on to argue that models-of allow the researcher to negotiate the gulf between a "limited and selective consciousness" on the one hand and "the unlimited complexity and 'richness' of the object" on the other (1972: 10). This negotiation happens, Shanin notes, "by purposeful simplification and by transformation of the object of study inside consciousness itself." In other words, a model-of is made in a consciously simplifying act of interpretation. Although this kind of model is not necessarily a physical object, the goal of simplification is to make *tractable* or *manipulable* what the modeler regards as interesting about it.

A fundamental principle for modeling-of is the exact correspondence between model and object with respect to the webs of relationships among the selected elements in each. Nevertheless, such *isomorphism* (as it is called) may be violated deliberately in order to study the consequences. In addition to distortions, a model-of may also require "properties of convenience," such as the mechanism by which a model airplane is suspended in a wind-tunnel. Thus a model-of is fictional not only by being a representation, and so not the thing itself, but also by selective omission and perhaps by distortion and inclusion as well.

Taxonomies of modeling differ, as noted. Among philosophers and historians of science there seems rough agreement on a distinction between theoretical and physical kinds, which are expressed in language and material form respectively (Black 1962: 229). Computational modeling, like thought-experiment, falls somewhere between these two, since it uses language but is more or less constrained by characteristics of the medium of its original.

From physical modeling we can usefully borrow the notion of the "study" or "tinker-toy" model – a crude device knowingly applied out of convenience or necessity (Achinstein 1968: 209). Indeed, in the humanities modeling seems as a matter of principle to be crude, "a stone adze in the hands of a cabinetmaker," as Vannevar Bush said (Bush 1967: 92). This is not to argue against progress, which is real enough for technology, rather that deferral of the hard questions as solutions inevitably to be realized – a rhetorical move typical in computing circles – is simply irresponsible.

Theoretical modeling, constrained only by language, is apt to slip from a consciously makeshift, heuristic approximation to hypothesized reality. Black notes that in such *"existential use of modeling"* the researcher works *"through* and by means of" a model to produce a formulation of the world as it actually is (1962: 228f). In other words, a theoretical model can blur into a theory. But our thinking will be muddled unless we keep "theory" and "model" distinct as concepts. Shanin notes that modeling may be useful, appropriate, stimulating, and significant – but by definition never true (1972: 11). It is, again, a pragmatic strategy for coming to know. How it contrasts with theory depends, however, on your philosophical position. There are two major ones.

To the realist theories are true. As we all know, however, theories are overturned. To the realist, when this happens – when in a moment of what Thomas Kuhn called "extraordinary science" a new theory reveals an old one to be a rough approximation of the truth (as happened to Newtonian mechanics about 100 years ago) – the old theory becomes a model and so continues to be useful.

To the anti-realist, such as the historian of physics Nancy Cartwright, the distinction collapses. As she says elegantly in her "simulacrum account" of physical reality, *How the Laws of Physics Lie*, "the model is the theory of the phenomenon" (1983: 159). Since we in the humanities are anti-realists with respect to our theories (however committed we may be to them politically), her position is especially useful: it collapses the distinction between theory and theoretical model, leaving us to deal only with varieties of modeling. This, it should be noted, also forges a link between on our terms between humanities computing and the theorizing activities in the various disciplines.

Since modeling is pragmatic, the worth of a model must be judged by its fruitfulness. The principle of isomorphism means, however, that for a model-of, this fruitfulness is meaningful in proportion to the "goodness of the fit" between model and original, as Black points out (1962: 238). But at the same time, more than a purely instrumental value obtains. A model-of is not constructed directly from its object; rather, as a bridge between theory and empirical data, the model participates in both, as Shanin says. In consequence a good model can be fruitful in two ways: either by fulfilling our expectations, and so strengthening its theoretical basis, or by violating them, and so bringing that basis into question. I argue that from the research perspective of the model, in the context of the humanities, failure to give us what we expect is by far the more important result, however unwelcome surprises may be to granting agencies. This is so because, as the philosopher of history R. G. Collingwood has said, "Science in general . . . does not consist in collecting what we already know and arranging it in this or that kind of pattern. It consists in fastening upon something we do not know, and trying to discover it. . . . That is why *all science begins from the knowledge of our own ignorance*: not our ignorance of everything, but our ignorance of some definite thing . . ." (1993/1946: 9). When a good model fails to give us what we expect, it does precisely this: it points to "our ignorance of some definite thing."

The rhetoric of modeling begins, Achinstein suggests, with analogy – in Dr Johnson's words, "resemblance of things with regard to some circumstances or effects." But as Black has pointed out, the existential tendency in some uses of modeling pushes it from the weak statement of likeness in simile toward the strong assertion of identity in metaphor. We know that metaphor paradoxically asserts identity by declaring difference: "Joseph is a fruitful bough" was Frye's favorite example. Metaphor is then characteristic not of theory to the realist, for whom the paradox is meaningless, but of the theoretical model to the anti-realist, who in a simulacrum-account of the world will tend to think paradoxically. This is, of course, a slippery slope.

But it is also a difficult thought, so let me try again. Driven as we are by the epistemological imperative, *to know*; constrained (as in Plato's cave or before St Paul's enigmatic mirror) to know only poor simulacra of an unreachable reality – but aware somehow that they are shadows *of* something – our faith is that as the shadowing (or call it modeling) gets better, it approaches the metaphorical discourse of the poets.

If we are on the right track, as Max Black says at the end of his essay, "some interesting consequences follow for the relations between the sciences and the humanities," namely their convergence (1962: 242f). I would argue that the humanities really must meet the sciences half-way, on the common ground that lies between, and that we have in humanities computing a means to do so.

In Humanities Computing: an Example

Let me suggest how this might happen by giving an example of modeling from my own work modeling personification in the Roman poet Ovid's profoundly influential epic, the *Metamorphoses*. Personification – "the change of things to persons" by rhetorical means, as Dr Johnson said – is central to Ovid's relentless subversion of order. His primary use of this literary trope is not through the fully personified characters, such as Envy (in book 2), Hunger (in book 8) and Rumor (in book 12), rather through the momentary, often incomplete stirrings toward the human state. These figures are contained within single phrases or a few lines of the poem; they vanish almost as soon as they appear. Many if not most of the approximately 500 instances of these tend to go unnoticed. But however subtle, their effects are profound.

Unfortunately, little of the scholarship written since classical times, including James Paxson's study of 1994, helps at the minute level at which these operate. In 1963, however, the medievalist Morton Bloomfield indicated an empirical way forward by calling for a "grammatical" approach to the problem. He made the simple but profoundly consequential observation that nothing is personified independently of its context, only when something ontologically unusual is predicated of it. Thus Dr Johnson's example, "Confusion *heard* his voice." A few other critics responded to the call, but by the early 1980s the trail seems to have gone cold. It did so, I think, because taking it seriously turned out to involve a forbidding amount of *Sitzfleisch*. Not to put too fine a point on it, the right technology was not then conveniently to hand.

It is now, of course: software furnishes a practical means for the scholar to record, assemble, and organize a large number of suitably minute observations, to which all the usual scholarly criteria apply. That much is obvious. But seeing the methodological forest requires us to step back from the practical trees. The question is, what kind of data-model best suits the situation? Unfortunately, the two primary requirements of modeling literature – close contact with the text, and rapid reworking of whatever model one has at a given moment – are not well satisfied by the two obvious kinds of software, namely text-encoding and relational database design. The former keeps one close to the text but falls short on the manipulatory tools; the latter supplies those tools but at the cost of great distance from the text. (Given a choice, the latter is preferable, but clearly the right data-model for this kind of work remains to be designed.) The lesson to be learned here, while we stumble along with ill-suited tools, is that taking problems in the humanities seriously is the way forward toward better tools. Adding features or flexibilities to existing tools is not.

But let us notice where we are with the literary problem. We begin with a theoretical model of personification – let us call it **T** – suitable to the poem. **T** assumes a conventional *scala naturae*, or what Arthur Lovejoy taught us to call "the great chain of being," in small steps or links from inanimate matter to humanity. In response to the demands of the *Metamorphoses* personification is defined within **T** as *any* shift up the chain to *or toward* the human state. Thus **T** focuses, unusually, on ontological change per se, not achievement of a recognizable human form. **T** incorporates the Bloomfield hypothesis but says nothing more specific about how any such shift is marked. With **T** in mind, then, we build a model by analyzing personifications according to the linguistic factors that affect their poetic ontology.

But what are these factors? On the grammatical level the most obvious, perhaps, is the verb that predicates a human action to a non-human entity, as in Dr Johnson's example. But that is not all, nor is it a simple matter: different kinds of entities have different potential for ontological disturbance (abstract nouns are the most sensitive); verbs are only one way of predicating action, and action only one kind of personifying agent; the degree to which an originally human quality in a word is active or fossilized varies; and finally, the local and global contexts of various kinds affect all of these in problematic ways. It is, one is tempted to say, all a matter of context, but as Jonathan Culler points out, "one cannot oppose text to context, as if context were something other than more text, for context is itself just as complex and in need of interpretation" (1988: 93f).

Heuristic modeling rationalizes the ill-defined notion of context into a set of provisional but exactly specified factors through a recursive cycle. It goes like this. Entity X seems to be personified; we identify factors A, B, and C provisionally; we then encounter entity Y, which seems not to qualify even though it has A, B, and C; we return to X to find previously overlooked factor D; elsewhere entity Z is personified but has only factors B and D, so A and C are provisionally downgraded or set aside; and so on. The process thus gradually converges on a more or less stable phenomenology of personification. This phenomenology is a model according to the classical criteria: it is representational, fictional, tractable, and pragmatic. It is a computational model because the analysis that defines it obeys two fundamental rules: total explicitness and absolute consistency. Thus everything to be modeled must be explicitly represented, and it must be represented in exactly the same way every time.

The imaginative language of poetry doesn't survive well under such a regime. But this is only what we expect from modeling, during which (as Teodor Shanin said) the "limited and selective consciousness" of the modeler comes up against "the unlimited complexity and 'richness' of the object." In the case of poetry the result can only be a model of the tinker-toy variety, Vannevar Bush's "stone adze in the hands of a cabinetmaker." Nevertheless, with care, scholarly furniture may be made with this adze. In return for "suspension of ontological unbelief," as Black said about models generally (1962: 228), modeling gives us manipulatory power over the data of personification. With such a model we can then engage in the second-order modeling of these data by adjusting the factors and their weightings, producing different results and raising new questions. The model can be exported to other texts, tried out on them in a new round of recursive modeling, with the aim of producing a more inclusive model, or a better questions about personification from which a better model may be constructed. This is really the normal course of modeling in the sciences as well: the working model begins to converge on the theoretical model.

At the same time, Edward Sapir famously remarked, "All grammars leak" (1921: 47). The failures of the model – the anomalous cases only special pleading would admit – are the leaks that reflect questioningly back on the theoretical model of the *Metamorphoses* and so challenge fundamental research. They point, again as Collingwood said, to our ignorance of a particular thing.

This is, I think, what can now come of what Northrop Frye had in mind, when he suggested in 1989 that were he writing the *Anatomy of Criticism* afresh he'd be paying a good deal of attention to computational modeling.

Experimental Practice

As I have defined and illustrated it, modeling implies the larger environment of experimentation and so raises the question of what this is and what role it might have in the humanities. I have argued elsewhere that our heuristic use of equipment, in modeling, stands to benefit considerably from the intellectual kinship this use has with the experimental sciences (McCarty 2002). Since Paul Feyerabend's attack on the concept of a unitary scientific method in *Against Method* (1975) and Ian Hacking's foundational philosophy of experiment in *Representing and Intervening* (1983), two powerful ideas have been ours for the thinking: (1) experiment is an epistemological practice of its own, related to but not dependent on theory; and (2) experiment is not simply heuristic but, in the words the literary critic Jerome McGann borrowed famously from Lisa Samuels, is directed to "imagining what we don't know" (2001: 105ff), i.e., to making new knowledge. This is the face that modeling turns to the future, that which I have called the "model-for," but which must be understood in Hacking's interventionist sense.

In the context of the physical sciences, Hacking argues that we make hypothetical things real by learning how to manipulate them; thus we model-for them existentially in Black's sense. But is this a productive way to think about what happens with computers in the humanities? If it is, then in what sense are the hypothetical things of the humanities realized? – for example, the "span" in corpus linguistics; the authorial patterns John Burrows, Wayne McKenna, and others demonstrate through statistical analysis of the commonest words; Ian Lancashire's repetends; my own evolving phenomenology of personification. Ontologically, where do such entities fit between the reality of the object on the one hand and the fiction of the theoretical model on the other? They are not theoretical models. What are they?

Models-for do not have to be such conscious things. They can be the serendipitous outcome of play or of accident. What counts in these cases, Hacking notes, is not observation but being observant, attentive not simply to anomalies but to the fact that something is fundamentally, significantly anomalous – a bit of a more inclusive reality intruding into business as usual.

Knowledge Representation and the Logicist Program

The conception of modeling I have developed here on the basis of practice in the physical sciences gives us a crude but useful machine with its crude but useful tools and a robust if theoretically unattached epistemology. It assumes a transcendent, imperfectly accessible reality for the artifacts we study, recognizes the central role of tacit knowledge in humanistic ways of knowing them and, while giving us unprecedented means for systematizing these ways, is pragmatically anti-realist about them. Its fruits are manipulatory control of the modeled data and, by reducing the reducible to mechanical form, identification of new horizons for research.

Jean-Claude Gardin's logicist program, argued in his 1989 lecture and widely elsewhere, likewise seeks to reduce the reducible – in his case, through field-related logics to reduce humanistic discourse to a Turing-machine calculus so that the strength of particular arguments may be tested against expert systems that embed these structures. His program aims to explore, as he says, "where the frontier lies between that part of our interpretative constructs which follows the principles of scientific reasoning and another part which ignores or rejects them" (1990: 26). This latter part, which does not fit logicist criteria, is to be relegated to the realm of literature, i.e., dismissed from scholarship, or what he calls "the science of professional hermeneuticians" (1990: 28). It is the opposite of modeling in the sense that it regards conformity to logical formalizations as the goal rather than a useful but intellectually trivial byproduct of research. Whereas modeling treats the ill-fitting residue of formalization as meaningfully problematic and problematizing, logicism exiles it – and that, I think, is the crucial point.

The same point is emerges from the subfield of AI known as "knowledge representation," whose products instantiate the expertise at the heart of expert systems. In the words of John Sowa, KR (as it is known in the trade) plays "the role of midwife in bringing knowledge forth and making it explicit," or more precisely, it displays "the implicit knowledge about a subject in a form that programmers can encode in algorithms and data structures" (2000: xi). The claim of KR is very strong, namely to encode all knowledge in logical form. "Perhaps," Sowa remarks in his book on the subject, "there are some kinds of knowledge that cannot be expressed in logic." Perhaps, indeed. "But if such knowledge exists," he continues, "it cannot be represented or manipulated on any digital computer in any other notation" (2000: 12).

He is, of course, correct to the extent that KR comprises a far more rigorous and complete statement of the computational imperatives I mentioned earlier. We must therefore take account of it. But again the problematic and problematizing residue is given short shrift. It is either dismissed offhandedly in a "perhaps" or omitted by design: the first principle of KR defines a representation as a "surrogate," with no recognition of the discrepancies between stand-in and original. This serves the goals of aptly named "knowledge engineering" but not those of science, both in the common and etymological senses. The assumptions of KR are profoundly consequential because, the philosopher Michael Williams has pointed out, "'know' is a success-term like 'win' or 'pass' (a test). Knowledge is not just a factual state or condition but a particular *normative status*." "Knowledge" is therefore a term of judgment; projects, like KR, which demarcate it "amount to proposals for a map of culture: a guide to what forms of discourse are 'serious' and what are not" (2001: 11–12). So again the point made by Winograd and Flores: "that in designing tools we are designing ways of being" and knowing.

I have used the term "relegate" repeatedly: I am thinking of the poet Ovid, whose legal sentence of *relegatio*, pronounced by Augustus Caesar, exiled him to a place so far from Rome that he would never again hear his beloved tongue spoken. I think that what is involved in our admittedly less harsh time is just as serious.

But dangerous to us only if we miss the lesson of modeling and mistake the artificial for the real. "There is a pernicious tendency in the human mind," Frye remarked in his 1989 lecture, "to externalize its own inventions, pervert them into symbols of objective mastery over us by alien forces. The wheel, for example, was perverted into a symbolic wheel of fate or fortune, a remorseless cycle carrying us helplessly around with it" (1991: 10). Sowa, who has a keen historical sense, describes in *Knowledge Representation* the thirteenth-century Spanish philosopher Raymond Lull's mechanical device for automated reasoning, a set of concentric wheels with symbols imprinted on them. We must beware that we do not pervert our wheels of logic into "symbols of objective mastery" over ourselves but use them to identify what they cannot compute. Their failures and every other well-crafted error we make are exactly the point, so that (now to quote the Bard precisely) we indeed are "Minding true things by what their mock'ries be" (*Henry V* iv.53).

Note

1 This essay is a substantial revision of a plenary address delivered at the conference of the Consortium for Computers in the Humanities/Consortium pour ordinateurs en sciences humaines (COSH/COCH), May 26, 2002, at Victoria College, University of Toronto, and subsequently published in *Text Technology* 12.1 (2003) and *Computers in the Humanities Working Papers* A.25.

References

Achinstein, Peter (1968). *Concepts of Science: A Philosophical Analysis*. Baltimore MD: Johns Hopkins Press.

Black, Max (1962). *Models and Metaphors: Studies in Language and Philosophy*. Ithaca, NY: Cornell University Press.

Brown, John Seely, and Paul Duguid (2000). *The Social Life of Information*. Boston MA: Harvard Business School Press.

Bush, Vannevar (1967). "Memex Revisited." In *Science is Not Enough*. New York: William Morrow and Company, pp. 75–101.

Cartwright, Nancy (1983). *How the Laws of Physics Lie*. Oxford: Clarendon Press.

Collingwood, R. G. (1993 [1946]). *The Idea of History*, rev. edn. (Ed. Jan van der Dussen). Oxford: Oxford University Press.

Culler, Jonathan (1988). *Framing the Sign: Criticism and its Institutions*. Oxford: Basil Blackwell.

Feyerabend, Paul K. (1993 [1975]). *Against Method*, 3rd edn. London: Verso.

Frye, Northrop (1991). "Literary and Mechanical Models." In Ian Lancashire (Ed.). *Research in Humanities Computing 1. Selected Papers from the 1989 ACH-ALLC Conference*. Oxford: Clarendon Press, pp. 3–12.

Gardin, Jean-Claude (1990). "L'interprétation dans les humanités: réflexions sur la troisième voie/Interpretation in the humanities: some thoughts on the third way." In Richard Ennals and Jean-Claude Gardin (Eds.). *Interpretation in the Humanities: Perspectives from Artificial Intelligence*. Boston Spa: British Library Publications, pp. 22–59.

—— (1991). "On the Way We Think and Write in the Humanities: A Computational Perspective." In Ian Lancashire (Ed.). *Research in Humanities Computing 1. Papers from the 1989 ACH-ALLC Conference*. Oxford: Clarendon Press, pp. 337–45.

Geertz, Clifford (1993 [1973]). *The Interpretation of Cultures: Selected Essays*. London: Fontana Press.

Groenewold, H. J. (1961). "The Model in Physics." In Hans Freudenthal (Ed.). *The Concept and the Role of the Model in Mathematics and Natural and Social Sciences*. Dordrecht: D. Reidel, pp. 98–103.

Hacking, Ian (1983). *Representing and Intervening: Introductory Topics in the Philosophy of Natural Science*. Cambridge: Cambridge University Press.

McCarty, Willard (2002). "A Network with a Thousand Entrances: Commentary in an Electronic Age?" In Roy K. Gibson and Christina Shuttleworth Kraus (Eds.). *The Classical Commentary: Histories, Practices, Theory*. Leiden: Brill, pp. 359–402.

—— (2005). *Humanities Computing*. Basingstoke: Palgrave.

McGann, Jerome (2001). *Radiant Textuality: Literature after the World Wide Web*. New York: Palgrave.

Sapir, Edward. 1921. *Language: An Introduction to Speech*. New York: Harcourt, Brace and World.

Shanin, Teodor (1972). "Models in Thought." In Teodor Shanin (Ed.). *Rules of the Game: Cross-Disciplinary Essays on Models in Scholarly Thought*. London: Tavistock, pp. 1–22.

Sowa, John F. (2000). *Knowledge Representation: Logical, Philosophical, and Computational Foundations*. Pacific Grove CA: Brooks/Cole.

Williams, Michael (2001). *Problems of Knowledge: A Critical Introduction to Epistemology*. Oxford: Oxford University Press.

Winograd, Terry, and Fernando Flores (1987). *Understanding Computers and Cognition: A New Foundation for Design*. Boston: Addison-Wesley.

22
Digital and Analog Texts
John Lavagnino

We have all been asked in the past few decades to consider the advances offered in our lives by digital sound and image recording. Some must have felt that listening, seeing, and reading didn't always seem so different in this digital world when compared to the analog world; that a change that goes all the way down to the most fundamental aspects of representation ought to be more noticeable. Is this distinction between two modes of representation something fundamental that matters for how we read and interpret? Much of the talk of digital and analog comes from work on cybernetics and cognitive science; are these fundamental categories of thought that shape our experiences?

My approach to these questions is through the history of their use in twentieth-century engineering, cybernetics, and cognitive science. It is a history of metaphorical transfers, in which conceptual tools from one field are reused in others, and along with the spur to thought comes the potential for error. As I will show, the origin of the digital/analog distinction is in the practicalities of building machinery rather than in the fundamental nature of things. And the significance of the distinction also depends on the context. In the realm of engineering, the concepts of digital and analog are exact descriptions of how machinery is designed to operate; in studies of the body and brain, some functions may fit one category or the other, but the whole picture does not contain the same kind of sharp definitions and boundaries; and in the realm of cultural productions, some common practices may be usefully related to these concepts, but many other practices do not abide by those boundaries.

The concepts of digital and analog are helpful to readers and interpreters of texts insofar as they can help us describe some practices in the use of texts more precisely. But these concepts do not control the way texts work, nor do they exhaust the range of things texts can do. Systems are digital or analog because they were designed to act that way; the concepts are less pertinent for application to a system without overt design, explicit boundaries, or rules for interpretation.

Digital and Analog Systems

The common habit is to refer to *data* as being digital or analog; but it is only as a property of whole *systems* that the terms are meaningful. A body of data in either form means nothing outside the system that is engineered to perform operations on it. References to digital and analog data suggest that this is an essential property of such data, when it is instead a way to describe how the systems using such data are built to work.

John Haugeland's definitions of digital and analog devices remain the best, and are those I will follow. His principal point about digital devices is that they are based on data defined so that it can be copied exactly: such a system can read, write, and transfer data with perfect preservation of exactly the same content. That is achieved by defining a closed set of distinct tokens that may appear, and requiring all data to be a sequence of such tokens; in most present-day computer systems these basic tokens are bits that may be either 0 or 1 and nothing else, but a system may be based on many more values. (Some early computer systems were intrinsically decimal, for example; and a three-valued notation is more efficient for storage than binary [Hayes 2001].) A copy of digital data is indistinguishable from the original, and within digital computer systems such copying happens with great frequency: the reliability of copying in such systems is not a potential property but one that is exercised constantly. Analog systems involve continuous ranges, not discrete ones: there could always be more gradations between two selected values on a scale. Analog data cannot be copied perfectly, so the criterion in building an analog system is not making perfect copying happen every time, but reducing the accumulation of error and minor changes. The *n*th-generation-copy problem is a problem of an analog system; a digital system must be designed so that it doesn't have that problem in the slightest degree.

Analog and digital systems embody different sorts of rules for interpretation of data, but they are both built on rules, and the data they process is defined in terms of those rules. Removed from the systems and from the rules for interpretation, the data may also change from analog to digital or vice versa. A famous example due to Nelson Goodman is the clock dial: this looks like an analog system, because you can read off the time to any degree of precision in measuring the position of the hands. In actual practice, we often treat this as a digital device, and only read it to full minutes. The clock might have a digital or an analog mechanism, which affects whether the information is really there to be measured at arbitrary precision. But in any case, this stage of interpretation of something outside the system is an occasion when information often changes from digital to analog or vice versa.

A system of either type cannot regard the data as stable and unproblematic; both digital and analog systems must be engineered to preserve the data. We have some familiarity with that effort from daily life when using analog systems: here again, practical familiarity with operations such as photocopying gives us the intuition that an analog copy may be better or worse and that some effort can improve the result.

In analog systems, the crucial need is to avoid introducing noise as data moves about within the system. In computer systems the provisions for keeping data stable are internal and rarely visible to users, but they are there all the same. In discussions of computing it's common to read that switches are either on or off and therefore digital bits naturally have two values, 0 or 1; this analogy seems to go back to an essay by Alan Turing, but Turing's point that it is a simplified picture is usually omitted (1950: 439). The simplification is flatly wrong about how present-day computers actually work, since they use high and low voltages and not open or closed circuits, and their circuitry at many points works to push signals to the high or low extremes, and away from the intermediate range where one value could be mistaken for another. (Hillis 1998 is one of the rare popular accounts of computer hardware that touches on these provisions.) Peter Gutmann's account of the problems of erasing hard disk drives helps to illustrate the work behind the scenes to produce those perfect bits, a complex but ultimately very reliable process – and also the possibility of studying the history of what a drive has stored if you analyze it using analog equipment:

> ... truly deleting data from magnetic media is very difficult. The problem lies in the fact that when data is written to the medium, the write head sets the polarity of most, but not all, of the magnetic domains. This is partially due to the inability of the writing device to write in exactly the same location each time, and partially due to the variations in media sensitivity and field strength over time and among devices....
>
> In conventional terms, when a one is written to disk the media records a one, and when a zero is written the media records a zero. However the actual effect is closer to obtaining a 0.95 when a zero is overwritten with a one, and a 1.05 when a one is overwritten with a one. Normal disk circuitry is set up so that both these values are read as ones, but using specialised circuitry it is possible to work out what previous "layers" contained. The recovery of at least one or two layers of overwritten data isn't too hard to perform by reading the signal from the analog head electronics with a high-quality digital sampling oscilloscope, downloading the sampled waveform to a PC, and analysing it in software to recover the previously recorded signal....
>
> Deviations in the position of the drive head from the original track may leave significant portions of the previous data along the track edge relatively untouched.... Regions where the old and new data coincide create continuous magnetization between the two. However, if the new transition is out of phase with the previous one, a few microns of erase band with no definite magnetization are created at the juncture of the old and new tracks....
>
> When all the above factors are combined it turns out that each track contains an image of everything ever written to it, but that the contribution from each "layer" gets progressively smaller the further back it was made. Intelligence organisations have a lot of expertise in recovering these palimpsestuous images.

The difference between digital and analog systems, then, is best understood as an *engineering* difference in how we choose to build systems, and not as resulting from an intrinsic property of data that somehow precedes those systems. Outside such systems, the status of data is less definite, because there is no longer the same specification about what is and is not significant. John Haugeland remarked: *"digital*, like *accurate, economical,* or *heavy-duty,* is a mundane engineering notion, root and branch. It only makes sense as a practical means to cope with the vagaries and vicissitudes, the noise and drift, of earthly existence" (1981: 217). It has become common in popular usage to talk about the analog as the category that covers everything that isn't digital; but in fact most things are neither. The images, sounds, smells, and so on that we live among have mostly not been reduced to information yet. Both analog and digital systems require some stage of choice and reduction to turn phenomena from the world into data that can be processed. The most common error about digital systems is to think that the data is effortlessly stable and unchanging; the most common error about analog systems is to think they're natural and simple, not really encoded.

Minds and Bodies

Both approaches were embodied in machinery long before the rise of digital computers: the abacus is digital, the slide rule is analog. As technology, then, the digital is not something that only arose in the twentieth century. But it was in the later twentieth century that digital computers came to provide an almost inescapable model for thinking about the mind. (On the longer history of such technological analogies, see Wiener 1948; Marshall 1977; Bolter 1984.) How the digital computer came to eclipse the analog computer in such thinking, even though careful study suggested that both kinds of processing were probably among those used in the brain, is one key element of that story, and one that illuminates some of the cultural associations of our current ideas of the digital and analog.

Although the use of both approaches and an awareness of their differences go back a long way, the standard distinction between the two, their names and their pairing, all came in the mid-twentieth century, when substantial advances were made in machinery for both kinds of systems, and there was a serious choice between building one kind of system or the other for many communications and computational applications. (The best available account of that moment is in Mindell 2002.) That was also the moment when the new fields of cybernetics and information theory arose, and seemed to offer remarkable insights into human bodies and minds. Cybernetics in particular proposed understandings of systems that responded to the environment, without strong distinctions between machinery and living beings. In that context, it was a natural question to ask whether human minds and bodies were digital or analog. The thinking of that era is worth revisiting because its perspective is so different from today's assumptions – and so suggests other paths of thought; this earlier perspective has the merit of pointing out complexities that are lost when we focus primarily on the digital.

Cybernetics, today, is a field that lingers on in small pockets of activity but does not matter. But in its day, roughly from 1943 to 1970, it was a highly interdisciplinary field, which encompassed topics now split up among medicine, psychology, engineering, mathematics, and computing, and one of its most persuasive claims to importance was its ability to bring so much together productively. Today its achievements (quite substantial ones) have been merged back into the subject matter of those separate disciplines, and in a broader cultural context its nature and ideas have been mostly forgotten – so that (to give one example) a recent editor of Roland Barthes's work assumes that the term "homeostat" was invented by Barthes, though in Barthes's writings of the 1950s its source in cybernetics is clearly indicated (Barthes 2002: 83).

Although cybernetics included much that is now classified under the heading of cognitive science, it did not give cognition primacy as the object of study. Definitions of cybernetics usually focused on the idea of "control systems," which could respond to the environment and achieve results beyond what it was normally thought machines could do; as Norbert Wiener wrote in his influential book *Cybernetics; or, Control and Communication in the Animal and the Machine* in 1948:

> The machines of which we are now speaking are not the dream of the sensationalist, nor the hope of some future time. They already exist as thermostats, automatic gyro-compass ship-steering systems, self-propelled missiles – especially such as seek their target – anti-aircraft fire-control systems, automatically controlled oil-cracking stills, ultra-rapid computing machines, and the like. (1948: 55)

The workings of the body were as important a subject as anything cognitive. The interest more recently in "cybernetic organisms" reflects the perspective of cybernetics, which did not distinguish sharply between biological and mechanical systems, and also did not emphasize thought. The excitement associated with the field goes back to earlier discoveries that showed how (for example) the body maintained its temperature by means that were natural but also not cognitive: we don't *think* about how to keep our body temperature stable, but it is also not a supernatural effect. Previous doubts that the body could be described as a machine had been based on too limited an understanding of the possibilities of machinery; cybernetics showed that a "control system" could achieve a great deal without doing anything that looked like thinking. Wiener's book, which at times has whole pages of mathematical equations, also includes a cultural history of the idea of building "a working simulacrum of a living organism" (1948: 51), leading up to the way cybernetics proposed to do it.

> To sum up: the many automata of the present age are coupled to the outside world both for the reception of impressions and for the performance of actions. They contain sense-organs, effectors, and the equivalent of a nervous system to integrate the transfer of information from the one to the other. They lend themselves very well to description in physiological terms. It is scarcely a miracle that they can be subsumed under one theory with the mechanisms of psychology. (1948: 55)

The word "cybernetic" today is most often just a synonym for "computational"; but in the early thinking of the field computation was only one subject, and being effectively "coupled to the outside world" seemed more important. Peter Galison has traced the role played by Wiener's war work in the development of his thinking – in particular, he had actually been involved in building "anti-aircraft fire-control systems." They could be thought of "in physiological terms" by analogy with reflexive actions of the body, not with thought or calculation. Galison mounts a critique of the dehumanizing tendency of cybernetic thought, but that doesn't seem to be the only way people took it at the time. Theodore Sturgeon's science-fiction novel *More than Human* (1953) is very clearly influenced by cybernetic thinking (one scene involves "a couple of war-surplus servo-mechanisms rigged to simulate radar-gun directors" that happen to appear as part of a carnival's shooting-gallery attraction [1953: 169]), and it follows cybernetics in assigning conscious thought a role that does not direct everything else. The novel describes the genesis of a being made up of several people with different abilities: "a complex organism which is composed of Baby, a computer; Bonnie and Beanie, teleports; Janie, telekineticist; and myself, telepath and central control" (1953: 142). Computing was quite distinct from "central control."

Cybernetics did include a chapter entitled "Computing Machines and the Nervous System," specifically concerned with how you might build a computer to do what the brain does; though it spends as much time on memory and reflex action as on calculation. Wiener talks about digital and analog representation, but the stress is on the engineering question of what would work best in building a computer, and he argues for binary digital computers for reasons broadly similar to those behind their use today. The neuron, he observes, seems to be broadly digital in its action, since it either fires or does not fire; but he leaves mostly open the question of just what sort of representation the brain uses, and is instead trying to consider very generally how aspects of the brain could be realized in machinery. The importance of the digital-or-analog question here is practical: if you are going to do a lot of computation and data storage, digital has more advantages; but analog representation for other purposes is not ruled out. (In contexts where not very much information needed to be preserved, and detection and reaction were more important, the issue might be quite marginal. W. Ross Ashby's *Introduction to Cybernetics* has only the barest mention of digital and analog representation.)

The writings of John von Neumann and Gregory Bateson are the two principal sources for the idea that the choice of digital or analog representation is not merely an engineering choice for computer builders, but had real consequences for thought; and that it was a choice that is built into the design of the brain. Von Neumann's views appeared in a posthumously published book, *The Computer and the Brain*, which in its published form is closer to an outline than to a fully elaborated text. (The review by von Neumann's associate A. H. Taub is a very helpful supplement.) The title characterizes the contents very exactly: Part I describes how computers (both digital and analog) work; Part II describes how the brain works, so far as that was known at the time, and then tries to conclude whether it's a digital or an analog system. Like Wiener he sees the neuron as mainly digital because it either fires or it doesn't; but he too sees that the question is actually more complicated because that activity is

influenced by many factors in the brain which aren't on/off signals. This leads to a
conclusion that is often cited as the book's main point: that the brain uses a mixture of
digital and analog representation (Taub 1960: 68–9). But a substantial part of the
book follows that passage, and here von Neumann develops a quite different conclusion: that the brain works in a way fundamentally different from computers analog
and digital – it's statistical. Nothing like the precision of mechanical computers in
storage or computation is available given the brain's hardware, yet it achieves a high
degree of reliability. And von Neumann concludes that the logic used within the
brain must be different from that of mathematics, though there might be some
connection: a striking conclusion from a mathematician strongly associated with
the development of digital computers. But in the end, von Neumann's account of
computers is present to highlight what's different about the brain, not to serve as the
complete foundation for understanding it.

Gregory Bateson, like von Neumann, was active in cybernetics circles from the
1940s onward; but unlike Wiener and von Neumann he did not work in the physical
sciences, but instead in anthropology and psychology. His *Steps to an Ecology of Mind:
Collected Essays in Anthropology, Psychiatry, Evolution, and Epistemology* (1972) collects
work that in some cases dates back to the 1940s. It is perhaps best known today as the
apparent source of the definition of information as "a difference which makes a
difference" (1972: 315, 459). The breadth of concerns surpasses even that of cybernetics: few other books combine analyses of schizophrenia with accounts of communicating with dolphins. But looking for fundamental principles that operated very
broadly was a habit of Bateson's:

> I picked up a vague mystical feeling that we must look for the same sort of processes in
> all fields of natural phenomena – that we might expect to find the same sort of laws at
> work in the structure of a crystal as in the structure of society, or that the segmentation
> of an earthworm might really be comparable to the process by which basalt pillars are
> formed. (1972: 74)

Bateson's criticism of much work in psychology in his day was that it lacked an
adequate conceptual basis; so he sought to find fundamental principles and mechanisms on which to build in his work. The difference between digital and analog
representation seemed to him one such fundamental distinction: he argued that the
two modes entailed different communicative possibilities with different psychological
consequences. Analog communication, in his view, did not support the kinds of
logical operations that digital communication facilitated, and in particular negation
and yes/no choices were not possible; that led to a connection with Freudian concepts
that also did not work in accordance with traditional logic (as in "The Antithetical
Meaning of Primal Words," for example), and to new theories of his own (of the
"double bind," for example).

Bateson's work mirrors one feature of cybernetics in its advantages and disadvan-
tages: he seeks to talk about whole systems rather than about artificially isolated parts;

but it is then difficult to find places to start in analysis. The analog/digital pairing is important in his work because of the resulting ideas about different cognitive and communicative possibilities. The distinction had some connection with the difference between people and animals: nonverbal communication was necessarily analog, in Bateson's view, and so could not have the digital features he saw in verbal communication. But, like von Neumann, he concluded that digital and analog representation were both used in thinking – though von Neumann's account was based on a consideration of brain physiology, and Bateson's on the nature of different forms of communication. In both cases, the answers to the question track rather closely the answers current in the 1940s and 1950s to questions about how you'd engineer practical control systems using the available technology. The accounts by Wiener and von Neumann are only clearer than Bateson's about how thought is being seen in the light of current technology, because of their deeper understanding of that technology and fuller awareness of how open the choice still was.

In all of these accounts, then, the mind is not just a digital computer, and its embodiment is a major concern in developing a scientific account. Of course, the course of subsequent technological history was one in which digital computing grew far faster than analog computing, and also began to take over applications that had originally been handled using analog technology. We also have more and more an equation of the analog with the physical and the digital with the cognitive, an alignment that wasn't there in the 1940s and 1950s; popular ideas about the digital/analog pairing in general are narrower in their field of application. While work continues on all the topics that cybernetics addressed, attempts to bring them all together as cybernetics did are now much rarer, and as a result there is (for example) a good deal of work in cognitive science and artificial intelligence that is about ways to make computers think, without reference to how the body works, and with the assumption that only digital techniques are necessary. This approach results, of course, from the remarkable development in the speed and capacity of digital computers: this line of work is attractive as a research program, even if it remains clear that the brain doesn't actually work that way.

One stage along that path may be seen in work from the 1970s by the social anthropologist Edmund Leach, who absorbed influences from cybernetics and structuralism, among other things. In Wiener the choice of binary representation was an engineering decision; but the connection with structuralist thinking was probably inevitable:

> In practice, most structuralist analysis invokes the kind of binary algebra which would be appropriate to the understanding of the workings of a brain designed like a digital computer. This should not be taken to imply that structuralists imagine that human brains really work just like a digital computer. It is rather that since many of the products of human brains can be shown to have characteristics which appear also in the output of man-made computers it seems reasonable to attribute computer-like qualities to human brains. This in no way precludes the probability that human brains have many other important qualities which we have not yet been able to discern. (1972: 333)

Leach's is what by now is a common move: to state that the compelling analogy with digital computing is of course partial, but then to go on to assume it is total. This essay was a contribution to a symposium on nonverbal communication, and unlike most of the other contributors Leach saw nonverbal communication as very similar to verbal communication:

> The "yes"/"no" opposition of speech codes and the contrasted signals of non-speech codes are related to each other as metaphors; the structuralist hypothesis is that they are all alike transforms of a common algebraic opposition which must be assumed to occur as "an abstract element of the human mind" in a deep level structure. The relation between this abstraction and the physical organisation of human brain tissue is a matter for later investigation.
>
> Incidentally it is of interest that the internationally accepted symbolism of mathematics represents this binary opposition either as 0/1 or as $-/+$. The second of these couplets is really very similar to the first since it consists of a base couplet $-/-$ with the addition of a vertical stroke to the second half of the couplet. But if a student of primitive art, who could free himself from our assumptions about the notations of arithmetic, were to encounter paired symbols 0/1 he would immediately conclude that the opposition represented "vagina"/"penis" and was metonymic of female/male. A structuralist might argue that this fits very well with his assumptions about the deep structure algebra of human thought. (1972: 334)

As we have seen, Bateson's view of nonverbal communication was that it involved a kind of logic that was basically different from the digital and the verbal; but Leach doesn't respond to his views (though he cites one of his books on the subject), or to those of the other speakers at the symposium.

Like cybernetics, structuralism has come and gone. But just as anything binary looked like the right answer to Leach, today anything digital has the same appeal for many. Thus it is now common to read scrupulous and thoroughly researched books on cognitive science – such as Daniel C. Dennett's *Consciousness Explained* (1991) and Steven Pinker's *How the Mind Works* (1997) – in which considerations of brain anatomy are only a secondary matter. Once the point is established that there is a good case for seeing the brain as performing computations, though in ways different from conventional digital computers, there is a shift of emphasis to the computational level alone: with the idea that (as both writers put it) most of what matters can be seen as happening in a layer of "software" whose nature doesn't depend very strongly on the brain "hardware" whose details are yet to be established. Though the non-digital features of the brain are fully acknowledged, everything shows a tendency to revert to a digital mode. Some are highly critical of the digital emphasis of this kind of approach: Jerry Fodor, for example, commented in 1983: "If someone – a [Hubert] Dreyfus, for example – were to ask us why we should even suppose that the digital computer is a plausible mechanism for the simulation of global cognitive processes, the answering silence would be deafening" (129). It is nevertheless a strong program for research: it has produced good work, it makes it possible to draw on the power of digital computers as research tools, and it does not require waiting around for a resolution of the many outstanding questions about brain anatomy.

But it doesn't prove that all thinking is digital, or that the situation of the program on the digital computer, involved from start to finish in processing digital data, is a complete model for the mind. The imbalance is far greater in popular culture, where the equation of the digital with thought and a disembodied computational world, and of the analog with the physical world, is inescapable (Rodowick 2001). In the era of cybernetics, the body was both digital and analog, and other things too; not only was the anatomy of the brain significant in a consideration of the mind, but the anatomy of the body offered useful analogies. Now we find ourselves needing to make an effort to defend the idea that the body has something to do with thinking, so strong is the idea of the division.

The Nature of Texts

In the mid-1960s, Nelson Goodman used the ideas of digital and analog representation to help develop a distinction between artworks expressed through "notations" – systems such as writing or musical scoring for specifying a work, with the digital property of being copyable – and art objects such as paintings that could be imitated but not exactly copied. The alphabet, on this view, is digital: every A is assumed to be the same as every other A, even if differences in printing or display make some particular instances look slightly different. There is a fixed set of discrete letters: you can't make up new ones, and there is no possibility of another letter halfway between A and B. A text is readily broken down into its component letters, and is readily copied to create something just as good as the original. But a painting is not based on juxtaposing elements from a fixed set, and may not be easy to decompose into discrete parts. Like von Neumann and Bateson, Goodman found that the modes could be mixed: "A scale model of a campus, with green papier-mâché for grass, pink cardboard for brick, plastic film for glass, etc., is analog with respect to spatial dimensions but digital with respect to materials" (1968: 173).

The idea that text is in this sense a digital medium, a perfect-copy medium, is now widespread. And this view also fits many of our everyday practices in working with texts: we assume that the multiple copies of a printed book are all the same, and in an argument at any level about the merits of a recent novel it would not be persuasive if I objected, "But you didn't read *my copy* of it." In the world of art history, though, that kind of argument does have force: it is assumed that you need to see originals of paintings, and that someone who only saw a copy was seeing something significantly different. In discussions of texts we also assume that it is possible to quote from a text and get it right; you could make a mistake, but in principle it can be done and in frequent practice it is done. The digital view of text offers an explanation of what's behind these standard practices.

The digital view of text also suggests reasons why it works so well in digital computer systems: why text does not in general pose as many technical difficulties as graphics, and is at the heart of some outstandingly successful applications, most notably digital publishing and full-text searching. Written language is pre-analyzed into letters, and because those letters can be treated as digital data it is straightforward to make digital texts, and then to search them. The limitations of full-text searching are familiar: above all, the problem that it's only particular word forms that are easy to search, and not meanings. But that is still far ahead of the primitive state of searching digital images: because there is no easy way to decompose digital images into anything like an alphabet of visual components, even the most limited kind of image searching is a huge technical problem. And while we have many tools for working with digital texts and images, it is for texts that we have tools like spelling correctors that are able to get somewhere near the meaning, without any special preparation of the data. Image manipulation cannot do that unless the image has been created in a very deliberate manner, to keep its components separate from the beginning (as with the "layering" possible in some programs).

But digital computers and written texts are digital in different ways. Digital computer systems are engineered to fit that definition: data in them is digital because it is created and maintained that way. Goodman's definition of a "notation" is an exact description of such data. But the same description is an idealized view of our practice with texts, one that helps explain many of its features but is wrong about others. A digital system has rules about what constitutes the data and how the individual tokens are to be recognized – and nothing else is to be considered significant. With texts we are free to see any other features as significant: to decide that things often considered as mere bearers of content (the paper, the design, the shapes of the letters) do matter. Such decisions are not merely arbitrary whims, as we internalize many assumptions about how particular sorts of texts should be presented. Jonathan Gibson has demonstrated the importance of blank space in seventeenth-century English letters: the higher the status of the addressee, the more blank space there was supposed to be on the page. And most readers of the present chapter would find their response to it affected by reading a text written in green crayon on yellow cardboard, rather than in a printed Blackwell *Companion*. Examples are not difficult to multiply once you try to examine implicit assumptions about how texts are appropriately *presented* and not merely *worded*. Though many of our practices assume that text is only the sequence of alphabetic letters, is only the "content," the actual system involves many other meaningful features – features which as readers we find it difficult to ignore. These issues about copying are ones that may well seem to lack urgency, because along with knowledge of the alphabet we've absorbed so much about the manner of presentation that we don't normally need to think about it: the yellow cardboard is not something you even consider in thinking about academic writing. But a description of what reading actually is must take these issues into account.

The digital trait of having an exact and reliable technique for copying does not in practice apply to texts on paper: it is not hard to explain how to copy a contemporary printed text letter-for-letter, but getting it letter-perfect is in fact difficult for a text of any length, unless you use imaging methods that essentially bypass the digitality of the alphabet. But the bigger problem is knowing what matters besides the letters: To what level of detail do we copy? How exactly do we need to match the typefaces? Does it need to be the same kind of paper? Do the line breaks need to match? Some of these features are ones that could be encoded as digital data, some as analog; but the core problem is that there is not a clearly bounded set of information we could identify as significant, any more than with a painting. Once we attend to the whole object presented to our senses every feature is potentially significant.

Texts *created* in digital form to some extent avoid these problems. They're digital and so can be exactly copied. Languages such as PostScript can specify what is to be displayed with great specificity (though the more specific such languages are, the more complex they are: PostScript is vastly larger than HTML). But actual presentations still wind up being variable because machinery is: a reader still sees the text on a particular screen or paper, and those interfaces are features that still matter for the reception of what's written.

It is not, of course, absurd to say to readers: look at what I've said, not at the way it's written down! It remains true that many practices in working with texts fit the digital view, in which only the sequence of letters is significant, and this view of their work is often what authors intend. The experience of using the World Wide Web has bolstered that view, as we now often see work of scholarly value presented in a typographically unattractive manner that we ought to disregard. But that bracketing is a step we have to choose to take: our normal mode of reading just isn't to read the letters alone and abstract them in the digital way; we normally take in much more than that. We may think of ourselves as working with text as computers do, but it is not a way of working that comes naturally.

The constitution of digital and analog data is a function of the whole system in which it is embedded, rather than of data as an independent entity; the problem with texts is that the system does not have the built-in limits of a computer system, because we as readers don't always follow the digital rules. Just as it is appealing and even useful to think about the mind in digital-computer terms, it is also appealing and useful to think about text that way: so long as we remember that it is a partial view. You are not *supposed* to be paying attention to the typography of this chapter in reading it and extracting its informational content; as a piece of scholarly writing it is not supposed to have an aesthetic dimension at all. But, as Gérard Genette argued, there are ample empirical and theoretical reasons to think that any text has the potential to be regarded aesthetically, even this one; some writing by its form (such as poetry) makes a direct claim to literary status, but readers choose to regard other writing as literary despite its nonliterary genre. And beyond this, there does not seem to be a human operation of reading that works the way digital reading has to: by making a copy of the data as defined within the system, and nothing more. That bracketing may to a degree become habitual for us, to the extent that it seems like the proper way to read, but it never becomes quite complete. Reading remains a practice that is not reducible to information or to digital data.

REFERENCES

Ashby, W. Ross (1956). *An Introduction to Cybernetics.* London: Chapman and Hall.

Barthes, Roland (2002). *Comment vivre ensemble: Simulations romanesques de quelques espaces quotidiens. Notes de cours et de séminaires au Collège de France, 1976–1977.* Paris: Seuil.

Bateson, Gregory (1972). *Steps to an Ecology of Mind: Collected Essays in Anthropology, Psychiatry, Evolution, and Epistemology.* San Francisco: Chandler.

Bolter, Jay David (1984). *Turing's Man: Western Culture in the Computer Age.* Chapel Hill: University of North Carolina Press.

Dennett, Daniel C. (1991). *Consciousness Explained.* Boston: Little, Brown.

Fodor, Jerry A. (1983). *The Modularity of Mind: An Essay on Faculty Psychology.* Cambridge, MA: MIT Press.

Freud, Sigmund (1957). "The Antithetical Meaning of Primal Words." In James Strachey (Ed.). *The Standard Edition of the Complete Psychological Works of Sigmund Freud, Volume XI* (Alan Tyson, Trans.). London: Hogarth Press and the Institute of Psycho-Analysis, pp. 155–61 (Original work published 1910).

Galison, Peter (1994). "The Ontology of the Enemy: Norbert Wiener and the Cybernetic Vision." *Critical Inquiry* 21: 228–66.

Genette, Gérard (1991). *Fiction et diction.* Paris: Seuil.

Gibson, Jonathan (1997). "Significant Space in Manuscript Letters." *The Seventeenth Century* 12: 1–9.

Goodman, Nelson (1968). *Languages of Art: An Approach to a Theory of Symbols.* Indianapolis: Bobbs-Merrill.

Gutmann, Peter (1996). "Secure Deletion of Data from Magnetic and Solid-state Memory." Sixth USENIX Security Symposium Proceedings, San Jose, California, July 22–25, 1996. <http://www.cs.auckland.ac.nz/~pgut001/pubs/secure_del.html>.

Haugeland, John (1981). Analog and Analog. *Philosophical Topics* 12: 213–25.

Hayes, Brian (2001). "Third Base." *American Scientist* 89: 490–4.

Hillis, W. Daniel (1998). *The Pattern on the Stone: The Simple Ideas that Make Computers Work.* New York: Basic Books.

Leach, Edmund (1972). "The Influence of Cultural Context on Non-verbal Communication in Man." In R. A. Hinde (Ed.). *Non-Verbal Communication.* Cambridge: Cambridge University Press, pp. 315–44.

Marshall, John C. (1977). "Minds, Machines and Metaphors." *Social Studies of Science* 7: 475–88.

Mindell, David A. (2002). *Between Human and Machine: Feedback, Control, and Computing before Cybernetics.* Baltimore: Johns Hopkins University Press.

Pinker, Steven (1997). *How the Mind Works.* New York: Norton.

Rodowick, D. N. (2001). "Dr. Strange Media; or, How I Learned to Stop Worrying and Love Film Theory." *PMLA* 116: 1396–404.

Sturgeon, Theodore (1953). *More than Human.* New York: Farrar.

Taub, A. H. (1960). "Review of *The Computer and the Brain.*" *Isis* 51: 94–6.

Turing, Alan (1950). "Computing Machinery and Intelligence." *Mind,* NS 59: 433–60.

von Neumann, John (1958). *The Computer and the Brain.* New Haven: Yale University Press.

Wiener, Norbert (1948). *Cybernetics; or, Control and Communication in the Animal and the Machine.* New York: Wiley.

23
Cybertextuality and Philology
Ian Lancashire

What is Cybertextuality?

Employed sometimes as a synonym for "digital text" and "reading machine," the term "cybertext" is any document viewed from the perspective of the theory or study of communication and control in living things or machines. This theory emerged in 1948 in a book titled *Cybernetics* by the American mathematician Norbert Wiener (1894–1964). Cybernetics derives from the Greek *kubernetes*, meaning "steersman." Wiener calls it "the theory of messages" (Wiener 1950: 106; Masani 1990: 251–2) because it theorizes communications among animals and machines. I refer to Wienerian messages in any cybernetic system as cybertexts (Lancashire 2004). They come in pairs, an utterance-message and its feedback-response, both of them transmitted through a channel from sender (speaker/author) to receiver (listener/reader) through an ether of interfering noise. Five control modules (sender, channel, message, noise, and receiver) affect forward-messaging (the utterance) and messaging-feedback (the model) through this cybernetic channel. Wiener's insight, and the raison-d'être of cybernetics, is that anyone authoring a message steers or governs its making by feedback from those who receive it. Norbert Wiener defined the mechanics of cybernetics, and Claude Shannon, who founded information science, devised its equations.

Many sciences, having lionized the brainchild of Wiener and Shannon for a time, went on with their business as usual, and the digital humanities have been no exception. The postmodernist François Lyotard in *The Postmodern Condition* derived his "agonistic" model for communication and his "theory of games" (Galison 1994: 258) from cybernetics. Donna Haraway's cyborg manifesto also builds on cybernetics. Postmodernists tend to draw on cybernetics as a fund of metaphors, but the mechanics of messages, whether they are instructions relayed to a missile system by radar, or poems, have measurable feedback. Under a decade ago, Espen Aarseth coined the term "cybertext" in his book of the same name. All cybertexts, Aarseth says, are "ergodic," a word that Wiener uses and that etymologically means "path of energy or work": a cybertext requires a reader to do physical work aside from turning pages and focusing his eyes. By throwing stalks (if reading the I Ching) or managing a computer process with a mouse or a keyboard, the human operator-reader partners with an active and material medium and so becomes part of a figurative reading "machine for the production of variety of expression" (1997: 3). To Aarseth, the cybertext is that machine. It includes the reader, his request, and a computer that parses his request, sends it to a "simulation engine" that assembles digital objects for a "representation engine" that passes it along to a synthesizer or interface device, which returns feedback to the reader. There is no author or noise in Aarseth's diagram. It cuts Wiener's system in half.

Another computing humanist who cites Norbert Wiener is Katherine N. Hayles. In her *How We Became Posthuman: Virtual Bodies in Cybernetics, Literature, and Informatics* (1999), Hayles also drops Wiener's sender/author in order to focus on his receiver/observer, following the concept of autopoesis, a self-organizing principle that she finds in the cybernetic research of the South American scientist, Humberto Maturana. He observes that, in seeing things, a frog "does not so much register reality as construct it," a theme he generalizes in the maxim, "Everything said [in a cybernetic system] is said by an observer" (xxii, cited by Hayles 1999: 135). That is, living things do not receive messages passing through a noiseless channel in the state that they were sent. In constructing or modeling messages, readers change what authors utter: new messages result. Maturana, Hayles, and many others neglect the sender/author, although authors and readers are one and the same because authors receive and construct their own utterances.

Cybertextuality systematically applies cybernetics to speaking and writing as well as listening and reading. Consider how the five things studied by literary researchers parallel the five modules of cybernetics. There are *authors* of texts (studied in stylistics, biography, and authorship attribution; Lancashire 2005), *readers* of texts (studied in theory, criticism, and usability studies), *texts* themselves (studied in close reading and encoding), and the language technologies and media, which together form a channel, that govern their transmission through wear-and-tear that might be called literary *noise* (studied in stemmatics, textual criticism, and media).

This five-part model supports two kinds of messages or cybertexts: an outward message, from author to reader, that is encoded with redundancy to resist the damaging effects of noise; and a feedback response that variously reflects the state in which the original message arrived. Authors bring to bear all the techniques of grammar and rhetoric to repeat and vary what they want to say so that the reader can understand it. Cybertextually speaking, authors encode redundant data in their cybertexts so that they can withstand interference by noise and can reach readers comprehensibly. The thought that an author hopes to communicate is the content of a cybertext, and the degree of its rhetorical treatment (the encoding) marks how dense that content or information will be. (Sometimes the content is its encoding.) As redundancy increases, the information density of a cybertext (in information science, its entropy) lessens. Inadequate encoding, and persistent extraneous noise, may lead a reader to mistake or doubt what a dense, underspecified text says. Textual criticism studies noise, that is, the effects that the channel itself (e.g., a scriptorium, a printing press, a noisy room) and extraneous interference (e.g., the interpretative readings that scribes and compositors sometimes impose on texts that they are copying) have on cybertexts. The complementary feedback cybertext, which registers that the outgoing message has been received, can be used to detect errors in transmission. The humanities enshrine this reader-to-writer, receiver-to-sender feedback in teaching, discussion, and peer-review. The digital humanities supplement the human reader-receiver by developing text-analysis software that feeds back semi-automatic analyses of its texts. Working with the information sciences, the digital humanities do not leave the reader-receiver to chance but build one. In this respect, computing humanists bring together human and machinic communications to form a cybernetic package.

Cybertextual Simulations

Cybertextuality, to recapitulate, is a subset of cybernetics that studies the messaging and feedback modules – author, text, channel/media, noise, and reader – of languages and literatures. It is difficult to analyze this system directly because authors create reclusively. Computing humanists, for that reason, employ purpose-built simulations. Simulators enable us experimentally to test the theory and practice of cybertexts. Because this is an unusual way of thinking about what we are doing, I will break down the simulations by cybernetic module: cybertext, receiver/reader, noise, channel, and author/sender.

Poetry generators, some computer text games, and chatterbots are artificial or simulated author-agents. We can study how they implement natural language or we can analyze the cybertexts that they make, which include poems, stories, and conversation. The software simulates authors and outputs algorithmic cybertexts. The last Loebner Prize for the best chatterbot, in 2005, went to Rollo Carpenter for his *Jabberwacky*. Authoring software often spoofs writing. For instance, three MIT students, Jeremy Stribling, Max Krohn, and Dan Aguayo, devised SCIgen – An Automatic CS Paper Generator, "a computer program to generate nonsensical research papers, complete with 'context-free grammar,' charts and diagrams." They submitted "Rooter: A Methodology for the Typical Unification of Access Points and Redundancy" to the ninth World Multi-Conference on Systematics, Cybernetics, and Informatics, which initially accepted it as a non-reviewed paper.

Media studies treat the cybernetic channel. Marshall McLuhan conflated the Wienerian cybertext with the channel when he said that the medium was the message. Mark Federman of the McLuhan Program explains this equation: "We can know the nature and characteristics of anything we conceive or create (medium) by virtue of the changes – often unnoticed and non-obvious changes – that they effect." Within cybertextuality, most research on the channel's impact on the utterances it carries takes place in usability studies. What affordances, an information scientist asks, does the channel have with respect to the communication of a message? Computer-mediated mail, webcasting, cell phone, printed book, posted letter, meeting, and lecture instantiate differently this cybernetic channel. The Knowledge Media Design Institute (Toronto) produces software named *ePresence Interactive Media* that enables remote viewers to take part in webcasts. Because computer workstations are themselves a channel, cybertextuality mainly analyzes how novel electronic media affect authoring and reading. Simulation of non-electronic channels by software is uncommon.

The digital humanities applies what we know of cybertext noise to model how a text metamorphoses over time. Computer-based stemmatics reconstructs the timeline of a work as noise alters it, state by state, in moving through the channel we call manuscript scriptoria and printed editions. Cladograms from Phylogenetic Analysis using Parsimony, software devised by the Canterbury Tales project, gives a schematic tree of snapshots of a cybertext as it falls through time from one state to another (Dunning 2000). Stephen E. Sachs' *The Jumbler*, which algorithmically mixes up every letter in a word but the first and the last, simulates noise. A sentence muddled in this way can still be read. (*A snceente muldded in tihs way can sltil be raed.*) If our subject of research were noise itself, we would study how living scribes alter their exemplars in copying them. When people retell events from memory after a time, they suffer from another kind of noise, what psychologists name the post-event misinformation or retelling effect. Collational software can readily identify and time-stamp the emergence and reworking of textual variants. This cybertextual experiment would help classify the kind of errors that scribes make and complicate over time.

We create text-analysis programs that act as artificial or simulated readers to give feedback on cybertexts. By running Robert Watt's *Concordancer* on any work, for example, we act as stand-ins for the work's author in remitting it to a computer reader for feedback. In both simulations, we control, as far as possible, the noise of the simulated channel by choosing the most error-free common carrier of our time: the workstation. For all our complaining, it is a reliable device, enabling many people to repeat the same cybertextual experiment many times, in many places. This reliability allows us to do experiments together and to agree on criteria whereby our research can be falsified.

Some cybertextual simulators appear impoverished when compared to human beings. Concordances output indexes and rearrange a text rather than respond, like a reader, to one. The Jumbler, Jabberwacky, and SCIgen play word-games. Other simulators devised by artificial intelligence and computational linguistics teach us much about communication and can stand in routinely for human beings. Machine-translation (MT) systems read text in one language and feed back a version of that text in another language. The morphological, lexical, syntactic, and semantic analyzers in a classical MT system have helped us understand how language works. Recent story-generation programs like MakeBelieve from MIT Media Lab use Open Mind, a web database of 710,000 common-sense facts, as well as ConceptNet, a semantic network built on top of it (Liu and Singh 2002). The infrastructure by which it assembles little coherent stories from sample opening sentences uses a constituent structure parser, fuzzy matching, and a sentence generator. If these simulations or modeling programs had access to the same high-performance computing resources employed in protein-folding, cosmology, weather prediction, and airframe design, the results might be still more impressive.

The Cybertextual Cycle

The digital humanities have a helpful cognate discipline in cognitive psychology, which experimentally analyzes how the living speaker-writer and the living listener-reader manage their language, both message and feedback, in a noisy world. The digital humanities also analyze this process, but only indirectly, through our stored cybertexts alone.

The journal *Brain* last year published Peter Garrard's remarkable study of works by the English novelist Iris Murdoch as she succumbed to Alzheimer's disease. Tests during her final years revealed a mild impairment of working memory (in digit span). After her death in 1999, an autopsy found "profound bilateral hippocampal shrinkage." A healthy hippocampus is necessary for working memory. By generating the simplest form of text analysis – word-frequency lists from early, middle, and last novels – Garrard found an increasing lexical and semantic "impoverishment." Although *Jackson's Dilemma*, her last novel, showed no deterioration in syntax, it had a "more restricted vocabulary," that is, a smaller number of word-types (different words) and, thus, a greater rate of lexical repetition. Her earliest novel exhibited about 5,600 word-types per 40,000 words, but in *Jackson's Dilemma* that ratio had fallen to 4,500, a drop of 20 percent. The final novel was not unreadable but critics described it as transparent, economical, scant of explanation, and "distrait" in narrative. The medical tests and autopsy make predictions that the computer text substantiates. Together, they tie semantic complexity and information density to the size of working memory and to the hippocampus. Garrard's case study shows that evidence of cognitive affects in language processing, those backed up experimentally, help explain the lexical minutiae of authoring at work, whether in making or remaking/reading text. These low-level mechanics are beyond our ability to observe consciously in ourselves as we utter phrases and sentences, but we can access them experimentally with the help of special tools.

The language powers movingly described in the case of Iris Murdoch have two cognitive staging grounds: working memory, where we consciously recall spoken language and written images of text so that we can work with them; and the big black box of unconscious neurological functions that working memory accesses but that we cannot access directly. Alan Baddeley, an English cognitive psychologist, proposed working memory in the mid-1970s. It remains today the standard theoretical model. In 2003 he published a schematic flowchart of how we consciously use working memory to speak aloud something we have read or heard (Figure 23.1).

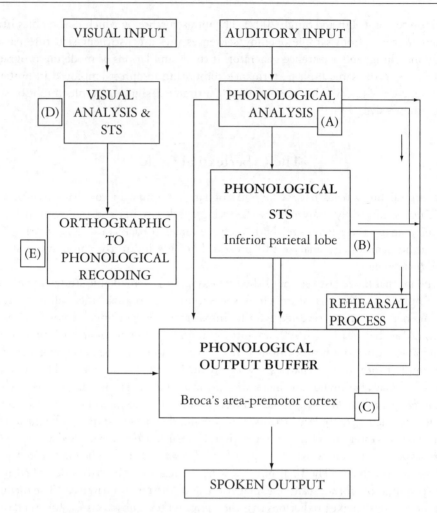

Figure 23.1 Baddeley's proposed structure for the phonological loop. *Source*: Baddeley, Alan, 2003, "Working Memory and Language: An Overview." *Journal of Communication Disorders* 36.3: 189–203. Reprinted with permission from Elsevier.

We consciously place or retrieve a visually seen sentence into a visual short-term store, recode it elsewhere into phonological form, and then send that recoded data to an output buffer for pronouncing. The visual short-term store is a visuo-spatial sketchpad in working memory. Nothing in this visual short-term store can be processed as speech unless it is converted to auditory form. Mentally, we process language as speech, not writing. That is why sudden heard speech always gains our immediate attention: auditory data do not need to be re-encoded to access working memory. When we hear speech, we place it in another short-term store, this time a phonological one that Baddeley called the phonological loop. An utterance enters this short-term store and exits from it after a short time, unless we consciously rehearse or refresh it, as if memory were a loop. Then we send it to an output buffer for pronouncing.

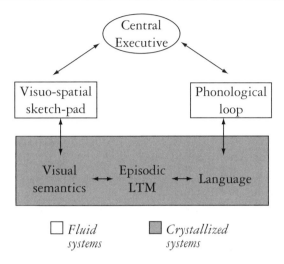

Figure 23.2 Baddeley's three-component model of working memory. *Source*: Baddeley, Alan, 2003, "Working Memory and Language: An Overview." *Journal of Communication Disorders* 36.3: 189–203. Reprinted with permission from Elsevier.

Another schematic by Baddeley identifies the model's functions – input, analysis, short-term store, recoding, and output buffer – as being fluid (Figure 23.2). The contents come and go dynamically. However, the model draws on the brain's crystallized systems, which interpret what images signify linguistically, give long-term memory of events, and enable phonological, lexical, grammatical, and syntactic analysis. We store the content in these systems and it is available for use over a long period of time. In the classical model, Baddeley's language functions correspond, more or less, to locations in the brain. These locations and their language functions have been disputed. The classical Lichtheim-Geschwind model has the angular gyrus recoding phonologically visual data from the visual cortex at the back of the brain, passing it to Wernicke's area, which processes phonemic language semantically and in turn sends it to Broca's area, which shapes semantic text into syntactic form in preparation for articulation (Geschwind 1979). Recently, however, subcortical areas in the basal ganglia have been shown to regulate cognitive sequencing, including the motor controls that produce speech. Thus the phonological loop in working memory, which represents words as articulated, depends on the basal ganglia. Working memory uses multiple locations simultaneously, but it is associated with the hippocampus in the forebrain.

Baddeley's flowchart is a torus, a looping cybernetic channel for cybertext. What goes out as uttered speech authored by us in turn enters working memory as received heard speech to which we will give, in turn, feedback. Cognitive language processing is thus a cybertextual message-feedback system.

Creating takes place in the black box outside working memory. Normally we are not conscious of what we say before we say it. Few people script an utterance in working memory before uttering. The same holds true for written output, for although we may hear silently the text as we are storing it on screen or paper, we seldom preview it in working memory before typing it. There is often surprise in discovering what we have just said. As Baddeley's first flowchart shows, we are also not aware of what goes on in boxes A and D, the visual and phonological analyses of input sense data, before we store those analyses in working memory. Between the visual and auditory input, and our conscious reception of image and speech in working memory, there are two black boxes in which we actively construct what we think we see and hear. The so-called McGurk effect tells us that we unconsciously subvocalize a model of what someone else is saying. We then "hear" only what we analyze we are hearing. The last one to utter any heard utterance, in effect, is the hearer-observer. The McGurk experiment is described by Philip Lieberman (2000: 57, citing McGurk and MacDonald 1976):

> The effect is apparent when a subject views a motion picture or video of the face of a person saying the sound [ga] while listening to the sound [ba] synchronized to start when the lips of the speaker depicted open. The sound that the listener "hears" is neither [ba] or [ga]. The conflicting visually-conveyed labial place-of-articulation cue and the auditory velar place of articulation cue yield the percept of the intermediate alveolar [da]. The tape-recorded stimulus is immediately heard as a [ba] when the subject doesn't look at the visual display.
>
> The listener hears a sound that no one uttered. Cybertextually, a receiver co-authors, by virtue of his cognitive interpretation of auditory and visual inputs, a message from the sender.

It is not unreasonable to believe that the McGurk effect applies to all heard and seen words, from whatever source. If we utter speech unselfconsciously, not knowing what it will be until we experience it ourselves – that is, if we do not script our words in working memory before we say them (and to do so would be to reduce our conversation to an agonizingly slow, halting process) – and if we receive our own utterance auditorily (listening to our words as we speak them), then our brain must unconsciously model those words before they fall into our working memory. Whenever we author speech, therefore, we hear it at the same time as our listeners. Or, when we write something down, that utterance also reaches us through the visual cortex and must be decoded and analyzed cognitively before we can receive it in working memory. Cybertextually, the speaker receives his own message at the same time that his listener or his reader does. A message is always cognitively constructed by its receivers, and the author is always one of these constructing observers. A message passes through, simultaneously, different cybernetic channels for its sender and for every receiver. One goes back to the author, and others to audience members and readers.

The author's self-monitoring is not much studied. Feedback for every utterance is of two kinds. The author's initial cognitive construction of what he hears himself say or sees himself write, on paper or screen, is published in a moment of conscious recognition in his working memory. Second, the author's response to his own self-constructed message then helps him to revise his last utterance and to shape his next utterance. Thus, cybertextually, authors steer or govern their speech internally by a recursive message-feedback cycle. Unconsciously, the author creates a sentence and utters it (a messaging). By witnessing the utterance through his senses, in iconic memory, he first recognizes what he has created. That moment of recognition leads him to construct what he hears or sees (a feedback response). His construction of his own utterance, by reason of being held in working memory, becomes in turn another message to his mind's unselfconscious language-maker that enables him to rewrite or to expand on what he has just uttered. If we fully knew what we were saying in advance of saying it, if we were aware of our entire composition process consciously as it unfolded, there would be no moment of recognition and hence no internal cognitive feedback.

The McGurk effect complicates basic cybernetics by showing that every reader authors all messages received by him. Once we realize that every author also gives feedback to all his own messages, that authors and readers behave identically, then cybernetic process becomes cyclic. Uttering, viewed cybertextually, is cognitively recursive, complex, and self-regulatory (or, in Hayles' term, homeostatic). It is recursive because every utterance to the senses (vocalized or written), just by reason of being cognitively modeled, sets in motion an internal mimicking utterance in the speaker's mind. Uttering is complex because a single cybertext proceeds through different channels, one internal and many external, each of which is vulnerable to different types of noise. Uttering is self-regulatory by tending to dampen positive feedback, which accelerates a process beyond what is desired, with negative feedback, which brakes or reverses an action. Positive feedback in cybernetics urges that information density be increased. Negative feedback urges that information density be reduced. Authors govern this density by adding or deleting redundancy. Mechanically, James Watt's flyball governor receives information on the speed of the engine, information that can trigger its slowing down. Even so, the feedback that authors receive from themselves tells them how to revise what they are saying to make it more effective. Positive feedback tells us to repeat and vary; negative feedback, to simplify and condense. This self-monitoring, I argue, is partly available for study with text-analysis tools.

The Author's Self-monitoring

We now know a great deal about the cognitive mechanics of authoring. It is largely unconscious. Because we cannot remember explicitly how it utters sentences, we have concocted fugitive agents like the Muse to explain creativity. Etymologically, "muse" comes from the Indo-European base for "mind," that is, memory, of which we have several kinds. There is associative long-term episodic and semantic memory, from which we can extract information but can never read through as we do a book. Try as we may by probing long-term memory, in particular, we cannot recover the steps of the uttering process that creates a sentence. On occasion, we make one painstakingly in working memory, a short-term, explicit phonological store with a known capacity, 4 ± 2 items in Cowan (2000), revising George Miller's 7 ± 2 items, only as many words as we can utter aloud in two seconds, and confirmed by many experiments since then. The gist behind a sentence taking shape consciously in working memory, however, still comes from a cognitive unknown, "through a glass darkly." We use working memory to rearrange words in such semi-memorized sentences, but the authoring process that suggests them must be queried by a type of memory that we cannot recover as an episode or a semantic meaning. We know from experimentation that people absorb, in the short term, a non-recallable but influential memory of sensory experience. This is not the brief iconic or echoic memory of experience that lasts about 100 microseconds, the space of time between two claps of a hand. We are conscious of these traces. It is the residue they leave in the unconscious, a residue called priming, which is a form of implicit memory lasting several weeks. When we have implicit memory lasting indefinitely in perma-store, we call it procedural memory instead of priming. Here cognitive language processing and other motor skills (like bicycle riding) are stored. Although procedural memories are powerful, we can only recall them by performing them. Why can we not remember, step-by-step, how we make a sentence? The answer seems to be that there is no place in our brain to put the protocol, and maybe no names to identify what goes into it. Its complexity would likely overwhelm working memory many times over. Because we utter easily, we don't really need to know how we do it unless we enjoy frustration and take up stylistics and authorship attribution.

The only window of consciousness we have on our language processing is the phonological loop in working memory. Cowan's magic number, "four, plus or minus two" items (2000; cf. Baddeley 1975), governs all our speaking, listening, writing, and reading. What do we know about this humiliating limit? Reading-span tests show that we can recall a range of from 2 to 5.5 final words of a group of unrelated sentences (Just and Carpenter (1992)): a smaller number, but then we have to deselect all initial words in each sentence. The "word-length" effect shows that the number of items in working memory lessens as their length in syllables increases. We can be confounded at first by garden-path sentences such as "The horse raced past the ancient ruined barn fell" because a key word at the end of a clause (here the verb "fell") takes as subject, not the opportunistic word just preceding, but a noun at the beginning, on the very edge of working-memory capacity. The "articulatory suppression" effect confounds us in another way. If I repeat aloud a nonsense word, "rum-tum, rum-tum, rum-tum," it subvocally captures the working memory of my listeners and prevents them consciously attending to other words. We process words in working memory by drawing on the motor instructions that Broca's area gives to articulate them aloud. Another effect, termed "acoustic similarity," describes our difficulty in recalling a list of similar-sounding words. We can remember semantically related groups like "ghost," "haunt," "sprite," "poltergeist," "specter," "balrog," and "revenant" more easily than simple terms that sound alike, such as "lake," "rack," "trick," "rock," "cake," "coke," and "make." If working memory did not encode words acoustically, we would not experience this trouble.

Self-monitoring is partly conscious when taking place in working memory today, principally while we read what we have just written onto a page or word-processed onto a screen. We can only read, however, from five to nine acoustically-encoded items at a time. Baddeley (2004: 26) shows that recall errors, fewer than two for 9-letter words, more than double for 10-letter words (which must exceed working-memory limits). Only when we can chunk the items into larger units, as in real English words, does the error rate fall. Empirical research into the psychology of reading and writing, which teaches the teachers how to make children literate, reveals that our eyes read by saccades (jumps), fixations, and gazes, that a typical saccade takes twenty milliseconds and covers six–eight letters, and that fixations have a perceptual span of about three characters to the right and fifteen to the left (or four–five words in length) and last 200–300 milliseconds unless they settle into a gaze. College-level students jump and fix their eyes 90 times for every 100 words; one-quarter of those jumps go backwards (Crowder and Wagner 1992: table 2.1). Function words get briefer fixations than content words (Gleason and Ratner 1998: fig. 5.4). We evidently use iconic memory to keep a continuing image of a cybertext before ourselves so that we can free up our working memory for other items, such as higher-level entities than words. It is thought that these entities are propositions, each of which holds an argument and a predicate. Examples of propositions are subject–verb and adjective–noun combinations such as "The sun is a star" and "bright as Venus." The average reading span, calculated to be between six and twelve propositions, that is, between twelve and twenty-four arguments and predicates, can pack a lot into working memory because we can chunk words into higher-level entities. In other words, we form concept maps in which high-level propositions are placeholders for many lower-level items. An item can be a word (argument or predicate), a proposition (a combined argument-predicate), or one or more related propositions.

Consider the first two lines in the first quatrain of Shakespeare's sonnet 73. The 18 words in the first two lines cannot fit separately into the phonological loop (PL) working memory (WM) unless they are chunked. Six propositions can do the job (Figure 23.3).

The absolute maximum size of working memory can be as much as ten times four, plus or minus two, but only if words and propositions are fused into a schema. Although these two lines have at least twenty argument-predicate propositions, they can be fitted into the average reading span with some chunking, if working memory handles only propositions 1, 2, 3, 8, 9, and 10, but these are spread out over six levels, some more deeply encoded than others. Of course, chunking becomes easier if the text appears constantly before one's eyes in iconic memory for ready reference. Three quatrains and a couplet would have $21 + 21 + 21 + 10 + 3$ propositions, or 76 in all (within about 125 words), well inside the maximum size of working memory, 40, plus or minus 20 basic items, heavily chunked. See Figure 23.4.

That time of year thou mayst in me behold
When yellow leaves, or none, or few, do hang
Upon those boughs which shake against the cold,
Bare ruin'd choirs, where late the sweet birds sang.

Line	Argument	Predicate	Proposition No.
1	time	year	→ p1
	thou	behold	→ p2
	p1	p2	→ p3
2	yellow	leaves	→ p4
	none	leaves	→ p5
	p4	p5	→ p6
	few	leaves	→ p7
	p6	p7	→ p8
	p8	hang	→ p9
	p3	p9	→ p10

* 18 words are twice the size of the PL in WM
        BUT

* 6 propositions fit within the PL:

line 1   = p1, p2, p3
line 2   = p8, p9
line 1-2   = p10

Figure 23.3   The first quatrain of Shakespeare's sonnet.

Three-digit area code and exchange (if chunked to one each), and local number, fall just within working memory for unrelatable numbers. Cybertexts are more heavily redundant than numbers and are integrated syntactically. The maximum reading span for meaningful text would appear to be sonnet-sized, that is, about the length of the Lord's Prayer or the Ten Commandments. The average reading span would cover a shorter span, perhaps a quarter of that, about the amount of text in the 20-word oath like "I do solemnly swear to tell the truth, the whole truth, and nothing but the truth, so help me God."

The quantitative limits of working memory in authoring and reading serve an important purpose for cybertextuality: they define the dynamic playing field for an author's *currente calamo* revisions of his work. In size, this cognitive field covers a quatrain-to-sonnet-sized window of text that shifts forward in jumps, as the author is uttering a text. If we examine how the author manipulates text within this window, we may find some new measures for authorship. They might include the size of the author's uttering window (how many words the author inputs without looking up to

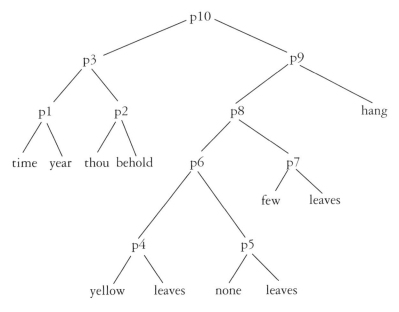

Figure 23.4   Propositions in the first quatrain of Shakespeare's sonnet 73.

absorb them and to generate internal feedback), the types of editorial changes the author carries out inside that window (are they transformative in a syntactic sense, or are they just diction-related?), and the speed with which he moves through the composing process.

Computer Text Analysis and the Cybertextual Cycle

Traditional stylistics investigates a text spatially as a chain of words that, though it may take time for the reader to traverse, exists complete in a single moment. It has a three-dimensional size on the page but is frozen in time. Most text-analysis programs count the number and frequency of words, phrases, and sentences but do not analyze the text's dynamics as it unfolds. In both making and reading, however, an author has dynamic strategies in revising what he utters, moment by moment. Quantitative information about the frequency and proximity of words and phrases to one another characterizes a whole flat text, or samples of it that are judged representative. However, a text-analysis method captures aspects of the author's cognitive idiolect, such as the ways in which he reacts, positively or negatively, to the feedback that his unselfconscious cognitive modeling gives him. Thus style is partly a function of the author's internal cybertextual message-feedback cycles.

My traditional text-analysis studies of Chaucer and Shakespeare highlight features that cognitive processing can explain. Phrase concordancers identify repeated fixed phrases and unfixed collocations in Chaucer's The General Prologue that recur elsewhere in the entire *Canterbury Tales*. The same holds true of Shakespeare's *Troilus and Cressida* in his body of work. Their natural vocabularies appear to have been phrasal in nature, comprising units no longer than four, plus or minus two terms, which I called phrasal repetends. *Collgen*, a program included within *TACT*, detected them. No repeated phrases exceed in length the capacity of the phonological store of working memory. Their phrasal repetends also form clusters. If we recursively concord a concordance of their repeated words and phrases, we find associative networks. Such clusters must arise from the structure of their long-term memory. I found unusual peaks of overlap in phrasal repetitions between Chaucer's General Prologue and the last tale in the work, the Manciple's (Lancashire 1993a, 1993b). These clustered repetitions did not arise from subject matter specific to either poem; they belonged to Chaucer's free-floating, current language pool. The shared phrasal repetitions suggest that he wrote the first and the last poem in the *Canterbury Tales* at about the same time. A comparable overlap ties Shakespeare's *Troilus* to *Hamlet* and other plays written in the same period.

I analyzed one speech in particular from Shakespeare's problem play, *Troilus and Cressida*, the Greek leader Agamemnon's disgruntled address to his generals before the walls of Troy (Lancashire 1999). Without looking for authorial self-monitoring, I found it. This perplexing speech breaks into two mirroring sonnet-sized passages, lines 1–16 and 16–29. Repeated collocations appear in bold, words that occur only once in Shakespeare's vocabulary are in large capital letters, and words that occur twice in small capitals (Figure 23.5).

Shakespeare anchors this two-part speech on five words, all repeated in each part: "princes" and "cheeks," "trial," "action" or "works," and "matter." Each part begins with a question. The right-hand glosses highlight the similar sequence of propositions mirrored in both parts. Despite the novel Latinate words, Shakespeare drew much from associational clusters in his long-term memory. Ten collocations here, each occurring four or more times in his works, form two clusters. One centers on the node word "grow" (7), which collocates with "cheeks" (14), "sap" (7), "knot" (6), "pine" (5), "prince" (5), "veins" (5), and "check" (4) and is found in the first part of his speech. Another centers on the words "winnows" (5) and "wind" (4) in the second part. The word "trial" connects the two parts. Shakespeare seems to have created lines 1–16 in a single dash, then paused, taking it in. His dynamic cognitive field appeared to be about a sonnet in length. Seeing the difficulty of what he had written, he then "explained" it to himself again. Feedback led to repetition with variation within a second identified structured segment, steered by feedback, his recognition and reconstruction of lines 1–16.

Feedback governs the information richness of the Agamemnon speech. The first part has six strange words, an acoustic pun ("check" and "cheek"), and almost no repetitions. It is vulnerable to misconstruction by Shakespeare's audience. His satisfaction with the dense imagery and novel language gave him positive feedback and led him to add six neologisms to the second part. Yet doubts about meaning led Shakespeare to negative feedback. And so he introduced redundancy in the form of restatement. He adjusted the rate of information, a cybertext's "entropy" (Pierce

1 **Princes**, what **grief** hath **set** these JAUNDIES o'r your **cheeks?**   (1a) queries
princes'cheeks
  2 The **ample** PROPOSITION that **hope makes**
  3 In all designs begun on **earth below**
  4 Fails in the promised LARGENESS. **Checks** and **disasters**
  5 **Grow** in the **veins** of **actions highest reared,**   (1b) their actions are
  6 As **knots**, by the CONFLUX of meeting **sap,**
  7 **Infects** the sound **pine** and diverts his **grain**
  8 TORTIVE and errant from his course of growth.
  9 Nor, **princes**, is it **matter new** to us   (1c) the matter;
10 That we **come short** of our suppose so far
11 That after **seven years'** siege yet **Troy walls** stand,
12 Sith every **action** that hath gone before,   (1b) each action
13 Whereof we have **record, trial** did **draw**   (1d) in trial
14 **Bias** and thwart, not **answering** the aim
15 And that UNBODIED figure of the **thought**   (1e) lacks body or shape.
16 That **gave** 't surmised **shape.**

                  Why then, you **princes,**   (2a) queries princes'
cheeks;
17 Do you with **cheeks ABASHED behold** our **works,**   (2b) their works
(=actions)
18 And **call** them **shames,** which are indeed naught else
19 But the PROTRACTIVE **trials** of **great Jove**   (2d) are trials that make
the
20 To **find PERSISTIVE constancy** in **men?**
21 The FINENESS of which **metal** is not found
22 In **fortune's love,** for then the bold and coward,
23 The **wise** and **fool**, the artist and UNREAD,
24 The **hard** and **soft**, seem all affined and kin.
25 But in the **wind** and **tempest** of her **frown**
26 Distinction with a broad and powerful **fan,**
27 **Puffing** at all, **winnows** the **light** away,
28 And what hath **mass** or **matter** by itself   (2c) the matter
29 Lies **rich** in **virtue** and UNMINGLED.   (2e) visible.

Figure 23.5   Chunked six-proposition schema of Shakespeare's sonnet 73.

1961: 80) by simultaneously accelerating and braking the passage's information density. Because written speech lifts the capacity constraints of working memory, and everything Shakespeare wrote remained accessible to his eyes long after uttering, he could allow density to increase. Shakespeare's cybertextual style uses repetition with variation of large units to counterbalance the unrelenting lexical strangeness he cultivates, devising new words, fixing them in striking metaphors. He combines positive and negative feedback.

A New Philology

Central to old philology are historical linguistics and a literary scholarship that applies what we know about language to the understanding of literature in its historical period. Typical old-philology tools include the concordance and the dictionary. Both read homogeneous, flat, unchanging material texts; and computerized concordancers do not change that fact. New philology supplements this traditional text analysis with tools from cognitive psychology and information science. These include brain-imaging devices and word-processing software like Tech Smith *Morae*, which records keystrokes, mouse actions, screens, the writer's face, and other events that take place in a composing session. These read dynamic, non-material texts of authors at work in composing. Both old and new philology, when employing computer tools, are cybertextual to the extent that they apply evidence of the author's use of his memory systems, as in self-monitoring and cognitive-feedback processing, to interpret the flat material text that he utters.

The most promising applications of the new philology are in the future. It is because the computer workstation can supplement the capacity of working memory that we can observe and measure how an author today responds to his own in-progress, window-by-window uttering of a work. Access to brain-imaging technology is beyond the means of literary researchers without medical qualifications. However, the word-processor enables a writer to solve garden-path sentences, to transform large verbal units (sentences, paragraphs) on the fly, and rapidly to adjust the redundancies he builds into his work. And every event in a word-processed document – continuations, deletions, additions, transpositions – can be time-stamped and counted. Lexical events, especially ones resulting from using online thesauri and lexicons, can be tabulated. Phrasal- and clausal-level events can be described grammatically: passive constructions made active, verb tenses altered, conjuncts replaced by subjuncts, and so on. A new cybertextual stylistics can be based on quantitative information available from the archived word-processing sessions that go into creating a text. Usability software undertakes the kind of archiving that John B. Smith, a pioneer in thematic criticism in English studies, and a process-based writing researcher, applied in his protocol analysis of living writers. Smith believed that asking writers to think aloud as they wrote, a technique Linda Flower introduced, injected noise into that process, and so he used instead a writer's keystrokes, sequences of which he interpreted as actions (Hayes and Flower 1980). Tracking, replaying, parsing, and displaying the writing process replaced Flower's thinking-aloud protocol. Santos and Badre inferred 73 percent of a writer's mental chunks through automatic analysis of keystrokes (1994: 75). Only semi-automatic analysis could tame the mass of data from such recording sessions.

Morae offers some of the functionality that Smith describes. Its name, from the Latin term for "delay," names a unit of sound in natural language. The software records keystrokes, mouse actions, screens, the writer's face, and other events that take place in a composing session. This protocol can log each keystroke (including modifying keys) with its elapsed time, and its time of day and date, and can link it to a video of the computer screen as well as to the image of the author at work, at that very moment. A distribution graph of that activity log shows the density of keystrokes at any instant during the keyboarding session. A partial spreadsheet, image, and graph of a *Morae* session in which I worked on this essay (Figure 23.6) reveals a rhythmic chunking in the uttering process.

A *Morae* graph can be exported to a spreadsheet for analysis; and one can play back, in a sequence of recorded sessions, the making of an entire work. These record cybertextual self-monitoring at work.

Even one recording session by a Shakespeare or a James Joyce would be invaluable evidence of the author's cognitive self-monitoring while composing. Their habits, of course, can only be inferred from texts and foul papers. For most writers, we do not even have the equivalent of Joyce's extraordinary notebooks, such as the well-known "Circe 3" (1972: 278–83) from *Ulysses*, which holds his brief notes in vertical and horizontal lists, many crossed out in colored crayon after he used them in revision. It is hard to resist interpreting Joyce's notes, most of which fall between one and nine words, as direct, cognitively chunked deposits from his limited-capacity, very human working memory. Short lyrics, especially the 14-line sonnet, may also remain the

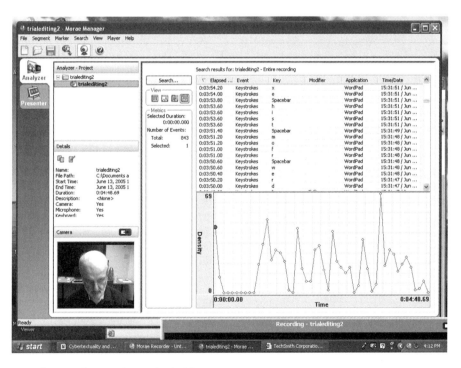

Figure 23.6   Part of my writing session in Morae.

most popular verse forms because of cognitive chunking: they can hold the maximum number of propositions that we can consciously encode in memory. Yet the truth is that we will never know how the minds of these writers worked. If present and future writers, however, record their authoring sessions and donate them, with their letters and papers, for study, critics bent on text analysis, close reading, and stylistics will inherit a windfall of data and new measures. Cybertextuality then will be a widely testable theory.

SELECTED REFERENCES

Aarseth, Espen J. (1997). *Cybertext: Perspectives on Ergodic Literature*. Baltimore: Johns Hopkins University Press.

Baddeley, Alan (2003). "Working Memory and Language: An Overview." *Journal of Communication Disorders* 36.3: 189–203.

—— (2004). *Your Memory: A User's Guide*. New Illustrated Edition. Richmond Hill, Ontario: Firefly Books.

——, Neil Thomson, and Mary Buchanan (1975). "Word Length and the Structure of Short-term Memory." *Journal of Verbal Learning and Verbal Behavior* 14.6: 575–89.

Carpenter, Rollo (2006). *Jabberwacky*. Icogno. URL: <http://www.jabberwacky.com>. Accessed May 8, 2006.

Cowan, Nelson (2000). "The Magical Number 4 in Short-term Memory: A Reconsideration of Mental Storage Capacity." *Behavioural and Brain Sciences* 24: 87–185.

Crowder, Robert G., and Richard K. Wagner (1992). *The Psychology of Reading: An Introduction*. New York: Oxford University Press.

Dunning, Alastair (2000). "Recounting Digital Tales: Chaucer Scholarship and The Canterbury Tales Project." Arts and Humanities Data Service. <http://ahds.ac.uk/creating/case-studies/canterbury/>.

ePresence Consortium (2006). *ePresence Interactive Media*. University of Toronto: Knowledge Media Design Institute. <http://epresence.tv/mediaContent/default.aspx>. Accessed May 8, 2006.

Federman, Mark (2004). "What is the Meaning of The Medium is the Message?" <http://individual.utoronto.ca/markfederman/article_mediumisthemessage.htm>. Accessed May 8, 2006.

Galison, Peter (1994). "The Ontology of the Enemy: Norbert Weiner and the Cybernetic Vision." *Critical Inquiry* 21: 228–66.

Garrard, Peter, L. M. Maloney, J. R. Hodges, and K. Patterson (2005). "The Effects of Very Early Alzheimer's Disease on the Characteristics of Writing by a Renowned Author." *Brain* 128.2: 250–60.

Geschwind, Norman (1979). "Specializations of the Human Brain." *The Brain*. A Scientific American Book. San Francisco: W. H. Freeman, pp. 108–17.

Gleason, Jean Burko, and Nan Bernstein Ratner (Eds.) (1998). *Psycholinguistics*, 2nd edn. Fort Worth: Harcourt Brace.

Haraway, Donna (1985). "A Manifesto for Cyborgs: Science, Technology, and Socialist Feminism in the 1980s." *Socialist Review* 80: 65–108.

Hayes, J. R., and L. S. Flower (1980). "Identifying the Organization of Writing Processes." In L. W. Gregg and E. R. Steinberg (Eds.). *Cognitive Processes in Writing*. Hillsdale, NJ: Lawrence Erlbaum.

Hayles, N. Katherine (1999). *How We Became Posthuman: Virtual Bodies in Cybernetics, Literature, and Informatics*. Chicago: University of Chicago Press.

Just, Marcel A., and Patricia A. Carpenter (1992). "A Capacity Theory of Comprehension: Individual Differences in Working Memory." *Psychological Review* 99: 122–49.

Lancashire, Ian (1993a). "Chaucer's Phrasal Repetends and *The Manciple's Prologue and Tale*." In *Computer-Based Chaucer Studies*. CCHWP 3. Toronto: Centre for Computing in the Humanities, pp. 99–122.

—— (1993b). "Chaucer's Repetends from The General Prologue of *The Canterbury Tales*." In *The*

Centre and its Compass: Studies in Medieval Literature in Honor of Professor John Leyerle. Kalamazoo, MI: Western Michigan University, pp. 315–65.

—— (1999). "Probing Shakespeare's Idiolect in *Troilus and Cressida* I.3.1–29." *University of Toronto Quarterly* 68.3: 728–67.

—— (2004). "Cybertextuality." *TEXT Technology* 2: 1–18.

—— (2005). "Cognitive Stylistics and the Literary Imagination." *Companion to Digital Humanities*. Cambridge: Cambridge University Press, pp. 397–414.

Lieberman, Philip (2000). *Human Language and Our Reptilian Brain: The Subcortical Bases of Speech, Syntax, and Thought*. Cambridge, MA: Harvard University Press.

Liu, Hugo, and Push Singh (2002). "MAKEBE-LIEVE: Using Commonsense Knowledge to Generate Stories." *Proceedings of the Eighteenth National Conference on Artificial Intelligence*, AAAI 2002. Edmonton: AAAI Press, pp. 957–58. <http://agents.media.mit.edu/projects/make believe/>.

Lyotard, Jean François (1984). *The Postmodern Condition: A Report on Knowledge* (Geoff Bennington and Brian Massumi, Trans.). Minneapolis: University of Minnesota Press.

Masani, R. P. (1990). *Norbert Wiener 1894–1964*. Basel: Birkhäuser.

McGurk, H., and J. MacDonald (1976). "Hearing Lips and Seeing Voices." *Nature* 263: 747–8.

Miller, G. A. (1956). "The Magical Number Seven, plus or minus Two: Some Limits on our Capacity for Processing Information." *Psychological Review* 63: 89–97.

Pierce, John R. (1961). *An Introduction to Information Theory: Symbols, Signals & Noise*, 2nd edn. New York: Dover, 1980.

Sachs, Stephen (2006). *The Jumbler*. <http:// www.stevesachs.com/jumbler.cgi>. Accessed May 8, 2006.

Santos, Paulo J., and Albert N. Badre (1994). "Automatic Chunk Detection in Human-computer Interaction." *Proceedings of the Workshop on Advanced Visual Interfaces*. New York: ACM, pp. 69–77.

Smith, John B., Dana Kay Smith, and Eileen Kupstas (1993). "Automated Protocol Analysis." *Human–computer Interaction* 8: 101–45.

Stribling, Jeremy, Max Krohn, and Dan Aguayo (2006). *SCIgen – An Automatic CS Paper Generator*. Cambridge, MA: Computer Science and Artificial Intelligence Laboratory, MIT. <http://pdos.csail.mit.edu/scigen/>. Accessed May 8, 2006.

TechSmith (2006). *Morae Usability Testing for Software and Web Sites*. Okemos, MI. <http://www.tech-smith.com/morae.asp>. Accessed May 8, 2006.

Watt, Robert (2004). *Concordance*. Version 3.2. <http://www.concordancesoftware.co.uk/>. Accessed May 8, 2006.

Wiener, Norbert (1948). *Cybernetics or Control and Communication in the Animal and the Machine*, 2nd edn. Cambridge, MA: MIT Press, 1961.

—— (1950). *The Human Use of Human Beings: Cybernetics and Society*. New York: Hearst, 1967.

24

Electronic Scholarly Editions

Kenneth M. Price

Many people have commented on the ongoing transformation of scholarly publication, with some fearing and some exulting over the move to digital production and dissemination. It seems inevitable that an ever-increasing amount of scholarly work will take digital form. Yet if we assess the current moment and consider key genres of traditional print scholarship – articles, monographs, collections of essays, and scholarly editions – we find that digital work has achieved primacy only for editions. The turn toward electronic editions is remarkable because they are often large in scope, requiring significant investments in time and money. Moreover, although editions are monuments to memory, no one is expressing great confidence in our ability to preserve *them*. Marilyn Deegan notes the challenge librarians face in preserving digital scholarly editions – this "most important of scholarly tools" – and suggests steps scholars may take "in order to ensure that what is produced is preserved to the extent possible" (Deegan 2006: 358). Morris Eaves candidly acknowledges the uncertain future of the project he co-edits: "We plow forward with no answer to the haunting question of where and how a project like [*The William Blake Archive*] will live out its useful life" (Eaves 2006: 218). Given the apparent folly of investing huge amounts of time and money in what cannot be preserved with certainty, there must be sound reasons that make this medium attractive for scholarly editors. This chapter explores some of those reasons.

Jerome McGann has argued that the entirety of our cultural heritage will need to be re-edited in accord with the new possibilities of the digital medium (McGann 2002: B7). He laments that the academy has done little to prepare literary and historical scholars for this work, thus leaving the task, he fears, to people less knowledgeable about the content itself: librarians and systems engineers. In general, humanities scholars have neglected editorial work because the reward structures in the academy have not favored editing but instead literary and cultural theory. Many academics fail to recognize the theoretical sophistication, historical knowledge, and analytical strengths necessary to produce a sound text or texts and the appropriate scholarly apparatus for a first-rate edition. In this fraught context, it seems useful to clarify the key terms and assumptions at work in this chapter. By *scholarly edition*, I mean the establishment of a text on explicitly stated principles and by someone with specialized knowledge about textual scholarship and the writer or writers involved. An edition is *scholarly* both because of the rigor with which the text is reproduced or altered and because of the expertise brought to bear on the task and in the offering of suitable introductions, notes, and textual apparatus. Mere digitizing produces information; in contrast, scholarly editing produces knowledge.

Many prominent electronic editions are referred to as digital *archives*, and such terminology may strike some people as loose usage. In fact, electronic editorial undertakings are only imperfectly described by any of the terms currently in use: edition, project, archive, thematic research collection. Traditionally, an archive has referred to a repository holding material artifacts rather than digital surrogates. An archive in this traditional sense may well be described in finding aids but its materials are rarely, if ever, meticulously edited and annotated as a whole. In an electronic environment, *archive* has gradually come to mean a purposeful collection of digital surrogates. Words take on new meanings over time, of course, and *archive* in a digital context has come to suggest something that blends features of editing and archiving. To meld features of both – to have the care of treatment and annotation of an edition and the inclusiveness of an archive – is one of the tendencies of recent work in electronic editing. One such project, the *William Blake Archive*, was awarded an MLA prize recently as a distinguished scholarly edition. The *Walt Whitman Archive* also contains a fair amount of matter that, in the past, ordinarily would not be included as part of an edition focused on an "author's" writings: we have finding guides to manuscripts, a biography, all reviews of Whitman's work, photographs of the poet, selected criticism from his contemporaries and from our own time, an audio file of what is thought to be the poet's voice reading "America," encoding guidelines, and other information about the history and technical underpinnings of the site. In other words, in a digital context, the "edition" is only a piece of the "archive," and, in contrast to print, "editions," "resources," and "tools" can be interdependent rather than independent.

Why Are People Making Electronic Editions?

One distinguishing feature of electronic editions is their capaciousness: scholars are no longer limited by what they can fit on a page or afford to produce within the economics of print publishing. It is not as if economic problems go away with electronic editing, but they are of a different sort. For example, because color images are prohibitively expensive for most book publications, scholars can usually hope to have only a few black and white illustrations in a book. In an electronic edition, however, we can include as many high-resolution color images as can be procured, assuming adequate server space for storage and delivery, and assuming sufficient staff to carry out the laborious process of scanning or photographing materials and making them available to users. A group of scholars who have sufficient resources (and who work with cooperative repositories) can create an edition of extraordinary depth and richness, an edition that provides both the evidence and the final product – a transcribed text and the images of the material they worked from in producing the edition. They can include audio and video clips, high-quality color reproductions of art works, and interactive maps. For multimedia artists such as William Blake and Dante Gabriel Rossetti the benefits are clear: much more adequate representation of their complex achievements. Likewise it is now possible to track and present in one convenient place the iconographic tradition of *Don Quixote*, a novel that has been repeatedly illustrated in ways rich with interpretive possibilities (<http://www.csdl.tamu.edu/cervantes/english/images_temp.html>). The non-authorial illustrations of this novel are part of the social text and provide an index to the culturally inscribed meanings of Cervantes' novel. Electronic editions have also deepened interest in the nature of textuality itself, thus giving the field of scholarly editing a new cachet.

The possibility of including so much and so many kinds of material makes the question of where and what is the text for an electronic edition every bit as vexed (if not more so) than it has been for print scholarship. For example, we might ask: what constitutes the text of an electronic version of a periodical publication? *The Making of America* project, collaboratively undertaken by Cornell University (<http://cdl.library.cornell.edu/moa/>) and the University of Michigan (<http://www.hti.umich.edu/m/moagrp/>), is a pioneering contribution of great value, but it excludes advertising, thereby implying that the authentic or real text of a periodical excludes this material of great importance for the study of history, popular culture, commerce, and so on.[1] A similar disregard of the material object is seen also in editions that emphasize the *intention* of the writer over the actual documents produced. This type of edition has been praised, on the one hand, as producing a purer text, a version that achieves what a writer ideally wanted to create without the intervening complications of overzealous copyeditors, officious censors, sloppy compositors, or slips of the writer's own pen. For these intentionalist editors, any particular material manifestation of a text may well differ from what a writer meant to produce. On the other hand, the so-called "critical" editions they produce have been denigrated in some quarters as being ahistorical, as producing a text that never existed in the world. The long-standing debate between, say, critical and documentary editors won't be resolved because each represents a legitimate approach to editing.

A great deal of twentieth-century editing – and, in fact, editing of centuries before – as G. Thomas Tanselle notes, was based on finding an authoritative text based on "final intentions" (Tanselle 1995: 15–16). Ordinarily editors emphasized the intentions of the "author" (a contested term in recent decades) and neglected a range of other possible collaborators including friends, proofreaders, editors, and compositors, among others. A concern with final intentions makes sense at one level: the final version of a work is often stronger – more fully developed, more carefully considered, more precisely phrased – than an early or intermediate draft of it. But for poets, novelists, and dramatists whose work may span decades, there is real question about the wisdom of relying on last choices. Are people at their sharpest, most daring, and most experimental at the end of life when energies (and sometimes clarity) fade and other signs of age begin to show? Further, the final version of a text is often even more mediated by the concerns of editors and censors than are earlier versions, and the ability of anyone to discern what a writer might have hoped for, absent these social pressures, is open to question.

The long-standing concern with an author's final intentions has faced a significant challenge in recent years. Richard J. Finneran notes that the advent of new technologies "coincided with a fundamental shift in textual theory, away from the notion of a single-text 'definitive edition' " (Finneran 1996: x). Increasingly, editors have wanted to provide multiple texts, sometimes all versions of a text. Texts tend to exist in more than one version, and a heightened concern with versioning or fluidity is a distinctive trait of contemporary editing (Bryant 2002; Schreibman 2002: 287). Electronic editing allows us to avoid choosing, say, the early William Wordsworth or Henry James over the late. Even if there were unanimous agreement over the superiority of one period over another for these and other writers, that superiority would probably rest on aesthetic grounds open to question. And of course we often want to ask questions of texts that have nothing to do with the issue of the "best version."

New developments in electronic editing – including the possibility of presenting all versions of some especially valuable texts – are exciting, but anyone contemplating an electronic edition should also consider that the range of responsibilities for an editorial team has dramatically increased, too. The division of labor that was seen in print editing is no longer so well defined. The electronic scholarly edition is an enterprise that relies fundamentally on collaboration, and work in this medium is likely to stretch a traditional humanist, the solitary scholar who churns out articles and books behind the closed door of his office. Significant digital projects tend to be of a scope that they cannot be effectively undertaken alone, and hence collaborations with librarians, archivists, graduate students, undergraduate students, academic administrators, funding agencies, and private donors are likely to be necessary. These collaborations can require a fair amount of social capital for a large project, since the good will of many parties is required. Editors now deal with many issues they rarely concerned themselves with before. In the world of print, the appearance of a monograph was largely someone else's concern, and the proper functioning of the codex as an artifact could be assumed. With regard to book design, a wide range of options were available, but these choices customarily were made by the publisher. With electronic work, on the other hand, proper functionality cannot be assumed, and design choices are wide open. Collaboration with technical experts is necessary, and to make collaboration successful some knowledge of technical issues – mark-up of texts and database design, for example – is required. These matters turn out to be not merely technical but fundamental to editorial decision-making.

The electronic edition can provide exact facsimiles along with transcriptions of all manuscripts and books of a given writer. At first glance, it might be tempting to think of this as unproblematic, an edition without bias. Of course, there are problems with this view. For one thing, all editions have a perspective and make some views more available than others. An author-centered project may imply a biographical framework for reading, while a gender-specific project like the Brown University Women Writers Project (<http://www.brown.edu/>) implies that the texts should be read with gender as a key interpretive lens. Neutrality is finally not a possibility. Peter Robinson and Hans Walter Gabler have observed that "experiments with the design of electronic textual editions suggest that mere assembly does not avoid the problem of closing off some views in order to open up a particular view" (Robinson and Gabler 2000: 3). Even an inclusive digital archive is both an amassing of material and a shaping of it. That shaping takes place in a variety of places, including in the annotations, introductions, interface, and navigation. Editors are shirking their duties if they do not offer guidance: they are and should be, after all, something more than blind, values-neutral deliverers of goods. The act of *not* overtly highlighting specific works is problematic in that it seems to assert that all works in a corpus are on the same footing, when they never are. Still, there are degrees of editorial intervention; some editions are thesis-ridden and others are more inviting of a multitude of interpretations.

A master database for a project may provide a unique identifier (id) for every document created by a writer. In this sense all documents are equal. Lev Manovich has commented interestingly on the role of the database in digital culture:

> After the novel and subsequently cinema privileged narrative as the key form of cultural expression in the modern age, the computer age introduces its correlate – the database. Many new media objects do not tell stories; they don't have beginning or end; in fact, they don't have any development, thematically, formally or otherwise which would organize their elements into a sequence. Instead, they are collections of individual items, where every item has the same significance as any other. As a cultural form, the database represents the world as a list of items and it refuses to order this list. In contrast, a narrative creates a cause-and-effect trajectory of seemingly unordered items. Therefore, database and narrative are natural enemies. Competing for the same territory of human culture, each claims an exclusive right to make meaning out of the world. (Manovich 2005)

Manovich's remarks notwithstanding, the best electronic editions thrive on the combined strengths of database and narrative. William Horton has written that creators of digital resources may feel

> tempted to forego the difficult analysis that linear writing requires and throw the decision of what is important and what to know first onto the user. But users expect the writer to lead them through the jungle of information. They may not like being controlled or manipulated, but they do expect the writer to blaze trails for them ... Users don't want to have to hack their way through hundreds of choices at every juncture. (Horton 1994: 160)

The idea of including everything in an edition is suitable for writers of great significance. Yet such an approach has some negative consequences: it can be seen as damaging to a writer (and might be seen as counterproductive for readers and editors themselves). In fact, the decision to include everything is not as clear a goal or as "objective" an approach as one might think. Just what is "everything," after all? For example, are signatures given to autograph hunters part of what is everything in a truly inclusive edition of collected writings? Should marginalia be included? If so, does it comprise only words inscribed in margins or also underlinings and symbolic notations? Should address books, shopping and laundry lists be included? When dealing with a prolific writer such as W. B. Yeats, editors are likely to ask themselves if there are limits to what *all* should be construed to be. What separates wisdom and madness in a project that sets out to represent everything?

This section started by asking why people are making electronic editions, and to some extent the discussion has focused on the *challenges* of electronic editing. I would argue that these very challenges contribute to the attraction of working in this medium. At times there is a palpable excitement surrounding digital work stemming in part from the belief this is a rare moment in the history of scholarship. Fundamental aspects of literary editing are up for reconsideration: the scope of what can be undertaken, the extent and diversity of the audience, and the query potential that – through encoding – can be embedded in texts and enrich future interpretations. Electronic editing can be daunting – financially, technically, institutionally, and theoretically – but it is also a field of expansiveness and tremendous possibility.

Digital Libraries and Scholarly Editions

It is worthwhile to distinguish between the useful contributions made by large-scale digitization projects, sometimes referred to as digital library projects, and the more fine-grained, specialized work of an electronic scholarly edition. Each is valuable, though they have different procedures and purposes. The *Wright American Fiction* project can be taken as a representative digital library project (<http://www.letrs. indiana.edu/web/w/wright2/>). Such collections are typically vast. *Wright American Fiction* is a tremendous resource that makes freely available nearly 3,000 works of American fiction published from 1851 to 1875. This ambitious undertaking has been supported by a consortium of Big Ten schools plus the University of Chicago. As of September 2005 (the most recent update available) nearly half the texts were fully edited and encoded; the rest were unedited. "Fully edited" in this context means proofread and corrected (rather than remaining as texts created via optical character recognition (OCR) with a high number of errors). The "fully edited" texts also have SGML tagging that enables better navigation to chapter or other divisions within the fiction and links from the table of contents to these parts. Not surprisingly, *Wright American Fiction* lacks scholarly introductions, annotations, and collation of texts. Instead, the collection is made up of full-text presentations of the titles listed in Lyle

Wright's *American Fiction 1851–1875: A Contribution Toward a Bibliography* (1957; rev. 1965). The texts are presented as page images and transcriptions based on microfilm originally produced by a commercial firm, Primary Source Media. It is telling that the selection of texts for *Wright American Fiction* was determined by a pre-existing commercial venture and was not based on finding the best texts available or by creating a fresh "critical" edition. The latter option was no doubt a practical impossibility for a project of this scale. In contrast to *Wright American Fiction*'s acceptance of texts selected and reproduced by a third party, the editor of a scholarly edition would take the establishment of a suitable text to be a foundational under-taking. Moreover, as the MLA "Guidelines for Editors of Scholarly Editions" indicate, any edition that purports to be scholarly will provide annotations and other glosses.

Wright American Fiction, in a nutshell, has taken a useful bibliography and made it more useful by adding the content of the titles Wright originally listed. One might think of the total record of texts as the great collective American novel for the period. *Wright American Fiction* has so extended and so enriched the original print bibliog-raphy that it has become a fundamentally new thing: the difference between a title and a full text is enormous. As a searchable collection of what approaches the entirety of American fiction for a period, *Wright American Fiction* has a new identity quite distinct from, even if it has its basis in, the original printed volume.

Wright American Fiction's handling of Harriet Jacobs (listed by her pseudonym Linda Brent) demonstrates some of the differences between the aims of a digital library project and a scholarly edition. The key objective of *Wright American Fiction* has been to build a searchable body of American fiction. Given that between the creation of the bibliography and the creation of the full-text electronic resource, an error in the original bibliography has been detected (a work listed as fiction has been determined not be fictional), it seems a mistaken policy to magnify the error by providing the full text of a non-fictional document. *Incidents in the Life of a Slave Girl* was listed as fiction by the original bibliographer, Lyle Wright – at a time when Jacobs's work was thought to be fictional – and it remains so designated in the online project even though the book is no longer catalogued or understood that way. This would seem to be a mechanical rather than a scholarly response to this particular problem. The collection of texts in the Wright project is valuable on its own terms, but it is different from an edition where scholarly judgment is paramount. *Wright American Fiction* consistently follows its own principles, though these principles are such that the project remains neutral on matters where a scholarly edition would be at pains to take a stand. *Wright American Fiction* is a major contribution to scholarship without being a scholarly edition per se.

In contrast to the digital library collection, we also see a new type of scholarly edition that is often a traditional edition and more, sometimes called a thematic research collection. Many thematic research collections – also often called archives – aim toward the ideal of being all-inclusive resources for the study of given topics. In an electronic environment, it is possible to provide the virtues of both a facsimile and a critical or documentary edition simultaneously. G. Thomas Tanselle calls "a newly keyboarded rendition (searchable for any word)" and "a facsimile that shows the original typography or handwriting, lineation, and layout . . . the first requirement of an electronic edition" (1995: 58). A facsimile is especially important for those who believe that texts are not separable from artifacts, that texts are fundamentally linked to whatever conveys them in physical form. Those interested in bibliographic codes – how typeface, margins, ornamentation, and other aspects of the material object convey meaning – are well served by electronic editions that present high-quality color facsimile images of documents. Of course, digital facsimiles cannot convey *every* physical aspect of the text – the smell, the texture, and the weight, for example.

An additional feature of electronic editions deserves emphasis – the possibility of incremental development *and* delivery. If adequate texts do not exist in print then it is often advisable to release work-in-progress. For example, if someone were to undertake an electronic edition of the complete letters of Harriet Beecher Stowe, it would be sensible to release that material as it is transcribed and annotated since no adequate edition of Stowe's letters has been published. It has become conventional to release electronic work before it reaches fully realized form, and for good reason. Even when a print edition exists, it can be useful to release electronic work-in-progress because of its searchability and other functionality. Of course, delivering work that is still in development raises interesting new questions. For example: when is an electronic edition stable? And when is it ready to be ingested into a library system?

Electronic editing projects often bring into heightened relief a difficulty confronted by generations of scholarly editors. As Ian Donaldson argues in "Collecting Ben Jonson," "*The collected edition* [a gathering of the totality of a writer's oeuvre, however conceived] is a phrase that borders upon oxymoron, hinting at a creative tension that lies at the very heart of editorial practice. For collecting and editing – gathering in and sorting out – are very different pursuits, that often lead in quite contrary directions" (Donaldson 2003: 19). An "electronic edition" is arguably a different thing than an archive of primary documents, even a "complete" collection of documents, and the activities of winnowing and collecting are quite different in their approaches to representation. Is a writer best represented by reproducing what may be most popular or regarded as most important? Should an editor try to capture all variants of a particular work, or even all variants of all works? As Amanda Gailey has argued, "Each of these editorial objectives carries risks. Editors whose project is selection threaten to oversimplify an author's corpus, [and to] neglect certain works while propagating overexposed ones . . . Conversely, editors who seek to collect an author's work, as Donaldson put it, risk 'unshap[ing] the familiar canon in disconcerting ways'" (2006: 3).

Unresolved Issues and Unrealized Potentials

Much of what is most exciting about digital scholarship is not yet realized but can be glimpsed in suggestive indicators of what the future may hold. We are in an experimental time, with software and hardware changing at dizzying speeds and the expectations for and the possibilities of our work not yet fully articulated. Despite uncertainty on many fronts, one thing is clear: it is of the utmost importance that electronic scholarly editions adhere to international standards. Projects that are idiosyncratic are almost certain to remain stand-alone efforts: they have effectively abandoned the possibility of interoperability. They cannot be meshed with other projects to become part of larger collections and so a significant amount of the research potential of electronic work is lost. Their creators face huge barriers if they find they want to integrate their work with intellectually similar materials. As Marilyn Deegan remarks, "Interoperability is difficult to achieve, and the digital library world has been grappling with it for some time. Editors should not strive to ensure the interoperability of their editions but make editorial and technical decisions that do not preclude the possibility of libraries creating the connections at a later date" (Deegan 2006: 362). Deegan perceives that tag sets such as the Text Encoding Initiative (TEI) and Encoded Archival Description (EAD) make possible interoperability, though they do not guarantee it. Figuring out how to pull projects together effectively will be a challenging but not impossible task. We face interesting questions: for example, can we aggregate texts in ways that establish the necessary degree of uniformity across projects without stripping out what is regarded as vital by individual projects? An additional difficulty is that the injunction to follow standards is not simple because the standards themselves are not always firmly established.

Many archivists refer to eXtensible Markup Language (XML) as the "acid-free paper of the digital age" because it is platform-independent and non-proprietary. Nearly all current development in descriptive text markup is XML-based, and far more tools (many of them open-source) are available for handling XML data than were ever available for SGML. Future versions of TEI will be XML-only, and XML search engines are maturing quickly. XML and more particularly, the TEI implementation of XML, has become the de facto standard for serious humanities computing projects. XML allows editors to determine which aspects of a text are of interest to their project and to "tag" them, or label them with markup. For example, at the *Whitman Archive*, we tag structural features of the manuscripts, such as line breaks and stanza breaks, and also the revisions that Whitman made to the manuscripts, as when he deleted a word and replaced it with another. Our markup includes more information than would be evident to a casual reader. A stylesheet, written in Extensible Stylesheet Language Transformations (XSLT), processes our XML files into reader-friendly HTML that users see when they visit our site. A crucial benefit of XML is that it allows for flexibility, and the application of XSLT allows data entered once to be transformed in various ways for differing outputs. So while some of the information that we have embedded in our tagging is not evident in the HTML display, later, if we decide that the information is valuable to readers, we can revise our stylesheet to include it in the HTML display.

The combination of XML-encoded texts and XSLT stylesheets also enables projects to offer multiple views of a single digital file. This is of considerable importance in scholarly editing because editors (or users) may want to have the same content displayed in various ways at different times. For example, the interface of the expanded, digital edition of *A Calendar of the Letters of Willa Cather*, now being prepared by a team led by Andrew Jewell, will allow users to dynamically reorder and index over 2,000 letter descriptions according to different factors, such as chronology, addressee, or repository. Additionally, the Cather editorial team is considering giving users the option of "turning on" some of the editorial information that is, by default, suppressed. In digitizing new descriptions and those in Janis Stout's original print volume, such data as regularized names of people and titles often takes the form of a mini-annotation. In the digital edition, the default summary might read something like, "Going to see mother in California"; with the regularization visible, it might read, "Going to see mother [Cather, Mary Virginia (Jennie) Boak] in California."

These multiple views of the *Calendar* are enabled by the rich markup adopted by this project and point to some of the issues that editors must consider. Even while adhering to the same TEI standard used on many other digital editing projects, these editors' choices of which textual characteristics to mark up may nonetheless differ significantly from choices made by other project editors. When an effort is made to aggregate material from *The Willa Cather Archive* (<http://cather.unl.edu>) with that of other comparable sites, how will differences in markup be handled? Of course, unless projects make their source code available to interested scholars and expose their metadata for harvesting in accordance with Open Archives Initiative (OAI) protocols, it won't be easy now or in the future even to know what digital objects make up a given edition or how they were treated.

Clearly, then, issues of preservation and aggregation are now key for editors. In looking toward the future, the *Whitman Archive* is attempting to develop a model use of the Metadata Encoding and Transmission Standard (METS) for integrating metadata in digital thematic research collections. A METS document enables the *Whitman Archive* – and all entities that subsequently ingest the Whitman materials into larger collections – to describe administrative metadata, structural metadata, and descriptive metadata. For example, the *Whitman Archive* uses thousands of individual files in our project to display transcriptions and digital images of Whitman's manuscripts and published works. These files – TEI-encoded transcriptions, archival TIFF images, derived JPEG images, EAD finding guides – could be more formally united through the use of a METS document to record their specific relationships. The use of METS will help preserve the structural integrity of the *Whitman Archive* by recording essential relationships among the files. Additionally, we think that using METS files which adhere to a proper profile will promote accessibility and sustainability of the *Archive* and other projects like it, making them prime candidates for ingestion into library collections.

The proper integration of metadata is important because large sites are likely to employ more than one standard, as the example of the *Walt Whitman Archive* suggests. Redundant data is at least a workflow problem when it involves unnecessary labor.

There is also the matter of figuring out what the canonical form of the metadata is. Currently, no METS Profile for digital thematic research collections has been developed, and there has not been a demonstration of the effectiveness of METS as an integration tool for such collections. In a report to the UK Joint Information Systems Committee, Richard Gartner argues that what prohibits "the higher education community [from] deriving its full benefit from METS is the lack of standardization of metadata content which is needed to complement the standardization of format provided by METS" (Gartner 2002). Specifically, he calls for new work to address this gap so that the full benefits of METS can be attained. In short, practices need to be normalized by user communities and expressed in detailed and precise profiles if the promise of METS as a method for building manageable, sustainable digital collections is to be realized.

Researchers and librarians are only just beginning to use the METS standard, so the time is right for an established humanities computing project, like the *Whitman Archive*, to develop a profile that properly addresses the complicated demands of scholar-enriched digital documents. In fact, a grant from the Institute for Museum and Library Services is allowing the *Whitman Archive* to pursue this goal, with vital assistance from some high-level consultants.[2]

Cost

A significant amount of scholarly material is now freely available on the web, and there is a strong movement for open access. As I have observed elsewhere, scholarly work may be free to the end user but it is not free to produce (Price 2001: 29). That disjunction is at the heart of some core difficulties in digital scholarship. If one undertakes a truly ambitious project, how can it be paid for? Will granting agencies provide editors the resources to make costly but freely delivered web-based resources?

The comments of Paul Israel, Director and General Editor of the Thomas A. Edison Papers, highlight the problem; his comments are all the more sobering when one recalls that the Edison edition recently was honored with the Eugene S. Ferguson Prize as an outstanding history of technology reference work:

> It is clear that for all but the most well funded projects online editions are prohibitively expensive to self publish. The Edison Papers has been unable to fund additional work on our existing online image edition. We have therefore focused on collaborating with others. We are working with the Rutgers Library to digitize a small microfilm edition we did of all extant early motion picture catalogs through 1908, which we are hoping will be up later this year. The library is doing this as part of a pilot project related to work on digital infrastructure. Such infrastructure rather than content has been the focus [of] funding agencies that initially provided funding for early digital editions like ours. We are also now working with the publisher of our book edition, Johns Hopkins

University Press, to do an online edition of the book documents with links to our image edition. In both cases the other institution is both paying for and undertaking the bulk of the work on these electronic editions. (Israel 2006)

Over recent decades, grant support for the humanities in the US has declined in real dollars. By one estimate, "adjusted for inflation, total funding for NEH is still only about 60% of its level 10 years ago and 35% of its peak in 1979 of $386.5 million" (Craig 2006). If development hinges on grant support, what risks are there that the priorities of various agencies could skew emphases in intellectual work? Some have worried about a reinstitution of an old canon, and others have expressed concern about the possible dangers of political bias in federally awarded grants. Some worry that canonical writers may be more likely to be funded by federal money and that writers perceived to be controversial might be denied funding.

One possible strategy for responding to the various funding pressures is to build an endowment to support a scholarly edition. The National Endowment for the Humanities provides challenge grants that hold promise for some editorial undertakings. One dilemma, however, is that the NEH directs challenge grants toward support of institutions rather than projects – that is, toward ongoing enterprises rather than those of limited duration. Thus far, some funding for editorial work has been allocated via "We the People" challenge grants from NEH, but this resource has limited applicability because only certain kinds of undertakings can maintain that they will have ongoing activities beyond the completion of the basic editorial work, and only a few can be plausibly described as treating material of foundational importance to US culture.[3]

Presses and Digital Centers

University presses and digital centers are other obvious places one might look for resources to support digital publication, and yet neither has shown itself to be fully equipped to meet current needs. Oxford University Press, Cambridge University Press, and the University of Michigan Press all expressed interest in publishing electronic editions in the 1990s, though that enthusiasm has since waned. On the whole, university presses have been slow to react effectively to the possibilities of electronic scholarly editions. University presses and digital centers have overlapping roles and interests, and there may well be opportunities for useful collaborations in the future, and some collaborations have already been effective. Notably, it was the Institute for Advanced Technology in the Humanities (IATH), under John Unsworth's leadership, that secured grant funding and internal support for an electronic imprint, now known as Rotunda, at the University of Virginia Press. It is too early to tell whether or not the Electronic Imprint at the University of Virginia will flourish – either way it is already an important experiment.

Digital Centers such as IATH, the Maryland Institute for Technology in the Humanities (MITH), and the Center for Digital Research in the Humanities at the

University of Nebraska–Lincoln (CDRH) in a sense have been acting as publishers for some of their projects, though they are really research and development units. They ordinarily handle some publisher functions, but other well-established parts of the publishing system (advertising, peer review, cost-recovery) are not at the moment within their ordinary work. Nor are these units especially suited to contend with issues of long-term preservation. They can nurture projects with sustainability in mind, but the library community is more likely to have the people, expertise, and the institutional frameworks necessary for the vital task of long-term preservation. As indicated, many scholars promote open access, but not all of the scholarship we want to see developed can get adequate support from universities, foundations, and granting agencies. Presses might one day provide a revenue stream to support projects that cannot be developed without it. What we need are additional creative partnerships that build bridges between the scholars who produce content, the publishers who (sometimes) vet and distribute it, and the libraries who, we hope, will increasingly ingest and preserve it. A further challenge for editors of digital editions is that this description of roles suggests a more clearly marked division of responsibilities than actually exists. Traditional boundaries are blurring before our eyes as these groups – publishers, scholars, and librarians – increasingly take on overlapping functions. While this situation leaves much uncertainty, it also affords ample room for creativity, too, as we move across newly porous dividing lines.

Audience

Having the ability, potentially, of reaching a vast audience is one of the great appeals of online work. Most of us, when writing scholarly articles and books, know we are writing for a limited audience: scholars and advanced students who share our interests. Print runs for a book of literary criticism are now rarely more than 1,000 copies, if that. A good percentage of these books will end up in libraries, where fortunately a single volume can be read over time by numerous people. In contrast, an online resource for a prominent writer can enjoy a worldwide audience of significant size. For example, during the last two months of the past academic year (March–April 2006), *The Willa Cather Archive* averaged about 7,700 hits a day, or about 230,000 hits a month. In that period, there was an average of 7,639 unique visitors a month. The *Journals of the Lewis and Clark Expedition* (<http://lewisandclarkjournals.unl.edu>), which, interestingly, has numbers that correspond less to the academic year, had its peak period of the last year during January–March 2006. For those three months, *Lewis and Clark* averaged 188,000 hits a month (about 6,300 hits a day), and an average of 10,413 unique visitors a month.

In the past the fate of the monumental scholarly edition was clear: it would land on library shelves and, with rare exceptions, be purchased only by the most serious and devoted specialists. Now a free scholarly edition can be accessed by people all over the world with vastly different backgrounds and training. What assumptions about audience should the editors of such an edition make? This is a difficult question since the audience may range widely in age and sophistication and training, and the answer of how best to handle the complexity is unclear. A savvy interface designer on a particular project might figure out a way to provide levels of access and gradations of difficulty, but unless carefully handled, such an approach might seem condescending. Whatever the challenges are of meeting a dramatically expanded readership – and those challenges are considerable – we should also celebrate this opportunity to democratize learning. Anyone with a web browser has access, free of charge, to a great deal of material that was once hidden away in locked-up rare-book rooms. The social benefit of freely available electronic resources is enormous.

Possible Future Developments

Future scholarship will be less likely than now to draw on electronic archives to produce paper-based scholarly articles. It seems likely that scholars will increasingly make the rich forms of their data (rather than the HTML output) open to other scholars so that they can work out of or back into the digital edition, archive, or project. An example may clarify how this could work in practice. The *Whitman Archive*, in its tagging of printed texts, has relied primarily on non-controversial markup of structural features. Over the years, there have been many fine studies of *Leaves of Grass* as a "language experiment." When the next scholar with such an interest comes along, we could provide her with a copy of, say, "Song of Myself" or the 1855 *Leaves* to mark up for linguistic features. This could be a constituent part of her own free-standing scholarly work. Alternatively, she could offer the material back to the *Archive* as a specialized contribution. To take another example, in our own work we have avoided thematic tagging for many reasons, but we wouldn't stand in the way of scholars who wished to build upon our work to tag Whitman for, say, racial or sexual tropes.

Translation

In an intriguing article, "Scales of Aggregation: Prenational, Subnational, Transnational," Wai Chee Dimock points out that "humanistic fields are divided by nations: the contours of our knowledge are never the contours of humanity." She further notes that

> nowhere is the adjective American more secure than when it is offered as American literature; nowhere is it more naturalized, more reflexively affirmed as inviolate. American literature is a self-evident field, as American physics and American biology are not. The disciplinary form of the humanities is "homeland defense" at its deepest and most unconscious. (Dimock 2006: 223)

We might be able to adjust our fields of inquiry if we, through editorial work on translations, highlighted the limitations of "humanistic fields . . . divided by nations." For example, we could approach Whitman via a social text method – where versions produced by non-US societies are key objects of interest. The remaking of a writer to suit altered cultural contexts is a rich and largely untapped field of analysis. A truly expansive electronic edition – one more expansive than any yet realized – could make this possibility a reality.

Whitman said to one of his early German translators: "It has not been for my country alone – ambitious as the saying so may seem – that I have composed that work. It has been to practically start an internationality of poems. The final aim of the United States of America is the solidarity of the world. . . . One purpose of my chants is to cordially salute all foreign lands in America's name" (quoted in Folsom 2005: 110). As Ed Folsom has remarked, Whitman "enters most countries as both invader and immigrant, as the confident, pushy, overwhelming representative of his nation . . . *and* as the intimate, inviting, submissive, endlessly malleable immigrant, whose work gets absorbed and rewritten in some surprising ways" (Folsom 2005: 110–11). Scholarly editions, especially with the new possibilities in their electronic form, can trouble the nationally bounded vision so common to most of us.

In the near future, the *Walt Whitman Archive* will publish the first widely distributed Spanish language edition of *Leaves of Grass*. One of our goals is to make a crucial document for understanding Whitman's circulation in the Hispanophone world available, but an equally important goal is to make available an edition that will broaden the audience for the *Archive*, both in the US and abroad, to include a huge Spanish-speaking population. Foreign-language editions of even major literary texts are hard to come by online, and in many cases the physical originals are decaying and can barely be studied at all.[4] Translations and other "responses" (artistic, literary) can be part of a digital scholarly edition if we take a sociological view of the text. In this social text view a translation is seen as a version. The translation by Álvaro Armando Vasseur that we are beginning with is fascinating as the work of a Uruguayan poet who translated Whitman not directly from English but via an Italian translation (apparently Luigi Gamberale's 1907 edition), and our text is based on the 1912 F. Semper issue. These details are suggestive of the development of a particular version of modernism in South America, and of the complex circulation of culture.

The translation project serves as an example of the expansibility of electronic editions. Electronic work allows an editor to consider adding more perspectives and materials to illuminate texts. These exciting prospects raise anew familiar issues: who pays for expansive and experimental work? Given that not all of the goals imaginable by a project can be achieved, what is the appropriate scope and what are the best goals? Scholars who create electronic editions are engaged in the practice of historical criticism. Editing texts is a way to preserve and study the past, to bring it forward into the present so that it remains a living part of our heritage. How we answer the difficult questions that face us will to a large extent determine the past we can possess and the future we can shape.

NOTES

1 It could be argued that the *Making of America* creators didn't so much make as inherit this decision. That is, librarians and publishers made decisions about what was important to include when issues were bound together into volumes for posterity. One could imagine a project less given to mass digitization and more devoted to the state of the original material objects that would have searched more thoroughly to see how much of the now "lost" material is actually recoverable.

2 Daniel Pitti, Julia Flanders, and Terry Catapano.

3 The *Whitman Archive* is addressing the question of cost by building an endowment to support ongoing editorial work. In 2005 the University of Nebraska–Lincoln received a $500,000 "We the People" NEH challenge grant to support the building of a permanent endowment for the *Walt Whitman Archive*. The grant carries a 3 to 1 matching requirement, and thus we need to raise $1.5 million dollars in order to receive the NEH funds. The *Whitman Archive* is the first literary project to receive a "We the People" challenge grant. What this may mean for other projects is not yet clear. In a best-case scenario, the *Whitman Archive* may use its resources wisely, develop a rich and valuable site, and help create a demand for similar funding to support the work of comparable projects.

4 A Brazilian scholar, Maria Clara Bonetti Paro, recently found that she needed to travel to the Library of Congress in order to work with Portuguese translations of *Leaves of Grass* because the copies in the national library in Brazil were falling apart and even scholars had only limited access to them.

REFERENCES AND FURTHER READING

Bryant, John (2002). *The Fluid Text: A Theory of Revision and Editing for Book and Screen*. Ann Arbor: University of Michigan Press.

Craig, R. Bruce (2006). Posting for the National Coalition for History to SEDIT-L, June 30.

Deegan, Marilyn (2006). "Collection and Preservation of an Electronic Edition." In Lou Burnard, Katherine O'Brien O'Keeffe, and John Unsworth (Eds.). *Electronic Textual Editing*. New York: Modern Language Association.

Dimock, Wai Chee (2006). "Scales of Aggregation: Prenational, Subnational, Transnational." *American Literary History* 18: 219–28.

Donaldson, Ian (2003). "Collecting Ben Jonson." In Andrew Nash (Ed.). *The Culture of Collected Editions*. New York: Palgrave Macmillan.

Eaves, Morris (2006). "Multimedia Body Plans: A Self-Assessment." In Lou Burnard, Katherine O'Brien O'Keeffe, and John Unsworth (Eds.). *Electronic Textual Editing*. New York: Modern Language Association.

Finneran, Richard J. (1996). *The Literary Text in the Digital Age*. Ann Arbor: University of Michigan Press.

Folsom, Ed (2005). " 'What a Filthy Presidentiad!': Clinton's Whitman, Bush's Whitman, and Whitman's America." *Virginia Quarterly Review* 81: 96–113.

Gailey, Amanda (2006). "Editing Whitman and Dickinson: Print and Digital Representations." Dissertation, University of Nebraska–Lincoln.

Gartner, Richard (2002). "METS: Metadata Encoding and Transmission Standard." Techwatch report TSW 02–05. <http://www.jisc.ac.uk/index.cfm?name=techwatch_report_0205>.

Horton, William (1994). *Designing and Writing Online Documentation*, 2nd edn. New York: John Wiley.

Israel, Paul (2006). Email message to Kenneth M. Price and other members of the Electronic Editions Committee of the Association for Documentary Editing. August 7.

Manovich, Lev (2005). "Database as a Genre of New Media," /AI & Society/<http://time.arts.ucla.edu/AI_Society/manovich.html>.

McCarty, Willard (2005). *Humanities Computing*. Basingstoke, England: Palgrave Macmillan.

McGann, Jerome (2002). "Literary Scholarship and the Digital Future." *The Chronicle Review* [*The Chronicle of Higher Education* Section 2] 49: 16 (December 13), B7–B9.

Price, Kenneth M. (2001). "Dollars and Sense in Collaborative Digital Scholarship." *Documentary Editing* 23.2: 29–33, 43.

Robinson, Peter M. W., and Gabler, Hans Walter (2000). "Introduction" to *Making Texts for the Next Century*. Special issue of *Literary and Linguistic Computing* 15: 1–4.

Schreibman, Susan (2002). "Computer Mediated Texts and Textuality: Theory and Practice." *Computers and the Humanities* 36: 283–93.

Smith, Martha Nell (2004). "Electronic Scholarly Editing." In Susan Schreibman, Ray Siemens, and John Unsworth (Eds.). *A Companion to Digital Humanities*. Oxford: Blackwell Publishing, pp. 306–322.

Tanselle, G. Thomas (1995). "The Varieties of Scholarly Editing." In D. C. Greetham (Ed.). *Scholarly Editing: A Guide to Research*. New York: Modern Language Association, pp. 9–32.

Wright, Lyle H. (1957; 1965). *American Fiction, 1851–1875: A Contribution Toward a Bibliography*. San Marino, CA: Huntington Library.

The Text Encoding Initiative and the Study of Literature

James Cummings

Introduction

The Text Encoding Initiative (TEI) is an international consortium which is dedicated to maintaining the TEI Guidelines as a recommended standard for textual markup (see TEI website). The TEI grew out of a recognized need for the creation of international standards for textual markup that resulted in a conference at Vassar College, Poughkeepsie, in November 1987. Participants representing text archives, scholarly societies, research projects, and academic institutions met at this conference to examine the existing methods of text encoding, to discuss the feasibility of an international standard for such encoding, and to make recommendations for its scope, structure, content, and drafting (Ide and Sperberg-McQueen 1995). The initial sponsors of the TEI as a project were the Association of Computers in the Humanities (ACH), the Association for Computational Linguistics (ACL), and the Association of Literary and Linguistic Computing (ALLC). Although the TEI is now mostly maintained as an international consortium by four institutional hosts, as well as institutional members and individual subscribers, over the years it has received support from sources including the US National Endowment for the Humanities (NEH), the European Union, the Andrew W. Mellon Foundation, and the Social Science and Humanities Research Council of Canada (SSHRCC). The overall purpose of the project was to produce a set of guidelines for the creation and use of electronic texts in the majority of linguistic and literary disciplines (Renear, Mylonas, and Durand 2004: 232–5). Now, a couple of decades later, the TEI Guidelines are used for many text-encoding projects, especially in the Arts and Humanities. Moreover, as the TEI existed before the World Wide Web its recommendations have influenced the development of a number of web standards, most notably XML and XML-related standards. This chapter will examine some of the history and theoretical and methodological assumptions embodied in the text-encoding framework recommended by the TEI. It is not intended to be a general introduction to the TEI or XML markup more generally, nor is it exhaustive in its consideration of issues concerning the TEI. The first the TEI does admirably itself, the second would take much more space than is allowed here. Instead, this chapter includes a sampling of some of the history, a few of the issues, and some of the methodological assumptions, for the most part unavoidable, that the TEI makes.

The TEI Guidelines, officially titled *Guidelines for Electronic Text Encoding and Interchange*, are a continually revised set of proposals of suggested methods for text encoding (see TEI Guidelines). At time of writing they have reached their fifth major version, "P5," and provide recommendations for methods of markup for a broad range of textual, physical, literary, and linguistic phenomena of interest to those in the TEI community. The TEI Guidelines are not only a guide to best practice, but are also an evolving historical record of the concerns of the field of Humanities Computing.

The TEI Guidelines are divided into chapters and cover a wide range of topics, beginning with four introductory chapters: a description of the Guidelines them-selves, a gentle introduction to XML, an overview of the TEI infrastructure, and a discussion of the use of languages and character sets. Following these introductory materials are chapters on the structure of TEI documents, the manner in which metadata is stored in a TEI document's header, and a description of the large number of elements which are available for use in any TEI document. These are followed by chapters on more specific topics such as TEI elements for verse, performance texts, transcriptions of speech, print dictionaries, terminological databases, manuscript description, methods of linking, segmenting or aligning texts, simple analytic mechanisms, and feature structures. Further chapters make recommendations on the encoding of certainty and responsibility, the transcription of primary sources, the creation of a critical apparatus, the recording of names and dates, the creation of language corpora, as well as methods for recording graphs, networks, trees, tables, formulae, and graphics. In addition, there are chapters on the relationship of the TEIs Header elements with other metadata standards, the representation of non-standard characters and glyphs, feature system declarations, and elements for documentation used in the creation of the TEI Guidelines (the Guidelines are themselves a valid TEI document). Finally, there are chapters on what conformance to the TEI Guidelines implies, how one can modify the TEI schema to suit individual needs, rules for the interchange of documents, and methods for overcoming the problem of overlapping XML hierarchies. All these chapters are supplemented by various appendices of reference material.

In addition to publishing the TEI Guidelines, the TEI consortium also provides a method for projects to produce customized schemas (currently in RelaxNG, W3C, and DTD formats) in order to validate their TEI documents. Moreover, they produce various free software packages, including a set of XSLT Stylesheets to transform TEI XML into HTML and PDF (see TEI Stylesheets).

The TEI Guidelines have gained a reputation for having both broad coverage, addressing the needs of many fields in the humanities generally, as well as in-depth coverage for more specialized concerns/applications. TEI XML is, where applicable, the format recommended for preservation and interchange of electronic textual resources by a number of funding bodies for arts and humanities projects (for example, the UK's Arts and Humanities Research Council). As such, it is important for us not only to understand the TEI Guidelines as an evolving set of recommendations, but also to understand the technological and theoretical background, assumptions, and biases that have influenced this evolution.

Principles of the TEI

As mentioned above, TEI was formed as a project at a conference at Vassar College, Poughkeepsie, in November 1987. The conference participants drafted an initial set of principles to guide the project, titled "The Poughkeepsie Principles." What is surprising is that very few of the concerns expressed in this document now seem dated in the face of technological advances. Instead, many of the goals of the TEI Guidelines remain the same, if slightly expanded, from what is found in this early manifesto. Overall, it is these principles that form the theoretical and methodological basis from which the TEI has developed.

The Poughkeepsie Principles
Closing Statement of Vassar Conference
The Preparation of Text Encoding Guidelines

Poughkeepsie, New York
13 November 1987

1. The guidelines are intended to provide a standard format for data interchange in humanities research.
2. The guidelines are also intended to suggest principles for the encoding of texts in the same format.
3. The guidelines should
    1. define a recommended syntax for the format,
    2. define a metalanguage for the description of text-encoding schemes,
    3. describe the new format and representative existing schemes both in that meta-language and in prose.
4. The guidelines should propose sets of coding conventions suited for various applications.
5. The guidelines should include a minimal set of conventions for encoding new texts in the format.
6. The guidelines are to be drafted by committees on
    1. text documentation
    2. text representation
    3. text interpretation and analysis
    4. metalanguage definition and description of existing and proposed schemes, coordinated by a steering committee of representatives of the principal sponsoring organizations.
7. Compatibility with existing standards will be maintained as far as possible.

8. A number of large text archives have agreed in principle to support the guidelines in their function as an interchange format. We encourage funding agencies to support development of tools to facilitate this interchange.
9. Conversion of existing machine-readable texts to the new format involves the translation of their conventions into the syntax of the new format. No requirements will be made for the addition of information not already coded in the texts.

(see TEI EDP01)

While the scope of the TEI has certainly evolved outside of the four committees suggested above (point 6), and it has succeeded in proposing widely used "sets of coding conventions suited for various applications" (point 4), there is much which is still germane to the TEI's central mission. While many of these goals have been accomplished, it is interesting to note that twenty years later we are still encouraging "funding agencies to support development of tools to facilitate" (point 8) the interchange, interoperability, creation, and analysis of TEI-encoded texts. Certainly some tools have been developed for the creation, editing, and presentation of TEI documents, but many of these have evolved from very specific uses relating to the projects for which they have been created.

The most beneficial decision, with regard to the availability of tools, has been the migration of the TEI from Standard Generalized Markup Language (SGML) to Extensible Markup Language (XML) as the TEI format for TEI P4 (and later versions). Since XML has received worldwide support from all manner of disciplines, many commercial applications exist for the creation of XML in general, and tools which support XML also are usable for TEI XML. It is indeed true that a "number of large text archives have agreed in principle to support the Guidelines in their function as an interchange format" (point 8), and the Oxford Text Archive and the University of Virginia's Electronic Text Center are two such archives which have helped to establish TEI as a standard for interchange and preservation. A number of data services, set up to preserve the outcomes of funded digital projects, list TEI XML as one of their preferred archival formats and encourage its use as suitable for long-term preservation.[1]

Although the history of the TEI has been driven by the needs of its members, it has also been directed by, and taken on the assumptions inherent in, the technologies it employs. The TEI Guidelines are the prime deliverable of the TEI (see TEI Guidelines). They describe the principles to use in marking up texts, and these principles can be expressed in electronic schemas or document type definitions (DTDs) which can be used to validate a document instance against this form of these principles. While the formulation of the Guidelines into machine-readable schemas is an extremely useful by-product created from the same files which also produce the Guidelines, it is the Guidelines themselves that take priority. Likewise, the technologies involved are also secondary to the recommendations. There are suggestions detailed in the prose of the Guidelines that are unable to be constrained adequately in some schema languages; in these cases, the prose of the Guidelines always takes precedence. Currently the TEI Guidelines express the description of what elements are allowed in any particular location, that is, the content models of elements, in RelaxNG Compact Syntax; previously they used DTD language. These are both accepted electronic formulations of the more abstract concepts codified within the Guidelines. Technologies continue to develop, and the manner in which the concerns of the TEI Guidelines are expressed will evolve as well.

That the TEI Guidelines currently use XML is simply a reflection that "compatibility with existing standards will be maintained as far as possible" (point 7). Previous to P4, the TEI recommended the use of SGML, an ISO standard (ISO 8879:1986). In a family tree of markup languages, SGML is often thought of as the parent of both HTML and XML. SGML is itself a descendant of IBM's Generalized Markup Language (GML) which was a milestone system based on character flagging, enabling basic structural markup of electronic documents for display and printing (Renear 2004: 225–31). SGML was originally intended for the sharing of documents throughout large organizations, especially governmental, and in the legal and aerospace industries which were required to preserve and provide access to documents for at least a few decades. As solutions for creating and printing these documents developed, SGML was increasingly adopted in the printing and publishing industries. However, the support for the processing of SGML documents existed in relatively few applications, and specialism in learning SGML markup meant that it was not the universal answer for the markup of texts that many hoped it would become. XML, however, has become an international success in a very short period of time. It is used in many fields, academic and commercial, for documents, data files, configuration information, temporary and long-term storage, for transmitting information locally or remotely, by new start-ups and multinational conglomerates. It is used as a storage format for almost everything, including word processing documents, installation scripts, news articles, product information, and web pages. More recently XML has been increasingly popular as a temporary storage format for web-based user interfaces. Its all-pervasive applicability has meant not only that there are numerous tools which read, write, transform, or otherwise manipulate XML as an application-, operating-system- and hardware-independent format, but also that there is as much training and support available. The contrast with SGML is significant. It should also be noted that one of the editors of the XML specification, Sperberg-McQueen, was prior to this an editor of the TEI Guidelines, and that his experience with the TEI helped to shape the format which the TEI now uses.

While the TEI Guidelines will inevitably change, they will overall stay true to the initial design goals:

4. Design Goals

The following design goals are to govern the choices to be made by the working committees in drafting the guidelines. Higher-ranked goals should count more than lower-ranked goals. The guidelines should

1. suffice to represent the textual features needed for research
2. be simple, clear, and concrete
3. be easy for researchers to use without special-purpose software

4. allow the rigorous definition and efficient processing of texts
5. provide for user-defined extensions
6. conform to existing and emergent standards

Throughout the changes and revisions the TEI makes to the recommendations, the versions of the TEI Guidelines themselves chronicle the development of methodologies and assumptions concerning the nature of text encoding more broadly. These have been not only influenced by, but intentionally shaped to answer, the needs of the text encoding community at the time. But this TEI community is in itself extremely broad and diverse, ranging across all disciplines in the Arts and Humanities and even extending into more scientific domains (see TEI Projects). This reach has resulted in a deliberate design decision to enable, wherever possible, the most general of encoding structures, but often complementing these with more detailed data models intended for specialist use. The TEI caters to these specialized areas either where there has been a belief in their centrality to the mission of the TEI in developing standards for text encoding, or where the TEI community has lobbied for improvement in these areas. For examples, basic textual modules exist for drama, verse, and prose, but more specialized modules exist for print dictionaries, corpus linguistics, and manuscript description.

At its heart the TEI is a community-led organization, and this is reflected in all areas of its activity. It is members (whether institutional hosts, funded projects, or individuals) who pay for the consortium's continuation, and a desire to further the goals of the TEI prompts members to stand for election to the Board or Technical Council. Likewise, members working in particular areas, or with specific techno-logical solutions or concerns, often gather themselves together into special interest groups which may eventually produce suggestions for improving the TEI Guidelines.

That the nature of the TEI is to be directed by the needs of its users is not surprising given that it is as a result of the need for standardization and interoperability that the TEI was formed. However, this community-led focus does have certain theoretical implications. Aside from the areas which seem to the TEI to be central to most forms of text encoding and so covered by the Guidelines early on, the most sophisticated developments have taken place in those areas where there are active users wanting to use the TEI Guidelines for their specific discipline. For example, in developing recommendations for the creation of linguistic corpora, the TEI defined a <person> element to record information about the participants in a linguistic interaction. However, once it existed it began to be used by others to record information about the people mentioned in texts. Moreover, the extended use highlighted several limita-tions with the data model of <person>. Since it was originally intended for people whose speech had been transcribed, while there was a <birth> element to record details of the speaker's birth, there was no <death> element since the conversations are assumed to have taken place while the speaker was alive. And yet, as soon as people started to use the <person> element to record more detailed prosopographical infor-mation, having a <death> element to record the date and place of the subject's (not necessarily speaker's) death became an obvious addition. That the TEI did not include this to begin with is entirely understandable given that they had created the <person> element solely with speech corpora in mind (see TEI CC).

This example highlights both the drawbacks and benefits of a community-led standards organization. In response to a perceived need, the TEI created elements for metadata relating to linguistic corpora for a particular community, when a different community adopted these elements for a different use the TEI generalized and developed the Guidelines to make the elements more applicable to a greater number of users. That the TEI has added a much more detailed prosopographical markup in their P5 release is only partly the point. More importantly, it has created a mixture of the specialized elements retained from its use with linguistic corpora (such as <socecStatus> to record socio-economic status) while adding newer, more generalized elements (such as <persTrait> to record personal traits) – extending from the specific to the general. The community helped develop a specialized tag-set and then later decided to generalize it for applicability in other areas. This is only one example out of many. Over the years this method of development has produced an extremely useful, but occasionally erratic set of recommendations with multiple ways to solve some problems, and only a single generalized solution for others. While this is generally perceived to be one of the strengths of the TEI, it can make it confusing for new users who may be uncertain when to use the specialized or more generalized forms of markup described in the TEI Guidelines.

The continued development of the TEI to become more useful to various disciplines will only continue this process of simultaneous specialization and generalization. While this is not necessarily a bad thing, it can encourage methodological inequality where detailed specialized markup is used for some aspects of a project, while more generalized solutions are used for others. This in turn can lead to inaccurate or otherwise skewed impressions of the content of the document. While this should, of course, be avoided with detailed document analysis and careful schema creation, the willingness of projects to seize on whichever elements seem to provide the most detail for their immediate concerns can lead to inequalities that (even when properly documented) may escape the notice of later users. To guard against this, rigorous local encoding guidelines should be developed to increase overall consistency.

The theoretical implications of the application of markup to a text are a subject of much discussion and too large to treat in depth here (see Landow 2006; Hayles 2005; McGann 2001). It is needless to say that many involved with the very earliest efforts to create systems of markup for computer systems were not literary theorists, but this is not the case with the development of the TEI, which has often benefited from rigorous debate on the very nature of what constitutes a text (McGann 2001: 187). While the history of textual markup obviously pre-dates computer systems, its application to machine-readable text was partly influenced by simultaneous developments in literary theory and the study of literature. Textual theories from Barthes, Foucault, Bakhtin, and Derrida all have a concept of interlinking which both pre-dates and almost anticipates the later development of hypertextual linking in electronic documents (Landow 2006: 53–68). New Criticism was intent on the close reading of a text with a rejection of any extra-textual information as a source for one's understanding of that text. Authorial biography or information understood by comparative analysis with other texts could not be relied upon to illuminate the text under consideration. This matches well with the notion of textual markup providing interpretative information about the structure and content of the text. What might jar slightly is the notion of a text's ambiguity that informs most of New Critical thought; it is inconceivable from such a theoretical position that a text might have a single incontrovertible meaning or indeed structure.

That the intelligent application of markup to a text is itself an interpretative act is quite straightforward. And while this occasionally has to be re-emphasized, it is less theoretically interesting than what the application of that markup tells us about our understanding of a text (Renear 1999). One of the TEI's enduring legacies has been in being a catalyst for the development of many, sometimes conflicting, understandings of what constitutes a text.

> This crucial understanding – that print textuality is not language but an operational (praxis-based) theory of language – has stared us in the face for a long time, but seeing we have not seen. It has taken the emergence of electronic textualities, and in particular operational theories of natural language like TEI, to expose the deeper truth about print and manuscript texts. (McGann 2004: 205)

That the TEI has helped us to greater understanding concerning the nature of text is unsurprising given its nature. Although the structure of any text is open to debate, it is questionable how much this understanding of markup as interpretation should apply to the basic structural markup applied to an electronic text. The problematic notion is whether marking a paragraph with the TEI element for paragraphs (the <p> element) does anything more than mark that there is a structural unit of some sort there. It is arguable that the application of structural markup does not necessarily imply specific semantic meaning, that <p> does not necessarily mean a paragraph or that while <title> may mark a title, it does not say what constitutes a title. A possible problem with such arguments in relation to the TEI Guidelines is that the meaning of these elements is indeed defined in the prose of the Guidelines. The <title> element is said to contain "the full title of a work of any kind," but since it does not further define what a "title" means, this only strengthens the argument of markup as an act of interpretation. It is up to the researcher applying the markup to decide what portion of the text to wrap a <title> element around. It could be argued that what the TEI provides is phenomenology, not ontology (cf. Sartre 1943: 40–3):

> Texts do not have an unproblematic objective existence; they are not self-identical, even if more-or-less transparent page designs have traditionally catered to the illusion that they are. Their encoding for computer analysis and presentation is therefore doomed to remain problematic, incomplete, and perspectival. In a sense, a phenomenology of texts has replaced an ontology. (Eggert 2005: 429)

The TEI does not tell us what a "title" is, it simply gives us a means of recording the current beliefs and practices about what a title may be through indicating how and where they are used. While this may indeed doom the TEI to continue to remain "problematic, incomplete, and perspectival," to do otherwise, while remaining useful in an age of increasing internationalization and diversification of semantic concepts for the creation of electronic resources intended for a wide range of end purposes, would be impossible.

While the application of markup to computerized text may have been influenced by New Critical thought, there are many later developments in literary theory which have influenced, most likely unintentionally, the development of the TEI's under-standing of markup. In reacting against the structuralism and the new critical concentration on the text itself, the poststructuralist movement's destabilization of meaning placed the act of interpretation on the reader and viewed the text as a cultural product necessarily embedded in the culture from which it originates. It could be argued that the TEI's development of text encoding standards is an attempt to enable greater comparative study between such texts. But, with deconstructionist analysis especially critiquing the assumptions of structuralist binary opposition and ultimately rejecting that a text can have a consistent structure, it would be more sensible to view the TEI's assumptions of markup theory as basically structuralist in nature as it pairs record (the text) with interpretation (markup and metadata).

> Although most of these researchers thought of themselves as practitioners rather than theorists, their decisions [. . .] constituted a de facto theory of textuality that was reinforced by their tacit assumptions that the "Platonic reality" of a text really is its existence as an ordered hierarchy of content objects. (Hayles 2005: 95)

The belief that texts are able to be divided into consistent understandable struc-tures is central to the TEI Guidelines. While, for the purpose of text encoding, the units the TEI suggests are hardly controversial, they do imply a particular theoretical understanding of what constitutes a text.

> A text is not an undifferentiated sequence of words, much less of bytes. For different purposes, it may be divided into many different units, of different types or sizes. A prose text such as this one might be divided into sections, chapters, paragraphs, and sen-tences. A verse text might be divided into cantos, stanzas, and lines. Once printed, sequences of prose and verse might be divided into volumes, gatherings, and pages. (See TEI SG)

This very literal view of what constitutes a text derives partly from the notion that text is hierarchical, more specifically that it is "an ordered hierarchy of content objects" (Renear 1993). While the original authors may have retreated from this position slightly, it still underlies much of the theoretical background to the TEI. This holds that the hierarchy of these content objects "is essential to the production of the text and so must occupy centre stage in transforming print text into digital code"

(Hayles 2005: 95). Yet others have argued that this treatment reduces imaginative works solely to computational data:

> TEI is now a standard for humanities encoding practices. Because it treats the humanities corpus – typically works of imagination – as informational structures, it ipso facto violates some of the most basic reading practices of the humanities community, scholarly as well as popular. (McGann 2001: 139)

But it could equally be argued that any process of creating texts in their physical embodiment has always involved this treatment of the text. Whether with medieval scribes or modern publishing, the text itself is accommodated, shaped, and treated as a separate structure from the work of imagination that it is in order to complete the process of the creation of its physical manifestation.

While the TEI Guidelines clearly recognizes both that major structural divisions are not the only phenomena of interest and that there are problematic text structures such as those which overlap with their physical manifestations, they are less concerned with the theoretic understanding of these structures than with the interplay between them:

> These textual structures overlap with each other in complex and unpredictable ways. Particularly when dealing with texts as instantiated by paper technology, the reader needs to be aware of both the physical organization of the book and the logical structure of the work it contains. Many great works (Sterne's *Tristram Shandy* for example) cannot be fully appreciated without an awareness of the interplay between narrative units (such as chapters or paragraphs) and page divisions. For many types of research, it is the interplay between different levels of analysis which is crucial: the extent to which syntactic structure and narrative structure mesh, or fail to mesh, for example, or the extent to which phonological structures reflect morphology. (See TEI SG)

The desire to have markup be of use in helping to elucidate the nature of the text is entirely reasonable. While XML allows the easy marking of most textual structures of interest to the study of literature, the specification which defines XML creates certain limitations with regard to the encoding of multiple overlapping hierarchies. This is problematic when one structure runs concurrently with another and the encoder wishes to record both of these structures simultaneously. These can be quite common, for example where paragraphs run over pages and the both the intellectual structure of the document and its physical structure are to be marked up. The markup for paragraphs may split over pages, or in verse drama different characters' speeches may truly be one metrical line. For example one cannot do:

```
<div type="page" n="1">
<p>This is a paragraph where there is a page-break
</div>
<div type="page" n="2">
in the middle of it</p>
</div>
```

This is illegal XML because it is not well-formed, that is, the elements are not properly nested, but it also concentrates on the physical structure of the document. In most cases, the hierarchy which constitutes the physical structure conflicts or overlaps with the intellectual structure of the document. The usual method of dealing with this is simply to decide which is most important for the reasons you are encoding the document and prioritize one hierarchy over another, and this is sufficient for many users. Usually, in an ordered hierarchy of content objects (OHCO) model it is the understood intellectual structure of the document that is thought to be more important than the physical structure of the work.

> The model in question postulates that text consists of objects of a certain sort, structured in a certain way. The nature of the objects is best suggested by example and contrast. They are chapters, sections, paragraphs, titles, extracts, equations, examples, acts, scenes, stage directions, stanzas, (verse) lines, and so on. But they are *not* things like pages, columns, (typographical) lines, font shifts, vertical spacing, horizontal spacing, and so on. The objects indicated by descriptive markup have an intrinsic direct connection with the intellectual content of the text; they are the underlying "logical" objects, components that get their identity directly from their role in carrying out and organizing communicative intention. (Renear 2004: 224–5)

But the assumptions made in this model are that such an intellectual structure exists separately from its physical embodiment. Others have argued against this:

> There is no Platonic reality of texts. There are only physical objects such as books and computers, foci of attention, and codes that entrain attention and organize material operations. (Hayles, 2005: 97)

However, most encoding practice finds it useful to de-prioritize the physicality of texts, even their electronic texts, and understand the primacy of an intellectual structure reflecting this Platonic ideal. In the example above, of encoding paragraphs which break over pages, the TEI uses so-called "empty" elements. Although these are restricted to attribute content only, as opposed to element content, to refer to them as empty – implying they have no content whatsoever – is theoretically dangerous. In the TEI's case these are milestone pointers which indicate where a change of state happens in the text, for example that the text runs from one page to another, but these milestones do not enclose the content of that page itself. The above example would be shown as:

```
<p>This is a paragraph where there is a page-break <pb n="2"/> in the
middle of it</p>
```

This, as a solution to competing hierarchies, is perfectly feasible and has had much support (Barnard 1995). The use of empty milestone-like elements to indicate the start of a phenomenon, and then later to mark its end, mimics the similar use of specialized characters in certain forms of printed editions. For example, differentiating between areas of the text written by different scribes – areas that may overlap with the intellectual structure of the text. The Records of Early English Drama project uses a small superscript circle in this manner to indicate the change of hand in its printed volumes. And, indeed, the TEI also enables this with an empty element <handShift/>. What is interesting about the use of this for page-breaks (as opposed to line or column breaks) is that one is marking up a break or gap in the physical media. That is, marking an absence through the use of a presence – an element in the document itself (Sartre 1943: 30–6). And yet, it is just as reasonable to see such a page or folio break as a very real structure. Certainly, it can be seen to be so when one moves away from codex-based forms and look, for example, at inscribed tablets, sectioned wall decoration, and other text-bearing objects where the physical break itself may also contain data. But the physicality of an object could be described or recorded in an infinite number of ways:

> The physical instantiation of a text will in this sense always be indeterminate. What matters for the understanding of literature, however, is how the text creates possibilities for meaning by mobilizing certain aspects of its physicality. These will necessarily be a small subset of all possible characteristics. (Hayles 2005: 103)

It is this small subset of characteristics, those most common in the physical representation of source texts, which the TEI attempts to encode. In any case, the transformation of TEI-encoded documents from one hierarchy of encoding to another, as long as both have been recorded, is certainly possible, though not always easy depending on what features overlap.

The TEI in its most recent version includes recommendations for encoding conflicting hierarchies in an expanded milestone method. There has been a great deal of discussion recently among markup experts concerning both the problems of overlapping hierarchies and solutions for them in XML and other possible options. While this is a very real problem, and concurrent hierarchies are certainly needed in some specialized applications, the majority of projects using TEI get along just fine without using complicated solutions for resolving these conflicts. Why is this? Simply, they are content to prioritize one hierarchy over the other. In most cases they have the creation of an end resource in mind, which will be easier with one of these hierarchies and simply refers to the other as an extra source of information. For example, most projects encode the intellectual structure of the document and simply record its physical manifestation as milestone references, but if their end product needs individual pages they would choose to prioritize this hierarchy instead. Relying on milestone elements does not necessarily mean that one hierarchy is inaccessible, but certainly makes it marginally less prominent than the enclosing hierarchy. There are, however, many disciplines, such as corpus and computational linguistics, where the problems of overlap for annotation cannot be so easily ignored.

If the prioritization of one hierarchy over another is unsuitable, some of the possible methods to mark up overlapping hierarchies are noted by the TEI (See TEI NH). These include:

- redundantly encoding the same information in multiple forms;
- remodeling the document structure to merge the competing hierarchies into a non-TEI form;
- element fragmentation and virtual re-creation of single elements into multiple parts, with each properly nested;
- boundary marking of starting and ending element locations using milestones to form a non-nesting structure;
- stand-off markup where the text is separated from the annotation and virtual re-creation of elements;
- a number of competing non-XML solutions.

Basic element fragmentation (where attributes then indicate the other parts of the element) is perhaps the most straightforward for encoding and processing. However, there is more theoretical interest in the use of forms of boundary marking or stand-off markup, or various non-XML solutions (such as LMNL or MECS).

Although there is no standardized solution to this problem, that possible methods of encoding this information (where it is deemed necessary) exist is a good sign. The creation of these methods, however, has involved a great deal of theoretical debate, and indeed it is an interesting theoretical problem which raises numerous issues about how we understand text and our relationship to it. In addition, because of the popular adoption of XML as such a worldwide markup system in many different disciplines, it is a problem which will continue to affect XML use. However, that there is an interesting problem with many intriguing possible solutions should not itself detract from the use of XML, as many users will find it entirely unproblematic in prioritizing one hierarchy over another, or make use of one of the existing solutions.

The concentration on structural encoding is understandable given that TEI markup is a form of structural descriptive markup. However, this concentration on structure could be seen to be in preference to thematic interpretation of the text itself. Although the TEI provides recommendations for encoding interpretations of a passage's meaning, importance, or other thematic analysis of a part of a text in relation to its whole, these are less frequently used compared to the basic structural information. Partly this is because some amount of structure is always necessary and the TEI has chosen a book-like infrastructure for its basic recommendations, but overall the encoding is used by many to provide a basic electronically searchable text, which they then use to assist them in their research. They use it to speed up a manual form of analysis by hard-coding the basic aspects (structure, names, dates, etc.) that they want to retrieve quickly. It is more unusual for someone to encode the inter-pretative understanding of passages and use the electronic version to retrieve an aggregation of these (Hockey 2000: 66–84). It is unclear whether this is a problem with the TEI's methods for indicating such aspects, the utility of encoding such interpretations, or the acceptance of such methodology by those conducting research with literature in a digital form (Hayles 2005: 94–6).

Textual Criticism and the Electronic Edition

The theoretical movements which have had a more direct influence on the development of the TEI are those which more directly involve either computational linguistics or textual (so-called "lower") criticism (Sperberg-McQueen 1994). This is understandable given the nature and uses of electronic texts when the TEI was founded – long before the World Wide Web and the revolution in computing technology that accompanied it. Aggregating electronic texts to form corpora is central to computational linguistics and that the TEI caters for this with an alternative corpus structure (the <teiCorpus> element) and other specialized elements for linguistic analysis and metadata is unsurprising.

The notion that text encoding can help to explicate our understanding of a document is generally attractive to various branches of textual criticism. The TEI provides a set of critical apparatus elements to record varying witnesses to any single text. The methodological assumption here is that usually there is a single text from which all these witnesses diverge. Textual criticism is often seen to have three basic parts: cladistics, eclecticism, and stemmatics (Van Reenen and Van Mulken 1996). Cladistics involves the use of statistical analysis to attempt to determine which readings are more likely to be correct (Salemans 1996: 3–51). Textual eclecticism consists of an editor choosing those readings as the critical text which explains with the least complexity the other extant variants. Another branch of textual criticism is that of stemmatics, where the more likely readings of a text are determined through the classification of the witnesses into groupings or "family trees" based on perceived phylogenetic relationships of the readings they contain (Robinson 1996: 71–101). The TEI enables the markup of texts with the aims of facilitating such forms of textual criticism. It is implicit in the critical apparatus markup that it is intended to enable a greater understanding of the text, even if initially this is to problematize readings through avoiding settling on one reading as a preferred reading. Partly this is inherent with a move from the assumptions of print culture to that of digital textuality:

> It is particularly ironic or simple poetic justice – take your pick – that digital technology so calls into question the assumptions of print-associated editorial theory that it forces us to reconceive editing texts originally produced for print as well as those created within earlier information regimes. (Landow 2006: 104)

A consideration of the nature of textual criticism and its relationship to electronic markup, and indeed the TEI, is nothing new. At the Modern Language Association

(MLA) conference in 2002, at an announcement of a volume of essays entitled "Electronic Textual Editing" John Unsworth introduced two sessions on "Electronic Textual Editing and the TEI" (Unsworth 2002). In his examination not only of the need for such a volume, but the history of the TEI's interaction with textual criticism, he referred to an even more seminal presentation given at the same conference in 1994 by Michael Sperberg-McQueen examining how appropriate the recommendations of the TEI were for the production of electronic scholarly editions (Sperberg-McQueen 1994). As the assumptions that he makes concerning the nature of such editions are crucial in understanding not only the assumptions behind the text-critical provision by the TEI but also the foundations of modern electronic scholarly editions, like Unsworth I quote them in full here:

1. Electronic scholarly editions are worth having. And therefore it is worth thinking about the form they should take.
2. Electronic scholarly editions should be accessible to the broadest audience possible. They should not require a particular type of computer, or a particular piece of software: unnecessary technical barriers to their use should be avoided.
3. Electronic scholarly editions should have relatively long lives: at least as long as printed editions. They should not become technically obsolete before they are intellectually obsolete.
4. Printed scholarly editions have developed their current forms in order to meet both intellectual requirements and to adapt to the characteristics of print publication. Electronic editions must meet the same intellectual needs. There is no reason to abandon traditional intellectual requirements merely because we are using a different medium to publish them.
5. On the other hand, many conventions or requirements of traditional print editions reflect not the demands of readers or scholarship, but the difficulties of conveying complex information on printed pages without confusing or fatiguing the reader, or the financial exigencies of modern scholarly publishing. Such requirements need not be taken over at all, and must not be taken over thoughtlessly, into electronic editions.
6. Electronic publications can, if suitably encoded and suitably supported by software, present the same text in many forms: as clear text, as diplomatic transcript of one witness or another, as critical reconstruction of an authorial text, with or without critical apparatus of variants, and with or without annotations aimed at the textual scholar, the historian, the literary scholar, the linguist, the graduate student, or the undergraduate. They can provide many more types of index than printed editions typically do. And so electronic editions can, in principle, address a larger audience than single print editions. In this respect, they may face even higher intellectual requirements than print editions, which typically need not attempt to provide annotations for such diverse readers.
7. Print editions without apparatus, without documentation of editorial principles, and without decent typesetting are not acceptable substitutes for scholarly editions. Electronic editions without apparatus, without documentation of editorial principles, and without decent provision for suitable display are equally unacceptable for serious scholarly work.

8. As a consequence, we must reject out of hand proposals to create electronic scholarly editions in the style of Project Gutenberg, which objects in principle to the provision of apparatus, and almost never indicates the sources, let alone the principles which have governed the transcription, of its texts.

In sum: I believe electronic scholarly editions must meet three fundamental requirements: accessibility without needless technical barriers to use; longevity; and intellectual integrity. (Sperberg-McQueen 1994)

These three requirements, accessibility, longevity, and integrity, are the foundation of many of the intentions behind the creation of electronic scholarly editions and repositories of knowledge to disseminate them. Sadly, there are still many electronic editions produced to this day which fail to meet modern standards of accessibility: they often require a particular operating system and version of software (e.g., editions which function properly only in the Microsoft Internet Explorer web browser). This in turn jeopardizes their longevity as, being dependent on market forces for continued support, there is no guarantee that they shall continue to function in the future. This is slowly improving as funding bodies realize the need for proper accessibility and longevity from those resources produced with public money.

The need for intellectual integrity is highlighted in several of the points above. Sperberg-McQueen reminds us that the point of producing a scholarly edition – whether electronic or otherwise – is to meet the intellectual needs of those who will be using the edition. The quality and academic credibility which one finds in reputable print editions are just as important (if not arguably more so) in an electronic edition. While certain conventions have developed in print editions solely because of the limitations of the media, we do not need to perpetuate those in our digital editions (Hockey 2000: 124–45). However, a note of caution should be sounded here: although we do not need to adopt the scholarly traditions enforced by media-dependent requirements, we must be careful not to just depart from them without reflection. Instead we should be careful to build upon them to exploit the benefits of the chosen media in a manner which furthers the goals of a scholarly edition. One of the most salient points above (number 7) reminds us that just as printed editions without proper apparatus, editorial documentation, and reasonable publication should not be considered a substitute for a proper scholarly edition, neither should an electronic edition without similar equivalents.

Sperberg-McQueen's list of assumptions is partly intended to suggest how the TEI facilitates the creation and preservation of such electronic editions. He further expands on this by suggesting the kinds of apparatus and editorial documentation that should be a basic requirement for any such edition. In doing so he lists the textual phenomena which editors of such editions have been interested in recording in printed editions. It is unsurprising that these items can all be successfully encoded in TEI markup. In addition to the elements necessary to create a multi-source critical edition, the TEI also reflects the scholarly concerns in the transcription of primary sources. The elements provided include (with the TEI element also supplied), abbreviations (<abbr>), expansions (<expan>), additions (<add>), deletions (<del>), corrections (<corr>), apparent errors (<sic>), omitted material (<gap>), previously deleted text restored (<restore>), editorially supplied text (<supplied>), highlighted material (<hi>), changes of scribal hand (<handShift>), damage in the source (<damage>), illegibility (<unclear>), and unexpected spaces (<space>) amongst others. There are of course more elements to deal with other issues, and that the TEI is an appropriate choice for the textual encoding of such material is hardly in doubt (see TEI PH).

When it comes to transcription of primary sources, however, there is a significant new development in the TEI P5 version of the Guidelines in the removal of attributes containing textual data. There had been a misplaced notion by some that only text which was in the original should form element content proper, and that all metadata relating to that element (if outside the header) should be contained in that element as attributes. In a major move in their modification of the TEI Guidelines for their P5 version, the TEI recognized that many attributes contained text (rather than specific datatypes such as dates), and furthermore that this text might have elements inside it which an editor may wish to further mark up. One good example of this is that this text may contain non-Unicode characters which have need of the <g> element to record them properly. As a result the TEI made a large number of these elements into children of the elements to which they used to be attributes.

At the same time the TEI introduced the <choice> element as a method to indicate a divergence of possibilities in the original text-stream at a given point. This "groups a number of alternative encodings for the same point in a text," but is a significant editorial departure from previous versions of the recommendations (see TEI CO). This allowed the simultaneous encoding of abbreviations along with their expansions, or combinations of original, corrected readings, regularized, incorrect or unclear readings. Previously one might have used so-called janus tags, which allowed one to foreground one of the two pairs of abbr/expan, orig/reg, corr/sic. So while one might have done this by prioritizing either the original:

```
<l>So hath myn <orig reg="herte">hert</orig> caught in
remembraunce</l>
```

or the regularized form:

```
<l>So hath myn <reg orig="hert">herte</reg> caught in
remembraunce</l>
```

in TEI P4, under TEI P5 one is allowed to indicate both of these simultaneously. And, more importantly, without necessarily judging which of these is to be preferred by an end application or user. The first line of this poem above would now be encoded as:

```
<l>So hath myn
<choice>
```

```
<orig>hert</orig>
<reg>herte</reg>
</choice> caught in remembraunce</l>
```

This enables not only for the simultaneous encoding of the original and regularized version, but also the possibility of further markup of these items which would be impossible if one of them was forced to be an attribute. Moreover, a single <choice> could contain an abbreviation, an expansion and different forms of regularization among other possibilities. In addition, <choice> is self-nestable, that is, it can contain itself as a child in order to allow for choices between sets of possible alternatives.

The use of <choice> should not be confused with the ability to indicate variant readings between witnesses and thus construct a scholarly critical apparatus with the <app> element. Although there are some similarities, in that the linear text-stream is split at this point to provide a number of alternatives, with <choice> these are different possible interpretations or variants of a single witness, whereas <app> is a more specialized encoding of a point of divergence between various witnesses. The intention with one is to provide a clearer understanding of a single text, and with the other the reconciliation of a number of witnesses to that text. That the chapter on transcription from primary sources and that on the creation of a critical apparatus follow each other in the Guidelines is no mere coincidence. Although not explicitly stated, the transcription from primary sources could be seen to encompass the foundation of "non-critical editing," which they intentionally set aside from the creation of a critical edition in stating at the outset that it "is expected that this module will also be useful in the preparation of critical editions, but the module defined here is distinct [. . .] and may be used independently of it" (see TEI PH).

Those examining the influence of the theoretical schools of textual editing on the TEI's methodology have noticed that this may indicate that the TEI feels this form of editing could be considered less important or interpretative than the creation of critical apparatus, and that this in turn indicates the influence of conservative textual editing theories on the TEI (Vanhoutte 2006: 170). Whether this is the case or not, the use of these tags separately is certainly less powerful than when they are used in combination.

In indicating the variant readings of different sources for a text, the TEI enables the ability to construct a full critical apparatus in a straightforward manner. In a fictitious set of manuscripts referred to as manuscripts A, B, C, D, and E, the first line of the poem used earlier could present the readings for each of these manuscripts:

```
<l>So hath myn <app>
  <rdg wit="#msA">hert</rdg>
  <rdg wit="#msB">herte</rdg>
  <rdg wit="#msC">herte</rdg>
  <rdg wit="#msD">minde</rdg>
```

```
  <rdg wit="#msE">mynde</rdg>
</app> caught in remembraunce</l>
```

As the manuscripts B and C (the "wit" attribute simply points to the document's header where more information concerning these manuscripts is stored) have the same reading, these <rdg> tags could be merged into one, with multiple values for the wit attribute. Or indeed, since this is our preferred reading we could use the lemma (<lem>) element to indicate that this is the base text we are working from to create our critical edition.

```
<l>So hath myn <app>
  <lem wit="#msB #msC">herte</lem>
  <rdg wit="#msA">hert</rdg>
  <rdg wit="#msD">minde</rdg>
  <rdg wit="#msE">mynde</rdg>
</app> caught in remembraunce</l>
```

The benefit here is that the TEI enables an editor to foreground a particular reading as a lemma, or not. Moreover, the variant readings can be grouped for whatever theoretical reason, here suggesting possible relationships in the history of their textual transmission. This is an extremely flexible system which enables encoding according to a variety of theoretical perceptions as to the purpose and nature of a critical edition (Cover and Robinson 1995). The avoidance of the suggestion of a base-text here is important because it allows a variety of user interactions with this text. Any reading based on these can be seen as only one synchronous structure that is unprivileged in comparison with any other possible reading (Gabler 1981). The amount of power and flexibility inherent in a system which simultaneously encodes the textual variants along with possibility of indicating editorial treatment of these texts is what will allow for the creation of significantly more enhanced and flexible scholarly editions.

```
<l>So hath myn <app>
  <rdgGrp>
    <rdg wit="#msB #msC">herte</rdg>
    <rdg wit="#msA">
      <choice><orig>hert</orig><reg>herte</reg></choice>
    </rdg>
  </rdgGrp>
  <rdgGrp>
    <rdg wit="#msD">
      <choice><orig>minde</orig><reg>mind</reg></choice>
    </rdg>
    <rdg wit="#msE">
      <choice><orig>mynde</orig><reg>mind</reg></choice>
```

```
    </rdg>
   </rdgGrp>
 </app> caught in remembraunce</l>
```

One of the continual arguments in textual criticism concerns our relationship with a possible base-text and its relationship to putative copy-texts. Whether it is "the old fallacy of the 'best text'" (Greg 1950: 24), the necessity of the process "being appreciated with the finished and familiar product" (Eggert 1990: 21), that a study should not be constrained only to authorial changes, but also posthumous editing by publishers (McGann 1992), possibly as a form of continuous production text (McGann 1991: 20–1), or that developments in text encoding have coincided with a paradigm shift away from the concept of a definitive edition (Finneran 1996: ix–xi), the encoding provided by the TEI enables the creation of a sophisticated textual resource which is of use to the end user. After all, this is one of the intended goals in creating a scholarly edition. As a result, some have argued that it is not a critical mass of variants that we need to display to the users, rather we should return to the practice of providing a logical edited text which rationalizes the differences, we should re-create a reading text from whatever (possibly fragmentary) witnesses remain. This in no way does away with the need for detailed text critical markup; if this is done properly, of course, a reading text can be created from a base of critical editorial decisions which should also be available for further consultation by readers if they desire:

> There is a theoretical purity in unedited, unreconstructed texts that is comforting to editors. But our aim as editors should not be to achieve our own comfort. It should be to make editions that will be useful to the readers: editions that will help them read. Parker's *Living Text of the Gospels* is an eloquent plea for a connection between textual criticism (treating texts as editorial problems to be solved) and cultural criticism (treating the texts as resources for our knowledge of the culture from which they came). This is a division that runs very deep in textual scholarship. (Robinson 2000: 13)

That this divide exists in textual scholarship is undeniable. The creation of editions which fully embody the text, both as output of editorial decisions and as variants which also act as a method of access for historical knowledge, will be useful to anyone studying that text and its time-period. The reason some editors shy away from this idea is in an attempt to preserve the perception of some mythical editorial objectivity.

> By highlighting the most crucial points of textual variation, and by leading the reader into an understanding of how and why this variation arose at these points, we can make this connection between variation and meaning in the most useful way. In the context of electronic editions, with all their variant texts, a single reconstructed, and eclectic text may provide the best means to do just this. (Robinson 2000: 13)

If we view the TEI as interested in enabling the codification of texts for the benefit of creating such textual editions, then it certainly is beneficial in creating such a reconstructed text while fully conscious that this is not the "original" text but a reading edition for the benefit of the user of the resource. However, increasingly there is not necessarily a non-digital source text from which the resource has been digitized, but the text is a modern born-digital text which may still be subject to many of the textual phenomena that the TEI enables editors to encode. Likewise, TEI-encoded texts should not necessarily be viewed as static, for there is the possibility that the text may undergo not only successive revisions but annotations and comments by readers, all of which could be displayed as a single evolving resource. One possible model for this was proposed as an ongoing collaborative "work-site":

> The work-site is text-construction site for the editor and expert reader; and it is the site of study of the work (of its finished textual versions and their annotation) for the first-time reader, as well as any position in between. Because the building of such textual and interpretative work-sites will be piece by piece, collaborative and ongoing, we are starting to look at a future for humanities, work-oriented research that is, if not scientific exactly, then more *wissenschaftlich*, in the German sense, than what literary critics, historians, and others are used to. (Eggert 2005: 433)

Such as system would be dependent on stand-off markup to provide the annotations and alternative readings on any aspect of the text (or indeed the ongoing annotations). It would certainly possible to encode the texts and annotations produced in the study of digital literature as TEI, and indeed given the provision for stand-off markup in the TEI Guidelines, the TEI would be a good choice for such an application.

Customization: Fragmentation or Consolidation?

The increasing popularity of the TEI as a system for text encoding in humanities projects does bring with it certain problematic aspects. Since the TEI is conceived as a generalized system, it contains much more than any individual project will ever need to accomplish its goals. It is not that the TEI seeks to become monolithic, having an encoding recommendation for all possibilities – that is naturally impossible – but it intends to be customized and modified. Indeed, it is expected that, especially in creation of a local encoding format, individual projects will remove elements, constrain attribute value lists, add new elements, and even import schemas from other namespaces. And yet, this aspect of the TEI has often been ignored or misunderstood. John Unsworth, in comparing the MLA's Committee on Scholarly Editing (CSE) and the TEI, noted that one of the central missions of the TEI is to cope with the differing needs of scholars:

> While it would be foolish to assert that the CSE and the TEI are without critics, sceptics, and detractors, they do in fact represent a broad, community-based consensus, and they are, in their respective arenas, the only credible institutions attempting to develop, disseminate and maintain general (rather than project-specific) guidelines.

Both organizations have been accused, at various points in the past, of promoting a monologic orthodoxy, but in fact each organization has devoted significant time and effort to accommodating difference – the CSE in the evolution of its guidelines over the last decade to accommodate a greater variety of editorial methods and a broader range of materials and periods, as well as editions in electronic media, and the TEI, most importantly, in its extension mechanism, as well in its consistent insistence, over its fifteen-year history, on international and interdisciplinary representation in its governing bodies, its workgroups, its funding sources, and its membership. (Unsworth 2002)

Indeed, the extension and customization of the TEI is listed earlier in this chapter as one of its original design goals. In promoting the need for individual customization of the TEI, they have created examples of such customization (see TEI Custom). It is in some ways unfortunate that one of these, so-called TEI-Lite, has been adopted wholesale by many projects who do not need the entirety of the TEI Guidelines, and which instead simply adopt this subset of the TEI (see TEI Lite). While this is very useful for large-scale projects which need a basic light encoding, it is equally unfortunate, because the intellectual integrity which Sperberg-McQueen hoped for in the creation of electronic editions (Sperberg-McQueen 1994) benefits greatly from the constraint of a schema to just the needs of the project. The advantages of customizing the TEI for the needs of the project in question is that greater consistency and less human error find their way into the resulting files.

The method by which the TEI allows the customization of the overall TEI schema is through the use of a specialized form of TEI document referred to as a TEI ODD, "One Document Does (it all)." ODD uses TEI descriptive markup to produce a file which can then be used as a base to generate not only a schema to validate document instances (in RelaxNG compact or XML format, W3C Schema, or DTD language), but a variety of accompanying subset of the descriptive documentation concerning the elements it describes. The TEI Guidelines themselves are written in this TEI ODD XML format, and this generates the overall TEI schemas, the prose of the Guidelines themselves, as well as the element references available. This would be an extremely beneficial format for any project to use in producing a set of local encoding Guidelines based on the TEI. An additional benefit is that the documentation produced reflects any changes of name, added or deleted elements, or changes of content model. More information concerning ODD is available as part of the Guidelines in the chapter on "Documentation Elements" (see TEI TD).

One can either write these documents directly in XML (the TEI provides a number of example customizations (see TEI Custom)), or use the web front-end to Roma, the TEI's ODD processor (see TEI Roma). Roma provides a user-friendly method of selecting modules, adding, removing, or customizing the elements they contain, and producing schemas and the accompanying documentation. In addition, this front-end allows you to save the TEI ODD file you have created for further modification at a later date.

Although customization and extension of the TEI are a necessary reality because the needs of the community they serve is so vast and disparate, it does bring with it some theoretical complications. The very first of the Poughkeepsie Principles, never mind the use of the word in the Guidelines' full title, indicates that the TEI as an interchange format is one of the prime goals for its existence. And yet, the continual divergence from the TEI through customization and modification of the schema inherently problematizes this. If one makes very minor changes to the TEI through limiting the elements which are available, or providing a fixed list of attribute values, then there are no implications for the interchange of a document encoded according to this schema. It will validate against the tei_all schema which contains all available TEI elements. Even if some of the elements or attributes are renamed, but follow the recommended methods to do so and provide TEI equivalences for them, then the document is still suitable for interchange because there is a documented method of returning it to a state where it would validate against tei_all. However, once new elements with no TEI equivalences are added, the content model of elements is significantly changed, or elements are imported from another XML namespace, then the document instance which validates against this schema will not necessarily be able to be transformed into a document which could validate against the tei_all schema. Thus, these kinds of changes – although encouraged and considered TEI documents – must necessarily be viewed as significantly different from those which leave a pure subset of the TEI.

The importance of this point is reflected in the fear that instead of encouraging community and interoperability, the ease of customization that the TEI now allows may in fact result in greater divergence and fragmentation of the document instances created by projects using the TEI. If, however, we accept that it is a necessarily evil for projects to customize their schemas, then this is not as problematic as it first appears. Although the customization will result in document instances that are not directly interoperable, they retain the benefit of having diverged from a common source. At least the documents will have some relationship to the TEI as a standard encoding format. Moreover, if they have followed the instructions on creating conformant customizations given in the Guidelines, then the accompanying TEI ODD file will provide an electronic record of exactly how the new schema differs from standard TEI. If customization is a necessary evil, then the recording of the details of a customization in a standardized format is the best one can hope for, and even if this causes problems for interchange, it still has appreciable benefits for long-term preservation. Whether this will result in a greater fragmentation of the compatibility of TEI documents, or a consolidation around specific customizations, will be seen with time.

While there is no reason necessarily to customize the TEI if one of the publicly available schemas will suffice for the needs of the project, the temptation to customize, and in particular extend the TEI is difficult to resist. When presented with an encoding problem it is far easier to simply add a new element to deal with the problem than it is to undertake the proper document analysis and see if there is an applicable existing solution. For those less familiar with the TEI Guidelines, this temptation for unbridled customization can be overwhelming, yet should be avoided if possible.

Conclusions

The TEI provides a substantial framework upon which scholars and editors can undertake the study of literature through digital means. It is inevitable that more digital editions will continue to be produced, and that the TEI has a role in assisting these to be accessible and interoperable. It is, however, a duty of those creating them to ensure their intellectual integrity. If the study of literature is increasingly to become digital then we have an academic duty to ensure as much as possible that this is based on truly scholarly electronic editions which not only uphold the quality and reliability expected from such editions, but simultaneously capitalize upon the advantages that publication in a more flexible media affords:

> It follows then that all major series of scholarly editions, including those now published by the major academic presses, also will become digital. There will be exceptions: there always will be a place for a printed "reader's edition" or similar. But we should expect that for most of the purposes for which we now use editions, the editions we use will be electronic. We should do this not just to keep up with the rest of the world, but because indeed electronic editions make possible kinds of reading and research never before available and offer valuable insights into and approaches to the texts they cover. (Robinson 2005)

We are not yet at the point where the creation of digital editions is either unproblematic or fully exploits the benefits of the media in which they are published. We still need to encourage funding bodies to produce better tools to enable the digital study of literature, as the TEI foresaw in point 8 of the Poughkeepsie Principles (see TEI EDP01). This period of digital incunabula will eventually pass, and the efforts of organizations like the TEI are laudable in attempting to produce a standard base on top of which increasingly sophisticated software, publication frameworks, and virtual research environments designed specifically for the study of literature can be, and hopefully will soon be, created.

NOTE

1 For example: the Oxford Text Archive <http://www.ota.ox.ac.uk/>, the Electronic Text Center at University of Virginia <http://etext.lib. virginia.edu/>, and the United Kingdom's Arts and Humanities Data Service <http://www.ahds.ac.uk/>.

REFERENCES AND FURTHER READING

Barnard, David, Lou Burnard, Jean-Pierre Gaspart, et al. (1995). "Hierarchical Encoding of Text: Technical Problems and SGML Solutions." In Nancy Ide and Jean Véronis (Eds.). *Text Encoding Initiative: Background and Context.* Dordrecht: Kluwer Academic Publishers. Repr. from (1995) *Computers and the Humanities* 29: 211–231.

Cover, Robin, and Robinson, Peter M. W. (1995). "Encoding Textual Criticism." In Nancy Ide and Jean Véronis (Eds.). *Text Encoding Initiative: Background and Context*. Dordrecht: Kluwer Academic Publishers. Repr. from (1995) *Computers and the Humanities* 29: 123–36.

Eggert, Paul (1990) "Textual Product or Textual Process: Procedures and Assumptions of Critical Editing." In P. Eggert (Ed.). *Editing in Australia*. Canberra: University College ADFA, pp. 19–40.

—— (2005). "Text-encoding, Theories of the Text and the 'Work-site.'" *Literary and Linguistic Computing* 20.4: 425–35.

Finneran, R. J. (Ed.) (1996). *The Literary Text in the Digital Age*. Editorial Theory and Literary Criticism. Ann Arbor: University of Michigan Press.

Gabler, H. W. (1981). "The Synchrony and Diachrony of Texts: Practice and Theory of the Critical Edition of James Joyce's *Ulysses*." *TEXT* 1: 305–26.

Greg, W. W. (1950–1). "The Rationale of Copy-text." *Studies in Bibliography* 3: 19–37.

Hayles, N. Katherine. (2002). *Writing Machines*. Cambridge. MA: MIT Press.

—— (2005). *My Mother Was a Computer: Digital Subjects and Literary Texts*. Chicago: University of Chicago Press.

Hockey, Susan (2000). *Electronic Texts in the Humanities: Principles and Practices*. Oxford: Oxford University Press.

Ide, Nancy, and C. M. Sperberg-McQueen (1995). "The Text Encoding Initiative: Its History, Goals, and Future Development." In Nancy Ide and Jean Véronis (Eds.). *Text Encoding Initiative: Background and Context*. Dordrecht: Kluwer Academic Publishers. Repr. from (1995) *Computers and the Humanities* 29: 5–15.

Landow, George P. (2006). *Hypertext 3.0: Critical Theory and New Media in an Era of Globalization*, 3rd edn. Baltimore: John Hopkins University Press.

McGann, J. J. (1991). *The Textual Condition*. Princeton: Princeton University Press.

—— (1992). *Critique of Modern Textual Criticism*. Chicago: University of Chicago Press. Repr. (1992). Charlottesville, VA: University Press of Virginia.

—— (1996). The rationale of hypertext. <http://www.iath.virginia.edu/public/jjm2f/rationale.html>; repr. *TEXT* 9: 11–32; repr. (1997)

Electronic Text: Investigations in Method and Theory (Kathryn Sutherland, Ed.). Oxford: Clarendon Press, pp. 19–46; repr. (2001). *Radiant Textuality: Literature after the World Wide Web*. New York: Palgrave, pp. 53–74.

—— (2001). *Radiant Textuality: Literature after the World Wide Web*. New York: Palgrave.

—— (2004). "Marking Texts of Many Dimensions." In Susan Schreibman, Ray Siemens, and John Unsworth (Eds.). *A Companion to Digital Humanities*. Oxford: Blackwell Publishing, pp. 98–217.

Renear A. (1999). Paper abstract for panel participation on: "What is text? A debate on the philosophical and epistemological nature of text in the light of humanities computing research" at the conference of the Association of Computing in the Humanities/Association of Literary and Linguistic Computing.

—— (2004). "Text Encoding." In Susan Schreibman, Ray Siemans and John Unsworth (Eds.). *A Companion to Digital Humanities*. Oxford: Blackwell Publishing, pp. 218–39.

——, E. Mylonas, and D. Durand (1993). *Refining our Notion of What Text Really Is: The Problem of Overlapping Hierarchies*. <http://www.stg.brown.edu/resources/stg/monographs/ohco.html>. Accessed August 1, 2006.

Robinson, Peter M. W. (1996). "Computer-Assisted Stemmatic Analysis and 'Best-Text' Historical Editing." In Pieter Van Reenen and Margot van Mulken (Eds) *Studies in Stemmatology*. Amsterdam: John Benjamins, pp. 71–104.

Robinson, P. (2000). "The One and the Many Text." *Literary and Linguistic Computing* 15.1: 5–14.

—— (2005). "Current Issues in Making Digital Editions of Medieval Texts – or, Do Electronic Scholarly Editions Have a Future?" *Digital Medievalist* 1:1. <http://www.digitalmedievalist.org/article.cfm?RecID=6>. Accessed August 1, 2006.

Salemans, Ben J. P. (1996). "Cladistics or the Resurrection of the Method of Lachmann." In Pieter Van Reenen and Margot van Mulken (Eds.). *Studies in Stemmatology*. Amsterdam: John Benjamins, pp. 3–70.

Sartre, J-P. (1943). *Being and Nothingness: an Essay on Phenomenological Ontology* (H. E. Barnes, Trans. 1956). NY: Philosophical Library.

Sperberg-McQueen, C. M. (1994). *Textual Criticism and the Text Encoding Initiative*. Annual Convention of the Modern Language Association. <http://www.tei-c.org/Vault/XX/mla94.html>. Accessed August 1, 2006. Repr. in Finneran, R. J. (Ed.) (1996) *The Literary Text in the Digital Age*. Editorial Theory and Literary Criticism. Ann Arbor: University of Michigan Press, pp. 37–62.

TEI CC. "Language Corpora." In C. M. Sperberg-McQueen and L. Burnard (Eds.). *TEI P5: Guidelines for Electronic Text Encoding and Interchange*. Oxford: Text Encoding Initiative Consortium. <http://www.tei-c.org/P5/Guidelines/CC.html>. Accessed August 1, 2006.

TEI CO. "Elements Available in All TEI Documents." In C. M. Sperberg-McQueen and L. Burnard (Eds.). *TEI P5: Guidelines for Electronic Text Encoding and Interchange*. Oxford: Text Encoding Initiative Consortium. <http://www.tei-c.org/P5/Guidelines/CO.html>. Accessed August 1, 2006.

TEI Custom. *TEI Example Customizations*. <http://www.tei-c.org/release/xml/tei/custom/>. Accessed August 1, 2006.

TEI EDP01. *New Draft of Design Principles*. <http://www.tei-c.org/Vault/ED/edp01.gml>. Accessed August 1, 2006.

TEI Guidelines (2005). C. M. Sperberg-McQueen and L. Burnard (Eds.). *TEI P5: Guidelines for Electronic Text Encoding and Interchange*. Oxford: Text Encoding Initiative Consortium. <http://www.tei-c.org/P5/>. Accessed August 1, 2006.

TEI NH. "Multiple Hierarchies." In C. M. Sperberg-McQueen and L. Burnard (Eds.). *TEI P5: Guidelines for Electronic Text Encoding and Interchange*. Oxford: Text Encoding Initiative Consortium. <http://www.tei-c.org/P5/Guidelines/USE.html#NH>. Accessed August 1, 2006.

TEI PH. "Transcription of Primary Sources." In C. M. Sperberg-McQueen and L. Burnard (Eds.). *TEI P5: Guidelines for Electronic Text Encoding and Interchange*. Oxford: Text Encoding Initiative Consortium. <http://www.tei-c.org/P5/Guidelines/PH.html>. Accessed August 1, 2006.

TEI Projects. *Projects using the TEI*. <http://www.tei-c.org/Applications/>. Accessed August 1, 2006.

TEI Roma. *Roma: Generating Validators for the TEI* (A. Mittlebach and S. P. Q. Rahtz, Creators and Maintainers). <http://www.tei-c.org/Roma/>. Accessed August 1, 2006.

TEI SG. "A Gentle Introduction to XML." In C. M. Sperberg-McQueen and L. Burnard (Eds.). *TEI P5: Guidelines for Electronic Text Encoding and Interchange*. Oxford: Text Encoding Initiative Consortium. <http://www.tei-c.org/P5/Guidelines/SG.html>. Accessed August 1, 2006.

TEI Stylesheets. *XSL Stylesheets for TEI XML* (S. P. Q. Rahtz, Maintainer). <http://www.tei-c.org/Stylesheets/teic/>. Accessed August 1, 2006.

TEI TC. "Critical Apparatus." In C. M. Sperberg-McQueen and L. Burnard (Eds.). *TEI P5: Guidelines for Electronic Text Encoding and Interchange*. Oxford: Text Encoding Initiative Consortium. <http://www.tei-c.org/P5/Guidelines/TC.html>. Accessed August 1, 2006.

TEI TD. "Documentation Elements." In C. M. Sperberg-McQueen and L. Burnard (Eds.). *TEI P5: Guidelines for Electronic Text Encoding and Interchange*. Oxford: Text Encoding Initiative Consortium. <http://www.tei-c.org/P5/Guidelines/TD.html>. Accessed August 1, 2006.

TEI Website. *TEI: Yesterday's Information Tomorrow*. <http://www.tei-c.org/>. Accessed August 1, 2006.

Unsworth, J. (2002). *Electronic Textual Editing and the TEI*. Annual Convention of the Modern Language Association. <http://www3.isrl.uiuc.edu/~unsworth/mla-cse.2002.html>. Accessed August 1, 2006.

——, K. O'Keefe, and L. Burnard (Eds.) (2006). *Electronic Textual Editing*. New York: Modern Language Association of America.

Vanhoutte, E. (2006). "Prose Fiction and Modern Manuscripts: Limitations and Possibilities of Text-encoding for Electronic Editions." In J. Unsworth, K. O'Keefe, and L. Burnard (Eds.). *Electronic Textual Editing*. New York: Modern Language Association of America, pp. 161–80.

Van Reenen, Pieter, and Margot van Mulken (Eds) (1996). *Studies in Stemmatology*. Amsterdam: John Benjamins, pp. 3–70.

26

Algorithmic Criticism

Stephen Ramsay

Digital Humanities, like most fields of scholarly inquiry, constituted itself through a long accretion of revolutionary insight, territorial rivalry, paradigmatic rupture, and social convergence. But the field is unusual in that it can point both to a founder and to a moment of creation. The founder is Roberto Busa, an Italian Jesuit priest who in the late 1940s undertook the production of an automatically generated concordance to the works of St. Thomas Aquinas using a computer. The founding moment was the creation of a radically transformed, reordered, disassembled and reassembled version of one of the world's most influential philosophies:

> 00596 in veniale peccatum non cadat; ut sic hoc verbum habemus non determinatum, sed confusum praesens importet   -003(3SN)3.3.2.b.ex/56
> 00597 intellegit profectum scientiae christi quantum ad experientiam secundum novam conversionem ad sensibile praesens,   -S-003(3SN)14.1.3e.ra4/4
> 00598 ita quot apprehenditur ut possibile adipisce, aprehenditur ut jam quodammodo praesens: et ideo spec delectationem   -003(3SN)26.1.2.ra3/8
> 00599 operationibus: quia illud quod certudinaliter quasi praesens tenemus per intellectum, dicimur sentire, vel videre;   -003(3Sn)26.1.5.co/11 (Index 65129)

Undertaking such transformations for the purpose of humanistic inquiry would eventually come to be called "text analysis," and in literary study, computational text analysis has been used to study problems related to style and authorship for nearly sixty years. As the field has matured, it has incorporated elements of some of the most advanced forms of technical endeavor, including natural language processing, statistical computing, corpus linguistics, and artificial intelligence. It is easily the most quantitative approach to the study of literature, the oldest form of digital literary study, and, in the opinion of many, the most scientific form of literary investigation.

But "algorithmic criticism" – *criticism* prompted by the algorithmic manipulation of literary texts – either does not exist, or exists only in nascent form. The digital revolution, for all its wonders, has not penetrated the core activity of literary studies, which, despite numerous revolutions of a more epistemological nature, remains mostly concerned with the interpretive analysis of written cultural artifacts. Texts are browsed, searched, and disseminated by all but the most hardened Luddites in literary study, but seldom are they transformed algorithmically as a means of gaining entry to the deliberately and self-consciously subjective act of critical interpretation. Even text analysis practitioners avoid bringing the hermeneutical freedom of criticism to the "outputted" text. Bold statements, strong readings, and broad generalizations (to say nothing of radical misreadings, anarchic accusations, agonistic paratextual revolts) are rare, if not entirely absent from the literature of the field, where the emphasis is far more often placed on methodology and the limitations it imposes.

It is perhaps not surprising that text analysis would begin this way. Busa's own revolution was firmly rooted in the philological traditions to which modern criticism was largely a reaction. Reflecting on the creation of the Index some forty years after the fact, Busa offered the following motivations:

> I realized first that a philological and lexicographical inquiry into the verbal system of an author has to precede and prepare for a doctrinal interpretation of his works. Each writer expresses his conceptual system in and through his verbal system, with the consequence that the reader who masters this verbal system, using his own conceptual system, has to get an insight into the writer's conceptual system. The reader should not simply attach to the words he reads the significance they have in his mind, but should try to find out what significance they had in the author's mind. (Annals 83)

Such ideas would not have seemed unusual to nineteenth-century biblical scholars for whom meaning was something both knowable and recoverable through careful, scientific analysis of language, genre, textual recension, and historical context. Nor would it, with some rephrasing, have been a radical proposition either for Thomas himself or for the Dominican Friars who had produced the first concordance (to the Vulgate) in the thirteenth century. We do no injustice to Busa's achievement in noting, however, that the contemporary critical ethos regards Busa's central methodological tenets as grossly naive. Modern criticism, entirely skeptical of authorial intention as a normative principle and linguistic meaning as a stable entity, has largely abandoned the idea that we could ever keep from reading ourselves into the reading of an author and is, for the most part, no longer concerned with attempting to avoid this conundrum.

But even in Busa's project, with its atomized fragmentation of a divine text, we can discern the enormous liberating power of the computer moving against the sureness of philology. In the original formation of Thomas's text, "presence" was a vague leitmotif. But on page 65129 of the algorithmically transformed text, "presence" is that toward which every formation tends, the central feature of every utterance, and the pattern that orders all that surrounds it. We encounter "ut sic hoc" and "ut possibile," but the transformed text does not permit us to complete those thoughts.

Even Busa would have had to concede that the effect is not the immediate apprehension of knowledge, but instead what the Russian Formalists called *ostranenie* – the estrangement and defamiliarization of textuality. One might suppose that being able to see texts in such strange and unfamiliar ways would give such procedures an important place in the critical revolution the Russian Formalists ignited; which is to say, the movement that ultimately gave rise to the ideas that would supplant Busa's own hermeneutics.

But text analysis would take a much more conservative path. Again and again in the literature of text analysis, we see a movement back toward the hermeneutics of Busa, with the analogy of science being put forth as the highest aspiration of digital literary study. For Roseanne Potter, writing in the late 1980s, "the principled use of technology and criticism" necessarily entailed criticism becoming "absolutely comfortable with scientific methods" (Potter 1988: 91–2). Her hope, shared by many in the field, was that the crossover might create a criticism "suffused with humanistic values," but there was never a suggestion that the "scientific methods" of algorithmic manipulation might need to establish comfort with the humanities. After all, it was the humanities that required deliverance from the bitter malady that had overtaken modern criticism:

> In our own day, professors of literature indulge in what John Ellis (1974) somewhat mockingly called "wise eclecticism" – a general tendency to believe that if you can compose an interesting argument to support a position, any well-argued assertion is as valid as the next one. A scientific literary criticism would not permit some of the most widespread of literary critical practices. (Potter 1998: 93)

Those not openly engaged in the hermeneutics of "anything goes" – historicists old or new – were presented with the settling logic of truth and falsehood proposed by computational analysis:

> This is not to deny the historical, social, and cultural context of literature (Bakhtin, 1981), and of language itself (Halliday, 1978). Nor can one overlook the very rich and subtle elaborations of literary theory in the forty years since Barthes published *Le degre zero de l'ecriture* (1953). In point of fact, most of these elaborations have the technical status of hypothesis, since they have not been confirmed empirically in terms of the data which they propose to describe – literary texts. This is where computer techniques and computer data come into their own. (Fortier 1993: 376)

Susan Hockey, in a book intended not only to survey the field of humanities computing, but to "explain the intellectual rationale for electronic text technology in the humanities," later offered a vision of the role of the computer in literary study to which most contemporary text analysis practitioners fully subscribe:

> Computers can assist with the study of literature in a variety of ways, some more successful than others. [. . .] Computer-based tools are especially good for comparative work, and here some simple statistical tools can help to reinforce the interpretation of

the material. These studies are particularly suitable for testing hypotheses or for verifying intuition. They can provide concrete evidence to support or refute hypotheses or interpretations which have in the past been based on human reading and the somewhat serendipitous noting of interesting features. (Hockey 2000: 66)

It is not difficult to see why a contemporary criticism temperamentally and philosophically committed to intuition and serendipity would choose to ignore the corrective tendencies of the computer against the deficiencies of "human reading." Text analysis arises to assist the critic, but only if the critic agrees to operate within the regime of scientific methodology with its "refutations" of hypotheses.

The procedure that Busa used to transform Thomas into an alternative vision is, like most text analytical procedures, algorithmic in the strictest sense. If science has repeatedly suggested itself as the most appropriate metaphor, it is undoubtedly because such algorithms are embedded in activities that appear to have the character of experiment. Busa, in the first instance, had formed a hypothesis concerning the importance of certain concepts in the work. He then sought to determine the parameters (in the form of suitable definitions and abstractions) for an experiment that could adjudicate the viability of this hypothesis. The experiment moved through the target environment (the text) with the inexorability of a scientific instrument creating observable effects at every turn. The observations were then used to confirm the hypothesis with which he began.

Some literary critical problems clearly find comfort within such a framework. Authorship attribution, for example, seeks definitive answers to empirical questions concerning whether a work is by a particular author or not, and programs designed to adjudicate such questions can often be organized scientifically with hypotheses, control groups, validation routines, and reproducible methods. The same is true for any text analysis procedure that endeavors to expose the bare empirical facts of a text (often a necessary prelude to textual criticism and analytical bibliography). Hermeneutically, such investigations rely upon a variety of philosophical positivism in which the accumulation of verified, falsifiable facts forms the basis for interpretive judgment. In these particular discursive fields, the veracity of statements like "The tenth letter of *The Federalist* was written by James Madison," or, "The 1597 quarto edition of Romeo and Juliet is a memorial reconstruction of the play" are understood to hinge more or less entirely on the support of concrete textual evidence. One might challenge the interpretation of the facts, or even the factual nature of the evidence, but from a rhetorical standpoint, facts are what permit or deny judgment.

For most forms of critical endeavor, however, appeals to "the facts" prove far less useful. Consider, for example, Miriam Wallace's discussion of subjectivity in Virginia Woolf's novel *The Waves*:

In this essay I want to resituate *The Waves* as complexly formulating and reformulating subjectivity through its playful formal style and elision of corporeal materiality. *The Waves* models an alternative subjectivity that exceeds the dominant (white, male, heterosexual) individual western subject through its stylistic usage of metaphor and metonymy. [...] Focusing on the narrative construction of subjectivity reveals the pertinence of *The Waves* for current feminist reconfigurations of the feminine subject. This focus links the novel's visionary limitations to the historic moment of Modernism. (Wallace 2000: 295–6)

Wallace frames her discourse as a "resituation" of Woolf's novel within several larger fields of critical discourse. This will presumably involve the marshaling of evidence and the annunciation of claims. It may even involve offering various "facts" in support of her conclusions. But hermeneutically, literary critical arguments of this sort do not stand in the same relationship to facts, claims, and evidence as the more empirical forms of inquiry. There is no experiment that can verify the idea that Woolf's "playful formal style" reformulates subjectivity or that her "elision of corporeal materiality" exceeds the dominant western subject. There is no control group that can contain "current feminist reconfigurations." And surely, there is no metric by which we may quantify "pertinence" either for Woolf or for the author's own judgment.

The hermeneutical implications of these absences invoke ancient suspicions toward rhetoric, and in particular, toward the rhetorical office of *inventio*: the sophistic process of seeking truth through "the dialectical interplay of trust, emotion, logic, and tradition which has, since the seventeenth century, contended with the promises of empiricism" (Bold 1988: 543–4). In some sense, humanistic discourse seems to lacks methodology; it cannot describe the ground rules of engagement, the precise means of verification, or even the parameters of its subject matter. Still, as Gadamer pointed out in *Truth and Method*:

> The hermeneutic phenomenon is basically not a problem of method at all. It is not concerned with a method of understanding by means of which texts are subjected to scientific investigation like all other objects of experience. It is not concerned primarily with amassing verified knowledge, such as would satisfy the methodological ideal of science – yet it too is concerned with knowledge and with truth. In understanding tradition not only are texts understood, but insights are acquired and truths known. But what kind of knowledge and what kind of truth? (1996: 544)

Though Gadamer's question is not easily answered, we may say that from a purely cultural standpoint, literary criticism operates at a register in which understanding, knowledge, and truth occur outside of the narrower denotative realm in which scientific statements are made. It is not merely the case that literary criticism is concerned with something other than the amassing of verified knowledge. Literary criticism operates within a hermeneutical framework in which the specifically scientific meaning of fact, metric, verification, and evidence simply do not apply. The "facts" of Woolf – however we choose to construe this term – are not the principal objects of study in literary criticism. "Evidence" stands as a metaphor for the delicate building blocks of rhetorical persuasion. We "measure" (as in prosody) only to establish webs of interrelation and influence. "Verification" occurs in a social community of scholars whose agreement or disagreement is almost never put forth without qualification.

All of this leaves the project of text analysis in a difficult position. For even if we are willing to concede the general utility of computational methods for the project of humanistic inquiry, we must nonetheless contend with a fundamental disjunction between literary critical method and computational method. The logic that underlies computation, though not scientific in the strict sense of the term, conforms easily to the methodologies of science. Computers are, as Hockey noted, good at counting, measuring, and (in a limited sense) verifying data, and we judge the tractability of data by the degree to which it can be made to conform to these requirements. When it comes to literary criticism, however, we find that the "data" is almost entirely intractable from the standpoint of the computational rubric.

Paper-based textual artifacts must either be transformed from a continuous field into some more quantized form (i.e., digitized), or else accompanied, as in the case of markup, with an elaborate scaffolding by which the vagaries of continuity can be flattened and consistently recorded. We accept the compromises inherent in such transformations in order to reap the benefits of speed, automation, and scale that computational representations afford, but the situation is considerably more complicated in the case of the analysis that is undertaken with these objects. Not a single statement in Wallace's précis, and indeed, very few of the statements one encounters in literary critical discourse, can be treated in this way. No extant computer can draw the conclusions that Wallace does by analyzing the links between "the novel's visionary limitations" and "the historic moment of Modernism" – particularly since the Modernism being invoked here is not a matter of shifting consumer prices or birth statistics. Literary critical interpretation is not just a qualitative matter, but an insistently subjective manner of engagement.

Given the essential properties of computation, we might conclude that text analysis is precisely designed to frame literary critical problems in terms of something analogous to consumer prices and birth statistics, and in general, text analysis has chosen low-level linguistic phenomena as its primary object of study. Doing so would seem to demand that we assume the methodological posture of computational linguistics, with its (entirely appropriate) claims toward scientific rigor. According to this hermeneutical vision, text analysis is simply incapable of forming the sorts of conclusions that lie outside of a relatively narrow range of propositions.

It is not at all uncommon to encounter explicit statements of such interpretive limitation in text analytical scholarship. John Burrows and Hugo Craig's use of principle component analysis for comparing Romantic and Renaissance tragedy – a masterful work of text-analytical scholarship by any measure – is typical in the way it commits itself to an essentially scientific vision of permissible conclusion. The goal of the study is to elucidate the stylistic differences between the two periods of drama – one widely considered to have produced some of the greatest works in English, and another that is almost universally regarded as one of the low points of English literary drama. They draw a number of conclusions from their use of sophisticated statistical clustering methods, but in the end, they confidently state that the sort of insight offered by George Steiner, who felt that the loss of a "redemptive world-view" had rendered Romantic tragedy an impossibility, is "well beyond the ambit of present computational stylistics" (Burrows and Craig 1994: 64).

For an algorithmic criticism to emerge, it would have to come to a philosophical decision concerning statements like these. But the question is less about agreement or disagreement, and more about a willingness to inquire into the hermeneutical foundations that make such statements seem necessary. The computer is certainly incapable of offering "the shift to a redemptive world-view" as a solution to the problem at hand; it is wholly incapable of inferring this from the data. But is it likewise the case that computational results – the data and visualizations that the computer generates when it seeks to quantize and measure textual phenomena – cannot be used to engage in the sort of discussion that might lead one to such a conclusion?

It is useful to put the question this way, because in doing so we refocus the hermeneutical problem away from the nature and limits of computation (which is mostly a matter of methodology) and move it toward consideration of the nature of the discourse in which text analysis bids participation. Burrows and Craig's statement of limitation is valid if we consider computational stylistics to be essentially a scientific pursuit, because within this hermeneutical framework, it makes sense to frame conclusions in terms of what the data allows. But in literary criticism – and here I am thinking of ordinary "paper based" literary criticism – conclusions are evaluated not in terms of what propositions the data allows, but in terms of the nature and depth of the discussions that result. The scientist is right to say that the plural of anecdote is not data, but in literary criticism, an abundance of anecdote is precisely what allows discussion and debate to move forward.

Wallace's essay concerns what many consider to be Virginia Woolf's most experimental work. The novel consists of a series of monologues that trace the lives of six friends from early childhood to old age, with each monologue (beginning always with "Susan said" or "Bernard said") telling the characters' stories at seven distinct stages of their lives. Yet "story" is far too strong a word for their ruminations. The characters recount only a few of the sorts of events one would expect to see forming the basis of plot in a conventional narrative. They speak about different things and have different perspectives on the world, but they employ roughly the same manner of speaking, and do so from childhood to adulthood – employing, as one critic puts it, "the same kind of sentence rhythms and similar kinds of image patterns" throughout (Rosenthal 1979: 144). Some critics have suggested that there are differences that lie along the axis of gender or along a rift separating the more social characters from the more solitary ones, but in the end, one has the sense of an overall unity running against the perspectival conceit that frames the narrative.

It is natural for a Modernist critic to pursue patterns of difference amid this apparent unity, in part because, as Wallace points out, subjectivity is a major concern for "the historic moment of Modernism." Are Woolf's individuated characters to be understood as six sides of an individual consciousness (six modalities of an idealized Modernist self?), or are we meant to read against the fiction of unity that Woolf has created by having each of those modalities assume the same stylistic voice?

It is tempting for the text analysis practitioner to view this as a problem to be solved – as if the question was rhetorically equivalent to "Who wrote *Federalist* 10?" The category error arises because we mistake questions about the properties of objects with questions about the phenomenal experience of observers. We may say that Woolf's novel "is" something or that it "does" something, but what we mean to capture is some far less concrete interpretive possibility connected with the experience of reading. We may ask "What does it mean?" but in the context of critical discourse this is often an elliptical way of saying "Can I interpret (or read) it this way?"

It is reasonable to imagine tools that can adjudicate questions about the properties of objects. Tools that can adjudicate the hermeneutical parameters of human reading experiences – tools that can tell you whether an interpretation is permissible – stretch considerably beyond the most ambitious fantasies of artificial intelligence. Calling computational tools "limited" because they cannot do this makes it sound as if they might one day evolve this capability, but it is not clear that human intelligence can make this determination objectively or consistently. We read and interpret, and we urge others to accept our readings and interpretations. When we strike upon a reading or interpretation so unambiguous as to remove the hermeneutical questions that arise, we cease referring to the activity as reading and interpretation. We may even come to refer to it as the annunciation of fact.

If text analysis is to participate in literary critical endeavor in some manner beyond fact-checking, it must endeavor to assist the critic in the unfolding of interpretive possibilities. We might say that its purpose should be to generate further "evidence," though we do well to bracket the association that term holds in the context of less methodologically certain pursuits. The evidence we seek is not definitive, but suggestive of grander arguments and schemes. The "problem" (to bracket another term) with Woolf's novel is that despite evidence of a unified style, one suspects that we can read and interpret the novel using a set of underlying distinctions. We can uncover those distinctions by reading carefully. We can also uncover them using a computer.

It is possible – and indeed, an easy matter – to use a computer to transform Woolf's novel into lists of tokens in which each list represents the words spoken by the characters ordered from most distinctive to least distinctive term. $Tf - idf$, one of the classic formulas from information retrieval, endeavors to generate lists of distinctive terms for each document in a corpus. We might therefore conceive of Woolf's novel as a "corpus" of separate documents (each speaker's monologue representing a separate document), and use the formula to factor the presence of a word in a particular speaker's vocabulary against the presence of that word in the other speakers' vocabularies.

Criticism drifts into the language of mathematics. Let tf equal the number of times a word occurs within a single document. So, for example, if the word "a" occurred 194 times in one of the speakers in *The Waves*, the value of tf would be 194. A term frequency list is therefore the set of tf values for each term within that speaker's vocabulary. Such lists are not without utility for certain applications, but they tend to follows patterns that are of limited usefulness for our purposes. Since the highest frequency terms in a given document are almost always particles ("the" can account for as much as seven percent of a corpus vocabulary), and the lower-frequency words are almost always single-instance words (or "hapax legomena," as they are referred to in the field), we often end up with a list of words that is better at demonstrating the general properties of word distribution in a natural language than it is at showing us the distinctive vocabulary of an author.

If, however, we modulate the term frequency based on how ubiquitous the term is in the overall set of speakers, we can diminish the importance of terms that occur widely in the other speakers (like particles), and raise the importance of terms that are peculiar to a speaker. *Tf − idf* accomplishes this using the notion of an inverse document frequency:

$$tf - idf = tf \cdot \left(\frac{N}{df}\right)$$

Let *N* equal the total number of documents and let *df* equal the number of documents in which the target term appears. We have six speakers. If the term occurs only in one speaker, we multiply *tf* by six over one; if it occurs in all speakers, we multiply it by six over six. Thus, a word that occurs 194 times, but in all documents, is multiplied by a factor of one (six over six). A word that occurs in one document, but nowhere else, is multiplied by a factor of six (six over one).

Here are the first twenty-five lines of output from a program designed to apply the *tf − idf* formula to the character of Louis.[1] In addition to providing the weighted scores, the program also generates the number of times Louis uses the term:

Table 26.1   First twenty-five terms (with *tf − idf* weights)
for the character Louis in Virginia Woolf's *The Waves*.

Weight	Term
5.917438	mr
5.7286577	western
5.5176187	nile
5.0021615	australian
5.0021615	beast
5.0021615	grained
5.0021615	thou
5.0021615	wilt
4.675485	pitchers
4.675485	steel
4.2756658	attempt
4.2756658	average
4.2756658	clerks
4.2756658	disorder
3.9164972	accent
3.7602086	beaten
3.7602086	bobbing
3.7602086	custard
3.7602086	discord
3.7602086	eating-shop
3.7602086	england
3.7602086	eyres
3.7602086	four-thirty
3.7602086	ham
3.7602086	lesson

Few students of *The Waves* would fail to see some emergence of pattern in this list. Many have noted that Louis seems obsessed with Egypt and the Nile. The list indicates that such terms are indeed distinctive to Louis, but the second most distinctive term in his vocabulary is the word "western." Louis is also very conscious of his accent and his nationality (he's Australian; all the other characters are English), and yet the fact that "accent" is a distinctive term for Louis would seem to indicate that the other characters aren't similarly concerned with the way he talks. Further analysis revealed that only one other character (Neville) mentions it. Louis is likewise the only character in the novel to speak of "England."

Similar convergences appear in the other lists:

Table 26.2 First twenty-four terms for all characters in *The Waves*.

Bernard		Louis		Neville	
thinks	rabbit	mr	clerks	catullus	loads
letter	tick	western	disorder	doomed	mallet
curiosity	tooth	nile	accent	immitigable	marvel
moffat	arrive	australian	beaten	papers	shoots
final	bandaged	beast	bobbing	bookcase	squirting
important	bowled	grained	custard	bored	waits
low	brushed	thou	discord	camel	stair
simple	buzzing	wilt	eating-shop	detect	abject
canopy	complex	pitchers	england	expose	admirable
getting	concrete	steel	eyres	hubbub	ajax
hoot	deeply	attempt	four-thirty	incredible	aloud
hums	detachment	average	ham	lack	bath
Jinny		Rhoda		Susan	
tunnel	cabinet	oblong	immune	setter	cabbages
prepared	coach	dips	many-backed	washing	carbolic
melancholy	crag	bunch	minnows	apron	clara
billowing	dazzle	fuller	pond	pear	cow
fiery	deftly	moonlight	structure	seasons	cradle
game	equipped	party	wonder	squirrel	eggs
native	eyebrows	them	tiger	window-pane	ernest
peers	felled	allowed	swallow	kitchen	hams
quicker	frightened	cliffs	africa	baby	hare
victory	gaze	empress	amorous	betty	lettuce
band	jump	fleet	attitude	bitten	locked
banners	lockets	garland	bow	boil	maids

For Jinny, whose relationships with men form the liminal background of her narrative, words like "billowing" (a sexually charged word almost always used in reference to her skirts), "fiery," "victory," and "dazzle" appear in the top twenty-five. For Bernard, the aspiring novelist whom some say is modeled on Woolf herself, the top word is "thinks." Susan becomes a housewife and frequently invokes the virtues of a pastoral life in the country; nearly every word in her vocabulary seems directly related to the domestic. Neville, the brilliant unrequited lover of Percival (a mutual friend of all the characters who dies while serving in India), has the word "doomed" in second place.

We might begin to wonder how vocabulary plays out along the gender axis. For example, we might modify the program so that it gives us lists of words that are only spoken by the women in the novel and another that lists words only spoken by men. When we do that, we find that the women possess fourteen words in common:

Table 26.3   Terms held in common by the female characters in *The Waves* with *tf – idf* weights.

Weight	Term
1.8087245	shoes
1.1736002	lambert
1.1736002	million
1.1736002	pirouetting
0.6931472	antlers
0.6931472	bowl
0.6931472	breath
0.6931472	coarse
0.6931472	cotton
0.6931472	diamonds
0.6931472	rushes
0.6931472	soften
0.6931472	stockings
0.6931472	wash

The men have 90 words in common:

Table 26.4   Terms held in common by the male characters in *The Waves* with *tf – idf* weights.

2.1345062	boys	1.1736002	possible	0.6931472	ends
1.8087245	church	1.1736002	sentences	0.6931472	everybody
1.8087245	larpent	1.1736002	tortures	0.6931472	feeling
1.8087245	office	1.1736002	united	0.6931472	felt
1.8087245	rhythm	1.1736002	weep	0.6931472	heights
1.8087245	wheel	0.6931472	able	0.6931472	however
1.6540532	banker	0.6931472	accepted	0.6931472	hundred
1.6540532	brisbane	0.6931472	act	0.6931472	included
1.6540532	ourselves	0.6931472	alas	0.6931472	inflict
1.6540532	poetry	0.6931472	approach	0.6931472	irrelevant
1.6540532	power	0.6931472	background	0.6931472	knew
1.4546472	arms	0.6931472	baker	0.6931472	language
1.4546472	destiny	0.6931472	banks	0.6931472	latin
1.4546472	letters	0.6931472	became	0.6931472	meeting
1.4546472	lord	0.6931472	block	0.6931472	neat
1.4546472	poet	0.6931472	board	0.6931472	novel
1.4546472	reason	0.6931472	brake	0.6931472	observe

(Continued)

Table 26.4   (*Continued*)

1.4546472	respect	0.6931472	burnt	0.6931472	oppose
1.4546472	telephone	0.6931472	central	0.6931472	pointing
1.4546472	waistcoat	0.6931472	certainly	0.6931472	sensations
1.1736002	beak	0.6931472	chose	0.6931472	sheer
1.1736002	chaos	0.6931472	cinders	0.6931472	story
1.1736002	difficult	0.6931472	clamour	0.6931472	suffering
1.1736002	endure	0.6931472	course	0.6931472	torture
1.1736002	forgotten	0.6931472	crucifix	0.6931472	troubling
1.1736002	friend	0.6931472	distinctions	0.6931472	use
1.1736002	god	0.6931472	distracted	0.6931472	waste
1.1736002	king	0.6931472	doctor	0.6931472	watched
1.1736002	notice	0.6931472	ease	0.6931472	willows
1.1736002	ordinary	0.6931472	edges	0.6931472	works

These are provocative results, but the provocation is as much about our sense of what we are doing (the hermeneutical question) as it is about how we are doing it (the methodological question).

We might want to say that the purpose of these procedures is to confirm or deny the "serendipitous reading" of literary critics. Is Louis obsessed with his accent? Yes. The data confirms that he is. Critics who have argued for a deep structure of difference among the characters – one perhaps aligned along the gender axis – might also feel as if the program vindicates their impressions. Is there a gender divide? Yes. The characters are divided along the gender axis by a factor of 6.4285 to 1.

To level such arguments, however, is to turn the hermeneutical question back into a methodological one. To speak of the procedure as "verifying" some other finding is to beg questions of the procedure itself. And here, we are on somewhat shaky ground. *Tf – idf* "works" in the context of information retrieval because it appears to match our general expectations. When we undertake a search for the term "baseball" with a search engine, we want to rule out passing references in favor of documents that are substantially about this topic. If we get back relevant hits, we could say that the *tf – idf* formula has done its job. In the case of Woolf, we might say that we are getting back results that conform to our general expectations of what distinguishes the characters. But in both cases, *tf – idf* itself has no more claim to truth value than any ordinary reading procedure. Manning and Schütze, in their magisterial work on statistical natural language processing, note that the "the family of [tf − idf] weighting schemes is sometimes criticized because it is not directly derived from a mathematical model of term distribution or relevancy" (1999: 544). The full version of the formula (the one used to generate the results above) includes a *log* function and an addition:

$$tf - idf = 1 + tf \cdot \log\left(\frac{N}{df}\right)$$

The main purpose of these additions, however, is not to bring the results into closer conformity with "reality," but merely to render the weighting numbers more sensible to the analyst. The logarithm dampens the function so that one term isn't a full six times more important than another; the -1 keeps the end of the curve from trailing off into negative territory.

Some text analytical procedures do rely on empirical facts about language (or on statistical and mathematical laws in general). But even when they do, we often find ourselves unable to point to the truth of the procedure as the basis for judgment. We might say that this is because computational literary criticism is insufficiently scientific. We might even long for a "scientific literary criticism." We would do better to recognize that a scientific literary criticism would cease to be criticism.

It is no longer controversial to point out that science involves interpretation, rhetoric, social construction, and politics – as if this exposure of science's hidden humanism could somehow discredit the achievements of one of the world's greatest epistemological tools. No serious scientist could ever deny that interpretation, disagreement, and debate are at the core of the scientific method. But science differs significantly from the humanities in that it seeks singular answers to the problems under discussion. However far-ranging a scientific debate might be, however varied the interpretations being offered, the assumption remains that there is a singular answer (or a singular set of answers) to the question at hand. Literary criticism has no such assumption. In the humanities, the fecundity of any particular discussion is often judged precisely by the degree to which it offers ramified solutions to the problem at hand. Woolf critics are not trying to solve Woolf. They are trying to ensure that discussion of *The Waves* continues into further and further reaches of intellectual depth.

Critics often use the word "pattern" to describe what they're putting forth, and that word aptly connotes the fundamental nature of the data upon which literary insight relies. The understanding promised by the critical act arises not from a presentation of facts, but from the elaboration of a gestalt, and it rightfully includes the vague reference, the conjectured similitude, the ironic twist, and the dramatic turn. In the spirit of *inventio*, the critic freely employs the rhetorical tactics of conjecture – not so that a given matter might be definitely settled, but in order that the matter might become richer, deeper, and ever more complicated. The proper response to the conundrum posed by Steiner's "redemptive worldview" is not the scientific imperative toward verification and falsification, but the humanistic prerogative toward disagreement and elaboration.

If algorithmic criticism is to have a central hermeneutical tenet, it is this: that the narrowing constraints of computational logic – the irreducible tendency of the computer toward enumeration, measurement, and verification – are fully compatible with the goals of criticism set forth above. For while it is possible, and in some cases useful, to confine algorithmic procedures to the scientific realm, such procedures can be made to conform to the methodological project of *inventio* without transforming the nature of computation or limiting the rhetorical range of critical inquiry. This is possible, because critical reading practices already contain elements of the algorithmic.

Any reading of a text that is not a recapitulation of that text relies on a heuristic of radical transformation. The critic who endeavors to put forth a "reading," puts forth not the text, but a new text in which the data has been paraphrased, elaborated, selected, truncated, and transduced. This basic property of critical methodology is evident not only in the act of "close reading," but in the more ambitious project of thematic exegesis. In the classroom, one encounters the exegete instructing his or her students to turn to page 254, and then to page 16, and finally to page 400. They are told to consider just the male characters, or just the female ones, or to pay attention to the adjectives, the rhyme scheme, images of water, or the moment in which Nora Helmer confronts her husband. The interpreter will set a novel against the background of the Jacobite Rebellion, or a play amid the historical location of the theater. He or she will view the text through the lens of Marxism, or psychoanalysis, or existentialism, or postmodernism. In every case, what is being read is not the "original" text, but a text transformed and transduced into an alternative vision, in which, as Wittgenstein put it, we "see an aspect" that further enables discussion and debate.

It is not that such matters as redemptive world views and Marxist readings of texts can be arrived at algorithmically, but simply that algorithmic transformation can provide the alternative visions that give rise to such readings. The computer does this in a particularly useful way by carrying out transformations in a rigidly holistic manner. It is one thing to notice patterns of vocabulary, variations in line length, or images of darkness and light; it is another thing to employ a machine that can unerringly discover every instance of such features across a massive corpus of literary texts and then present those features in a visual format entirely foreign to the original organization in which these features appear. Or rather, it is the same thing at a different scale and with expanded powers of observation. It is in such results that the critic seek not facts, but patterns. And from pattern, the critic may move to the grander rhetorical formations that constitute critical reading.

It might still make sense to speak of certain matters being "beyond the ambit of present computational stylistics." Research in text analysis continues to seek new ways to isolate features and present novel forms of organization. But the ambit of these ways and forms need not be constrained by a hermeneutics that disallows the connotative and analogical methods of criticism. Algorithmic criticism would have to retain the commitment to methodological rigor demanded by its tools, but the emphasis would be less on maintaining a correspondence or a fitness between method and goal, and more on the need to present methods in a fully transparent manner. It would not be averse to the idea of reproducibility, but it would perhaps be even more committed to the notion of "hackability." For just as one might undertake a feminist reading of a text by transporting a set of heuristics from one critical context to another, so might the algorithmic critic undertake a particular type of reading by transforming a procedure that has been defined in terms of that most modern text, the computer program.

Algorithmic criticism undoubtedly requires a revolution of sorts, but that revolution is not one of new procedures and methods in contradistinction to the old ones. Algorithmic criticism seeks a new kind of audience for text analysis – one that is less concerned with fitness of method and the determination of interpretive boundaries, and one more concerned with evaluating the robustness of the discussion that a particular procedure annunciates. Such an audience exists, of course, and has existed for the better part of a century in the general community of literary critics from which text analysis has often found itself exiled. For this reason, text analysis practitioners should view the possibility of such a revolution as both welcome and liberating – not a critique of their methods, but a bold vote of confidence in the possibilities they hold.

NOTE

1 I am indebted to Sara Steger at the University of Georgia, who was a co-investigator in the work on computational analysis of Woolf's novel that forms the basis of the following examples. The electronic edition used is from The University of Adelaide Library (<http://etext.library.adelaide.edu.au/w/woolf/virginia/w91w/>).

REFERENCES AND FURTHER READING

Bold, S. C. (1988). "Labyrinths of Invention from the New Novel to OuLiPo." *Neophilologus* 82: 543–57.

Burrows, J. F., and D. H. Craig (1994). "Lyrical Drama and the 'Turbid Montebanks': Styles of Dialogue in Romantic and Renaissance Tragedy." *Computers and the Humanities* 28: 63–86.

Fortier, P. A. (1993). "Babies, Bathwater and the Study of Literature." *Computers and the Humanities* 27: 375–85.

Gadamer, H. (1996). *Truth and Method*. New York: Continuum.

Hockey, S. (2000). *Electronic Texts in the Humanities*. Oxford: Oxford University Press.

Manning, C. D., and H. Schütze (1999). *Foundations of Statistical Natural Language Processing*. Cambridge: MIT Press.

Potter, R. G. (1988). "Literary Criticism and Literary Computing: the Difficulties of a Synthesis." *Computers and the Humanities* 22: 91–7.

Ramsay, S. (2003). "Toward an Algorithmic Criticism." *Literary and Linguistic Computing* 18: 167–74.

Rosenthal, M. (1979). *Virginia Woolf*. London: Routledge.

Wallace, M. L. (2000). "Theorizing Relational Subjects: Metonymic Narrative in *The Waves*." *Narrative* 8: 294–323.

27

Writing Machines

William Winder

> They used to say, my friend, that the words of
> the oak in the holy place of Zeus at Dodona
> were the first prophetic utterances. The people
> of that time, not being so wise as you young
> folks, were content in their simplicity to hear
> an oak or a rock, provided only it spoke the
> truth. (*Phaedrus* 275b–c)

Writing

Writing in a new key

It has been the fleets of humming word processors, not the university mainframe computers nor the roaring newspaper printing presses of the turn of the nineteenth century, that have drawn humanists to writing machines and their industrialized texts (Winder 2002). We write perhaps less and less, but we process more and more, with computers working quietly in the background. And only in the dead silence of a computer crash where hours of work have disappeared do we understand clearly how much our writing depends on machines. Formatters, spell checkers, thesauri, grammar checkers, and personal printers support our writing almost silently. Yet we suspect that today's ubiquitous editing and display functions will seem quaint in ten years' time, perhaps as quaint and mysterious as the thump of a typewriter's carriage shift.

Computers are necessarily writing machines. When computers process words, they generate text and a great deal of it. Library catalogues over the globe spew out countless replies to queries (author, keyword, call number, title, subject heading, year, language, editor, series, . . .); banking machines unabashedly greet us, enquire discreetly about our password in hushed tones, and remind us not to leave our banking card in the machine when we leave (would you like a receipt?). From the internet come waves of pages crafted for each visitor's communicative needs. Computers, however much they calculate, write even more relentlessly.

But are computers typists or writers? We can understand the constant growth of writing, by or through computers, as the effect of two complementary cultural compulsions, each tunneling toward the other from opposing positions and destined to meet ultimately somewhere in an unknown middle ground. The first driving force is the grassroots improvement of computer-assisted writing; the second is artificial intelligence.

From the "**accelerated writing**" paradigm will come the next generation of word processors – true text processors – that will give us advanced tools for automatic generation of text. The computer is much too powerful to remain a simple word processor, offering only word changes such as spelling and thesaurus functions; it can do much more, such as understanding text well enough to propose radical changes in composition.

Tools for boilerplate construction are good candidates for the text processor of the near future. If I write a reference letter for one student, Sarah, and then have another student, Ralph, who followed much the same program of study and requires a letter as well, I might cut and paste relevant parts of Sarah's letter into Ralph's. At present I would have the tedious task of making sure all occurrences of "Sarah" are replaced by "Ralph" and that no "she" referring to Sarah is left in the pasted text. The text processor of the future should check the coherence of my discourse and transform the pasted text for me automatically, just as even now grammar checkers automatically suggest changes for agreement between verbs and their subjects. In many languages, such text transformations would not be trivial at all: in French it would require changing all the numerous gender agreements ("son professeur de mathématiques l'a décrite comme une bonne étudiante"); in English, though simpler, it might mean transforming gender-specific adjectives or nouns ("pretty"/"handsome," "waiter"/ "waitress") and possessive adjectives ("him," "his"). At present, crude search and replace functions lead to embarrassing slips: in one republished thesis all the occurrences of "thesis" had been replaced with "book," even in the case of "hypothesis," which became the curious neologism "hypobook" throughout the published text.

Creating texts in this accelerated writing paradigm is more about writing text-generating code and using functions that recycle texts into boilerplate components than it is about writing any of the final versions themselves. Separation of content and form is a standard approach for some editing software such as *Tex* and bibliographic software that generates citations and bibliography. The new text processor will extend this approach by becoming a spreadsheet equivalent for writing: instead of cutting and pasting blocks of text, we will cut and paste text formulae that generate programmatically the final text (see the discussion of a "textual *Excel*" in Winder forthcoming). We find the infrastructure for this coded text in present-day applications such as automatic translation (increasingly online, such as *Babel Fish*), formalisms developed in text encoding projects (Unicode standard, *Text Encoding Initiative*), and programming languages that are increasingly closer to human language (Perl, Ruby, Python; see Malsky 2006, chapter 3, "Language and I MEAN Language"[1]).

The other, complementary orientation does not have as its goal an incremental enhancement of writers' tools; rather, the goal of the **artificial intelligence** approach is to construct directly the components of a writing intelligence – machines that have personality and thoughts like humans, not unlike the robots we know from science fiction.

These two projects, accelerated writing and artificial intelligence, seem destined to meet. Writers will become increasingly wedded to programming, to code-generating programmer tools (such as databases and version control), and to the industrial production of text, on the one hand, and computers will become increasingly human on the other.

But there is a third paradigm, a third perspective, less overtly commercial, but perhaps just as focused on that eventual meeting of minds and machines as the first two: **automatic generation of art**. What is most human is not just the body's artifacts (enhanced by the versatile printing of the accelerated writing paradigm) nor the calculating mind (studied and re-created in artificial intelligence), but as well that elusive creative spirit that traverses all our endeavors. These three orientations are destined to meet because human value ultimately has its source in precisely what is peculiarly human: a certain confluence of mind, body, and spirit.

Our focus here is on automatically produced written art. This is clearly a narrow view of how people communicate in the electronic medium (by definition a multi-media environment) and a radical reduction of the field of generated art. Written language has, however, a singular place in computational systems, if only because writing and reading program code is a faculty shared by both human programmers and computers. As well, generation is perhaps best defined as a reading out of instructions. Printing, as the ultimate and most general reading and writing out of instructions, is where writing, thinking, and creating converge (Winder 2004: 449).

Printing, writing, and art

Printing and writing are clearly related. Like printing, writing is machine-mediated language, though the machine may be as simple as a pencil. (Is there writing without printing?) And though we may understand writing as something more than printing, it is often not clear what precisely distinguishes the two. Such is the point that Plato brings home in Socrates's retelling of the myth of the birth of writing. Theuth invents writing as a remedy for memory loss, as if the mind could extend to the page. Thamus, the king of the gods, claims that Theuth's invention is not a tonic for memory but rather a poison, the death of the mind (see the *Perseus* library (Crane 2006) for *Phaedrus*; discussion in Derrida 1992). Socrates debates the question of the soul of discourse that writing is supposed to capture, that precise place where discourse takes on its own life. He finds there something we will call art.

The word "art" has many meanings, which reflect that same liveliness of meaning we find in artistic objects themselves:

- *Mercantile art*: The "pricelessness" of art reflects the fact that it is not produced in the same way as other commercial products (the value of the means of production is not commensurate with the value of the artistic object) and thus art seems to belong to an entirely different economy (the slogan "art for art's sake" is perhaps a reflection of that otherness of art). It is also other in that its uniqueness is seemingly borrowed from the uniqueness and pricelessness of the very life of the artist. Within the commercial system, art is **arbitrary** because ultimately everything is tied to a unique human existence; anything can be bought and sold as art (witness the "readymade" art of Marcel Duchamp).

- *Inspirational art*: The "liveliness" of art lies in an overabundance made possible by a surprising efficiency, an efficiency (analogous to Freud's economy principle for wit) that does not make sense with respect to the mercantile economy. For example, Francis Ponge (1999: 346) notes that the French word "oiseau" contains all the vowels (such poetic "trouvailles" generally do not translate; the word in Spanish with all the vowels, written and pronounced, is "murciélago", bat). This is a surprising efficiency in the sense that the otherwise arbitrary word for bird seems to reflect the vocal dimension of its object: a bird is in fact a "vowel" creature. The artistic reflex we cultivate and from which derive a feeling of joy, freedom, generosity, and community, is to recognize and cultivate this "graceful" dimension of the universe, a grace that seems to conspire to harmonize the world in an abundant, costless economy. The artistic vision, as a lay version of the religious experience, adds a layer of meaning that harmonizes the way things are. In the artistic world, nothing is arbitrary, nothing is without meaning, and everything is given freely – if not, it would not be art, it would not be grace. Inspirational art is therefore not arbitrary, but rather **motivated** by the surprising generosity of the world.
- *Living art*: Art is not only lively, it is "alive" in that, like a living organism, it assimilates other forms of art, adapts itself to new environments, and reproduces itself in derivative works. Unlike living things, however, art has no "fixed address." It does not need any particular material envelope and by nature tends to bleed into all things at all levels of organization, including the spectator. An artistic organization such as Shakespearean style can find itself just as easily in a play as in a novel, in a style of dress, or in a person. Art is universal **form**.

As a universal principle of combination, art's most general aesthetic effect is a feeling of vivifying inclusion – connectedness – that attaches the spectator to the grace (costless harmony) of the world. The artistic text must be coherent and alive at the same time. It is an adaptive structure that is stubbornly the same in spite of the constant changing or shimmering of its being. Art is both process and product: through art we capture open-ended productivity (generation) in a closed system (product).

The question we must deal with here is the relation between artful generation and machines. Just as Socrates concluded that writing is discourse without a soul, so we might suspect that machines are writers without creativity. What is artful generation? How do machines simulate, at least, generation? Is there a special kind of artistic generation? A special use of technique?

Transmutations: things that go generate in the night

Criticizing a poorly organized discourse, Socrates points out that the lines of Midas's epitaph, delivered by the bronze statue of a maiden and reported in Plato's text, can be read in any order:

> Bronze maiden am I and on Midas's mound I lie.
> As long as water flows and tall trees bloom,
> Right here fixed fast on the tearful tomb,
> I shall announce to all who pass near: Midas is dead and buried here.
>
> (*Phaedrus* 264d; cited and translated in Carson 1986: 134)

How many permutations are there and do they all truly make sense? (There are $n!$ permutations of n things. Here there are 4 sentences and therefore 4! permutations: $4*3*2*1 = 24$ altogether.) Does Socrates know how many there really are? Did he actually generate all permutations (etched in stone? on "papyrus"? in his head?) or can he simply "tell" from each sentence? Are some better than others? How are we to judge?

We can generate all of the permutations easily enough (see Winder 2006, *Robotic Poetics*, for an online generator), but are there not many more "versions" we might want to consider? For instance, the original Greek is certainly a version:

> χαλκῆ παρθένος εἰμί, Μίδα δ' ἐπὶ σήματι κεῖμαι.
> ὄφρ' ἂν ὕδωρ τε νάῃ καὶ δένδρεα μακρὰ τεθήλῃ,
> αὐτοῦ τῇδε μένουσα πολυκλαύτου ἐπὶ τύμβου,
> ἀγγελέω παριοῦσι Μίδας ὅτι τῇδε τέθαπται.
>
> ("Phaedrus" 264d[2])

And the transliterated Greek:

> chalkê parthenos eimi, Mida d' epi sêmati keimai.
> ophr' an hudôr te naêi kai dendrea makra tethêlêi,
> autou têide menousa poluklautou epi tumbou,
> angeleô pariousi Midas hoti têide tethaptai.
>
> ("Phaedrus" 264d[3])

And perhaps we should even consider the Greek transliteration of the English translation of the Greek!:

> Βρονζε μαιδεν αμ I ανδ ον Μιδασ μουνδ I λιε.
> Ασ λονγ ασ ωατερ φλοωσ ανδ ταλλ τρεεσ βλοομ,
> Ριγητ ηερε φιξεδ φαστ ον τηε τεαρφυλ τομβ,
> I σηαλλ αννουνχε το αλλ ωηο πασσ νεαρ: Μιδασ ισ δεαδ ανδ βυριεδ ηερε.
>
> (Symbol font)

The latter is generated simply by a switch of fonts in a word processor (see Balpe "Imagination" 16–18). Word processors have a "Midas touch" we are all familiar with (whether they produce gold or not is another question). Text is malleable; one text can be transformed into another; the same thing can be said in different ways. Here is the same English epitaph in the BookDings font:

✎onwe m✓ iden ✓ m 🚕 ✓nd on ⬇ld✓ ?' mo🗟nd 🚕 lie ◂
📔? long ✓ ? 🗟✓ 🗟e✗ flo🗟? ✓ nd 🗟 ✓ll 🗟✗ee? ✗loom☉
🗟igh🗟 he✗e fl⬌ed f✓ ?🗟 on 🗟he 🗟e ✓ ✗f🗟l 🗟om✗☉
🚕 ?h✓ll ✓nno🗟nce 🗟o ✓ll 🗟ho p✓ ?? ne✓✗🗝 ⬇id✓ ? i? de✓d
✓nd ✗🗟✗ied he✗e.

(BookDings font)

JanusNode (Westbury) has an "ee cummings" mode, along with a sophisticated generation scripting language (see below), which will lay out a text in an ee cummings fashion:

> Bronze maiden
>   am
> I
>   and
>   on Midas' mound
> I lie.
> As
> long as water flows
>   and
>   tall
>   trees bloom,
> Right
>   here
>   fixed fast on
>   the tearful
> tomb,
> I
>   sh
> all announce
> to
>   all
>   who
> pass
>   near:
>   Midas
>   is
>   dead
>   and
> buried
>   here.
> (*JanusNode* "ee cummings" style)

Such transmutations are perhaps not of themselves art, but they are certainly starting points of creativity. Whether automatic or human, transmutation is most often simply the source of humor and obfuscation. Luis d'Antin van Rooten's *Mots d'heures: Gousses, Rames* are phonetic transliterations of English "Mother Goose rhymes" into French, which he then presents, with "serious" exegesis, as a critical edition of a collection of medieval French verse. Here is "Humpty Dumpty":

> Un petit d'un petit
> S'étonne aux Halles
> Un petit d'un petit
> Ah! degrés te fallent [3]
> Indolent qui ne sort cesse
> Indolent qui ne se mène
> Qu'importe un petit d'un petit
> Tout Gai de Reguennes.
>   ("Poem 1")

Exegesis is given in copious footnotes to this "medieval" poem; here is the third annotation [3], an interpretation of line 4:

Since this personage [the "petit," offspring of the child marriage ("d'un petit") mentioned in the first line] bears no titles, we are led to believe that the poet writes of one of those unfortunate idiot-children that in olden days existed as a living skeleton in their family's closet. I am inclined to believe, however, that this is a fine piece of misdirection and that the poet is actually writing of some famous political prisoner, or the illegitimate offspring of some noble house. The Man in the Iron Mask, perhaps? ("Poem 1", note 3; pages unnumbered)

Russell Horban makes use of the prolific number of graphemes in English (1,120 graphemes for 40 sounds; compared with Italian, which has 33 graphemes for 25 sounds) to transliterate present-day English into a futuristic newspel: "What ben makes tracks for what wil be. Words in the air pirnt foot steps on the groun for us to put our feet in to" (121). In Dunn's *Ella Minnow Pea* letters of the alphabet are progressively banned from all writings and the eponymous protagonist is reduced to expressing herself in baby talk – "No mo Nollop poo poo!" ["No more Nollop mess"] – and signing her name as "LMNOP" (2001: 197).

Transliteration in a more practical vein is found in spelling reform projects such as *Truespel*. The online *Truespel Converter* transforms our epitaph into:

> Braanz maedin am Ie and aan Miedis's mound Ie lie.
> Az laung az wauter floez and taul treez bluem,
> Riet heer fiksd fast aan thu teerfool tuem,
> Ie shal unnounts tue aul hue pas neer: Miedis iz ded and baireed heer.
>   (Davidson 2006)

Transmuted versions proliferate in the machine (the Unicode specification for character sets has over 2^{32} possible characters). Word processors can transmute text so effectively because each character is represented by a specific number or "code point" that can be mapped to any other code point. All word processor text is represented in fundamentally the same way: a set of points that can be dressed up in different font garb. Underlying the word processor's transmutations and Socrates's permutations is a very abstract machine, the fundamental machine of transmutation, a mapping between code points: a permutation is a mapping of one line onto another (for instance, mapping line 1 to 2 and line 2 to 1 gives one combination); a symbol transmutation is a mapping of one alphabet onto another.

Topographies for Transmutation

For mapping to be coherent, automatic techniques depend on the formally described topographies of the source and target texts. Beyond characters, more important linguistic topographies are syntax, lexical meaning, and narrative. Each of these dimensions brings with it its own processing difficulties. We will look at each in turn.

One fundamental method of generation is through **syntactic templates**, essentially the boilerplate texts of word processors. Any number of variant epitaphs can be generated by substituting equivalent terms at appropriate positions in the text (Table 27.1).

This "combinatory of combinations" codes for 4^6 sentences, for a total of 4,096. Here all the combinations are acceptable, but generally syntactic and perhaps semantic constraints will be limiting factors (see Winder 2004: 458ff and the *Robotic Poetics* site). As syntactic constraints are reduced, generation becomes increasingly simple. Divinatory systems, such as *I Ching*, are typically built on units that combine freely, with few or no syntactic constraints: a single narrative unit is attached to each free combination of rods. There are no natural languages that are combinatorially complete in this way, i.e., not all combinations of words make grammatical utterances. Even declined languages like Latin, which have very flexible word order, require a particular mix of nouns and verbs. Perhaps only artificial languages such as *I Ching* can achieve the ideal of a combinatorially complete language.

The systematic choices that are driven by referential and stylistic constraints are part of language use, not of the linguistic system. Syntactic templates are useful

Table 27.1 Syntactic templates.

Bronze	maiden	am	I	and	on	Midas's	mound	I	lie
Silver	missy				above	Goldfinger's	heap		repose
Gold	miss				outside	Buster's	pile		perch
Metal	girl				supra	Bambi's	stack		recline

starting points for generation because they largely resolve the major systemic linguistic constraints and so set the stage for a free stylistic and referential combinatory. Using such templates Roubaud (1985: 191, cited in Braffort 2006) imagined chimeric poetry which combines the style of two poets. One example is the Rimbaudelaire, a set of poems built from templates extracted from Rimbeau's poems and lexical items from Baudelaire's (or vice versa). Roubaud and Lusson developed combinatory software that automatically generates all the permutations of the lexical items within a template (Roubaud and Lusson 2006; refreshing the page or clicking on "poème" will generate a new poem). *JanusNode*'s textual "DNA" are similarly syntactic templates that are randomly filled with a given vocabulary.

Formally, such chimeric poetry is possible because it is an easy step to abstract away the syntactic structure of a text and then combine the resulting template with a lexicon. Most of the text's linguistic constraints are managed in the templates (though here too there are some stylistic influences); lexical choice, on the other hand, reflects stylistic and referential constraints which are informed by the author's discursive practices and the world the text describes. Roubaud and Lusson's software automates the combining of templates and lexicons (no doubt the method used in the Malvole (Round 2006) and Kurzweil (2006) generators as well, with probabilistic improvements in the latter), but it is clear that template construction and lexicon building could be easily automated as well. From the corpora of two poets, it is possible to generate automatically the two lexicons and templates. What is more challenging is selecting semantically **relevant** combinations from all the possibilities. A **semantic templating system** requires a different set of linguistic resources.

Semantic templates

A semantic template is a systematic lexical choice that reflects either the state of an imaginary world or a particular way to express statements about that world. For instance, from "She likes pink dresses," where the semantic marker "feminine" is repeated in many of the lexical items, we may wish to generate a second, gender-bent sentence "He likes blue pants," where the semantic markers "masculine" systematically replace (as far as possible) the feminine markers. Both sentences, as well as many others such as "It likes tall trees," correspond to the general syntactic template "<pronoun> likes <adjective> <noun>." But we do not want such a large range in meaning; we would like to modulate sentence generation more finely by systematically choosing semantically related words. That requires considerably more information about the relation between lexical items than do the Rimbaudelaire poems.

To illustrate some of the difficulties and possibilities of semantic templating, we will explore here the programming that would allow us to move from Midas's epitaph to another version which is considerably more abstract in its expression (Table 27.2).

These automatic transformations replace nouns and verbs (marked with asterisks) with words that are doubly more abstract than the target word. Adjectives (and past

Table 27.2 Double abstraction of Midas's epitaph.

*Bronze *maiden am I and on Midas's *mound I *lie.	*Alloy *young female that I am and on Midas's *artifact I *be
As + long as *water *flows and + tall *trees *bloom,	As long as *fluid *covers and + long-stalked *tracheophytes *grow,
Right here + fixed fast on the tearful *tomb,	Right here + immobile fast on the + sniffly *point,
I shall *announce to all who *pass near: Midas is + dead and + buried here.	I shall *inform to all who *change near: Midas is + defunct and + belowground here.

participles used as adjectives; both marked with a plus sign) are replaced with words that are similar, but not necessarily more abstract. The procedure requires (1) tagging all the words with their part of speech and then (2) making a programmed walk in the *WordNet* dictionary that leads from one word to another. This set of programmed walks in *WordNet* is a semantic template in the sense that there is an overall logic in the shift in meaning that affects the entire text; here, the paradigmatic choice at each syntactic spot in the template is under the same "abstracting" influence. Any given generated text is therefore the product of a semantic template, where word choice is regulated, and a syntactic template, where syntactic agreement is established.

Automatic syntactic template building through POS tagging

There are a growing number of public domain packages for creating and manipulating text and its linguistic infrastructure. Text generation systems (e.g., *KMPL* (Reiter 2002) and *Vinci* (Lessard and Levison, described in Winder 2004: 462ff)) allow for a detailed specification of text structure. Part-of-speech taggers (e.g., *TreeTagger* (Stein 2006)), have become fairly robust and simple to operate. General text engineering systems (e.g., *OpenNLP* (Baldridge and Morton 2006) and *NLTK* (Bird et al. n.d.)) are considerably more difficult to master, but accessible even to inexperienced users (with patience!). The pedagogical, well-documented *NLTK* is built on the humanist-friendly programming language Python. We will use *NLTK* to tag each word of the text with a part of speech. *NLTK* has a number of tagging algorithms that can be combined. This is the part-of-speech template that *NLTK* produces, using several taggers trained on the accompanying Brown corpus:

> Bronze/jj maiden/nn am/bem I/ppss and/cc on/in Midas/nnp 's/poss mound/nn I/ppss lie/vb ./.
> As/ql long/rb as/ql water/nn flows/vbz and/cc tall/jj trees/nns bloom/vb , /,
> Right/ql here/rn fixed/vbn fast/rb on/in the/at tearful/jj tomb/nn
> I/ppss shall/md announce/vb to/in all/abn who/wps pass/vb near/rp :/:
> Midas/nnp is/bez dead/jj and/cc buried/vbn here/rb ./.

Codes for parts of speech are found in the *NLTK* documentation;[4] those that interest us are the adjective (jj), past participle (vbn), noun (nn, nns), and verb (vb). *NLTK* tagging routines use a set of tagged texts from the Brown Corpus included with *NLTK* to make a lexicon with parts of speech, frequencies, and POS contexts. Variations in cases ("Bronze" vs. "bronze"), punctuation (all punctuation is tagged as itself here), affix and prefixes ("tearful"/"tear") are analyzed by preprocessors that tokenize the input text. To correctly choose a tag for a given word requires several steps:

- The default tagger tags all tokenized words with the proper noun tag (nnp), since most unrecognized words will be in the open class of proper nouns.
- Then the unigram tagger finds the most frequent tags in the reference corpus associated with each word and applies them accordingly. "Bronze" will go from nnp to nn, since in the *NLTK* Brown corpus nn is its most frequent tag for "bronze."
- A bigram tagger then looks at what tag **pairs** are in the database: as it turns out, the Brown corpus has tagged occurrences as both jj+nn and nn+nn: "bronze wreath" is analyzed as "bronze/nn wreath/nn" (vs. "bronze/jj neck/nn"):

```
attern/nn in/in blue/jj ,/, pink/jj ,/, bronze/jj and/cc gold/jj and/
cc a/at rimson/nn ,/, gold/nn ,/, purple/nn ,/, bronze/nn ,/, blue/nn
and/cc vermili /, inscriptions/nns on/in the/at Han/np bronze/nn
mirrors/nns ,/, as/ql well le/nn saw/nn ./. Besides/rb flathead/nn
bronze/nn screws/nns ,/, silicon/nn /nn bronze/nn screws/nns ,/,
silicon/nn bronze/nn Stronghold/nn-tl nails/nns that/cs an/at
eight-and-a-half-foot/jj bronze/nn statue/nn of/in William/np
at memorial/nn ./. There/ex is/bez a/at bronze/nn wreath/nn on/
in the/at wal s in/in gold/nn ,/, ivory/nn ,/, and/cc bronze/nn
grow/vb more/ql numerous/j bn yellow/jj and/cc black/jj ,/, the/at
bronze/jj cannon/nn at/in the/at por snake/nn wrapped/vbn around/
in his/pp$ bronze/jj neck/nn ./. The/at yout t/ppo against/in
the/at circle/nn of/in bronze/nn ;/. ;/. but/cc the/at spir
```
                                                    ("bronze" in the Brown corpus)

The bigram tagger understands, however, that the frequency of jj+nn (as in "bronze cannon") is far greater in the corpus than the frequency of nn+nn ("bronze statue") and assumes that since "bronze" is also jj, it can retag it so that the more frequent tag combination is respected. (The tagger is logical, though this is not the standard analysis of "bronze.")

NLTK includes other taggers (i.e., different algorithms and databases for tagging texts) such as the Brill tagger and Hidden Markov Model tagger that make a more thorough analysis of tag probabilities. For our purposes, the default tagging (with nnp), the unigram tagger, and the bigram tagger are sufficient, in spite of certain errors which we will correct manually. All taggers break down in places, and some sentences are simply not analyzable (to experiment with tagging, see UCREL for the online version of the *CLAWS* tagger).

The basic problem faced by a tagger algorithm is that linguistic information is typically not layered in a homogeneous fashion. For example, though the nn+nn combination is relatively infrequent, in some cases, such as "lawn tennis," it is the only possibility (since "lawn" is not an adjective). Taggers must work not only on a given "horizontal" relation with units at the same level, such as tag combination, but as well they must take into account the idiosyncratic influence of one level on another, such as the influence of a particular lexical choice. Such idiosyncratic "vertical" influences are cited as one justification for tree adjoining grammar formalism, which encapsulate information at different levels using a tree structure – see Abeillé and Rambow 2000: 8.

Automatic semantic template building: navigating between senses

The POS tagged text is the syntactic half of generation. A semantic template is the complementary organization of the word meanings that are chosen to fill the slots in the syntactic template. Words and their meanings have an intrinsic organization that does not concern syntax at all. *WordNet* (see Fellbaum 1998) groups words of like meaning into synsets, i.e., into "a set of words that are interchangeable in some context without changing the truth value of the proposition in which they are embedded" (Miller 2006[5]). Synsets are themselves related according to several semantic relations, among which: hypernymy/hyponymy (the more general type of the source word; e.g., "color" is the hypernym of "red"; inversely, "red" is the hyponym of "color"); holonymy/meronymy (the whole of which the source word is a part; e.g., "crowd" is the holonym of "person"); antonyms (extreme opposites such as "good" and "bad"), similar to (adjectives that mean something similar; e.g., "immobile" is similar to "fixed"), and entailment (the source word has as a logical consequence another: e.g., "snoring" entails "sleeping").

Just as our syntactic template is built out of the general syntactic categories (like "noun" and "verb"), our semantic template will use general relations, like "antonym" and "similar to", to describe in general terms the meaning structures of a generated sentence.

Double hypernyms

Each word of our epitaph has a position in the *WordNet* meaning universe which is defined by its synset membership. The word "bloom" belongs to 6 noun synsets and 1 verb synset:

Noun

- S: (n) blooming, **bloom** (the organic process of bearing flowers) *"you will stop all bloom if you let the flowers go to seed"*
- S: (n) flower, **bloom**, blossom (reproductive organ of angiosperm plants especially one having showy or colorful parts)
- S: (n) **bloom**, bloom of youth, salad days (the best time of youth)
- S: (n) **bloom**, blush, flush, rosiness (a rosy color (especially in the cheeks) taken as a sign of good health)

- S: (n) <u>flower</u>, <u>prime</u>, <u>peak</u>, <u>heyday</u>, **bloom**, <u>blossom</u>, <u>efflorescence</u>, <u>flush</u> (the period of greatest prosperity or productivity)
- S: (n) <u>efflorescence</u>, **bloom** (a powdery deposit on a surface)

Verb
- S: (v) **bloom**, <u>blossom</u>, <u>flower</u> (produce or yield flowers) *"The cherry tree bloomed"*

("bloom" in Miller *WordNet*[6])

The synset for the verb "bloom" contains "bloom, blossom, flower". The lexical relations that that synset entertains with other synsets can be displayed by clicking on the synset ("S"). The first-level direct hypernym of the verb "bloom" is thus "develop" (a blooming is a kind of developing) and the hypernym of "develop" is "grow" (a developing is a kind of growing):

- S: (v) **bloom**, <u>blossom</u>, <u>flower</u> (produce or yield flowers) *"The cherry tree bloomed"*
  - *direct hypernym*
    - S: (v) <u>develop</u> (grow, progress, unfold, or evolve through a process of evolution, natural growth, differentiation, or a conducive environment) *"A flower developed on the branch"; "The country developed into a mighty superpower"; "The embryo develops into a fetus"; "This situation has developed over a long time"*
      - ***direct hypernym***
        - S: (v) <u>grow</u> (become larger, greater, or bigger; expand or gain) *"The problem grew too large for me"; "Her business grew fast"*

("bloom" in Miller 2006[7])

The abstracting algorithm will take all the nouns and verbs in our epitaph and navigate to their second-level direct hypernyms (a double hypernym) and put that double hypernym (or the first word of the synset, if the synset has more than one word) in place of the original word of the epitaph. In a similar way, adjectives and past participles will be replaced with "similar to" words. In the case of the verb "bloom," the replacement word is "grow."

Word sense disambiguation

WordNet comes with an assortment of tools for navigating the database (in many programming languages, but the Python modules are perhaps the most compatible with *NLTK*). In our double hypernym navigation we will generally have to choose between different senses, just as when we syntactically parsed the text we had to decide which part of speech was appropriate. In the case of navigating the sense tree of "bloom", there is no confusion; only one sense is under verb and only one hypernym at each level (bloom→develop→grow). The adjective "dead", on the other hand, has 21 senses (i.e., it belongs to 21 different synsets). We need a method for disambiguating different meanings.

Sense disambiguation depends on context, both syntactic and semantic. For example, to disambiguate "lie" it is useful to know that the subject is a person; in our text, "I" is a personified object, so "I" can tell a lie, lie down, but rarely will "I" lie in a certain position, as in "the mountains lie in the west." Semantic clues also come from the set of words that are in the same passage, whatever their syntactic relation. "Mound" could be a baseball mound, but since in the same context we find "tomb," "dead," and "tearful," our choice would favor a burial mound (though that sense is not found in *WordNet*).

SenseRelate (Pedersen) is a Perl package that attempts to compare all such relations and disambiguate words according to their immediate context, their position in the *WordNet* ontology, and a corpus of sense tagged texts. *SenseRelate*, properly configured, will semantically tag our text as follows (*WordNet* only tags nouns, adverbs, adjectives and verbs) (Table 27.3).

The online version of *SenseRelate*[8] shows how meanings are selected according to several algorithms that quantify how semantically close entries are in the *WordNet* network. The Lesk algorithm, for example, evaluates word overlaps in the glosses for each meaning. As we can see above, "tomb" and "mound" are related by the words "**earth**" and "**stone**" (in the gloss of "mound") and "**ground**" and "**tombstone**" (in "tomb"; "ground" has for gloss "the solid part of the **earth's** surface"); "dead" and "tomb" are linked by the relation between "life" and "**dead man**" (in "dead") and

Table 27.3   *SenseRelate* meaning selection (excerpt).

Word POS Sense	*WordNet* Gloss
BRONZE n 1	an alloy of copper and tin and sometimes other elements; also any copper-base alloy containing other elements in place of tin
MAIDEN n 1	an unmarried girl (especially a virgin)
	. . .
MIDAS n 1	(Greek legend) the greedy king of Phrygia who Dionysus gave the power to turn everything he touched into gold
MOUND n 4	a structure consisting of an artificial heap or bank usually of **earth** or **stones**; "they built small mounds to hide behind"
	. . .
TEARFUL a 1	filled with or marked by tears; "tearful eyes"; "tearful entreaties"
TOMB n 1	a place for the burial of a **corpse** (especially beneath the **ground** and marked by a tombstone); "he put flowers on his mother's grave"
	. . .
DEAD a 1	no longer having or seeming to have or expecting to have **life**; "the nerve is dead"; "a dead pallor"; "he was marked as a **dead man** by the assassin"
	. . .
BURY v 2	place in a grave or tomb; "Stalin was buried behind the Kremlin wall on Red Square"; "The pharaohs were entombed in the pyramids"; "My grandfather was laid to rest last Sunday"
HERE r 1	in or at this place; where the speaker or writer is; "I work here"; "turn here"; "radio waves received here on Earth"

Table 27.4   *SenseRelate* word relatedness comparison ("dead" and "tomb").

Measure	Word 1	Word 2	Score
lesk	dead#a#1	tomb#n#1	6
lesk	dead#n#1	tomb#n#1	4
lesk	dead#n#2	tomb#n#1	3
lesk	dead#r#2	tomb#n#1	2
lesk	dead#a#2	tomb#n#1	1
lesk	dead#a#14	tomb#n#1	1
lesk	dead#a#3	tomb#n#1	0
....			

"corpse" (in "tomb"; the gloss of "corpse" is "the **dead** body of a **human** being"). Table 27.4 shows the Lesk values for the latter pair (top values only; the rest are 0), as generated by the online tool; sense 1 of the adjective "dead" is most closely related to sense 1 of the noun "tomb".

We use such sense relatedness measures to choose between alternative hypernyms or "similar to" adjectives in our abstracting algorithm.

Automatic narrative

Narrative represents the third major topography. Most generators do not deal directly with that topography; rather, narrative generation is generally approached in the same manner as syntactic and semantic generation, with a few enhancements. Table 27.5 shows some sample generation from *JanusNode*.

The French site *Charabia* (see Reyes 2006) has a generator which subscribers use to produce various texts. Here is the start of a (long) philosophical essay that one user programmed:

Tribalisme vs tribalisme
1. Prémisses du tribalisme idéationnel.

Si on ne saurait ignorer la critique bergsonienne du primitivisme substantialiste, Montague systématise néanmoins la destructuration primitive du tribalisme et il en identifie, par la même, l'aspect transcendental en tant que concept primitif de la connaissance.

Cependant, il identifie le primitivisme de la société tout en essayant de le resituer dans toute sa dimension sociale, et le tribalisme ne se borne pas à être un primitivisme existentiel comme concept rationnel de la connaissance.

(Reyes at *Charabia*[9])

Both these generators script narrative through different kinds of syntactic templating. *Charabia* uses a simplified transition network (Figure 27.1).[10]

Table 27.5 *JanusNode* sample story plot output.

(none)	Possible title: The Hostility of Erroneous Hate	Possible title: Baggaging Bros
This story has two main characters. The first is Noel, a dogged air traffic controller. The second is named Erna. Erna is a dead angel. This is their story, of sex and solitude.	This story has two main characters. The first is a cold master named Una. The second is named Alonso. Alonso is a drunk master.	Your protagonist is a brown skin broke bro named Larissa. Your antagonist is a kindhearted agent named Griselda. Their story is one of creativity and open-heartedness.
Noel and Erna meet in an useful motel. Noel wants to discuss personalizing and hugging. Erna is tired of being dead and needing. She knows that Noel is neither dead nor needing. Noel is only after one thing: contents. Erna needs to get contents. The well-intentioned air traffic controller explains to the thrilling angel that the difficult animation is like an atmosphere. Erna feels confused. The moral is worth remembering. Clairvoyant sex is not the same as optimal solitude.	Una and Alonso meet in a boisterous crimson hospital waiting room. Alonso is thinking of giving up being a master to study epitaphs with Una. Una takes out a hostility, and advises Alonso to be more quarrelsome. The penniless master reveals the hostility to the master. Alonso becomes less drunk.	Larissa and Griselda meet in an alien furthest sitting room. Larissa and Griselda have been brought together by their common friendship with a third character named Nicola. Griselda is thinking of giving up being an agent in order to pursue an interest in studying intentional metaphysics. Larissa gives benumbed information about the importance of weakness and destruction. The illiterate agent steals the baggage from the brown skin bro. Larissa becomes more brown skin. The moral is instructive. Interesting creativity is only xenophobic open-heartedness.

Generation passes through each node in a random fashion, text is written out, variables are set that select the lexicon ($theme_dtd qualifies the chosen thematic word, $theme), loops are defined, and control is passed to subnetworks (comp2, a complement such as "au regard du maximalisme", and adj1_fs, a feminine singular adjective, are described in other networks).

JanusNode uses the same techniques for the most part, but the network is implemented with scripts called TextDNA:

```
100 Subject(AnimalPoemSetUp) < assign(Cur,"dog,cat,pig") 100 >
100 Subject(ShortAnimalPoem) "A" 100 < GetRhyme(Cur,noun) 100 >
"likes to" 100 < GetRhyme(Cur,verb) 100 > "!" 100

A pig likes to jig!
A cat likes to bat!
```

(TextDNA and sample output from *JanusNode* documentation)

The numbers indicate the probability that a given function will fire (100 means that the function will fire 100% of the time); the *assign* function chooses a word randomly

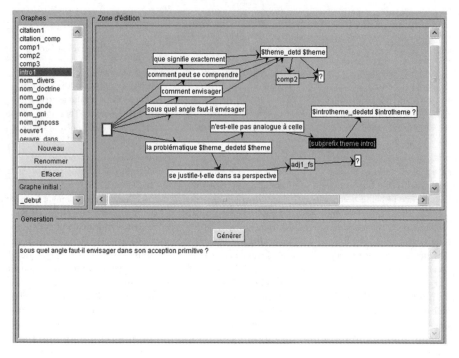

Figure 27.1   Intro1 node of the *Charabia* generator.

in a set or file of words given in the second argument and assigns it to the variable given in the first argument. *JanusNode* has some built-in linguistic functionality: a rhyming function (GetRhyme) and minimal morphology. It also has a rudimentary TextDNA generation system which will make scripts from source text. Properly configured, *JanusNode* scripts are more powerful than *Charabia*'s networks, but are more tedious to write.

One significant variation on this basic template framework for generation are systems that are designed for dialogue, such as *A.L.I.C.E.* (and the *AIML* scripting language). Narrative is developed "on the fly" in response to the user's input. In such cases the input text is transformed into data for generation.

Narrative topology: chaining events

Generating truly creative narrative poses a particular problem. The template systems we have dealt with so far only concern the most combinable units of language – words – through word-centered syntax (POS tagging) and semantics (dictionary meanings). Programming narrative is difficult because the fundamental topography of narrative is not linguistic, but rather a topography of events. **Grammars** offer much accumulated knowledge about syntax that is formalized; **dictionaries** describe word meaning in a very clear fashion; **encyclopedias** describe events, but with almost no formalization. No convincing narrative can be made without a large database of our commonsense understanding of events. Narrative does have a linguistic component as well, which dictates how information will be parceled out to the reader. For instance, it is a purely linguistic fact that the order of sentences typically represents the order of events. We understand differently "Paul broke down in tears. Mary broke his channel changer" and "Mary broke his channel changer. Paul broke down in tears." However, it is a fact of the world, not of language, that the destruction of an object might have an emotional impact on a person. Neither a grammar nor a dictionary has that fundamental knowledge, knowledge that a story generator must inevitably orchestrate.

The lightweight templating systems we have seen so far require the user to build events through language. On the contrary, an ideal story generator would either generate events automatically, selected from an events database, or take a general description of an event and generate the appropriate language. **Good** narrative, the most general topography and the one that connects language most directly to reality, is particularly difficult to master because it is at this level that all the underlying topologies are given a final meaning. Narrative is where information at different levels is **evaluated**. Poetry shows this most clearly, since even the simple sound or spelling of a word might be the focus of the text. Thus a story generator about birds in French might need to know something about the character level of the word "oiseau" (that it has all the vowels). Similarly, in our epitaph it is perhaps important, or not, that the maiden be bronze, rather than silver. Ultimately, the pertinence of a lexical choice can only be determined by the goal of the narrative; narrative establishes a general logic and hierarchy for all the other kinds of information in the text.

Heavyweight narrative generators (see Mueller 2006 for a bibliography and resources) depend on large databases of encyclopedic knowledge. *MIT*'s *Open Mind Common Sense* (*OMCS*; see Singh et al. 2002) was conceived to collect a database of common sense reasoning from internet users and distill it into a computer-usable form. General event scripts are added to these databases or generated from the encyclopedic knowledge. *Thought Treasure* (Mueller 2000[11]) is a well-documented, pioneering reasoning database that was used as a model for the *OMCS* database. Here is one of the handcrafted scripts from *Thought Treasure*:

```
2. (sleep) [frequent] sleep; [English] sleep; [French] dormir
[ako ^ personal-script]
[cost-of ^ NUMBER:USD:0]
[duration-of ^ NUMBER:second:28800]
[entry-condition-of ^ [sleepiness sleeper]]
[event01-of ^ [strip sleeper]]
[event02-of ^ [ptrans-walk sleeper na bed]]
```

[event03-of $^\wedge$ [set sleeper alarm-clock]]
[event04-of $^\wedge$ [lie-on sleeper bed]]
[event05-of $^\wedge$ [groggy sleeper]]
[event06-of $^\wedge$ [sleep-onset sleeper]]
[event07-of $^\wedge$ [asleep sleeper]]
[event07-of $^\wedge$ [dream sleeper]]
[event08-of $^\wedge$ [ring alarm-clock]]
[event08-of $^\wedge$ [wake alarm-clock sleeper]]
[event09-of $^\wedge$ [awake sleeper]]
[event10-of $^\wedge$ [rise-from sleeper bed]]
[goal-of $^\wedge$ [s-sleep sleeper]]
[performed-in $^\wedge$ bedroom]
[period-of $^\wedge$ NUMBER:second:86400]
[result-of $^\wedge$ [restedness sleeper]]
[role01-of $^\wedge$ sleeper]
[role02-of $^\wedge$ bed]
[role03-of $^\wedge$ alarm-clock]

(Mueller 1999)

The sleep script describes the event as being personal, costing nothing (in US dollars!) and having a duration of 28,800 seconds (the conventional 8 hours), requiring a sleeper and sleepiness, having a series of subevents, such as stripping, the sleeper walking (from n/a) to bed, setting the alarm clock, lying on the bed, feeling groggy, beginning to go to sleep, being asleep and dreaming, the alarm clock ringing, etc.

This handcrafted script gives the barest understanding of the sleep event. The *Open Mind* project collected 700,000 commonsense statements (the *OMCS* raw data) about the human experience, deduced some 1.7 million formal relations, and compiled them in the *ConceptNet* application (Lui et al. 2006). Over 2,000 sentences of the *OMCS* raw data use the word "sleep" or its direct derivatives; here is an arbitrary sample:

1. If a person is bored he may fall asleep
2. Jake has two states – awake and asleep
3. You are likely to find a cat in front of a fireplace, sleeping
4. Sometimes viewing a film at home causes you to fall asleep on the sofa
5. A motel is a place where you can rent a room to sleep in
6. Many people have schedules that allow them to sleep later on weekends than on weekdays
7. The effect of attending a classical concert is falling asleep
8. Something you might do while watching a movie is falling asleep
9. A sofa hide-a-bed is for sleeping
10. Sometimes taking final exams causes sleepiness
11. Ken fell asleep

12. Studies have shown that **sleep** deprivation leads to impaired consolidation of both declarative and procedural memories
13. Something you might do while **sleep**ing is fall out of bed
14. An activity someone can do is **sleep** in a hotel
15. You would relax because you want to go to **sleep**
16. Cindy Lou has a home to **sleep** in
17. You would **sleep** at night because you had a busy day

(OMCS raw data)

Heavyweight story generators (such as *Make Believe* (Liu and Singh 2002); for others see Meuller 2006) will use such information to create a narrative topography. A character sleeping in bed might be in her home, and she may fall out, dream, snore, it could be at the end of a busy day, etc. Simply ordering a selection of the sentences given above and making adjustments gives a rough narrative sequence describing Jake's falling asleep and then falling out of bed (words inserted are in bold; words deleted are struck out):

1. Jake has two states – awake and asleep
17. You **too** would sleep at night ~~because~~ **if** you had a busy day
15. You would relax because you want to go to sleep
4. Sometimes viewing a film at home causes you to fall asleep on the sofa
9. A sofa hide-a-bed is for sleeping
11. ~~Ken~~ **Jake** fell asleep **on the hide-a-bed**
13. Something you **too** might do while sleeping is fall out of bed

. . .

ConceptNet's database is a network of the abstract rendering of such messy statements about the world. Every node of the network will have "incoming" and "outgoing" relations with other concepts (Figure 27.2).

Automatic generation with *ConceptNet* consists in following event links, playing out the combinatory of their subevents, and creatively developing descriptions based on the other types of relations in the network.

Art

The techniques described here do not produce very comprehensible nor artistic narrative. There is little chance that computers will figure soon on the list of best selling authors. At the same time, these techniques are prerequisites for creative writing by computers or computer-assisted writing by people. Text processors will soon offer thesaurus-like functions that produce variants of a sentence, a paragraph, or perhaps even a text. But what makes **good** writing?

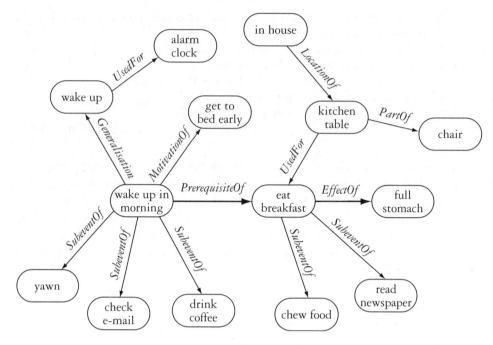

Figure 27.2   ConceptNet's network of concepts (Liu and Singh).

According to one successful writer, Stephen King, good writing is not about the mechanics of plot:

> Stories are found things, like fossils in the ground [...]. Stories aren't souvenir tee-shirts or *GameBoys*. Stories are relics, part of an undiscovered pre-existing world. The writer's job is to use the tools in his or her toolbox to get as much of each one out of the ground as intact as possible. Sometimes the fossil you uncover is small; a seashell. Sometimes it's enormous, a *Tyrannosaurus Rex* with all those gigantic ribs and grinning teeth. Either way, short story or thousand-page whopper of a novel, the techniques of excavation remain basically the same. (2000: 163)

Getting a fossil out of the ground requires delicate tools, like a palm-pick, airhose, or toothbrush. Plot is the jackhammer of writers: "a good writer's last resort and the dullard's first choice" (2000: 164). As an exercise for the aspiring writer King describes (in his own good style) a bare-bones narrative about a woman who is stalked in her home by her estranged husband:

> It's a pretty good story, yes? I think so, but not exactly unique. As I've already pointed out, ESTRANGED HUBBY BEATS UP (OR MURDERS) EX-WIFE makes the paper every other

week, sad but true. What I want you to do in this exercise is change the sexes of the antagonist and the protagonist before beginning to work out the situation in your narrative [. . .]. Narrate this without plotting – let the situation and that one unexpected inversion carry you along. I predict you will succeed swimmingly... if, that is, you are honest about how your characters speak and behave. Honesty in story telling makes up for a great many stylistic faults, as the work of wooden-prose writers like Theodore Dreiser and Ayn Rand shows, but lying is the great unrepairable fault. (2000: 173)

The great gap between printing and writing seems indeed to concern that "honesty in story telling"; writers must use the finest brush to extract from the mass of our beliefs about the world a single compelling image of the way things inescapably are. But how can the writer be honest about **fictional** characters!? King's honesty is about what our understanding of the world will allow us to put together reasonably (in his exercise, it is understanding the difference between the sexes in their manner of stalking). How things cohere **in principle** is a truth that writer and reader must both possess in order to understand each other. That coherence is no more nor less than who writer and reader are together, as one being. It defines the single honest way to set about thinking and speaking.

Let us assume, then, that the artistic text captures the higher truth of the way things are. It is priceless, lively, and live because, by being intensely, exactly itself, it subsumes the many variants of itself. A gender-bent text is artistic only when it implicitly says the straight text and underlines the inescapable reasoning that brings both texts under a same denomination and so subsumes by the same stroke the many possible variations on the theme. By showing what stalking **might** be, it shows what stalking **must** be, however the situation may vary. Artistic texts, clearly departing from the norm by a twist or a wriggle, scintillate with meaning and show dramatically the principle of how they came to be – their "makedness." The deepest truth about anything is the way it comes to be, because there lies the secret of how it might continue to be.

If poetic art is indeed "impeded form" or "roughened language" (Shklovsky), it is because narrative leads the reader to tease out a synthetic position – a higher ground – that explains the world of perplexing opposites. Artistic narrative is "roughened reasoning" that leads up to a communal, true way to seeing as one the perplexing opposites of the world. Socrates's complaint about Midas's epitaph is that it does not go anywhere: there is no excavation project to exhume the truth of Midas. There is only the clanking tongue of a bronze maiden, just as petrified as Midas in his grave. Combinatory is not art. Narrative goes somewhere specific: up.

Can computers really write? Only if they can fly. They must move up out of their clanking linguistic machinery to a general truth about the world and to a vantage point that captures the text's fundamental generativity. **A good** text – an artistic text – is the one that represents best many other texts.

Remarkable steps have been made to give machines the resources needed to build higher meaning, but it will take still more accumulation of data about how people see the world. Minsky estimates that even simple commonsense "is knowing maybe 30 or 60 million things about the world and having them represented so that when something happens, you can make analogies with others" (Dreifus 1998, cited in Liu and Singh forthcoming: 2). We will only see computers generate art from all that commonsense when they can be programmed to tell us something true.

NOTES

1 <http://www.poignantguide.net/ruby/chapter-3.html>, section 1. "Language and I MEAN Language."

2 <http://www.perseus.org/cgi-bin/ptext?doc=Perseus:text:1999.01.0173:text=Phaedrus:section=264d> and "Greek display."

3 <http://www.perseus.org/cgi-bin/ptext?doc=Perseus:text:1999.01.0173:text=Phaedrus:section=264d> and "Greek transliterated display."

4 <http://nltk.sourceforge.net/tutorial/tagging/section-a1189.html>.

5 <http://wordnet.princeton.edu/man/wngloss.7WN>.

6 <http://wordnet.princeton.edu/perl/webwn?o2=&o0=1&o7=&o5=&o1=1&o6=&o4=&o3=&s=bloom>.

7 <http://wordnet.princeton.edu/perl/webwn?o2=&o0=1&o7=&o5=&o1=1&o6=&o4=&o3=&s=bloom&i=12&h=00000010110000000#c>.

8 <http://marimba.d.umn.edu/cgi-bin/similarity.cgi>.

9 <http://www.charabia.net/gen/gendisp.php?gen=1\&big=1>.

10 <http://www.charabia.net/gen/gendisp.php?gen=1\&big=1\&fonc=1>.

11 <http://www.signiform.com/tt/python/query.cgi>.

BIBLIOGRAPHY

Abeillé, A. and O. Rambow (2000). "Tree Adjoining Grammar: An Overview." In A. Abeillé and O. Rambow (Eds.). *Tree Adjoining Grammars: Formalism, Linguistic Analysis and Processing*. Stanford: CSLI Publications, pp. 1–68.

A.L.I.C.E. AI Foundation (2006). <http://www.alicebot.org/>. Accessed August 2006.

Babel Fish Translation (2006). <http://babelfish.altavista.com/>. Accessed August 2006.

Baldridge, Jason and Tom Morton (Eds.) (2006). *OpenNLP*. <http://opennlp.sourceforge.net/>. Accessed August 2006.

Bird, Steven, Edward Loper, and Rob Speer (Eds.) *NLTK: Natural Language ToolKit*. <http://nltk.sourceforge.net/>. Accessed August 2006.

Balpe, J.-P., and B. Magné (Eds.) (1991). *L'Imagination informatique de la littérature*. Saint-Denis: Presses Universitaires de Vincennes.

Braffort, P. (2006). "L'ALAMO: en avant 'post-'." <http://paulbraffort.free.fr/litterature/alamo/alamo_avant_post.html>. Accessed August 2006.

Carson, A. (1986). *Eros the Bittersweet*. Princeton: Princeton UP.

Crane, G. (Ed.) (2006). *The Perseus Digital Library*. <http://www.perseus.org>. Accessed August 2006.

D'Antin Van Rooten, L. (1968). *Mots D'Heures: Gousses, Rames The D'Antin Manuscript*. London: Angus & Robertson.

Davidson, J. (2006). *Truespel Converter*. <http://www.truespel.com/en/>. Accessed August 2006.

Derrida, J. (1992). "La Pharmacie de Platon" [Plato's Pharmacy]. In L. Brisson (Ed.). *Phèdre suivi de La Pharmacie de Platon*. Paris: Gallimard.

Dreifus, C. (1998). "Got Stuck for a Moment: An Interview with Marvin Minsky." *The International Herald Tribune* August.

Dunn, M. (2001). *Ella Minnow Pea*. New York: Anchor Books.

Fellbaum, C. (Ed.) (1998). *WordNet: An Electronic Lexical Database*. Cambridge, MA: MIT Press.

Hoban, R. (1980). *Riddley Walker*. New York: Summit Books/Simon & Schuster.

King, Stephen (2000). *On Writing: A Memoir of the Craft*. New York: Scribner.

Kurzweil, R. (2006). "Kurzweil CyberArt Technologies." <http://www.kurzweilcyberart.com/>. Accessed August 2006.

Lessard, Greg, and Levison, Michael. *VINCI Laboratory*. <http://www.cs.queensu.ca/CompLing/>. Accessed August 2006.

Liu, H., and P. Singh (2002). "MAKEBELIEVE: Using Commonsense to Generate Stories." In *Proceedings of the Eighteenth National Conference on Artificial Intelligence, AAAI 2002, July 28 – August 1, 2002,* Edmonton, Alberta, Canada, 2002, pp. 957–8.

——, and P. Singh (forthcoming). "ConceptNet: A Practical Commonsense Reasoning Toolkit." *BT Technology Journal* 22, forthcoming, Kluwer Academic Publishers. <http://web.media.mit. edu/~hugo/publications/papers/BTTJ-Concept Net.pdf>. Accessed August 2006.

——, P. Singh, and I. Eslick (2006). *ConceptNet v.2.1*. <http://web.media.mit.edu/~hugo/conceptnet/>. Accessed August 2006.

Malsky, W. (2006). *Why's (Poignant) Guide to Ruby*. <http://www.poignantguide.net/ruby/>. Accessed August 2006.

Miller, George (Ed.) (2006). *WordNet: An Electronic Lexical Database*. <http://wordnet.princeton.edu/>. Accessed August 2006.

Mueller, E. T. (1999). "A Database and Lexicon of Scripts for *Thought Treasure*." <http://www.signiform.com/tt/htm/script.htm>. Accessed August 2006.

—— (2000). *Thought Treasure*. <http://www.signiform.com/tt/htm/tt.htm>. Accessed August 2006.

—— (2006). "Story Understanding Resources." <http://xenia.media.mit.edu/~mueller/storyund/storyres.html>. Accessed August 2006.

Pedersen, T. (2006). *SenseRelate*. <http://www.d.umn.edu/~tpederse/senserelate.html> and <http://senserelate.sourceforge.net/>. Accessed April 2007.

Ponge, F. (1999). *Tome Premier*. Paris: Gallimard.

Reiter, E. (2002). *KPML*. <http://www.fb10.uni-bremen.de/anglistik/langpro/kpml/README.html>. Accessed August 2006.

Reyes, R. (2006). "*Charabia*: Essais philosophiques." <http://www.charabia.net/gen/gendisp.php?gen=1&big=1&font=l>. Accessed August 2006.

Roubaud, J. (1985). "Prothèse." in J.-F. Lyotard and T. Chaput (Eds.). *Épreuves d'écriture*. Paris: Éditions du Centre Georges Pompidou.

——, and P. Lusson (2006). *Rimbaudelaire*. <http://alamo.mshparisnord.net/rialt/rimbaud.html>. Accessed August 2006.

Round, M. (2006). *Malvole Text Generator*. <http://www.malevole.com/mv/misc/text/>. Accessed August 2006.

Singh, P. (2006a). "Open Mind Common Sense Data." <http://csc.media.mit.edu/omcsraw_id.txt.gz>. Accessed August 2006.

—— (2006b). "Open Mind Experiences." <http://csc.media.mit.edu/OMEXHome.htm>. Accessed August 2006.

——, T. Lin, E. T. Mueller, G. Lim, T. Perkins, and W. L. Zhu (2002). "Open Mind Common Sense: Knowledge Acquisition from the General Public." In *Proceedings of the First International Conference on Ontologies, Databases, and Applications of Semantics for Large Scale Information Systems,* Irvine, California. <http://web.media.mit.edu/push/ODBASE2002.pdf>. Accessed August 2006.

Stein, A. (2006). *TreeTagger*. <http://www.uni-stuttgart.de/lingrom/stein/forschung/resource.html>. Accessed August 2006.

UCREL: University Centre for Computer Corpus Research on Language at the University of Lancaster (2006). *CLAWS*. <http://www.comp.

lancs.ac.uk/ucrel/claws/>. Accessed August 2006.

Westbury, C. (2006). *JanusNode*. <http://www.janusnode.com>. Accessed August 2006.

Winder, W. (2002). "Industrial Text and French Neo-structuralism." *Computers and the Humanities* 36.3: 295–306.

—— (2004). "Robotic Poetics." In S. Shreibman, R. Siemens, and J. Unsworth (Eds.). *Blackwell* *Companion to Digital Humanities*. Oxford: Blackwell, pp. 448–68.

—— (2006). *Robotic Poetics*. <http://edziza.arts.ubc.ca/winder/rp>. Accessed August 2006.

—— (forthcoming). "Linking Fancy unto Fancy: Towards a Semantic IDE for Cascading Summaries." In G. Shawver and R. Siemens (Eds.). *New Paths for Computing Humanists*. Toronto: University of Toronto Press.

Quantitative Analysis and Literary Studies

David L. Hoover

History, Goals, and Theoretical Foundation

Modern quantitative studies of literature begin about 1850, with periods of intense activity in the 1930s and the 1980s. Fortunately, several excellent overviews discuss earlier work in the context of computers and literary studies (Burrows 1992a), stylometry (Holmes 1998), and authorship attribution (Holmes 1994; Love 2002). We can thus concentrate here on recent advances, driven primarily by the huge growth in the availability of electronic texts, increasingly sophisticated statistical techniques, and the advent of much more powerful computers that have produced much more accurate and persuasive analyses.

Quantitative approaches to literature represent elements or characteristics of literary texts numerically, applying the powerful, accurate, and widely accepted methods of mathematics to measurement, classification, and analysis. They work best in the service of more traditional literary research, but recent and current work often necessarily concentrates much of its effort on the development of new and improved methodologies. The availability of large numbers of electronic literary texts and huge natural language corpora has increased the attractiveness of quantitative approaches as innovative ways of "reading" amounts of text that would overwhelm traditional modes of reading. They also provide access to kinds of information that are not available even in principle without them. Quantitative approaches are most naturally associated with questions of authorship and style, but they can also be used to investigate larger interpretive issues like plot, theme, genre, period, tone, and modality.

A concrete example will suggest some of the benefits of quantitative analysis. In *To the Lighthouse*, Virginia Woolf describes a vacation house that has been closed up for the winter:

> Nothing it seemed could break that image, corrupt that innocence, or disturb the swaying mantle of silence. . . . Once only a board sprang on the landing; once in the

middle of the night with a roar, with a rupture, as after centuries of quiescence, a rock rends itself from the mountain and hurtles crashing into the valley, one fold of the shawl loosened and swung to and fro.

A critic struck by the comparison of a rock hurtling into a valley with a shawl loosening and swinging might also be interested in the apparent self-agency of the rock, the board, and the shawl, and might want to investigate Woolf's use of inanimate objects where animates are expected, a type of personification. The critic would normally deploy a series of supporting examples selected from the novel through careful reading, perhaps including some striking examples like these:

all round the table, beginning with Andrew in the middle, like a <u>fire</u> leaping from tuft to tuft of furze, her children laughed

It was as if the <u>water</u> floated off and set sailing thoughts which had grown stagnant on dry land, and gave to their bodies even some sort of physical relief.

And now in the heat of summer the <u>wind</u> sent its spies about the house again.

The list might be expanded with similar examples involving body parts:

His <u>hands</u> clasped themselves over his capacious paunch, his <u>eyes</u> blinked, as if he would have liked to reply kindly to these blandishments

Indeed she had been keeping guard over the dish of fruit . . . hoping that nobody would touch it. . . . until, oh, what a pity that they should do it – a <u>hand</u> reached out, took a pear, and spoilt the whole thing.

For how could one express in words these emotions of the <u>body</u>? . . . It was one's <u>body</u> feeling, not one's mind.

Most readers will agree that Woolf's personifications are striking, but their literary functions seem quite varied. In the first, the comparison of laughter and fire seems an apt and vivid way of characterizing the spontaneous, variable, and contagious out-break of humor, while the personification of the hand in the fifth example, by removing the agency, focuses our attention on the fruit basket still life.

A careful enough reading can examine all the uses of inanimate objects and body parts in the novel. If the goal is merely to point out the personifications or to categorize them, there may be little gain in quantifying the analysis, though cat-egorizing the personifications would seem peculiar without any indication of the frequencies of the various categories. Examples are rarely significant, however, unless they are either unusual or characteristic of the novel or the author – otherwise why analyze them? And the unusual and the characteristic must be validated by counting and comparison: the bare claim that Woolf uses a great deal of personification is without value and nearly meaningless unless it is quantified. In rare cases the quantification can be implicit: no mathematical demonstration is necessary to show that a novel without the word "the" is unusual, but Woolf's use of inanimate subjects is another matter. A single remarkable use of personification can certainly be significant and noteworthy, but most stylistic and interpretive observations rest upon patterns, and, therefore, upon repetition. Basing an argument about *To the Lighthouse* on the prevalence of personification, then, requires counting those personifications and at least a rough comparison of their frequency with some kind of norm or reference point. Finding dozens of odd inanimate subjects in *To the Lighthouse* and only a few in other modernist novels of roughly the same length might be sufficient.

Readers who know Woolf's novel well may doubt the centrality of personification to its interpretation: in *To the Lighthouse*, the personification seems to be an aesthetic literary device rather than an important and integral stylistic characteristic. The same cannot be said of *The Inheritors* (Golding 1955). In that strange novel, the extreme prevalence of body parts and inanimate objects as agents and subjects of verbs of motion (and even verbs of perception) is central to Golding's creation of the imagined Neanderthal world-view of the text (see Hoover 1999 for discussion). Many stylistic and interpretive patterns, however, are far more pervasive or far more subtle, and they require more sophisticated, more powerful, and more explicit quantification.

Methods

Almost any item, feature, or characteristic of a text that can be reliably identified can be counted, and most of them have been counted. Decisions about what to count can be obvious, problematic, or extremely difficult, and poor initial choices can lead to wasted effort and worthless results. Even careful planning leaves room for surprises, fortunately often of the happy sort that call for further or different quantification. The frequencies of various letters of the alphabet and punctuation marks, though not of obvious literary interest, have been used successfully in authorship attribution, as have letter n-grams (short sequences of letters). Words themselves, as the smallest clearly meaningful units, are the most frequently counted items, and syntactic categories (noun, verb, infinitive, superlative) are also often of interest, as are word n-grams (sequences) and collocations (words that occur near each other). Thematic or semantic categories (angry words, words related to time), while more difficult to count, have the advantage of being clearly relevant to interpretation, and automated semantic analysis may reduce the effort involved. Phrases, clauses, syntactic patterns, and sentences have often been counted, as have sequences or subcategories of them (prepositional phrases, subordinate clauses, passive sentences). Many of the items listed above are also used as measures of the lengths of other items: word length in characters, sentence or clause length in letters or words, text length in words, sentences, paragraphs, and so forth. Nonlinguistic textual divisions ranging from small units like lines and couplets to larger structural units like paragraphs, stanzas, scenes, acts, and chapters can also sometimes be usefully counted, as can literary categories like narrators and characters (including subcategories like first-person and third-person narrators, and characters divided by age, ethnicity, nationality, class, and gender), and plot elements (marriages, deaths, journeys, subplots).

The most obvious place to count whatever is counted is a single literary text that is of interest, as with the example from Woolf above. The need for some kind of comparative norm suggests that counting more than one text will often be required and the nature of the research will dictate the appropriate comparison text. In some cases, other texts by the same author will be selected, or contemporary authors, or a natural language corpus. In other cases, genres, periods, or parts of texts may be the appropriate focus. Counting may be limited to the dialogue or narration of a text, to one or more speakers or narrators, or to specific passages.

In the simplest quantifications, the numbers are merely presented and interpreted or offered as evidence that further investigation is likely to be productive. A critic interested in how writers differ in their vocabularies may find the raw counts of the numbers of different words (word types) in the first 50,000-word sections of a group of novels worth studying. In the first section of Sinclair Lewis's *Main Street*, for example, about 8,300 different words appear, but only 4,400 in Faulkner's *Light in August*, where the localization of the story may make the huge difference seem comprehensible. The 5,200 different words in the first section of James's *The Ambassadors* and the 6,600 in London's *The Sea Wolf* will require different explanations, and few readers would predict that *Main Street* has an exceptionally large vocabulary or *Light in August* an exceptionally small one.

Quantification does not end with counting or measurement and presentation, of course, and many different kinds of mathematical operations have been applied to the numbers. Among the simplest of these is comparing frequencies or averages among a group of texts, often using an appropriate statistical test of significance, such as Student's T-test or Chi-square, to gauge the likelihood that the observed difference could have arisen by chance. Authorship or style cannot reasonably be analyzed if the differences observed are likely to occur without the author's intervention. Fortunately, the patterns found in literary texts are often so obviously significant that no statistical testing is required, but it is easy to overestimate the oddity of a pattern, and statistical tests help to avoid untenable claims.

The standard deviation (roughly, the average difference, in either direction, of all frequencies from the mean), which measures how widely scattered the values are, and the z-score, which measures the distance of any given value from the mean in standard deviations, are often valuable for questions of textual difference. For example, in a corpus of 46 Victorian novels by six authors, the average rate of occurrence per 10,000 words is about 11 for "upon" and 63 for "on." In *Silas Marner* the frequencies are 4 "upon," 72 "on," and in *Vanity Fair* 17 "upon" and 50 "on," so that the difference between these two novels seems more extreme for "upon" than for "on." The standard deviations for the two words tell a different story: "upon" is quite variable in these six authors, with a standard deviation of about 9 words per 10,000 (not far below its average frequency of 11), but "on" is distributed much more evenly, with a standard deviation of about 15 (less than one-fourth its average frequency). Thus the frequencies of these words in the two novels are well within a single standard deviation from the mean, with z-scores between -0.84 and 0.71. Because they differ less than the average difference from the mean, frequencies in this range are quite likely to occur by chance, though the combination of the differences between the two words is suggestive.

Another simple operation is dividing the frequency of an item in one text by its frequency in another, yielding the distinctiveness ratio (DR), a measure of the difference between the texts. Ratios below 0.67 or above 1.5 are normally considered worth investigating. Returning to inanimate subjects in Woolf, even my example of 24 such subjects in one novel and 8 in another gives a distinctiveness ratio of 3. But note that in the example of "upon" above the DR between the novels is greater than 4, so that some care should be taken not to over-interpret a DR when the frequencies of the words vary a great deal. Some measures of vocabulary richness or concentration, such as Yule's characteristic constant K, take into account the frequencies of all the word types in a text and require more complex calculations, as do other measures of vocabulary richness based on probabilistic models.

Recent years have seen a trend toward multivariate methods that are especially designed to deal with large amounts of data – methods such as principal components analysis, cluster analysis, discriminant analysis, correspondence analysis, and factor analysis. Statistical programs have made these methods much more practical by performing long sequences of required computations rapidly and without error. Principal components analysis, the most popular of these methods, allows the frequencies of many different items with similar distributions in a group of texts to be combined into a single component. The result is a small number of unrelated measures of textual difference that account for most of the variation in the texts. The first two of these components are typically used to create a scatter plot in which the distance between any two texts is a simple visual measure of their similarity. This technique provides a graphical method of "reading" a large number of frequencies at once, and is much easier to interpret than the list of frequencies themselves.

Delta, a promising new measure of textual difference based on word frequency, has stirred a great deal of interest (Burrows 2002a). Delta is designed to pick the likeliest author of a questioned text from among a relatively large number of possible authors. Burrows begins by recording the frequencies of the most frequent words of a primary set of texts by the possible authors and calculating the mean frequency and standard deviation for each word in this set of texts. He then uses z-scores to compare the difference between the mean and each of the primary authors with the difference between the mean and the questioned text for each of the words. He completes the calculation by averaging the absolute values of the z-scores of all the words to produce Delta, a measure of the difference between the test text and each primary-set author. The primary set author with the smallest Delta is suggested as the author of the test text. A further innovation in Delta is that Burrows expands the set of words analyzed to the 150 most frequent rather than the 30–100 used in earlier work with PCA, and I have shown that further expansion of the list to the 800 or even the 4,000 most frequent words often produces even stronger results on long texts (Hoover 2004a).

Recently Burrows has introduced two further measures, Zeta and Iota, which concentrate on words of moderate and low frequencies, respectively (2006). For both measures, a word frequency list is created for a sample of text by a primary author, and then the sample is divided into several sections of equal size. The heart of the procedure is to record the number of these sections that contain each of the words and then record which of the words occur in samples by other authors and in texts to be tested for authorship. By sorting the word list on the basis of how many of the primary author's text sections contain each word, Burrows eliminates the very frequent words that occur in most texts and concentrates on different parts of the word frequency spectrum. For Zeta, he retains only moderately frequent words, ones that occur in a subset of the primary author's sections. Where only two poets are being compared, he then further reduces the list of words by removing those that exceed a specific frequency in the works of the second poet. Where many authors are being compared, he removes words that appear in the text samples of most of the other authors. Whether there are two or many authors, the result is a list of words that are moderately frequent in the primary author and very infrequent in the other author(s). For Iota, words are removed that appear in most of the sections by the primary author. For two authors, words are also removed that do not appear in the second author's sample, and, where many authors are being tested, the second step removes words that appear in about half or more of the other authors. Both of these methods are remarkably effective in attributing poems as short as 1,000 words, and the discussion of methodology and substance is rich enough to provoke another wave of interest in authorship attribution and stylometry.

Techniques related to artificial intelligence are also increasingly being applied, including neural networks, machine learning, and data mining (see, for example, Waugh, Adams, and Tweedie 2000). These methods, which require more computing power and expertise than many other methods, are sometimes used in authorship attribution, but more often in forensic than in literary contexts. One reason for this is that they treat authorship attribution as a classification problem, and their results are more difficult to extend to traditional literary questions. Many of these techniques, as well as key word analysis, are well suited to the analysis of content, especially in the context of the huge amounts of text being produced on the World Wide Web.

Applications

Many kinds of studies of literary texts use quantitative methods. Quantitative thematic analysis can trace the growth, decay, or development of vocabulary within a thematic domain, or study how authors differ in their expressions of a theme (see Fortier 2002). Many empirical studies of literature translate readers' judgments into numerical scales to study literary response using techniques borrowed from the social sciences. Metrical analysis, because of the inherent reliance of meter on pattern, is a natural area for quantitative study, though there has been less research in this area than one might have expected.

A growing area of research is in the study of manuscript relationships, where techniques designed for the study of genetic relationship among organisms have been ingeniously and fruitfully applied to the study of the manuscripts of Chaucer's *Canterbury Tales* (see, for example, Spencer et al. 2003). These studies take literally the metaphor of genetic relationships among manuscripts, treating differences among them as if they were differences in DNA sequences. The huge amount of data involved in some manuscript traditions invites and practically requires sophisticated statistical techniques, whether those of evolutionary biology or other multivariate techniques. Genre and period definition and classification also benefit from quantitative approaches, especially factor analysis and other multivariate techniques.

Authorship attribution and statistical stylistics (or stylometry), currently two of the most important areas of quantitative analysis of literature, deserve a fuller treatment. They share many basic assumptions and methods, though some techniques that are effective in distinguishing authors may have no clear interpretive value. A discussion of authorship attribution in the present context necessarily forces a distinction between forensic and literary authorship attribution that is sometimes without a difference. Determining who wrote a text generally requires much the same methodology whether the text is ransom note, a threatening letter, a legal opinion, the federalist papers, a contemporary political novel like Joe Klein's *Primary Colors*, an anonymous eighteenth-century verse satire, or play by Shakespeare.

Yet two differences between the forensic and literary attribution must be kept in mind. First, in many forensic contexts, the identity of the person who produced the language of the text may be irrelevant, while the identity of the person responsible for sending it may be crucial. A kidnapper may force a victim to write a ransom note, and a manifesto may be cribbed from a series of websites; determining these facts may or may not help to solve the crime. Second, the text in a forensic problem typically has little intrinsic value and becomes irrelevant once the attribution is made and the crime solved. In the case of literary attribution, however, and preeminently for Shakespeare's plays, the aesthetic and contested cultural value of the texts lies at the heart of the problem. One consequence of these differences is that literary attribution is often only a first step, so that methods easily turned to stylistic or interpretive purposes tend to be favored.

Only when external evidence fails is it reasonable to apply quantitative methods, and the presence or absence of a closed set of possible authors and differences in the size and number of documents available for analysis are usually more significant than the kind of text involved. Here I will concentrate on reasonably tractable kinds of literary authorship problems in which the questioned text is of a reasonable size and similar texts by the claimant authors are available.

Authorship attribution has often been based on a single variable like word length, sentence length, or vocabulary richness, and some researchers continue to achieve good results using a small number of such variables. Most current research, however, has turned to more robust multivariate methods such as principal components analysis and cluster analysis, often combining the results of more than one method to solve a problem. In his excellent overview of computers and the study of literature, Burrows (1992a) uses principal components analysis (PCA) of the fifty most frequent words to argue against the possibility that Lady Vane had a hand in the "Memoirs of a Lady of Quality" which Smollet includes in his *Peregrine Pickle*. In other work, he shows that the seventy-five most frequent words can successfully distinguish 4,000-word sections of novels by the Brontë sisters and that the twenty most frequent words can distinguish 500-word sections of letters by Scott and Byron (Burrows 1992b). Even more remarkable, when statistical tests are used to select the words that most effectively discriminate between Scott and Byron, the ten most effective of these do an excellent job of separating the works of Scott and Byron even across several genres. A good recent example of this methodology, using a careful approach that also takes into account traditional methods, persuasively adds additional shore journalism to Stephen Crane's small oeuvre (Holmes et al. 2001). Principal components analysis (PCA) of the fifty most frequent words of the texts shows that Crane's fiction can be distinguished from Conrad's, that his fiction can be distinguished from his shore journalism and New York City journalism, and that these two kinds of journalism are different from his war journalism. The same method shows that Crane's shore and New York journalism are different from that of his brother Townley and two other contemporary journalists. Both PCA and cluster analysis strongly suggest that seventeen pieces of previously unattributed shore journalism (known to be by one of the brothers) is Stephen's rather than Townley's.

Authorship attribution based on n-grams, sequences of various numbers of letters or words, has become increasingly popular, sometimes performing better than word frequency alone, especially on small texts. In a wide-ranging and provocative article, Clement and Sharp (2003) show that both letter and word n-grams perform marginally better than methods based on words. For these experiments, the frequencies of the various items in the known documents are transformed into probabilities of randomly extracting them from the text, and the test document is assigned to the author whose training set maximizes the probability of generating the text. Besides presenting many different methods and varieties of results, Clement and Sharp raise important questions about the relationship between content and style, the effects of text size, and apparently random differences that alter the accuracy of analyses. Although letter n-grams lack any transparent relationship to the meaning or style of a text, and are unlikely to be attractive to researchers who are interested in broader literary questions, word n-grams are likely to become increasingly popular because they may both improve accuracy and allow the critic to focus on meaningful word groups.

Four Exemplary Studies

Statistical stylistics or stylometry is the broadest of the areas in which quantitative analysis intersects with literary study, and it might be said to subsume parts or all of the applications just discussed. Its central concerns are closest to those of literary studies in general, with a special emphasis on the patterns that comprise style and how those patterns are related to issues of interpretation, meaning, and aesthetics. Rather than surveying or describing various kinds of stylometric studies, I will focus in a more detail on four recent articles that exemplify some of the most central concerns and methods while treating important literary problems and questions.

"Cicero, Sigonio, and Burrows" (Forsyth, Holmes, and Tse 1999) is about authorship, but it also treats issues of chronology and genre. It applies methods first proven on English to classical Latin and neo-Latin (inflected languages) and examines not only words, but also word length (in syllables) and some information about transitions between words of different lengths. These variables are analyzed using PCA, cluster analysis, and discriminant analysis, and the authors combine careful analysis with useful methodological observations. The central question asked is whether it is likely that the *Consolatio Ciceronis*, which was edited and published by Sigonio in 1583, is really the lost work known to have been written by Cicero about 45 BC and existing only as fragments quoted in other works, or, as was suggested shortly after its publication, a forgery by Sigonio himself. Can authorship attribution methods distinguish "between Cicero and Ciceronianism" (Forsyth, Holmes, and Tse 1999: 378)?

After collecting more than 300,000 words of classical and neo-Latin by eleven authors and dividing them into 70 sample texts, the authors use PCA based on the 46 most frequent function words to show that Cicero's oratory is distinct from his prose – that, as has often been noted, genre effects sometimes overwhelm authorship effects. The same method distinguishes Cicero well from six other classical authors, as does cluster analysis, and both produce slightly weaker but still broadly accurate results when Sigonio is tested against the other sixteenth-century authors.

Turning to Sigonio, Cicero, and the *Consolatio*, the authors use stepwise discriminant analysis of known texts by Sigonio and Cicero to determine the words that are most effective in distinguishing the two authors. This technique is especially appropriate in cases like this one where some samples belonging to distinct groups are available. It identifies a small group of discriminators that are quite effective in distinguishing Sigonio and Cicero: they classify only two Ciceronian texts as by Sigonio and attribute both sections of the *Consolatio* to him. Discriminant analysis is also used to discover variables that distinguish effectively between classical and neo-Latin, discriminators that classify the *Consolatio* as neo-Latin. Adding information about word length and syllable transition improves the accuracy of the analyses and more firmly identifies the *Consolatio* as neo-Latin. Finally, discriminant analysis also shows that the *Consolatio* is enough like Sigonio's other work to suggest that he is its author.

The authorship of this disputed work is inherently significant, and this article does an exceptionally clear job of describing the literary and cultural situation in which the authorship question is to be asked. The careful division of the problem into sub-problems provides clarity, and the variety and methodological sophistication of the analyses both strengthen the case against Cicero as the author and serve as a guide to future work.

In "Jonsonian Chronology and *A Tale of a Tub*," one of several careful and important studies, Hugh Craig also uses discriminant analysis, but he applies it to a very different literary problem (1999). His central question is the position of Ben Jonson's *A Tale of a Tub* in the chronology of his work, and thus the context in which the play is read. Whether, "it is a late work of pastiche or is in origins an early, naively conventional one" (230–31) has important implications for its significance and its interpretation.

The existence of several datable early, middle, and late comedies allows Craig to set up a discriminant analysis based on the 58 most frequent function words, more heavily weighting those words that discriminate best among the three periods. When the plays are divided into 2,000-word segments, those segments separate clearly into clusters, with very little overlap. Craig's methodology, like the PCA analysis popularized by Burrows, allows a scatter plot of the play segments to be compared with a scatter plot of the variables that produced it, and this in turn allows him to discuss the words and their stylistic and chronological implications.

Analyzing segments of *A Tale of a Tub* in the same way shows that its segments are very widely dispersed: some appear among the earliest segments, some in the middle, some among the late segments, and one outside all three of these clusters. Though this is consistent with an early play later revised, Craig wisely tests other late plays, showing that the scatter is not an artifact of the analysis and that *A Tale of a Tub* is much more widely scattered than the others. The sectioning of the plays also allows a discussion of plot and content in relationship to the scattered segments.

Next, the play is repeatedly re-segmented at 100-word intervals and subjected to the same analysis to pinpoint abrupt changes in style, which are discussed with reference to the boundaries between acts and scenes. Finally, rolling segments of *A Tale of a Tub* are compared with those of other plays, showing that the fluctuations in *A Tale of a Tub* are much more extreme. Although no firm conclusions can be reached, this careful, innovative, and thorough analysis strongly suggests an early play reworked by Jonson near the end of his career. Craig's frequent and insightful return to the text and to questions of serious literary significance marks this as model stylometric analysis.

In taking up "Charles Brockden Brown: Quantitative Analysis and Literary Inter-pretation" (Stewart 2003) we shift genres, continents, centuries, and focus, but retain a strong relationship between quantitative analysis and more traditional literary questions. Rather than authorship or chronology, Stewart focuses on the styles of narration in two novels by Charles Brockden Brown (1771–1810), *Wieland or The Transformation* and the unfinished *Memoirs of Carwin, the Biloquist*. He investigates whether Brown successfully creates distinct narrative voices for the four narrators of *Wieland* and a consistent voice for Carwin, who is both one of those narrators and also the narrator of the unfinished *Memoirs of Carwin*.

Burrows used PCA successfully in distinguishing the dialogue of Jane Austen's various characters in his classic *Computation into Criticism* (1987), treating the characters as if they were literally the "authors" of their own speech. One interesting question is whether or not a writer of more modest gifts can successfully create distinct and consistent narrative styles. However important Brown may be to the origins of American literature, he is no Jane Austen. I have investigated a similar question regarding Hannah Webster Foster's 1797 American epistolary novel, *The Coquette* (Hoover et al. forthcoming), and, in a discussion of *Nineteen Eighty-Four*, *The Inheritors*, and *The Picture of Dorian Grey*, have suggested revisions to the standard methodology that may improve analyses of parts of texts by a single author (2003).

Stewart uses both PCA and cluster analysis and bases them not only on the frequencies of the 30 most frequent words, but also on the frequencies of various punctuation marks, and on the frequencies of words, sentences, and paragraphs of different lengths. He shows that the chapters of *Wieland* narrated by Clara, Pleyel, and Theodore are generally quite distinct from the chapter narrated by the villainous Carwin, which clusters with his chapters from *Memoirs of Carwin*. The analysis reveals an anomaly that provides the impetus for a discussion of more traditional literary concerns: both Pleyel's chapter of *Wieland* and the final chapter of that novel, which is narrated by Clara, cluster with *Memoirs of Carwin*, and Carwin's chapter of *Wieland*. (In an article in a similar spirit, McKenna and Antonia [2001] probe the differences among interior monologue, dialogue, and narrative in Joyce's *Ulysses*, arguing that multivariate analysis of Gerty McDowell's language can contribute to the interpretation of form, meaning, and ideology in that complex and difficult novel.)

There is no space here to do justice to the subtlety of Stewart's integration of these quantitatively anomalous results into the larger critical debate surrounding the interpretation of the early American novel, but he produces some very suggestive reasons for the similarity of the voices of Pleyel and Carwin, including their long years spent in Europe – quite significant in an early American novel – and the fact that both want to dominate and possess Clara. Stewart also suggests connections between Clara's narration of the final chapter of *Wieland*, a kind of "happy ending" postscript written from Europe after her marriage to Pleyel, and critical views of Brown as a skeptic about the American experiment. He also makes intriguing suggestions of a connection between Carwin's ventriloquism and the similarity between Clara's voice and his own in the final chapter of *Wieland*. This study not only uses statistics effectively to provide insight into important questions of interpretation, but also "suggests that traditional critical interpretation has a real bearing on how we understand the meaning of those statistics" (138). There is, of course, always the danger of arguing a specious excuse for a real anomaly after the fact, but that is the nature of interpretation, and such speciousness often leads to its own correction.

I conclude this selection of exemplary articles with "The Englishing of Juvenal" (Burrows 2002b), which contrasts in topic and methodology with the three articles just discussed, but continues their serious engagement with traditional literary concerns. Its focus is on translation and style, with a twist of authorship and chronology, and the method is Delta analysis, described above. (For another very interesting look at translation and authorship attribution, see Rybicki 2006.) To a database of more than half a million words of English Restoration poetry, Burrows adds fifteen translations of Juvenal's tenth satire dating from 1646 to 1967. When Delta is used to attribute the translations to their authors, it is not very successful. D'Urfey is ranked first and Dryden second as the author of Dryden's translation; Johnson is strongly identified as the author of his translation, but Vaughan and Shadwell both rank well down the list of possible authors of theirs. Tests involving other translations give similar spotty results, suggesting that some authors effectively suppress their own styles and others do not; for his other translations, for example, Dryden often appears far down the list of likely authors.

Characteristically, Burrows goes on to a second analysis. This time, rather than asking who is the likeliest author of each translation, this analysis focuses on the authors, asking which of the fifteen Juvenal translations is most like the original work of each translator. In three of the four tests, the results are correct; in the fourth Dryden's comes in a very close second to Higden's as the most similar to the work of Dryden. These impressive results on a very difficult problem show that Delta is capable of capturing subtle authorial markers that persist even when submerged beneath the style of a translation. Another interesting fact is that D'Urfey, who ranks first as author of Dryden's Juvenal X, appears as the most likely author of five of the fifteen translations and as second or third most likely of eight others. Burrows shows that this is not the phenomenon often seen in authorship studies, where the lowest common denominator is, by default, the likeliest author when the true author is not present. The phenomenon is limited to the translations of Juvenal, suggesting that there are real similarities in style between D'Urfey's English and Juvenal's Latin.

Burrows then alters Delta slightly by using the averages of the word frequencies in all of the translations as the test text, treating this average text as a model of Juvenalism, but also retaining the average frequencies as the means against which Delta is calculated. (For other, more extensive alterations to Delta that I have suggested, see Hoover 2004b.) This naturally results in a complete set of zero z-scores for the test text and the mean, but it allows all fifteen translations to be measured against the "model." Shadwell's translation is the most similar to the mean and Johnson's the most different, even more different than the twentieth-century translations and the prose translations. Burrows concludes by using the differences between Johnson and the model to illuminate some of the important characteristics of Johnson's style, noting that Dryden and Johnson lie at opposite ends of a spectrum from versatility to consistency, a spectrum that all students of style would do well to remember. The emphasis on comparison in this article and the telling applications of statistical methods are particularly valuable. The concluding comments about the contrast between close reading and computer analysis emphasize the use of the computer to enhance and extend our ability to "read" literary texts in new ways:

> The close reader sees things in a text – single moments and large amorphous movements – to which computer programs give no easy access. The computer, on the other hand, reveals hidden patterns and enables us to marshal hosts of instances too numerous for our unassisted powers. Even in the common case where we do not have fifteen versions of one original to bring into comparison, these principles hold good. (Burrows 2002b: 696)

A Small Demonstration: Zeta and Iota and Twentieth-Century Poetry

Given the rapid developments in this field, a small demonstration of the potential of Burrows's newest measures of textual difference, Zeta and Iota, seems appropriate. I began with some Delta tests on very different data, samples of poetry by forty twentieth-century poets, using large samples by twenty-six poets as the primary set and thirty-nine long poems as the secondary set. Twenty-five of these were by poets in the primary set and fourteen by other poets (these poems by primary authors were removed from their main samples). Delta is very accurate on these texts, correctly identifying the authors of all but three of the long poems by members of the primary set. I then took the few errors that occurred and looked for circumstances where a single author erroneously ranks first as the author of one poem and also ranks among the likeliest authors of another poem by the same poet. Among the most similar of the poets in my study using these criteria are Wallace Stevens, Archibald MacLeish, and T. S. Eliot. Burrows's tests of Waller and Mavell using Zeta and Iota were based on main sets of about 13,000 and 20,000 words, and my set for Eliot is about the same size; the sets for Stevens and MacLeish are much larger, more than 70,000 words. The individual poems to be tested are roughly the same size as those Burrows tested, about 2,000 to 6,000 words.

The results of tests of MacLeish against Stevens using both Zeta and Iota were impressive. The new measures had no difficulty distinguishing the two poets, whether MacLeish or Stevens formed the primary sample. There is space here to discuss only the results of Zeta, which is based on the middle of the word frequency spectrum – words that have largely been ignored in earlier studies. Zeta is even more effective in distinguishing MacLeish and Stevens than it was in distinguishing Waller and Marvell, with the lowest Zeta for the primary author typically twice as large as that for the second author. As Burrows found, the poems by another author, here Eliot, sometimes narrowly outscore some of those of the primary author. Although this may seem disconcerting, it actually suggests that Zeta is narrowly and appropriately tuned to the difference between the authors being tested.

On this set of texts, I found that much more stringent stipulations than those used by Burrows produced some fascinating results: the 26 words that are found in all five sections of MacLeish's sample but do not occur in the Stevens sample seem to be good potential MacLeish authorship markers. Their total frequency is 321 in the five MacLeish sections and 40 in the two individual long MacLeish poems, but only 2 in the Stevens sample and his two long poems combined. Relaxing the restriction to retain words if they appear in more than three, more than two, or more than one section gradually reduces the amount of difference between the poems by MacLeish and Stevens, though all of these analyses are completely accurate. The 40 words remaining based on the same stipulations in the Stevens sample, with a total frequency of 545 in Stevens and 60 in Stevens's two long poems, but only 3 in the MacLeish sample and his two long poems combined, in turn seem to be good potential Stevens authorship markers.

Selecting words that occur in all of the sections of the primary sample seems to violate Burrows's intention of avoiding the 30–150 most frequent words that are so often used in other methods, but the stipulation of a maximum frequency of 3 in Stevens accomplishes this in any case. For example, "answered" is the most frequent of the 26 potential MacLeish markers, but it ranks only 323rd among the most frequent words in the MacLeish samples, and "reality" is the most frequent of the 40 potential Stevens markers, but it ranks only 184th among the most frequent words in the Stevens samples. Both are thus beyond the range normally used in tests of frequent words. The 26 MacLeish words range in rank from 323 to 1,422 and the 40 Stevens words from 184 to 1,378, placing all of them well within the range of words that I normally now include in Delta analyses and placing most of them within the range I normally include in cluster analyses. The presence of powerful discriminators like these may help to explain why expanding the size of the word list that is analyzed so often increases the accuracy of the results.

Finally, a glance at the 26 MacLeish words and the 40 Stevens words suggests that Zeta and Iota may provide useful ways of focusing our attention on interesting words:

Ubiquitous Stevens – Rare MacLeish

reality, except, centre, element, colors, solitude, possible, ideas, hymns, essential, imagined, nothingness, crown, inhuman, motions, regard, sovereign, chaos, genius, glittering, lesser, singular, alike, archaic, luminous, phrases, casual, voluble, universal, autumnal, café, inner, reads, vivid, clearest, deeply, minor, perfection, relation, immaculate

Ubiquitous MacLeish – Rare Stevens

answered, knees, hope, ways, steep, pride, signs, lead, hurt, sea's, sons, vanish, wife, earth's, lifted, they're, swing, valleys, fog, inland, catch, dragging, ragged, rope, strung, bark

Besides the obviously greater length and abstractness of the Stevens words, especially the nouns, the Stevens list is saturated with adjectives, while the MacLeish list has very few adjectives and proportionally more verbs and concrete nouns. A search for some of the most frequent of these marker words in each poet's work yields an interesting pair of short poems: MacLeish's "'Dover Beach' – A Note to that Poem" and Stevens's "From the Packet of Anacharsis." Forms of no less than 7 of MacLeish's 26 marker words appear in his short poem (215 tokens, 123 types), including the 3 italicized in the following brief passage:

> ...It's a fine and a
> Wild smother to *vanish* in: pulling down –
> Tripping with outward ebb the urgent inward.
>
> Speaking alone for myself it's the *steep* hill and the
> Toppling *lift* of the young men I am toward now...

Forms of 6 of Stevens's 40 marker words appear in his even shorter poem (144 types, 91 tokens), including the 3 italicized in the brief passage below (internal ellipsis present in the original):

> And Bloom would see what Puvis did, protest
>
> And speak of the floridest *reality*...
> In the punctual *centre* of all circles white
> Stands truly. The circles nearest to it share
>
> Its *color*...

One of the most difficult challenges for quantitative analyses of literature is preventing the huge numbers of items being analyzed from overwhelming our ability to see the results in insightful ways. By reducing the numbers of words to be examined and selecting sets of words that are particularly characteristic of the authors, Zeta and Iota seem likely to prove very useful for literary analysis as well as authorship attribution, whatever the further developments of them may be once they have been tested and refined. (Zeta and Iota sometimes produce anomalous results in tests including many authors; Burrows suggests [personal communication] that they are better reserved for head-to-head comparisons.)

The Impact, Significance, and Future Prospects for Quantitative Analysis in Literary Studies

As has often been noted, quantitative analysis has not had much impact on traditional literary studies. Its practitioners bear some of the responsibility for this lack of impact because all too often quantitative studies fail to address problems of real literary significance, ignore the subject-specific background, or concentrate too heavily on technology or software. The theoretical climate in literary studies over the past few decades is also partly responsible for the lack of impact, as literary theory has led critics to turn their attention away from the text and toward its social, cultural, economic, and political contexts, and to distrust any approach that suggests a scientific or "objective" methodology. There are, however, signs of progress on both these fronts. The recent increased interest in archives within literary criticism will almost necessarily lead to the introduction of quantitative methods to help critics cope with the huge amount of electronic text now becoming available. Some quantitative studies have also begun to appear in mainstream literary journals, a sure sign of their growing acceptance. The increasing frequency of collaborations between literary scholars and practitioners of quantitative methods of many kinds also promises to produce more research that strikes an appropriate balance between good methodology and significant results. Prospects for the emergence of quantitative approaches as a respected, if not central, branch of literary studies seem bright.

References

Burrows, J. F. (1987). *Computation into Criticism*. Oxford: Clarendon Press.

—— (1992a). "Not Unless You Ask Nicely: The Interpretative Nexus between Analysis and Information." *LLC* 7: 91–109.

—— (1992b). "Computers and the Study of Literature." In C. S. Butler (Ed.). *Computers and Written Texts*. Oxford: Blackwell, pp. 167–204.

—— (2002a). "'Delta': a Measure of Stylistic Difference and a Guide to Likely Authorship." *LLC* 17: 267–287.

—— (2002b). "The Englishing of Juvenal: Computational Stylistics and Translated Texts." *Style* 36: 677–99.

—— (2006). "All the Way Through: Testing for Authorship in Different Frequency Strata." *LLC* 22: 27–47.

Clement, R., and D. Sharp (2003). "Ngram and Bayesian Classification of Documents." *LLC* 18: 423–47.

Craig, H. (1999). "Jonsonian Chronology and the Styles of *A Tale of a Tub*." In M. Butler (Ed.). *Re-Presenting Ben Jonson: Text, History, Performance*. Houndmills: Macmillan, pp. 210–32.

Forsyth, R. S., D. Holmes, and E. Tse. (1999). "Cicero, Sigonio, and Burrows: Investigating the Authenticity of the *Consolatio*." *LLC* 14: 375–400.

Fortier, P. (2002). "Prototype Effect vs. Rarity Effect in Literary Style." In M. Louwerse and W. van Peer (Eds.). *Thematics: Interdisciplinary Studies*. Amsterdam: Benjamins, pp. 397–405.

Golding, W. (1955). *The Inheritors*. London: Faber & Faber.

Holmes, D. (1994). "Authorship Attribution." *Computers and the Humanities* 28: 87–106.

—— (1998). "The Evolution of Stylometry in Humanities Scholarship." *LLC* 13: 111–17.

Holmes, D. I., M. Robertson, and R. Paez (2001). "Stephen Crane and the New York Tribune: A Case Study in Traditional and Non-Traditional Authorship Attribution." *Computers and the Humanities* 35.3: 315–31.

Hoover, D. L. (1999). *Language and Style in The Inheritors*. Lanham, MD: University Press of America.

—— (2003). "Multivariate Analysis and the Study of Style Variation." *LLC* 18: 341–60.

—— (2004a). "Testing Burrows's Delta." *LLC* 19: 453–75.

—— (2004b). "Delta Prime?" *LLC* 19: 477–95.

——, J. Culpeper, B. Louw, and M. Wynne (forthcoming). *Approaches to Corpus Stylistics*. London: Routledge.

Love, H. (2002). *Attributing Authorship: An Introduction*. Cambridge: Cambridge University Press.

McKenna, C. W. F., and A. Antonia (2001). "The Statistical Analysis of Style: Reflections on Form, Meaning, and Ideology in the 'Nausicaa' Episode of *Ulysses*." *LLC* 16: 353–73.

Rybicki, J. (2006). "Burrowing into Translation: Character Idiolects in Henryk Sienkiewicz's Trilogy and its Two English Translations." *LLC* 21: 91–103.

Spencer, M., B. Bordalejo, P. Robinson, and C. J. Howe (2003). "How Reliable is a Stemma? An Analysis of Chaucer's *Miller's Tale*." *LLC* 18: 407–22.

Stewart, L. (2003). "Charles Brockden Brown: Quantitative Analysis and Literary Interpretation." *LLC* 18: 129–38.

Waugh, S., A. Adams, and F. Tweedie (2000). "Computational Stylistics using Artificial Neural Networks." *LLC* 15: 187–98.

29
The Virtual Library
G. Sayeed Choudhury and David Seaman

Introduction

Literary studies are all over the net. A Google search on the term yields several million results, and combining "literary studies" with "online," "digital," or "web" still keeps the count in the hundreds of thousands. Closer examination reveals that many of these sites are library-based and point to primary texts, items digitized from special collections, and digital archives directed by faculty through initiatives, centers, and services that often have a library component. Syllabi and other materials are also widely available, and the blogosphere bristles with literary studies discussions. Data repositories and open-access journals relevant to literary studies are appearing by the dozen. Still more material is available for fee online, and is often purchased by university libraries or their consortia – publishers began in the late 1980s to sell massive full-text databases of materials germane to literary studies, and this trend continues today.

And yet, after fifteen years of digital library production and enormous purchasing of commercial content, there is still little sign of literary disciplines and departments being transformed by new modes of inquiry, new publishing opportunities, or new textual editing paradigms. There are individuals who stand out as landmark adopters of digital content and related technologies, but – as several of the pioneers in the field have observed in recent years (McGann 2004; Ayers and Grisham 2003) – there has not yet been a change in the discipline or its scholarly communications to the degree we are seeing in science, technology, medicine, and business.

As this chapter will demonstrate, libraries can provide literary scholars and students with collections that are increasingly a rich and complex hybrid of analog and digital resources, and librarians can function as willing allies in the exploration of new teaching techniques, research collaborations, analytical tools, and scholarly communications channels.

Discovery

Literary studies in the virtual library can be found through a local library catalog, an online bibliography or aggregation service (in the case of journal articles in particular), and the usual web-searching tools. In the case of a search of the entire web, the sheer volume of material can make discovery difficult for a popular and populous topic such as English literature; much easier, say, for "classical Japanese literature" where there are rich online holdings in the original language and in translation, but where there is a better chance of Google having the most relevant items in the top twenty returns. A web search, of course, is likely to miss many of the commercially published resources that libraries license, and even some of the freely available material (especially for webpages that are generated dynamically from a database, as many are).

No definitive single guide to literary studies online exists, but various collecting points list rich subsets according to their collecting criteria, including the Western European Studies Section of the Association of College and Research Libraries (<http://www.dartmouth.edu/~wessweb/>); the University of Pennsylvania Library's Online Books Page (<http://onlinebooks.library.upenn.edu/>); the Voice of the Shuttle (<http://vos.ucsb.edu/>); OAIster (<http://oaister.umdl.umich.edu/o/oaister/>), and – on a smaller scale – the emerging Digital Library Federation's Collections Registry (<http://dlf.grainger.uiuc.edu/DLFCollectionsRegistry/browse/>). Disciplinary gateways cover topic areas such as Irish Resources in the Humanities (<http://irith.org/>) or the broader Humbul Humanities Hub (<http://www.humbul.ac.uk/>). Sometimes it is also possible to find environmental scans that provide high-level analytical guides to a disciplinary area: a good recent example is *A Kaleidoscope of Digital American Literature* by Martha L. Brogan (<http://www.diglib.org/pubs/dlf104/>). Its purpose is twofold: to offer a sampling of the types of digital resources currently available in support of American literature, and to identify the prevailing concerns of specialists in the field as expressed during interviews conducted between July 2004 and May 2005. The report also classifies the major types of resource one is likely to find online for literary studies:

> (1) quality-controlled subject gateways, (2) author studies, (3) public domain e-book collections and alternative publishing models, (4) proprietary reference resources and full-text primary source collections, (5) collections by design, and (6) teaching applications. (p. 1)

There are still too few places where such resources get promoted, reviewed, and critiqued, although some online journals are getting better at featuring them, such as *D-Lib magazine* (<http://www.dlib.org/>).

Mass: Virtual Library Collections

Published collections

Libraries are purchasing electronic texts, collections of digital images, and now digital audio and video titles in ever-increasing numbers, either to load on local servers for use with software provided by the library, or – more usually – by subscription to a web service produced by the publisher of the material. The holdings of primary materials in digital form for literary studies are impressive indeed; for example, three recent undertakings are providing access to several hundred thousand early American and English books:

1. *Archive of Americana* (including Evans Early American Imprints Collection): 100,000 titles, from seventeenth and eighteenth century America. NewsBank/Readex Co. <http://www.readex.com/readex/index.cfm?content=93>.
2. *Early English Books Online*: Most of the 125,000 titles listed in Pollard and Redgrave's *Short-Title Catalogue (1475–1640)* and Wing's *Short-Title Catalogue (1641–1700)*. ProQuest Information & Learning. <http://eebo.chadwyck.com/home>.
3. *Eighteenth Century Collections Online (ECCO)*: 150,000 titles. Thomson-Gale. <http://www.gale.com/EighteenthCentury/>.

One common feature of collections such as these is less than ideal for some types of literary inquiry: the texts are often digital images of the pages of the books, with the searchable text that lies behind them created by machine recognition (optical character recognition, or OCR) and left uncorrected. This limits the user's ability to perform searches across the corpus that yield reliable results, and complicates machine-aided textual analysis. When the page images are digitally photographed in black and white (rather than utilizing color or grayscale imaging) there is the additional problem that book features such as illustrations can be difficult to decipher, as they require a tonal variation that is absent in a binary black or white digital rendition. Other online versions of multi-volume printed collections such as *Harper's Weekly* (1862–1912) or ProQuest's *Literature Online*, which gives access to huge amounts of British and American poetry, prose, and drama (350,000 works, plus supporting material), are accurately keyboarded and encoded, fully supporting machine-aided literary analysis. The publishers' willingness to undertake such expensive and ambitious projects bodes well for future such endeavors, assuming that use and improved scholarly output justifies the continuing production and purchase of this type of expensive publication.

University, college, and even some school libraries who can subscribe to these collections are likely to have in digital form many books that they will never have in print, and library subscriptions also bring many online versions of leading journals to the desktop. So prevalent are electronic journals in other disciplines, especially science, technology, and medicine (STM), that it is impossible to imagine them functioning without electronic access to most scholarly communication relevant to their daily work. It is not clear that we are close to a similar situation in literary studies, although the economic impact on the humanities of STM online journals and their frequent price rises is evident: libraries are spending more and more on electronic STM journals and less and less on the traditional scholarly monograph that is the backbone of the humanistic disciplines. Consequently, university and other academic presses are publishing fewer book-length studies in print, and literary scholars are having real problems finding a publisher for a book that would have been relatively easily published a decade ago. As much as any other force, the need to publish a book for scholarly communication and for professional advancement combined with the paucity of presses willing to publish in the traditional manner may compel the humanities to move to the wholesale adoption of electronic publishing. There are signs that certain university presses are readying themselves for this eventuality: The University Press of Virginia, for example, has a Digital Rotunda imprint, producing works of scholarly editing, and Rice University has just resurrected its press as an electronic-only publisher.

Freely available collections

We are seeing a steady increase in libraries digitizing their own materials, which are often of particular relevance to literary studies. Many of these items are available freely on the web and often concentrate on rare books and unique manuscripts, including author or theme-centered collections. In some notable cases, these collections are built by librarians who are driven by their own sense of the worth of the material and a desire to make it more accessible to facilitate better pedagogy and scholarship. Many excellent online archives are also being compiled and annotated by scholars around an author or a topic. This is a rich area of scholarly engagement and often of productive partnerships with librarians. The motivations for these sites are various:

- access to rare materials in the classroom;
- combinations of print and manuscript materials;
- research with new digital tools;
- collaborative work with teams at other institutions;
- virtual collections that bring together in one place digital versions of physical objects that will remain geographically dispersed;
- and new forms of textual scholarship and enquiry.

These sites can change the way the scholar teaches, researches, or thinks about his or her discipline; they can be widely used resources in the work of others; and they can reach out to very large international and general public audiences who rarely benefit from the scholarly and pedagogical expertise of subject experts. The final chapter in this *Companion*, 'ANNOTATED OVERVIEW OF SELECTED ELECTRONIC RESOURCES,' gives a flavor of some of the extraordinary scholar-driven sites available for literary studies, resources of distributed material built by distributed teams (such as *The Blake Archive*), emerging online scholarly journals (*Southern Spaces*), and the ambitious experiments in scholarly communications that are under way for the discipline, most notably Jerome McGann's NINES:

> [NINES is] a project to found a publishing environment for aggregated, peer-reviewed online scholarship centered in nineteenth-century studies, British and American. NINES was created as a way for excellent work in digital scholarship to be produced, vetted, published, and recognized by the discipline. (<http://www.nines.org/>)

Still others exist not in literary studies but in closely allied disciplines such as history, and provide good examples of what can be done in the humanities more generally – excellent examples include *The Valley of the Shadow: Two Communities in the American Civil War* (<http://valley.vcdh.virginia.edu/>) and *The Salem Witch Trials Documentary Archive* (<http://www.salemwitchtrials.org/>). One thing that they all have in common is a close connection with their libraries, not just as a source of material to digitize, but as a source of expertise, sometimes of project management space, and even of funding. Certain funding sources are available to literary scholars when in partnership with a library or museum, such as the US Federal funding agency the Institute for Museum and Library Services (IMLS) (<http://www.imls.gov/>). The recently announced grants given jointly by the IMLS and the US National Endowment for the Humanities (NEH) indicate that the granting community wants to foster more collaboration between the scholarly and library communities (<http://www.neh.gov/>).

Mass Ambitions

In recent years, we have seen a general acceleration in the ambitions of publishers, not-for-profit consortiums, federal agencies, and commercial internet companies to create digital content on larger and larger scale. While not focused on literary studies, these real and planned undertakings will have a transformational impact on the materials available for the study of literature. One of the early signs of this willingness to think in massive terms in the US was the proposal for a *Digital Opportunity Investment Trust* (DO IT), a multi-billion dollar "digital gift to the nation" as a transformational federal investment:

> The Digital Opportunity Investment Trust (or "DO IT") would be financed by billions of dollars in revenue from auctions of unused, publicly-owned telecommunications spectrum, as mandated by Congress. Funded by five major national foundations, the project proposes to do for education in the U.S. what the National Science Foundation does for science, the National Institutes of Health do for health, and DARPA does for

defense. DO IT would enable the nation's schools, universities, libraries and museums to reach outside their walls to millions of people in the U.S. and throughout the world. (<http://www.digitalpromise.org/>)

Whatever finally happens with these ongoing and ambitious plans, the arrival on the scene of DO IT in 2001 spurred librarians and others to think about what we would do in the face of a massive investment in digital content, tools, evaluation, and learning systems. One could also point to ongoing projects such as Carnegie Mellon's *Million Books Project* (<http://www.library.cmu.edu/Libraries/MBP_FAQ.html>) as examples of this willingness to digitize large amounts of content, or the new Open Content Alliance championed by the Internet Archive and finding some support in North American university libraries (<http://www.opencontentalliance.org/>).

Currently looming over all of these projects, however, is Google Book Search (<http://books.google.com/>), the ongoing massive digital production that Google is undertaking in partnership with publishers and with the university libraries of Harvard, Oxford, Stanford, Michigan, Virginia, Wisconsin-Madison, the University Complutense of Madrid, the University of California, and The New York Public Library. These plans call for the digitizing of millions of volumes across these libraries, and the aim is to make Google a search tool not only for online materials but for printed books too. Google Book Search is a discovery tool that searches the content of books, but once an item is found its aim is to connect users to the *physical book itself* – either via a publisher or bookseller, or by referring one to a local library where the book can be borrowed or read. It is not at present a "virtual library service" as we typically think of one, although out-of-copyright texts can be viewed in their entirety online. But the service is of great value as a discovery tool for books that are in copyright, even if one cannot make use of that content online.

The latter point highlights an issue for literary studies that has hitherto gone unaddressed here – the virtual library for literary studies is relatively well-stocked with material published up to the 1920s, and many commercial offerings focus on this material too, although in the area of literary studies Alexander Street Press in particular has shown a strong willingness to create products relevant to literary studies in theater, song, women writers, African-American or Latino fiction that contain much licensed content from the twentieth century. Innovative publishers notwithstanding, scholars of twentieth-century literature have less opportunity to engage with the virtual library than their colleagues studying writers of earlier periods. (See Van Hulle, Chapter 7, HYPERTEXT AND *AVANT-TEXTE* IN TWENTIETH-CENTURY AND CONTEMPORARY LITERATURE, in this volume.)

Many literary scholars and the libraries that serve them have ambitions to create digital archives of twentieth-century materials. If the publisher is extant, there is someone to contact for permission – say, for the non-commercial use of that book on a public website – and there are good indications of some success in this type of request, as Denise Troll-Covey's work at Carnegie Mellon University on the Million Books Project has recorded. But what to do if something is in copyright but the owner cannot be found? The item is of great intellectual and pedagogical value but it is long out of print and the publisher no longer exists. In the absence of no discoverable press or author, the response too often is to do nothing, but in the US at least, there are public policy trends that give us some hope that the "permissions problem" may be on its way to being solved. The proposed Orphan Works legislation under investigation by the US Copyright Office has great prospects for literary scholars of twentieth-century materials by providing us a legal process through which to seek permission and the ability to proceed (with new legal safeguards in place) if no owner can be discovered from whom permission can be sought. There is an opportunity and arguably a necessity for humanists to have a voice in legislation and issues that are central to literary studies, such as this *Report on Orphan Works* (U.S. Copyright Office. 2006 <http://www.copyright.gov/orphan/>) or 2005's "Urgent Action Needed to Preserve Scholarly Electronic Journals" edited by Donald J. Waters (<http://www. diglib.org/pubs/waters051015.htm>). The American Council of Learned Societies has taken up this opportunity in *Our Cultural Commonwealth: The Report of the American Council of Learned Societies' Commission on Cyberinfrastructure for Humanities and Social Sciences* 2006 (<http://www.acls.org/cyberinfrastructure/>), echoing the hugely influential *Revolutionizing Science and Engineering Through Cyberinfrastructure: Report of the National Science Foundation Blue Ribbon Advisory Panel on Cyberinfrastructure* (Washington, DC 2003) (<http://www.communitytechnology.org/nsf_ci_report/>).

Malleability

As our familiarity with the use of digital content grows, so too does our realization that we can do more with this material than search it and browse it. There are a growing number of software tools that allow for the sort of scholarly behaviors that are natural to us in the print world: gathering up copies of things, annotating them, and arranging them into personal libraries (virtual filing cabinets). We are seeing the emergence of personal library organization and publishing tools (Greenstone from the University of Waikato, New Zealand <http://www.greenstone.org/>) and The Scholar's Box from UC Berkeley's Interactive University Project <http:// scholarsbox.net>; multimedia annotation tools (MediaMatrix, from Michigan State University <http://matrix.msu.edu/~mmatrix/>); geographic information systems (Google Earth <http://earth.google.com/>); data visualization software (Grokker <http://www.grokker.com/>); and many more. The library tends to keep up with such developments and is a natural and willing partner with the humanities departments as they explore the possibilities such tools have for data mining and the display of results. Add to these software packages the blogs, wikis, and virtual communities that are being adopted, the digital tools for collaborative scholarship, for innovative ways of interrogating text, and for new teaching possibilities, and it is not difficult to see increasing potential for transformative change in the way that literary scholars research, publish, and teach.

The Library as Laboratory

For scientists, the laboratory represents a major hub of scholarly activity. In the laboratory, scientists acquire, gather, combine, analyze, and process data that allows them to test hypotheses and construct new lines of inquiry. These data and findings are subsequently used as the foundation for scholarly communication, most often in the form of journal articles. The laboratory can range from the entire universe to more controlled settings such as a chemistry laboratory to simulated environments that exist only within a computer.

While the modes of scholarship and dissemination differ between humanists and scientists, it is useful to consider how a similar concept might apply for humanists – with the library as one form of laboratory. The library can provide a welcome space in which to innovate and experiment, and its subject librarians, digital specialists, catalogers, and programmers can all be valuable allies in exploring new forms of publication, production, and dissemination. Most library patrons can recall moments of exploration, serendipitous discovery, and purposeful construction of new ideas regarding research while browsing and reading within the stacks. In the physical environment, such exploration and discovery is "constrained" by realities of space and resources. How much does such exploration change in the digital environment? The emergence of "mashups," which reflect one of the unique capabilities of the digital environment, provides an interesting example of combining digital content and services without physical constraints. Craigslist.com represents a well-known classifieds service and Google Maps offers a visual interface for information presentation. A mashup of the two resulted in a visually based service for housing (<http://www.housingmaps.com/>). Will humanists begin to "mashup" scholarly content and services across a distributed network? On the other hand, the physical library provides a sense of context that is difficult to emulate in the digital environment. Will it be important to maintain context and, if so, how will this be managed in digital literary studies?

Scientists and engineers often believe that their disciplines are "data rich" whereas the humanities are "data poor." However, even a casual examination of primary materials such as manuscripts will reveal that the humanities are rich with content that is difficult to extract into digital form. At Johns Hopkins, the Sheridan Libraries are conducting research into automated transcription from medieval manuscripts. Even before such a capability can be considered, the research team concluded that it is essential to digitally "straighten" the lines from the manuscripts. This realization demonstrates some of the difficulty in extracting "data" from humanities content. At the most recent Document Image Analysis for Libraries (DIAL) conferences, there has been an increasing awareness of the difficult image recognition challenges for the Computer Science community as they consider digital humanities content.

Additionally, if one considers the scale of the entire printed record and newer forms of media such as television programs or movies, it becomes clear that humanists have voluminous quantity of data, which remain untapped for deep exploration or examination because the infrastructure and services to use them effectively in digital form remain in nascent form. As initiatives such as the Open Content Alliance and Google Book Search gain momentum, the amount of digital content that becomes available will increase exponentially. The challenge for libraries lies in the realm of building infrastructure and services to support large datasets such that humanists might work in the laboratory of the digital library.

Humanists are not accustomed to imagining medieval manuscripts as "data" but interesting developments from the *Roman de la Rose Project* (<http:// rose.mse.jhu.edu>) led by Johns Hopkins University lend evidence to the idea that digital manuscripts should not be viewed as surrogates but rather as a new form of data to be examined, analyzed, and processed in new ways. In particular, the lead scholar for this project, Stephen G. Nichols, has asserted that working in the digital environment allows medievalists to "break free" of the constraints of traditional literary studies. For example, Lecoy's line-numbering scheme has been used as a canonical method for comparisons between Roman de la Rose manuscripts. Nichols is developing a scene-based methodology that does not rely on "lines" but rather upon semantic information for comparison. The Library is playing a key role in "mapping" this scene-based protocol into a technology framework that will support new forms of searching and comparison.

Greg Crane, the Editor-in-Chief of the *Perseus Digital Library*, has raised thought-provoking ideas related to the theme of "What Do You Do with a Million Books?" With the growing array of tools, it becomes increasingly likely that humanists will look upon collections and content as sources of data to be analyzed, queried, re-purposed, shared, disseminated, and preserved. These and several other projects offer an unusual view for humanists, but one that strikes a chord with some scientists. Alex Szalay of the US National Virtual Observatory has stated that with large-scale, digital astronomy, "data are fuzzy and answers are approximate." For the Virtual Observatory, tools to navigate this fuzzy space and issues such as provenance, annotation, and preservation – which have long interested humanists – have become of paramount importance.

Libraries can play an integral role in supporting both scientists and humanists with data-driven scholarship by digitizing collections and by developing appropriate infrastructure (both human and technological) and services to support new modes of inquiry. At the heart of the digital library that can support this type of digital scholarship lies the concept of a repository.

The Library as Repository and Publisher

Libraries have been the eventual home of scholars' archives, and the place that safeguards the published scholarly record over time. Increasingly, the rise of the institutional repository extends this role to digital content and to a wider variety of material. Whether as a service built on top of a repository or as a separate endeavor, the virtual library is often also a publishing space, partnering with faculty and departments to launch electronic journals, host faculty-driven collections and disseminate scholarship around a theme or an author.

In the physical environment, the library represents a repository of content, with associated services and infrastructure to support the collections. This concept translates into the digital environment with some important distinctions. In the digital realm, the previously distinct elements of collections, services, and infrastructure have become blurred. Robin Chandler of the California Digital Library has indicated that the Open Content Alliance views digital content as infrastructure. OCA intends to build a repository of content as a foundation for services and tools that will augment the capability of the digital collections to support scholarship. The aforementioned Virtual Observatory is a good example of how collections and services work together seamlessly. Digital astronomers acquire data with an explicit consideration of what services can be applied to these data and build services with an a priori understanding of applications for existing data.

As digital capabilities grow, the roles of scholars, libraries, and publishers have also become more fluid. Roles that were distinct and separable in the past are open to renegotiation in the digital age, providing opportunities to strengthen existing partnerships and to form new collaborative efforts – both Cornell University (<http://cip.cornell.edu/webdocs/>) and Rice University (<http://cnx.org/>) have launched new electronic publishing initiatives with strong involvement from their libraries. Cornell's initiative emphasizes cost-effective, customized options for specific communities or user needs. Rice's all-digital effort extends their repository-based technology infrastructure, Connexions, which is already used for e-learning applications, into the e-publishing domain. The Sheridan Libraries at The Johns Hopkins University continue to collaborate with *Project Muse* and other electronic publishing initiatives; the aforementioned *Perseus Digital Library* could be considered a novel form of publication produced directly by scholars. Each of these approaches provides interesting models to consider for digital publishing, either through open access or fee-based approaches.

These new models raise important questions regarding roles and division of labor for libraries and publishers, and for modes of scholarly communication for humanists. With print-based scholarship and publishing, the roles of library and publisher evolved over time into familiar relationships, which may be re-examined for digital scholarship. As for literary studies, the "traditional" form of publishing – the monograph – influenced the way in which research has been conducted and conveyed. With new avenues for publishing, it is possible, even probable, that humanists will begin to explore new forms of research and dissemination. As an example, if humanists begin to embrace the concept of data-driven scholarship, the traditional monograph does not easily support direct connections to digital data. The "fixed" presentation format, however, lends itself to a certain stability and line of thought. How humanists emphasize these attributes – and how academic reward structures change – will affect digital publishing and the roles of libraries and publishers.

This dynamic nature of digital scholarship also raises significant implications for the development of digital libraries. The repository forms the foundation of digital libraries that comprise collections, services, and infrastructure to support learning, research, dissemination, and preservation. In many discussions regarding the repository, it is often described in terms of the form of particular software, content types, discipline, or institution. While each of these lenses is useful, perhaps the most important aspect of repositories relates to the support of services. In an Association of Research Libraries (ARL) report, Clifford Lynch offered the following definition: "a university-based institutional repository is a set of services that a university offers to the members of its community for the management and dissemination of digital materials created by the institution and its community members" (<http://www.arl.org/newsltr/226/ir.html>). This definition is compelling precisely because it avoids discussions of specific technology or organizational schemes, and emphasizes the provision of services, which will undoubtedly change over time (and therefore the repository systems will also evolve).

Access-related services such as search or metadata harvesting often attract greater attention, perhaps because of the direct impact on scholars. Metadata harvesting efforts such as the Open Archives Initiative Protocol for Metadata Harvesting (OAI-PMH) allow discovery of a vast array of materials within repositories that might otherwise remain undiscovered or untapped for literary studies. Both individually customized search interfaces for particular collections and wide-scale, federated searches across distributed repositories facilitate greater discovery. Such discovery is undeniably important for scholarship, but without a commitment to long-term curation of digital content, there is a risk that digital scholarship will become unpredictable or even unreliable.

In this context, it is worth considering that one of the most important adjectives to describe repositories is *persistent*. Digital preservation is an essential service that has received relatively little attention until recently, despite concerns over long-term persistence of digital materials over a decade ago. Most recently, the call for "urgent action" to preserve electronic scholarly journals has garnered some notable interest and activity, but it is worth mentioning that electronic journals are the proverbial tip of the iceberg in the important realm of digital preservation. Given that libraries, archives, and museums are charged with recording and preserving cultural heritage, it is important for these memory institutions to embrace the responsibility of digital preservation.

Librarians often mention that preservation is long-term access. However, with physical items, there is an undeniable tradeoff in the sense that when an item is being preserved, it remains temporarily inaccessible. This tradeoff need not be realized in the digital environment. As digital objects are ingested and managed within repositories to begin the process of digital preservation, parallel pipelines can process these objects to support direct access or transfer into learning environments and publishing systems. While this opportunity offered through repository-based infrastructure bolsters the opportunity for digital preservation, it is essential to consider explicitly such needs from the inception of the digital object life-cycle. Digital collections and services that support literary studies need to be created with an understanding that creation of the object represents the first step in a long-term commitment. Preservation "after the fact" raises significant difficulties that are much more easily addressed at the point of creation. As an example, technologists can use a machine-generated number ("checksum") to validate a digital image. If this checksum is not calculated at the point of creation, it becomes difficult, if not impossible, to determine if a particular digital image has been compromised.

The relatively familiar, stable, library settings to support physical collections evolved over centuries. The models for libraries in the digital age have only begun to be formed. There is little doubt that in future scholars will access new forms of content and services that are unimaginable today. By creating repositories as part of an overall digital architecture that preserves digital content without requiring it to be fixed into a rigid format, libraries offer the pathway toward long-term access in a variety of contexts. Rather than assume or predict scholarly needs, libraries can use repositories as the foundation for frameworks that will facilitate use of digital content in multiple settings, within multiple applications, and through various interfaces.

With a degree of flexibility, and an ongoing commitment to focus on scholarly needs, digital libraries based on repositories will continue to ensure that the library remains a hub of scholarly activity.

Conclusion

In all of this discussion of virtual collections and tools that are accessible wherever you are, it is important to remind ourselves of the enduring role of the library as a physical place in the life of the literary scholar. The library buildings with their collections and related services are central to the working life of the literary scholar, whose engagement with material not yet digitized and with the physical book and literary manuscript as an object of study is greater than in many other disciplines. Inescapably, however, the research collection is increasingly a hybrid of physical and electronic sources, with more and more contemporary journal literature available through electronic publication only. For convenience, for utility, and for the myriad teaching and research possibilities that the combination of digital content and the computer-aided analysis and dissemination affords, the digital library is moving slowly to the center of literary scholarship just as it has – much more rapidly and with greater initial transformational effect – in many of the sciences.

The virtual library is a tale of mass and malleability, and much of the turmoil and opportunity of the present decade in the digital library centers around these twin themes (or their lack). Current copyright restrictions and the inability even to buy access to digital versions of many books, journals, and manuscripts central to literary studies all hamper our deep and daily immersion into the digital library in the manner we are used to doing with the print library. This is changing, as dramatic increases in digitized content from local initiatives, from commercial publishers, and from Google's planned digitizing of entire academic libraries takes us closer to the point where most of what we want to use is available in digital form (although not necessarily without fee).

There is a growing realization that in order to encourage the innovative uses we as librarians want to enable in our users, we need electronic content that is not simply available on a website but which encourages innovation by being easily gathered, personalized, re-purposed, and delivered out again to an audience. This malleability goes to the heart of much scholarly endeavor – gather, annotate, analyze, and re-publish are the so-called "scholarly primitive behaviors" that characterize our work (Unsworth 2000) – and in partnership with their libraries we can look forward to literary scholars increasingly realizing the power of the virtual library in the coming years.

REFERENCES

Ayers, Edward L., and Charles M. Grisham (2003). "Why IT Has Not Paid Off As We Hoped (Yet)." *EDUCAUSE Review* 38:6 (November/December): 40–51. <http://www.educause.edu/pub/er/erm03/erm0361.asp>.

McGann, Jerome (2004). "A Note on the Current State of Humanities Scholarship." *Critical Inquiry* 30:2 (Winter). <http://www.uchicago.edu/research/jnl-crit-inq/issues/v30/30n2.McGann.html>.

Unsworth, John (2000). "Scholarly Primitives: What Methods Do Humanities Researchers Have in Common, and How Might Our Tools Reflect This?" *Humanities Computing: Formal Methods, Experimental Practice*. A symposium sponsored by King's College, London, May 13, 2000. <http://www.iath.virginia.edu/~jmu2m/Kings.5-00/primitives.html>.

30
Practice and Preservation – Format Issues
Marc Bragdon, Alan Burk, Lisa Charlong, and Jason Nugent

Introduction

Text analyses, project collaborations, and the myriad other research activities of humanities computing center largely on the use of artifacts in various digital formats. As containers through which content is engaged and transformed, these formats are currencies for scholarly trade. They must inspire confidence, evidenced by broad use, in their ability to meet present and future research needs. To each format its purpose, though, regardless of respective uses, they must meet common criteria to be considered appropriate to a given task. Not surprisingly, these criteria are very much identified with standard application support. Community and cross-community use of artifacts, and the long-term preservation of digital content, demand of formats a high level of interoperability across platforms and applications as well as the sort of version compatibility identified with industry-based standards.

The formats discussed herein – eXtensible Markup Language (XML), Portable Document Format (PDF), Tagged Image File Format (TIFF), Joint Photographic Experts Group (JPEG), and JPEG 2000 – are all either de facto or emerging standards for formatting many of the digital objects employed in humanities computing research. Each is discussed in light of their facility in promoting associated discipline goals.

XML is a file format used by many humanist researchers and scholars for the creation, description, and exchange of textual materials. While use of XML is often in the areas of text description, text analysis, and processing, XML is also used for methods of storing or preserving texts. It is this point, XML as a text storage or archival format, which is the focus of XML in this chapter.

Unlike XML, PDF and PDF/A are not formats that digital humanists normally employ for capturing and distributing literary texts or other genres. Still, examining the strengths and weaknesses of PDF is important because of its prevalence on the web and for assessing its place relative to the use of other formats for digital humanities.

TIFF and JPEG are the de facto standards for digitally representing visual matter – the former for preservation and the latter for access enablement. JPEG 2000 is an emerging standard that strives to combine the richness of TIFF with the portability of JPEG to create a single standard that accommodates multiple purposes on multiple platforms.

XML

Discussion about XML as a file format for preservation generally refers to two distinct yet overlapping contexts: XML as a file format for describing text and XML as a format and mechanism for describing information *about* that text or *metadata*. Both contexts are addressed in this section.

Before discussing preservation and XML as a preservation file format, it may be useful to look at XML's predecessor, SGML, as well as the syntax and general principles within each language. SGML (SGML, ISO 8879:1986) is a descendant of Generalized Markup Language (GML), developed in the 1960s at IBM by Charles Goldfarb, Edward Mosher, and Raymond Lorie. A fundamental feature of GML was its separation of a document's *structure* from its *presentation*. In word processing software, for example, a text's structure, such as title, paragraphs, and bibliography, is implicitly recognized through presentation styles. Titles are generally separated from paragraphs with line breaks as well as font style and size. In descriptive markup such as SGML and, later, XML, textual elements such as titles are marked or encoded *as* titles. Any presentation information is separated from the document and is expressed in a stylesheet using Cascading Style Sheets (CSS) or eXtensible Stylesheet Language (XSL), to name but two. In focusing on structure and semantics and not formatting, XML enables re-purposing of texts to multiple output scenarios. For example, one XML text can be converted to PDF for printing or distributing over the web in HTML. In the same way, a bibliography encoded using XML can be presented according to a number of different styles of documenting sources. The original XML does not change; a different stylesheet is applied for different purposes or audiences.

SGML is not a markup language in itself but is instead "meta" language used for defining markup languages such as Text Encoding Initiative (TEI) and Hypertext Markup Language (HTML). User communities such as the TEI define sets of tags based on user needs as well as guidelines for using those tags. Tags are declared and described in Document Type Definitions or DTDs, a second distinct feature of SGML besides descriptive markup. By introducing the concept of a document *type*, texts can be more easily processed and checked for errors in structural descriptions. A program called a *parser* checks the validity of a document or document instance against the definition of the document's structure as defined in the DTD. A third feature of SGML essential for preservation, character entities and data independence, or data that is not tied to proprietary software, will be examined later.

XML is a simplified subset of SGML. Like SGML, XML's primary purpose is to facilitate the description and sharing of data across different systems and across the web. It has some of the same features of SGML. However, where SGML requires that structured documents reference a DTD to be "valid," XML allows for "well-formed" data and can be delivered without a DTD. With XML new associated standards evolved, such as XML Schema and associated technologies including: XSL, XML Linking Language (XLink) for creating hyperlinks in XML texts, XML Path Language (XPath) for addressing points in an XML document, and XML Pointer Language (XPointer) which allows XLink hyperlinks to point to more specific parts in the XML document. It is outside the scope of this chapter to go into these technologies and their associated parts in detail here. For more information on the status, use, and development of these technologies see the World Wide Web Consortium (W3C) (<www.w3c.org>). However, it may be useful to describe the differences between a DTD and Schema. It is also useful to identify the consistent mechanisms or conventions that SGML and XML use to encode or mark up various textual features or units.

Here is an example of poetry, "Every Man In His Humour," expressed using TEI Lite. For those unfamiliar with TEI Lite, it is manageable subset of the full TEI encoding scheme. (See Cummings, Chapter 25, THE TEXT ENCODING INITIATIVE AND THE STUDY OF LITERATURE, in this volume.) The example is taken from the working files of *The Cambridge Edition of the Works of Ben Jonson*:

```
<div1 id="f5104-005-d101" type="prologue">
  <stage id="f5104-005-st01" type="business">
  <hi>After the second sounding</hi>.</stage>
  <stage id="f5104-005-st02" type="character">ENVIE.</stage>
  <stage id="f5104-005-st03" type="entrance">
  <hi>Arising in the<lb/>midst of the<lb/>stage</hi>.</stage>
  <sp id="f5104-005-sp01" rend="speech">
    <p id="f5104-005-p01" rend="para">
    <figure entity="fig104-005-2" rend="inline"/>
    </p>
    <l id="f5104-005-vl01" rend="verseline">
      <app id="f5104-005-ap01">
        <rdg wit="gr01" type="variant"><orig reg="Light">
        Ight</orig>, I salute thee; but with wounded nerues:</rdg>
        <rdg wit="gr02" type="variant"><orig reg="Light">
        Ight</orig>, I salute thee, but with wounded nerues:</rdg>
      </app>
    </l>
```

```
<l  id="f5104-005-vl02"  rend="verseline">Wishing  thy  golden
splendor, pitchy <orig reg="darknesse">dark-</orig>
</l>
<l id="f5104-005-vl03" rend="verseline">
. . . </sp>
. . .
</div1>
```

In this example the following textual structures are encoded: a division <div1>, a stage direction <stage>, graphically distinct text <hi>, speeches <sp>, paragraphs <p>, verse lines <l>, critical apparatus <app>, and readings within textual variations <rdg>. Each of these structures is called an "element," demarcated by start tags and end tags using angle brackets. The above example also shows that elements can be further described using "attributes." For example, the <stage> element can take the attribute "character" or "entrance" and if one of the goals of text encoding is to express the structural reality of a text, using attributes enables a granular description of a number of properties of particular elements.

The element <div> has a declaration in the DTD that lists elements and attributes that the <div> element can contain as well as their relationship to one another. The syntax used in DTDs is not XML. XML Schemas, on the other hand, are expressed in XML grammar. One of the most significant differences between XSD and DTDs is that a Schema is expressed using XML syntax whereas a DTD uses an entirely different grammar. In addition, XSD has the capability to create and use data types in conjunction with element and attribute declarations. A date like: "08-11-2004" can be interpreted as the 8th of November. However, an XML element with this data type <date type="date">2004-08-11</date> enables an agreed-on understanding of the content, because the XML data type "date" requires the format "YYYY-MM-DD."

No matter what the preservation strategy employed by scholars or institutions, a cornerstone of that strategy should be the reliance on standard and open file formats. As was mentioned in the introduction, formats should also be backward compatible in their versions, enjoy widespread use, encourage interoperability, and lead to a range of platform- and device-independent applications that use the format.

XML is an ideal file format in each of these respects and is used by many literary scholars in text creation, preservation, and interchange. It is an open standard, supported by the World Wide Web Consortium as well as by community-led standards, such as the TEI and HTML. It is also portable and non-proprietary. All XML documents, whatever language or writing system they employ, use the same underlying character encoding, known as Unicode. Texts can move from one hardware and software environment to another without loss of information, and because XML is stored in plain text files it is not tied to any proprietary software. Finally, XML documents are self-describing and human readable, as evident in the Jonson example. These are XML's most significant strengths in a preservation and storage context.

A large number of digital projects and collections transform propriety formats to XML for both text processing and preservation purposes. One project at the University of New Brunswick, *The Atlantic Canada Virtual Archives* (<http://atlanticportal. hil.unb.ca/>), has developed a series of scripts that converts texts in word processing formats to TEI XML. The XML is then stored in a MySQL database and is transformed to HTML using XSL on the fly for web distribution. For this or other digital projects at UNB, XML-based tools are used for editing, transformations, indexing, and searching.

In addition to the factors listed above, long-term stability of any file format should be assessed in terms of metadata support. Metadata can have enormous value both during the subsequent active use of the data and for long-term preservation, where it can provide information on both the provenance and technical characteristics of the data. Many text-focused XML applications such as HTML, TEI, and DocBook have metadata elements as central components of their markup tag sets. In the case of TEI, the metadata element set in the TEI Header is robust, as seen in Cummings, Chapter 25, THE TEXT ENCODING INITIATIVE AND THE STUDY OF LITERATURE, in this volume. In others, such as HTML, it is less so.

There are metadata applications that have been developed expressly for preservation such as the Metadata Encoding & Transmission Standard (METS) and the Dublin Core Metadata Initiative (DCMI), expressed in XML. The Encoded Archival Description (EAD) is another XML-based metadata application, describing the structure(s) of archival finding aids. METS is a flexible XML framework designed for storing administrative, structural, and descriptive metadata about digital objects. In addition to encapsulating the metadata itself, the framework provides elements for describing the relationship among the metadata and the pieces of the complex objects. In short, it is an XML-based container for all types of metadata, for the relationships among them and the objects they are about, and for the behaviors associated with the objects.

The Modernist Journals Project at Brown University (<http://dl.lib.brown. edu:8080/exist/mjp/index.xml>) recently moved to a metadata-driven architecture, employing METS to describe its digital serials. The full architecture includes storage of text files in TEI XML, and use of the Metadata Object Description Schema (MODS) for encoding bibliographic elements for each resource as well as the Metadata Authority Description Schema (MADS) for describing named authorities. The Berkeley Art Museum and Pacific Film Archive (<http://www.bampfa.berkeley. edu/>) has developed a software tool that has as one of its primary functions, the ability to export EAD and METS XML documents that include metadata about museum collections. The California Digital Library (<http://www.cdlib.org/>) has developed a simple content management system that is based on METS. There are four profiles of METS in production: EAD finding aids, simple image objects extracted from EAD, and two profiles of TEI text objects.

In terms of limitations for using XML as a preservation file format, some would say XML applications are too time-consuming or complicated, especially where deep, granular encoding is required. However, a number of tools and initiatives are available today to lessen the complexity of using XML. A second limitation is with regards to presentation. While XML describes the structural and semantic aspects of a text, its ability to represent the physical appearance of a text is more challenging. For this reason, a number of collections and repositories choose to store an XML copy of a text for preservation and processing as well as a PDF or other image-based version for physical presentation and printing.

Portable Document Format (PDF)

PDF texts are ubiquitous in the web environment. Just about everyone who frequents the web has used Adobe's Acrobat Reader or a web plug-in to display a PDF text and has probably employed one of a number of utilities to convert documents to PDF. PDF is a format for the capture, display, and now, through a version of PDF known as PDF/A, the preservation of texts. PDF/A is a recently published International Standards Organization (ISO) standard, ISO 19005-1. However, unlike XML, TIFF, and some other open formats, PDF and PDF/A are not formats that digital humanists normally employ for capturing and distributing literary texts or other genres. Some humanities scholarly journals published electronically and large text repositories may be the exception. But, these initiatives tend to be associated more with the digital library and publishing communities than with digital humanities. Still, understanding the strengths and weaknesses of PDF is important if for no other reasons than its prevalence on the web and gauging its place relative to the use of other more accepted formats for digital humanities. Some digital humanities applications may warrant the use of PDF and several of these applications will be looked at in this chapter segment. For the purposes of this discussion of the PDF format, the term "text" is being used in a broad sense to include images and texts as both simple and complex documents, comprised of text and other media objects. The term "document" is used interchangeably with "text."

The PDF format was developed by Adobe in the early 1990s in order to solve the fundamental problem of communicating texts and other visual material between different computer operating systems and applications. At that time, there was no common way of viewing these electronic resources across different computer hardware. In developing the PDF format, Abobe based it on their already released PostScript language, a hardware-independent page description language for printing (Warnock 1991). By Adobe's estimates, there are currently greater than 200 million PDF documents available on the web, and since its release, users have downloaded over 500 million copies of the company's free PDF Acrobat Reader. PDF is an open format by virtue of its published specification, *PDF Reference: Adobe Portable Document Format Version 1.6* (Adobe 2005). This Specification provides the necessary information for understanding and interpreting the format and for building PDF applications and plug-ins. Adobe allows the creation of applications that read, write, and transform PDF files and makes use of certain of its patents for this purpose royalty free.

However, PDF is not completely open. Adobe authors the specification and decides what will go into each release, including functionality of the format.

PDF is a complex but versatile format. A PDF document is comprised of one file, yet that file may be any document from a simple one-page text to a multi-part text, comprised of chapters and other segments, along with a range of fonts, images, and other subordinate digital objects. Using one of Adobe's proprietary editors it is relatively easy to transform a mixed set of digital objects, including images and texts, into one document of properly arranged segments, such as an image appearing in the upper right-hand corner of the first page of a text. PDF also currently supports interactive features, such as hyperlinks, and the inclusion of metadata and XML markup for describing document structure, semantics, and layout. A PDF file may be either image or character based. For example, a book may be scanned, producing a series of TIFF images. These images can then be transformed into PDF images and wrapped into one document. Like TIFF or any other image format, individual characters are neither differentiated nor encoded in image PDF. This means that the text cannot be manipulated or even searched unless optical character recognition is first applied to the document. A PDF document can also be text where the text is defined by such properties as character strings, font, and point size. In theory PDF text documents can be transformed into character-based formats such as Word, HTML, or ASCII. In reality, given the design of PDF, a transformation may not be completely accurate in character representation or layout. This can be problematic in situations where it is necessary to deconstruct a PDF text for machine analysis or for other purposes, including editing.

Given the large amount of digital information being web published each year, a number of organizations with publishing and preservation mandates, such as electronic publishers, government departments, and libraries, are employing PDF as a storage, archival, and presentation format. A Berkeley information science research project looking at the information explosion estimates that on a yearly basis upwards of 1,986,000 terabytes of new information is being stored on hard disks alone (UC Berkeley 2003). In this ever-expanding web environment, PDF offers, in addition to being an extremely portable format, an easy and inexpensive solution to publishing extremely large numbers of texts. In the 1990s, many were dismissive of PDF as a proprietary, complex format and one that was unsuitable for purposes of long-term preservation. But, the format has evolved with the development of PDF/A for document preservation, as has PDF software for rendering and creating PDF documents, including editors, readers, and browser plug-ins.

Most digital humanists are working on relatively contained, focused research projects that require limited digitization of source materials, not on massive digitization projects, which cry out for the use of a format supporting low production costs. Digital humanists are instead focusing on formats that are open, promote information interchange, textual analysis and interpretation, and the preservation of electronic texts. PDF supports all these desiderata but only to a limited degree. PDF is a proprietary format but with an open specification. However, the specification is complex and, unlike XML, the PDF code is not human readable. PDF supports information interchange by being device independent and having an open metadata protocol. PDF/A may in the future provide a practical, standards-based preservation path once the necessary conversion applications are developed and become available. PDF texts can be used with some text analysis tools once the PDF text is extracted into an ASCII format. Nevertheless, the format will see limited use in the future by digital humanities centers and digital humanists for building and publishing electronic literary collections. This is in light of the strengths of XML and the image formats TIFF and JPG2000 and the relatively small numbers of texts being digitized by digital humanists, which allow a more labor-intensive approach to text creation. However, PDF may be used by humanists as a secondary and supplementary approach to distributing and rendering texts in a collection.

The interplay between PDF and more accepted formats for digital humanities are explored briefly in the two case studies below.

Early Canadiana Online (ECO) (<http://www.canadiana.org/eco.php?doc= home>): ECO is a large Canadian digital library project with over two million pages scanned in a 1-bit compressed TIFF format. The images were originally scanned from Canadian heritage materials on microfiche, dating from the sixteenth up to the early twentieth century. ECO includes a number of literary texts. Because the source material for this project was microfiche or photographic images, project administrators needed to develop a cost-effective approach to making the texts highly searchable, both within the text and bibliographically, at a work level. One approach would have been to make accurate transcriptions of the texts but the cost was prohibitive, given the number of pages involved. As an alternative, optical character recognition software was used to automatically scan the texts and create searchable texts. The OCR text was found to be approximately 90% free of errors or have a 90% confidence level. Because the OCR texts were to be used only for searching and the costs of correcting the OCR were not affordable within the parameters of the project, the OCR was left uncorrected and not published. It was used only for creating indexes for searching. Metadata was also created for searching at a work level. Once a licensed ECO user selects a text for viewing through the ECO interface, he or she has the choice of retrieving any of its pages in GIF, in image PDF, or retrieving the entire volume in PDF. The PDF for a page or volume and the GIF page images are created on the fly for delivery to the desktop. The GIF images are converted from the archival TIFF images, using an open-source utility. There are a number of these image conversion utilities available. ImageMagick (<http://netpbm.sourceforge.net/>) is one that is widely used, an open-source software suite for editing images and converting them to any of approximately 100 formats, including PDF, GIF, JPEG, JPEG 2000, PNG, PhotoCD, and Tiff. ImageMagick runs on most operating systems. For converting the TIFF images to image PDF, ECO employs a series of filters for UNIX. In the process, the requested TIFF images are converted to PBM or the Portable Bitmap Format, then in turn to PostScript and finally to PDF, with PDF providing a cost-effective way of delivering electronic volume surrogates to the desktop. The Acrobat reader plug-in for browsers offers extra functionality, such as the ability to navigate pages within a multi-page work and for increasing or decreasing the size of a page or pages. This functionality can also be provided for the delivery of TIFF or JPEG images, but this necessitates server-side programming.

Digital humanities initiatives focusing on different editions of a single work or on a much smaller number of works than ECO in all likelihood would employ XML and XSLT to deliver in XHTML pages and volumes to the desktop. In such applications, if there were no acceptable electronic versions of the works in a text format, this would call for making accurate transcriptions of the original texts and then adding markup to a predetermined level in TEI. But, these projects could, with little additional overhead, offer readers a choice of XHTML or PDF. PDF would give readers a facsimile of the original work and the ability to size and navigate through the text.

PDF and Humanities Scholarly Journal Publishing: The digital world is opening up rich possibilities for scholarly journal publishing. These include reaching a larger, worldwide audience for print journals struggling with declining print subscriptions; by reducing production costs, allowing journals to move to an open-access model of publishing; and, offering new publishing models, like the use of citation linking, incorporation of multimedia into articles, and providing rich searching across aggregations of journals. Many journals in the humanities are small operations, cash strapped and struggling with their evolution to the electronic. Editors realize that if their journals are to survive, they will need a digital presence. To assist editors and publishers in this transformation process, there is a wide range of open source software available, from journal-specific DTDs, such as the Journal Publishing Document Type Definition (<http://dtd.nlm.nih.gov/publishing/>), developed by the National Library of Medicine, to complete systems for the management, distribution, and archiving of journals, for example the Open Journal Systems (OJS) (<http://pkp.sfu.ca/?q=ojs>) and the Digital Publishing System (DPuBS) (<http://dpubs.org/>). OJS, one example of an open source solution to journal publishing, currently has 550 installations worldwide. OJS is part of a wider initiative known as the Public Knowledge Project and is a collaborative research and development project by the University of British Columbia, the Canadian Center for Studies in Publishing, and the Simon Fraser University Library. The software allows journal editors with minimal technical support to customize the look of their journal and to configure and manage the peer review process, online submission and management of the content. OJS also provides a number of services, basic Dublin Core (<http://dublincore.org/>) metadata, full text article searching, and reading tools. Like DPuBS and other similar packages, OJS does have a limitation. The journal management system does not provide the software necessary to transform word processing files into HTML or PDF for web delivery. That processing is left to the layout editor to do outside the system. PDF rather than HTML appears to be the format of choice for a large proportion of the journals which are employing OJS or a similar system. It is extremely easy to convert from an article in, say, Word to PDF, proof the result, and then upload it into OJS. A majority of these journals do not have the necessary expertise or financial support to invoke a production cycle using XML as opposed to PDF.

Journal publishing in PDF does have its drawbacks. PDF is an excellent format for print on demand or for rendering a text on a screen in a print layout. It is much less amenable to supporting new publishing models that are taking advantage of the possibilities of the electronic medium. PDF does support hyperlinks and there are some journals that use this feature. PDF also allows incorporating multimedia, such as video and sound, into an article, but these features are not often employed in scholarly journals because of the extra overhead involved. There are also concerns about the PDF generated by Acrobat and by other conversion tools as a preservation format. PDF/A theoretically addresses this problem but PDF/A will not be widely adopted until there are the utilities necessary for efficiently transforming documents and images into PDF/A.

There are options open to humanities journals for managing and distributing a journal in PDF other than establishing a self-managed local site with an OJS or DPubS implementation behind it. A scholarly communication initiative at the University of New Brunswick is one example. This multi-million-dollar research publishing project is part of a larger Pan-Canadian initiative known as Synergies (<http://www.synergies.umontreal.ca/>). It is being funded by the Canada Innovation Fund (<http://dtd.nlm.nih.gov/publishing/>). For this project, five institutions, along with fifteen partner institutions, will be establishing five regional publishing and research nodes across Canada for scholarly journals and other forms of scholarly communication in the humanities and social sciences. The nodes will feed the research texts and data produced at these nodes into a national distribution portal. The purpose of the initiative is ambitious, to effect on a national scale a transformation of scholarly publishing in the humanities and social sciences from print to digital.

Like a number of initiatives, such as Project Muse (<http://muse.jhu.edu/>), Euclid (<http://projecteuclid.org/Dienst/UI/1.0/Home>), and Erudit (<http://www.erudit.org/>), the Electronic Text Centre at the University of New Brunswick offers a range of electronic publishing services to journal editors, primarily, in the humanities. One aspect of its publishing efforts is the production and delivery of back files of journal articles. Many of these retrospective issues do not have surviving digital copies. This presents challenges. Echoing the situation of Early Canadiana Online, neither the Centre nor the journals is in the financial position to produce accurate, marked-up transcriptions of the print copies to support delivery of XHTML to users and for full text searching.

The Centre's approach to a solution is two-fold, to build XML files for search purposes and PDF for document delivery. The production process begins with scanning the original print issues and converting articles and other contributions to PDF, employing a flatbed scanner with built-in conversion software. The resulting PDF documents are then run through an optical character recognition package. The uncorrected OCR is marked up in an established XML document structure or DTD developed by the Érudit publishing consortium. This is used for encoding an article's basic structure along with extensive, journal-specific metadata. The XML files are then used to build within an Open Journals System or OJS implementation search indices for searching metadata elements, such as <title>, <author>, and which describe the articles and for searching full text within multiple issues and journals. Employing scripts, the metadata and structured content is extracted and uploaded into OJS. Currently, a full text search will only take readers to the start of an article and not to a page or line. However, the XML markup performed on the OCR could provide that capability in the future.

This approach of combining uncorrected OCR with an image-based format, like image PDF, has several advantages over PDF alone for large collections of print texts. Full search capability is one benefit, and this has been discussed. The other is preservation. A very simple XML encoding scheme can be used to mark up an OCR text's basic structure, including, for example, Sections, Pages, and Paragraphs. This encoded content combined with a metadata header into one XML file provides valuable archiving and preservation information to accompany the image PDF file. The files can then be bundled together and archived in a repository, whether it be a trusted institutional repository based at a university, a LOCKSS (Lots Of Copies Keep Stuff Safe) (<http://www.lockss.org/lockss/Home>) solution, or a repository service like Portico (<http://www.portico.org/about/>).

TIFF and JPEG

In building digital still images, one tries to match and, in some cases, exceed the functionality afforded by analog. The first step is to assess source characteristics – color, detail, and dimensions – and then weigh mapping options for output to target media. Since media ultimately drive benchmarks for output, working with formats has everything to do with striking the right balance between fidelity and portability. This often means generating files in a number of formats to represent a single document since media – and uses – will differ.

Digital image formats are distinguished principally by: (1) how they represent color, detail, and size, and (2) application support. Choice of formats depends on understanding how these factors bear on particular image management scenarios. Using a combination of encoding and compression techniques, digital image formats bend visual matter to particular purposes. Though purposes may differ, the imperative for standard application support is universal. Standards ensure mobility, and mobility is everything to a digital object. The more applications that support a given format, the more likely will its content be usable now and in the future.

TIFF

For over a decade now, the Tagged Image File Format (TIFF) has been the de facto standard for producing photographic-quality digital image master files. TIFF was developed in the middle of the 1980s by the document imaging industry in a successful bid to develop a common standard for desktop scanning. It is perhaps the most widely supported format for image processing applications across platforms – whether Windows, Mac, or UNIX. TIFF offers exhaustive color support (up to 64 bit) and supports a variety of standard color working spaces in both RGB and CMYK varieties.

TIFF is the format of choice for creating preservation-quality digital master files true to the original document's color, detail, and dimensions. Detail-intensive optical character recognition and high-quality printing applications often require source documents in TIFF format in order to function optimally. When storage space is not an issue, uncompressed TIFFs are the best choice for archiving to long-term storage media.

Image compression: Compression techniques run the full range of the fidelity–portability spectrum. These are algorithmic processes whereby images are transformed and bundled for optimum portability. Compression works by detecting what it considers either irrelevant or redundant data patterns and then expresses them more efficiently via mathematical formulae. Compression techniques come in lossless or lossy varieties, the latter amounting to better space savings. While there is a compression option for TIFF (the notorious patented LZW compression process usually identified with GIF), preservation imperatives and document characteristics limit the use of compression in TIFF to documents with minimal tonal variance.

Another strength of TIFF, particularly for long-term preservation, is its header option. The TIFF header accommodates technical, structural, and descriptive metadata about the component image and provides some flexibility in their elaboration. Encoded in ASCII format, TIFF header metadata is potentially useful in providing a record of conversion decisions specific to the image. While certain technical data fields are required for baseline processing, there are provisions for creating custom tags (courtesy of its Image File Directory framework) for project- or institution-specific purposes. Application support for editing headers is not extensive, however, particularly when generating tags that fall outside the standard.

While application support for reading and writing TIFF is extensive, actual manipulation – especially in batches – demands higher-end processing and memory capacities. File sizes, especially for larger items with extensive color information and detail, can climb into the several Gigabytes. TIFF files do, however, work well as authoritative sources from which any number of purpose-specific surrogates can be derived. For example, they often act as master files for web delivery where monitor, processing, and bandwidth constraints necessitate less discriminating encoding and compression techniques.

JPEG

JPEG is a popular standard for transforming source files into portable, photographic-quality images for networked applications. Strictly speaking, JPEG is a compression technique upon which a format is based. Around the time TIFF was standardized, a consortium of photographic industry players, known collectively as the Joint Photographic Experts Group, developed the JPEG compression standard (and corresponding JFIF–Jpeg File Interchange Format) for use in photographic digital image production and interchange.

JPEG's lossy compression employs an irrelevancy reduction algorithm based on the characteristics of human visual perception. Since brightness is more important than color in determining visibility, JPEG focuses its compression on the color aspects of an image. Building a JPEG image is a three-part process beginning with a lossless mathematical transformation known as Discrete Cosine Transform (DCT) and a subsequent compression process known as quantization. Together they simplify and round an image's color values in 8×8 pixel blocks. The higher the desired output quality, the less simplification and rounding are applied, and the less blockiness (visible boundaries between 8×8 blocks) is introduced in the output.

JPEG is important primarily for delivering images over the web, for previewing master files, and for printing at lower sizes and resolutions. It supports 24-bit color depth, which is more than adequate in preserving important color information in a photographic image. Since some detail is bound to be lost in translating images for network delivery and monitor display, JPEG's tremendous space-saving transformations offer an acceptable compromise between image fidelity and network portability. Software support for writing and reading JPEG is near universal.

Evolving technologies, expanding promise: JPEG 2000: As bandwidth, processing power, and network delivery models evolve, so too do demands for suitable digital formats. Less encumbered by technical limitations, developers and end users alike are very interested in image coding systems that suit multiple purposes and can combine rather than just balance fidelity and portability.

The JPEG 2000 compression standard is JPEG's effort to create such a coding system. The main motivator for a new standard was a desire to accommodate a much broader range of image data types with different color, resolution, and dimensional characteristics (such as medical, scientific, remote sensing, text, etc.) and to incorporate several delivery models (client/server, real-time transmission, image archiving, limited buffer and bandwidth resources, etc.) under a single system.

JPEG 2000 relies on wavelet compression technology to produce high-quality, scalable output. Wavelet-based compression transforms images into continuous waves or signals. The waves are iteratively decomposed into simplified versions by averaging the distances between adjacent points of the wave along a plotted median. The result is a multi-resolved image. JPEG 2000's wavelet transformations are applied to individual tiles or blocks, the sizes of which are largely user-defined. Tiling reduces memory load and can be used for later decoding sections rather than an entire image.

All the information necessary to reconstruct the original is efficiently stored in the image.

A crucial side effect to JPEG 2000's implementation of the wave transform process is that progressive decomposition in the forward transform allows for progressive display in the inverse. The parsable bit stream and file format allow regions, resolution levels, quality layers, color channels, or combinations of these to be extracted from a master file *without* having to decode the entire file.

In decompressing a single image, one can have it either grow in size or increase in specific detail without necessarily affecting bit transfer rates. A full color map, for example, measuring one meter in height by two meters in length, at a resolution of 300 dots per inch (dpi), could exceed sizes of 75 Gigabytes in uncompressed TIFF format. The resultant high-fidelity image may be excellent for archival purposes, but is practically useless for real-time processing. Though a JPEG 2000 version will still be of little practical use and may only halve storage requirements at similar resolution, a server-side extraction process could deliver a monitor-ready full image sample at 800×600 dpi that takes up no more than a few Megabytes, and then build incrementally higher resolution data for zooming in on or panning across image regions, all the while maintaining constant image transfer and display sizes.

The implications of progressive transformation for image use and management are compelling. From an end-user standpoint, content previously unsuitable for network and computing environments is easily manipulated. From an archival perspective, JPEG 2000's capacity for selective transformation would enable detailed study without risk of damaging fragile originals. The key advantage from a workflow perspective is that target bit rates/sizes need not be specified at the time of compression. Optimized master files can serve as the basis for thumbnails, real-time web versions, archival versions, and print masters.

JPEG 2000 also offers interesting encoding options that afford a good deal of control over the compression process. One can single out regions of interest (ROI) for special handling during the decomposition process, so that areas of particular concern are not subject to as much transformation. In the case of progressive image transmission, such regions can be transmitted at a higher priority. The process can amount to significant space savings for applications where storage is at a premium.

All features discussed above are part of the baseline JPEG 2000 implementation, known as Part 1. Parts 2 and 3, currently in use but still under development, provide support for basic and advanced forms of image metadata, including intellectual property rights, embedded full-text (in either XML or PDF), audio files, etc. They include advanced color profiling options, and there are plans for a moving image implementation for Part 3. Coupled with the control JPEG 2000 affords over encoding and decoding, the advanced management features of Parts 2 and 3 could effect significant changes in how images are described, stored, and transmitted in the near future.

Reality check: Does JPEG 2000 sound too good to be true? Then it probably is – for now. Though an ISO standard since 2000, application support for JPEG 2000 is limited. Its inherent features and functionality mean little if software to encode them is not readily available.

For web delivery, JPEG 2000 requires special software on the server side (and, depending on the implementation, on the client side as well) to manipulate files. To date, there are no standard delivery mechanisms or open source tools to facilitate networked manipulation. Built on an open architecture, the JPEG 2000 development model encourages specialized development efforts that optimize the system for different image types and applications. But the development process, inclusive as it may be, is very slow and the resultant applications do not necessarily implement all features, nor do they implement features in the same manner.

To further complicate matters, Parts 2 and 3 contain patented technologies that may prohibit implementation except under very specialized circumstances. Ironically, although standards with patented and/or proprietary technologies are potential barriers to interoperability and to the temporal mobility one associates with preservation imperatives, commercial interest and accompanying investments are often sufficient to deliver impressive application support. With sufficient industry buy-in, such standards as Adobe's PDF can overtake well-intentioned rivals to become a preferred receptacle for serving certain digital ends.

Evidently there are standards, and then there are *standards*. For now, TIFF remains the standard format for photograph-quality master images and will still require post-processing transformation to other formats, including JPEG, for specialized delivery purposes. JPEG 2000 will likely continue to develop and expand in use as applications exploit the format's potential. Cautious adopters will not want to throw away their TIFFs just yet, as the appeal of any format rests as much on buy-in – the sine qua non of portability – as it does on functionality.

REFERENCES AND FURTHER READING

Acharya, Tinky, and Ping-Sing Tsai (2005). *JPEG 2000 Standard for Image Compression: Concepts, Algorithms, and VLSI Architectures*. Hoboken, NJ: Wiley-Interscience. <http://proxy.hil.unb.ca/login?url=http://site.ebrary.com/lib/unblib/Doc?id=10114023>. Accessed June 12, 2006.

Adams, Michael David (1998). *Reversible Wavelet Transforms and Their Application to Embedded Image Compression*. MSc. Thesis. The University of Victoria Department of Electrical and Computer Engineering website. <http://www.ece.uvic.ca/~mdadams/publications/mascthesis.pdf>. Accessed May 22, 2006.

Adobe Developers Association. *TIFF Revision 6.0*. <http://partners.adobe.com/public/developer/en/tiff/TIFF6.pdf>. Accessed May 12, 2006.

Adobe Systems Incorporated (2005). *PDF Reference: Adobe Portable Document Format Version 1.6*, 5th edn. Adobe Systems Incorporated. <http://partners.adobe.com/public/developer/en/pdf/PDFReference16.pdf>.

Anderson, Richard et al. (2005). "The AIHT at Stanford University Automated Preservation Assessment of Heterogeneous Digital Collections." *D-Lib Magazine* 11.12 (December). <http://www.dlib.org/dlib/december05/

johnson/12johnson.html>. Accessed June 8, 2006.

Brown, Adrian. Digital Archives Analyst, Digital Preservation Guidance Note 1: Selecting file formats for long-term preservation. The National Archives (2003) The National Archives of England, Wales and the United Kingdom. <http://www.nationalarchives.gov.uk/docu ments/selecting_file_formats.rtf>. Accessed June 1, 2006.

Boucheron, Laura E., and Charles D. Creusere (2005). "Lossless Wavelet-based Compression of Digital Elevation Maps for Fast and Efficient Search and Retrieval." *IEEE Transaction of Geoscience and Remote Sensing* 43.5: 1210–14.

Clark, James (1997). World Wide Web Consortium. *Comparison of SGML and XML. World Wide Web Consortium Note 15-December-1997.* <http://www.w3.org/TR/NOTE-sgml-xml-971215>.

Cornell University Department of Preservation and Conservation. *Digital Preservation Management – Implementing Short-term Strategies for Long-term Problems.* <http://www.library.cornell.edu/iris/tutorial/dpm/index.html>. Accessed June 1, 2006.

Cornell University Library (2003). *Digital Preservation Management. Obsolescence: File Formats and Software.* <http://www.library.cornell.edu/iris/tutorial/dpm/oldmedia/obsolescence1.html>. Accessed June 19, 2006.

Cover Pages (2002). *Standard Generalized Markup Language (SGML). SGML and XML as (Meta-) Markup Languages.* <http://xml.coverpages.org/sgml.html)>. Accessed June 17, 2006.

Janosky, James S., and Rutherford W. Witthums (2003). *Using JPEG 2000 for Enhanced Preservation and Web Access of Digital Archives – A Case Study.* Accessed from The University of Connecticut Libraries website: <http://charlesolson.uconn.edu/Works_in_the_Collection/Melville_Project/IST_Paper3.pdf>.

Kenney, Anne R., and Stephen Chapman (1995). *Tutorial: Digital Resolution Requirements for Replacing Text-Based Material: Methods for Benchmarking Image Quality.* Council on Library and Information Resources.

——, and Oya Y. Rieger (2000). *Moving Theory into Practice: Digital Imaging for Libraries and Archives.* Research Libraries Group, Mountain View, California.

LeFurgy, William G. (2003). "PDF/A: Developing a File Format for Long-term Preservation." *RGL DigiNews* 7.6 (December 15). <http://www.rlg.org/preserv/diginews/v7_n6_feature1.html#congress>. Accessed June 25, 2006.

Padova, Ted (2005). *Adobe Acrobat 7 PDF Bible.* Indianapolis: Wiley Publishing, Inc.

Technical Committee ISO/TC 171 (2005). *Document Management – Electronic Document File Format for Long-term Preservation – Part 1: Use of PDF 1.4 (PDF/A-1).* Geneva: ISO.

Text Encoding Guidelines (TEI) to Document Creation and Interchange. "A Gentle Introduction to XML." <http://www.tei-c.org/P4X/SG.html>. Accessed June 19, 2006.

Ramesh, Neelamani, RicardoDe Queiroz, Zhigang Fan, Sanjeeb Dash, and Richard G. Baraniuk (2006). "JPEG Compression History Estimation for Color Images." *IEEE Transactions on Image Processing* 15.6: 1365–78.

UC Berkeley, School of Information Management and Systems (2003). Website: *How Much Information? 2003 – Executive Summary.* <http://www2.sims.berkeley.edu/research/projects/how-much-info-2003/execsum.htm>. Accessed July 2006.

Van Horik, Rene (2004). "Image Formats, Practical Experiences." *ERPANET Training File Formats for Preservation*, Vienna, May 10–11, 2004. <http://www.erpanet.org/events/2004/vienna/presentations/erpaTrainingVienna_Horik.ppt>. Accessed June 11, 2006.

Walker, F., and G. Thomas (2005). "Image Preservation through PDF/A." *Proceedings of IS&T's 2005 Archiving Conference.* Washington, DC, pp. 259–63. <docmorph.nlm.nih.gov/docmorph/publicationsmymorph.htm>.

Warnock, John (1991). White Paper: *The Camelot Project. Adobe Systems Incorporated.* <http://www.planetpdf.com/planetpdf/pdfs/warnock_camelot.pdf>. Accessed April 20, 2006.

About Referenced Standards

DocBook   <http://www.docbook.org/>.

EAD   <http://www.loc.gov/ead/>.

JPEG   <http://www.jpeg.org/>.

JPEG 2000   <http://www.jpeg.org/jpeg2000/>.

MADS   <http://www.loc.gov/standards/mads/>.

METS   <http://www.loc.gov/standards/mets/>.

MODS   <http://www.loc.gov/standards/mods/>.

PDF/A   <http://www.digitalpreservation.gov/formats/fdd/fdd000125.shtml>.

TEI   <http://www.tei-c.org/>.

TIFF   <http://home.earthlink.net/~ritter/tiff/>.

XML   <http://www.w3.org/XML/>.

XSL   <http://www.w3.org/Style/XSL/>.

31

Character Encoding

Christian Wittern

Introduction

Character encoding is an issue that mostly arises in the context of information processing and digital transcriptions of texts. To be precise, the honor of having created the first character encoding, long before the digital revolution, goes to Samuel Finley Breese Morse (1791–1872) for his Morse alphabet used in telegraphic transmissions. Texts are written by creating marks on some kind of medium. Since these written marks, characters as they are usually called, form part of the writing systems they are used in, they came to be analyzed and encoded within the context of that writing system.

While there are different ways for a text to become digital (for some discussion of this, please see Price, Chapter 24, ELECTRONIC SCHOLARLY EDITIONS, in this volume), the present chapter will be concerned only with texts transcribed in some way to form a digital text. There are many ways of how such a transcription might be achieved, either by converting a scanned image with some specialized software, or simply by typing the text in a way very similar way to how typing was done on a typewriter. However the input is done, the result will be a digital text that has been encoded.

A direct relationship exists between the written marks on a paper and how they are read. In a computer, however, there is no such fixed relationship. All characters that are typed by pressing a key will be mapped to some internal numeric representation of that character. The details of this internal representation, e.g., which number will represent which character, is determined by the coded character set used in the computing system convention, and is spelled out in the standard document and thus defines the *encoding* of that character.

Character encoding might seem arcane and a kind of specialized technical knowledge unnecessary, for example, for the transcription of modern English. The truth is, to the contrary, that every digital text has to use a character encoding in its internal representation and anybody setting out to work with digital texts had better have at least a basic understanding of what character encoding is and what the basic issues are.

There is another sense of the word encoding when used in connection with digital texts, namely in the combination "text encoding." Text encoding is the process of transcribing a text in digital form. It is sometimes confused with character encoding, which is the act of assigning distinct numeric values to the individual items (characters) observed in the stream of text. Text encoding comprises character encoding, but goes beyond that, since it is also concerned with re-creating the structure of a text in electronic form. Text encoding is sometimes also confused with markup, which is a methodology used in text encoding to express information about structure, status, or other special features of a text.

This chapter will first look at the relationship of character encoding and writing systems in a very general sense, will shortly look at as much of the history of character encoding as is needed to understand the following, and then look at the single most important coded character set in use today, namely Unicode. The intricacies of Unicode will then occupy most of the remaining part of the chapter, except for a short discussion of what is to be done if a character is not to be found in Unicode.

Character Encoding and Writing Systems

The study of writing systems within a framework of a scientifically sound theory is now usually called "Grammatology" (not Graphology, which is the practice of analyzing a person's handwriting), a designation adopted by I. J. Gelb in his seminal study *A Study of Writing: The Foundations of Grammatology* (1952). The philosopher Jacques Derrida later famously took over this term with acknowledgment in quite a different sense, yet the original sense should be kept, at least in the current context. The name is modeled on "phonology" and "morphology," the linguistic designations for the study of sounds and meaningful units.

Characters serve their function as a part of a writing system. While, in everyday language, writing system and script are frequently used interchangeably, we will need to distinguish them. A writing system needs a script for its graphical representation, but they are conceptually independent. The same writing system might be written in a number of different scripts, for example Cyrillic, Greek, and Russian are different graphic instantiations of the same writing system. A script thus is the graphic form of a writing system.

What is a Character?

A character is the smallest atomic component of a script that has a semantic value. If used to distinguish from "glyph," it refers to an abstract character, whereas glyph refers to the specific shapes that are used as a visual representation of a character. In the English alphabet, there are 26 letters that can be written with uppercase or lowercase characters. There is, however, a virtually unlimited form of glyph shapes that can be used to represent these characters. These shapes can vary considerably, but they have to maintain their ability to be distinguished from other characters.

Characters do not have to be separate typographic entities. Some Indic scripts and Tibetan, for example, write their characters in a continuum, as is usually done in western handwriting. Even in printing, adjacent characters are sometimes connected (for example, "f" followed by "I") to form a ligature, but they continue to exist as separate characters.

However, since characters are distinguished not only by their shape but also by their semantic value, the meaning of a character has also to be taken into consideration, which might lead to complications. For more on this, please see the section below on "Characters, not glyphs."

History of Character Encoding

As long as the processing of information from end to end occurs only in a single machine, there is no need for a standardized character encoding. Early computers up to the beginning of the 1960s thus simply used whatever ad-hoc convention to represent characters internally seemed appropriate; some distinguished upper- and lowercase letters, most did not.

However, information exchange very soon came to be seen as an important consideration, so a standard code that would allow data to move between computers from different vendors and subsequent models of computers from the same vendor became necessary; thus the development of ASCII (American Standard Code for Information Interchange), generally pronounced "æski," began.

The American Standards Association (ASA, later to become ANSI) first published ASCII as a standard in 1963. ASCII-1963 lacked the lowercase letters, and had an up-arrow (↑) instead of the caret (^) and a left-arrow (←) instead of the underscore (_). In 1967, a revised version added the lowercase letters, together with some other changes. In addition to the basic letters of the English alphabet, ASCII also includes a number of punctuation marks, digits, and an area of 33 code points reserved for "control codes"; this includes, for example, code points that indicated a "carriage return," "line feed," "backspace," or "tabulator move" and even a code point to ring a bell, thus bringing the total of code points assigned in ASCII to 127.

As can be learned immediately even from a cursory look at a table of the ASCII code, the repertoire of characters is suitable for almost no other language except English (one could theoretically also write Latin and Swahili, but in fact one would be hard pressed to write even a moderate essay with this repertoire, since it does not allow for foreign loan words, smart quotes, and other things that are frequently seen in modern English texts), since it defines no accented characters used in other European languages, not to mention languages like Arabic, Tibetan, or Chinese.

ASCII is the ancestor and common subset of most character codes in use today. It was adopted by ISO (International Organization for Standardization) as ISO 646 in

1967; in 1972, country-specific versions that replaced some of the less frequently used punctuation characters with accented letters needed for specific languages were introduced. This resulted in a babylonic situation where French, German, Italian, and the Scandinavian languages all had mutually exclusive, incompatible adaptations which made it impossible to transfer data to other areas without recoding.

Several attempts where made to improve this situation. In 1984, the Apple Macintosh appeared with the so-called MacRoman character set that allowed all languages of Western Europe to be used in the same document. The IBM codepage 850 (one of a variety of so-called codepages that could be used in DOS (disk operating system) environments) later achieved something similar. In the 1980s, an effort within the ISO finally succeeded in the publication of an international standard that would allow the combination of these languages, the group of ISO 8859 standards. This is a series of standards all based on ASCII, but they differ in the allocation of code points with values in the range 128–255. Of these, the first one, ISO 8859-1 (also known as Latin-1), is (albeit with some non-standard extensions) the "ANSI" used in the versions of the Microsoft Windows operating systems sold in Western Europe and the Americas. With the introduction of the European common currency, the euro, it became necessary to add the euro symbol to this character code; this version, with some additional modifications, has been adopted as ISO 8859-15, also known as Latin-0 or Latin-9.

As can be seen, even in the latter half of the 1980s, text encoding that involved more than one language (which is the norm, rather than the exception, for most literary works) was highly platform dependent and no universally applicable standard for character encoding was available.

For non-European languages, a mechanism similar in spirit was introduced with the framework of ISO 2022, which allowed the combined usage of different national character standards in use in East Asia. However, this was rarely fully implemented and, more importantly did not address the problem of combining European and Asian languages in one document.

Unicode

Software vendors and the ISO independently worked toward a solution to this problem that would allow the emerging global stream of information to flow without impediments. For many years, work was continuing in two independent groups. One of these was the Unicode Consortium, which was founded by some major software companies interested in capitalizing on the global market; the other was the charac-ter-encoding working groups within the ISO, working toward ISO 10646. The latter were developing a 32-bit character code that would have a potential code space to accommodate 4.3 billion characters, intended as an extension of the existing national and regional character codes. This would be similar to having a union catalog for libraries that simply allocates some specific areas to hold the cards of the participating libraries, without actually combining them into one catalog. Patrons would then have to cycle through these sections and look at every catalog separately, instead of having one consolidated catalog in which to look things up.

Unicode, on the other hand, was planning one universal encoding that would be a truly unified repertoire of characters in the sense that union catalogs are usually understood: Every character would occur just once, no matter how many scripts and languages made use of it.

Fortunately, after the publication of the first version of Unicode in the early 1990s, an agreement was reached between these two camps to synchronize development. While there are, to this day, still two different organizations maintaining a universal international character set, they did agree to assign new characters in the same way to the same code points with the same name, so for most practical purposes the two can be regarded as equivalent. Since ISO standards are sold by the ISO and not freely available online, whereas all information related to the Unicode standard is available from the website of the Unicode consortium (www.unicode.org), I will limit the discussion below to Unicode, but it should be understood that it also applies to ISO 10646.

Objectives and history

The latest version of Unicode published in book form as *The Unicode Standard* is version 5.0 at the time of this writing, in the following abbreviated as TUS with a number following indicating the version; TUS5 in this case. The design principles of Unicode are stated there as follows:

> The design of the Unicode Standard reflects the 10 fundamental principles stated in Table 2-1. Not all of these principles can be satisfied simultaneously. The design strikes a balance between maintaining consistency for the sake of simplicity and efficiency and maintaining compatibility for interchange with existing standards.

Table 2-1.

Universality	The Unicode Standard provides a single, universal repertoire.
Efficiency	Unicode text is simple to parse and process.
Characters, not glyphs	The Unicode Standard encodes characters, not glyphs.
Semantics	Characters have well-defined semantics.
Plain text	Unicode characters represent plain text.
Logical order	The default for memory representation is logical order.
Unification	The Unicode Standard unifies duplicate characters within scripts across languages.
Dynamic composition	Accented forms can be dynamically composed.
Equivalent sequences	Static precomposed forms have an equivalent dynamically composed sequence of characters.
Convertibility	Accurate convertibility is guaranteed between the Unicode Standard and other widely accepted standards.

(TUS5 2006: 13)

Most of these principles should be immediately obvious. The last principle ensures backward compatibility with existing standards, which is a very important consideration for the acceptance of Unicode. This means also that many accented characters, which had been encoded as they are in previous standards ("statically precomposed forms"), have more than one representation, since they can also be "dynamically composed sequences"; this means that accents and base characters are assembled when rendering a text, but stored as separate code points. To reduce character proliferation, the latter is the preferred way of encoding new characters. We will return to this problem later under the heading of "Normalization" below.

Unification is only applied within scripts, not across different scripts. The LATIN CAPITAL LETTER A (U+0041) (Unicode characters are referred to by their standard name, which is usually given in capital letters, followed in parentheses by the code point value in hexadecimal notation, prefixed with "U+") and the CYRILLIC CAPITAL LETTER A (U+0410) are thus not unified although they look identical, since they belong to different scripts.

Not surprisingly, in the close to twenty years of its development, the objectives and principles underlying the development have changed considerably. For example, in TUS3 2000: 12 the first principle was "Sixteen-bit character codes: Unicode character codes have a width of 16 bits." This is not true anymore, but this fact by itself is not of a major importance. This change has led, however, to problems for the early adaptors of Unicode, for example the Java programming language or Microsoft Windows NT. As with many other undertakings, important considerations had to be modified while working on the task as new information became available and the whole environment and, with it, many of the tacit assumptions on which earlier decisions were based had to be modified. However, since a standard can only modify earlier versions in limited ways (namely, it is extremely difficult to remove characters that have already been allocated, although this has happened on occasion), the current version (5.0, published in the fourth quarter of 2006) shows some degree of variation in application of the basic principles. Character unification proved to be at times politically controversial and hindered the adoption of Unicode, especially in East Asia.

Since Unicode aimed at maintaining compatibility with existing national and vendor-specific character encodings, it started out as a superset of the previously mentioned earlier character sets. Any encoded entity that existed in these earlier sets was also incorporated into Unicode, regardless of its conformance with the Unicode design principles.

To give just one example of what kind of practical problems are encountered as a result, units of measurement are frequently expressed with ordinary letters, for example the Ångström unit which was assigned the Unicode value ANGSTROM SIGN (U+212B), although the LATIN CAPITAL LETTER A WITH RING ABOVE (U+00C5) would have been perfectly suitable for this purpose. This example is just one of several types of duplicated encodings in Unicode of which text encoders have to be aware. Implications of this duplication and related recommendations for text-encoding projects will be discussed in a later section. A good start for a technical, but nevertheless accessible introduction to the Unicode Standard is the Technical Introduction at <http://www.unicode.org/standard/principles.html>.

Layout and overall architecture

As of version 5, there are 98,890 graphical characters defined in Unicode. In addition, there are 134 format characters, 65 control characters, and 137,468 code points set aside for characters in private use.

The encoded characters of the Unicode Standard are grouped by linguistic and functional categories, such as script or writing system. There are, however, occasional departures from this general principle, as when punctuation associated with the ASCII standard is kept together with other ASCII characters in the range U+0020 . . . U+007E, rather than being grouped with other sets of general punctuation characters. By and large, however, the code charts are arranged so that related characters can be found near each other in the charts.

The Unicode code space consists of the numeric values from 0 to 10FFFF, but in practice it has proven convenient to think of the code space as divided up into planes of characters, each plane consisting of 65,536 code points.

The Basic Multilingual Plane (BMP, or Plane 0) contains all the characters in common use for all the modern scripts of the world, as well as many historical and rare characters. By far the majority of all Unicode characters for almost all textual data can be found in the BMP.

The Supplementary Multilingual Plane (SMP, or Plane 1) is dedicated to the encoding of lesser-used historic scripts, special-purpose invented scripts, and special notational systems, which either could not be fit into the BMP or would be of very infrequent usage. Examples of each type include Gothic, Shavian, and musical symbols, respectively. While few scripts are currently encoded in the SMP in Unicode 5.0, there are many major and minor historic scripts that do not yet have their characters encoded in the Unicode Standard, and many of those will eventually be allocated in the SMP.

The Supplementary Ideographic Plane (SIP, or Plane 2) is the spillover allocation area for those Chinese, Japanese, or Korean (conventionally abbreviated as CJK) characters that could not be fit in the blocks set aside for more common CJK characters in the BMP. While there are a small number of common-use CJK characters in the SIP (for Cantonese usage, but also for Japanese), the vast majority of Plane 2 characters are extremely rare or of historical interest only. The barrier of Han unification that prevented many of these variant characters from being considered for inclusion into the BMP has been considerably lowered for the SIP. At the moment, there are more than 40,000 Han characters allocated here, whereas the BMP holds less than 30,000.

Within the planes, characters are allocated within character blocks, grouping together characters from a single script, for example the Greek or Arabic script, or for a similar purpose like punctuation, diacritics, or other typographic symbols.

Characters, not glyphs

As noted above, Unicode is encoding characters, not glyphs. While this has been employed to unify characters that look fairly similar and are semantically equivalent, occasionally it works the other way around and requires the encoding of similar, even indistinguishable characters separately. A "dash" character, for example, might look identical to a "hyphen" character as well to a "minus" sign. The decision which one is going to be used needs to be based on the function of the character in the text and the semantics of the encoded character. In Unicode, there is for example a HYPHEN-MINUS (U+002D), a SOFT HYPHEN (U+00AD), a NON-BREAKING HYPHEN (U+2011) and of course the HYPHEN (U+2010), not to mention the subscript and superscript variants (U+208B and U+207B). There are also compatibility forms at SMALL HYPHEN-MINUS (U+FE63) and FULLWIDTH HYPHEN-MINUS (U+FF0D), but these should never be considered for newly encoded texts, since they exist only for the sake of roundtrip conversion with legacy encodings. The "hyphen" character is sometimes lumped together with the "minus" character, but this is basically a legacy of ASCII, which has been carried over to Unicode; there now exists also MINUS SIGN (U+2212) plus some compatibility forms. As for the "dash" character, Unicode gives four encodings in sequence upfront: FIGURE DASH (U+2012), EN DASH (U+2013), EM DASH (U+2014), and HORIZONTAL BAR (U+2015). The last one might be difficult to find by just looking at the character name, but as its old name "QUOTATION DASH" reveals, this is also a dash character. TUS5 has a note on this character, explaining that it is a "long dash introducing quoted text," while the note for U+2014 says that it "may be used in pairs to offset parenthetical text."

Normalization

It was mentioned earlier that for a variety of reasons there are situations where a single character has two or more code points or sequences of code points assigned. Frequently used accented letters, for example, have been given separate Unicode values (TUS 5.0 calls these "precomposed" characters or forms), although the accents and the base characters also have been encoded, so that these could be used to assemble the same character. The character LATIN SMALL LETTER U WITH DIAERESIS (U+00FC ü) could also be expressed as a sequence of LATIN SMALL LETTER U (U+0075 u) and COMBINING DIAERESIS (U+0308 ü).

The way Unicode addresses this problem is by introducing the concept of "Normalization" of a text. A normalized text has all its characters in a known form of representation; other operations, for example search or string comparison, can then successfully be applied to this text. The *Unicode Standard Annex #15 Unicode Normalization Forms* (see <http://www.unicode.org/unicode/reports/tr15/>) explains the problem in greater detail and gives some recommendations. In many cases, it is most convenient to use the shortest possible sequence of Unicode characters ("Normalization Form C (NFC)" in the notation of the above-mentioned Unicode document). This will use precomposed accented characters where they exist and combining sequences in other cases. Many current software applications and operating systems are not capable of rendering combining sequences as a single visual unit. To overcome this problem, some encoding projects took refuge in defining new code points in the area of the Unicode code space set aside for private usage and created fonts accordingly. This will make it easier for encoders to work with these characters, but care should be taken to convert these private-use characters back to the standard representation of Unicode prior to electronic publication of the texts.

How to find Unicode characters?

Unicode characters are identified by their names; these names are in turn mapped to the numeric values used to encode them. The best strategy to find a character is therefore to search through the list of characters, also called the Unicode Character Database (UCD). As the examples of Unicode character names given so far will have shown, an individual name is usually derived by assigning names to the components of a character and then combining them if necessary in a systematic way. While the specific names for some of the diacritical marks may not be obvious, a look at the section where these are defined (U+0300 to U+0362) will quickly reveal how they are named in Unicode.

Not all characters, however, do have individual names. Han characters used for Chinese, Japanese, Korean, and old Vietnamese, and precomposed Hangul forms do only have generic names which do not allow identification of characters. However, there are still a large number of characters that are identified by individual names. Such characters can be looked up in the character tables of TUS5 or ISO 10646, but this process tends to be rather cumbersome. Unicode provides an online version of its character database, which can be downloaded from the Unicode Consortium's website at <http://www.unicode.org> by following the link to "Unicode Code Charts." There is also an online query form provided by the Institute of the Estonian language (<http://www.eki.ee/letter>), which allows more convenient searches.

Encoding forms of Unicode

Understanding how Unicode is encoded and stored in computer files requires a short treatment of some technical details. This section is especially intended for those who run into trouble with the default mechanism of their favorite software platform, usually designed to hide these details.

Unicode allows the encoding of about one million characters – the theoretical upper limit – but at present less than 10 percent of this code space is actually used. As noted above, the code space is arranged in 17 "planes" of 65,536 code points each, of which only 4 are used at the moment, with Plane 0, the "Basic Multilingual Plane (BMP)," being the one where most characters are defined. This architecture was finalized in Unicode 2.1. Before that, Unicode was considered to be limited to the BMP. Unicode 3.1, released in March 2001, was the first version to assign characters to code points outside of the BMP. Modern operating systems like Mac OS X (since version 10.3) or Windows (since version Vista) do provide full support even for the additional planes; in some cases there are patches available for older versions. It should be noted, however, that this provides only the basic foundation for handling these code points; in addition to this, applications and fonts have to be updated to allow actual display of the characters.

The numeric values of the code points have to be serialized in order to store them in a computer. Unicode defines three encoding forms for serialization: *UTF-8, UTF-16,* and *UTF-32.* UTF-16 simply stores the numerical value as a 16-bit integer, while characters with higher numerical values are expressed using two UTF-16 values from a range of the BMP set aside for this purpose, called "Surrogate Pairs." UTF-32, on the other hand, simply stores the whole 32-bit integer value for every single character. Since most computers store and retrieve numeric values in bundles of 8 bits ("bytes"), the 16 bits of UTF-16 and UTF-32 values have to be stored in two separate bytes. Preferences for the byte with the higher value ("Big-Endian") or the lower value ("Little-Endian") differ in the same way and for the same reasons as the egg openers in Jonathan Swift's *Gulliver's Travels.* There are thus two storage forms of UTF-16 and UTF-32: UTF-16-LE or UTF-32-LE and UTF-16-BE or UTF-32-BE. If they are used without any further specification, it is usually the *-BE form, which is the default, for example, on Microsoft Windows platforms.

UTF-8 avoids the whole issue of endian-ness by serializing the numbers in chunks of single bytes. In so doing, it uses sequences of multiple single bytes to encode a Unicode numeric value. The length of such sequences depends on the value of the Unicode character; values less than 128 (the range of the ASCII or ISO 646 characters) are just one byte in length, *hence identical to ASCII.* This means that English text and also the tags used for markup do not differ in UTF-8 and ASCII, one of the reasons why UTF-8 is rather popular. It is also the default encoding for XML files in the absence of a specific encoding declaration and is for most cases the recommended encoding to use. Most accented characters require a sequence of two bytes, East-Asian characters need three, and the characters beyond the BMP need four or more bytes.

Characters not in Unicode

Even with close to 100,000 characters in the current version, there are bound to be cases where some of the symbols found in a text cannot be readily transcribed into digital form. In anticipation of this problem, Unicode has set aside a rather large portion (of more than 137,000 characters) that can be used for private purposes.

This comes in useful in many cases, especially for in-house processing, data preparation, and print. However, as has been said in the beginning, the whole point of digital text is information interchange, which in turn requires a common character set as the basis. These private characters are thus *not* suitable for use in texts published digitally.

A frequent way to work around this problem is to use small graphics that represent the characters and are added to the text inline; if they resemble the selected font style and size, they can serve as a very good substitute. In the pre-publication workflow, a mechanism like the "TEI Gaiji module" (see *TEI P5. Guidelines for Electronic Text Encoding and Interchange*, chapter 25: Representation of non-standard characters and glyphs, at <http://www.tei-c.org/P5/Guidelines/WD.html>) can be used to encode these characters.

Representing Characters in Digital Documents

As discussed above, there are different encoding forms of Unicode for different purposes. In digital documents, it is best practice to indicate what encoding is being used, otherwise a software processing these will need to fall back to default values or use heuristics to determine what was being used, which might cause the documents to become unreadable. Since there are too many document formats in use today, it would make no sense to try to mention them all. I will only discuss some aspects of character representation in XML documents (and, only in passing, also SGML documents) here; for more information see Harold 1999 and Harold and Means 2001. In XML documents there is the optional encoding part of the xml declaration like `<?xml version=''1.0'' encoding=''utf-8'' ?/>`. The values allowed for encoding are not limited to the Unicode encoding forms mentioned above, but can also include other character encodings, provided they are a proper subset of Unicode. XML processors are only *required* to recognize Unicode encoding forms, but most *do* support a wide range of widely used character encodings.

The declaration `<?xml version=''1.0'' encoding=''ISO-8859-1'' ?/>` would thus declare that the characters used in the document are only a subset of Unicode, namely those defined in ISO-8859-1. This does not change the fact that all XML documents use Unicode as their internal encoding and will be converted to this upon being parsed. All Unicode characters can still be used in such a document, but they cannot be represented directly, that is, typed into the document as such. Instead, they have to use an escape mechanism to represent these characters, which is built into XML, the "numerical character references" (NCR). They take a form similar to entity references (see Harold and Means 2001: 18) in SGML and XML, but do not refer to something else; instead they contain a number which identifies the Unicode character represented with this NCR. For example, the character NON-BREAKING HYPHEN (U+2011) mentioned above could be represented in such a document by the sequence `&#8209;` or `&#x2011;`. Although this is a sequence of seven or eight characters when written like this, to any XML processor this is just one character. Like entity references, NCRs start with a "&" and end with a ";" character. The "#" character identifies this sequence as an NCR, rather than a standard entity reference. What follows is either a decimal integer indicating the Unicode code point or the "x" for "Hex," indicating that the integer is represented in hexadecimal notation. Since the latter is commonly used in code tables, a rarely used character can be looked up in a code table and inserted into the document with this mechanism, even on systems that do not support the wide range of Unicode characters available.

XML's predecessor SGML did define a special type of entity references called SDATA (for "system data," see Goldfarb 1990: 341) to allow the separation of system-specific and generic representations; however, this mechanism has not been carried over to XML and is thus rarely used today.

HTML, an SGML application, defines "entity references" (they are called "character entity references" in HTML:1997, Section 5.3.3, but this is not a formal designation) for a number of characters (a full list is here: <http://www.w3.org/TR/html4/sgml/ entities.html>). This allows the use of mnemonic references like £ to refer to the currency symbol for pound Sterling £. Since this requires a list of characters predefined as part of a document's DTD (document type definition) and is thus not available for all XML documents, it is gradually falling out of use outside HTML documents; this trend is further accelerated by the increasing availability of systems capable of editing and displaying Unicode directly.

Conclusions

Character encoding literally lies at the very basis of any digital text. While it is now technically well understood and has a stable foundation with Unicode 5.0, the history of earlier character encoding standards continues to play a role through legacy encodings and will continue to do so for some years to come.

This chapter has attempted to clarify some of the underlying concepts and show how to deal with them in practice. It should have become clear that even the most modest project involving digital texts needs to make informed use of the character encodings available, which in most cases will be Unicode encoded as UTF-8.

REFERENCES AND FURTHER READING

Coulmas, Florian (2003 [1989]). *The Writing Systems of the World*. Malden, MA: Blackwell Publishing.

—— (2004 [1996]). *The Blackwell Encyclopedia of Writing Systems*. Malden, MA: Blackwell Publishing.

deFrancis, John (1989). *Visible Speech: the Diverse Oneness of Writing Systems*. University of Hawaii Press: Honolulu.

Gelb, I. J. (1952). *A Study of Writing: the Foundations of Grammatology*. London: Routledge and Kegan Paul.

Goldfarb, Charles (1990). *The SGML Handbook*. Oxford: Clarendon Press.

Harold, Elliotte Rusty (1999). *XML Bible*. Foster City, CA: IDG Books Worldwide.

Harold, Elliotte Rusty, and W. Scott Means (2001). *XML in a Nutshell: A Desktop Quick Reference*. Sebastopol, CA: O'Reilly & Associates.

ISO (International Organization for Standardization) (1986). *ISO 8879 Information processing – Text and Office Systems – Standard Generalized Markup Language (SGML)*, 1st edn. Geneva: ISO.

ISO (International Organization for Standardization) (2000). *ISO/IEC 10646 Information technology – Universal Multiple-Octet Coded Character Set (UCS)*. Geneva: ISO.

Sperberg-McQueen, Michael, and Lou Burnard (Eds.) (2002). *Guidelines for Text Encoding and Interchange (TEI P4)*. Oxford: Text Encoding Initiative Consortium.

The Unicode Consortium (2006). *The Unicode Standard 5.0*. Boston: Addison Wesley.

World Wide Web Consortium (1999). *HTML 4.01 Specification*. Boston: World Wide Web Consortium. <http://www.w3.org/TR/html4/>.

Annotated Overview of Selected Electronic Resources

Tanya Clement and Gretchen Gueguen

Introduction

The materials reviewed in this bibliography have been carefully selected as a sampling of resources covering a wide range of genres, methods, perspectives, and literary traditions in digital literary studies. Limited to resources in English, these have been chosen because each resource is freely available online with few or no areas of restricted access and represents best practices reflecting time-honored scholarly traditions and current digital standards. In particular, each resource:

- contains rich, multi-layered content that is current and has been thoroughly referenced and vetted by the creators and/or the appropriate scholarly community;
- clearly reflects a guiding principle or theory that is in keeping with current standards of scholarly literary practice (both traditional and digital);
- uses the digital medium to facilitate a discovery-based, synthesized experience with its content, above and beyond providing access to digitized texts or a compilation of resources. These resources are *essentially* digital: each, at some level, engages with literature in ways not possible before the digital age.

This annotated overview is divided into three main sections based on content: Digital Transcriptions and Images; Born-Digital Texts and New Media Objects; and Criticism, Reviews, and Tools.

Digital Transcriptions and Images

One of the primary goals of digital literary resources has been to provide access to large bodies of related texts in a systematic way. In addition to providing access to digital transcriptions and images, the digital research archives included here present edited and encoded texts, contextual essays, and tools that help users discover new texts or make new connections within and between familiar ones. The exemplary nature of all these resources is reflected in the way that they examine or expose the differences in the very nature of analog and digital resources and research.

One key feature shared by some of these resources is a unique interface for discovery and analysis of the comprised materials. For example, many resources allow for easy navigation through side-by-side comparisons of text, multimedia objects, translations, commentary, and notes. Among the resources that have emphasized alternative viewing choices are *The Rossetti Archive, Princeton Dante Project, Internet Shakespeare Editions*, and *Hap Hazard*. In addition to reading interfaces, some projects offer advanced searching capabilities that are designed around textual features (*The Rossetti Archive, Princeton Dante Project, The Blake Archive*). Still other resources emphasize the physical organization of the original work through hypertext naviga-tion as in *The Early Stuart Libels* and *The Electronic Edition of John Ruskin's Modern Painters I*.

The resources listed here also emphasize the means by which the digital medium may be used to convey particular interpretations of text in novel ways. Both *Mark Twain In His Times* and *Uncle Tom's Cabin & American Culture: A Multimedia Archive* underscore a particular "interpretive" stance through interactive exhibits. These features highlight key themes such as the cultural impact of *Uncle Tom's Cabin* on race relations and book publishing or how the persona of "Mark Twain" was "created and defined, marketed and performed, reviewed and appreciated." In *The Thomas MacGreevy Archive* interpretation is guided through the "Browse" menu through which a user may explore "the life, writings, and relationships" of the author with and beyond his published texts through various media and from different perspec-tives. Other resources combine different types of materials to build a fuller context for their research. Resources such as *The Decameron Web, The Walt Whitman Archive*, and *Jónas Hallgrímsson: Selected Poetry and Prose* are not limited to primary texts; these combine textual, visual, and audio features to facilitate the exploration of the life and works of their subjects.

Many of these resources explicitly address the digital scholarly community through research articles, scholarly tools, and forums for scholarly discussion. From the "samplers" of the *Dickinson Electronic Archives* – digital articles that serve as examples of "what can be accomplished when shaping critical arguments via new media" – to the extensive documentation of editorial choices, digital design, and tools for literary analysis in *The Blake Archive* to the robust suite of user-oriented features in *Romantic Circles* (including a weblog and MOO alongside more traditional outlets for scholarly discussion), these resources not only provide access to primary materials but serve as an outlet for shaping the discipline through scholarly debate, presentation of research, and the establishment of practices and methods.

Finally, many of these resources bring together different communities in a new collaborative scholarly space. Literary scholars and libraries have long collaborated to provide easily accessible and thoughtfully collected resources to the larger community (*The Library of Southern Literature, British Women Romantic Poets*, and *Beowulf: A New Translation for Oral Delivery*). Other new bonds are being forged between traditional academic – the Early English Texts Society (EETS) – and digital literature communities through resources like *Ancrene Wisse Preface*. Likewise, *The Diary of Samuel Pepys* is an innovative weblog-based re-creation of the 1660 text that reflects a collective work-in-progress in which regular user comments provide for historical context and editorial analysis.

Ancrene Wisse Preface (eets e-edition)

<http://www.tei-c.org.uk/Projects/EETS/>

Editor: Bella Millet; Technical Assistance: Lou Burnard and Sebastian Rahtz; Design Input: Scott Agass

Ancrene Wisse was a guide written in the thirteenth century for "female recluses" in the West Midlands of England. This digital edition comprises the preface to the work. All texts are encoded in XML using the TEI (Text Encoding Initiative) markup schema. A simple full-text search function is available for the text which is available both as Middle English and modern English translation for comparison viewing. Manuscript facsimiles, critical apparatus, and textual commentary are also available.

Beowulf: A New Translation for Oral Delivery

<http://digicoll.library.wisc.edu/Literature/subcollections/RinglBeowulfAbout. shtml>

Translator: Dick Ringler; Encoder: Peter C. Gorman

An original translation of *Beowulf* created by Dick Ringler and published through the University of Wisconsin Library's digital collection, this edition contains scholarly apparatus, introduction, notes, and commentary encoded with TEI. The edition is available as a part of Wisconsin's digital collections online.

British Women Romantic Poets

<http://digital.lib.ucdavis.edu/projects/bwrp/>

Founding Editor: Nancy Kushigian; Managing Editor: Charlotte Payne

This resource aims to create an archive of scholarly texts of poetry by British and Irish women written during the Romantic period, between 1789 and 1832. Texts are chosen which are of interest to the scholarly community from the Kohler Collection at the University of California, Davis.

The Complete Writings and Pictures of Dante Gabriel Rossetti: a Hypermedia Archive

<http://www.rossettiarchive.org/>

General Editor: Jerome McGann

The Rossetti Archive features a broad spectrum of Rossetti's works including pictures, poems, and prose in both transcribed, translated, and manuscript forms. These primary texts are presented with editorial commentary, notes, and glosses.

Decameron Web

<http://www.brown.edu/Departments/Italian_Studies/dweb/dweb.shtml>

Coeditors: Michael Papio and Massimo Riva; Director: Christiana Fordyce

The Decameron Web explores the life of Boccacio and the historical and cultural context in which he created *The Decameron*. A text search of the XML version provides access to the primary text, and an advanced site search provides access to the secondary contextual materials.

The Diary of Samuel Pepys

<http://www.pepysdiary.com/>

Editor: Phil Gyford

Samuel Pepys's 1660 diary is re-created in the digital realm as a weblog updated with new entries that correspond to the date and month of Pepys's original text. The weblog format allows users to add annotations and folksonomic tags (used for browsing) to the text.

Dickinson Electronic Archives

<http://www.emilydickinson.org>

Executive Editor: Martha Nell Smith

The primary focus of the *Dickinson Electronic Archives* are writings that Emily Dickinson "published" via distribution through the postal service, through family, through friendly courier, and in handmade books. Resources include images and transcriptions of letters and poetry manuscripts, writings by members of her family, sound recordings of current poets reading Dickinson's work, other secondary scholarly materials, and a discussion space.

Early Stuart Libels: An edition of poetry from manuscript sources

<http://www.earlystuartlibels.net/htdocs/index.html>

Editors: Alastair Bellany, Andrew McRae

Early seventeenth-century political poetry is the focus of *Early Stuart Libels*. More than 350 poems, many of which had not been previously published, are included in the edition highlighting a range of traditional libel such as satire and invective as well as more orthodox anti-libel pieces. The texts are searchable by author and source and each poem is fully annotated in both an HTML hypertext and PDF edition.

The Electronic Edition of John Ruskin's Modern Painters I

<http://www.lancs.ac.uk/fass/centres/ruskin/empi/>

Editors: Lawrence Woof, Ray Halsam; Software Director: Roger Garside

The Electronic Edition of John Ruskin's Modern Painters I presents a digital edition of the first volume of Ruskin's five-volume work. Reading editions are presented as high-resolution facsimiles while transcribed texts are used to create annotations and hypertext links between images of the texts. Scholarly apparatus include information about Ruskin and his times and the impact and reception of *Modern Painters*.

The Internet Shakespeare Editions (ISE)

<http://ise.uvic.ca>

Coordinating Editor: Michael Best

The goal of the *Internet Shakespeare Editions* is to "create and publish works for the student, scholar, actor, and general reader." These take the form of annotated texts of the plays and other multimedia contextual materials about Shakespeare's life and works.

Hap Hazard: a manuscript resource for Spenser studies

<http://www.english.cam.ac.uk/ceres/haphazard/>

Editor: Andrew Zurcher

Part of COPIA, the CERES (Cambridge English Renaissance Electronic Sources) Online Publications Inter-Active, *Hap Hazard* features heavily annotated resources for the study of Edmund Spenser including his letters and the text of *A View of the Present State of Ireland*. Other contextual supplementary resources provide insight particularly into the study of manuscript materials relating to Spenser's writing.

Jónas Hallgrímsson: Selected Poetry and Prose

<http://www.library.wisc.edu/etext/Jonas/>

Editor and Translator: Dick Ringler; Developer: Peter C. Gorman

This site comprises poetry and prose of the Icelandic author along with biographical and scholarly resources. Fifty works of poetry and prose by Hallgrímsson with images of manuscripts and first editions, a biographical sketch, commentary, photos, and a bibliography make up the primary resources.

Library of Southern Literature

<http://docsouth.unc.edu/southlit/index.html>

Scholarly advisers: Dr. Robert Bain, Dr. Joseph M. Flora, Dr. William L. Andrews; Digitization Librarian: Natalia Smith

The *Library of Southern Literature* focuses on 100 works of Southern literature published before 1920 as part of the larger University of North Carolina libraries initiative *Documenting the American South*, which strives to make available primary materials from the university's southern collections in digitized form (text, images, and audio).

Mark Twain in His Times

<http://etext.lib.virginia.edu/railton/index2.html>

Writer and Director: Stephen Railton

The creator of *Mark Twain in His Times* argues that the author's career can best be understood through contemporary contextual evidence. To this end, the site provides access and searching capabilities into a mix of primary and secondary materials including images of manuscripts, contemporary reviews, articles, advertisements, the sales prospectus for and editions of Twain's works among many other objects.

Princeton Dante Project

<http://etcweb.princeton.edu/dante/pdp/>

Editor: Robert Hollander

Offering a hypertextual interface for Dante's *Commedia* and other minor works in English and Italian as well as numerous multimedia features, this project also offers lectures and commentary on Dante and his works by Robert Hollander.

Romantic Circles

<http://www.rc.umd.edu>

General Editors: Neil Fraistat, Steven E. Jones, and Carl Stahmer

Refereed scholarly content pertaining to Romantic period literature and culture is the main feature of *Romantic Circles*. This site comprises both primary and secondary materials and space for scholarly discussion and information exchange.

The Thomas MacGreevy Archive

<http://www.macgreevy.org/>

General Editor: Susan Schreibman

The Thomas MacGreevy Archive facilitates the exploration of "the life, writings, and relationships of the Irish poet and critic Thomas MacGreevy." The archive combines fully searchable, transcribed texts of articles by and about MacGreevy, with letters from MacGreevy and his contemporaries, a bibliography, biography, timeline, image gallery, and biographical database of people associated with his work.

Uncle Tom's Cabin & American Culture: a Multimedia Archive

<http://www.iath.virginia.edu/utc/>

Director: Stephen Railton

This collection's central theme is based on exploring interpretive modalities of *Uncle Tom's Cabin*. Many interpretive materials are included, with images from various editions of the book including articles and newspaper clippings, advertisements, playbills, and illustrations from the time period.

The Walt Whitman Archive

<http://www.whitmanarchive.org/>

Editors: Ed Folsom, Kenneth M. Price

The Walt Whitman Archive presents materials related to every poem in *Leaves of Grass*, including those poems that were never published, along with photographs and audio of what is thought to be Whitman's voice. Contemporary reviews and works by Whitman disciples are featured along with secondary scholarly materials about the author.

The William Blake Archive

<http://www.blakearchive.org/>

Editors: Morris Eaves, Robert Essick, and Joseph Viscomi

The William Blake Archive includes fully searchable and scalable electronic editions of all of Blake's nineteen illuminated works replete with contextual information and diplomatic transcriptions. A searchable electronic version of the standard printed edition, and other essential scholarly information, plus representations of Blake's works in other artistic media are also included.

Born-Digital Texts and New Media Objects

As diversified as any genre of literary works, the "born-digital" resources included here take on an amalgamation of various programming languages and electronic forms presented in a variety of digital environments. All of these resources are currently in use and include recent additions by the editors and authors. Some of the material associated with each entry is archived on the listed URL and some is linked from the site, but all of these resources function as thoughtful representations of a particular perspective or artist of digital media and literature. For example, some entries function much like literary journals and are associated with various works and artists. *Arras*, Brian Kim Stefans's contribution to new media poetry and poetics, is "devoted to exploring how digital technology has impacted the field of experimental poetics"; *blackice* showcases work "modeled after the great avant-garde literary writing of past" by "publishing some of the most offensive, sexy, and formally adventurous writing of the last fifteen years"; and the *Electronic Literature Organization* (ELO) is committed to providing access to a wealth of archived electronic literature and also to the Preservation, Archiving, and Dissemination (PAD) project (which seeks to "maintain accessibility, encourage stability, and ensure availability of electronic works" for future readers).

Other entries function as author sites that archive, link to, and comment on pieces by particular authors whose works have helped elevate digital literature to its current status as a well-regarded literary genre. Deena Larsen, Shelley Jackson, Stuart Moulthrop, M. D. Coverley, and Mark Amerika represent some "first wave" electronic literature with hypertext pieces such as Amerika's *Grammatron*, Jackson's "My Body," Larsen's "Disappearing Rain," Moulthrop's award-winning *hegirascope*, and Coverley's many pieces of early fiction in now-archived digital journals such as *Beehive* (<http://beehive.temporalimage.com/>) and subscription-based *Web Conjunctions* (<http://www.conjunctions.com/webconj.htm>). "Second Wave" electronic literature is represented by the flash pieces of Stefans, Talan Memmott, and Jason Nelson (*secrettechnology* and *Heliozoa*); JavaScript work by Stuart Moulthrop; collaborative new media poems directed by Thomas Swiss; and the game narratives of Michael Mateas and Andrew Stern. Other perspectives include John Cayley's work with pro-grammable, digital movies (*P=R=O=G=R=A=M=M=A=T=O=L=O=G=Y*), Nick Montfort's experiments with interactive fiction, and mez's "mezangelle" texts.

Mark Amerika

<http://www.markamerika.com/>

Author: Mark Amerika

Named a *"Time* Magazine 100 Innovator" as one of the most influential artists, scientists, entertainers, and philosophers into the twenty-first century, Amerika is now known for performances and demonstrations on all aspects of new media art and theory including live multimedia performances in which he produces narrative by integrating video sampling and experimental music with on-stage, live writing. His site includes links to all his work, past and present.

Arras: new media poetry and poetics

<http://arras.net/>

Author: Brian Kim Stefans

The site includes links to the author's own work in Flash, Shockwave, Director, JavaScript, and hypertext (including his best-known piece "Dreamlife of Letters"); it also includes Stefan's "gallery of digital poetry," annotated links to digital literary resources by other writers and artists who are "devoted to exploring how digital technology has impacted the field of experimental poetics," and use "multi-media, interactivity, algorithmic processes, and digital typefaces" to produce poetry and criticism.

Thomas Swiss

<http://bailiwick.lib.uiowa.edu/swiss/>

Author: Thomas Swiss

Currently a professor at the University of Iowa, Swiss's work includes scholarly criticism and new media poems. In keeping with Swiss's theory that web-based poetry has its "roots in the shared notion of community that was integral to the development of internet," most of these Flash pieces are created by collaborative teams and include designs by Motomichi Nakamura, Michael Cina, and Skye Giordano and audio by Aaron Day, Seb Chevrel, and Randy Schoen.

blackice

<http://www.altx.com/profiles/>

Publisher: Mark Amerika; Editors: Mark Amerika, Matt Samet

An integral section of the Alt-X network (which also includes the *electronic book review*), *blackice* includes electronic fiction and poetry, and literary criticism about electronic literature.

M. D. Coverley

<http://califia.us>

M. D. Coverley (aka Marjorie Coverley Luesebrink)

A professor at the School of Humanities and Languages, Irvine Valley College, Coverley includes on her site links to many of her award-winning hypertexts published in new media magazines and journals throughout the 1990s. She also includes her critical, academic work and excerpts from her longer fiction, *Califia* and *Egypt: the Book of Going Forth by Day*.

Electronic Literature Organization

<http://www.eliterature.org/>

ELO President: Thomas Swiss

The Electronic Literature Organization (ELO) is a nonprofit organization established "to promote and facilitate the writing, publishing, and reading of electronic literature." This site features a database-driven directory of electronic literature maintained by authors; information on the ELO coordination of readings and outreach events across the US including information about the Preservation, Archiving, and Dissemination (PAD) project.

Façade: a one-act interactive drama

<http://www.interactivestory.net/>

Authors: Michael Mateas, Andrew Stern

Winner of many game awards, *Façade* is "an artificial intelligence-based art/research experiment in electronic narrative" that was created by integrating artistry and artificial intelligence technologies. With this collaboration, Mateas and Stern have succeeded in engineering an environment in which a real-time 3D virtual world is inhabited by both AI characters and the player who experiences this text from the first-person perspective.

Heliozoa

<http://www.heliozoa.com/>

Author: Jason Nelson

This site features over sixteen pieces of this award-winning author's hypermedia work from 2000–2005, including e-literature and poetry that incorporates hypertext, Flash, various game interfaces, sound, and content of high literary quality.

Hyperfiction

<http://hyperfiction.org/>

Author: Noah Wardrip-Fruin

This author (co-editor with Nick Montfort of *The New Media Reader*) includes news and links to his new media work (both creative and scholarly) on his site. Here the reader finds *The Impermanence Agent* (1998–2002), which (created with Adam Chapman, Brion Moss, and Duane Whitehurst) is a web agent that "monitors" a reader's browser and then uses this material to create a different story for each reader. The site also includes other literary digital works and links to exhibitions as well as current events and news.

The Ineradicable Stain

<http://www.ineradicablestain.com/>

Author: Shelley Jackson

Jackson (known for her seminal hypertext *Patchwork Girl*) includes excerpts from and explanations of her work, including her most recent work *Skin: A Mortal Work Of Art* in which the author commissions "readers" to tattoo a word on their skin in "book font." The site also comprises much of Jackson's critical work such as "Stitch Bitch" and two of her major fictional works "My Body" and "The Doll Games."

Deena Larsen

<http://www.deenalarsen.net/>

Author: Deena Larsen

Larsen (author of the hypercard work *Marble Springs* and the hypertext *Samplers*) includes links to all aspects of her work: syllabi, writing exercises, articles, Flash collaborations and imagery, a matrix poem, and structural works (which explore a structural theme using layout, imagery, words, and navigation). Her works include well-known pieces such as the Flash piece "Firefly" available from the archived site *Poems that Go* (<http://www.poemsthatgo.com/>).

Talan Memmott

<http://www.memmott.org/talan/>

Author: Talan Memmott

This site serves as both an archive and a portal to Memmott's new media works including poetry, sound work, and Flash artistry (including his well-known *Lexia to Perplexia* – a piece which has received much critical attention from theorists). It also includes his critical work, interviews, and reviews.

mez

<http://www.hotkey.net.au/~netwurker/>

Author: mez (a.k.a. Mary Anne Breeze)

This site features the work of the award-winning new media artist mez who focuses on examining language by creating and using her "mezangelle" language (a combination of natural language and code). Major works include "pro][tean][.lapsing.txts," "_][s][hut][ters][of d.funct meat_," and "The data][h!][bleeding T.ex][e]ts" among others. The site also includes an introduction on reading, especially reading the mezangelle text.

Nick Montfort

<http://nickm.com/>

Author: Nick Montfort

A programmer and writer, Montfort is best known for his work with interactive fiction such as his collaborative piece *Mystery House Taken Over* (with Dan Shiovitz and Emily Short) and his book of scholarly criticism *Twisty Little Passages: An Approach to Interactive Fiction*. The site also includes his most recent work *Book and Volume*, the award-winning work *Ad Verbum*, presentations, reviews, and critical articles.

Stuart Moulthrop

<http://iat.ubalt.edu/moulthrop/>

Author: Stuart Moulthrop

Author of *Victory Garden* and a professor at the School of Information Arts and Technologies in the Yale Gordon College of Liberal Arts at the University of Baltimore, Moulthrop's most recent work focuses on "Instruments and Playable Texts" (reflected in a special 2006 issue of *Iowa Review Web* of which he was guest editor). "Pax" is his 2003 piece in which he explores these same issues "of what else we might play in addition to games." His site also includes syllabi, critical essays, and many of his hypertext work from the 1990s.

$$P=R=0=G=R=A=M=M=A=T=0=L=0=G=Y$$

<http://www.shadoof.net/in/>

Author: John Cayley

Winner of the *Electronic Literature Organization*'s first annual award in digital poetry in 2001, Cayley could be termed the "digital writer's digital writer" for his innovative use of "text movies" which combine literature and programmable technology (such as QuickTime) and his critical work on new media art in his essays "literal art" and "the code is not the text (unless it is the text)." He is also a frequent object of and contributor to scholarly, critical debates on the *electronic book review*.

Criticism, Reviews, and Tools

The following list comprises resources that function in a secondary capacity to the texts presented in the first two sections of this bibliography. The primary goal of these resources is to reflect on, engage with, and explore electronic texts of both transcription-based resources and born-digital literary objects. Many of these resources are sponsored and supported by established digital and literary associations and organizations, such as the Association of Literary Scholars and Critics (*The Valve*); the Alliance of Digital Humanities Organizations (*Digital Humanities Quarterly*); the Society for Digital Humanities/Société pour l'étude des médias interactifs (*Text Technology*; McMaster University), and the PEN American Center (*Words Without Borders*). Other resources were created and are maintained by other traditional cultural institutions such as the New Museum of Contemporary Art (*Rhizome.Org*), The New Media Group in English at George Mason University (*://English Matters*), Universities such as Nottingham Trent University (*trAce Online Writing Centre*) and the Graduate College and the Department of English at the University of Iowa and the School of Journalism and Mass Communication at the University of Minnesota (*The Iowa Review Web*). Others (*Web Del Sol* and Alt-X's *electronic book review*) were created by "born digital" organizations.

Also included in this section are digital tools which are meant to aid scholarly interpretations of literary texts through the digital medium. Some are built to "crunch" text in the manner of traditional computational linguistics, whether it be through creating co-occurrence and distribution lists with a tool like *HyperPo* or through determining "morphological, lexical, prosodic, and narratological criteria" with *WordHoard*. In addition to these functions, *TAPoR* (Text Analysis Portal for Research) provides a user "workbench" where the user can login, find help documentation about text analysis in general, upload her texts, use a variety of any tool the tool creators have made available to the *TAPoR* open-source environment, and save work for the next visit. Other types of tools facilitate the user's analysis and display of encoded XML and SGML texts. The resources *Juxta* and the *Versioning Machine* allow users to compare, collate, and display variant versions of digital texts while the *teiPublisher* facilitates the user's ability to create a searchable digital text repository, including metadata ontology development and indexing that may be displayed on the web. Still more tools included in this section include resources that incorporate innovative representations of texts that facilitate interpretive strategies unimaginable in the traditional text environment. The resources include single digital editions that incorporate image comparison (*John Lydgate's Fall of Princes* and *Extracts from the Diary of Robert Graves*) and an interactive timeline (*Absalom! Absalom!*). Other "tools" represented here are analysis tools incorporated into multiple-text archives like GIS plotting in *The Perseus Project* and an innovative visual interpretation of an entire text on a single screen in *TextArc*. All of the tools listed here are the creations of well-regarded institutions associated with the highest digital literary standards, traditions, and innovative practices and in many cases source code is also made available.

All of these sites maintain the goal to respond to, reflect, and engage the digital literary community at large. These resources include commentary on digital literary issues through more formal scholarly critiques and debates (*Digital Humanities Quarterly, electronic book review, Grand Text Auto, Postmodern Culture, Text Technology*, and *the Valve*) and informal book reviews and exchanges (*trace, Web Del Sol*, and *Words without Borders*). In addition, some of these digital resources have a focus on primary materials usually in the form of electronic literature, interviews, and teaching modules (:// *English Matters, The Iowa Review Web, trAce*, and *Rhizome.org*). Beyond presenting and commenting on digital literature, these resources use the digital medium as a platform for exchange, whether the implementation is a weblog (*The Valve*), an exhibition or installation (*Rhizome.org*), or a message board (*ebr*), and most of these sites use underlying databases and innovative interface designs to augment both the access to and the interaction with their content.

Digital Humanities Quarterly

<http://www.digitalhumanities.org/dhq/>

Editor in Chief: Julia Flanders

Produced by ADHO (the Alliance of Digital Humanities Organizations), the *DHQ* is an experiment in community journal publication committed to "experimenting with publication formats and the rhetoric of digital authoring," collaborating with a variety of scholarly groups and publications in a variety of languages, and using open standards. Its peer-reviewed materials include scholarly articles, editorials and feature articles, experiments in interactive media, and reviews of born-digital texts and tools.

Absalom, Absalom! Electronic Interactive! Chronology

<http://etext.lib.virginia.edu/railton/absalom/index2.html>

Creators: Stephen Railton, Will Rourk

This resource, supported by the University of Virginia's Institute for Advanced Technology in the Humanities (IATH), is a Flash-based timeline of the major events in William Faulkner's novel *Absalom, Absalom!* Based on Faulkner's own chronology (a manuscript of which is featured), the tool is primarily intended as a teaching resource to help readers become acquainted with the events of the novel through an interface that allows users to navigate these events in various ways.

electronic book review

<http://www.electronicbookreview.com/>

Publisher: Mark Amerika; Editor: Joseph Tabbi

This resource's primary purpose is to host debates on electronic textuality, cyberculture, and digital design literacy in scholarly and critical writing by some of today's leading scholars in these various fields. The threads are called "first person," "techno capitalism," "end construction," "music, sound, noise," "webarts," "writing under constraint," "internet nation," "image + narrative," "electro poetics," "critical ecologies," and "writing (post) feminism."

://English Matters

<http://chnm.gmu.edu/ematters/>

New Media Group in English Director: Devon Hodges

Organized around a central theme, each issue contains scholarly articles, exhibits, electronic poetry, and teaching modules to explore new genres of digital literature and poetry. Each issue is produced by the New Media Group in English

An Episode from John Lydgate's Fall of Princes

<http://web.uvic.ca/hrd/lydgate/>

Creators: Undine Bruckner, Martin Holmes

This experimental resource features an interface that allows users to compare a manuscript facsimile and a transcription of an excerpt from John Lydgate's *Fall of Princes* with side-by-side comparison and navigation within lines of both the image and the text. It is supported by the Humanities Computing and Media Center at the University of Victoria.

Extracts from the Diary of Robert Graves

\<http://web.uvic.ca/hrd/graves/\>

Creators: Undine Bruckner, Martin Holmes
   This resource uses several extracts from the diary of Robert Graves to experiment with integrating multiple texts into one display as an attempt to encode a multi-layered document like a diary with publicly available DTDs. The finished interface includes images and annotations in addition to the text of the diary and other texts that were enclosed with the original entries.

Grand Text Auto

\<http://grandtextauto.gatech.edu/\>

Contributors: Mary Flanagan, Michael Mateas, Nick Montfort, Scott Rettberg, Andrew Stern, Noah Wardrip-Fruin
   With contributors such as Flanagan (software artist, technoculture theorist, and activist), Mateas (professor at Georgia Tech in the School of Literature, Communication, and Culture and in the College of Computing), Montfort (poet and author of interactive fiction and other literary works for the computer), Rettberg (professor of new media studies in the literature program at Richard Stockton College of New Jersey), Stern (designer, writer and engineer of AI-based interactive characters and stories), and Wardrip-Fruin (professor at the University of California, San Diego), this weblog is updated frequently with scholarly and artistic critiques and announcements on many topics of interest to the digital literary community.

HyperPo: Text analysis and exploration tools

\<http://hyperpo.mcmaster.ca/\>

Designer and writer: Stéfan Sinclair
   HyperPo is a text exploration and analysis program that facilitates creating frequency lists of characters, words and series of words, KWIC (Keyword in Context), co-occurrence and distribution lists and comparing data from multiple texts while using external resources such as Google and other content repositories.

The Iowa Review Web

\<http://www.uiowa.edu/~iareview/mainpages/tirwebhome.htm\>

Advising Editor: Thomas Swiss; Editor and Programmer: Benjamin Basan
   This site features electronic literature, a variety of other types of experimental writing and art, author interviews and scholarly articles and essays.

Juxta

<http://www.patacriticism.org/juxta/>

Applied Research in Patacriticism team at the University of Virginia

Juxta is a tool for collating and analyzing text. Users have access to various methods of visualization such as "a heat map of textual differences and a histogram that can expose the filtering results." In addition, users may save collations and annotations for future use.

Perseus Project

<http://www.perseus.tufts.edu/>

Editor-in-chief: Gregory Crane

This resource, affiliated with the Department of the Classics at Tufts University, focuses on creating tools to facilitate the access to and the presentation and analysis of ancient, classical and Renaissance texts as well as art and architectural images. Some of these tools include word searches, atlas tools for creating maps, tools for morphological analysis and generating tables of contents, and a virtual reality interface.

Rhizome.Org

<http://rhizome.org/>

Executive Director: Lauren Cornell

Literary artworks are just one factor of this multifaceted archive, which includes new featured resources, online exhibitions and installations, archives such as "Artbase" (a database of new media resources by various international artists) and "Textbase" (which includes the site's archived conversations, commentary and listings of events and opportunities from the past decade), and services such as a calendar of events, employment, grant, and fellowship opportunities in new media work.

TAPoR

<http://tapor.humanities.mcmaster.ca/home.html>

Project Leader: Geoffrey Rockwell

This portal is a gateway to resources and tools "for sophisticated analysis and retrieval, along with representative texts for experimentation." A key feature is a user-interface that allows for uploading, deleting, and storing texts to an individual user account. In addition, users can store settings such as "favorite" tools and text analysis results alongside access to a more global interface that represents the "best practices of experienced computing humanists available to the larger humanities research community." Based at McMaster University, this project comprises a network of six Humanities computing centers in Canada: McMaster, University of Victoria (in collaboration with Malaspina UC), University of Alberta, University of Toronto, Université de Montreal (law) and University of New Brunswick.

<teiPublisher>

<http://teipublisher.sourceforge.net>

Creators: Amit Kumar, Susan Schreibman, Stuart Arneil, Martin Holmes, John A. Walsh

Building on the native XML database eXist and the text engine search library Lucene, this modular tool is designed to help repository managers with limited technical knowledge manage their repositories with modules that facilitate uploading and deleting, storing, searching, browsing, and displaying TEI documents on the web in HTML and PDF among other formats.

Text Technology

<http://texttechnology.mcmaster.ca/>

Co-editors: Geoffrey Rockwell and Alexandre Sévigny

The "journal of computer text processing," *TT* is meant for academics and professionals who are interested in articles devoted to computer-assisted text acquisition, creation, analysis, editing, or translation. It is the journal of the Society for Digital Humanities/Société pour l'étude des médias interactifs.

TextArc

<http://www.textarc.org>

Creator: W. Bradford Paley

This tool allows a user to display a text and make visual connections between individual words. It makes explicit concordances while also serving as an index and summary tool. It uses human visual processing to reveal patterns and concepts in textual works. Its designer sees it as a complement to Statistical Natural Language Processing and Computational Linguistics.

trAce Online Writing Centre

<http://trace.beds.ac.uk/>

[Keith Jebb and Lesley McKenna]

This site promotes "an accessible and inclusive approach to the internet with the focus on creativity, collaboration and training." Inviting writers to meet online and in person, *trAce* features an archive of new media writing, online courses, feature and scholarly articles, and a wide range of links to resources on the web at large.

Web Del Sol

<http://www.webdelsol.com/>

Founder and Chief Editor: Michael Neff

This site functions as a portal to literary magazines, journals, and weblogs published and hosted at *WDS* and on the web at large, chapbooks by writers and poets, and feature columns.

Words without Borders

<http://www.wordswithoutborders.org/>

Founding Editor: Alane Salierno Mason

This international literary journal contains pieces about and of international literature translated into English. It includes forums, fiction, book reviews, a weblog with a variety of regular contributors, and reflects collaborative scholarship on an international scale.

The Valve

<http://www.thevalve.org/go>

Editor: John Holbo

This resource comprises a literary weblog that seeks "to foster debate and circulation of ideas in literary studies and contiguous academic areas." *The Valve* features contributions by a range of authors on various subjects, a searchable archive of constantly updated entries/articles and reader comments, and online "Book Events" or ongoing reviews and discussions about featured books.

Versioning Machine (version 2.1)

<http://v-machine.org/>

Founding Editor: Susan Schreibman

This tool, "designed by a team of programmers, designers, and literary scholars," allows for the display and comparison of multiple versions of texts by reconstructing multiple witnesses from a single XML-encoded document and displaying them, side by side, as individual documents with annotations and introductory materials. It is supported and maintained by Digital Collections and Research at the University of Maryland.

WordHoard

<http://wordhoard.northwestern.edu>

A joint project of the Northwestern University departments of English and Classics and NU-IT Academic Technologies

   WordHoard serves as "an application for the close reading and scholarly analysis of deeply tagged literary texts" through corpus linguistics techniques, which the user accesses through an interface designed for the non-technical user.

Index